PARALLEL
COMPUTING
THEORY AND PRACTICE

McGraw-Hill Series in Computer Science

SENIOR CONSULTING EDITOR

C. L. Liu, *University of Illinois at Urbana-Champaign*

CONSULTING EDITOR

Allen B. Tucker, *Bowdoin College*

Fundamentals of Computing and Programming
Computer Organization and Architecture
Systems and Languages
Theoretical Foundations
Software Engineering and Database
Artificial Intelligence
Networks, Parallel and Distributed Computing
Graphics and Visualization
The MIT Electrical Engineering and Computer Science Series

Networks, Parallel and Distributed Computing

Ahuja: Design and Analysis of Computer Communication Networks
Filman and Friedman: Coordinated Computing: Tools and Techniques for Distributed Software
Hwang: Advanced Computer Architecture: Parallelism, Scalability, Programmability
Keiser: Local Area Networks
Kershenbaum: Telecommunications Network Design Algorithms
Lakshmivarahan and Dhall: Analysis and Design of Parallel Computers
Quinn: Parallel Computing: Theory and Practice

PARALLEL COMPUTING

THEORY AND PRACTICE

SECOND EDITION

Michael J. Quinn

Oregon State University

DISCARD

McGRAW-HILL, INC.

New York   St. Louis   San Francisco   Auckland   Bogotá   Caracas
Lisbon   London   Madrid   Mexico City   Milan   Montreal   New Delhi
San Juan   Singapore   Sydney   Tokyo   Toronto

This book was set in Times Roman by Electronic Technical Publishing Services.
The editor was Eric M. Munson;
the production supervisor was Annette Mayeski.
The cover was designed by Carla Bauer.
Project supervision was done by Electronic Technical Publishing Services.
R. R. Donnelley & Sons Company was printer and binder.

Figure Credits

Figures 1-2 and 3-27: Reprinted from *Computer Architecture: A Quantitative Approach* by John L. Hennessy and David A. Patterson, © 1990, with the permission of the publisher, Morgan Kaufmann Publishers, Inc.,

Figure 2-1: Aho, Hopcroft, and Ullman, *The Design and Analysis of Computer Algorithms*, © 1974, Addison-Wesley, Reading, Massachusetts, page 5, Figure 1.3. Reprinted with permission.

Figure 3-5: Reprinted from *Computational Aspects of VLSI* by Jeffrey D. Ullman, © 1984, with the permission of the publisher, Computer Science Press, Inc., 1803 Research Blvd., Rockville, MD 20850 USA.

Figure 3-16, 3-21, 4-3, 4-9, 4-12, 10-32, and 10-33: Reprinted from *Data-Parallel Programming on MIMD Computers* by Philip J. Hatcher and Michael J. Quinn, © 1991, with the permission of the publisher, The MIT Press.

Figure 8-6: Reprinted from *Introduction to Algorithms* by Thomas H. Cormen, Charles E. Leiserson, and Ronald L. Rivest, © 1990, with the permission of the publisher, McGraw-Hill, Inc.

Figure 9-1: David Halliday and Robert Resnick, *Fundamental of Physics, Revised Printing*, © 1974, John Wiley & Sons, Inc. Reprinted by permission of John Wiley & Sons, Inc.

Figure 10-15: Robert Sedgewick, *Algorithms*, © 1983, Addison-Wesley, Reading, Massachusetts, page 465 (figure). Reprinted with permission.

Figure 10-18: Donald E. Knuth, *The Art of Computer Programming, Volume 3, Sorting and Searching*, © 1973, Addison-Wesley, Reading, Massachusetts, page 237, Figure 56. Reprinted with permission.

Quotation at beginning of Chapter 6: *Zorba the Greek*, COPYRIGHT © 1953 by Simon & Schuster. © Renewed by Simon & Schuster. Reprinted by permission from Simon & Schuster, Inc.

PARALLEL COMPUTING
Theory and Practice

 This book is printed on recycled, acid-free paper containing a minimum of 50% recycled de-inked fiber.

1 2 3 4 5 6 7 8 9 0 DOH   DOH 9 0 9 8 7 6 5 4 3

ISBN 0-07-051294-9

Library of Congress Cataloging-in-Publication Data

Quinn, Michael J. (Michael Jay)
  Parallel computing: theory and practice / Michael J. Quinn.—
2nd ed.
    p. cm. — (McGraw-Hill series in computer science. Networks,
parallel and distributed computing)
  Rev. ed. of: Designing efficient algorithms for parallel
computers. c1987.
  Includes index.
  ISBN 0-07-051294-9
  1. Parallel computers. I. Quinn, Michael J. (Michael Jay).
Designing efficient algorithms for parallel computers. II. Title.
III. Series: McGraw-Hill computer science series. Networks,
parallel and distributed computing.
QA76.5.Q56 1994
004'.35—dc20   93-29813

ABOUT
THE AUTHOR

MICHAEL J. QUINN is an associate professor of computer science at Oregon State University. He received his Ph.D. in computer science from Washington State University. He has also taught at the University of New Hampshire, and he worked for two years at Tektronix, Inc. as a software engineer before earning his doctorate. He is author of *Designing Efficient Algorithms for Parallel Computers* (McGraw-Hill, 1987) and co-author (with Philip J. Hatcher) of *Data-Parallel Programming on MIMD Computers* (The MIT Press, 1991). Dr. Quinn has published dozens of technical papers in the areas of parallel algorithms and data-parallel programming environments. Currently he is editor-in-chief of *IEEE Parallel and Distributed Technology: Systems and Applications* magazine.

Doubt thou the stars are fire;
Doubt that the sun doth move;
Doubt truth to be a liar;
But never doubt I love.

Hamlet, Act II

**To Victoria,
my wife and best friend**

CONTENTS

PREFACE xv

1 Introduction 1

1.1	COMPUTATIONAL DEMANDS OF MODERN SCIENCE	2
1.2	ADVENT OF PRACTICAL PARALLEL PROCESSING	4
1.3	PARALLEL PROCESSING TERMINOLOGY	5
	1.3.1 Contrasting Pipelining and Data Parallelism	7
	1.3.2 Control Parallelism	8
	1.3.3 Scalability	9
1.4	THE SIEVE OF ERATOSTHENES	9
	1.4.1 Control-Parallel Approach	10
	1.4.2 Data-Parallel Approach	12
	1.4.3 Data-Parallel Approach with I/O	16
1.5	SUMMARY	18
1.6	BIBLIOGRAPHIC NOTES	19
1.7	PROBLEMS	20

2 PRAM Algorithms 25

2.1	A MODEL OF SERIAL COMPUTATION	26
2.2	THE PRAM MODEL OF PARALLEL COMPUTATION	27
2.3	PRAM ALGORITHMS	30
	2.3.1 Parallel Reduction	31
	2.3.2 Prefix Sums	32
	2.3.3 List Ranking	34
	2.3.4 Preorder Tree Traversal	36
	2.3.5 Merging Two Sorted Lists	40
	2.3.6 Graph Coloring	42
2.4	REDUCING THE NUMBER OF PROCESSORS	43

2.5   PROBLEMS DEFYING FAST SOLUTIONS ON PRAMS   46
2.6   SUMMARY   48
2.7   BIBLIOGRAPHIC NOTES   48
2.8   PROBLEMS   50

3   Processor Arrays, Multiprocessors, and Multicomputers   52

3.1   PROCESSOR ORGANIZATIONS   53
       3.1.1   Mesh Networks   53
       3.1.2   Binary Tree Networks   54
       3.1.3   Hypertree Networks   55
       3.1.4   Pyramid Networks   56
       3.1.5   Butterfly Networks   57
       3.1.6   Hypercube (Cube-Connected) Networks   57
       3.1.7   Cube-Connected Cycles Networks   58
       3.1.8   Shuffle-Exchange Networks   59
       3.1.9   de Bruijn Networks   60
       3.1.10   Processor Organization Summary   61
3.2   PROCESSOR ARRAYS   61
       3.2.1   Connection Machine CM-200   63
3.3   MULTIPROCESSORS   67
       3.3.1   Uniform Memory Access (UMA) Multiprocessors   67
       3.3.2   Non-Uniform Memory Access (NUMA)
                Multiprocessors   70
3.4   MULTICOMPUTERS   72
       3.4.1   nCUBE 2   74
       3.4.2   Connection Machine CM-5   75
       3.4.3   Paragon XP/S   76
3.5   FLYNN'S TAXONOMY   78
3.6   SPEEDUP, SCALED SPEEDUP, AND PARALLELIZABILITY   80
       3.6.1   Can Speedup Be Greater than Linear?   80
       3.6.2   Scaled Speedup   81
3.7   SUMMARY   84
3.8   BIBLIOGRAPHIC NOTES   85
3.9   PROBLEMS   88

4   Parallel Programming Languages   90

4.1   PROGRAMMING PARALLEL PROCESSES   91
       4.1.1   An Illustrative Example   91
       4.1.2   A Sample Application   93
4.2   FORTRAN 90   95
       4.2.1   Fortran 90 Programmer's Model   96
       4.2.2   Fortran 90 Language Features   96
       4.2.3   Sample Program   98
4.3   C*   99

		4.3.1	C* Programmer's Model	99
		4.3.2	Language Features	100
		4.3.3	Sample Program	103
	4.4	SEQUENT C		104
		4.4.1	Parallel Programming under DYNIX	104
		4.4.2	Monitors	106
		4.4.3	Sample Program	106
	4.5	nCUBE C		109
		4.5.1	The Run-Time Model	109
		4.5.2	Extensions to the C Language	110
		4.5.3	Sample Program	110
	4.6	OCCAM		113
		4.6.1	Programmer's Model	113
		4.6.2	Language Constructs	114
		4.6.3	Sample Program	
	4.7	C-LINDA		118
		4.7.1	Programmer's Model	118
		4.7.2	C-Linda Language Constructs	118
		4.7.3	Sample Programs	119
	4.8	A NOTATION FOR EXPRESSING PARALLEL ALGORITHMS		122
	4.9	SUMMARY		126
	4.10	BIBLIOGRAPHIC NOTES		127
	4.11	PROBLEMS		129
5	**Mapping and Scheduling**			**131**
	5.1	MAPPING DATA TO PROCESSORS ON PROCESSOR ARRAYS AND MULTICOMPUTERS		132
		5.1.1	Ring into 2-D Mesh	134
		5.1.2	2-D Mesh into 2-D Mesh	134
		5.1.3	Complete Binary Tree into 2-D Mesh	135
		5.1.4	Binomial Tree into 2-D Mesh	136
		5.1.5	Embedding Graphs into Hypercubes	137
		5.1.6	Complete Binary Tree into Hypercube	137
		5.1.7	Binomial Tree into Hypercube	138
		5.1.8	Rings and Meshes into Hypercube	139
	5.2	DYNAMIC LOAD BALANCING ON MULTICOMPUTERS		142
	5.3	STATIC SCHEDULING ON UMA MULTIPROCESSORS		143
		5.3.1	Deterministic Models	144
		5.3.2	Graham's List Scheduling Algorithm	145
		5.3.3	Coffman-Graham Scheduling Algorithm	146
		5.3.4	Nondeterministic Models	147
	5.4	DEADLOCK		151
	5.5	SUMMARY		152
	5.6	BIBLIOGRAPHIC NOTES		153
	5.7	PROBLEMS		154

6   Elementary Parallel Algorithms   **157**

   6.1   CLASSIFYING MIMD ALGORITHMS   157
   6.2   REDUCTION   159
          6.2.1   Hypercube SIMD Model   160
          6.2.2   Shuffle-Exchange SIMD Model   160
          6.2.3   2-D Mesh SIMD Model   162
          6.2.4   UMA Multiprocessor Model   165
   6.3   BROADCAST   170
   6.4   PREFIX SUMS   172
   6.5   SUMMARY   175
   6.6   BIBLIOGRAPHIC NOTES   176
   6.7   PROBLEMS   176

7   Matrix Multiplication   **178**

   7.1   SEQUENTIAL MATRIX MULTIPLICATION   179
   7.2   ALGORITHMS FOR PROCESSOR ARRAYS   180
          7.2.1   Matrix Multiplication on the 2-D Mesh SIMD Model   180
          7.2.2   Matrix Multiplication on the Hypercube SIMD Model   183
          7.2.3   Matrix Multiplication on the Shuffle-Exchange SIMD
                   Model   186
   7.3   ALGORITHMS FOR MULTIPROCESSORS   187
   7.4   ALGORITHMS FOR MULTICOMPUTERS   191
          7.4.1   Row-Column-Oriented Algorithm   191
          7.4.2   Block-Oriented Algorithm   193
   7.5   SUMMARY   196
   7.6   BIBLIOGRAPHIC NOTES   196
   7.7   PROBLEMS   197

8   The Fast Fourier Transform   **198**

   8.1   INTRODUCTION   198
   8.2   THE DISCRETE FOURIER TRANSFORM   201
          8.2.1   Inverse Discrete Fourier Transform   202
          8.2.2   Sample Application: Polynomial Multiplication   203
   8.3   THE FAST FOURIER TRANSFORM   205
          8.3.1   Implementation on a Hypercube Multicomputer   207
   8.4   SUMMARY   211
   8.5   BIBLIOGRAPHIC NOTES   213
   8.6   PROBLEMS   214

9   Solving Linear Systems   **217**

   9.1   TERMINOLOGY   218
   9.2   BACK SUBSTITUTION   220
   9.3   ODD-EVEN REDUCTION   224
   9.4   GAUSSIAN ELIMINATION   229

9.5   THE JACOBI ALGORITHM   237

     9.5.1   Sparse Linear Systems   239

9.6   THE GAUSS-SEIDEL ALGORITHM   244

9.7   JACOBI OVERRELAXATION AND SUCCESSIVE OVERRELAXATION   245

9.8   MULTIGRID METHODS   246

9.9   CONJUGATE GRADIENT   248

9.10   SUMMARY   251

9.11   BIBLIOGRAPHIC NOTES   252

9.12   PROBLEMS   253

10   Sorting   255

10.1   ENUMERATION SORT   256

10.2   LOWER BOUNDS ON PARALLEL SORTING   257

10.3   ODD-EVEN TRANSPOSITION SORT   258

10.4   BITONIC MERGE   260

     10.4.1   Bitonic Merge on the Shuffle-Exchange Network   264

     10.4.2   Bitonic Merge on the Two-Dimensional Mesh Network   267

     10.4.3   Bitonic Merge on the Hypercube Network   271

10.5   QUICKSORT-BASED ALGORITHMS   272

     10.5.1   Parallel Quicksort   273

     10.5.2   Hyperquicksort   276

     10.5.3   Parallel Sorting by Regular Sampling   281

10.6   RANDOM READ AND RANDOM WRITE   286

10.7   SUMMARY   288

10.8   BIBLIOGRAPHIC NOTES   290

10.9   PROBLEMS   292

11   Dictionary Operations   294

11.1   COMPLEXITY OF PARALLEL SEARCH   295

11.2   SEARCHING ON MULTIPROCESSORS   296

     11.2.1   Ellis's Algorithm   297

     11.2.2   Manber and Ladner's Algorithm   302

11.3   SUMMARY   306

11.4   BIBLIOGRAPHIC NOTES   307

11.5   PROBLEMS   307

12   Graph Algorithms   309

12.1   SEARCHING A GRAPH   309

     12.1.1   P-Depth Search   310

     12.1.2   Breadth-Depth Search   312

     12.1.3   Breadth-First Search   312

12.2   CONNECTED COMPONENTS   313

12.3	ALL-PAIRS SHORTEST PATH	318
12.4	SINGLE-SOURCE SHORTEST PATH	318
12.5	MINIMUM-COST SPANNING TREE	325
	12.5.1 Sollin's Algorithm	326
	12.5.2 Kruskal's Algorithm	329
12.6	SUMMARY	332
12.7	BIBLIOGRAPHIC NOTES	332
12.8	PROBLEMS	334

13 Combinatorial Search **336**

13.1	INTRODUCTION	337
13.2	DIVIDE AND CONQUER	338
13.3	BRANCH AND BOUND	339
	13.3.1 Traveling Salesperson Problem	342
13.4	PARALLEL BRANCH-AND-BOUND ALGORITHMS	346
	13.4.1 Multiprocessor Algorithms	346
	13.4.2 Multicomputer Algorithms	347
	13.4.3 Anomalies in Parallel Branch and Bound	352
13.5	ALPHA-BETA SEARCH	354
13.6	PARALLEL ALPHA-BETA SEARCH	359
	13.6.1 Parallel Move Generation and Position Evaluation	359
	13.6.2 Parallel Aspiration Search	359
	13.6.3 Parallel Subtree Evaluation	360
	13.6.4 Distributed Tree Search	361
13.7	SUMMARY	364
13.8	BIBLIOGRAPHIC NOTES	364
13.9	PROBLEMS	365

	APPENDIXES	
A	Graph Theoretic Terminology	367
B	Review of Complex Numbers	371
C	Parallel Algorithm Design Strategies	375

	GLOSSARY	376
	CALL NUMBERS	389
	BIBLIOGRAPHY	391
	INDEX	435

PREFACE

This book began as a revision of *Designing Efficient Algorithms for Parallel Computers*. I have changed the title for three reasons. First, two-thirds of the material in this edition is new. I have discarded the chapters on logic programming and pipelined vector processors, updated and enhanced the remaining material from the original book, and added chapters on PRAM algorithms, mapping and scheduling, and parallel imperative programming languages. Second, substantial organizational changes were made to improve the pedagogy. Third, the title *Parallel Computing: Theory and Practice* is more appropriate for an introductory text. My goal in writing this book has been to provide seniors and graduate students in computer science and engineering with an easy to understand introduction to the field of parallel computing.

Chapter 1 provides the motivation for the study of parallel computing. It explains why higher performance computers are needed and why commercial parallel computers have appeared over the past decade. It introduces basic parallel processing terminology and highlights the difference between control parallelism and data parallelism. Chapter 2 describes parallel algorithms for the PRAM, a theoretical model of parallel computation.

Chapter 3 begins with a discussion of nine fundamental processor organizations and continues with a description of three parallel computer architectures: the processor array, the multiprocessor, and the multicomputer. Several commercial parallel computers are presented as case studies. Chapter 4 summarizes the features of six parallel imperative programming languages. Both low-level and high-level languages are described. Chapter 5 concludes the introductory portion of the text with some important theoretical results in the areas of mapping and scheduling.

Chapters 6 through 13 cover the design, analysis, and implementation of parallel algorithms on parallel computers. The chapters are organized by problem domain. As much as possible, I have ordered the chapters by increasing level of difficulty. Chapter 6 describes three elementary parallel algorithms:

reduction, broadcast, and prefix sums. Chapter 7 discusses parallel implementations of matrix multiplication and Chapter 8 covers the parallelization of the Fast Fourier transform.

Chapter 9 follows with the parallelization of a wide variety of algorithms to solve systems of linear equations. Chapter 10 presents some important results in parallel sorting. Chapter 11 discusses dictionary operations and illuminates trade-offs between the complexity of the underlying sequential algorithm and the potential for keeping a large number of processors busy doing useful work. Chapter 12 describes parallel graph algorithms. Chapter 13 contains both theoretical and practical results in the area of parallel algorithms for combinatorial search. These problems occur in artificial intelligence, operations research, and graph theory, as well as in other areas.

A number of features make this book attractive for classroom use. Parallel algorithms are presented in a machine-independent, high-level pseudocode. Experimental results from implementations of parallel algorithms appear frequently. Each chapter ends with a set of exercises with the more difficult exercises denoted by an asterisk (*). Appendix A contains a review of the basic terminology of graph theory. Appendix B is a review of complex numbers. It can be used as a supplement to the chapter on the fast Fourier transform. A summary of parallel algorithm design strategies is given in Appendix C. I have also provided a glossary of parallel computing. The bibliography is large and facilitates further exploration of topics surveyed in this book. A directory of Library of Congress call numbers, which appears immediately before the bibliography, makes articles from the most frequently cited journals and conference proceedings easier to locate. Finally, an instructor's manual is available, which contains answers to most of the exercises.

This book is a reflection of my nine years' experience teaching parallel computing to undergraduate and graduate students at the University of New Hampshire and Oregon State University. I recommend that instructors augment the exercises with actual programming assignments on a parallel computer, computer network, or simulator. Programming a parallel computer is a new, difficult, and exciting experience for most students, and they learn a great deal from their efforts. In addition, graduate students should read recent journal articles and conference papers. With these supplements, there is more than enough material for a one-semester course. I recommend Chapters 1, 3, and 6 be covered in their entirety. Section 4-8 is a prerequisite for the material in the rest of the chapters. The instructor must decide whether to cover a few of the remaining chapters in their entirety or pick and choose interesting sections. For example, if I were teaching a one-semester course to undergraduates with access to a Sequent multiprocessor, I would lecture on Chapters 1 through 3, Sections 4-1, 4-4, 4-8, 5-3, and 5-4, and Chapters 6, 7, 9, and 10. If time permitted, I would also cover Sections 13-5 and 13-6.

I am grateful to Eric Munson, my editor at McGraw-Hill, for encouraging me to complete this project. Holly Stark, his editorial asistant, provided me with many valuable reviews that led to significant improvements in the quality of the text. I thank the reviewers for their efforts: Marc Abrams, Virginia Tech; Johnnie Baker, Kent State University; Moon Jung Chung, Michigan State University; Clyde Kruskal, University of Maryland; S. Lakshmivarahan, University of Oklahoma; Donald Miller, Arizona State University; Russ Miller, SUNY, Buffalo; Bruce Parker, New Jersey Institute of Technology; Oberta A. Slotterbeck, Hiram College; Pradip K. Srimani, Colorado State University; Boleslaw K. Szymanski, Rensselaer Polytechnic Institute; Pearl Wang, George Mason University; Layne Watson, Virginia Polytechnic Institute.

Many students at Oregon State University read drafts of the manuscript and provided me with corrrections and suggestions. Two students made particularly important contributions to the book. Teri Rohne helped me complete the Bibliography by tracking down dozens of missing references. Phyl Crandall carefully read the galley proofs and pointed out numerous errors.

Phil Hatcher deserves much of the credit for the cover. He suggested the orchestra analogy during a brainstorming session in Boulder, Colorado.

Finally, thanks to everybody who thought enough of the first edition of this book to ask me when the second edition was going to appear. Your confidence helped me find the energy to complete the job.

Michael J. Quinn

INTRODUCTION

What king marching to war against another king would not first sit down and consider whether with ten thousand men he could stand up to the other who advanced against him with twenty thousand?

Luke 14:31

For those interested in high-speed computing, studying parallel algorithms is no longer an academic exercise; it is a necessity. Many problems can be solved by massive parallelism. For these problems the fastest computers in the world are built of numerous conventional microprocessors. The emergence of high-performance, massively parallel computers demands the development of new algorithms to take advantage of this technology.

This book discusses designing, analyzing, and implementing parallel algorithms for computers that have numerous processors. These steps are not always easy. Many algorithms suitable for conventional, single-processor computers are not appropriate for parallel architectures. Many algorithms with inherent parallelism have a higher computational complexity than the best sequential counterpart. In either case, implementing an inappropriate algorithm wastes a parallel computer's resources. We will examine these trade-offs in later chapters and discuss how to choose a parallel algorithm that makes good use of the target architecture.

In the remainder of Chap. 1 we place our exploration of parallel algorithms in context. Section 1.1 describes how science relies upon numerical simulation and gives examples of problems that could benefit from faster computers. In Section 1.2 we see why, after 20 years in research laboratories, parallel computers finally entered the commercial market. Section 1.3 introduces some important terminology and gives examples of pipelining, data parallelism, and control parallelism. Section 1.4 is devoted to a sample application—the Sieve of Eratosthenes. Designing control-parallel and data-parallel algorithms in this application reveals problems that arise whenever a parallel program is developed.

Parallel computing has come of age. Let's begin our study.

1.1   COMPUTATIONAL DEMANDS OF CONTEMPORARY SCIENCE

Classical science is based on observation, theory, and experimentation. Observation of a phenomenon leads to a hypothesis. The scientist develops a theory to explain the phenomenon and designs an experiment to test that theory. Usually the results of the experiment require the scientist to refine the theory, if not completely reject it. Here, observation may again take center stage.

Classical science is characterized by physical experiments and models. For example, many high school physics students have explored the relationship between mass, force, and acceleration using paper tape, pucks, and an air table. Physical experiments allow the scientist to test a theory—e.g., Newton's first law of motion—against reality.

Unfortunately, we cannot always use physical experiments to test theories because they may be too expensive or time-consuming, because they may be unethical, or because they may be impossible to perform. High-speed computers allow scientists to test their hypotheses in another way by developing a numerical simulation of a phenomenon. The scientist compares the behavior of the numerical simulation, which implements the theory, to observations of "real world" phenomena. The differences cause the scientist to revise the theory and/or make more observations.

Contemporary science, then, is characterized by observation, theory, experimentation, and numerical simulation. Numerical simulation is an increasingly important tool for scientists. Many important scientific problems are so complex that solving them via numerical simulation requires extraordinarily powerful computers. These complex problems, often called "grand challenges" for science, fall into several categories (Levin 1989):

1 Quantum chemistry, statistical mechanics, and relativistic physics

2 Cosmology and astrophysics

3 Computational fluid dynamics and turbulence

4 Materials design and superconductivity

5 Biology, pharmacology, genome sequencing, genetic engineering, protein folding, enzyme activity, and cell modeling

6 Medicine, and modeling of human organs and bones

7 Global weather and environmental modeling

Consider three practical examples.

Oceanographers at Oregon State University are developing a numerical simulation of global ocean circulation. Their goal is to learn how the southern oceans transport heat to the south pole, an important step toward understanding the global warming problem (Fig. 1-1). To obtain accurate results, the scientists plan to divide the ocean into 4,096 regions running east to west and 1,024 regions running north to south. In addition, they will divide the ocean into 12 layers, with deeper layers containing sea water with greater density. In all, their model ocean will have about 50 million three-dimensional cells. A single iteration of their model simulates ocean circulation for 10 minutes and requires about 30 billion floating-point calculations. The oceanographers want to use the model to simulate ocean circulation over a period of years.

High temperature superconductivity may bring about many revolutionary developments, including highly energy-efficient power transmission and ultra-sensitive instrumentation. The development of new high-temperature superconducting materials is being slowed by the lack of an accepted theory. Researchers at Oak Ridge National Laboratory have used laws of quantum mechanics to develop a computer program that can predict the structural, vibrational, and electronic properties of new materials. More than 150 trillion floating-point operations must be performed to complete a single computational experiment.

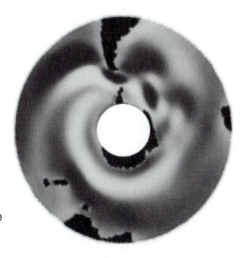

FIGURE 1-1   Sample output of a southern ocean circulation model developed at Oregon State University by Andrew F. Bennett and Boon Chua. The image shows ocean pressure (elevation) between the latitudes 32° S and 75° S. (Courtesy John A. Gregor.)

Finally, consider this example from molecular dynamics (Levin 1990). About one hour of Cray X/MP time is needed to model a one-picosecond interaction between a protein and its surrounding water molecules. An actual physical process of interest may continue for almost a second. Modeling such an interaction on the same machine, using the same algorithm, would require 31,688 years.

For decades computer architects have incorporated parallelism into various levels of hardware in order to increase the performance of computer systems. To achieve the extremely high speeds demanded by contemporary science, architectures must now incorporate parallelism at the highest levels of the system. Today, the fastest computers in the world use high-level parallelism. These computers are leading to new scientific discoveries.

1.2 ADVENT OF PRACTICAL PARALLEL PROCESSING

It took more than 20 years for parallel computers to move from the laboratory to the marketplace. Daniel Slotnick at the University of Illinois designed two early parallel computers: Solomon, constructed by Westinghouse Electric Company in the early 1960s, and the ILLIAC IV, assembled at Burroughs Corporation in the early 1970s. At Carnegie-Mellon University, two well-documented parallel computers—C.mmp and Cm*—were constructed during the 1970s. In the early 1980s researchers at Caltech built the Cosmic Cube, the ancestor of multicomputers built by Ametek, Intel, and nCUBE.

Still, it was not until the mid-1980s that commercial parallel computers constructed with microprocessors became available. A study of the performance growth in various computer classes reveals why microprocessor-based parallel processing finally became practical. Examine Fig. 1-2. The performance-growth

FIGURE 1-2   Performance growth of four classes of computers since 1965. (Courtesy Hennessy and Patterson 1990.)

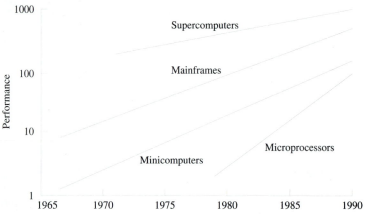

rate for minicomputers, mainframes, and traditional supercomputers has been just under 20% a year, while the performance growth rate for microprocessors has averaged 35% a year.

Why has the performance of microprocessors increased faster than the performance of other kinds of processors? The performance of a single processor can be improved through either architectural or technological advances. Architectural improvements can increase the amount of work performed per instruction cycle, while technological advances can reduce the time needed per instruction cycle. By the mid-1970s the fundamental architectural advances—bit-parallel memory, bit-parallel arithmetic, cache memory, channels, interleaved memory, instruction lookahead, instruction pipelining, multiple functional units, pipelined functional units, and data pipelining—had already been incorporated into supercomputer designs. Since then, improving the performance of individual processors has meant reducing the instruction-cycle time. This has become increasingly difficult, since the speed of electronic circuits is limited by the speed of light.

In contrast, microprocessors have been able to achieve more impressive performance gains, because they have had so far to go. Early microprocessors did not incorporate all the architectural advances already present in supercomputers, and their clock speeds were much slower. Architectural advances, coupled with reduced instruction-cycle times, have led to impressive performance gains for this class of computer.

The convergence in relative performance between microcomputers and traditional supercomputers has led to the development of commercially viable parallel computers consisting of tens, hundreds, or even thousands of microprocessors. At peak efficiency, microprocessor-based parallel computers such as Intel's Paragon XP/S™, MasPar's MP-2™, and Thinking Machines' CM-5™, exceed the speed of traditional single-processor supercomputers, such as the Cray Y/MP™ and the NEC SX-3™.

Harnessing the power latent in massively parallel microprocessor-based computers, however, requires the development of reasonable architectures, operating systems, programming languages, and algorithms. Poor design choices can lead to dismal performance. This book addresses the problem of designing efficient algorithms for real parallel computers.

1.3 PARALLEL PROCESSING TERMINOLOGY

Most high-performance modern computers exhibit concurrency. For example, multiprocessing is a method used to achieve concurrency at the job or program level, while instruction prefetching is a method of achieving concurrency at the interinstruction level. However, it is not desirable to call every modern computer a parallel computer. The concurrency of many machines is invisible to the user. Hence we adopt the following definitions.

Parallel processing is information processing that emphasizes the concurrent manipulation of data elements belonging to one or more processes solving *a single problem*. A **parallel computer** is a multiple-processor computer capable of parallel processing.

A **supercomputer** is a general-purpose computer capable of solving individual problems at extremely high computational speeds, compared with other computers built during the same time. Of course, "extremely high" is a relative term. By this definition supercomputers have always existed. All contemporary supercomputers are parallel computers. Some have a relatively small number of extremely powerful processors; others are made up of a relatively large number of microprocessors.

The **throughput** of a device is the number of results it produces per unit time. There are many ways to improve the throughput of a device. The speed at which the device operates can be increased, or the concurrency—the number of operations that are being performed at any one time—can be increased.

Pipelining and data parallelism are two ways to increase the concurrency of a computation. A **pipelined** computation is divided into a number of steps, called **segments**, or **stages**. Each segment works at full speed on a particular part of a computation. The output of one segment is the input of the next segment. If all the segments work at the same speed, once the pipe is full the work rate of the pipeline is equal to the sum of the work rates of the segments. A pipeline is analogous to an assembly line: the flow of results is simple and fixed, precedence constraints must be honored, and it takes time to fill and drain the pipe. If we assume that each segment of the pipe requires the same amount of time, the multiplicative increase in the throughput is equal to the number of segments in the pipeline. Figure 1-3 illustrates pipelining in the context of a high-performance photocopier.

Data parallelism is the use of multiple functional units to apply the same operation simultaneously to elements of a data set. A k-fold increase in the number of functional units leads to a k-fold increase in the throughput of the system, if there is no overhead associated with the increase in parallelism.

Speedup is the ratio between the time needed for the most efficient sequential algorithm to perform a computation and the time needed to perform the same computation on a machine incorporating pipelining and/or parallelism. (This definition of speedup is intuitive, but informal. We will formalize the definition in Chap. 3.)

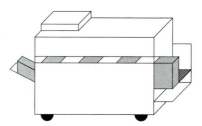

FIGURE 1-3   A high-performance photocopier is an example of a pipelined processor. By dividing the copy process into three pipelined stages, the throughput of the copier is increased threefold without increasing processing speed.

1.3.1   Contrasting Pipelining and Data Parallelism

An example will illuminate the difference between pipelining and data parallelism as well as provide a practical demonstration of speedup. Assume that it takes three units of time to assemble a widget. Furthermore, assume that this assembly consists of three steps—A, B, and C—and each step requires exactly one unit of time. A sequential widget-assembly machine makes a widget by spending one unit of time performing step A, followed by one unit of time performing step B, and one unit of time performing step C. Clearly a sequential widget-assembly machine produces one widget in three time units, two widgets in six time units, and so on, as shown in Fig. 1-4a. Consider how the output could be increased if the assembly were pipelined. Figure 1-4b illustrates a three-segment pipeline. Each of the subassembly tasks has been assigned to a separate machine. The first machine performs subassembly task A on a new widget every time unit and passes the partially assembled widget to the second machine. In a similar way the second machine performs subassembly task B, and the third machine performs subassembly task C. The pipelined widget-assembly machine produces one widget in three time units, as does the sequential machine; but after the initial time to fill the pipe (assembly line),

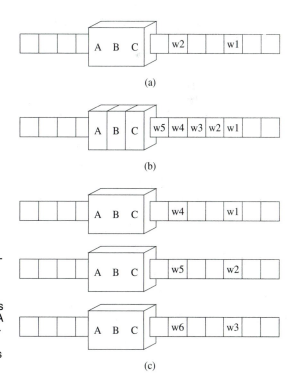

FIGURE 1-4   Three methods to assemble widgets. (a) A sequential widget-assembly machine produces one widget every three units of time. (b) A three-segment pipelined widget-assembly machine produces the first widget in three units of time and successive widgets every time unit thereafter. (c) A three-way data-parallel widget-assembly machine produces three widgets every three units of time.

one widget appears every time unit. Hence the second widget appears at time unit four, the third widget at time unit five, and so on.

Figure 1-4c shows a group of three data-parallel widget-assembly machines. Each machine performs every subassembly task, as does the sequential widget assembler. Throughput is increased by replicating machines. Another three widgets appear every three time units. Note that the time needed to produce four widgets is the same as the time needed to produce five or six widgets.

Figure 1-5 illustrates the speedup achieved by the pipelined and data-parallel widget machines. The x axis represents the number of widgets assembled; the y axis represents the speedup achieved. For any particular number of widgets i, the speedup is computed by dividing the time needed for the sequential machine to assemble i widgets by the time needed for the pipelined or data-parallel machine to assemble i widgets. For example, the sequential machine requires 12 time units to assemble four widgets, while the pipelined machine requires six time units to assemble four widgets. Hence the pipelined machine exhibits a speedup of two for the task of assembling four widgets.

1.3.2 Control Parallelism

Our discussion has focused on data-parallel and pipelined algorithms. Pipelining is actually a special case of a more general class of parallel algorithms, called control-parallel algorithms. In contrast to data parallelism, in which parallelism is achieved by applying a single operation to a data set, **control parallelism** is achieved by applying different operations to different data elements simultaneously. The flow of data among these processes can be arbitrarily complex. If the data-flow graph forms a simple directed path, then we say the algorithm is pipelined.

Most realistic problems can exploit both data parallelism and control parallelism. Realistic problems also have some precedence relations between different tasks. For example, consider the problem of performing an estate's weekly landscape maintenance as quickly as possible (Fig. 1-6). Suppose four chores must be performed: mowing the lawn, edging the lawn, checking the sprinklers, and weeding the flower beds. With the exception of checking the sprinklers,

FIGURE 1-5 Speedup achieved by pipelined and parallel widget-assembly machines. Note that speedup is graphed as a function of problem size (number of widgets assembled). This is unusual. Speedup is typically graphed as a function of number of processors used.

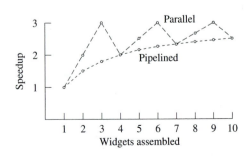

FIGURE 1-6   Most realistic problems have data parallelism, control parallelism, and precedence constraints between tasks. In this example, there are four tasks to complete. Three of the tasks—mowing the lawn, edging the lawn, and weeding the garden—may be undertaken simultaneously, an example of control parallelism. Each of these tasks viewed in isolation is data parallel. Finally, all three tasks must be finished before the fourth task—checking the sprinklers—can begin. Since everyone must be finished before the sprinklers are checked, any one of the employees performing the other tasks can also check the sprinklers.

SPEEDY LANDSCAPE, INC.
Work Assignments—Medici Manor

Mow lawn	Edge lawn
Allan	Francis
Bernice	Georgia
Charlene	**Weed garden**
Dominic	Hillary
Edward	Irene
Check sprinklers	Jose
Allan	

which is easily performed by a single person, each of the remaining chores can be done more quickly by multiple workers. Increasing the lawn-mowing speed by creating a lawn-mowing team and assigning each team member a portion of the lawn is an example of data parallelism. Since there is no reason why the flower beds cannot be weeded at the same time the lawn is being mowed, we can assign another team to the weeding. Concurrent weeding and lawn mowing is an example of control parallelism. Precedence relations exist between checking the sprinklers and the three other tasks, since all of the other tasks must be completed before the sprinklers are tested.

1.3.3 Scalability

An algorithm is **scalable** if the level of parallelism increases at least linearly with the problem size. An architecture is scalable if it continues to yield the same performance per processor, albeit used on a larger problem size, as the number of processors increases. Algorithmic and architectural scalability are important, because they allow a user to solve larger problems in the same amount of time by buying a parallel computer with more processors.

Data-parallel algorithms are more scalable than control-parallel algorithms, because the level of control parallelism is usually a constant, independent of the problem size, while the level of data parallelism is an increasing function of the problem size. Almost every problem we will study in this book has a data-parallel solution.

1.4 THE SIEVE OF ERATOSTHENES

In this section we will explore methods to parallelize the Sieve of Eratosthenes, the classic prime-finding algorithm. We will design and analyze both control-parallel and data-parallel implementations of this algorithm.

We want to find the number of primes less than or equal to some positive integer n. A prime number has exactly two factors: itself and 1. The Sieve of

Eratosthenes begins with a list of natural numbers 2, 3, 4, ..., n, and removes composite numbers from the list by striking multiples of 2, 3, 5, and successive primes (see Fig. 1-7). The sieve terminates after multiples of the largest prime less than or equal to $\sqrt{n}$ have been struck.

Note: The Sieve of Eratosthenes is impractical for testing the primality of "interesting" numbers—those with hundreds of digits—because the time complexity of the algorithm is $\Omega(n)$, and n increases exponentially with the number of digits. However, more reasonable factoring algorithms make use of sieve techniques in other ways.

A sequential implementation of the Sieve of Eratosthenes manages three key data structures: a boolean array whose elements correspond to the natural numbers being sieved, an integer corresponding to latest prime number found, and an integer used as a loop index incremented as multiples of the current prime are marked as composite numbers (Fig. 1-8a).

1.4.1 Control-Parallel Approach

First let's examine a control-parallel algorithm to find the number of primes less than or equal to some positive integer n. In this algorithm every processor

FIGURE 1-7   Use of the Sieve of Eratosthenes to find all primes less than or equal to 30. (a) Prime is next unmarked natural number—2. (b) Strike all multiples of 2, beginning with 2^2. (c) Prime is next unmarked natural number—3. (d) Strike all multiples of 3, beginning with 3^2. (e) Prime is next unmarked natural number—5. (f) Strike all multiples of 5, beginning with 5^2. (g) Prime is next unmarked natural number—7. Since 7^2 is greater than 30, algorithm terminates. All remaining unmarked natural numbers are also primes.

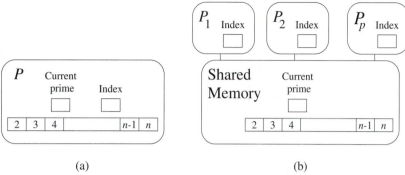

FIGURE 1-8   Shared memory model for parallel Sieve of Eratosthenes algorithm. (a) Sequential algorithm maintains array of natural numbers, variable storing current prime, and variable storing index of loop iterating through array of natural numbers. (b) In parallel model each processor has its own private loop index and shares access to other variables with all processors.

repeatedly goes through the two-step process of finding the next prime number and striking from the list multiples of that prime, beginning with its square. The processors continue until a prime is found whose value is greater than $\sqrt{n}$. Using this approach, processors concurrently mark multiples of different primes. For example, one processor will be responsible for marking multiples of 2 beginning with 4. While this processor marks multiples of 2, another may be marking multiples of 3 beginning with 9.

We will base the control-parallel algorithm on the simple model of parallel computation illustrated in Fig. 1-8b. Every processor shares access to the boolean array representing the natural numbers, as well as the integer containing the value of the latest prime number found. Because processors independently mark multiples of different primes, each processor has its own local loop index.

If a group of asynchronously executing processors share access to the same data structure in an unstructured way, inefficiencies or errors may occur. Here are two problems that can occur in the algorithm we just described. First, two processors may end up using the same prime value to sieve through the array. Normally a processor accesses the value of the current prime and begins searching at the next array location until it finds another unmarked cell, which corresponds to the next prime. Then it updates the value of the integer containing the current prime. If a second processor accesses the value of the current prime before the first processor updates it, then both processors will end up finding the same new prime and performing a sieve based on that value. This does not make the algorithm incorrect, but it wastes time.

Second, a processor may end up sieving multiples of a composite number. For example, assume processor A is responsible for marking multiples of 2, but before it can mark any cells, processor B finds the next prime to be 3, and processor C searches for the next unmarked cell. Because cell 4 has not yet been marked, processor C returns with the value 4 as the latest "prime" number. As in the previous example, the algorithm is still correct, but a processor sieving multiples of 4 is wasting time.

In later chapters we will discuss ways to design parallel algorithms that avoid such problems.

For now, let's explore the maximum speedup achievable by this parallel algorithm, assuming that none of the time-wasting problems described earlier happen. To make our analysis easier, we'll also ignore the time spent finding the next prime and concentrate on the operation of marking cells.

First let's consider the time taken by the sequential algorithm. Assume it takes 1 unit of time for a processor to mark a cell. Suppose there are k primes less than or equal to $\sqrt{n}$. We denote these primes $\pi_1, \pi_2, \ldots, \pi_k$. (For example, $\pi_1 = 2$, $\pi_2 = 3$, and $\pi_3 = 5$.) The total amount of time a single processor spends striking out composite numbers is

$$\left\lceil \frac{(n+1) - \pi_1^2}{\pi_1} \right\rceil + \left\lceil \frac{(n+1) - \pi_2^2}{\pi_2} \right\rceil + \left\lceil \frac{(n+1) - \pi_3^2}{\pi_3} \right\rceil + \cdots + \left\lceil \frac{(n+1) - \pi_k^2}{\pi_k} \right\rceil$$

$$= \left\lceil \frac{n-3}{2} \right\rceil + \left\lceil \frac{n-8}{3} \right\rceil + \left\lceil \frac{n-24}{5} \right\rceil + \cdots + \left\lceil \frac{(n+1) - \pi_k^2}{\pi_k} \right\rceil$$

There are $\lceil (n-3)/2 \rceil$ multiples of 2 in the range 4 through n, $\lceil (n-8)/3 \rceil$ multiples of 3 in the range 9 through n, and so on. For $n = 1,000$ the sum is 1,411.

Now let's think about the time taken by the parallel algorithm. Whenever a processor is unoccupied, it grabs the next prime and marks its multiples. All processors continue in this fashion until the first prime greater than $\sqrt{n}$ is found. For example, Fig. 1-9 illustrates the time required by one, two, and three processors to find all primes less than or equal to 1,000. With two processors the parallel algorithm has speedup 2 (1,411/706). With three processors the parallel algorithm has speedup 2.83 (1,411/499). It is clear that the parallel execution time will not decrease if more than three processors are used, because with three or more processors the time needed for a single processor to sieve all multiples of 2 determines the parallel execution time. Hence an upper bound on the execution time of the parallel algorithm for $n = 1,000$ is 2.83.

Increasing n does not significantly raise the upper bound on speedup imposed by a single processor striking all multiples of 2 (see Prob. 1-10).

1.4.2   Data-Parallel Approach

Let's consider another approach to parallelizing the Sieve of Eratosthenes. In our new algorithm, processors will work together to strike multiples of each newly found prime. Every processor will be responsible for a segment of the

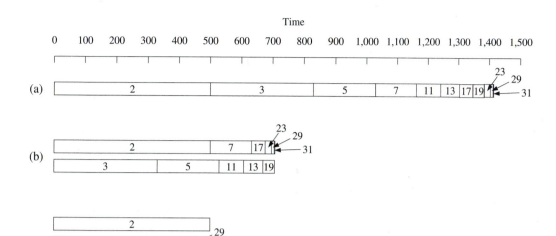

FIGURE 1-9   Study of how adding processors reduces the execution time of the control-parallel Sieve of Eratosthenes algorithm when $n = 1,000$. The number in the bar represents the prime whose multiples are being marked. The length of the bar is the time needed to strike these multiples. (a) Single processor strikes out all composite numbers in 1,411 units of time. (b) With two processors execution time drops to 706 time units. (c) With three or more processors execution time is 499 time units, the time needed for a processor to strike all multiples of 2.

array representing the natural numbers. The algorithm is data parallel, because each processor applies the same operation (striking multiples of a particular prime) to its own portion of the data set.

Analyzing the speedup achievable by the data-parallel algorithm on the shared memory model of Fig. 1-8b is straightforward; we have left it as an exercise. Instead, we will consider a different model of parallel computation (Fig. 1-10). In this model there is no shared memory, and processor interaction occurs through message passing.

Assume we are solving the problem on p processors. Every processor is assigned no more than $\lceil n/p \rceil$ natural numbers. We will also assume that p is much less than $\sqrt{n}$. In this case all primes less than $\sqrt{n}$, as well as the first prime greater than $\sqrt{n}$, are in the list of natural numbers controlled by the first processor. Processor 1 will find the next prime and broadcast its value to the other processors. Then all processors strike from their lists of composite numbers all multiples of the newly found prime. This process of prime finding and composite number striking continues until the first processor reaches a prime greater than $\sqrt{n}$, at which point the algorithm terminates.

Let's estimate the execution time of this parallel algorithm. As in the previous analysis, we ignore time spent finding the next prime and focus on the time spent marking composite numbers. However, since this model does not

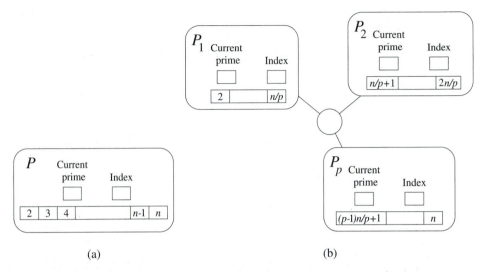

(a)   (b)

FIGURE 1-10   Private memory model for parallel Sieve of Eratosthenes algorithm. (a) Sequential algorithm maintains array of natural numbers, variable storing current prime, and variable storing index of loop iterating through array of natural numbers. (b) In parallel model each processor has its own copy of the variables containing the current prime and the loop index. Processor 1 finds primes and communicates them to the other processors. Each processor iterates through its own portion of the array of natural numbers, marking multiples of the prime.

have a shared memory, we must also consider the time spent communicating the value of the current prime from processor 1 to all other processors.

Assume it takes χ time units for a processor to mark a multiple of a prime as being a composite number. Suppose there are k primes less than or equal to $\sqrt{n}$. We denote these primes $\pi_1, \pi_2, \ldots, \pi_k$. The total amount of time a processor spends striking out composite numbers is no greater than

$$\left(\left\lceil \frac{\lceil n/p \rceil}{2} \right\rceil + \left\lceil \frac{\lceil n/p \rceil}{3} \right\rceil + \left\lceil \frac{\lceil n/p \rceil}{5} \right\rceil + \cdots + \left\lceil \frac{\lceil n/p \rceil}{\pi_k} \right\rceil \right) \chi$$

Assume every time processor 1 finds a new prime it communicates that value to each of the other $p - 1$ processors in turn. If processor 1 spends λ time units each time it passes a number to another processor, its total communication time for all k primes is $k(p - 1)\lambda$.

To bring this discussion down to earth, suppose we want to count the number of primes less than 1,000,000. It turns out that there are 168 primes less than 1,000, the square root of 1,000,000. The largest of these is 997. The maximum possible execution time spent striking out primes is

$$\left(\left\lceil \frac{\lceil 1,000,000/p \rceil}{2} \right\rceil + \left\lceil \frac{\lceil 1,000,000/p \rceil}{3} \right\rceil + \cdots + \left\lceil \frac{\lceil 1,000,000/p \rceil}{997} \right\rceil \right) \chi$$

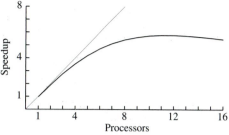

FIGURE 1-11   Estimated speedup of the data-parallel Sieve of Eratosthenes algorithm, assuming that $n = 1,000,000$ and $\lambda = 100\chi$. Note that speedup is graphed as a function of number of processors used. This is typical.

The total communication time is $168(p - 1)\lambda$.

If we know the relation between χ and λ, we can plot an estimated speedup curve for the parallel algorithm. Suppose $\lambda = 100\chi$. Figure 1-11 illustrates the estimated speedup of the data-parallel algorithm.

Notice that speedup is not directly proportional to the number of processors used. In fact, speedup is highest at 11 processors. When more processors are added, speedup declines. Figure 1-12 illustrates the estimated total execution time of the parallel algorithm along with its two components: computation time and communication time. Computation time is inversely proportional to the number of processors used, while communication time increases linearly with the number of processors used. After 11 processors, the increase in communication time is greater than the decrease in computation time, and the total execution time begins to increase.

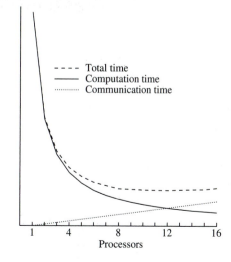

FIGURE 1-12   Total execution time of the data-parallel Sieve of Eratosthenes algorithm is the sum of the time spent computing and the time spent communicating. Computation time is inversely proportional to the number of processors; communication time is directly proportional to the number of processors.

1.4.3 Data-Parallel Approach with I/O

The prime-finding algorithms we have described are unrealistic, because they terminate without storing their results. Let's examine what happens when we execute a data-parallel implementation of the Sieve of Eratosthenes incorporating output on the shared-memory model of parallel computation.

The augmented shared memory model appears in Fig. 1-13. Assume only one processor at a time can access the I/O device. Let $i\beta$ denote the time needed for a processor to transmit i prime numbers to that device.

Let's predict the speedup achieved by the data-parallel algorithm that outputs all primes to the I/O device. Suppose $n = 1,000,000$. There are 78,498 primes less than 1,000,000. To find the total execution time, we take the total computation time,

$$\left(\left\lceil \frac{\lceil 1,000,000/p \rceil}{2} \right\rceil + \left\lceil \frac{\lceil 1,000,000/p \rceil}{3} \right\rceil + \cdots + \left\lceil \frac{\lceil 1,000,000/p \rceil}{997} \right\rceil \right) \chi$$

and add to it the total I/O time, $78,498\beta$.

The solid curve in Fig. 1-14 illustrates the expected speedup of this parallel algorithm for $1, 2, \ldots, 32$ processors, assuming that $\beta = \chi$. Figure 1-15

FIGURE 1-13 A shared-memory parallel model incorporating a sequential I/O device.

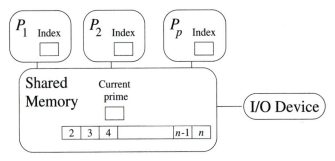

FIGURE 1-14 Expected speedup of data-parallel Sieve of Eratosthenes algorithm that outputs primes to an I/O device. Solid curve is speedup predicted from analysis. Dashed curve is maximum speedup as determined by Amdahl's law. This graph is for the case when $n = 1,000,000$ and $\beta = \chi$.

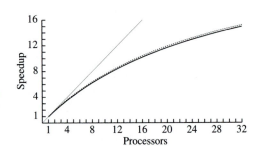

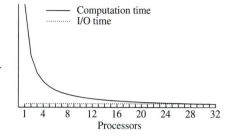

FIGURE 1-15   Total execution time of data-parallel output-producing Sieve of Eratosthenes algorithm as a function of its two components, computation time and I/O time. This graph is for the case when $n = 1,000,000$ and $\beta = \chi$.

illustrates the two components of the parallel execution time: computation time and output time. Because output to the I/O device must be performed sequentially, it puts a damper on the speedup achievable through parallelization. *Amdahl's law* is a way of expressing maximum speedup as a function of the amount of parallelism and the fraction of the computation that is inherently sequential.

Amdahl's law   (Amdahl 1967). Let f be the fraction of operations in a computation that must be performed sequentially, where $0 \leq f \leq 1$. The maximum speedup S achievable by a parallel computer with p processors performing the computation is

$$S \leq \frac{1}{f + (1 - f)/p}$$

For example, consider the algorithm we have just explored. When $n = 1,000,000$, the sequential algorithm marks $2,122,048$ cells and outputs $78,498$ primes. Assuming these two kinds of operations take the same amount of time, the total sequential time is $2,200,546$, and $f = 78,498/2,200,546 = .0357$. An upper bound on the speedup achievable by a parallel computer with p processors is

$$\frac{1}{.0357 + .9643/p}$$

The dotted curve in Fig. 1-14 plots the upper bound on the speedup of the algorithm as predicted by Amdahl's law.

Often, as the size of the problem increases, the fraction f of inherently sequential operations decreases, making the problem more amenable to parallelization. This phenomenon—called the **Amdahl effect**—is true for the application we have been considering. Figure 1-16 plots f as a function of n for the data-parallel sieve algorithm with output, assuming $\beta = \chi$.

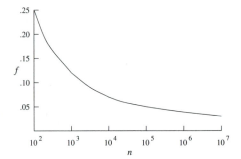

FIGURE 1-16   Fraction f of inherently sequential operations in data-parallel sieve algorithm with output, as a function of n, the size of the list of natural numbers, assuming $\beta = \chi$.

1.5   SUMMARY

Solving many important scientific problems demands computation rates that far exceed the capabilities of today's supercomputers. Because the speed of the fastest single processors is increasing more slowly than the speed of micro-processors, constructing supercomputers out of collections of microprocessors appears to be the surest route to achieving the incredibly high performance demanded by these problems.

Parallel algorithms can be categorized as either data parallel or control parallel. Data parallelism is the use of multiple functional units to apply the same operation to different elements of a data set. Control parallelism is achieved through the simultaneous application of different operations to different data elements. The flow of data among control-parallel processes may be complex. If the flow graph forms a simple, directed path, then we say the algorithm is pipelined. Scalable algorithms are desirable, because they permit larger problems to be solved on more massively parallel machines. As a rule, data-parallel algorithms are more scalable than control-parallel algorithms, because the level of control parallelism is usually a constant, independent of the problem size, while the level of data parallelism is an increasing function of the problem size.

In our examination of parallel algorithms to implement the Sieve of Eratosthenes, we encountered some typical design problems. In the control-parallel algorithm targeted to a shared-memory model, we saw problems that can result from the uncontrolled parallel access to shared resources. In the data-parallel algorithm targeted to a private-memory model, we saw that by increasing processors we increase the communication overhead of the parallel algorithm. Eventually the increase in communication time exceeds the decrease in computation time brought about by adding processors. When this point is reached, adding more processors increases, rather than decreases, total execution time.

In our third parallel algorithm we saw how a sequential component—in this case the time needed to access an output device—can put a damper on the speedup achievable through parallelization. Amdahl's law expresses maximum speedup as a function of the inherently sequential component and the number of processors executing a parallel algorithm. However, an ameliorating factor is that as the size of the problem increases, inherently sequential operations constitute a smaller fraction of the total computation, making the problem more amenable to parallelization.

1.6 BIBLIOGRAPHIC NOTES

All the references in this book can be found in the Bibliography at the end of the text.

Since the first edition of this book appeared in 1987, several other textbooks devoted to parallel algorithms and/or parallel computing have entered the market. These texts include Akl (1989), Anderson (1989), JáJá (1992), Lakshmivarahan and Dhall (1990), Leighton (1992), and Lewis and El-Rewini (1992). Besides providing different perspectives on parallel computing, these texts can also serve as a source of additional exercises.

Other books that devote attention to parallel algorithms include Evans (1982), Fox et al. (1988), and Jamieson et al. (1987).

The Turing lecture of Cocke (1988) discusses efforts to improve computer performance and includes his prediction that "the search for future scientific computing performance has to concentrate on gross parallelism." Another look into the future of high performance computers has been written by Bell (1989).

Hillis and Steele (1986, 1987) discuss data-parallel algorithms.

Several authors have described parallel implementations of the Sieve of Eratosthenes. Bokhari (1987) describes a control-parallel implementation that achieves modest speedup. Lansdowne et al. (1987) point out the weaknesses in Bokhari's algorithm and describe the implementation of a data-parallel version. Beck and Olien (1989) have implemented the algorithm of Lansdowne et al. (1987) on the Sequent Balance. Carriero and Gelernter (1989a) have compared several C-Linda implementations of the Sieve of Eratosthenes.

In the past, a number of arguments have been proposed against the merits of high-level parallelism. For instance, **Grosch's law** states that the speed of computers is proportional to the square of their cost (Grosch 1953, 1975). Modern studies of the price and performance of computer systems seem to indicate that Grosch's law no longer holds (Kang et al. 1986; Mendelson 1987).

Another argument against massive parallelism is **Minsky's conjecture**, which states that the speedup achievable by a parallel computer increases as the logarithm of the number of processing elements, thus making large-scale parallelism unproductive (Minksy and Papert 1971). In this book we will provide many examples to disprove Minsky's conjecture.

Developments in parallel computer architectures and parallel algorithms continue at an increasing pace. Journals and magazines regularly containing articles on parallel computing include *Communications of the ACM*; *Computer*; *Concurrency: Practice and Experience*; *Future Generations Computer Systems*; *IEEE Transactions on Computers*; *IEEE Parallel and Distributed Technology: Systems and Applications*; *IEEE Transactions on Parallel and Distributed Sys-*

tems; *IEEE Transactions on Software Engineering*; *International Journal of Parallel Programming*; *Journal of Parallel Algorithms and Applications*; *Journal of Parallel and Distributed Computing*; *New Generation Computing*; and *Parallel Computing*.

Conferences encompassing theoretical and/or practical aspects of parallel computing include the Annual Symposium on Foundations of Computer Science, the Annual Symposium on Computer Architecture, the Annual Symposium on Theory of Computing, Frontiers of Massively Parallel Computation, the International Conference on Parallel Processing, the International Parallel Processing Symposium, the SIAM Conference on Parallel Processing for Scientific Computing, Supercomputing '9X, and the Symposium on Principles and Practice of Parallel Programming.

1.7   PROBLEMS

1-1   Try this experiment with a few friends. Shuffle a deck of cards, then determine how long it takes one person to sort the cards into the order A♠, 2♠, ..., K♠, A♡, 2♡, ..., K♡, A♣, 2♣, ..., K♣, A◇, 2◇, ..., K◇. (Is it faster to sort the cards initially by suit or by value?) How long does it take p people to sort p decks of shuffled cards? How long does it take p people to sort one deck of cards? Try this experiment for $p = 1, 2, ..., 6$.

1-2   You have been assigned the task of computing the sum of one thousand 4-digit numbers as rapidly as possible. You hold in your hands a stack of 1,000 index cards, each containing a single number, and you are in charge of 1,000 expert accountants, each sitting at a desk in a cavernous room. Each accountant has a calculator.

  a   Describe a fast method of distributing cards to accountants.

  b   Describe a fast method of accumulating the subtotals generated by the active accountants into a grand total.

  c   Draw a graph that plots your best estimate of the time needed to compute the grand total as a function of the number of accountants you choose to use.

  d   Add another curve to the graph you drew in part **c**, estimating the time needed to compute the grand total of 10,000 numbers, given $1, ..., 1000$ accountants.

  e   Draw a speedup chart that plots speedup achieved on the two addition problems in parts **c** and **d** as a function of number of accountants.

  f   Explain why speedup does not reach 1,000 in either case.

1-3   Given a task that can be divided into m subtasks, each requiring 1 unit of time, how much time is required for an m-stage pipeline to process n tasks?

1-4   How many widgets must the pipelined widget-assembly machine of Fig. 1-4b assemble in order to achieve a speedup of 3 over the sequential machine? Justify your answer.

1-5   How many widgets must the parallel widget-assembly machine of Fig. 1-4c assemble in order to achieve a speedup of 3 over the sequential machine? Justify your answer.

1-6 Consider a parallel pipelined widget-assembly machine with three pipelines, each pipeline having three segments. Draw the speedup curve for this machine for $1, \ldots, 10$ widgets assembled.

1-7 A copy machine's feeder tray holds pages to be copied. Assume it takes 5 seconds to load a group of pages into the feeder before copying and 10 seconds to unload the originals and the copies after copying. If the copier takes 4 seconds to print a page and 1 second to print every subsequent page, what is the minimum capacity of the feeder tray necessary to ensure that the effective throughput of the copier asymptotically approaches 40 pages per minute as the length of the original document increases?

1-8 The task graph shown in Fig. 1-17 represents an image processing application. Each bubble represents an inherently sequential task. There are 12 tasks: an input task, 10 computation tasks, and an output task. Each of the 12 tasks can be accomplished in 1 unit of time on one processor. The input task must complete before any computational tasks begin. Likewise, all 10 computational tasks must complete before the output task begins. The input task consumes the entire bandwidth of the input device. The output task consumes the entire bandwidth of the output device.

a What is the maximum speedup that can be achieved if this problem is solved on two processors? (Hint: Processors do not have to receive the message elements in order.)

b What is an upper bound on the speedup that can be achieved if this problem is solved with parallel processors?

c What is the smallest number of processors sufficient to achieve the speedup given in part **b**?

d What is the maximum speedup that can be achieved solving five instances of this problem on two processors? Continue to assume that there is one input device and one output device.

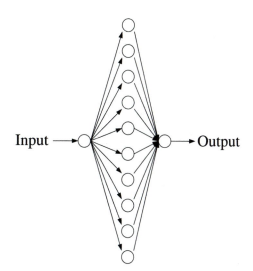

FIGURE 1-17   Task graph for Prob. 1-8.

e What is an upper bound on the speedup that can be achieved solving 100 instances of this problem with parallel processors? Continue to assume that there is one input device and one output device.

f What is the smallest number of processors sufficient to achieve the speedup given in part **e**?

1-9 Imagine a computer with p processors, each connected with every other processor by two unidirectional communication channels. (A four-processor system is shown in Fig. 1-18.) Suppose for any two processors i and j, it takes k units of time for processor i to send a k-element message to processor j, for all $k \geq 0$. In addition, suppose every processor has the ability to send and receive different messages concurrently on all its communication channels without slowing the communication rate on any channel. Determine how long it takes for an n-element message to be communicated from a single processor to every other processor in the network. In other words, how long does it take for one processor to broadcast an n-element message to the other $p - 1$ processors? (Hint: Processors do not have to receive the message elements in order.)

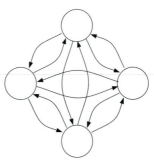

FIGURE 1-18   Processor organization for Prob. 1-9.

1-10 A sequential implementation of the Sieve of Eratosthenes marks about 2.2 million cells in order to compute all primes less than 1 million. Estimate the maximum speedup achievable by the control-parallel version of the Sieve of Eratosthenes as it finds all primes less than 1 million.

1-11 Figure 1-11 illustrates the estimated speedup of the data-parallel Sieve of Eratosthenes algorithm, assuming that $n = 1,000,000$ and $\lambda = 100\chi$. Augment this figure with two additional speedup curves, one for the case where $\lambda = 10\chi$ and one for the case where $\lambda = 1,000\chi$. Assume n is unchanged.

1-12 Estimate the speedup achievable by $1, 2, \ldots, 16$ processors executing the data-parallel Sieve of Eratosthenes program
a for $n = 1,000$, assuming the parallel model of Fig. 1-10 and $\lambda = 100\chi$.
b for $n = 1,000$, assuming the parallel model of Fig. 1-8.

1-13 Assume the communication network connecting the processors in Fig. 1-10b supports concurrent message passing. Propose a method faster than that described in this book for processor 1 to broadcast prime numbers to all other processors. Analyze the execution time and speedup on $1, 2, \ldots, 16$ processors of the new parallel algorithm, assuming $n = 1,000,000$ and $\lambda = 100\chi$.

1-14 The series of broadcast operations performed by the data-parallel Sieve of Eratosthenes algorithm on the model of Figure 1-10b can be reduced to a single broadcast operation. Processor 1 can compute all primes less than or equal to $\sqrt{n}$ and broadcast the entire list of values at once. Then every processor uses this list of primes to sieve its own set of, at most, $\lceil n/p \rceil$ values. No further communication is required. Assume it takes $\lambda + i\beta$ time units for a processor to send a message containing i prime numbers to another processor. Assume that $\lambda = 100\beta$. For $n = 1,000,000$ and $p = 16$, what is the smallest value of λ for which this single broadcast parallel algorithm is superior to the multiple broadcast algorithm?

1-15 Since 2 is the only even prime, one way to save memory and improve the speed of the sequential Sieve of Eratosthenes algorithm is to have the elements of the boolean array represent only odd numbers. In this scheme the first sieve step would mark multiples of the prime number 3.

    a Estimate the reduction in execution time of the sequential algorithm resulting from this improvement for $n = 1,000$ and $n = 1,000,000$.

    b The improved sequential algorithm can be used as the basis for an improved data-parallel algorithm. Using the machine model of Fig. 1-10b and assuming $\lambda = 100\chi$, estimate the execution time of the improved data-parallel algorithm for $1, 2, \ldots, 16$ processors.

    c Compute the speedup of the improved data-parallel algorithm over the improved sequential algorithm. Compare this speedup with the speedup estimated for the original data-parallel algorithm.

    d Why does the improved data-parallel algorithm achieve lower speedup than the original data-parallel algorithm?

    e Now that a better sequential algorithm exists, should the speedup figures in this chapter be modified?

1-16 In the control-parallel Sieve of Eratosthenes algorithm, a single processor is responsible for sieving all multiples of 2. For $n = 1,000$, sieving all multiples of 2 represents 35% of the total number of operations performed. By Amdahl's law the maximum speedup that can be achieved with $f = .35$ and $p = 2$ is $1/(.35 + .65/2) = 1.48$, yet our analysis showed a speedup of 2 with 2 processors. Where is the flaw in our reasoning?

1-17 Prove that if $(1/k)$th of the time spent executing an algorithm involves operations that must be performed sequentially, then an upper limit on the speedup achievable by executing the algorithm on parallel processors is k.

1-18 Name an algorithm (other than the Sieve of Eratosthenes) where the computational requirements grow faster than the I/O requirements. Name an algorithm where the computational requirements grow slower than the I/O requirements.

1-19 Define the following: microsecond (μs), millisecond (ms), nanosecond (ns), picosecond (ps), gigabyte (Gbyte), megabyte (Mbyte), and terabyte (Tbyte). A nanosecond is to a second as a second is to how many years?

1-20 If manufacturers of massively parallel computers are increasing the top performance of their systems by a factor of 100 every 5 years, how long does it take for performance to double?

1-21 Assume an implementation of the numerical ocean model described in Sec. 1.1 performs 30 billion floating-point operations to simulate 10 minutes of global ocean circulation.

a How many floating-point operations are needed to simulate 10 years of global ocean circulation?

b At what rate must the 10-year simulation execute, if it is to complete in 15 hours, e.g., between 5 P.M. and 8 A.M.?

c Assume that this application currently executes on a microprocessor-based parallel computer at the rate of 10 billion floating-point operations per second. If such architectures keep increasing in speed one-hundredfold every 5 years, when will a massively parallel supercomputer be capable of the execution rate computed in part **b**?

2

PRAM ALGORITHMS

Many hands make light work.

John Heywood, *Proverbs*

Perhaps some day students of algorithms and programming will see sequential computers as the exception, rather than the rule. Today, however, most students carry preconceived notions about algorithms and data structures from their experiences on sequential machines. New problem-solving techniques are needed in order to take full advantage of the power of parallel hardware.

This chapter provides a mental break from the von Neumann model and sequential algorithms. Our vehicle is the PRAM (parallel random access machine, pronounced "pea ram") model of parallel computation. The PRAM model allows parallel-algorithm designers to treat processing power as an unlimited resource, much as programmers of computers with virtual memory are allowed to treat memory as an unlimited resource. The PRAM model is unrealistically simple; it ignores the complexity of interprocessor communication. Because communication complexity is not an issue, the designer of PRAM algorithms can focus on the parallelism inherent in a particular computation.

For some important algorithms, such as reduction, cost-optimal PRAM solutions exist, meaning that the total number of operations performed by the PRAM algorithm is of the same complexity class as an optimal-sequential algorithm. In Chap. 6 we demonstrate how cost-optimal PRAM algorithms can serve as a foundation for efficient algorithms on real parallel computers.

This chapter begins with a review of the standard RAM model of sequential computation. Section 2.2 describes the PRAM model of parallel computation. In Sec. 2.3 we present five PRAM algorithms and analyze their complexity. We discuss Brent's theorem, used to determine when the number of processors used in a PRAM algorithm can be reduced without increasing the time complexity in Sec 2.4. In Sec. 2.5, we relate the PRAM model to complexity theory.

2.1   A MODEL OF SERIAL COMPUTATION

The **random access machine (RAM)** is a model of a one-address computer. A RAM consists of a memory, a read-only input tape, a write-only output tape, and a program (Fig. 2-1). The program is not stored in memory and cannot be modified. The input tape contains a sequence of integers. Every time an input value is read, the input head advances one square. Likewise, the output head advances after every write. Memory consists of an unbounded sequence of registers, designated $r_0, r_1, r_2, \ldots$. Each register can hold a single integer. Register r_0 is the accumulator, where computations are performed.

The exact instructions are not important, as long as they resemble the instructions found on an actual computer. Hence a RAM should have instructions along the lines of load, store, read, write, add, subtract, multiply, divide, test, jump, and halt.

The **worst-case time complexity** of a RAM program is the function $f(n)$, the maximum time taken by the program to execute over all inputs of size n. The **expected time complexity** of a RAM program is the average, overall inputs of size n, of the execution times. Analogous definitions hold for **worst-case space complexity** and **expected space complexity** by substituting the word "space" for "time" in the above definitions.

FIGURE 2-1   The random access machine (RAM) model of serial computation. (Aho, Hopcroft, and Ullman 1974.)

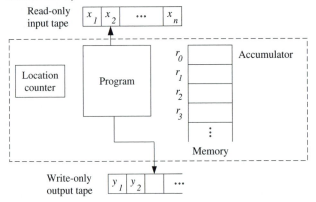

There are two ways of measuring time and space on the RAM model. The **uniform cost criterion** says each RAM instruction requires one time unit to execute and every register requires one unit of space. The **logarithmic cost criterion** takes into account that an actual word of memory has a limited storage capacity. The uniform cost criterion is appropriate if the values manipulated by the program always fit into one computer word. That is always the case in this text; hence we always use the uniform cost criterion when computing time and space complexity.

2.2 THE PRAM MODEL OF PARALLEL COMPUTATION

A **PRAM** consists of a control unit, global memory, and an unbounded set of processors, each with its own private memory (Fortune and Wyllie 1978) (see Fig. 2-2). Although active processors execute identical instructions, every processor has a unique index, and the value of a processor's index can be used to enable or disable the processor or influence which memory location it accesses.

A PRAM computation begins with the input stored in global memory and a single active processing element. During each step of the computation an active, enabled processor may read a value from a single private or global memory location, perform a single RAM operation, and write into one local or global memory location. Alternatively, during a computation step a processor may activate another processor. All active, enabled processors must execute the same instruction, albeit on different memory locations. The computation terminates when the last processor halts.

Definition 2.1. The **cost** of a PRAM computation is the product of the parallel time complexity and the number of processors used. For example, a PRAM algorithm that has time complexity $\Theta(\log p)$ using p processors has cost $\Theta(p \log p)$.

FIGURE 2-2   The PRAM model of parallel computation.

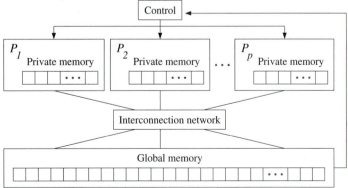

Various PRAM models differ in how they handle read or write conflicts; i.e., when two or more processors attempt to read from, or write to, the same global memory location. Most of the results in the research literature have been based upon one of the following models (Li and Yesha 1989):

1 EREW (Exclusive Read Exclusive Write): Read or write conflicts are not allowed.

2 CREW (Concurrent Read Exclusive Write): Concurrent reading allowed; i.e., multiple processors may read from the same global memory location during the same instruction step. Write conflicts are not allowed. (This is the default PRAM model.)

3 CRCW (Concurrent Read Concurrent Write): Concurrent reading and concurrent writing allowed. A variety of CRCW models exist with different policies for handling concurrent writes to the same global address. We list three different models:

a. COMMON. All processors concurrently writing into the same global address must be writing the same value.

b. ARBITRARY. If multiple processors concurrently write to the same global address, one of the competing processors is arbitrarily chosen as the "winner," and its value is written into the register.

c. PRIORITY. If multiple processors concurrently write to the same global address, the processor with the lowest index succeeds in writing its value into the memory location.

Let us examine the relative strengths of these models. The EREW PRAM model is the weakest. Clearly a CREW PRAM can execute any EREW PRAM algorithm in the same amount of time; the concurrent read facility is simply not used. Similarly, a CRCW PRAM can execute any EREW PRAM algorithm in the same amount of time.

The PRIORITY PRAM model is the strongest. Any algorithm designed for the COMMON PRAM model will execute with the same complexity on the ARBITRARY PRAM and PRIORITY PRAM models as well, for if all processors writing to the same location write the same value, choosing an arbitrary processor would cause the same result. Likewise, if an algorithm executes correctly when an arbitrary processor is chosen as the "winner," the processor with the lowest index is as reasonable an alternative as any other. Hence any algorithm designed for the ARBITRARY PRAM model will execute with the same time complexity on the PRIORITY PRAM model.

Because the PRIORITY PRAM model is stronger than the EREW PRAM model, an algorithm to solve a problem on the EREW PRAM can have higher time complexity than an algorithm solving the same problem on the PRIORITY PRAM model. Theorem 2.1 quantifies the increase in parallel time complexity that can occur when moving from the PRIORITY PRAM model to the EREW PRAM model. First, we state a lemma proven by R. Cole.

Lemma 2.1. (See Cole [1988].) A p-processor EREW PRAM can sort a p-element array stored in global memory in $\Theta(\log p)$ time.

Theorem 2.1. (See Eckstein [1979], Vishkin [1983].) A p-processor PRIORITY PRAM can be simulated by a p-processor EREW PRAM with the time complexity increased by a factor of $\Theta(\log p)$.

Proof. Assume the PRIORITY PRAM algorithm uses processors $P_1, P_2, \ldots, P_p$ and global memory locations $M_1, M_2, \ldots, M_m$. The EREW PRAM uses auxiliary global memory locations $T_1, T_2, \ldots, T_p$ and $S_1, S_2, \ldots, S_p$ to simulate each read or write step of the PRIORITY PRAM. See Fig. 2-3. When processor P_i in the PRIORITY PRAM algorithm accesses memory location M_j, processor P_i in the EREW PRAM algorithm writes the ordered pair (j, i) in memory location T_i. Then the EREW PRAM sorts the elements of T. This step takes time $\Theta(\log p)$ (Lemma 2.1). By reading adjacent entries in the sorted array, the highest priority processor accessing any particular location can be found in constant time. Processor P_1 reads memory location T_1, retrieves the ordered pair (i_1, j_1), and writes a 1 into global memory location S_{j_1}. The remaining processors P_k, where $2 \le k \le p$, first read memory location T_k and then read memory location T_{k-1}. If $i_k \ne i_{k-1}$, then processor P_k writes a 1 into S_{j_k}. Otherwise, processor P_k writes a 0 into S_{j_k}. At this point the elements of S with value 1 correspond to the highest priority processors accessing each memory location.

FIGURE 2-3   A concurrent write operation, which takes constant time on a p-processor PRIORITY PRAM, can be simulated in $\Theta(\log p)$ time on a p-processor EREW PRAM. (a) Concurrent write on the PRIORITY PRAM model. Processors P_1, P_2, and P_4 attempt to write values to memory location M_3. Processor P_1 wins. Processors P_3 and P_5 attempt to write values to memory location M_7. Processor P_3 wins. (b) To simulate concurrent write on the EREW PRAM model, each processor writes an (address, processor number) pair to a unique element of T. The processors sort T in time $\Theta(\log p)$. In constant time processors can set to 1 those elements of S corresponding to the winning processors. (c) Winning processors write their values.

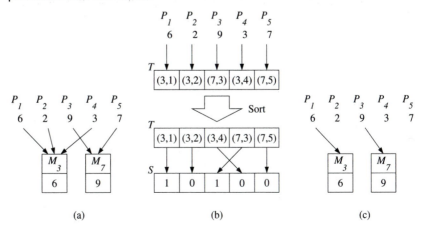

(a)   (b)   (c)

For a write instruction, the highest priority processor accessing each memory location writes its value. For a read instruction, the highest priority processor accessing each memory location reads that location's value, then duplicates the value in $O(\log p)$ time so there is a copy in a unique memory location for every processor to access the value.

2.3 PRAM ALGORITHMS

If a PRAM algorithm has lower time complexity than an optimal RAM algorithm, it is because parallelism has been used. Because a PRAM algorithm begins with only a single processor active, PRAM algorithms have two phases. In the first phase a sufficient number of processors are activated, and in the second phase these activated processors perform the computation in parallel.

Given a single active processor, it is easy to see that $\lceil \log p \rceil$ activation steps are both necessary and sufficient for p processors to become active, since the number of active processors can double by excuting a single instruction (Fig. 2-4). Unless otherwise noted, all logarithms in this book are to base 2. In our presentation of PRAM algorithms we use the meta-instruction

spawn (*<processor names>*)

to denote this logarithmic time generation of processors from a single active processor.

To make the second phase PRAM algorithm computations easier to read, we allow references to global registers to be array references. We assume there is a mapping from these array references to the appropriate global registers.

FIGURE 2-4 Exactly $\lceil \log p \rceil$ processor activation steps are necessary and sufficient to change from 1 active processor to p active processors.

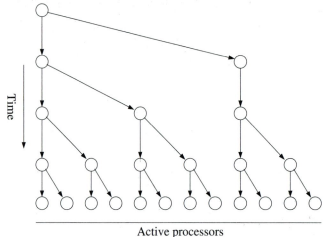

Active processors

The construct

for all *<processor list>* do *<{statement list>* endfor

denotes a code segment to be executed in parallel by all the specified processors.

Besides the special constructs already described, we express PRAM algorithms using the familiar control structures if ...then ...else ...endif, for ...endfor, while ...endwhile, and repeat ...until. The symbol $\leftarrow$ denotes assignment.

In the remainder of this section we present problems and solutions using the PRAM model.

2.3.1 Parallel Reduction

The binary tree is one of the most important paradigms of parallel computing (Fig. 2-5). In some algorithms data flows top-down from the root of the tree to the leaves. Broadcast and divide-and-conquer algorithms both fit this model. In **broadcast** algorithms the root sends the same data to every leaf. In **divide-and-conquer** algorithms the tree represents the recursive subdivision of problems into subproblems.

In other algorithms data flows bottom-up from the leaves of the tree to the root. These are called **fan-in** or **reduction** operations.

More formally, given a set of n values $a_1, a_2, \ldots, a_n$ and an associative binary operator $\oplus$, **reduction** is the process of computing $a_1 \oplus a_2 \oplus \cdots \oplus a_n$.

Parallel summation is an example of a reduction operation.

The processors in a PRAM manipulate data stored in global registers. To implement the summation algorithm illustrated in Figure 2-5, we represent each tree node with an element in an array. The mapping from the tree to the array is straightforward. Figure 2-6 illustrates how an array-based PRAM algorithm finds the sum of n values. Pseudocode for this algorithm appears in Fig. 2-7.

Let us analyze the complexity of this algorithm. The spawn routine requires $\lceil \log \lfloor n/2 \rfloor \rceil$ doubling steps. The sequential for loop executes $\lceil \log n \rceil$ times, and each iteration has constant time complexity. Hence the overall time complexity of the algorithm is $\Theta(\log n)$, given $\lfloor n/2 \rfloor$ processors.

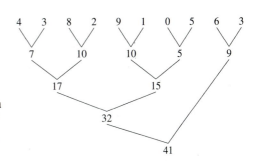

FIGURE 2-5 Parallel summation is an example of a reduction operation. Parallel reduction can be represented by a binary tree. A group of n values can be added in $\lceil \log n \rceil$ parallel addition steps.

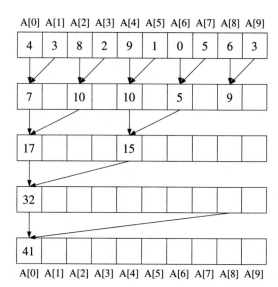

FIGURE 2-6   Example of operation of PRAM
algorithm to find sum of 10 values.

2.3.2   Prefix Sums

Given a set of n values $a_1, a_2, \ldots, a_n$ and an associative operation $\oplus$, the **prefix sums** problem is to compute the n quantities:

$$a_1$$
$$a_1 \oplus a_2$$
$$a_1 \oplus a_2 \oplus a_3$$
$$\cdots$$
$$a_1 \oplus a_2 \oplus a_3 \oplus \cdots \oplus a_n$$

For example, given the operation $+$ and the array of integers $\{3, 1, 0, 4, 2\}$, the prefix sums of the array are $\{3, 4, 4, 8, 10\}$.

FIGURE 2-7   EREW PRAM algorithm to sum n elements using $\lfloor n/2 \rfloor$ processors.

```
SUM (EREW PRAM)
Initial condition: List of n ≥ 1 elements stored in A[0···(n − 1)]
Final condition: Sum of elements stored in A[0]
Global variables: n, A[0···(n − 1)], j
begin
  spawn (P₀, P₁, P₂, ···, P⌊ n/2 ⌋−1)
  for all Pᵢ where 0 ≤ i ≤ ⌊ n/2 ⌋ − 1 do
    for j ← 0 to ⌈log n⌉ − 1 do
      if i modulo 2ʲ = 0 and 2i + 2ʲ < n then
        A[2i] ← A[2i] + A[2i + 2ʲ]
      endif
    endfor
  endfor
end
```

FIGURE 2-8   Packing elements is one application of prefix sums. (a) Array A contains both uppercase and lowercase letters. We want to pack uppercase letters into beginning of A. (b) Array T contains a 1 for every uppercase letter and a 0 for every lowercase letter. (c) Array T after prefix sums have been computed. For each element of A containing an uppercase letter, the corresponding element of T is that element's index in the packed array. (d) Array A after packing.

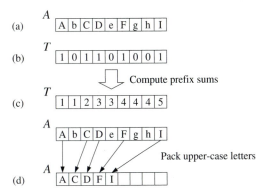

Prefix sums are also called **parallel prefixes** and **scans**. Prefix sums have many uses. For instance, suppose we are given an array A of n letters. We want to pack the uppercase letters in the initial portion of A while maintaining their order. See Fig. 2-8. First we initialize the elements of an auxiliary array T of size n. An element of T is 0 if the corresponding element of A is a lowercase letter, and an element of T is 1 if the corresponding element of A is an uppercase letter. Second, we compute the prefix sums of T using the addition operation. Now for every uppercase letter L located at $A[i]$, the value of $T[i]$ is the index of L in the packed array.

Figure 2-9 is a PRAM algorithm that computes prefix sums. The complexity of the algorithm is identical to the complexity of the parallel sum-finding algorithm. The **spawn** routine requires $\lceil \log(n-1) \rceil$ instructions. The sequential **for** loop executes $\lceil \log n \rceil$ times, and each iteration has constant time complexity. Hence the overall time complexity of the algorithm is $\Theta(\log n)$, given $n-1$ processors.

Figure 2-10 illustrates the prefix sums algorithm on a list of 10 values.

FIGURE 2-9   PRAM algorithm to find prefix sums of an n-element list using $n-1$ processors.

```
PREFIX.SUMS (CREW PRAM):
Initial condition: List of n ≥ 1 elements stored in A[0 ··· (n − 1)]
Final condition: Each element A[i] contains A[0] ⊕ A[1] ⊕ ··· ⊕ A[i]
Global variables: n, A[0 ... (n − 1)], j
begin
    spawn (P₁, P₂, ..., Pₙ₋₁)
    for all Pᵢ where 1 ≤ i ≤ n − 1 do
        for j ← 0 to ⌈log n⌉ − 1 do
            if i − 2ʲ ≥ 0 then
                A[i] ← A[i] + A[i − 2ʲ]
            endif
        endfor
    endfor
end
```

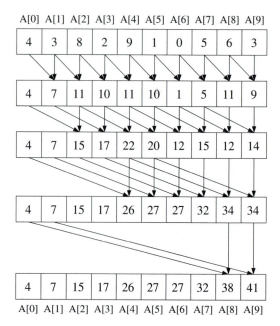

FIGURE 2-10   All prefix sums of a list of n values can be computed in $\lceil \log n \rceil$ addition steps on an EREW PRAM.

2.3.3 List Ranking

Consider the problem of finding, for each of n elements on a linked list, the *suffix sums* of the last i elements on the list, where $1 \leq i \leq n$ (Fig. 2-11). The **suffix sums** problem is a variant of the prefix sums problem, where an array is replaced by a linked list, and the sums are computed from the end, rather than from the beginning (Karp and Ramachandran 1990). (If the elements on the list are either 0 or 1, and the associative operation $\oplus$ is addition, the problem is usually called the **list ranking** problem. However, the algorithm in this section also works in the more general case.)

One way to determine list position is to count the number of links traversed between the list element and the end of the list. Only a single pointer can be followed in one step, and there are $n - 1$ pointers between the first list element and the end of the list. How can any algorithm traverse such a list in less than $\Theta(n)$ time?

If we associate a processor with every list element and jump pointers in parallel, the distance to the end of the list is cut in half through the instruction $next[i] \leftarrow next[next[i]]$.

Hence a logarithmic number of pointer-jumping steps are sufficient to collapse the list so that every list element points to the last list element. If a processor adds to its own link-traversal count, $position[i]$, the current link-traversal count of the successors it encounters, the list position will be correctly determined.

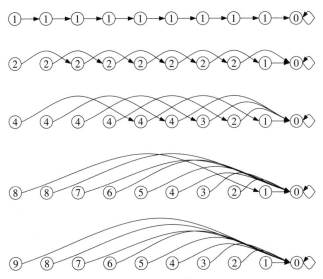

FIGURE 2-11   The position of each item on an n-element linked list can be determined in $\lceil \log n \rceil$ pointer-jumping steps.

The PRAM algorithm to determine the position of each element on a singly linked list appears in Fig. 2-12.

We have seen that spawning n processors has time complexity $\Theta(\log n)$. Because the constant time for loop executes at most $\lceil \log n \rceil$ times, the complexity of the parallel algorithm is $\Theta(\log n)$ using n processors.

FIGURE 2-12   PRAM algorithm to compute, for each element of a singly-linked list, its distance from the end of the list.

LIST.RANKING (CREW PRAM):
  Initial condition: Values in array *next* represent a linked list
  Final condition: Values in array *position* contain original distance
                 of each element from end of list
  Global variables: n, $position[0 \ldots (n-1)]$, $next[0 \ldots (n-1)]$, j
  begin
    spawn (P_0, P_1, P_2, ..., P_{n-1})
    for all P_i where $0 \leq i \leq n - 1$ do
      if $next[i] = i$ then $position[i] \leftarrow 0$
      else $position[i] \leftarrow 1$
      endif
      for $j \leftarrow 1$ to $\lceil \log n \rceil$ do
        $position[i] \leftarrow position[i] + position[next[i]]$
        $next[i] \leftarrow next[next[i]]$
      endfor
    endfor
  end

2.3.4   Preorder Tree Traversal

Sometimes it is appropriate to attempt to reduce a complicated-looking problem into a simpler one for which a fast parallel algorithm is already known. The problem of numbering the vertices of a rooted tree in preorder (depth-first search order) is a case in point. At first glance the problem of preorder traversal may seem inherently sequential. Consider its common recursive description:

```
PREORDER.TRAVERSAL (nodeptr) :

  begin
    if nodeptr≠ null then
        nodecount ← nodecount +1
        nodeptr.label ← nodecount
      PREORDER.TRAVERSAL (nodeptr.left)
      PREORDER.TRAVERSAL (nodeptr.right)
    endif
  end
```

Where is the parallelism? The fundamental operation assigns a label to a node. We cannot assign labels to the vertices in the right subtree until we know how many vertices are in the left subtree. We cannot assign labels to the vertices in the right subtree of the left subtree until we know how many vertices are in the left subtree of the left subtree, and so on. Viewed this way, the algorithm seems inherently sequential.

So let's take another view of the problem. Instead of focusing on the tree's *vertices*, let's think about the tree's *edges*. When we perform a preorder traversal, we systematically work our way through all the edges of the tree. In fact, we pass along every edge twice—once heading down from parent vertex to child vertex and once going back up. If we divide each tree edge into two edges, one corresponding to the downward traversal and one corresponding to the upward traversal, then the problem of traversing a tree turns into the problem of traversing a singly-linked list, which we have just seen in parallel.

This edge-oriented view of tree traversal leads to a fast parallel algorithm, first published by Tarjan and Vishkin (1984). Let us consider the algorithm in detail. The algorithm has four phases (Fig. 2-13). In step one the algorithm constructs a singly-linked list. Each vertex of the singly-linked list corresponds to a downward or upward edge traversal of the tree.

In step two the algorithm assigns weights to the vertices of the newly created singly-linked list. In the preorder traversal algorithm, a vertex is labeled as soon as it is encountered via a downward edge traversal. (The root vertex is an exception and must be handled differently.) For this reason every vertex in the singly-linked list corresponding to a downward edge gets the weight 1, meaning that the node count is incremented when this edge is traversed. List elements corresponding to upward edges have the weight 0, because the node

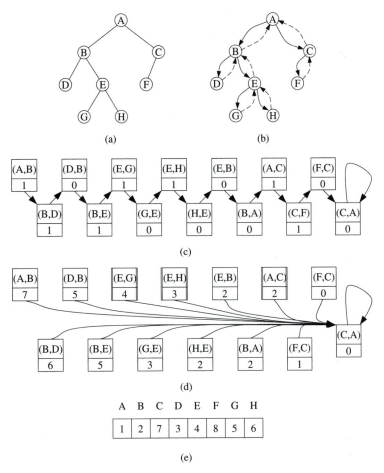

FIGURE 2-13   Preorder traversal of a rooted tree. (a) Tree. (b) Double tree edges, distinguishing downward edges from upward edges. (c) Build linked list out of directed tree edges. Associate 1 with downward edges and 0 with upward edges. (d) Use pointer jumping to compute total weight from each vertex to end of list. Bold elements of linked list correspond to downward edges. Processors managing these elements assign preorder values. For example, element (E, G) has weight 4, meaning tree node G is fourth node from end of preorder traversal list. The tree has 8 nodes, so we can compute that tree node G has label 5 in preorder traversal. (e) Preorder traversal values.

count does not increase when the preorder traversal works its way back up the tree through previously labeled nodes.

In the third phase of the parallel algorithm we compute, for each element of the singly-linked list, the rank of that list element.

In step four the processors associated with downward edges use the ranks they have computed to assign a preorder traversal number to their associated tree nodes (the node at the end of the downward edge).

Our implementation of the parallel preorder traversal algorithm uses an unusual data structure to represent the tree (see Fig 2-14). For every tree node, the data structure stores, the node's parent, immediate sibling to the right, and leftmost child. Representing the tree this way keeps the amount of data stored at a constant for each tree node and simplifies tree traversal.

Figure 2-15 contains the PRAM algorithm for preorder tree traversal. The algorithm associates a processor with each traversed edge. A tree with n nodes has $n - 1$ edges. Since we are dividing each edge into a downward edge and an upward edge, the algorithm needs $2(n - 1)$ processors to manipulate the $2(n - 1)$ elements of the singly-linked list of elements corresponding to the edge traversals.

Once all the processors have been activated, they construct a linked list of elements corresponding to edges in the preorder traversal. Given edge (i, j), each processor must compute the successor to that edge in the traversal. If $parent[i] = j$, the edge is moving upward in the tree, from a child node to its parent. Upward edges have three kinds of successors. If the child has a sibling, the successor edge goes from the parent node to the sibling. Otherwise, if the child has a grandparent, the successor edge goes from the parent node to the grandparent. If both of these conditions fail, the edge is at the end of the tree traversal, so we put a loop at the end of the element list. In this case we also know the identity of the root node, and we set its preorder number to 1.

Next we consider the case where $parent[i] \neq j$; that is, where the edge is moving downward in the tree, from a parent node to one of its children. There are only two kinds of successor edges. If the child node itself has children, the successor is the edge from the child to the grandchild. Otherwise, the child node is a leaf, and the successor is the edge from the child back to the parent.

After the processors construct the linked list, they assign a position value of 1 to those elements corresponding to downward edges and 0 to those elements corresponding to upward edges.

The pointer-jumping loop follows. The final position values indicate the number of preorder traversal nodes between the list element and the end of the list. To compute each node's preorder traversal label, each processor associated

FIGURE 2-14   We can represent a rooted tree with a data structure that stores, for every tree node, the node's parent, immediate sibling to the right, and leftmost child.

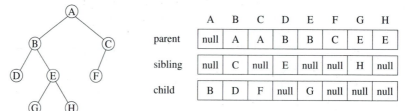

	A	B	C	D	E	F	G	H
parent	null	A	A	B	B	C	E	E
sibling	null	C	null	E	null	null	H	null
child	B	D	F	null	G	null	null	null

PREORDER.TREE.TRAVERSAL (CREW PRAM):
Global n {Number of vertices in tree}
          $parent[1 \ldots n]$ {Vertex number of parent node}
          $child[1 \ldots n]$ {Vertex number of first child}
          $sibling[1 \ldots n]$ {Vertex number of sibling}
          $succ[1 \ldots (n-1)]$ {Index of successor edge}
          $position[1 \ldots (n-1)]$ {Edge rank}
          $preorder[1 \ldots n]$ {Preorder traversal number}
begin
    spawn (set of all $P(i, j)$ where (i, j) is an edge)
    for all $P(i, j)$ where (i, j) is an edge do
      {Put the edges into a linked list}
      if $parent[i] = j$ then
        if $sibling[i] \neq$ null then
          $succ[(i, j)] \leftarrow (j, sibling[i])$
        else if $parent[j] \neq$ null then
          $succ[(i, j)] \leftarrow (j, parent[j])$
        else
          $succ[(i, j)] \leftarrow (i, j)$
          $preorder[j] \leftarrow 1$ {j is root of tree }
        endif
      else
        if $child[j] \neq$ null then $succ[(i, j)] \leftarrow (j, child[j])$
        else $succ[(i, j)] \leftarrow (j, i)$
        endif
      endif
      { Number of edges of the successor list }
      if $parent[i] = j$ then $position[(i, j)] \leftarrow 0$
      else $position[(i, j)] \leftarrow 1$
      endif
      {Perform suffix sum on successor list}
      for $k \leftarrow 1$ to $\lceil \log(2(n-1)) \rceil$ do
        $position[(i, j)] \leftarrow position[(i, j)] + position[succ[(i, j)]]$
        $succ[(i, j)] \leftarrow succ[succ[(i, j)]]$
      endfor
      {Assign preorder values}
      if $i = parent[j]$ then $preorder[j] \leftarrow n + 1 - position[(i, j)]$
      endif
    endfor
end

FIGURE 2-15   PRAM algorithm to label the nodes of a tree according to their position in a preorder traversal.

with a downward edge subtracts its value of *position* from $n + 1$. The added 1 causes the preorder traversal numbering to begin at 1, not 0.

We leave the complexity analysis of this algorithm as a simple exercise for the reader.

2.3.5   Merging Two Sorted Lists

Many PRAM algorithms achieve low time complexity by performing more operations than an optimal RAM algorithm. The problem of merging two sorted lists is another example.

One optimal RAM algorithm creates the merged list one element at a time. It requires at most $n - 1$ comparisons to merge two sorted lists of $n/2$ elements. Its time complexity is $\Theta(n)$. A PRAM algorithm can perform the task in $\Theta(\log n)$ time by assigning each list element its own processor. Every processor finds the position of its own element on the other list using binary search. Because an element's index on its own list is known, its place on the merged list can be computed when its index on the other list has been found and the two indices added. All n elements can be inserted into the merged list by their processors in constant time (see Fig. 2-16).

The pseudocode for the PRAM algorithm to merge two sorted lists appears in Fig. 2-17. In this version of the algorithm the two lists and their unions have disjoint values. Let's examine the algorithm in detail. As usual, the first step is to spawn the maximum number of processors needed at any point in the algorithm's execution. In this case we need n processors, one for each element of the two lists to be merged. After the processors are spawned, we immediately activate them. In parallel, the processors determine the range of indices they are going to search. The processors associated with elements in the lower half of the array will perform binary search on the elements in the upper half of the array, and vice versa.

FIGURE 2-16   Two lists having $n/2$ elements each can be merged in $\Theta(\log n)$ time.

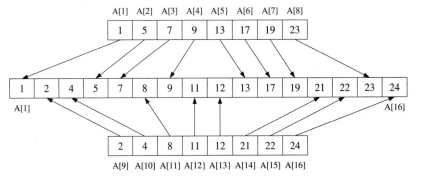

MERGE.LISTS (CREW PRAM):

Given: Two sorted lists of $n/2$ elements each, stored in
$A[1] \cdots A[n/2]$ and $A[(n/2)+1] \cdots A[n]$
The two lists and their unions have disjoint values
Final condition: Merged list in locations $A[1] \cdots A[n]$
Global $A[1 \cdots n]$
Local $x, low, high, index$
begin
  spawn $(P_1, P_2, \ldots, P_n)$
  for all P_i where $1 \leq i \leq n$ do
    { Each processor sets bounds for binary search }
    if $i \leq n/2$ then
      $low \leftarrow (n/2)+1$
      $high \leftarrow n$
    else
      $low \leftarrow 1$
      $high \leftarrow n/2$
    endif
    { Each processor performs binary search }
    $x \leftarrow A[i]$
    repeat
      $index \leftarrow \lfloor (low+high)/2 \rfloor$
      if $x < A[index]$ then
        $high \leftarrow index - 1$
      else
        $low \leftarrow index + 1$
      endif
    until $low > high$
    { Put value in correct position on merged list }
    $A[high + i - n/2] \leftarrow x$
  endfor
end

FIGURE 2-17 PRAM algorithm to merge two sorted lists. The two lists and their unions have disjoint values.

Every processor has a unique value of x, an element to be merged. The `repeat...until` loop implements binary search. When a processor exits the loop, its private value of *high* will be set to the index of the largest element on the list that is smaller than x.

Consider a processor P_i associated with value $A[i]$ in the lower half of the list. The processor's final value of *high* must be between $(n/2)$ and n. Element $A[i]$ is larger than $i - 1$ elements on the lower half of the list. It is also larger than $high - (n/2)$ elements on the upper half of the list. Therefore, we should put $A[i]$ on the merged list after $i + high - n/2 - 1$ other elements, at index $i + high - n/2$.

Now consider a processor P_i associated with value $A[i]$ in the upper half of the list. The processor's final value of *high* must be between 0 and $n/2$. Element $A[i]$ is larger than $i - (n/2 + 1)$ other elements on the upper half of the list. It is also larger than *high* elements on the lower half of the list. Therefore, we should put $A[i]$ on the merged list after $i + high - n/2 - 1$ other elements, at index $i + high - n/2$.

Since all processors use the same expression to place elements in their proper places on the merged list, every processor relocates its element using the same assignment statement at the end of the algorithm.

The total number of operations performed to merge the lists has increased from $\Theta(n)$ in the sequential algorithm to $\Theta(n \log n)$ in the parallel algorithm. This tactic is sensible only when the number of processors is unbounded. When we begin to develop algorithms for real parallel computers, with processors a limited resource, we must consider the cost of the parallel algorithm.

2.3.6 Graph Coloring

Determining if the vertices of a graph can be colored with c colors so that no two adjacent vertices are assigned the same color is called the **graph coloring problem**. To solve the problem quickly, we can create a processor for every possible coloring of the graph, then have each processor check to see if the coloring it represents is valid.

Assume the graph has n vertices. Given an $n \times n$ adjacency matrix and a positive constant c, a processor is created for every possible coloring of the graph. For example, processor $P(i_0, i_1, \ldots, i_{n-1})$ corresponds to a coloring of vertex 0 with color i_0, a coloring of vertex 1 with color i_1, ..., and a coloring of vertex $n - 1$ with color i_{n-1}.

Each processor initially sets its value in the n-dimensional *candidate* array to 1. It then spends $\Theta(n^2)$ time determining whether, for the particular assignment of colors to vertices it represents, two adjacent vertices have been given the same color. If $A[j, k] = 1$ and $i_j = i_k$, then the coloring is not valid, because $A[j, k] = 1$ means that vertices j and k are adjacent, and $i_j = i_k$ means that vertices j and k have the same color. If a processor detects an invalid coloring, it sets its value in the *candidate* array to 0. After the n^2 comparisons, if any element in the *candidate* array is still 1, then the coloring is valid. By summing over all c^n elements in the *candidate* array, it can be determined whether there exists a valid coloring (see Fig. 2-18). The CREW PRAM algorithm for graph coloring appears in Fig. 2-19.

Let us evaluate the time complexity of this algorithm. It takes $\Theta(\log c^n)$ time to spawn the c^n processors. Every processor executes the doubly-nested `for` loops in time $\Theta(n^2)$. Summing the c^n elements of answer requires time $\Theta(\log c^n)$ with the c^n processors we have available. The overall complexity of the algorithm, then, is $\Theta(\log c^n + n^2) = \Theta(n^2 + n \log c)$. Because $c < n$, the complexity expression reduces to $\Theta(n^2)$.

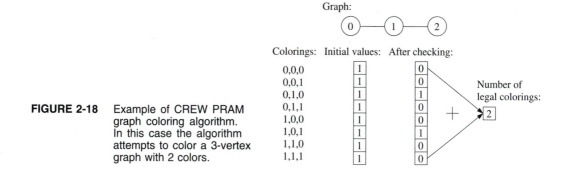

FIGURE 2-18   Example of CREW PRAM graph coloring algorithm. In this case the algorithm attempts to color a 3-vertex graph with 2 colors.

GRAPH.COLORING (CREW PRAM):

Global n {Number of vertices}
          c {Number of colors}
          $A[1...n][1...n]$ {Adjacency matrix}
          $candidate[1...c][1...c] \cdots [1...c]$ {n-dimensional boolean matrix}
          $valid$ {Number of valid colorings}
          j, k

begin
  spawn $(P(i_0, i_1, \ldots, i_{n-1}))$ where $0 \leq i_v < c$ for $0 \leq v < n$
  for all $P(i_0, i_1, \ldots, i_{n-1})$ where $0 \leq i_v < c$ for $0 \leq v < n$ do
    $candidate[i_0, i_1, \ldots, i_{n-1}] \leftarrow 1$
    for $j \leftarrow 0$ to $n-1$ do
      for $k \leftarrow 0$ to $n-1$ do
        if $A[j][k]$ and $i_j = i_k$ then
          $candidate[i_0, i_1, \ldots, i_n] \leftarrow 0$
        endif
      endfor
    endfor
    $valid \leftarrow \Sigma\ candidate$ {Sum of all elements of $candidate$}
  endfor
  if $valid > 0$ then print "Valid coloring exists"
  else printif "Valid coloring does not exist"
  endif
end

FIGURE 2-19   CREW PRAM algorithm to determine if a graph with n vertices can be colored with c colors.

2.4 REDUCING THE NUMBER OF PROCESSORS

Definition 2.2. A **cost optimal** parallel algorithm is an algorithm for which the cost is in the same complexity class as an optimal sequential algorithm.

None of the algorithms we presented in the previous section are cost optimal. For example, the parallel reduction algorithm has complexity $\Theta(\log n)$ given $\Theta(n)$ processors. This algorithm is not cost optimal because the product of its complexity and the number of processors is $\Theta(n \log n)$, which is greater than the complexity of an optimal sequential algorithm, $\Theta(n)$.

If, however, the total number of operations performed by the parallel algorithm is of the same complexity class as an optimal sequential algorithm, then a cost-optimal parallel algorithm does exist. Returning to our example, the parallel reduction algorithm performs about $n/2$ additions the first step, $n/4$ additions the second step, $n/8$ additions the third step, and so on, executing a total of $n - 1$ additions over the $\lceil \log n \rceil$ iterations. Since both the sequential and the parallel algorithms perform $n - 1$ additions, a cost-optimal variant of the parallel reduction algorithm exists.

Is there a cost-optimal parallel reduction algorithm that also has time complexity $\Theta(\log n)$? We can compute the minimum number of processors needed to perform the $n - 1$ operations in logarithmic time:

$$p = \frac{n-1}{\Theta(\log n)} \Rightarrow p = \Theta(n/\log n)$$

Once we have determined the appropriate number of processors, we need to verify that there is indeed a cost-optimal parallel-reduction algorithm with logarithmic time complexity. Theorem 2.2 lets us do that.

Theorem 2.2. (Brent's Theorem) (Brent 1974). Given A, a parallel algorithm with computation time t, if parallel algorithm A performs m computational operations, then p processors can execute algorithm A in time $t + (m - t)/p$.

Proof. Let s_i denote the number of computational operations performed by parallel algorithm A at step i, where $1 \leq i \leq t$. By definition $\sum_{i=1}^{t} s_i = m$. Using p processors we can simulate step i in time $\lceil s_i/p \rceil$. The entire computation A can be performed with p processors in time

$$\sum_{i=1}^{t} \left\lceil \frac{s_i}{p} \right\rceil \leq \sum_{i=1}^{t} \frac{s_i + p - 1}{p}$$

$$= \sum_{i=1}^{t} \frac{p}{p} + \sum_{i=1}^{t} \frac{s_i - 1}{p}$$

$$= t + (m - t)/p$$

Applying Brent's theorem to our parallel reduction algorithm, the execution time with $\lfloor \frac{n}{\log n} \rfloor$ processors is

$$\lceil \log n \rceil + \frac{n - 1 - \lceil \log n \rceil}{\lfloor \frac{n}{\log n} \rfloor} = \Theta\left(\log n + \log n - \frac{\log n}{n} - \frac{\log^2 n}{n} \right) = \Theta(\log n)$$

In this case reducing the number of processors from n to $\lfloor n/\log n \rfloor$ does not change the complexity of the parallel algorithm. Figure 2-20 illustrates how n values can be summed in $O(\log n)$ time using $\lfloor n/\log n \rfloor$ processors by associating no more than $\lceil \log n \rceil$ values per processor.

Let's consider another example. The prefix sums algorithm appearing in Sec. 2.3 executes in $\lceil \log n \rceil$ iterations. The number of operations performed in iteration i is $n - 2^i$. The total number of operations performed, then, is

$$\sum_{i=0}^{\lceil \log n \rceil - 1} n - 2^i = n \log n - (2^{\lceil \log n \rceil} - 1) = \Theta(n \log n)$$

This parallel algorithm is not cost optimal, because an optimal sequential algorithm can find all n prefix sums in $n - 1$ operations.

To reduce the cost, we must reduce the number of processors. However, if the processors simply emulate the current parallel algorithm—as they did in the modified parallel-sum algorithm—and do not change the the total number of operations performed, then the decrease in the number of processors will be offset by an increase in the execution time, and the cost will remain the same. If we are going to reduce the number of processors, we must make them work more efficiently.

When we reduce the number of processors, a single processor must manipulate a larger data set than in the original parallel algorithm. In many problems, including the computation of prefix sums, applying an optimal sequential algorithm will improve the efficiency of this portion of the parallel algorithm.

Figure 2-21 illustrates how we can use this idea to compute the prefix sums of n values given p processors, where $p < n - 1$. We divide the n values into p sets, each containing no more than $\lceil n/p \rceil$ values. The first $p - 1$ processors use the best sequential algorithm to find the sum of their $\lceil n/p \rceil$ values. This takes $\lceil n/p \rceil - 1$ steps. The processors compute the prefix sums of these subtotals in $\lceil \log(p - 1) \rceil$ time using the parallel algorithm described in Sec. 2.3. Finally,

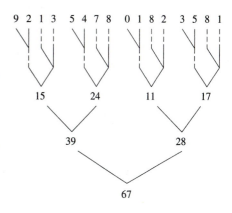

FIGURE 2-20   A PRAM can add n values in $\Theta(\log n)$ time using $\lfloor n/\log n \rfloor$ processors. During the first few iterations of the algorithm, each processor emulates a set of processors, adding to the execution time of the algorithm, but not increasing the overall complexity of the parallel algorithm beyond $\Theta(\log n)$. During later iterations, when no more than $\lfloor n/\log n \rfloor$ processors are needed, the algorithm is identical to the original PRAM algorithm.

FIGURE 2-21   Illustration of a cost-optimal parallel algorithm to find prefix sums. (a) Set of 14 values is divided into 4 subsets, 1 per processor. First 3 processors find sum of their values using best sequential algorithm. (b) First 3 processors compute prefix sums in parallel using algorithm of Sec. 2.3. (c) Each processor uses the sum of values in lower processors' blocks as base for computing prefix sums in its own block, using best sequential algorithm.

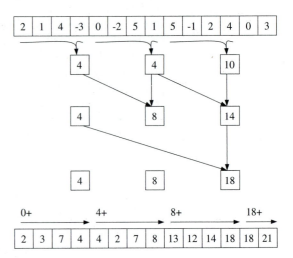

each processor uses the sum of the values in the lower blocks to compute the prefix sums of its block of values. This step requires $\lceil n/p \rceil$ additions. The execution time of the parallel algorithm is

$$\left\lceil \frac{n}{p} \right\rceil - 1 + \lceil \log(p-1) \rceil + \left\lceil \frac{n}{p} \right\rceil = \Theta \left(\frac{n}{p} + \log p \right)$$

The total number of addition steps performed is $\Theta(n + p \log p)$, meaning if p is small enough, the parallel algorithm will be cost-optimal.

Let's use Brent's theorem to explore the trade-off between processors and execution time. Executing this algorithm with p processors results in an execution time of

$$\Theta \left(\left(\frac{n}{p} + \log p \right) + \frac{n + p \log p - (\frac{n}{p} + \log p)}{p} \right) = \Theta \left(\frac{n}{p} + \log p \right)$$

Execution time is minimized when $p = \Omega(n/\log n)$. The parallel algorithm has optimal cost when $p = O(n/\log n)$. For this reason the value of p that ensures both optimal cost and minimum execution time is $p = \Theta(n/\log n)$.

2.5   PROBLEMS DEFYING FAST SOLUTIONS ON PRAMS

This section relates the PRAM model to the rest of complexity theory; it presumes the reader has a knowledge of standard complexity terms, such as $\mathcal{P}$, $\mathcal{NP}$, and $\mathcal{NP}$-complete.

Definition 2.3. The expression $T(n)^{O(1)}$ denotes polynomial functions of $T(n)$.

For example, the functions $log^2 n$ and $log^3 n$ are in the set $\log n^{O(1)}$, the functions n^2 and n^3 are in the set $n^{O(1)}$, and the functions e^{2x} and e^{3x} are in the set $(e^x)^{O(1)}$.

Definition 2.4. The set $(\log n)^{O(1)}$ is called the set of **polylogarithmic** functions.

Theorem 2.3. (Parallel Computation Thesis). The class of problems solvable in time $T(n)^{O(1)}$ by a PRAM is equal to the class of problems solvable in work space $T(n)^{O(1)}$ by a RAM, if $T(n) \geq \log n$.

The parallel computation thesis has been proven for those cases where $T(n)$ is a polynomial function of the problem size (von zur Gathen 1986).

Restating the case where the parallel computation thesis has been proven, a PRAM can recognize in polynomial time all languages recognized by a RAM in polynomial space. A consequence of this theorem is that a PRAM can solve $\mathcal{NP}$-complete problems in polynomial time. For example, the graph coloring problem considered in the previous section is $\mathcal{NP}$-complete, yet we gave an $O(n^2)$ algorithm to solve it. To do this, we used a number of processors exponential in the problem size.

Theorem 2.4. If the number of processors in a PRAM is restricted to some polynomial function of the size of the input, then the problems solvable in parallel polynomial time is $\mathcal{P}$, the set of problems solvable in sequential polynomial time.

Proof. This is left to the reader.

Definition 2.5. A parallel algorithm has **polylogarithmic time complexity** if its time complexity is a polylogarithmic function of the problem size.

Definition 2.6. $\mathcal{NC}$ is the class of problems solvable on a PRAM in polylogarithmic time using a number of processors that are a polynomial function of the problem size.

Many problems in $\mathcal{P}$ can be solved in parallel in polylogarithmic time. For example, hardware circuits perform many operations in time logarithmic in the number of bits in the operands. Other examples of problems in class $\mathcal{NC}$ include computing the transitive closure of a relation, boolean matrix multiplication, matrix inversion, and constructing the maximal independent set of vertices in a graph (Karp and Ramachandran 1990).

It is an open problem whether $\mathcal{NC} = \mathcal{P}$, but it seems unlikely that every problem in $\mathcal{P}$ is in $\mathcal{NC}$. In other words, there appear to be some problems in $\mathcal{P}$ that cannot be solved in polylogarithmic time on a PRAM using a polynomial number of processors.

Definition 2.7. (Gibbons and Rytter 1988) A problem $L \in \mathcal{P}$ is $\mathcal{P}$-**complete** if every other problem in $\mathcal{P}$ can be transformed to L in polylogarithmic parallel time using PRAM with a polynomial number of processors.

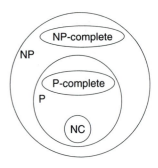

FIGURE 2-22   Conjectured relationship between the complexity classes
$\mathcal{NC}$, $\mathcal{P}$, $\mathcal{NP}$, $\mathcal{P}$-complete, and $\mathcal{NP}$-complete.

The $\mathcal{P}$-complete problems are those that seem to defy a fast (i.e., poly-logarithmic time) parallel solution. Problems in this class include depth-first search of an arbitrary graph, the maximum-flow problem, and the circuit value problem.

Figure 2-22 uses a Venn diagram to display the conjectured relationship between the sets $\mathcal{NC}$, $\mathcal{P}$, $\mathcal{NP}$, $\mathcal{P}$-complete, and $\mathcal{NP}$-complete. Remember that the questions $\mathcal{NC} = \mathcal{P}$ and $\mathcal{P} = \mathcal{NP}$ remain open.

2.6   SUMMARY

The PRAM is a parallel extension of the RAM model of serial computation. A PRAM allows algorithmic steps to be performed simultaneously on a large data set. PRAM models may or may not allow multiple processors to read from or write to the same memory location simultaneously, resulting in three model categories: EREW (exclusive read, exclusive write), CREW (concurrent read, exclusive write), and CRCW (concurrent read, concurrent write). CRCW PRAM models can be distinguished by how concurrent writes to the same memory location are resolved. In the COMMON PRAM model, concurrent writes to the same location are allowed only if all the values are identical. In the ARBITRARY PRAM model concurrent writes are resolved by letting the value of an arbitrary processor succeed. In the PRIORITY PRAM model the processor with highest priority wins a concurrent write to the same location.

Despite their popularity as bases for parallel algorithm design, no actual processor arrays have been built based on PRAM models because it is not feasible to allow p processors to access any p-memory locations simultaneously. Nevertheless, if a PRAM algorithm is cost optimal, it may be a suitable basis for the design of a parallel program targeted to a real machine. Brent's theorem can help identify those cases where cost-optimal parallel algorithms exist.

2.7   BIBLIOGRAPHIC NOTES

The primary sources for this chapter are Gibbons and Rytter (1988) and Karp and Ramachandran (1990).

We briefly described how one PRAM model can simulate another. For more information on the relationship between CREW PRAM models, see Fich et al. (1988).

We presented only the most common PRAM models in this chapter. The literature contains a variety of PRAM models. Some authors give different names to models we have discussed. Other authors have introduced models with unique capabilities. Here are a few references from the extensive literature on the subject.

Quinn and Deo (1984) and the first edition of this book, *Designing Efficient Algorithms for Parallel Computers*, referred to PRAM models as SIMD-SM: SIMD for the single instruction stream, multiple data-stream style of execution, and SM for shared memory. Perhaps for similar reasons, Akl (1989) refers to PRAM models as SM SIMD computers.

The SP-RAM (Shiloach and Vishkin 1982a) is identical to the ARBITRARY PRAM. The RP-RAM (Shiloach and Vishkin 1981) allows simultaneous reading and writing as well. If m processors attempt to write a value into the same memory location simultaneously, then exactly one processor succeeds, and the probability of each processor succeeding is $1/m$.

Goldschlager's SIMDAG model (1982) is identical to the PRIORITY PRAM.

The PP-RAM (Reif 1982) is a PRAM with processors having the added capability to perform independent probabilistic choices on a fixed input. Probabilistic parallel algorithms often have a much lower expected time complexity than nonprobabilistic parallel algorithms.

As we have noted, the PRAM is not a realistic model. Algorithms to simulate PRAM computations on parallel models giving processors more restricted access to memory locations have been published by Alt et al. (1987), Karlin and Upfal (1988), Melhorn and Vishkin (1984), Upfal (1984), and Upfal and Wigderson (1987). Valient (1990) has proposed the bulk-synchronous parallel (BSP) model as an efficient bridge between parallel software and parallel hardware.

Fisher (1988) and Vitányi (1988) have contested the PRAM model's assumption that the time needed for a value to travel from a processor to an arbitrary register is a constant. They show how the complexity of PRAM algorithms changes when we assume that processors occupy physical space and signal transmission speeds are finite.

In this chapter we have given an algorithm for performing a preorder tree traversal. He and Yesha (1988) present a parallel algorithm for constructing depth-first spanning trees in planar graphs. The model of computation is CRCW PRAM, the number of processors required is $O(n)$, and the time complexity is $O(log^2 n)$.

Guan and Langston (1991) have published a time-space optimal parallel-merge algorithm for the EREW PRAM model.

Atallah et al. (1989) describe how a divide-and-conquer method can be used to design parallel algorithms for the CREW PRAM.

Nick's Class $\mathcal{NC}$ was named for Nick Pippenger by Cook (1983).
A summary of parallel complexity classes appears in Cook.

2.8 PROBLEMS

2-1 Summarize the similarities and differences between the RAM model of serial computation and the PRAM model of parallel computation.

2-2 Given a COMMON (CRCW) PRAM algorithm with time complexity $O(t(n))$, what is an upper bound on the time complexity of an algorithm to solve the same problem on the CREW model? Given a CREW algorithm with time complexity $O(t(n))$, what is an upper bound on the time complexity of an algorithm to solve the same problem on the EREW model?

2-3 Given a PRAM model with a single active processor, prove that $\lceil \log p \rceil$ instructions are both necessary and sufficient for p processors to become active.

2-4 A variant of the original PRAM model often found in literature assumes that the computation begins with any number of processors active. In this model there is no need for a processor to activate another processor. Show that the complexities of all PRAM algorithms described in Sec. 2.3 are unchanged, given this new model.

2-5 Devise a PRAM algorithm to multiply two $n \times n$ matrices, where $n = 2^k$.

2-6 Modify the parallel-merge algorithm given in this book to accommodate each list having $n/2$ disjoint values, but the merged list having two identical values. Analyze the complexity of your algorithm.

2-7 Modify the parallel-merge algorithm given in this book to accommodate one list having n values and the other list having m values. Assume all $n + m$ values are distinct. Analyze the complexity of your algorithm.

2-8* Devise an $O(\log^2 n)$ PRAM algorithm to sort a list of n distinct elements. *Hint*: Use the parallel merge algorithm.

2-9 Analyze the complexity and determine the number of processors required for the preorder tree-traversal algorithm in Sec. 2.3.

2-10 Devise a PRAM algorithm to perform a postorder traversal of a rooted tree. Assume the same data structure as used by the algorithm in Fig. 2-15.

2-11* Devise a PRAM algorithm to perform a preorder traversal of a rooted tree, where the algorithm's input is a set of directed edges. Every vertex v other than the root has a corresponding edge (v, w), where w is the parent of v. The root vertex r is distinguished by its corresponding edge (r, r). Hence a graph with n vertices is represented by n vertex pairs.

2-12* Devise a PRAM algorithm to solve the graph coloring problem that has lower time complexity than the algorithm presented in the book. You may use a more powerful PRAM model.

2-13* Devise a PRAM algorithm to solve the vertex cover problem. (Given a graph with n vertices and a positive integer k, determine whether there is a set of k vertices such that every edge in the graph is incident upon at least one of the vertices.) Assume the inputs to your algorithm are n, k, and an $n \times n$ adjacency matrix A representing an undirected graph.

2-14* Devise a PRAM algorithm to solve the clique problem. (Given a graph with n vertices and a positive integer k, determine if there is a set of k vertices such that every pair of vertices in the set is connected by an edge.) Assume the inputs to your algorithm are n, k, and an $n \times n$ adjacency matrix A representing an undirected graph.

2-15 In Sec. 2.4 we learned that in order for a parallel algorithm to be cost optimal, the total number of operations it performs cannot be of a higher complexity class than an optimal sequential algorithm. In that case, why don't we simply choose any optimal sequential algorithm as the starting point for our parallel algorithm design?

2-16 For each problem listed below, design a cost-optimal polylogarithmic time PRAM algorithm and use Brent's theorem to determine the number of processors that minimizes parallel execution time.

    a List ranking

    b Preorder tree traversal

    c* List merging

2-17 Why is it unrealistic to expect to solve an $\mathcal{NP}$-complete problem on the PRAM in polylogarithmic time, using a polynomial number of processors?

2-18 Prove Theorem 2.4.

2-19 How could we formulate a polylogarithmic depth-first search algorithm in Sec. 2.3, when Sec. 2.5 says depth-first search is $\mathcal{P}$-complete?

3

PROCESSOR ARRAYS, MULTIPROCESSORS, AND MULTICOMPUTERS

E pluribus unum (Out of many, one)

From the Great Seal of the United States of America

The goal of this chapter is to introduce three important models of parallel computation and several associated parallel computer designs. The models are processor arrays, multiprocessors, and multicomputers, all of which have fostered actual parallel computers.

We present a number of processor organizations in Sec. 3.1; these are mesh, binary tree, hypertree, pyramid, butterfly, hypercube, cube-connected cycles, shuffle-exchange, and de Bruijn. These processor organizations are evaluated according to criteria that help determine their practicality and versatility. Section 3.2 surveys a number of processor array models including the Connection Machine CM-200™, a well-known processor array. Section 3.3 discusses multiprocessors, multiple-CPU computers with global address space. We describe two commercial multiprocessors—the Sequent Symmetry™ and the BBN Butterfly TC2000™. In Sec. 3.4 we examine multicomputers, multiple-CPU computers with no global address space. Our example architectures are the nCUBE 2™, Thinking Machines' CM-5™, and the Intel Paragon XP/S™. Section 3.5 presents Flynn's taxonomy, the most common classification of sequential and parallel computer architectures. In Sec. 3.6 we discuss the terms used to describe the performance of parallel algorithms. These terms include speedup, scaled speedup, and parallelizability.

52

3.1 PROCESSOR ORGANIZATIONS

This section defines nine important processor organizations—methods of connecting processors in a parallel computer. A processor organization can be represented by a graph in which the nodes (vertices) represent processors and the edges represent communication paths between pairs of processors. (For readers unfamiliar with graph theory, a brief introduction to graph theoretic terms is given in Appendix A.) We evaluate these processor organizations according to criteria that help us understand their effectiveness in implementing efficient parallel algorithms on real hardware. These criteria are:

1 Diameter. The **diameter** of a network is the largest distance between two nodes. Low diameter is better, because the diameter puts a lower bound on the complexity of parallel algorithms requiring communication between arbitrary pairs of nodes.

2 Bisection width of the network. The **bisection width** of a network is the minimum number of edges that must be removed in order to divide the network into two halves (within one). High bisection width is better, because in algorithms requiring large amounts of data movement, the size of the data set divided by the bisection width puts a lower bound on the complexity of the parallel algorithm.

3 Number of edges per node. It is best if the number of edges per node is a constant independent of the network size, because then the processor organization scales more easily to systems with large numbers of nodes.

4 Maximum edge length. For scalability reasons it is best if the nodes and edges of the network can be laid out in three-dimensional space so that the maximum edge length is a constant independent of the network size.

We now discuss the various type of processor organizations.

3.1.1 Mesh Networks

In a **mesh network**, the nodes are arranged into a q-dimensional lattice. Communication is allowed only between neighboring nodes; hence interior nodes communicate with $2q$ other processors. Figure 3-1a illustrates a two-dimensional (2-D) mesh. Some variants of the mesh model allow wrap-around connections between processors on the edge of the mesh. These connections can connect processors in the same row or column (Fig. 3-1b) or adjacent rows or columns (Fig. 3-1c).

Let's evaluate the mesh network according to our four criteria. We assume that the mesh has no wrap-around connections. The diameter of a q-dimensional mesh with k^q nodes is $q(k-1)$. Hence, from a theoretical point of view, mesh networks have the disadvantage that data routing requirements often prevent the

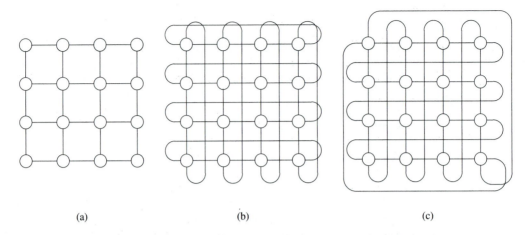

(a)   (b)   (c)

FIGURE 3-1 Two-dimensional meshes. (a) Mesh with no wrap-around connections. (b) Mesh with wrap-around connections between processors in same row or column. (c) Mesh with wrap-around connections between processors in adjacent rows or columns.

development of polylogarithmic time parallel algorithms. In practice, however, some computer architects would rather implement fewer, faster links than more, slower links.

The bisection width of a q-dimensional mesh with k^q nodes is k^{q-1}. The maximum number of edges per node is $2q$. The maximum edge length is a constant, independent of the number of nodes, for two- and three-dimensional meshes.

The two-dimensional mesh has been a popular topology for processor arrays, including Goodyear Aerospace's MPP™, the AMT DAP™, and MasPar's MP-1™. The Intel Paragon XP/S multicomputer connects processors with a two-dimensional mesh.

3.1.2 Binary Tree Networks

In a **binary tree network** the $2^k - 1$ nodes are arranged into a complete binary tree of depth $k - 1$ (Fig. 3-2). A node has at most three links. Every interior node can communicate with its two children and every node other than the root

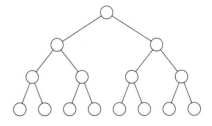

FIGURE 3-2 Binary tree network of size 15 and depth 3.

can communicate with its parent. The binary tree has low diameter, $2(k-1)$, but has a poor bisection width of one. Assuming nodes have volume, it is impossible to arrange the nodes of a binary tree in three-dimensional space such that as the number of nodes increases, the length of the longest edge is always less than a specified constant.

3.1.3   Hypertree Networks

A hypertree represents one approach to building a network with the low diameter of a binary tree but an improved bisection width. The easiest way to think of a **hypertree network** of degree k and depth d is to consider the network from two different angles (Fig. 3-3). From the front a hypertree network of degree k and depth d looks like a complete k-ary tree of height d (Fig. 3-3a). From the side, the same hypertree network looks like an upside down binary tree of height d (Fig. 3-3b). Joining the front and side views yields the complete network. Figure 3-3c illustrates a hypertree network of degree 4 and height 2.

A 4-ary hypertree with depth d has 4^d leaves and $2^d(2^{d+1}-1)$ nodes in all. The diameter of this network is $2d$ and its bisection width is 2^{d+1}. The number of edges per node is never more than six and the maximum edge length is an increasing function of the problem size.

FIGURE 3-3   Hypertree network of degree 4 and depth 2. (a) Front view. (b) Side view. (c) Complete network.

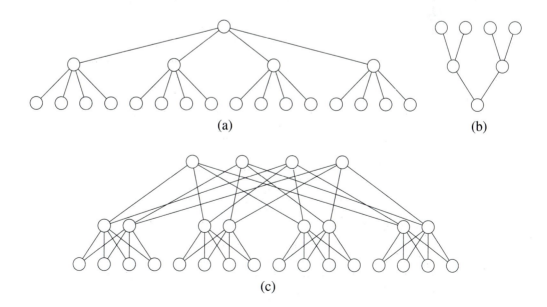

(a)

(b)

(c)

The data routing network of the Connection Machine CM-5 multicomputer is a 4-ary hypertree.

3.1.4   Pyramid Networks

The pyramid network can be seen as an attempt to combine the advantages of mesh networks with those of tree networks. A **pyramid network** of size k^2 is a complete 4-ary rooted tree of height $\log_2 k$ augmented with additional interprocessor links so that the processors in every tree level form a 2-D mesh network (Miller and Stout 1987). A pyramid of size k^2 has at its base a 2-D mesh network containing k^2 processors. The total number of processors in a pyramid of size k^2 is $(4/3)k^2 - (1/3)$. The levels of the pyramid are numbered in ascending order such that the base has level number 0, and the single processor at the apex of the pyramid has level number $\log_2 k$. Every interior processor is connected to nine other processors: one parent, four mesh neighbors, and four children. Figure 3-4 illustrates a pyramid network of size 16.

The advantage of the pyramid over the 2-D mesh is that the pyramid reduces the diameter of the network. For example, when a message must travel from one side of the mesh to the other, fewer link traversals are required if the message travels up and down the tree rather than across the mesh. The diameter of a pyramid of size k^2 is $2\log k$.

The addition of tree links does not give the pyramid a significantly higher bisection width than a 2-D mesh. The bisection width of a pyramid of size k^2 is $2k$.

The maximum number of links per node is no greater than nine, regardless of the size of the network. Unlike a 2-D mesh, however, the length of the longest edge in the pyramid network is an increasing function of the network size.

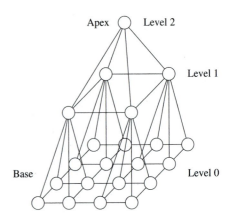

FIGURE 3-4   A pyramid network of size 16.

3.1.5 Butterfly Network

A **butterfly network** consists of $(k + 1)2^k$ nodes divided into $k + 1$ rows, or **ranks,** each containing $n = 2^k$ nodes (Fig. 3-5). The ranks are labeled 0 through k, although the ranks 0 and k are sometimes combined, giving each node four connections to other nodes.

Let node(i, j) refer to the jth node on the ith rank, where $0 \le i \le k$ and $0 \le j < n$. Then node(i, j) on rank $i > 0$ is connected to two nodes on rank $i - 1$, node$(i - 1, j)$ and node$(i - 1, m)$, where m is the integer found by inverting the ith most significant bit in the binary representation of j. Note that if node(i, j) is connected to node$(i - 1, m)$, then node(i, m) is connected to node$(i - 1, j)$. The entire network is made up of such "butterfly" patterns, hence the name. As the rank numbers decrease, the widths of the wings of the butterflies increase exponentially. For this reason the length of the longest network edge increases as the number of network nodes increases.

The diameter of a butterfly network with $(k + 1)2^k$ nodes is $2k$ and the bisection width of a network of that size is 2^{k-1}.

A butterfly network serves to route data from nonlocal memory to processors on the BBN TC2000 multiprocessor described later in this chapter.

3.1.6 Hypercube (Cube-Connected) Networks

A **cube-connected network**, also called a binary n-cube network, is a butterfly with its columns collapsed into single nodes. Formally, this network consists of 2^k nodes forming a k-dimensional **hypercube**. The nodes are labeled $0, 1, \dots, 2^k - 1$; two nodes are adjacent if their labels differ in exactly one bit position. A four-dimensional hypercube is shown in Fig. 3-6.

The diameter of a hypercube with 2^k nodes is k, and the bisection width of that size network is 2^{k-1}, the hypercube organization has low diameter and high bisection width at the expense of the number of edges per node and the

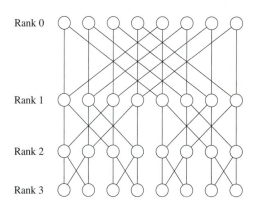

FIGURE 3-5   Butterfly network with 32 nodes. (Ullman [1984].)

Rank 0

Rank 1

Rank 2

Rank 3

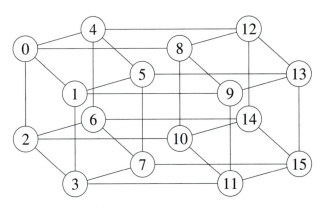

FIGURE 3-6   A four-dimensional (16 node) hypercube.

length of the longest edge.The number of edges per node is k—the logarithm of the number of nodes in the network. The length of the longest edge in a hypercube network increases as the number of nodes in the network increases.

The hypercube was the most popular processor organization for first- and second-generation multicomputers, and nCUBE continues to build systems based on this topology. In addition, processing element clusters on the Connection Machine CM-200 processor array are connected in a hypercube.

3.1.7 Cube-Connected Cycles Networks

The **cube-connected cycles network** is a k-dimensional hypercube whose 2^k "vertices" are actually cycles of k nodes formed by the columns of a butterfly network whose ranks 0 and k have been combined. For each dimension, every cycle has a node connected to a node in the neighboring cycle in that dimension. See Fig. 3-7 for a drawing of a 24-node cube-connected cycles network.

Formally, node(i, j) is connected to node(i, m) if and only if m is the result of inverting the ith most significant bit of the binary representation of j. Note that the connections are slightly different from those in the butterfly network, that is, if node(i, j) is connected to node($i - 1$, m) in the butterfly network, where $j \neq m$, then node(i, j) is connected to node(i, m) in the cube-connected cycles network. However, in the cube-connected cycles network, node(i, j) can still communicate with node($i - 1$, m) by following two links, since there is a direct path from node(i, m) to node($i - 1$, m).

Compared to the hypercube, the cube-connected cycles processor organization has the advantage that the number of edges per node is three—a constant independent of network size. However, the cube-connected cycles network has the disadvantage that the network diameter is twice that of a hypercube and the bisection width is lower. Given a cube-connected cycles network of size $k2^k$, its diameter is $2k$ and its bisection width is 2^{k-1}.

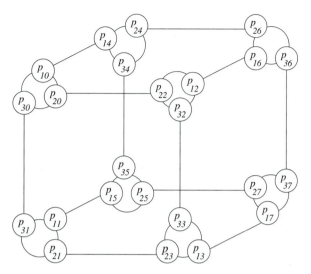

FIGURE 3-7   Cube-connected cycles network with 24 nodes. The first subscript of each node denotes the rank; the second subscript of each node denotes the column.

3.1.8 Shuffle-Exchange Networks

A **shuffle-exchange network** consists of $n = 2^k$ nodes, numbered $0, 1, \ldots, n - 1$, and two kinds of connections, called *shuffle* and *exchange*. **Exchange** connections link pairs of nodes whose numbers differ in their least significant bit. The **perfect shuffle** connection links node i with node $2i$ modulo $(n - 1)$, with the exception that node $n - 1$ is connected to itself. See Fig. 3-8 for a drawing of an eight-node shuffle-exchange network. Shuffle connections are indicated by the solid arrows and the exchange links are represented by the dashed arrows.

To understand the derivation of the name *perfect shuffle*, consider shuffling a deck of eight cards, numbered 0, 1, 2, 3, 4, 5, 6, 7. If the deck is divided into two exact halves and shuffled perfectly, then the result is the following order: 0, 4, 1, 5, 2, 6, 3, 7. Reexamine Fig. 3-8 and notice that the final position of the card that began at index i can be determined by following the shuffle link from node i.

Let $a_{k-1}a_{k-2} \cdots a_1 a_0$ be the address of a node in a perfect shuffle network, expressed in binary. A datum at this address will be at address $a_{k-2} \cdots a_1 a_0 a_{k-1}$

FIGURE 3-8   Shuffle-exchange network with eight nodes. Solid arrows denote shuffle connections. Dashed arrows denote exchange connections.

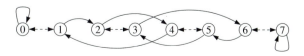

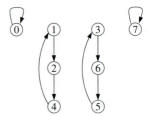

FIGURE 3-9   Necklaces of the shuffle-exchange network with eight nodes.

following a shuffle operation. In other words, the change in the address of a piece of data after a shuffle operation corresponds to a left cyclic rotation of the address by 1 bit (Prob. 3.4). If $n = 2^k$, then k shuffling operations move a datum back to its original location. The nodes through which a data item beginning at address i travels in response to a sequence of shuffles are called the **necklace** of i. No necklace is longer than k and a necklace shorter than k is called a **short necklace**. Figure 3-9 illustrates the necklaces of the perfect shuffle network with eight nodes.

Every node in a shuffle-exchange network has two outgoing and two incoming links. The length of the longest link increases as a function of network size. The number of long links has advantages with respect to network diameter and bisection width since the diameter of a shuffle exchange network is logarithmic in the number of nodes, that is, a network with 2^k nodes has diameter $2k - 1$. The bisection width is at least $2^{k-1}/k$.

Siegel (1979) has shown that a composition of k shuffle-exchange networks, called an **omega network**, is equivalent to a hypercube network with degree k. The same effect can be achieved by building only one stage of the network and cycling through it k times (Lawrie 1975).

3.1.9   de Bruijn Networks

A **de Bruijn network** consists of $n = 2^k$ nodes. Let $a_{k-1}a_{k-2} \cdots a_1 a_0$ be the address of a node in the de Bruijn network. The two nodes reachable via directed edges from that node are

$$a_{k-2}a_{k-3} \cdots a_1 a_0 0$$
$$a_{k-2}a_{k-3} \cdots a_1 a_0 1$$

Figure 3-10 illustrates an eight-processor de Bruijn network.

FIGURE 3-10   An 8–processor de Bruijn network.

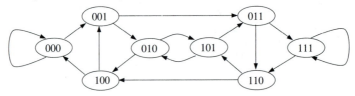

TABLE 3-1   CHARACTERISTICS OF VARIOUS PROCESSOR ORGANIZATIONS

Network	Nodes	Diameter	Bisection Width	Constant Number of Edges	Constant Edge Length
1-D mesh	k	$k-1$	1	Yes	Yes
2-D mesh	k^2	$2(k-1)$	k	Yes	Yes
3-D mesh	k^3	$3(k-1)$	k^2	Yes	Yes
Binary tree	$2^k - 1$	$2(k-1)$	1	Yes	No
4-ary hypertree	$2^k(2^{k+1} - 1)$	$2k$	2^{k+1}	Yes	No
Pyramid	$(4k^2 - 1)/3$	$2\log k$	$2k$	Yes	No
Butterfly	$(k+1)2^k$	$2k$	2^k	Yes	No
Hypercube	2^k	k	2^{k-1}	No	No
Cube-connected cycles	$k2^k$	$2k$	2^{k-1}	Yes	No
Shuffle-exchange	2^k	$2k-1$	$\geq 2^{k-1}/k$	Yes	No
de Bruijn	2^k	k	$2^k/k$	Yes	No

The number of edges per node is a constant independent of the network size. The bisection width of a network with 2^k nodes is $2^k/k$, and the length of the longest edge increases with the size of the network. As with shuffle-exchange networks, de Bruijn networks contain shuffle connections.

The diameter of a de Bruijn network with 2^k nodes is k, which is about half the diameter of a shuffle-exchange network with the same number of nodes.

The processors of the Triton/1™, a SIMD/MIMD parallel computer developed at the University of Karlsruhe, are connected with a de Bruijn network (Herter et al. 1992).

3.1.10 Processor Orginization Summary

Table 3.1 summarizes the characteristics of the processor organizations we have considered. Of the nine organizations, only the mesh has constant edge length. The hypercube is noteworthy as the only processor organization we have considered in which the number of edges per node is an increasing function of the network size.

3.2 PROCESSOR ARRAYS

A **vector computer** is a computer whose instruction set includes operations on vectors as well as scalars. Generally, there are two ways of implementing a vector computer. A **pipelined vector processor** streams vectors from memory to the CPU, where pipelined arithmetic units manipulate them. The Cray-1™ and Cyber-205™ are well known pipelined vector processors. We do not consider these architectures further.

A **processor array** is a vector computer implemented as a sequential computer connected to a set of identical, synchronized processing elements capable of simultaneously performing the same operation on different data. The sequential computer is usually called the **front end**.

The front end is a general-purpose CPU that stores the program and the data that are not manipulated in parallel and also executes the sequential portions of the program.

Each processing element has a small local memory that it can access directly. Collectively, the individual local memories of the processing elements store the vector data that are manipulated in parallel. When the front end computer encounters an instruction whose operand is a vector, it issues a command to the processing elements to perform the instruction in parallel. Although the processing elements execute in parallel, units may be programmed to ignore any particular instruction. This ability to mask processing elements allows synchronization to be maintained through the various paths of control structures, such as clauses of an `if...then...else` statement.

In the course of a normal computation, data flows from the front end to the processor array, between processing elements, and from the processor array to the front end. Processing elements communicate values to each other via an interconnection network (Fig. 3-11), which is usually based on one of the processor organizations we described in the previous section. Over the years, the 2–D mesh has been easily the most popular processor organization for

FIGURE 3-11 A realistic processor array model. Each processor has its own private memory, and processors can pass data only via a limited interconnection network.

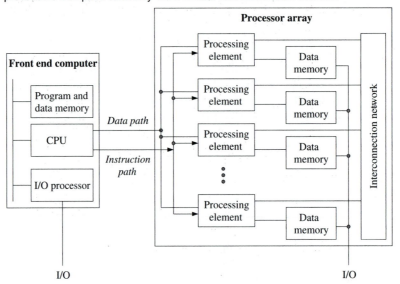

processor arrays. Processor arrays organized as hypercubes, shuffle-exchange networks, and cube-connected cycles networks have also been suggested. In later chapters we describe parallel algorithms based upon most of these models.

Processor arrays have an efficient mechanism for the front end to broadcast instructions and data items to the individual processing elements. In addition, processor arrays also support the efficient access of a particular memory location in the memory of an arbitrary processing element by the front end. The existence of fast operations for broadcast and arbitrary memory fetch plays an important role in many parallel algorithms.

3.2.1 Connection Machine CM-200

The Connection Machine CM-200 processor array is manufactured by Thinking Machines Corporation of Cambridge, Massachusetts. The primary source of information for our description of the CM-200 is Thinking Machines, 1989.

The CM-200 has three principal components: a front end computer, a parallel processing unit, and an I/O system (Fig. 3-12). The front-end computer, usually a Sun workstation, stores serial data and executes the sequential portions of programs. Parallel data are stored in the parallel processing unit. The front-end computer broadcasts parallel instructions to the parallel processing unit for

FIGURE 3-12   Block diagram of the Connection Machine CM-200 processor array. (Reprinted by permission of Thinking Machines Corporation.)

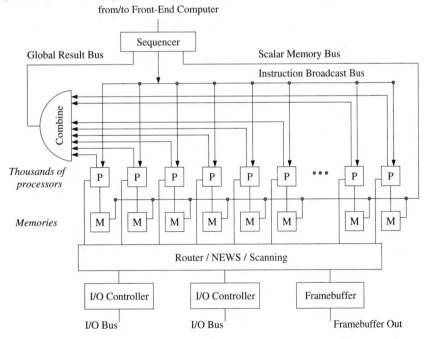

execution. A high speed I/O system allows efficient data transfers between the parallel processing unit and I/O devices, such as frame buffers and parallel disk drives.

The front end can exchange data with the processing elements in three ways. It can broadcast a single value to all of the processing elements. Through global combining, it can obtain the sum, maximum, global OR, etc., of one value from each processing element. By using the scalar memory bus, the front end processor can read or write 32-bit values stored in any processing element.

The parallel processing unit contains between 2,048 and 65,536 processing elements, an instruction sequencer, interprocessor communication networks, and I/O controllers and/or framebuffer modules.

The front end issues parallel processing instructions to the sequencer, which interprets each instruction and generates a series of "nanoinstructions." It broadcasts these nanoinstructions over an instruction bus to the processing elements, which execute them.

Paris, the PARallel Instruction Set of the Connection Machine, simplifies the development of compilers by providing a variety of operations similar to a more typical machine's instruction set. Some Paris instructions perform arithmetic operations on various data types, others facilitate communication between the processing elements, and still others facilitate communication between the processing elements and the front end computer.

By supporting virtual processors, Paris also serves the important function of insulating the user from the underlying processor array. A program can assume the existence of any number of processing elements, and these virtual processors are then mapped to the physical processing elements. This feature allows the same program to run on Connection Machine systems with different numbers of physical processors.

In general, whenever a Paris arithmetic operation is performed, each physical processing element may execute the operation many times, once for each virtual processor mapped to it. Virtual processor versions of the three hardware-supported routing mechanisms also exist in the Paris instruction set.

The individual processing elements of the Connection Machine are bit-serial processors. Each processing element has a context flag, indicating whether or not it is screened. Screened processing elements do not store the results of their computations. Every processing element also has three input bits (two from memory and one from a flag) and two result bits (one to memory and one to a flag).

A processing element can compute any two boolean functions on three inputs. These functions are specified as two 8-bit bytes representing the truth tables for the two functions. In other words, the processing element "computes" the result of the boolean function by consulting the truth table entry indexed by the three input bits.

For example, the truth table in Fig. 3-13 is used to perform bit-serial addition. In this case the two functions on three inputs are "carry-out" and "sum." To

INPUT BITS			OUTPUT BITS	
Memory	Memory	Flag	Memory	Flag
0	0	0	0	0
0	0	1	1	0
0	1	0	1	0
0	1	1	0	1
1	0	0	1	0
1	0	1	0	1
1	1	0	0	1
1	1	1	1	1

FIGURE 3-13   Truth table for bit-serial addition on CM-200 processor array. The sum bit is output to memory; the carry-out bit is output to a hardware flag.

add two k-bit integers stored in its local memory, a processing element first loads the virtual processor context flag into a hardware flag register. All ALU operations are conditional upon the state of this flag. Second, the processor clears a second flag that serves as the carry bit. Third, the processor iterates k times through a cycle in which it reads the carry bit and one bit of each operand and computes the sum bit and carry-out bit. The computation begins with the least significant bits of the operands and ends with their most significant bits.

A single VLSI chip contains 16 processing elements plus routing hardware. Each pair of processor chips shares a group of memory chips, a floating-point interface chip, and a floating-point execution chip (Fig. 3-14).

The memory chips provide a 44-bit wide data path, which translates into 32 data bits and 12 bits of error-correcting code. The 32 data bits can be sent to the 32 bit-serial processing elements, one bit per processing element. Alternatively, the 32 data bits can be directed to the floating-point interface chip. The floating-point interface chip may use this data for memory address control for indirect addressing, or it may send the data to the floating-point execution chip.

The floating-point execution chip produces results in 32-bit quantities. The interface unit stores these results back into memory. The maximum performance of this unit in performing 32-bit floating-point arithmetic is 20 megaflops. A maximally configured Connection Machine has 2048 floating-point chips and a peak performance of about 40 gigaflops.

The Connection Machine has three routing mechanisms. The most general routing mechanism, simply called the router, allows any processing element to communicate with any other processing element. Every processor chip contains one router node servicing all 16 processing elements on the chip. The router nodes are wired together to form a hypercube. In a fully configured Connection Machine having 65,536 processing elements on 4,096 (2^{12}) processor chips, the network is a 12-dimensional hypercube. Each message travels through the router nodes until it reaches the chip containing the destination processor. The

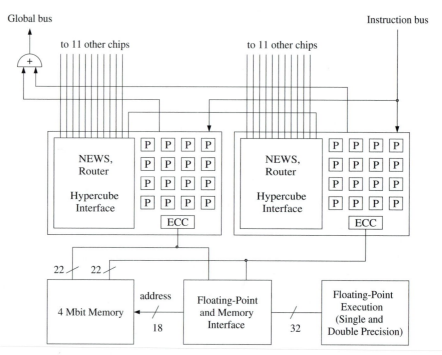

FIGURE 3-14   Architecture of processor chip pair on the Connection Machine CM-200. (Reprinted by permission of Thinking Machines Corporation.)

router nodes automatically forward messages and perform some dynamic load balancing. For example, the path a message takes may vary, depending upon which paths are available.

Each router node has an ALU capable of performing some arithmetic operations. The router checks to see if any messages share the same destination. If so, it combines the messages based upon the semantics of the parallel instruction being executed. For example, it may take the sum, maximum, or logical OR of the values, or it may simply discard all but one of the values.

The second routing mechanism is called the NEWS grid. A j-dimensional mesh can be embedded in a k-dimensional hypercube, if $j \leq k$. Hence, a subset of the wires that supports the router, can form a Cartesian mesh, which Thinking Machines calls a **NEWS grid**. If all communications between processing elements are neighbors in a NEWS grid of any dimension less than or equal to the dimension of the hypercube, then the message-passing speed is much higher than if the messages must be passed through the router. The system passes such messages using three special transfer methods, two of which are implemented in hardware.

To demonstrate the three transfer methods, suppose the system's 4096 processor chips are organized as a 64×64 grid. Assume each processor chip's

16 processing elements are organized as a 4×4 grid, and finally, assume each processing element has 64 virtual processors organized as a 8×8 grid.

Suppose each virtual processor must send a value to the virtual processor to the north. Within each group of 64 virtual processors, 56 of them are sending data to another virtual processor within the same processing element. The processing element "passes" the data values by copying the data within its own memory. Hence, the first specialized transfer method avoids interprocessor communication by rearranging data within local memory.

Each processing element must still send 8 data values to the processing element to the north. However, within each processor chip, 12 of the 16 processing elements are sending values to other processing elements in the same chip. The second specialized transfer method uses special permuation circuitry on the chip to perform these 12 data transfers.

Each processor chip must still send 32 data values (8 values times 4 processing elements) to its neighbor to the north along one hypercube wire and then receive 32 data values from its neighbor to the south along another hypercube wire. This third specialized transfer method used in NEWS grids takes advantage of the regular communication pattern to determine actual wires to be used.

Scans and spreads are the third kind of message routing. A **scan** is a NEWS operation that performs a prefix sum. A **spread** is a form of broadcast that allows a single processing element to send a value to every other processing element. Prefix sums or other scan operations may be incorporated into a spread.

A high-speed I/O capability increases the utility of a supercomputer. The Connection machine's DataVault™ is a parallel array of disk drives. A set of 8 DataVaults, connected to a 65,536-processor element Connection Machine, provides 480 gigabytes of secondary storage and data transfer rates above 100 megabytes per second. The Connection Machine also supports high speed output to a frame buffer driving a color monitor.

3.3 MULTIPROCESSORS

Multiple-CPU computers consist of a number of fully programmable processors, each capable of executing its own program. Multiprocessors are multiple-CPU computers with a shared memory. In a Uniform Memory Access (UMA, pronounced "you′ma") multiprocessor the shared memory is centralized. In a Non-Uniform Memory Access (NUMA, pronounced "new′ma") multiprocessor the shared memory is distributed.

3.3.1 Uniform Memory Access (UMA) Multiprocessors

The simplest processor intercommunication pattern assumes that all the processors work through a central switching mechanism to reach a centralized shared memory (Fig. 3-15). There are a variety of ways to implement this switching

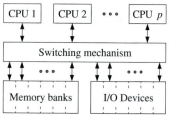

FIGURE 3-15 The uniform memory access (UMA) multiprocessor model. All the processors work through a central switching mechanism to reach a shared global memory and I/O devices.

mechanism, including a common bus to global memory, a crossbar switch, and a packet-switched network. The Encore Multimax™ and the Sequent Symmetry S81™ are examples of commercial **uniform memory access (UMA) multiprocessors**.

Systems using a bus, such as the Multimax or Symmetry, are limited in size, since only so many processors can share the bus before it becomes saturated. In the case of systems using a crossbar switch, the cost of the switch soon becomes the dominant factor, again limiting the number of processors which may be connected (Stone 1980).

UMA multiprocessors based on switching networks can conceivably contain a large number of processors, although no commercial computers using this architecture have yet appeared. The NYU Ultracomputer, an experimental UMA multiprocessor, is based on an omega switching network. The cost of an omega network for a p-processor system is $\Theta(p \log p)$—lower than the $\Theta(p^2)$ cost of a crossbar switch.

Symmetry The Symmetry is a UMA multiprocessor manufactured by Sequent Computer Systems, Inc., of Beaverton, Oregon. The Symmetry is not a supercomputer—some contemporary workstations have higher floating-point performance. We have included this section because it is a commercial example of a UMA multiprocessor. In addition, it is likely to be the only parallel computer that many readers can access.

The Symmetry uses a pipelined 64-bit bus to connect the system's CPUs, memory, and I/O devices. The Sequent System Bus (SSB) carries 32- or 64-bit data items and addresses up to 32 bits in length. Read and write operations on the SSB are pipelined, meaning that after the SSB has transmitted a read or write request to system memory, it can handle another transaction even before the memory has responded to the first request. The sustained data transfer rate on the bus is 53.3 Mbytes per second.

The processors use a second one-bit wide bus to exchange interrupts and other low-level control and error signals.

A Symmetry processor is based on the Intel 80386 CPU™, a 32-bit microprocessor, and an Intel 80387 floating-point coprocessor. An optional Weitek WTL 1167™ chip is available to enhance the speed of some floating-point operations. Since the Intel 80386 was not designed to be used as a multiprocessor

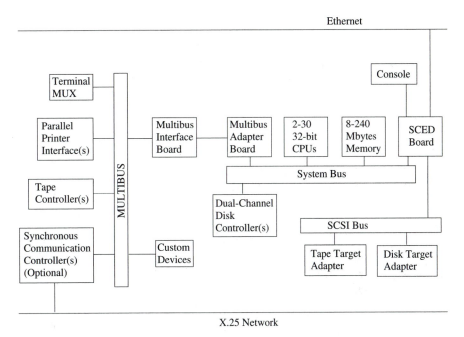

FIGURE 3-16   Block diagram of the Sequent Symmetry, a UMA multiprocessor. (Courtesy Hatcher and Quinn [1991].)

CPU, each processor has a System Link and Interrupt Controller to manage the interactions among processors. Additional hardware implements a cache memory.

The cache memories in the Symmetry multiprocessor play a vital role in keeping CPUs busy and reducing contention for the Sequent System Bus. The on-board cache memory responds quickly enough to allow the Intel 80386 CPU to operate at full speed. If the cache hit rate is high, then the burden each CPU puts on the system bus is light, allowing more processors to be active.

Each CPU has a 64-Kbyte cache. Whenever the CPU issues a read to an address in system memory that is not currently in the cache, the cache control suspends the CPU's execution and issues a 16-byte read request on the SSB to fetch the data from system memory. The least recently used 16-byte block in the selected row of the cache is swapped out to make room for the new block. At this point the cache controller resumes CPU execution and passes the requested data item to the CPU.

A central problem in the design of UMA multiprocessors is how to ensure cache consistency; that is, how to maintain consistency between copies of data in the main system memory and the local processor caches. To resolve this problem, a **write-through** caching policy was implemented in the older Sequent Balance™ multiprocessor. Every data write is sent directly to system memory, and all copies of the data item in the other processors' caches are invalidated.

The Symmetry uses a **copy-back** caching policy. When a processor modifies a data item in its own cache, it does not write the updated value to system memory until it swaps out the cache block or until another processor needs that data item. It does, however, signal the other processors that their copies of the data item are no longer up-to-date. The copy-back policy avoids the overhead of broadcasting all partial-block writes across the SSB into memory in those cases where no other processor accesses the modified data.

Single-byte load and store operations, as well as 16- and 32-byte loads and stores aligned on natural boundaries, always execute atomically. To ensure the atomic execution of any other operation, the operations must be protected with a locking routine that uses the Symmetry's hardware locking mechanism. The locking mechanism locks 16-byte regions of processor cache memory (corresponding to the cache block size). The system supports the concurrent locking of disjoint regions.

3.3.2   Non-Uniform Memory Access (NUMA) Multiprocessors

Like UMA multiprocessors, **non-uniform memory access (NUMA) multiprocessors** are characterized by a shared address space. Unlike UMA multiprocessors, NUMA multiprocessor memory is distributed. Every processor has some nearby memory, and the shared address space on a NUMA multiprocessor is formed by combining these local memories. The time needed to access a particular memory location on a NUMA multiprocessor depends on whether that location is local to the processor.

TC2000   The TC2000, manufactured by BBN Systems and Technologies of Cambridge, Massachusetts, is a NUMA multiprocessor that has up to 128 processor nodes. Each processor node contains a Motorola 88100 CPU, three Motorola 88200 chips providing separate instruction and data caches, between 4 and 16 Mbytes of primary memory, and interfaces to the Butterfly switch and a VME bus (see Fig. 3-17). The transaction bus connects these processor subsystems.

The maximum performance of a single processor is 20 megaflops. A fully figured 128-processor TC2000 would have a peak speed of about 2.5 gigaflops.

The hardware on each processor converts every 32-bit virtual address into a 34-bit physical address. The physical address may be in cache memory, the same processor's memory, or it may be in another processor's memory. Of course, cache memory accesses are the fastest. Private data and read-only shared data, such as program text, can be stored in cache memory. Data from the processor's own physical memory can be fetched over the transaction bus. Data from another processor's memory is retrieved by sending a request through the Butterfly switching network (Fig. 3-18).

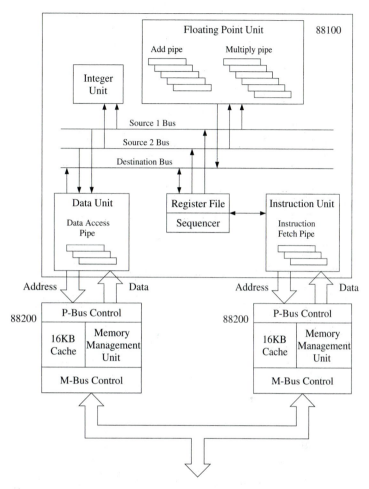

FIGURE 3-17   A processor node of the BBN TC2000. (Reprinted by permission of Bolt, Beranek, and Newman, Inc.)

Unlike UMA multiprocessors, such as the Sequent Symmetry, the TC2000 does not maintain cache consistency among all the processors' data caches. That is why the operating system puts restrictions on what data can be cached.

Figure 3-19 illustrates the butterfly switch shown in Fig. 3-18 in more detail. Imagine that the cylinder of Fig. 3-18 has been split down the side, between the processors and the memories, then flattened and rotated 90 degrees. Each node of the switch is a VLSI switching element with eight inputs and eight outputs. Hence the number of switching elements in a p-processor machine is $p \log_8 p$. Data flow through the switch in packets; and the address bits route the data from the source to the destination.

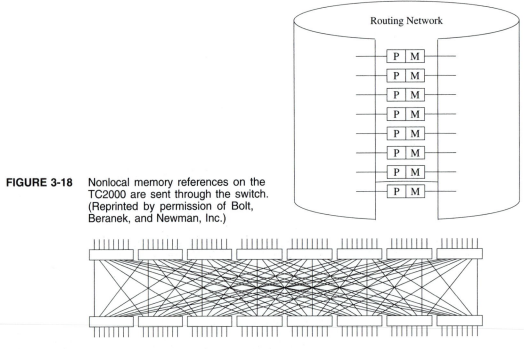

FIGURE 3-18 Nonlocal memory references on the TC2000 are sent through the switch. (Reprinted by permission of Bolt, Beranek, and Newman, Inc.)

FIGURE 3-19 Switching network for a 64–processor TC2000.

Since every processor has a VME interface, the I/O capability of the system grows at the same rate as the number of CPUs. The VME interface provides access to a wide variety of I/O devices, including A/D and D/A converters, secondary storage devices, and graphics processors. A 16-Mbyte window in each VME bus address space is mapped into the system's global address space, giving every processor in the system the potential to access to every I/O device.

Another computer, called the Test and Control System (TCS) master processor, provides several vital functions. The TCS master processor provides a user interface to the TCS. It also loads bootstrap programs into the processors' memories at system boot time, coordinates the activities of the slave processors, and receives messages sent by the slave processors. The TCS master processor is connected via a diagnostic bus to slave processors, which are located in the processor cards and in every pair of switch modules, and which continuously monitor the system for faults.

3.4 MULTICOMPUTERS

Another multiple-CPU architecture, the multicomputer, has no shared memory. Each processor has its own private memory and process interaction occurs through message passing. Commercial multicomputers include Intel's Paragon

XP/S, Meiko's Computing Surface™, nCUBE's nCUBE 2, Parsytec's SuperCluster™, and Thinking Machines' CM-5.

An important distinction between early multicomputers and contemporary systems is the change in how processors communicate. First generation multicomputers, such as the Intel iPSC™, the nCUBE/10™, and systems based on the T800 Transputer™, are characterized by software managed **store-and-forward message passing** (Fig. 3-20). In order to send a message from one processor to a nonadjacent processor, every intermediate processor along the message's path must store the entire message and then forward the message to the next processor down the line. Even if the data transfers are accomplished through DMA channels, the CPU is interrupted every time a DMA transfer is initiated.

In contrast, second generation multicomputers, such as the Intel iPSC/2™, Intel iPSC/860™, and nCUBE 2, have **circuit-switched message routing**. For example, every iPSC/2 and iPSC/860 node has a routing logic daughter card called the Direct-Connect Module. The Direct-Connect Modules set up a circuit from the source node to the destination node. Once the circuit is set up, the message flows in a pipelined fashion from the source node to the destination node— none of the intermediate nodes store the message. A message being passed from one node to a nonadjacent node does not interrupt the CPUs of the intermediate nodes and only the Direct-Connect Modules are involved (Fig. 3-21).

In a store-and-forward scheme, the time needed to send a message from one processor to another processor grows linearly with the number of "hops" the message must make to reach its destination. In contrast to a store-and-forward scheme, the time needed to send a message from one processor to another processor in a circuit-switched scheme is much less dependent on the distance between the processors.

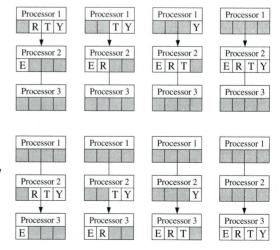

FIGURE 3-20   Early multicomputers used store-and-forward routing. Every intermediate processor along the message's path must store the entire message before forwarding the message to the next processor.

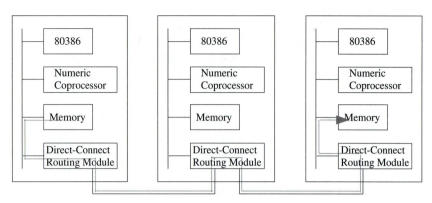

FIGURE 3-21   The Direct-Connect Modules on the Intel iPSC/2 multicomputer support circuit-switched message routing which allows a connection to be established between the sending and receiving processors and keeps the CPUs of intermediate nodes from being interrupted when a message passes through. (Courtesy Hatcher and Quinn [1991].)

3.4.1   nCUBE 2

The nCUBE 2 is manufactured by nCUBE Corporation of Foster City, California. The nCUBE 2 has three principal components: a front-end computer, a back-end array of processors, and parallel I/O devices (Fig. 3-22). Superficially, the nCUBE 2 resembles a processor array (compare Fig. 3-22 with Fig. 3.11). However, the two architectures have a fundamental difference. The front-end computer of a processor array controls the activities of the processing elements, which synchronously perform simple computations. In contrast, the back-end (or node) processors of the nCUBE are full-fledged CPUs, and these CPUs execute their own instruction streams in parallel.

The nCUBE 2 contains up to 8,192 node processors. Each node processor has a peak performance of 2.5 megaflops. Hence the theoretical peak perfor-

FIGURE 3-22   Block diagram an nCUBE 2 multicomputer with eight back-end processors and two parallel I/O devices.

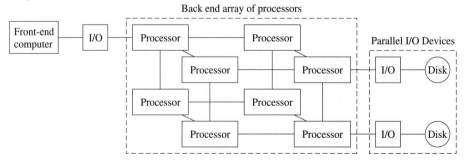

mance of a maximally-configured nCUBE 2 is about 20 gigaflops. Every node processor has between 1 and 64 megabytes of primary memory.

The back-end processors are organized into a hypercube. The nCUBE 2 is a second generation multicomputer in that hardware-routed, DMA communication channels form the edges of the hypercube. The peak data-transfer rate between processors is 2.2 Mbytes per second.

Each node has a DMA channel dedicated to the data transfers to and from I/O devices. These I/O channels have the same speed as the internode communication channels.

Many early multicomputers, including the nCUBE 2, have two problems related to the front-end processor. First, the power of the front-end processor does not scale with the number of back end processors. If the number of users scales with the number of processors, then at some point the front end will be unable to support the users. Second, the front-end processor is isolated from the back-end processors.

3.4.2   Connection Machine CM-5

The Connection Machine CM-5 is the first multiple-CPU computer manufactured by Thinking Machines Corporation of Cambridge, Massachusetts. Thinking Machines argues that since the CM-5 supports fast synchronization hardware as well as multiple CPUs, the CM-5 is a suitable architecture for executing both data-parallel and control-parallel programs.

Figure 3-23 is a block diagram of the CM-5. Processing nodes, labeled with a P, execute user programs. Control processors, labeled CP, act as partition managers—front ends for clusters of processing nodes. I/O control processors control I/O devices.

The CM-5 architecture remedies some of the problems associated with front-end processors of some earlier multicomputers. First, the system may contain multiple front-end processors, the partition managers. Second, these processors are based upon the SPARC CPU, the same processor as the back-end processors. Third, the partition managers are part of the same data routing network as the back-end processors.

The CM-5 processor organization is a 4-ary hypertree (Fig. 3-3). The processors are at the leaves of the tree and the interior nodes route data between the leaves. The minimum network bandwidth is 5 Mbytes/second.

Each CM-5 processing node consists of a SPARC CPU, network interface hardware, up to 32 megabytes of primary memory, and four pipelined vector processing units, each capable of performing up to 32 million double-precision floating-point operations per second. A fully configured CM-5 would have 16,384 processing nodes, 512 Gbytes of primary memory, and a theoretical peak performance of about 2 teraflops. (We should point out that a CM-5 built using 1991 technology would occupy about 10,000 square feet of floor space and would cost several hundred million dollars.)

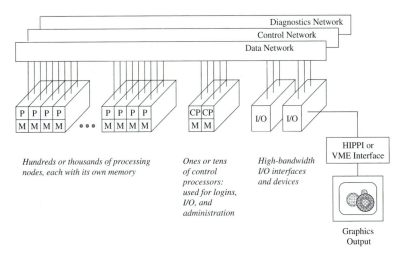

Hundreds or thousands of processing
nodes, each with its own memory

Ones or tens
of control
processors:
used for logins,
I/O, and
administration

High-bandwidth
I/O interfaces
and devices

Graphics
Output

FIGURE 3-23 Block diagram of the Connection Machine CM-5. Processing nodes, labeled with a *P*, execute user programs. Control processors, labeled *CP*, act as partition managers—front ends for clusters of processing nodes. I/O control processors control I/O devices. (Reprinted by permission of Thinking Machines Corporation.)

3.4.3 Paragon XP/S

The Paragon XP/S is the fourth in a series of commercial multicomputers manufactured by Intel Corporation in Beaverton, Oregon. A number of important hardware and software features distinguish the Paragon XP/S from the nCUBE 2 and the CM-5.

The first interesting feature of the Paragon is that its nodes are organized as a 2-D mesh (Fig. 3-24). Much of the hardware is dedicated to improving the communication speed of the system. Custom mesh-routing chips lie at each mesh intersection. Each of these chips can route more than 200 Mbytes of data per second. Inside the node a custom network interface chip serves as the interface between a node and its mesh routing chip. Finally, an i860 XP processor within each node, is dedicated to message passing, which frees the application processors from the details of message passing. Figure 3-25 illustrates a node of the Paragon XP/S.

A second distinguishing characteristic of the Paragon XP/S is that it goes even further than the CM-5 in eliminating barriers between the front-end and back-end processors. In the Intel scheme of things, a node can play one of three roles. A "service node" supports general user services such as text editors, compilers, and UNIX shells. A "compute node" executes users' application programs, usually in conjunction with other compute nodes. And finally, I/O nodes serve as intermediaries between service and compute nodes and the I/O devices. As in the CM-5, all of these node types are part of the same routing network. There are no arbitrary bottlenecks between service nodes and compute

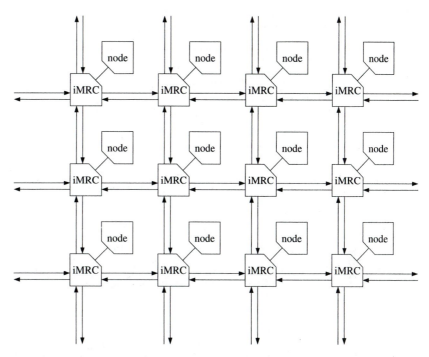

FIGURE 3-24   The Paragon XP/S uses a 2-D mesh processor organization. At each mesh point a mesh routing chip passes data at up to 200 Mbytes/second. (Reprinted by permission of Intel Corporation. Copyright ©Intel Corporation 1993.)

FIGURE 3-25   Architecture of a Paragon XP/S node. Each node contain at least one i860 XP application processor, one i860 XP message processor, performance monitoring hardware, and a network interface chip. Compute and service nodes can have between 16 and 128 Mbytes of primary memory. I/O nodes can have between 16 and 64 Mbytes of primary memory. I/O nodes also contain at least one I/O interface. (Reprinted by permission of Intel Corporation. Copyright ©Intel Corporation 1993.)

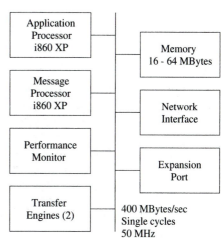

FIGURE 3-26   The role of nodes in a compute partition can change over time. In this figure the system's nodes are divided into three batch partitions (A, B, and C) between midnight and 8 AM. Between 8 AM and 5 PM the nodes are divided into one batch partition (D) and three interactive partitions (E, F, and G). The reallocation of nodes can be done as the system is running.

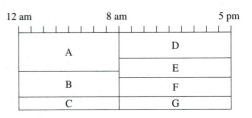

nodes or between compute nodes and I/O nodes. Unlike the CM-5, however, the XP/S can be reconfigured, altering the relative number of service and compute nodes.

For example, during the daytime the system may be configured so that it has a larger number of service nodes to support the number of people logged into the system, while at night the system may be reconfigured to have fewer support nodes and more compute nodes, so that production jobs may finish more quickly.

In addition, the nodes in the compute partition can be divided into a number of subpartitions. Some subpartitions can be used to execute batch jobs, while others use timesharing to support multiple users. Figure 3-26 illustrates how the subpartitioning of Paragon compute nodes can change over time.

A third distinguishing characteristic of the Paragon XP/S is that it supports virtual memory, which allows each process to access more memory than physically exists on a single node.

The theoretical peak performance of the i860 XP CPU is 75 million double-precision floating-point operations per second. If a Paragon XP/S system were constructed with 1024 nodes, each containing four i860 XP application processors, the theoretical peak performance of the system would be about 300 gigaflops. At 128 Mbytes primary memory per node, the aggregate primary memory of the system would be 128 Gbytes.

3.5 FLYNN'S TAXONOMY

Flynn's taxonomy is the best known classification scheme for serial and parallel computer architectures. In this section we present his scheme and use it to categorize the parallel architectures we have described in this chapter.

Flynn bases his taxonomy of computer architectures on the dual concepts of instruction stream and data stream (Flynn 1966, 1972). An **instruction stream** is a sequence of instructions performed by a computer; a **data stream** is a sequence of data manipulated by an instruction stream. Flynn categorizes an architecture by the multiplicity of hardware used to manipulate instruction and data streams. "The multiplicity is taken as the maximum possible number of simultaneous operations (instructions) or operands (data) being in the same phase of execution *at the most constrained* component of the organization" (Flynn's emphasis) (Flynn 1966). Four classes of computers result from the given multiplicity of instruction and data streams.

Single Instruction stream, Single Data stream (SISD) Most serial computers fall into this category. Although instruction execution may be pipelined, computers in this category can decode only a single instruction in unit time. A SISD computer may have multiple functional units, but these are under the direction of a single control unit.

Single Instruction stream, Multiple Data stream (SIMD) Processor arrays fall into this category. A processor array executes a single stream of instructions, but contains a number of arithmetic processing units, each capable of fetching and manipulating its own data. Hence in any time unit, a single operation is in the same state of execution on multiple processing units, each manipulating different data. The Connection Machine CM-200 is a SIMD computer.

Multiple Instruction stream, Single Data stream (MISD) Of the four categories in Flynn's taxonomy, MISD is the least intuitive. How can a computer have multiple instruction streams but only a single data stream? Some think **systolic arrays** fit into this category. The word "systolic" means a rhythmic contraction, especially of the heart muscle. A systolic array is a parallel computer that rhythmically "pumps" data from processor to processor. Each processor may modify the data before passing it on to the next processor, which may perform a different operation on the data (see Fig. 3-27).

Multiple Instruction stream, Multiple Data stream (MIMD) —This category contains most multiprocessor systems. Early multiprocessors were built to increase the throughput of multiprogrammed operating systems, and there was little interaction among the CPUs. In this book the label *MIMD* is reserved for multiple-CPU computers designed for parallel processing; that is, computers designed to allow efficient interactions among their CPUs. The Symmetry, TC2000, nCUBE 2, Paragon XP/S, and Connection Machine CM-5 are MIMD computers.

FIGURE 3-27   A comparison of a traditional SISD computation model with the systolic array computation model, which some consider an example of MISD processing. (Hennessy and Patterson [1990].)

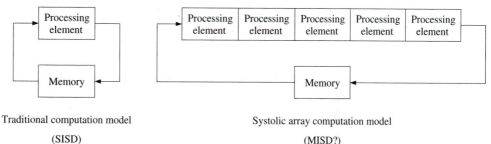

Traditional computation model

(SISD)

Systolic array computation model

(MISD?)

Flynn's classification scheme is too vague to allow iron-clad labeling of supercomputers. It is only natural, then, that there is some disagreement among experts as to how to classify certain architectures. For example, in what category does the Cray-1, a pipelined vector processor, belong? Because it is a vector computer, Hockney and Jesshope (1981) label the Cray-1 an example of an SIMD architecture. Because it does not have multiple processing elements, Hwang and Briggs (1984) put the Cray-1 into the SISD category. Hwang and Briggs' position seems more consistent with Flynn's definition that we quoted earlier, so we categorize the Cray-1 as a SISD computer. In this text the terms *SIMD computer* and *processor array* are synonymous.

3.6   SPEEDUP, SCALED SPEEDUP, AND PARALLELIZABILITY

Two important measures of the quality of parallel algorithms implemented on multiprocessors and multicomputers are speedup and efficiency. The **speedup** achieved by a parallel algorithm running on p processors is the ratio between the time taken by that parallel computer executing the fastest serial algorithm (on one processor) and the time taken by the same parallel computer executing the corresponding parallel algorithm using p processors. The **efficiency** of a parallel algorithm running on p processors is the speedup divided by p.

An example illustrates the terminology. If the best known sequential algorithm executes in 8 seconds on a parallel computer, while a parallel algorithm solving the same problem executes in 2 seconds when five processors are used, then we say that the parallel algorithm "exhibits a speedup of 4 with five processors." A parallel algorithm that exhibits a speedup of 4 with five processors "has an efficiency of 0.8 with five processors."

Some define the speedup of a parallel algorithm running on p processors to be the time taken by the parallel algorithm on one processor divided by the time taken by the parallel algorithm using p processors. This definition can be misleading since parallel algorithms frequently contain extra operations to facilitate parallelization. Comparing the execution time of a parallel algorithm running on many processors with that same algorithm running on one processor can exaggerate the speedup, because it masks the overhead of the parallel algorithm. In this book we use the term **parallelizability** to refer to the ratio between the time taken by a parallel computer executing a parallel algorithm on one processor and the time taken by the same parallel computer executing the same parallel algorithm on p processors.

3.6.1   Can Speedup Be Greater than Linear?

Is superlinear speedup possible? In other words, is it possible for the speedup achieved by a parallel algorithm to be greater than the number of processors used? The answer is that it depends upon the assumptions made.

Some people argue that speedup cannot be greater than linear (e.g., see Faber et al. 1986). They base their proof on the premise that a single processor can always emulate parallel processors. Suppose a parallel algorithm A solves an instance of problem Π in T_p units of time on a parallel computer with p processors. Then algorithm A can solve the same problem instance in $p \times T_p$ units of time on the same computer with one processor through time slicing. Hence the speedup cannot be greater than p. Since parallel algorithms usually have associated overhead, it is most likely there exists a sequential algorithm that solves the problem instance in less than $p \times T_p$ units of time, which means the speedup would be even less than linear.

We disagree with two assumptions made in the previous proof. One assumption is algorithmic, and the other is architectural. Let us first examine the questionable algorithmic assumption.

Is it reasonable to choose the algorithm after the problem *instance* is chosen? Speedup is intended to measure the time taken by the best sequential algorithm divided by the time taken by the parallel algorithm, but it is going too far to allow the definition of "best" to change every time the problem instance changes. In other words, it is more realistic to assume that the best sequential algorithm and the parallel algorithm be chosen before the particular problem instance is chosen. In this case it is possible for the parallel algorithm to exhibit superlinear speedup for some problem instances. For example, when solving a search problem, a sequential algorithm may waste a lot of time examining a dead-end strategy. A parallel algorithm pursues many possible strategies simultaneously, and one of the processes may "luck out" and find the solution very quickly.

The second questionable assumption is that a single processor can always emulate multiple processors without a loss of efficiency. There are often architectural reasons why this assumption does not hold. For example, each CPU in a UMA multiprocessor has a certain amount of cache. A group of p processors executing a parallel algorithm has p times as much cache memory as a single processor. It is easy to construct circumstances in which the collective cache hit rate of a group of p processors is significantly higher than the cache hit rate of a single processor executing the best sequential algorithm or emulating the parallel algorithm. In these circumstances the p processors can execute a parallel algorithm more than p times faster than a single processor executing the best sequential algorithm.

The reader may favor either side of the argument, but we have adopted the latter position. Later in the book examples of superlinear speedup are given where the problem instance is chosen after the sequential and parallel algorithms have been selected.

3.6.2 Scaled Speedup

Let f be the fraction of operations in a computation that must be performed sequentially, where $0 \le f \le 1$. Amdahl's law states that the maximum speedup S achievable by a parallel computer with p processors performing the computation is

$$S \leq \frac{1}{f + \frac{(1-f)}{p}}$$

A corollary follows immediately from Amdahl's law: a small number of sequential operations can significantly limit the speedup achievable by a parallel computer. For example, if 10 percent of the operations must be performed sequentially, then the maximum speedup achievable is 10, no matter how many processors a parallel computer has.

Amdahl's law is based upon the idea that parallel processing is used to reduce the time in which a problem of some particular size can be solved, and in some contexts this is a reasonable assumption. In many situations, however, parallel processing is used to increase the size of the problem that can be solved in a given (fixed) amount of time. For example, a design engineer checking the turbulence around an air foil may be willing to wait an hour for the computer to determine the solution. Increasing the speed of the computer allows the engineer to increase the resolution of the computed answer. Under these circumstances, Amdahl's law is not an accurate indicator of the value of parallel processing, because Amdahl's law assumes that the sequential component is fixed.

However, for many problems the proportion of the operations that are sequential decreases as the problem size increases. Every parallel program has certain overhead costs, such as creating processes, which are independent of the problem size. Other overhead costs, such as input/output and process synchronization, may increase with the problem size, but at a slower rate than the grain size. This phenomenon is called the **Amdahl effect** (Goodman and Hedetniemi 1977), and it explains why speedup is almost universally an increasing function of the size of the input problem (Fig. 3-28).

Scaled speedup is the ratio between how long a given optimal sequential program would have taken, had it been able to run on a single processor of a parallel computer, and the length of time that the parallel program requires when executing on multiple processors of the same parallel computer (Gustafson

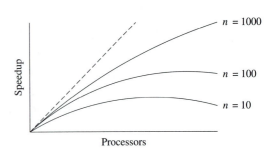

FIGURE 3-28 The Amdahl effect. As a general rule, speedup is an increasing function of the problem size.

1988; Gustafson et al. 1988). We define **scaled efficiency** to be scaled speedup divided by the number of processors used.

The difference between speedup and scaled speedup is subtle, yet important. In order to measure speedup, the algorithm must run on a single processor. On a multicomputer, that means the problem data must fit in the memory of that one processor. Far larger problems can be, and usually are, solved by systems with hundreds or thousands of processors, but the restriction that the problem be solvable by a single processor means that these large problems cannot be used to determine the speedup achieved by the parallel machine. The definition of scaled speedup allows the solution of these realistic, large problems on a multicomputer and an estimation of the execution time that would have been required if the same problems had been solved on a single processor with a massive primary memory.

For example, suppose we are interested in solving the largest system of linear equations we can in one minute. We would like to find out if we can make efficient use of a particular parallel computer to perform this task. A good sequential algorithm performs roughly $2n^3/3$ floating-point operations to solve a dense $n \times n$ system of linear equations. Given a processor capable of 100 million floating-point operations per second, the largest linear system we can solve in one minute is approximately

$$\frac{\left(2n^3/3\right) \text{ ops}}{100,000,000 \text{ ops/sec}} \leq 60 \text{ sec} \Rightarrow$$

$$n \leq 2,080$$

Now consider the implementation of a parallel linear system solver on a multicomputer system with 1024 processors. Assume that each processor performs 100 million floating point operations per second. Suppose sending or receiving a message requires 1 microsecond message initiation time plus 5 nanoseconds transmission time per floating-point value. A parallel linear system solver has each of the p processors performing roughly $2n^3/(3p)$ floating-point operations and sending or receiving about $4n \log p$ messages containing a total of about $n^2/2$ floating-point values. Given these assumptions, the largest system we can solve in one minute on the 1024–processor system is (maintaining 3 digits of precision)

$$\frac{\left(2n^3/3072\right) \text{ ops}}{1 \times 10^8 \text{ ops/sec}} + \frac{(40n) \text{ msgs}}{1 \times 10^6 \text{ msgs/sec}} + \frac{\left(n^2/2\right) \text{ floats}}{2 \times 10^8 \text{ floats/sec}} \leq 60 \text{ sec} \Rightarrow$$

$$6.51 \times 10^{-12}n^3 + 4.00 \times 10^{-5}n + 2.50 \times 10^{-9}n^2 \leq 60 \Rightarrow$$

$$n \leq 20,700$$

This calculation assumes, of course, that the entire system of equations fits in the aggregate primary memory of the multicomputer.

Now we can determine the scaled efficiency of the parallel implementation. A single 100-megaflop processor executing the sequential algorithm would require roughly 59,000 seconds to solve a system of size 20,700. The scaled speedup of this application is $59,000/60$ or about 983. The scaled efficiency of the processors is $983/1024$ or about 96%. In other words, the utilization of the 1024 processors is very high when solving a system of size 20,700 in 60 seconds.

3.7   SUMMARY

This chapter has discussed nine processor organizations and several parallel computer architectures. Processor organizations that have been suggested for parallel computers include the mesh, binary tree, hypertree, pyramid, butterfly, hypercube, cube-connected cycles, shuffle-exchange, and de Bruijn networks. We have evaluated these organizations according to four criteria: diameter, bisection width, number of connections per node, and whether or not increasing the number of nodes leads to an increase in the maximum connection length. These criteria help us determine both the suitability of the processor organization for supporting efficient parallel algorithms and the practicality of the organization from a manufacturing point of view.

Flynn's taxonomy divides all computers into four classes, based upon the serial/parallel processing of the instruction and data streams. Traditional sequential computers fall into the SISD category. Processor arrays are SIMD computers. Systolic arrays can be viewed as falling into the MISD category, while multiple-CPU computers, both multiprocessors and multicomputers, are MIMD.

A processor array is a practical implementation of a SIMD model of computation, in which parallel processing is achieved through the application of a single operation to a data set. It is not feasible to construct a processor array in which every processing element shares access to a common memory. In a real processor array, each processing element has its own local memory. The underlying processor organization determines the manner in which data are passed from processing element to processing element. For this reason we characterize SIMD models by the organization of the processing elements.

We described in some detail the Connection Machine CM-200, a well-known commercial processor array.

MIMD computers are a more general-purpose model of parallel computation, since they consist of a number of CPUs asynchronously executing independent instruction streams. MIMD computers can be categorized by the way that the CPUs access memory. UMA multiprocessors have a single, shared address space, and the distance from a CPU to any memory location is a constant.

NUMA multiprocessors also have a shared address space, but each memory cell is closer to one CPU than it is to the others. Multicomputers have no shared memory. Each CPU has its own private address space, and the processors interact through message passing.

In this chapter we described five commercial MIMD computers: the Sequent Symmetry, a UMA multiprocessor, the BBN TC2000, a NUMA multiprocessor, and the three multicomputers; the nCUBE 2, Thinking Machines CM-5, and Intel Paragon XP/S.

Speedup and efficiency are two important measures of the quality of a particular parallel algorithm implementation. Given the best sequential algorithm and a corresponding parallel algorithm, there may exist particular problem instances for which the parallel algorithm exhibits superlinear speedup (and hence efficiency greater than 1) for certain numbers of processors.

Amdahl's law assumes that parallel processing is used to reduce the time needed to solve a problems of a fixed size. However, parallel computers are often used to increase the size of a problem that can be solved in a fixed amount of time. In these circumstances scaled speedup is superior to speedup as a measure of the quality of a parallel algorithm.

3.8 BIBLIOGRAPHIC NOTES

The texts by Siegel (1985), Ullman (1984), and Uhr (1984) contain a wealth of information on processor interconnection methodologies. Feng (1981) also surveys connection methods.

Miller and Stout (1984b, 1985b, 1987) have described algorithms for pyramid computers. The shuffle-exchange network was introduced by Stone (1971). Additional references on shuffle-exchange networks include Kumar and Reddy (1987), Lang and Stone (1976) and Wu and Feng (1981). Lawrie (1975) introduced the omega network, a multistage network based on perfect shuffle connections. Siegel (1979a) shows how other interconnection networks can simulate the perfect shuffle.

The evaluation of interconnection networks for multicomputers is the subject of a paper by Agrawal et al. (1986). Reed and Grunwald (1987) discuss methods that can be used to choose the best interconnection network for a class of applications. Bhuyan et al. (1989) give a tutorial on evaluation tools to help designers evaluate network performance.

The April 1989 issue of *IEEE Transactions on Reliability* is a special issue focusing on the reliability of parallel and distributed computing networks. Other papers discussing fault tolerance of interconnection networks include Adams (1987) and Das et al. (1990)

Papers discussing de Bruijn networks include (Esfahanian and Hakimi 1985; Pradhan 1985; Samatham and Pradhan 1989, 1991; Sridar 1988).

Two other processor organizations, not discussed in this chapter, deserve mention. Rosenfeld (1985) has proposed the prism network as an alternative to the pyramid. A prism network contains as many levels as a pyramid network, but, unlike a pyramid, every level of the prism contains the same number of processors. Prisms have a number of interesting attributes. A prism can simulate a pyramid in linear time. In addition, a prism can compute a fast Fourier transform in linear time. Also, the mesh-of-trees network has captured the interest of some theoreticians. Properties of this topology are discussed in Ullman (1984).

A parallel model is **reasonable** if the number of processors each processor can communicate with is bounded by a constant (Goldschlager 1982). A natural question is whether each of these reasonable processor organizations—mesh, pyramid, butterfly, shuffle-exchange, de Bruijn, cube-connected cycles, binary tree, and hypertree—is superior for some class of problems or whether one of these is the best overall model. Galil and Paul (1981, 1983) show that a universal parallel model can simulate every reasonable parallel model "with only a small loss of time and with essentially the same number of processors." The heart of their universal computer is a sorting network that is used as a "post office" for sending and requesting information. Galil and Paul have shown that since cube-connected cycles are used as the sorting network, the cube-connected cycles network (and hence the butterfly) is an efficient general-purpose network. However, constants of proportionality are unimportant to a theoretician, yet are vital to a computer architect interested in building a supercomputer. This may be one reason why commercial parallel computer companies have not rushed to build computers based upon the cube-connected cycles network.

Books on parallel computer architecture include Almasi and Gottlieb (1989), Frenkel (1986), Hockney and Jesshope (1981), Hwang and Briggs (1984), Lipovski and Malek (1987), and Tabak (1990). The Hennessy and Patterson (1990) architecture book has an excellent chapter on parallel processing.

Duncan (1990, 1992) has surveyed parallel computer architectures, both SIMD and MIMD. Lubeck (1988) describes models and supercomputer performance and discusses benchmarking practices.

A large number of references exist for processor arrays. Books by Thurber (1976), Kuck (1978), Stone (1980), and Hwang and Briggs (1984) introduce the subject. Paul (1978), Thurber (1979), and Hwang, Su, and Ni (1981) have compared various processor array architectures. Hockney and Jesshope (1981) cover the DAP, a mesh-connected processor array, in their monograph. The DAP is also discussed by Reddaway (1979). Barnes et al. (1968) and Falk (1976) are references for the ILLIAC IV computer. Batcher (1980) and Fung (1977) describe Goodyear's Massively Parallel Processor.

Enslow (1977) is an early survey of multiprocessor architectures. Fuller and Oleinick (1976) and Mashburn (1979) have written about C.mmp, a multiprocessor developed at Carnegie-Mellon University in the 1970s. Gottlieb (1986) and Gottlieb et al. (1983) describe the New York University Ultracomputer. Mudge et al. (1987) argue that the number of CPUs in a UMA multiprocessor can be increased to a few hundred by replacing a single shared bus with a set of buses. Thakkar et al. (1990) also discuss methods to build larger UMA multiprocessors.

An important problem associated with UMA multiprocessors is cache coherency. Stenström (1990) has surveyed cache coherency schemes. Other articles discussing the cache coherency problem include (Archibald and Baer 1986; Chaiken et al. 1990; Cheong and Veidenbaum 1990; Eggers and Katz 1989; Gupta and Weber 1992; Hill and Larus 1990; Teller 1990).

Stenström (1988) surveys methods to reduce contention in UMA multiprocessors. Dinning (1989) and Graunke and Thakker (1990) describe synchronization algorithms for UMA multiprocessors.

Stone (1980) and Swan et al. (1977) are two of many sources of information on Cm*, a NUMA multiprocessor constructed at Carnegie-Mellon University. Cheriton et al. (1991) discuss Paradigm, a NUMA multiprocessor under development at Stanford University.

Seitz (1985) describes the implementation of the Cosmic Cube, a hypercube multicomputer built at the California Institute of Technology. Athas and Seitz (1988) describe contemporary multicomputer architectures and algorithms.

The February 1982 issue of *Computer* is dedicated to data-flow computing and it is a good place to start learning more about the subject. Particularly useful articles in this issue are those by Ackerman (1982), Davis and Keller (1982), Gajski et al. (1982), and Watson and Gurd (1981). Gurd, Kirkham, and Watson (1985) have described the prototype data-flow computer built at the University of Manchester.

Much attention has been given to designing parallel algorithms for VLSI circuits. A representative set of references includes Bilardi, Pracchi, and Preparata (1981); Chazelle and Monier (1981a, 1981b); Kung (1982); Mead and Conway (1980); Lang et al. (1983); Leighton (1983); Leiserson (1983); Shröder (1983); Thompson (1980, 1983); and Ullman (1984).

Kutti (1985) has proposed a taxonomy for parallel and distributed systems that uses "the address space or buffer type as the key identifying element." This classification scheme is able to distinguish multiprocessors from multicomputers, both of which fall into Flynn's MIMD category. Skillicorn (1988) has proposed an extension to Flynn's taxonomy that also serves to distinguish various MIMD computers. Yet another classification scheme has been proposed by Händler (1977).

Distributed shared memory is the implementation of the shared-memory abstraction on a multicomputer architecture. Nitzberg and Lo (1991) and Stumm and Zhou (1990) compare algorithms for implementing distributed shared memory.

Numerous papers describe models for predicting the speedup and/or scalability of parallel algorithms. A few references are Eager et al. (1989), Flatt and Kennedy (1989), Karp and Flatt (1990), and Nussbaum and Agarwal (1991).

3.9 PROBLEMS

3-1 What is the difference between a binary k-cube and a cube-connected network of degree k?

3-2 Given a d-dimensional hypercube and a designated source node s, how many nodes are distance i from s, where $0 \leq i \leq d$?

3-3* A shuffle-exchange network can simulate a hypercube network. Because not every pair of nodes connected in a hypercube is connected in a shuffle-exchange network, a single hop along a communication link in a hypercube may turn into several hops in a shuffle-exchange network. Derive an upper bound on the maximum number of communications necessary in a shuffle-exchange network to simulate a single communication in a hypercube.

3-4 Given a shuffle-exchange network, prove that if a shuffle link connects nodes i and j, then j is a single-bit left cyclic rotation of i.

3-5 Given a shuffle-exchange network with 2^k nodes, under what circumstances are nodes i and j exactly $2k - 1$ link traversals apart?

3-6* Prove that the number of necklaces in an n-node shuffle-exchange network is $O(2^k/k)$.

3-7 Show how to perform the perfect shuffle network's exchange operation on a de Bruijn network.

3-8 A bipartite graph is a graph G with the property that its set of vertices can be decomposed into two disjoint subsets V_1 and V_2 such that every edge in G connects a vertex in V_1 with a vertex in V_2. Which of the graphs described in Sec. 3.1 are bipartite?

3-9 Name two ways to implement vector computers.

3-10 What are the advantages and disadvantages of moving from the UMA multiprocessor model to the NUMA multiprocessor model?

3-11 Read this quote from Lillevik (1991): "The CSC Touchstone DELTA [multicomputer] System features a glass-like front door with an array of LEDs that indicate both processor and communication status. Physically, each node in the mesh is mapped to a corresponding position on the front door. At this location, there is both a red and green LED that the application can control. Between each set of node LEDs, a longer LED spans the distance and illuminates when a message traverses that position in the interconnect. As an application runs, the LEDs offer a rather unique picture or signature of node activity and this communication is useful for application debugging and performance tuning." What does this quote say about the state of application debugging and performance monitoring tools on some contemporary parallel computers?

3-12 The **bisection bandwidth** of a parallel computer is the bisection width of its underlying processor organization multiplied by the data transfer rate of each communication link. What is the bisection bandwidth of a Paragon XP/S configured as a 16×64 mesh? What is the bisection bandwidth of a CM-5 with 1024 nodes?

3-13 Suppose a multiprocessor is built out of individual processors capable of sustaining 50 megaflops. What is the largest fraction of a program's execution time that could be devoted to sequential operations if the parallel computer is to exceed the performance of a supercomputer capable of sustaining 1 gigaflops?

3-14 Is it possible for the average speedup exhibited by a parallel algorithm to be superlinear?

3-15 Calculate the speedup that would be achieved on a system of size 2,080 by the hypothetical parallel linear system solver described in Sec. 3.6 as a function of number of processors p, where $1 \le p \le 1024$.

4

PARALLEL
PROGRAMMING
LANGUAGES

There are many different languages in the world, yet none of them is without meaning. But if I do not know the language being spoken, the person who uses it will be a foreigner to me, and I will be a foreigner to him.

In this chapter we describe six of the languages used to program parallel computers and how these languages address the problems of parallel process allocation and coordination. In Sec. 4.1 we present a high-level view of parallel programming issues. In Sec. 4.2 through 4.7, we introduce six parallel programming languages. In Sec. 4.8, we describe the pseudocode we will use to represent parallel algorithms in the remainder of the text.

Our focus is on imperative languages, because the majority of sequential and parallel programs are written in the imperative style. Many parallel programmers will continue to use imperative languages, even if research in logic programming and functional programming languages leads to efficient implementations on parallel machines. See the bibliographic notes at the end of this chapter for more references regarding parallel implementations of functional and declarative languages.

4.1 PROGRAMMING PARALLEL PROCESSES

Every parallel language must address certain issues, either explicitly or implicitly. There must be a way to create parallel processes, and there must be a way to coordinate the activities of these processes. Sometimes the processes work on their own data and do not interact. But when processes exchange results, they must communicate and synchronize with each other. Communication and synchronization can be accomplished by sharing variables or by message passing.

There are two methods of synchronization: synchronization for precedence and synchronization for mutual exclusion. Precedence synchronization guarantees that one event does not begin until another event has finished. Mutual exclusion synchronization guarantees that only one process at a time enters a critical section of code where a data structure to be shared is manipulated.

4.1.1 An Illustrative Example

The way in which the creation, communication, and synchronization of processes are ultimately implemented depends upon the target architecture. To illustrate this point, let's consider the problem of computing, for a list of real numbers, the variance of the values: given $r_1, r_2, r_3, \ldots, r_n$, compute $\sum_1^n (r_i - m)^2/n$ where $m = \sum_1^n r_i/n$.

Suppose we want to implement a parallel algorithm to perform this task on a UMA multiprocessor with four processors. We store the n real numbers in shared memory. We also reserve four variables in shared memory: one will contain the grand total, another the mean, a third the global sum of squares, and a fourth the variance. In sequential code we initialize the two accumulator variables to zero. We create four processes, one per processor. Each process has a local temporary variable. Each process adds its share of the n values, accumulating the sum in its local temporary variable. When the process is through computing its subtotal, it adds its subtotal to the shared variable, accumulating the grand total. Since multiple processes are accessing the same global variable, that portion of code is a critical section, and the processes must enforce mutual exclusion. A **barrier synchronization** step, inserted in the algorithm after the critical section, ensures that no process continues until all processes have added their subtotals to the grand total. In sequential code one process computes the average by dividing the grand total by n. To compute the global sum of squares, the processes go through a process similar to that which computes the global sum. Again, the processes must enforce mutual exclusion as they add the sum of squares for their part of the list to the grand total. After another barrier synchronization, one process computes the variance by dividing the sum of squares by the number of values. We illustrate the procedure in Fig. 4-1.

Now let us consider how to solve the same problem on a four-node hypercube multicomputer. The program executing on the host processor allocates the

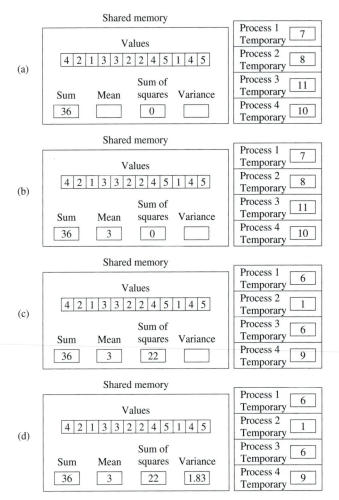

FIGURE 4-1 Computation of variance of a list of numbers on a UMA multiprocessor. (a) Each process totals its share of the values, accumulating the sum in its own temporary variable. When it has found its subtotal, it adds its subtotal to the grand total stored in a shared variable. (b) A single process computes the mean, given the sum. (c) Each process finds, for its set of three values, the sum of the square of the difference between each value and the mean, accumulating the sum of squares in its own temporary variable. When it has found its subtotal, it adds its subtotal to the grand total stored in a shared variable. (d) A single process divides the sum of squares by 12 to determine the variance.

hypercube (gaining access to the nodes) and starts a node process executing on each of the four nodes of the back end. There is no shared memory; the n values are distributed among the local memories of the nodes. Each node process has four variables: two to accumulate sums, one to store the mean, and another to store the variance. Each node process initializes the two accumulator variables to zero. It then accumulates the sum of its local portion of the list into the global sum variable. At this point every process has a subtotal; the four subtotals must be combined to find the grand total. After two exchange-and-add steps, every process has the grand total. Every process can divide the grand total by n to determine the mean.

A similar set of steps allows the processes to compute the variance of the list values. Every process has the result. One of the processes can pass the answer back to program running on the front end, which then deallocates the hypercube, surrendering access to the nodes. The procedure is illustrated in Fig. 4-2.

Low-level parallel languages present the programmer with constructs closely tied to the underlying architecture. For example, Sequent C, targeted to a UMA multiprocessor, enhances C by adding constructs for declaring shared variables, forking and killing parallel processes, locking and unlocking variables to enforce mutual exclusion, and enforcing barrier synchronizations. In contrast, nCUBE C, targeted to a hypercube multicomputer, enhances C by adding constructs for sending, receiving, and testing for the existence of messages between processors. We will examine both these low-level parallel languages later in this chapter.

High-level parallel languages present the programmer with a more abstract model of parallel computation. This can make programs shorter and easier to understand. Another advantage of a high-level parallel language is that it may be less dependent on the system architecture, increasing program portability. The disadvantage of a high-level language, of course, is that it makes compiler construction more challenging, since high-level languages increase the demands programmers make on the target hardware. We will explore four high-level parallel imperative languages in this chapter: the SIMD languages Fortran 90 and C*, and the MIMD languages occam and C-Linda.

Many have argued that the existence of billions of dollars' worth of programs written in sequential languages—particularly FORTRAN—implies that the most reasonable approach to programming parallel computers is to provide users with compilers to translate sequential programs into code that works on parallel machines. For more than 20 years researchers have continued to develop more sophisticated analysis techniques to facilitate the translation process. Whether or not the approach is sound, it is outside the scope of this book. The bibliographic notes list books devoted to automatic parallelization of sequential programs.

4.1.2   A Sample Application

We will implement a solution to a simple numerical integration problem using each language. The parallel program must compute an approximation to π by using numerical integration to find the area under the curve $4/(1+x^2)$ between 0 and 1 (Fig. 4-3).

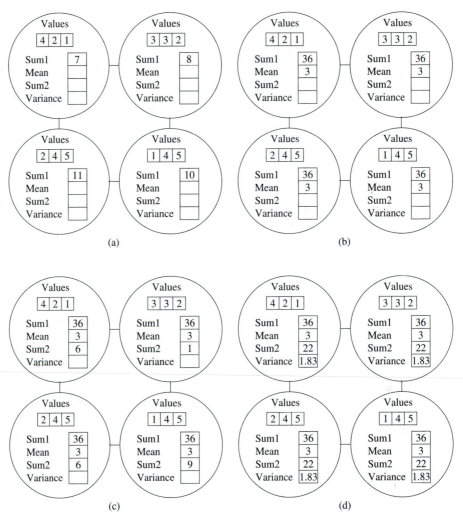

FIGURE 4-2   Computing the variance of a list of numbers on a four-node hypercube multicomputer. (a) Each process sums its own values. (b) Processes swap values and accumulate total. Each process divides total by 12 to get mean. (c) Each process computes, for its own set of values, the sum of the squares of the difference between each value and the mean. (d) Processes swap values and accumulate total sum of squares. Each process divides total by 12 to get variance.

The interval $[0, 1]$ is divided into n subintervals of width $1/n$. For each of these intervals the algorithm computes the area of a rectangle whose height is such that the curve $4/(1 + x^2)$ intersects the top of the rectangle at its midpoint. The sum of the areas of the n rectangles approximates the area under the curve. Increasing n reduces the difference between the sum of the rectangle's area and the area under the curve.

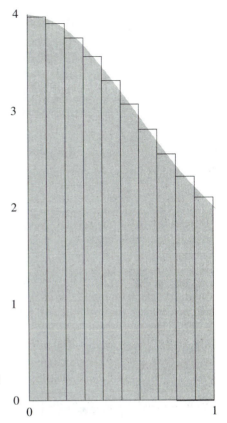

FIGURE 4-3   The area under the curve $4/(1 + x^2)$ between 0 and 1 is π. The area of the rectangles approximates the area under the curve. (Courtesy Hatcher and Quinn (1991).

This algorithm is data-parallel, since the areas of all the rectangles can be computed simultaneously. Computing the area of each rectangle requires the same amount of work: hence load balancing is insignificant. If the language requires us to divide the work among the processors, we can do so easily.

4.2 FORTRAN 90

In 1978 the ANSI-accredited technical committee, X3J3, began working on a new version of the FORTRAN language. In the early 1990s the resulting language, Fortran 90, was adopted as an ISO and ANSI standard. Fortran 90 is a superset of FORTRAN 77. It includes all the features of FORTRAN 77, plus

- Array operations
- Improved facilities for numerical computations
- Syntax to allow processors to support short integers, packed logicals, very large character sets, and high-precision real and complex numbers
- User-defined data types, structures, and pointers

- Dynamic storage allocation
- Modules to support abstract data types
- Internal procedures and recursive procedures
- Improvements to input-output facilities
- New control structures
- New intrinsic procedures
- Terminal-oriented source form

The committee also marked many language features as obsolete, including arithmetic `IF`, some `DO`-construct variations, assigned `GO TO`, assigned formats, and the `H` edit descriptor. The next revision of the FORTRAN standard may not contain these features.

In this section we will describe only a small portion of the language. For a more complete description of the Fortran 90 language, refer to Metcalf and Reid (1990), our primary source for the information and examples in this section.

4.2.1   Fortran 90 Programmer's Model

The Fortran 90 programmer has a model of parallel computation similar to a PRAM (Fig. 4-4). A CPU and a vector unit share a single memory. The CPU executes sequential instructions, accessing variables stored in the shared memory. To execute parallel operations, the CPU controls the vector unit, which also stores and fetches data to and from the shared memory.

4.2.2   Fortran 90 Language Features

Fortran 90 gives the programmer the ability to specify the type of variables through type declaration statements, such as

```
REAL A, B, C
INTEGER I
```

Each type may have several kinds. For example, a real variable may be stored in 4 bytes or 8 bytes. The Fortran 90 programmer may specify explicitly the kind, as well as the type of the variable, as in the following example:

```
REAL(KIND=LONG) PI
```

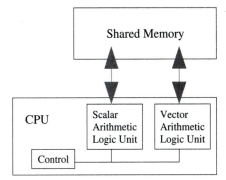

FIGURE 4-4   The Fortran 90 programmer's model of parallel computation.

Fortran 90 introduces the notion of an array constant. For example,

```
(/ 2, 3, 5, 7, 11 /)
```

denotes a one-dimensional array with five elements. It is possible to construct an array of higher dimension by declaring an array constant, then changing its dimension with the RESHAPE function.

An implied DO notation can simplify the specification of array constants. For example, the array constant

```
(/ 2, 4, 6, 8, 10 /)
```

may be specified as

```
(/ (I, I = 2, 10, 2) /)
```

Fortran 90 also allows operations on arrays. When applied to an array, the unary intrinsic operators + and − return an array of the same dimensions, where the elements in the result array are found by applying the operator to the corresponding elements in the operand array. Numerical, relational, and logical binary intrinsic operators can manipulate arrays having the same dimensions. Each element in the result array is found by applying the operator to the corresponding elements in the operand arrays. A binary intrinsic operator can also manipulate an array and a scalar variable, resulting in an array of the same dimensions as the array operand.

For example, given the array declarations

```
REAL, DIMENSION(100,50) :: X, Y
REAL, DIMENSION(100) :: Z
```

the following are examples of legal array expressions:

```
X + Y          ! Array of shape (100,50), elements X(I,J)+Y(I,J)
X + 1.0        ! Array of shape (100,50), elements X(I,J)+1.0
X .EQ. Y       ! Array of shape (100,50), elements having
               ! value .TRUE. if X(I,J).EQ.Y(I,J) and .FALSE.
               ! otherwise
X(1:100,3) + Z ! Array of shape (100),
               ! elements X(I,3)+Z(I)
```

Sometimes it is important to be able to perform an operation on a subset of the array elements. The WHERE statement allows the programmer to specify which array elements are to be active. For example, the statement

```
WHERE (A > 0.0) A = SQRT(A)
```

replaces every positive element of A with its square root. In its most general form, the WHERE statement divides the array elements into two sets, first performing one or more array assignments on the elements for which the expression is true, then performing one or more array assignments on the elements for which the expression is false. The syntax of the most general WHERE statement is

```
WHERE (logical-array-expression)
    array-assignment-statements

ELSEWHERE
    array-assignment-statements

END WHERE
```

Finally, new transformational functions allow the reduction of an array into a scalar value. For example, the function SUM returns the sum of the elements of the array passed to it as an argument.

4.2.3   Sample Program

Figure 4-5 contains a Fortran 90 program to compute π using numerical integration. The parameter N, declared in line 1, is the number of subintervals. In line 2 we declare parameter LONG, used to set up floating-point variables

```
 1.     INTEGER, PARAMETER :: N = 131072
 2.     INTEGER, PARAMETER :: LONG = SELECTED_REAL_KIND(13,99)
 3.     REAL(KIND=LONG) PI, WIDTH
 4.     INTEGER, DIMENSION(N) :: ID
 5.     REAL(KIND=LONG), DIMENSION(N) :: X, Y

 6.     WIDTH = 1.0_LONG / N
 7.     ID = (/ (I, I = 1, N) /)
 8.     X = (ID - 0.5) * WIDTH
 9.     Y = 4.0 / (1.0 + X * X)
10.     PI = SUM(Y) * WIDTH
11. 10  FORMAT (' ESTIMATION OF PI WITH ',I6, &
12.      'INTERVALS IS ',F14.12)
13.     PRINT 10, N, PI
14.     END
```

FIGURE 4-5   Fortran 90 program to compute π using numerical integration. The line numbers are for reference purposes only; they are not part of the program.

with at least 13 digits of precision and exponents covering at least the range 10^{-99} through 10^{99}. These high precision floating-point variables are declared in lines 3 and 5. In line 6 we compute the width of each subinterval. The array ID, declared in line 4 and initialized in line 7, represents the subinterval number associated with each array element. In line 8 we compute in parallel the midpoint of each of the subintervals, and in line 9 we compute in parallel the height of the function curve at each of these points. Line 10 contains the call to the SUM function, which adds the heights of all of the rectangles, then multiplies the total height by the rectangles' width to yield the area under the curve. In line 13 we print the result.

4.3   C*

In 1987, Thinking Machines Corporation announced the availablility of C*, a data-parallel extension of the C language suitable for programming the Connection Machine. In 1990, Thinking Machines announced C*, Version 6.0 with syntax and semantics radically different from the prior versions of C*. We describe a few ways in which C*, Version 6.0 supports the programming of SIMD algorithms, and we conclude with a sample program.

4.3.1   C* Programmer's Model

C* programmers imagine they are programming a SIMD computer consisting of a front-end uniprocessor attached to an adaptable back-end parallel processor (Fig. 4-6). The front-end processor stores the sequential variables and executes the sequential code. The back-end processors store the parallel variables and

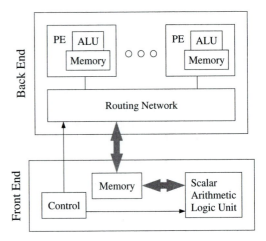

FIGURE 4-6 C* programmer's model of parallel computation.

execute the parallel portions of the program. Each processing element in the back end has its own local memory. There is a single flow of control; at any one time either the front-end processor is executing a sequential operation, or the back-end processors are executing a parallel operation.

The back-end processor array is adaptable—that is, programmers can select the size and shape of the processing elements they want to activate. These parameters are independent of the size and topology of the underlying physical machine. For this reason we sometimes refer to processing elements as **virtual processors**. Furthermore, the configuration of the back-end processor array is adaptable between different points in the same program.

4.3.2 Language Features

C* introduces the notion of a **shape**, which specifies the way in which parallel data are organized. By declaring a variable to be of some shape type, programmers indicate that they want the ability to perform parallel operations on that variable. For example, the variable declaration

```
shape [128][128]foo;
```

sets up a template for parallel data. The subsequent declaration

```
real:foo a, b, c;
```

specifies that variables a, b, and c are 128 × 128 arrays upon which parallel operations can be performed.

Parallel operations usually occur within the context of a with statement. The with statement activates the positions of a shape, setting up a context in which variables of that type can be manipulated in parallel.

For example, given the previous two declarations, the statement

```
with (foo) { a = b + c; }
```

performs an element-wise addition on each component of b and c and stores the resulting values in the corresponding components of a.

C* has a set of built-in reduction operators that reduce parallel values into sequential values. For example, the following C* segment computes the sum of all 16,384 values of a and stores it in sequential variable sum:

```
main () {
  real sum;
  with (foo) { sum = (+= a); }
}
```

The where statement gives C* programmers the ability to perform operations on a subset of the elements of a parallel variable.

For example, execution of the statements

```
with (foo) {
  where (a > 0.0) {
    a = b + c;
  }
}
```

results in the evaluation of the sum b + c and the assignment of the resulting value to a only at those positions in the shape where the value of a is greater than zero.

Sometimes the value of each element of a parallel variable depends upon its relative location within the shape. The function pcoord, passed a dimension number, returns each element of a parallel variable to its position within that dimension of the shape. Figure 4-7 illustrates the workings of function pcoord.

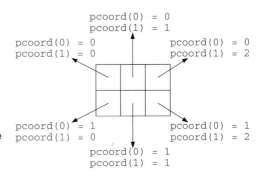

FIGURE 4-7 Function pcoord, passed a dimension number, returns to each element of a parallel variable its position within that dimension of the shape. In this example the shape has dimension [2][3].

As we have seen, the `with` statement selects the current shape. If an operation is to be performed on certain elements of a parallel variable, the `where` statement can be used to "set the context."

For example, given the following C* declarations:

```
shape [65536]students;
float:students credits, grade_points, gpa;
int:students count;
float upper_gpa, lower_gpa;
```

the code segment

```
with (students) {
  where (credits >= 64.0) {
    gpa = grade_points / credits;
    count = 1;
    upper_gpa = (+= gpa) / (+= count);
  }
}
```

computes the mean grade-point average of upper-division students (those who have at least 64 credits).

Nesting `where` statements conditionally shrinks the set of active positions.

The `where` statement has an `else` clause, which is analogous to the `else` clause of the C `if` statement. The meaning of the else clause is: "Perform the following operations on positions that were made inactive by the where condition" (Thinking Machines Corporation 1991). For example, given the previous declarations, the following code segment would compute the mean grade point average of both lower-division and upper-division students:

```
with (students) {
  where (credits > 0.0) {
    count = 1;
    gpa = grade_points / credits;
    where (credits >= 64.0)
      upper_gpa = (+= gpa) / (+= count);
    else
      lower_gpa = (+= gpa) / (+= count);
  }
}
```

Note the use of nested `where` statements. The outer `where` statement excludes students with zero credit hours, to prevent divide-by-zero errors. The inner `where` statement divides the students with credit hours into two groups; those with at least 64 hours, and those with fewer than 64 hours.

4.3.3 Sample Program

Figure 4-8 illustrates how to implement our numerical integration program in C*. The program is written for a Connection Machine with 8192 processing elements. In line 1 we define INTERVALS so that the number of rectangles is a multiple of the number of processing elements. The C* programmer thinks in terms of virtual processors, because the total number of elements in a shape can exceed the number of processing elements in the target machine. The compiler and operating system take care of virtual processor emulation.

In line 2 we declare a one-dimensional shape that corresponds to the set of subintervals into which we have divided the line segment [0, 1]. In lines 4 and 5 we declare two scalar double-precision variables. Line 6 is is the start of the with statement, which puts us in a parallel context. We declare a double precision variable x of shape type span in line 7. There is one value of x for each element of the shape. In line 8 we compute the midpoint of each rectangle on the *x* axis. Note the use of function pcoord, which returns a unique value in the range $0 \ldots 131071$ to each of the elements of x. In line 9 we compute the height of the function curve at each of the midpoints, add these heights, and store the result in scalar variable sum. We multiply the total height by the rectangles' width in line 11 to determine the total area, and print the result in line 12.

FIGURE 4-8 Pi computation program written in C*, Version 6.0. The program is written for a Connection Machine with 8192 processing elements. The line numbers are for reference purposes only; they are not part of the program.

```
1. #define INTERVALS (8192*16)

2. shape [INTERVALS] span;

3. main () {
4.    double sum;                /* Sum of areas */
5.    double width=1.0/INTERVALS; /* Width of rectangle */

6.    with(span) {
7.      double:span x;                 /* Midpoint of rectangle */
                                       /* on x axis */

8.      x = (pcoord(0)+0.5)*width;
9.      sum = (+= (4.0/(1.0+x*x)));
10.   }
11.   sum *= width;
12.   printf ("Estimation of pi is %14.12f\n", sum);
13. }
```

4.4   SEQUENT C

4.4.1   Parallel Programming Under DYNIX[†]

Sequent computers run the DYNIX™ operating system, a version of UNIX™ tailored for the multiprocessor environment. In addition to the operating-system calls typically found in a UNIX system, DYNIX provides a set of routines to facilitate parallel processing. The commercial parallel programming languages the Sequent hardware uses are simple extensions of sequential languages that allow programmers to declare shared variables that interact via mutual exclusion and barrier synchronization. The resulting languages are primitive. In this section we describe parallel programming from the perspective of Sequent C programmers. The primary source for this information is Osterhaug (1986).

Shared Data   Parallel processes on the Sequent coordinate their activities by accessing shared data structures. The keyword, `shared`, placed before a global variable declaration, indicates that all processes are to share a single instance of that variable. For example, if a 10-element global array is declared `int a[10]`, then every active process has its own copy of the array; if one process modifies a value in its copy of `a`, no other process's value will change. On the other hand, if the array is declared `shared int a[10]`, then all active processes share a single instance of the array, and changes made by one process can be detected by the other processes.

Parallel Processing Functions   The standard parallel programming model on the Sequent is straightforward and intuitive. A program begins execution as a single process. This process is responsible for executing those parts of the program that are inherently sequential. When control reaches a part of the computation that may be performed in parallel, the original process forks a number of other processes, each process performing its share of the work. The total number of processes accessing shared data cannot exceed the number of physical processors less one. Because there are at least as many CPUs as active processes, each process may execute on its own CPU. This allows a major reduction in the execution time, assuming that the computer is not executing any other jobs. When control reaches an inherently sequential portion of the computation, only the original process executes the code; the remaining processes wait until control reaches another portion of the computation that can be divided into pieces and executed concurrently. The program cycles through these two modes until termination (Fig. 4-9).

Parallel programs executing on the Sequent alternate between sequential and parallel execution. The transition from parallel to sequential execution is always delimited by a barrier synchronization. In addition, data dependencies may require the insertion of barrier synchronizations within parallel code. No

[†]This section is reprinted from Hatcher and Quinn (1991). Used by permission.

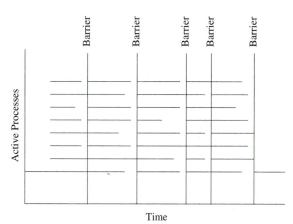

FIGURE 4-9   Sequent C programs alternate between a single thread of execution and multiple threads of execution. (Courtesy Hatcher and Quinn [1991].)

process may proceed beyond a barrier synchronization point until every process has reached the barrier.

The existence of a shared memory means that all process interactions can be performed through variables accessible to all the processes. For example, if a group of processes are working together to solve a large problem divided into numerous subproblems, the processes can share a variable that stores the index of the next unsolved subproblem.

Sequent's microtasking library has seven key functions:

m_set_procs(p): By calling m_set_procs with argument p, the parent process initializes to value p a shared variable that controls the number of processes created by a subsequent call to m_fork. The value of p cannot exceed the number of physical processors in the system minus one. The function also initializes barriers and locks.

m_fork(*name [,arg, ...]*): The parent process creates a number of child processes, then the parent process and the child processes begin executing function *name* with the arguments (if any) also specified by the call to m_fork. After all the processes (the parent and all the children) have completed execution of function *name*, the parent process resumes execution with the code after m_fork, while the child processes busy wait until the next call to m_fork. Therefore, the first call to m_fork is more expensive than subsequent calls, because only the first call entails process creation.

m_get_myid: A process calls function m_get_myid to get its unique process number. If the total number of active processes is p, then the process number of the parent is 0, while the process numbers of the child processes range from 1 to $p - 1$.

m_get_numprocs: Function m_get_numprocs returns the number of processes executing in parallel. Given the total number of processes and its own process number, a process can determine which portion of a computation is its responsibility.

m_lock, m_unlock: Functions m_lock and m_unlock ensure mutually exclusive execution of the code that the two calls surround. Once a process has entered a block of code delimited by m_lock and m_unlock, no other process may enter until the first process has left.

m_kill_procs: Function m_kill_procs kills the child processes created by the first call to m_fork.

4.4.2 Monitors

Most parallel algorithms implemented on multiprocessors require a process to perform a series of operations on a shared data structure, as if it were an atomic operation. For example, a process may need to fetch the value at the beginning of a linked list and advance the list pointer to the next list element. When the hardware cannot perform the entire series of operations as an atomic operation, the process must have some way to enforce mutual exclusion, keeping all other processes from referencing the resource while it is being modified. The piece of code in which mutual exclusion must be enforced is called a critical section.

Unfortunately, it is easy to miss critical sections, unless you think of the shared resource in a systematic way. One way to structure accesses to shared resources is by using a monitor. A **monitor** consists of variables representing the state of some resource, procedures that implement operations on that resource, and initialization code. The values of the variables are initialized before any procedure in the monitor is called; these values are retained between procedure invocations and may be accessed only by procedures in the monitor. Monitor procedures resemble ordinary procedures in the programming language with one significant exception. The execution of the procedures in the same monitor is guaranteed to be mutually exclusive. Hence monitors are a structured way of implementing mutual exclusion.

Programming languages that support monitors include Concurrent Pascal (Brinch Hansen 1975, 1977) and Modula (Wirth 1977a, 1977b, 1977c). Even if your parallel programming language does not support monitors, you can implement one yourself. For example, in the Sequent C language, you can implement a monitor by declaring a shared lock variable for each resource, putting an s_lock statement that accesses the variable at the start of each procedure, and putting an s_unlock statement at the end of each procedure (Fig. 4-10). You also must have enough self-discipline to use only these procedures to access the shared resource.

4.4.3 Sample Program[†]

We present a sample program written in Sequent C. The program computes an approximation to π by using numerical integration to find the area under the curve $4/(1 + x^2)$ between 0 and 1 (Fig. 4-11).

[†]This section is reprinted from Hatcher and Quinn (1991). Used by permission.

```
/* stack.h file included by modules calling stack func-
tions */
void stack_init();   /* Initialize stack */
int  stack_empty();/* Returns TRUE if stack is empty */
void push();         /* Pushes integer onto stack */
int  pop();          /* Pops integer from stack */



/* stack.c file implementing the monitor */
shared slock_t stack_lock;
shared int top_of_stack, stack[MAX_STACK_SIZE];

void stack_init() {
  s_init_lock (&stack_lock);
  top_of_stack = -1;
}

int stack_empty() {
  int result;
  s_lock(&stack_lock);
  result = (top_of_stack <  0);
  s_unlock(&stack_lock);
  return result;
}

void push (i)
  int i;
{
  s_lock(&stack_lock);
  stack[++top_of_stack] = i;
  s_unlock(&stack_lock);
}

int pop () {
  int result;
  s_lock(&stack_lock);
  result = stack[top_of_stack- -];
  s_unlock(&stack_lock);
  return result;
}
```

FIGURE 4-10   A primitive stack monitor implemented in Sequent C.

```
#include < stdio.h>
#include < parallel/microtask.h>
#include < parallel/parallel.h>

shared double pi; /* Approximation to pi */

main (argc, argv)
  int argc; char *argv[];
{
  void computepi ();
  int intervals;   /* Number of intervals */
  int numprocs;  /* Number of processes to be forked */

  numprocs = atoi (argv[1]);
  intervals = atoi (argv[2]);
  m_set_procs (numprocs);
  pi = 0.0;
  m_fork (computepi, numprocs, intervals);
  printf ("Estimation of pi is %14.12f.\n", pi);
  m_kill_procs ();
  return 0;
}


void computepi (numprocs, intervals)
  int numprocs, intervals;
{
  int id;  /* Index of this process */
  int i;
  double localsum, width, x;
  id = m_get_myid ();
  localsum = 0.0;
  width = 1.0/intervals;
  for (i = id; i < intervals; i += numprocs) {
    x = (i+0.5)*width;
    localsum += (4.0/(1.0+x*x));
  }
  localsum *= width;
  m_lock ();
  pi += localsum;
  m_unlock ();
}
```

FIGURE 4-11   Sequent C program to compute π using numerical integration.

The program begins with directives to the compiler to include standard header files. The header files stored in `microtask.h` and `parallel.h` contain information on the parallel library functions.

The double-precision floating-point variable `pi` will contain the approximation to π. Since all processes will need access to `pi` in order to store their subtotals, `pi` is declared resident in shared memory.

The main procedure parses the command line, calls `m_set_procs` to set the program's level of parallelism, initializes `pi`, and calls `m_fork` to initiate the parallel computation of `pi`. After all processes have finished executing function `computepi`, the parent process prints the current value of variable `pi`, kills the child processes, and terminates.

In function `computepi`, every process calls function `m_get_myid` to find its unique identifying number in the range `0...numprocs`. By setting the initial value of the loop index `i` to `id` and making the loop increment value `numprocs`, the processes as a whole cover every value of `i` in the range `0...intervals-1` exactly once.

Once every process has computed its share of the sum, it must add its subtotal to `pi`. Because the statement `pi += localsum` is not an atomic operation, the processes must mutually exclude each other when executing it. They create the necessary critical section through the calls to functions `m_lock` and `m_unlock`.

4.5   nCUBE C[†]

4.5.1   The Run-Time Model

An nCUBE programmer usually writes a single program that executes on every node processor. Each node program begins execution as soon as the operating system loads it into the node. To implement a data-parallel application, the programmer assigns each processor responsibility for storing and manipulating its share of the data structure. This is called programming in the **SPMD** (Single Program, Multiple Data) style (Karp 1987). Processors work on their own local data until they reach a point in the computation when they need to interact with other processors to: swap data items, communicate results, perform a combining operation on partial results, etc. If a processor initiates a communication with a partner that has not finished its own computation, then the initiator must wait for its partner to catch up. Once the processors have performed the necessary communications, they can resume work on local data. One way to view the entire computation is to consider the activities of the processors, as they cycle between computing and communicating, with occasional periods of waiting (Fig. 4-12).

A SPMD program executing on a multicomputer such as the nCUBE consists of alternating segments in which processors work independently on local data, then exchange values with other processors through calls to communication

[†]This section is reprinted from Hatcher and Quinn (1991). Used by permission.

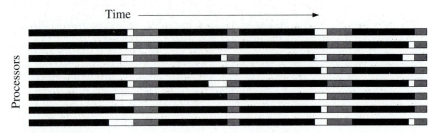

FIGURE 4-12   This figure gives an abstract view of the nCUBE C run-time model. Every processor begins execution as soon as the executable is loaded into its memory. Black represents time spent computing, white represents time spent waiting for a message, and gray represents time spent communicating with other processors. (Courtesy Hatcher and Quinn 1991.)

routines. In Fig. 4-12 black represents computing, white represents waiting, and gray represents communicating.

4.5.2 Extensions to the C Language

The C programs running on the nodes are inherently parallel, in the sense that every node is active from the time its program is loaded. For this reason there is no need for a process creation mechanism in nCUBE C. In fact, three new functions are sufficient for us to run our sample application on the nCUBE:

`whoami`: Returns information about the node process, including the dimension of the allocated hypercube and the position of the node in the allocated hypercube.

`nwrite`: Sends a message to another node. Arguments to this function include the destination node number, the address of the message to be sent, the length of the message, and the message type, an integer. Function `nwrite` is nonblocking.

`nread`: Receives a message from another node. Arguments to this function include the source node number, the message type, the address where the message is to be stored, and the maximum number of bytes to be read. The value returned from the function is the number of bytes actually read. The user has the option of specifying that the message to be read can be of any type or from any source, or both. Function `nread` blocks until a message fitting the source and type criteria has been read.

4.5.3 Sample Program

An nCUBE C program to perform the π computation appears in two parts (see Figs. 4-13 and 4-14). Look at the code in Fig. 4-13. The two "include" files allow the node program to call functions from the C I/O library. All messages sent by the fan-in function are of type `FANIN`.

```
/* Node program */
#include < special.h>
#include < stdio.h>
#include
#include

main (argc, argv)
  int argc; char *argv[];
{
  void fan_in();
  int cube_dim;      /* Dimension of allocated hypercube */
  int i;
  int intervals;     /* Number of intervals */
  int nodenum;       /* Position of node in */
                     /* allocated hypercube */
  int not_used;      /* Place holder */
  int num_procs;     /* Number of active processors */
  double sum;        /* Sum of areas */
  double width;      /* Width of interval */
  double x;          /* Midpoint of rectangle on x axis */

  /* argv[0] is name of file containing host program */
  /* argv[1] is name of file containing node program */
  /* argv[2] is dimensional of allocated hypercube */
  /* argv[3] is number of intervals */

  intervals = atoi(argv[3]);
  width = 1.0 / intervals;
  whoami (&nodenum, &not_used, &not_used, &cube_dim);
  num_procs = 1 < < cube_dim;
  sum = 0.0;
  for (i = nodenum; i < intervals; i+=num_procs) {
    x = (i+0.5)*width;
    sum += width*(4.0/(1.0+x*x));
  }
  fan_in (&sum, nodenum, cube_dim);

  if (!nodenum)
    printf ("Estimation of pi is %14.12f\n", sum);
}
```

FIGURE 4-13   First part of nCUBE C program to compute π using numerical integration.

```
void fan_in (value, nodenum, cube_dim)
  double *value; int nodenum, cube_dim;
{
  int dest, i, source, type;
  double tmp;
  type = FANIN;
  for (i = cube_dim-1; i >= 0; i- -)
    if (nodenum < (1 << i)) {
      source = nodenum ^ (1 << i);
      nread (&tmp, sizeof(double), &source, &type);
      *value += tmp;
    } else if (nodenum <  (1 << i  (i+1))) {
      dest = nodenum ^ (1 << i);
      nwrite (value, sizeof(double), dest, type);
    }
}
```

FIGURE 4-14   nCUBE C source code for function `fan_in`, which accumulates each node's subtotal into a sum stored on node 0.

Each node processor executes the function `main`. Every processor has its own local copy of each of the variables declared inside `main`.

The nodes will estimate π by approximating the area under the curve $4/(1 + x^2)$ between 0 and 1 with `intervals` rectangles.

The node process calls function `whoami` to determine the dimension of the allocated hypercube, as well as its position in the allocated hypercube. The number of processors is 2 raised to the power of the cube dimension.

Once a processor has computed the sum of the areas of its share of the rectangles, it participates in calling function `fan_in`. After completion of function `fan_in`, processor 0 has the total value, which it prints.

Function `fan_in` is shown separately in Fig. 4-14. Passed the address of a double-precision floating-point value, the node number, and the cube dimension, function `fan_in` computes the sum of every processor's value at that address, using a binomial tree communication pattern (Fig. 4-15). Initially all the processors are active. During each iteration the algorithm divides the active processors into two sets of equal size. The processors in the upper half send their values to the processors in the lower half. The processors in the lower half add the two values, while the processors in the upper half become inactive. If a processor is sending a value, variable `dest` contains the number of the processor receiving the value; if a processor is receiving a value, variable `source` contains the number of the processor sending the value. After one iteration per cube dimension, processor 0 is the only remaining active processor, and it contains the global sum in variable `value`. Other processors will have either the original value or a partial sum.

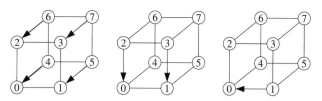

FIGURE 4-15 Function `fan_in` in Fig. 4-14 computes the sum of values stored on the hypercube nodes using the communication pattern shown by the arrows. Together, the arrows form a binomial tree.

4.6   OCCAM

Inmos Limited of Great Britain developed occam as a programming language for its Transputer series of processors. The design of occam was heavily influenced by the work done by Hoare on communicating sequential processes (Hoare 1978). Because the occam language has been closely associated with the evolution of the Transputer chip, it has improved as the hardware of successive Transputers has become more sophisticated. For example, the original occam language did not use floating-point data, because the T414 processor did not support it. This feature was added to the language with the introduction of the T800 processor, which used floating-point hardware.

4.6.1   Programmer's Model

At the macro level the occam programmer views a parallel computation as a collection of asynchronously executing processes communicating via a synchronous message-passing protocol. An occam program is built from three kinds of primitive process: assignment, input, and output. The programmer can assemble more complicated processes by specifiying when they must execute sequentially and when they can execute in parallel.

Figure 4-16 represents the structure of a hypothetical occam program. At the global level the program is one occam process, indicated by the ellipse E around the graph. In this example, the process has six subprocesses that must execute sequentially. (Control dependencies are shown with dashed arrows.) All but the fourth process are primitive processes, indicated by small circles. The fourth process is a built-up process, as indicated by ellipse D. Built-up processes can represent either a sequential or a parallel collection of simpler processes. The primitive process represented by a filled gray circle is an input process

inside a sequential collection of processes (A)
inside a parallel collection of processes (B)
inside a sequential collection of processes (C)
inside a parallel collection of processes (D)
inside a sequential collection of processes (E).

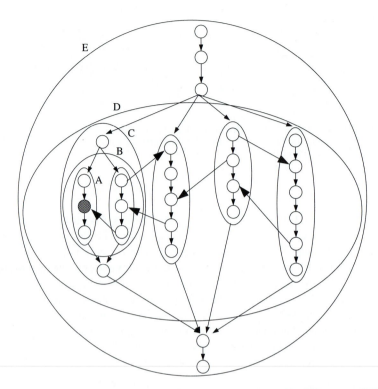

FIGURE 4-16   The occam programmer's model of parallel computation. Primitive processes appear as circles. Ellipses indicate processes built up as sequential or parallel collections of processes. Control dependencies are shown as dashed arrows. Communications appear as bold arrows between primitive processes.

The assignment process, one of the three primitive processes in an occam program, assigns the value of an expression to a variable. An input process assigns to a variable the value read from a channel. An output process evaluates an expression and writes the result to a channel.

A **channel** is a one-way, point-to-point, synchronous link from one process to another process. An occam channel is a logical entity independent of the underlying hardware.

4.6.2   Language Constructs

In this section we describe features of the occam language that are used in the sample program.

The assignment process allows the value of an expression with, at most, one operator assigned to a variable. For example,

```
sum := partial1 + partial2
```

assigns to variable `sum` the sum of the values of variables `partial1` and `partial2`.

The input process reads a value from a channel and assigns that value to a variable. For example,

```
channel1 ? partial1
```

assigns to variable `partial1` the value input from channel `channel1`.

The output process writes a value to a channel. For example,

```
channel3 ! sum
```

outputs value of `sum` to channel `channel3`.

All communication in occam is synchronous. A process performing output on a channel does not complete until the process performing input on the same channel executes.

The `SEQ` (pronounced "seek") construction specifies that a number of processes should execute sequentially. In the following piece of code, integers are input from two different channels, added, and the sum output to a third channel:

```
SEQ
  channel1 ? partial1
  channel2 ? partial2
  sum := partial1 + partial2
  channel3 ! sum
```

In occam, indentation indicates which processes are part of the `SEQ`. The indentation must be exactly two characters. A `SEQ` construction terminates when the final process in the sequence terminates.

The `PAR` construction specifies that a number of processes may execute in parallel. The following piece of code performs the same task as the previous example, but allows the two inputs to occur simultaneously:

```
SEQ
  PAR
    channel1 ? partial1
    channel2 ? partial2
  sum := partial1 + partial2
```

A `PAR` construction terminates when its last constituent process terminates.

The `IF` construct allows the conditional execution of processes. A boolean control expression precedes each process that may be executed. The control expressions are evaluated from top to bottom. The process associated with the first condition that evaluates to true is executed.

The following `IF` construct guarantees that variable `a` has a value in the range of 0 through 10. If the value of `a` is already inside that range, no work needs to be done (indicated by the `SKIP` process).

```
IF
    a > 10
      a := 10
    a < 0
      a := 0
    TRUE
      SKIP
```

`ALT`, the alternation construct, allows control to flow to the first alternative the system finds to be true. In an `ALT` the conditions of an alternation may depend upon input. A blocked input process in one condition of the alternation will not prevent a later condition from being evaluated.

Consider this ALT construct:

```
ALT
    temperature.channel ? value
        IF
            value > high.value
                high.value := value
            TRUE
                SKIP
    enable  report.channel ? check
        SEQ
            result.channel ! high.value
            high.value := -100
```

If the alternation process gets the next value from the input channel `temperature.channel`, then it checks to see if the input value is a new high value, and if so, the value is recorded. If the process first gets a value from the input channel `report.channel`, then the process outputs its recorded high value to `result.channel`. However, input from `report.channel` is ignored if the boolean variable enable is false.

The replicator construct allows the constructs `SEQ`, `PAR`, `IF`, and `ALT` to execute some number of times. For example, the construct

```
PAR i = [0 FOR 10]
```

creates 10 replicated parallel processes, each with a unique value of i in the range from 0 through 9.

The remaining features of occam used in the sample program are intuitive. We will explain them as we describe the sample code.

```
1. DEF N = 400000 :
2. DEF PROCESSES = 8 :
3. DEF CHUNK = N / PROCESSES :
4. CHAN sum[PROCESSES] :
5. PAR
6.    PAR i = [0 FOR PROCESSES]
7.       REAL64 x, localsum, width :
8.       SEQ
9.       localsum := 0.0
10.      width := 1.0 / N
11.      x := ((i * CHUNK) + 0.5) * width
12.      SEQ i = [0 FOR CHUNK]
13.         SEQ
14.         localsum := localsum + (4.0 / (1.0 + (x * x)))
15.         x := x + width
16.      localsum := localsum * width
17.      sum[i] ! localsum
18.   REAL64 pi :
19.   INT got[PROCESSES] :
20.   SEQ
21.      pi := 0.0
22.      SEQ i = [0 FOR PROCESSES]
23.         got[i] := FALSE
24.      SEQ i = [0 FOR PROCESSES]
25.         REAL64 y :
26.         SEQ
27.            ALT i = [0 FOR PROCESSES]
28.               (got[i] = FALSE) & sum[i] ? y
29.               got[i] := TRUE
30.            pi := pi + y
31.    output ! "Approximation to pi is "; pi
```

FIGURE 4-17   An occam program to compute π using numerical integration. The line numbers are not part of the program; they are for reference purposes only.

4.6.3 Sample Program

The occam program in Fig. 4-17 computes π using the numerical integration method already described. Lines 1–3 define constants. N is the number of intervals, PROCESSES is the number of processes we will create, and CHUNK is the number of intervals per process. (For the program to execute correctly, N must be a multiple of PROCESSES.) In line 4 we define one channel per process. The process will use this channel to output its partial sum to the process that is finding the grand total.

Lines 5–31 constitute a parallel construct with PROCESSES+1 processes. All but one of the processes execute lines 6–17. Each process computes the sum

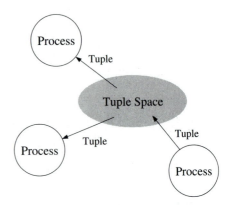

FIGURE 4-18 The Linda programmer's model of parallel computation.

of the areas of its share of rectangles. The last process executes lines 18–31 where it collects the output of the sum-finding processes, computes the grand total, and prints the result.

4.7 C-LINDA

Linda consists of several operations that work on **tuple space**, a shared associative memory. Incorporating Linda operations into a sequential base language yields a parallel programming language. For example, in C-Linda, Linda primitives have been added to C. In this section we describe the Linda programming model and present two C-Linda programs to solve the numerical integration problem.

4.7.1 Programmer's Model

Linda is a MIMD model of parallel computation. The Linda programmer envisions an asynchronously executing group of processes that interact by means of a associative shared memory, *tuple space*. Tuple space consists of a collection of logical tuples. Parallelism is achieved by creating process tuples, which are evaluated by processors needing work. Parallel processes interact by sharing data tuples. After a process tuple has finished execution, it returns to tuple space as a data tuple.

In many MIMD languages, such as occam, processes may interact with each other in complicated ways (see Fig. 4-16). Proponents of Linda say that forcing all process interactions to occur through tuple space simplifies parallel programming.

4.7.2 C-Linda Language Constructs

Six functions enable a process to interact with tuple space. Function out, passed tuple t as an argument, causes t to be added to tuple space. The process executing the out operation continues immediately.

Function `in`, passed template `s`, removes from tuple space a tuple `t` that matches template `s`. The values of the actual parameters in `t` are assigned to the formal parameters in `s`. The `in` operation blocks the process until a suitable matching tuple is found. If multiple tuples match, an arbitrary one is chosen.

Function `rd`, passed template `s`, behaves in the same way as function `in`, except that the matching tuple is not removed from tuple space.

Function `eval`, passed tuple `t`, forks a new process to evaluate `t`. Once `t` has been evaluated, it is placed in tuple space as an ordinary data tuple.

Function `inp` is a nonblocking version of `in`. It returns a 1 if a matching tuple is retrieved, 0 if not.

Function `rdp` is a nonblocking version of `rd`. It returns a 1 if a matching tuple is found, 0 if not.

4.7.3 Sample Programs

We will examine two C-Linda programs to solve the π computation problem. One program implements a master/worker algorithm; the other implements a divide-and-conquer algorithm.

The first C-Linda program appears in Fig. 4-19. Each process will execute function `work` (lines 3–16) to compute the area of its share of the rectangles.

Function `main`, the starting point for C programs, is reserved by the run-time system to start up C-Linda. Function `real_main` is the user function where execution begins. In line 21 we compute `len`, the maximum number of rectangles assigned to any process. Variable `left_overs`, computed in line 22, is the number of processes that will have to compute `len` intervals; the rest will compute `len-1` intervals.

The `for` loop in lines 23–26 spawns NUM_WORKERS-1 processes. Each process will execute function `work`, computing the sum of the heights of its share of rectangles, then returning the total area. When the process executes the return statement, it inserts into tuple space a tuple whose first field is "worker" and whose second field is the area. Then it terminates.

After forking off NUM_WORKERS-1 parallel processes in lines 23–26, the parent process executes function `work` itself. It assigns the value returned from the function to variable `sum`. In lines 28–31 the parent process collects from tuple space the subtotals generated by the other processes and adds each subtotal to `sum`. When it has added all these values, it prints the answer in line 32.

The second C-Linda program, listed in Fig. 4-20, implements a divide-and-conquer algorithm to solve the π computation problem. In this version of the program the original process, executing `real_main`, calls function `work` with arguments specifying the entire set of intervals.

Function `work` implements the parallel divide-and-conquer algorithm. If the number of intervals specified in the formal parameters to `work` is greater than INTERVAL_LIM, the process executing `work` uses the `eval` primitive to fork

```
/* Pi computation in C-Linda */

/* Compute the area under the curve 4/(1 + x*x) between
   0 and 1 */
1.  #define INTERVALS 4000000
2.  #define NUM_WORKERS 7
3.  double work (start, finish, width)
4.     int start, finish;
5.     double width; /* Width of interval */
6.  {
7.     int i;
8.     double sum;   /* Sum of areas */
9.     double x;     /* Midpoint of rectangle on x axis */
10.    sum = 0.0;
11.    for (i = start; i < finish; i++) {
12.      x = width * (i + 0.5);
13.      sum += 4.0/(1.0+x*x);
14.    }
15.    return (sum * width);
16. }

17. real_main() {
19.    int  i, left_overs, len, w;
20.    double result, sum;
21.    len = INTERVALS/NUM_WORKERS + 1;
22.    left_overs = INTERVALS%NUM_WORKERS;
       /* This process will do some work too,
          so start the worker count/id
          variable, w, at 1 rather than at 0. */
23.    for (i = 0, w = 1; w < NUM_WORKERS; i += len, ++w) {
24.      if (i == left_overs) --len;
25.      eval("worker", work(i, i+len, 1.0/INTERVALS));
26.    }
27.    sum = work(i, INTERVALS, 1.0/INTERVALS);
28.    for (w = 1; w < NUM_WORKERS; ++w) {
29.      in("worker", ? result);
30.      sum += result;
31.    }
32.    printf ("Estimation of pi is %14.12f\n", sum);
33. }
```

FIGURE 4-19   Master/worker-style C-Linda program to compute π. The line numbers are not part of the program; they are for reference purposes only. (This program was provided by Scientific Computing Associates, New Haven, Connecticut. Used by permission.)

```
/* Pi computation in C-Linda: divide and conquer approach. */

/* Compute the area under the curve 4/(1 + x*x) between 0 and 1 */

#define INTERVAL_LIM  50000
#define INTERVALS    400000

double work (id, start, finish, width)
   int   id, start, finish;
   double width;    /* Width of interval */
{
  int i;
  int length = finish - start;
  double sum, sum2;
  double x;

  if (length > INTERVAL_LIM) {
   eval("worker", id, work(id< < 1, start,
     start+(length >> 1), width));
   eval("worker", id, work((id< < 1)+1,
     start+(length >> 1), finish, width));
   in("worker", id, ?sum);
   in("worker", id, ?sum2);
   return (sum+sum2);
  }
  sum = 0.0;
  for (i = start; i < finish; i++) {
   x = width * (i + 0.5);
   sum += 4.0/(1.0+x*x);
  }
  return (sum * width);
}



real_main() {
 printf("Estimation of pi is %14.12f\n",
 work(1, 0, INTERVALS, 1.0/INTERVALS));
}
```

FIGURE 4-20   Divide-and-conquer-style C-Linda program to compute π. (This program was provided by Scientific Computing Associates, New Haven, Connecticut. Used by permission.)

off two parallel processes, each of which calls `work` recursively to compute the area under the curve for half the intervals. The forking process retrieves the results of the computations, sums them, and returns a data packet containing the total area to tuple space. If the number of intervals is less than or equal to `INTERVAL_LIM`, the process computes the area under the curve for these intervals and returns a data packet containing the area to tuple space.

Figure 4-21 illustrates the execution of this program. The figure shows how tuples enter and exit tuple space as the computation progresses. In part (a), a single process executing function `work` forks off two new processes using the `eval` primitive. Ready processors grab the `eval` tuples and start the execution of new processes (as indicated by the dashed arrows). (b) The two new processes spawn more processes using the eval primitive. (c) Processes 1, 2, and 3 are blocked executing the `in` primitive, since the tuples they want are not yet in tuple space. Processes 4, 5, 6, and 7 execute function `work`. Because the number of intervals is below the threshold, they do not spawn more processes. Instead, they compute the area under the curve for their intervals. As these processes terminate, tuples containing the sums are entered into tuple space. (d) Processes 2 and 3 are now able to "in" the tuples they need, and compute the total. When these processes terminate, tuples containing the totals are entered into tuple space. (e) The original process retrieves two tuples containing subtotals and adds them.

4.8   A NOTATION FOR EXPRESSING PARALLEL ALGORITHMS

In the remainder of this book we will present parallel algorithms in a machine-independent pseudocode. Some of the pseudocode constructs appeared in Chap. 2, where we examined a variety of PRAM algorithms. In this section we describe these constructs and introduce additional syntax that will enable us to present the parallel algorithms in Chaps. 5–13.

We represent variables with strings of characters and periods. The variable p always represents the level of parallelism, i.e., the number of processes executing the algorithm. For algorithms targeted to shared-memory models, we use the keyword **Global** to designate those variables accessible to all parallel processes. The keyword **Local** indicates each active process has its own copy of the variable. Distributed-memory machines do not have global memory, but in many cases it makes sense to assume that when the algorithm begins, certain values have been communicated to each process. We use the keyword **Parameter** to indicate such constants. Formal parameters to functions are labeled **Value** or **Reference**, depending upon whether the arguments are pass-by value or pass-by reference, respectively.

We can combine variables and constants with unary and binary operators to form expressions. The meaning of most of the operators is obvious. For example, we use + to denote addition and × to denote multiplication. Note, however, that we use superscripting, rather than an explicit operator, to indicate exponentiation.

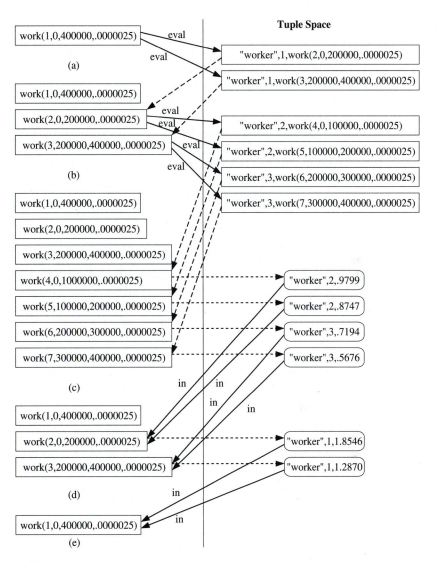

FIGURE 4-21   Execution of the C-Linda program shown in Fig. 4-20. Solid arrows indicate Linda primitives. Dashed arrows indicate places where `eval` tuples are removed from tuple space for execution. Dotted arrows indicte places where termination of an `eval`'ed function results in a tuple containing the return value being inserted into tuple space.

The ← symbol represents the assignment of an expression's value to a variable. Assignment is allowed only when the process performing the assignment has access to all variables referenced.

We use the syntax **if...else...endif, while...endwhile**, and **for...endfor** to represent the familiar control structures.

Data parallelism is indicated by the use of the **for all** statement. Unlike a conventional **for** loop, the **for all** statement activates a set of processes that execute the statements before the matching **endfor** in parallel. In the case of SIMD algorithms, we assume the processing elements execute the operations inside the statements in lock step. In the case of MIMD algorithms, we assume that the CPUs are executing asynchronously.

We use the $\Leftarrow$ symbol to denote places where a processor must store or retrieve a value local to another processor. There are two methods to indicate which value is being fetched. The first method uses left subscripts, a syntax taken from C*. For example, if every processor has a local value of a, the expression $[27]a$ refers to processor 27's value of a. The second method to refer to nonlocal values is to use special keywords that refer to neighboring processes. Usually the location of the processor whose value is being retrieved is at some fixed location relative to the fetching processor's position. We use keywords to represent these relationships. For example, in the context of pseudocode algorithms in which processors are organized as a one-dimensional mesh, the expression $successor(a)$ refers to the value of a controlled by the next processor in the ring. Figure 4-22 illustrates the communication keywords used in this text for data interchange among neighboring elements in when the processors are organized as a one-dimensional mesh. Figure 4-23 illustrates the communication keywords used when the processors are organized in a shuffle-exchange network. Figure 4-24 illustrates the communication keywords used for data interchange among neighboring processors when they are organized as a 2-D mesh.

The $\Leftarrow$ notation ignores the possiblity that both the process fetching the value and the process controlling the value to be fetched may have to be active. For example, in nCUBE C, if processor X needs a value in the local memory of processor Y, it is not sufficient that processor X call function **nread**. Processor Y must also call function **nwrite**. To simplify the algorithms presented in this text, we have ignored this possibility. But when implementing the pseudocode algorithms in a real programming language, consider the fact that both processors may have to be active.

Asynchronous algorithms targeted to shared memory architectures need mechanisms for synchronizing parallel processes. Recall there are two fundamental kinds of synchronization: synchronization for mutual exclusion and synchro-

FIGURE 4-22 Illustration of pseudocode communication macros for the one-dimensional mesh processor organization. (a) $B \Leftarrow predecessor(A)$ or $successor(B) \Leftarrow A$. (b) $B \Leftarrow successor(A)$ or $predecessor(B) \Leftarrow A$.

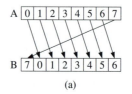

(a)

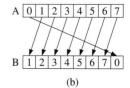

(b)

FIGURE 4-23 Illustration of pseudocode communication macros for the shuffle-exchange processor organization. (a) *shuffle(B)* ⇐ *A.* (b) *B* ⇐ *exchange(A)* or *exchange(B)* ⇐ *A.*

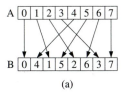
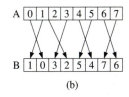

(a)   (b)

A
0	1	2	3
4	5	6	7
8	9	A	B
C	D	E	F

(a)

B
C	D	E	F
0	1	2	3
4	5	6	7
8	9	A	B

(b)

B
4	5	6	7
8	9	A	B
C	D	E	F
0	1	2	3

(c)

B
1	2	3	0
5	6	7	4
9	A	B	8
D	E	F	C

(d)

B
3	0	1	2
7	4	5	6
B	8	9	A
F	C	D	E

(e)

FIGURE 4-24 Illustration of pseudocode communication macros for the 2-D mesh processor organization. (a) Values of *A* in a 2-D array of 16 processes. (b) *B* values after the communication step *B* ⇐ *north(A)* or *south(B)* ⇐ *A.* (c) *B* values after the communication step *B* ⇐ *south(A)* or *north(B)* ⇐ *A.* (d) *B* values after the communication step *B* ⇐ *east(A)* or *west(B)* ⇐ *A.* (e) *B* values after the communication step *B* ⇐ *west(A)* or *east(B)* ⇐ *A.*

nization for precedence. We use the functions **lock** and **unlock** to delimit critical sections of code. The functions take a global variable as an argument. If there are two or more independent resources demanding mutually exclusive access, having different lock variables for each resource allows resources to be accessed simultaneously.

There is an implicit barrier synchronization at the end of every **for all** statement.

Finally, we delimit comments with curly brackets.

To illustrate our notation, we present two pseudocode versions of the π computation problem. The first algorithm, shown in Fig. 4-25, is targeted to the hypercube processor array model. The front-end processor stores the global variable area and executes the sequential portions of the algorithm (lines 22–23). Each processing element in the back end has a copy of the parameter and each of the local variables, and executes the parallel portion of the algorithm (lines 9–21). A communication step is required when a processing element needs the local value of another processing element (line 17).

PI CALCULATION (HYPERCUBE PROCESSOR ARRAY)
1. Global   *area*   {Estimation of area under curve}
2. Parameter *intervals*   {Number of intervals on x axis}
3. Local   *total.height* {Height of process's share of rectangles}
4.   *index*   {Rectangle number}
5.   *x*   {Midpoint of rectangle on x axis}
6.   *j*   {Dimension of current data swap}
7.   *tmp*   {Other processor's subtotal}
8. begin
9. for all P_i, where $0 \leq i < p$ do
10   *total.height* $\leftarrow$ 0
11.   for *index* $\leftarrow$ 0 to *intervals* $-$ 1 step p do
12. $x \leftarrow (index + 0.5) / intervals$
13.   *total.height* $\leftarrow$ *total.height* $+ 4 / (1 + x^2)$
14.   endfor
15.   for $j \leftarrow \log p - 1$ downto 0 do
16.   if $i < 2^j$ then
17. $tmp \Leftarrow total.height[i + 2^j]$
18.   *total.height* $\leftarrow$ *total.height* $+ tmp$
19.   endif
20.   endfor
21.   endfor
22.   *area* $\leftarrow$ $[0]total.height / intervals$
23.   print "Estimate of pi is ", *area*
24. end

FIGURE 4-25   Pseudocode version of the π-calculation problem.

The second pseudocode algorithm, illustrated in Fig. 4-26, is designed for a UMA multiprocessor. A single process executes the sequential code (lines 8, 19, and 20), while p processes execute the parallel code (lines 9–18). The sequential and the parallel processes can all access the global variables. Each of the parallel processes has its own copy of the local variables, and there is no way for another process to access them directly. Note the critical section in lines 15–17, where each process in turn adds its subtotal to the grand total.

4.9 SUMMARY

We began this chapter by describing the functions that parallel programming languages must provide, either explicitly or implicitly. These include facilities for the creation and termination of parallel processes, as well as facilities that enable the programmer to manage the process interactions.

We described six imperative parallel programming languages. Two of the languages (Fortran 90 and C*) assume a SIMD model of parallel computation. Two of the languages target particular MIMD computers. Sequent C targets the Sequent family of UMA multiprocessors, and nCUBE C is designed for

PI CALCULATION (UMA MULTIPROCESSOR)

1. Global *intervals* {Number of intervals on x axis}
2. *sum* {Sum of rectangle heights, then total area}
3. *p* {Number of processes}
4. Local *j* {Index of current rectangle}
5. *local.sum* {Sum of heights of process's share of rectangles}
6. *x* {Midpoint of rectangle on x axis}
7. begin
8. $sum \leftarrow 0$
9. for all P_i, where $0 \le i < p$ do
10. $local.sum \leftarrow 0$
11. for $j \leftarrow 0$ to $n - 1$ step p do
12. $x \leftarrow (j + 0.5) / intervals$
13. $local.sum \leftarrow local.sum + 4 / (1 + x^2)$
14. endfor
15. lock(*sum*)
16. $sum \leftarrow sum + local.sum$
17. unlock(*sum*)
18. endfor
19. $sum \leftarrow sum / intervals$
20. print "Estimation of pi is", *sum*
21. end

FIGURE 4-26 Second pseudocode version of the π-calculation problem. Target machine is a UMA multiprocessor.

the nCUBE family of hypercube multicomputers. Although the occam programming language was developed in concert with the Transputer chip, it is an architecture-independent programming language, since it can be ported to other machines. The occam programmer views parallel computation as a group of MIMD processes interacting through synchronous message passing. Linda is a set of primitives that can be used to transform a sequential language into a parallel language. The Linda model assumes a shared associative memory called tuple space, through which a collection of MIMD processes interact.

We have also described the syntax of the pseudocode we will use in the remainder of the text to express our parallel algorithms.

4.10 BIBLIOGRAPHIC NOTES

There are many papers, survey articles, and books in the general area of parallel programming languages. In this section we direct you to a few sources for further reading.

A good place to start is the August 1986 issue of *Computer*, a special issue dedicated to parallel programming languages. It includes articles on Concurrent Prolog (Shapiro 1986), Linda (Ahuja et al. 1986), Multilisp (Halstead 1986), and para-functional programming (Hudak 1986).

Karp (1987) provides a survey of language extensions for parallel Karp (1987) provides a survey of language extensions for parallel programming. Karp and Babb (1988) have compared twelve parallel FORTRAN dialects. Babb (1988) has edited a collection of papers describing the implementation of the π calculation algorithm on a variety of commercial parallel computers, using several imperative parallel programming languages. Perrott (1987) has written a book describing ten different parallel programming languages, including MIMD languages, SIMD languages, and VAL, a data flow language.

Pancake and Bergmark (1990) question if existing parallel languages meet the needs of scientific programmers.

A tremendous amount of energy has been spent over the past 20 years to develop compiler technologies that will allow sequential FORTRAN codes to execute efficiently on supercomputers. Some progress has been made in the area of vectorizing compilers, which generate code suitable for execution on pipelined vector processors. Parallelizing compilers, which can generate code for multicomputers, seem to be much more difficult to construct. Consult the monographs of Bannerjee (1988) and Wolfe (1989) for more details on this subject.

SIMD computers are not the only suitable targets for programs written in SIMD programming languages; Hatcher and Quinn have demonstrated that compilers can translate SIMD programs into code that executes efficiently on multiprocessors and multicomputers (Hatcher and Quinn 1991; Hatcher et al. 1991a, 1991b, 1991c). Other advocates of executing SIMD programs on a variety of parallel computers are Blelloch and Chatterjee (Blelloch 1990; Blelloch and Chatterjee 1990; Chatterjee et al. 1991).

More references to Linda in the literature are in Carriero and Gelernter (1988, 1989a, 1989b, 1990), Carriero et al. (1986), and Gelernter (1985). Leler (1990) describes the design of the QIX operating system, which is based on the Linda model.

In his Turing Award lecture, Backus (1978) outlines the advantages of functional programming languages over imperative languages. A number of functional programming languages have been proposed for parallel computers, including Crystal (Chen 1986, 1987; Saltz and Chen 1987), Nial (Glasgow et al. 1989), ParAlfl (Hudak 1986), and SISAL (Allan and Oldehoeft 1985; Lee et al. 1988).

A few years ago Japan's initiative in developing fifth-generation computer systems attracted a lot of attention. A **fifth-generation computer** is a computer system capable of knowledge processing. The preliminary report on fifth-generation computer systems appears in Moto-oka (1982). Journals concentrating on this topic include *Future Generations Computer Systems* and *New Generation Computing*.

Fifth-generation computers use logic programming. For an introduction to logic programming, see works by Kowalski (1979) and Lloyd (1984). A standard reference for the Prolog logic programming language is Clocksin and Mellish (1981).

Parallelism in logic programs is discussed in books by Conery (1987) and Tick (1991), as well as in dozens of papers, including Chang and Despain (1985), Chen and Wu (1991), Clocksin and Mellish (1981), Conery and Kibler (1981), Fagin and Despain (1990), Lin et al. (1986), Ng and Leung (1988), and Tanaka (1986).

The implementation of Flat Concurrent Prolog is described in Taylor et al. (1987); the implementation of Parlog is discussed in Foster (1988); Foster and Taylor (1988); and Gregory (1987). A distributed version of yet another parallel logical programming language, Flat GHC, is documented in Ichiyoshi et al., (1987).

Douglass (1984) has written a paper critiquing approaches to the parallelization of rule-based expert systems, including production systems as well as systems based on logic programming. His paper highlights the lack of empirical evidence that could help determine the parallelizability of expert systems.

4.11 PROBLEMS

4-1 In Sec. 4.1 we presented one formula to compute the variance of a set of values. Here is another formula. Given $r_1, r_2, r_2, \ldots, r_n$, the variance of the values is equal to $(\sum_1^n r_i^2)/n - m^2$, where $m = \sum_1^n r_i/n$. Explain how to use this formula to compute the variance (*a*) on a UMA multiprocessor and (*b*) on a multicomputer. Would the resulting parallel algorithms execute faster or slower than the algorithms presented in Sec. 4.1?

4-2 Is Fortran 90 a superset of FORTRAN 77? Is *every* FORTRAN 77 program a valid Fortran 90 program?

4-3 Write a Fortran 90 statement that initializes a 100-element array with the values $99, 98, 97, \ldots, 0$.

4-4 Imagine you have been assigned the job of writing a compiler to translate Fortran 90 programs into code that executes on a multicomputer. Explain why the Fortran 90 model of parallel computation makes it more difficult to generate code for a distributed-memory architecture than if the model were based on the C* model of parallel computation.

4-5 The current Thinking Machines C* compiler demands that the size of each dimension of a shape be a power of 2. Suppose we want to compute the integral using exactly 100,000 rectangles. Modify the program in Fig. 4-8 to effect this change.

4-6 Look at the Sequent Parallel C program in Fig. 4-11. What would happen at execution time if the programmer had forgotten to surround the statement `pi += localsum;` with the `m_lock` and `m_unlock` function calls? What would happen at execution time if the programmer had forgotten just `m_unlock`?

4-7 Differentiate between SIMD programming, SPMD programming, and MIMD programming.

4-8 Rewrite function `fan_in`, shown in Fig. 4-14, so that at the end of the function's execution, every node, not just node 0, will have the sum of every node's initial value.

4-9 In the occam program shown in Fig. 4-17, one process collects the subtotals generated by the other processes. Rewrite the program so that the processes accumulating the subtotals perform the addition fan-in style—in a logarithmic number of steps—without using another process.

4-10 Write a version of the divide-and-conquer style C-Linda program that uses a fixed number of processes.

4-11 Using the algorithm described in Sec. 4.1, implement a program to find the variance of n numbers. Write your program in

  a Fortran 90
  b C*
  c Sequent C
  d nCUBE C
  e occam
  f C-Linda

4-12 Simpson's Rule is a better numerical integration algorithm than the rectangle rule presented in this book, because it converges more quickly. Suppose we want to compute $\int_a^b f(x)dx$. We divide the interval $[a, b]$ into n subintervals, where n is even. Let x_i denote the end of the ith interval, for $1 \le i \le n$, and let x_0 denote the beginning of the first interval. According to Simpson's Rule:

$$\int_a^b f(x)dx \approx \frac{1}{3n}\left[fx_0 - fx_n + \sum_{i=1}^{n/2}(4f(x_{2i-1}) + 2f(x_{2i})) \right]$$

In the case of the π calculation problem presented in the book, $f(x) = 4/(1+x^2)$, $a = 0$, $b = 1$, and $n = 400,000$. Write a program to compute π using Simpson's Rule. Write your program in

  a Fortran 90
  b C*
  c Sequent C
  d nCUBE C
  e occam
  f C-Linda

4-13 We have called Fortran 90, C*, occam, and Linda high level parallel programming languages, but some parallel programming languages are more high level than others. Let us say a language is more high level if the programmer does not have to manage the number of processes explicitly, i.e., if the programmer can think in terms of parallelism of the problem, rather than the parallelism of the underlying architecture. Using this criteria, rank these four languages from most high level to least high level, and justify your ranking.

5

MAPPING AND SCHEDULING

Hail, memory, hail! in thy exhaustless mine
From age to age unnumbered treasures shine!
Thought and her shadowy brood thy call obey,
And Place and Time are subject to thy sway!

Samuel Rogers, *Pleasures of Memory Pt. II, L. 428*

This chapter addresses four problems related to implementing algorithms on parallel computers: the static mapping of processes to processors on multicomputers and processor arrays, dynamic load balancing on multicomputers, task scheduling on multiprocessors, and ways in which parallel processes can deadlock.

On multicomputers and processor arrays local variables are accessed faster than nonlocal variables, and the distribution of the data structures usually dictates which processors perform which operations. In Sec. 5.1 we consider four common graphs representing the communication pattern of the parallel elements and two common processor organizations. For each of eight potential algorithm-to-architecture mappings, we determine how well the algorithm graph can be embedded in the architecture graph.

The level of parallelism must be fixed in order to associate parallel data elements with particular processors. Some parallel algorithms dynamically create and destroy processes. In Sec. 5.2 we explore proposed algorithms for performing dynamic load balancing on multicomputers.

UMA multiprocessors usually have a single ready list that all processors access in order to get more work. As a result, there is usually no tight binding of processes to particular processors, and the operating system provides dynamic load balancing with no effort by the programmer. However, the scheduling problem still has interest in many cases. For example, static scheduling sometimes results in lower execution times than dynamic scheduling. In addition, a parallel program development system can use scheduling algorithms to predict the execution time and speedup of a parallel algorithm, assuming no preemption of processes occurs. Section 5.3 discusses the problem of scheduling processes to processors, given a task graph containing information about the lengths of the individual tasks and the precedence relations between tasks.

A more flexible, but more complicated, model of parallel computing assumes that the execution time of a task is not a constant, but is a random variable. At the end of Sec. 5.3 we show how to estimate the speedup of nondeterministic parallel algorithms for which the task graphs are well structured.

Finally, Sec. 5.4 describes how deadlock can occur in a parallel processing system. We discuss methods for detecting or preventing deadlock.

5.1 MAPPING DATA TO PROCESSORS ON PROCESSOR ARRAYS AND MULTICOMPUTERS

Processor arrays and multicomputers are characterized by a nonuniform memory structure: each processor is able to get data from local memory much faster than from nonlocal memory. When designing algorithms for these machines, it makes sense to have processors manipulate local data as much as possible. For this reason, the distribution of parallel data structures often dictates which processor is responsible for performing a particular operation. An algorithm's data manipulation patterns can be represented as a graph: each vertex represents a data subset allocated to the same local memory, and each edge represents a computation involving data from two data sets. These graphs are often regular. An important goal of a parallel algorithm designer is to map the algorithm graph into the corresponding graph of the target machine's processor organization (Bokhari 1981).

Performance may suffer if the algorithm graph is not a subgraph of the parallel architecture's processor organization. For example, suppose we are implementing a parallel algorithm on a multicomputer that uses store-and-forward routing, and two connected vertices in the algorithm graph map to a pair of vertices distance two apart on the machine (Fig. 5-1a). Passing a message from one processor to the other requires roughly twice the time it takes to pass a message between adjacent processors. Or, suppose we are implementing a parallel algorithm on a multicomputer with circuit-switched routing, and different edges in the algorithm graph map to a shared link on the machine (Fig. 5-1b).

FIGURE 5-1   If the algorithm graph is not a subgraph of the target architecture's processor organization, performance of the parallel algorithm may suffer. (a) Dilation: on a multicomputer with store-and-forward message passing, communication time is roughly proportional to the length of the path between the processors. (b) Congestion: on any distributed memory system, every communication link has a fixed bandwidth. Mapping multiple edges of a algorithm graph onto a single communication link can increase communication time.

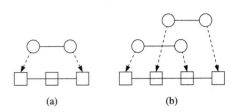

(a)   (b)

If simultaneous communications occur between both pairs of nodes, the speed of the communication will be affected by the shared use of the same link. On some systems one message would be blocked until the other message had finished. On other systems the physical link would be multiplexed between the two virtual links, cutting the bandwidth of each link in half. In either case, performance is lower because each message does not have exclusive use of a communication path.

In this section we discuss the problem of mapping four important algorithm graphs—complete binary tree, binomial tree, ring, and mesh—into two important processor organizations, the 2-D mesh and the hypercube (binary n-cube). Readers unfamiliar with the vocabulary of graph theory can find a review of graph theoretic terminology in Appendix A.

Definition 5.1. An **embedding** of a graph $G = (V, E)$ into a graph $G' = (V', E')$ is a function ϕ from V to V'.

Definition 5.2. Let ϕ be the function that embeds graph $G = (V, E)$ into graph $G' = (V', E')$. The **dilation** of the embedding is defined as follows: $dil(\phi) = \max\{dist(\phi(u), \phi(v))|(u, v) \in E\}$ where $dist(a, b)$ is the distance between vertices a and b in G'.

There exists a dilation-1 embedding of G into G' if G is a subgraph of G'. Figure 5-2 illustrates a dilation-1 embedding.

G G'

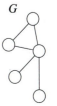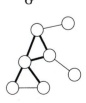

FIGURE 5-2   If graph G is a subgraph of G', there exists a dilation-1 embedding of G into G'.

G $\qquad$ G'

 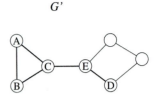

FIGURE 5-3 A dilation-3 embedding of graph G into graph G'. The edge (B,D) in G becomes a path of length 3 in G'.

Figure 5-3 illustrates a dilation-3 embedding of a graph G into another graph G'.

Definition 5.3. The **load** of an embedding $\phi : G \rightarrow G'$ is the maximum number of vertices of G that are mapped to a single vertex of G'.

For the rest of this chapter we will focus our attention exclusively on embeddings with load 1.

5.1.1 Ring into 2-D Mesh

Our first case is one of the simplest: embedding a ring into a 2-D mesh without wraparound connections. We assume that the ring and the mesh have the same number of vertices.

A dilation-1 embedding exists if the mesh has an even number of rows and/or columns. A mesh with an odd number of rows and columns has no Hamiltonian circuit (Prob. 5-1); hence there is no way to embed a ring in such a mesh without increasing the dilation.

Figure 5-4 illustrates one way to map a ring into a 2-D mesh.

5.1.2 2-D Mesh into 2-D Mesh

Under what circumstances can a 2-D mesh without wraparound connections be embedded with dilation 1 in another 2-D mesh without wraparound connections?

Let A_r denote the number of rows in the algorithm graph, A_c denote the number of columns in the algorithm graph, M_r denote the number of rows in the machine graph, and M_c denote the number of columns in the machine graph.

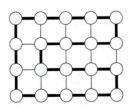

FIGURE 5-4 A dilation-1 embedding of a ring into a 2-D mesh having the same number of vertices exists if and only if the number of vertices is even.

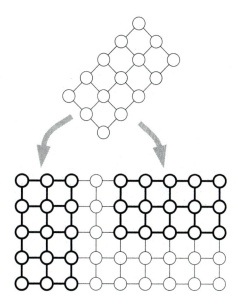

FIGURE 5-5   Two dilation-1 embeddings of a 2-D mesh into another 2-D mesh.

The algorithm graph can be embedded with dilation 1 in the machine graph if and only if (1) $A_r \leq M_r$ and $A_c \leq M_c$, or (2) $A_c \leq M_r$ and $A_r \leq M_c$. (See Fig. 5-5).

5.1.3   Complete Binary Tree into 2-D Mesh

Figure 5-6 illustrates a dilation-1 embedding of a complete binary tree of height 3 into a 2-D mesh.

Theorem 5.1. A complete binary tree of height greater than 4 cannot be embedded in a 2-D mesh without increasing the dilation beyond 1.

Proof. The total number of mesh points k or fewer jumps away from an arbitrary point in a 2-D mesh is $2k^2 + 2k + 1$ (Problem 5-5). The total number of nodes in a complete binary tree of depth k is $2^{k+1} - 1$. It is easy to show that $2^{k+1} - 1 > 2k^2 + 2k + 1$ for all $k > 4$.

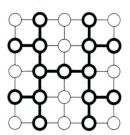

FIGURE 5-6   A dilation-1 embedding of a binary tree of height 3 into a 2-D mesh.

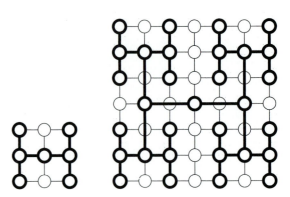

FIGURE 5-7   H-trees of height 2 and 4.

The H-tree is a common way of embedding a complete binary tree into a 2-D mesh. The name H-tree arises from the recursive "H" pattern used to construct a large H-tree out of four small H-trees (see Fig. 5-7).

Theorem 5.2. A complete binary tree of height n has a dilation $\lceil n/2 \rceil$ embedding in a 2-D mesh.

Proof. We use H-trees to map binary trees to nodes of a 2-D mesh. The longest edges in an H-tree are the edges from the root to its two children. These edges have the same length. The length of the root edges in an H-tree of height n is $\lceil n/2 \rceil$.

5.1.4   Binomial Tree into 2-D Mesh

Figure 5-8 illustrates a dilation-1 embedding of a binomial tree of height 4 into a 2-D mesh.

Theorem 5.3. A binomial tree of height greater than 4 cannot be embedded in a 2-D mesh without increasing the dilation beyond 1.

Proof. The root node of a binomial tree of height d tree is connected to d other nodes. No node in a 2-D mesh has more than 4 neighbors. Hence a binomial tree of height greater than 4 cannot be embedded in a 2-D mesh without increasing the dilation beyond 1.

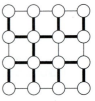

FIGURE 5-8   A binomial tree of height 4 embedded in a 2-D mesh. The dilation is 1.

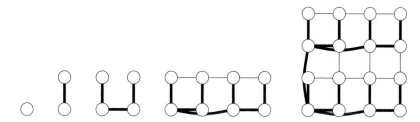

FIGURE 5-9   Embeddings of binomial trees into a 2-D mesh. In this scheme an embedding of a binomial tree of height n has dilation $\lceil n/2 \rceil$.

Theorem 5.4. A binomial tree of height n has a dilation $\lceil n/2 \rceil$ embedding in a 2-D mesh.

Proof. The construction is illustrated in Fig. 5-9.

5.1.5 Embedding Graphs into Hypercubes

Definition 5.4. A graph G is **cubical** if there is a dilation-1 embedding of G into a hypercube.

Theorem 5.5. The problem of determining whether an arbitrary graph G is cubical is $\mathcal{NP}$-complete (Afrati et al. 1985; Cybenko et al. 1986).

Theorem 5.6. A dilation-1 embedding of a connected graph G into a hypercube with n nodes exists if and only if it is possible to label the edges of G with the integers $\{1, \ldots, n\}$ such that:

1 Edges incident with a common vertex have different labels.
2 In every path of G at least one label appears an odd number of times.
3 In every cycle of G no label appears an odd number of times.

(See Havel and Morávek 1972; Livingston and Stout 1987).

Figure 5-10 illustrates those conditions that prevent a dilation-1 embedding of a graph into a hypercube.

5.1.6 Complete Binary Tree into Hypercube

Theorem 5.7. A dilation-1 embedding of a complete binary tree of height n into a hypercube of dimension $n + 1$ does not exist if $n > 1$.

Proof. A complete binary tree of height n has $2^{n+1} - 1$ nodes. A hypercube of dimension $n + 1$ has 2^{n+1} nodes. If a complete binary tree is to be embedded in a

FIGURE 5-10   A dilation-1 embedding of a graph G into a hypercube with n nodes does not exist if every possible labeling of edges of G with the integers $1, \ldots, n$ leads to at least one of the following conditions. (a) Two edges incident on the same vertex have the same label. (b) In some path of G no label appears an odd number of times. (c) In a cycle of G at least one label appears an odd number of times.

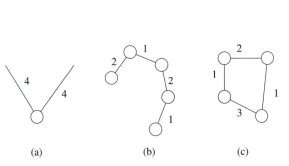

(a)   (b)   (c)

hypercube, the root of the tree must be mapped to a node X of the hypercube. The hypercube is a bipartite graph. Hence half the hypercube's nodes can be reached only by following an even number of edges from X. Likewise, half the hypercube's nodes can be reached only by following an odd number of edges from X. If k is odd, then more than half the nodes of the binary tree are an even distance away from the root of the binary tree. If k is even, then more than half the nodes of the binary tree are an odd distance away from the root of the binary tree. In either case, there is no way to embed the binary tree into the hypercube and keep the dilation at 1, because there are not enough hypercube nodes to accommodate the leaves of the tree while maintaining parity (odd or even) with the interior nodes.

Theorem 5.8. A balanced binary tree with of height n has a dilation-1 embedding into a hypercube of dimension $n + 2$ (see Nebesky 1974).

Theorem 5.9. A complete binary tree of height n has a dilation-2 embedding in a hypercube of dimension $n + 1$, for all $n > 1$ (see Leighton 1992).

5.1.7   Binomial Tree into Hypercube

Theorem 5.10. A binomial tree of height n can be embedded in a hypercube of dimension n such that the dilation is 1.

Proof. Organize the subtree so that the nodes that are roots of larger subtrees appear to the left of nodes that are the roots of smaller subtrees (Fig. 5-11). Give the edge to the leftmost child of the root node the label 1, the edge to the second child of the root node the label 2, and so on, to the edge to the last child, which gets label n. For all remaining interior nodes of the tree, if the edge above the node has label i, then the edges to the k children of the node should be given labels $i + 1, i + 2, \ldots, i + k$, from left to right.

To demonstrate this is an embedding with dilation 1, we must show we satisfy the conditions of Theorem 5.6.

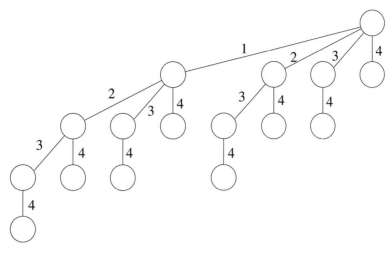

FIGURE 5-11   A numbering of the edges of a binomial tree of height 4 that proves the tree can be embedded with dilation 1 into a hypercube of dimension 4.

First, we must show that no two edges incident on the same vertex have the same label. This is clear by construction. Second, we must show that every path in the graph has at least one edge whose label appears an odd number of times. There are two kinds of paths: paths from ancestors to descendents and paths between vertices that share a common ancestor. Every edge on a path from a node to one of its descendents has a unique label, so there is at least one edge whose label appears an odd number of times. On a path between vertices that share a common ancestor, the edges work their way up the tree to the common ancestor, then back down the tree. Two edges on the path are incident upon the common ancestor. The label assigned to the left edge is smaller than any of the other edge labels on the path. Hence this label appears exactly once, and the condition is satisfied. The third condition is trivially satisfied, since trees contain no cycles.

5.1.8 Rings and Meshes into Hypercube

Assume the hypercube contains $p = 2^d$ processors. Let $G(i)$ be the number of the processor assigned to ring position i, where $0 \le i < p$. Note that the straightforward encoding $G(0) = 0$, $G(1) = 1$, $G(2) = 2$, ..., $G(p-1) = p-1$ will not work, since it would cause many pairs of adjacent ring processors, such as processors 1 and 2, to be not adjacent in the hypercube.

The encoding must have the following properties:

1 The values must be unique, in other words, $G(i) = G(j) \Rightarrow i = j$.

2 $G(i)$ and $G(i+1)$ must differ in exactly one bit position, for all i, where $0 \le i < p - 1$.

3 $G(p-1)$ and $G(0)$ must differ in exactly one bit position.

Students of combinatorics will recognize that these three criteria constitute a definition of a **Gray code**. There are many possible n-bit Gray codes. Here is a way to construct longer Gray codes from shorter Gray codes. A 1-bit Gray code is {0, 1}, that is, $G(0) = 0$ and $G(1) = 1$. Given a d-bit Gray code, a $(d + 1)$-bit Gray code can be constructed by listing the d-bit Gray code with the prefix 0, followed by the d-bit Gray code in reverse order with the prefix 1.

Using this technique, we build the following 2-bit Gray code:

```
00
01
11
10
```

From this 2-bit Gray code we generate the following 3-bit Gray code:

```
000
001
011
010
110
111
101
100
```

The inverse Gray code is defined as follows: $G^{-1}(i) = j$ if and only if $G(j) = i$. We use both the Gray code and the inverse Gray code to embed rings and meshes in the hypercube. For example, the following function defines the successor of processor i on a ring with 2^d nodes:

$$Successor(i) = \begin{cases} 0, & \text{if } i = 2^{d-1}; \\ G(G^{-1}(i) + 1), & \text{otherwise.} \end{cases}$$

C functions to compute $G(i)$ and $G^{-1}(i)$ appear in Figure 5-12.

Figure 5-13 illustrates a dilation-1 embedding of a ring in a three-dimensional hypercube. Node numbers listed in the order of a ring traversal are called a Gray code.

Mapping a ring onto a hypercube is an example of the problem of mapping a multidimensional mesh with wraparound connections onto a hypercube. Again, the use of Gray codes yields a straightforward solution, albeit with the constraint that the size of the mesh in each dimension must be a power of 2. Each dimension of the mesh is assigned an appropriate number of bit positions of the encoding string. Traversing mesh nodes along that dimension yields a cycle. Gray codes determine the values assigned to the bit field.

```
/* Passed ring position i, function gray returns
   the number of the processor occupying that position */
int gray (i)
  int i;
{
  return (i ^ (i/2)); /* Exclusive or */
}
/* Passed processor number i, function gray_inverse returns
   the position of that processor in a Gray code sequence */

int gray_inverse (i)
  int i;
{
  int answer, mask;
  answer = i;
  mask = answer / 2;
  while (mask > 0) {
    answer = answer ^ mask;  /* Exclusive or */
    mask = mask / 2;
  }
  return (answer);
}
```

FIGURE 5-12   C functions to compute Gray code and inverse Gray code.

For example, consider mapping a 4×8 mesh into a 32-node hypercube. Two bit positions are reserved for the row and three bit positions are set aside for the column. Let us assume that the first two bit positions are used for the row. The 2-bit Gray code {00, 01, 11, 10} corresponds to a traversal through rows 0, 1, 2, and 3. The 3-bit Gray code {000, 001, 011, 010, 110, 111, 101, 100} corresponds to a traversal through columns 0, 1, 2, 3, 4, 5, 6, and 7. Hence we have the following mapping of a 4×8 mesh into a 32-node hypercube:

```
00000  00001  00011  00010  00110  00111  00101  00100
01000  01001  01011  01010  01110  01111  01101  01100
11000  11001  11011  11010  11110  11111  11101  11100
10000  10001  10011  10010  10110  10111  10101  10100
```

FIGURE 5-13   A mapping of an 8-node ring into an 8-processor hypercube.

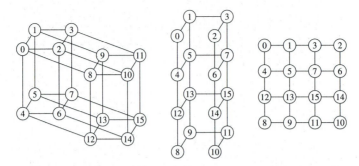

FIGURE 5-14   A dilation-1 embedding of a 4 × 4 mesh into a 4-dimensional hypercube exists because the mesh is a subgraph of the hypercube. We remove 12 edges from the hypercube and unfold it to reveal the mesh.

As another example, Fig. 5-14 illustrates a way to embed a 2-D mesh into a four-dimensional hypercube. Problem 5-13 explores conditions necessary for a mesh to be embedded in a hypercube with dilation 1.

Theorem 5.11. Any two-dimensional mesh with n vertices can be embedded in a $\lceil \log n \rceil$-dimensional hypercube with dilation 2 (Leighton 1992).

5.2   DYNAMIC LOAD BALANCING ON MULTICOMPUTERS

In Sec. 5.1 we assumed that if data were distributed evenly among the local memories of a multicomputer's processors, the processors' workloads would be balanced for the entire computation. In many cases this assumption is true, but not always.

For example, high-speed computing is used to solve partial differential equations resulting from fluid dynamics problems. For instance, you may wish to compute the velocity, density, and pressure of air as it passes by an air foil. An iterative solution method begins with a coarse grid around the air foil. The grid is refined at those places where the rate of change is particularly large, resulting in a highly irregular final grid. Assigning each processor to its share of the original grid elements results in poor load balance, once the algorithm has decomposed some of the grid elements into much smaller pieces.

Another example of a computation with changing load balance is a particle-in-cell simulation. If each processor is responsible for simulating the particles within an equal-sized area of the model space, and the particles are uniformly scattered throughout this space, then the workload is balanced at the beginning of the simulation. However, as the computation progresses, the distribution of the particles may become less uniform. If nothing is done to change the size of each processor's area of responsibility the processors' workloads may become severely imbalanced.

Dynamic load balancing is the process of making changes to the distribution of work among the processors at run time. The measure of success of dynamic load balancing is the net reduction of execution time achieved by applying the load balancing algorithm. Of course, dynamic load balancing may actually increase the execution time of the parallel algorithm if the time spent performing the load balancing is more than the time saved by reducing the variance in the execution time of tasks on the various processors.

Authors have proposed a variety of algorithms to perform dynamic load balancing. We follow Znati et al. (1991) and classify these algorithms as centralized, fully distributed, or semi-distributed.

Centralized load balancing algorithms make a global decision about the re-allocation of work to processors. Some centralized algorithms assign the maintenance of the system's global state information to a particular node. Global state information can allow the algorithm to do a good job balancing the work among the processors. However, this approach does not scale well, because the amount of information increases linearly with the number of processors. Dragon and Gustafson (1989) have implemented a centralized algorithm that distributes global state information throughout the system and demands only a constant amount of memory per processor.

Fully distributed load balancing algorithms let each processor build its own view of the state of the system. Processors exchange information with neighboring processors and use this information to make local changes in the allocation of work. A fully distributed algorithm has the advantage of lower scheduling overhead. However, since processors have only local state information, the workload may not be balanced as well as it would be by centralized algorithms.

A **semi-distributed load balancing algorithm** divides the processors into regions. Within each region a centralized algorithm distributes the workload among the processors. A higher level scheduling mechanism balances the workload between regions.

Load balancing may be either sender initiated or receiver initiated. In a **sender initiated load balancing algorithm**, a processor with too much work sends some work to another processor. In a **receiver initiated load balancing algorithm**, a processor with too little work takes some work from another processor. Two performance studies have shown that sender-initiated policies perform better in an environment with light to medium workload per processor, while receiver-initiated policies perform better in an environment with heavy workload per processor (Livny 1983; Tantawi and Towsley 1985). One disadvantage of a receiver-initiated policy is that task migration can be expensive if the receiver grabs a partially completed task.

5.3 STATIC SCHEDULING ON UMA MULTIPROCESSORS

The typical UMA multiprocessor provides dynamic scheduling of parallel processes as a matter of course. All processes in need of CPU cycles are stored in a single ready queue. Every physical processor accesses this ready queue to run the next process. The binding of processes to processors is not tight, and a single process may receive cycles from many different CPUs before eventually terminating. Because the operating system provides dynamic scheduling automatically, we will not consider it further.

However, there are three reasons why static scheduling is still of interest. First, static scheduling sometimes results in lower execution times than dynamic scheduling. Second, static scheduling can allow the generation of only one process per processor, reducing process creation, synchronization, and termination overhead. Third, static scheduling can be used to predict the speedup that can be achieved by a particular parallel algorithm on a target machine, assuming no preemption of processes occurs. In this section we describe the problem of static scheduling for both deterministic and nondeterministic models.

5.3.1 Deterministic Models

One way to view a parallel algorithm is as a collection of tasks, some of which must be completed before others begin. In a **deterministic model**, the execution time needed by each task and the precedence relations between the tasks are fixed and known before run time. This information can be represented by a directed graph called a **task graph**. For example, consider the task graph illustrated in Fig. 5-15. We are given a set of seven tasks and their precedence relations (i.e., information about what tasks must be completed before other tasks can be started).

A task graph is an idealized representation of a parallel algorithm's execution, which ignores variances in tasks' execution times due to interrupts, contention for shared memory, etc. Nevertheless, task graphs do provide a basis for the static allocation of tasks to processors.

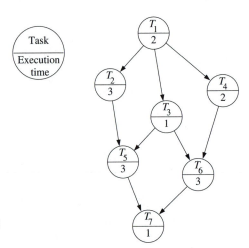

FIGURE 5-15   A task graph. Each node represents a task to be performed. A directed arc from T_i to T_j indicates that task T_i must complete before task T_j begins.

A **schedule** is an allocation of tasks to processors. Schedules are often illustrated with Gantt charts. A **Gantt chart** indicates the time each task spends in execution, as well as the processor on which it executes. For example, Fig. 5-16 is a Gantt chart of a schedule based on the task graph of Fig. 5-15. A desirable feature of Gantt charts is that they graphically illustrate the **utilization** of each processor (percentage of time spent executing tasks).

Given a task graph and some number of processors, an **optimal schedule** minimizes the total execution time. Some simple scheduling problems are solvable in polynomial time, while other problems, only slightly more complex, are intractable.

For example, if all of the tasks take unit time, and the task graph is a forest (i.e., no task has more than one predecessor), then a polynomial time algorithm exists to find an optimal schedule (Hu 1961).

If all of the tasks take unit time, and the number of processors is two, then a polynomial time algorithm exists to find an optimal schedule (Coffman and Graham 1972).

If the task lengths vary at all, or if there are more than two processors, then the problem of finding an optimal schedule is $\mathcal{NP}$-hard (Ullman 1975), meaning the only known algorithms that find an optimal schedule require exponential time in the worst case.

In general we are interested in scheduling arbitrary task graphs onto a reasonable number of processors, and we must be content with polynomial time scheduling algorithms that do a good, but not perfect, job.

Given a list of tasks ordered by their relative priority, it is possible to assign tasks to processors by always giving each available processor the first unassigned task on the list whose predecessor tasks have already finished execution. This list-scheduling algorithm was proposed by Graham (1966, 1969, 1972), and we formalize it next.

5.3.2 Graham's List Scheduling Algorithm

Let $T = \{T_1, T_2, \ldots, T_n\}$ be a set of tasks. Let $\mu : T \to (0, \infty)$ be a function that associates an execution time with each task. We are also given a partial order $\prec$ on T. Let L be a list of the tasks in T.

Whenever a processor has no work to do, it instantaneously removes from L the first ready task; that is, an unscheduled task whose predecessors under $\prec$

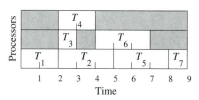

FIGURE 5-16   A Gantt chart illustrating a schedule for the task graph of Fig. 3-8.

have all completed execution. If two or more processors simultaneously attempt to execute the same tasks, the processor with the lowest index succeeds, and the other processors look for another suitable task.

The Gantt chart of Fig. 5-16 is the result of applying Graham's list-scheduling algorithm to the task graph of Fig. 5-15, given the priority list $L = \{T_1, T_2, T_3, T_4, T_5, T_6, T_7\}$.

Contrary to intuition, increasing the number of processors, decreasing the execution times of one or more tasks, or eliminating some of the precedence constraints can actually increase the length of the schedule generated using Graham's heuristic. See Fig. 5-17 for a clever set of examples invented by Graham (1972).

5.3.3 Coffman-Graham Scheduling Algorithm.

Graham's list-scheduling algorithm depends upon a prioritized list of tasks to execute. What is the best way to construct this list? A well-known and intuitive

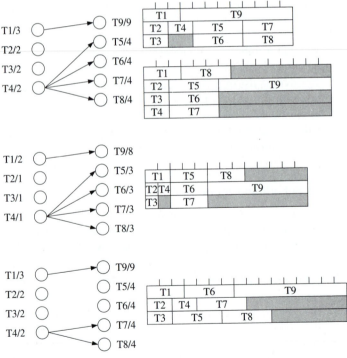

FIGURE 5-17   A series of examples illustrating that increasing the number of processors, decreasing the execution times of one or more tasks, or eliminating some of the precedence constraints can actually increase the length of the schedule generated using Graham's heuristic (Graham 1972). In each case the priority task list is the same: $L = \{T_1, T_2, \ldots, T_9\}$.

scheduling algorithm due to Coffman and Graham (1972) constructs the list of tasks for the simple case when all tasks take the same amount of time. Once this list L has been constructed, the algorithm applies Graham's list-scheduling algorithm, already described.

Let $T = T_1, T_2, \ldots, T_n$ be a set of n unit-time tasks to be executed on p processors, and let $\prec$ be a partial order on T that specifies which tasks must complete before other tasks begin. If $T_i \prec T_j$, then task T_i is an **immediate predecessor** of task T_j, and T_j is an **immediate successor** of T_i. Let $S(T_i)$ denote the set of immediate successors of T_i.

Let $\alpha(T)$ be an integer label assigned to T. $N(T)$ denotes the decreasing sequence of integers formed by ordering the set $\{\alpha(T')|T' \in S(T)\}$.

1. Choose an arbitrary task T_k from T such that $S(T_k) = \emptyset$, and define $\alpha(T_k)$ to be 1
2. for $i \leftarrow 2$ to n do
   a. R be the set of unlabeled tasks with no unlabeled successors
   b. Let $T*$ be the task in R such that $N(T*)$ is lexicographically smaller than $N(T)$ for all T in R (breaking ties arbitrarily)
   c. Let $\alpha(T*) \leftarrow i$
   endfor
3. Construct a list of tasks $L = (U_n, U_{n-1}, \ldots, U_2, U_1)$ such that $\alpha(U_i) = i$ for all i where $1 \leq i \leq n$
4. Given $(T, \prec, L)$, use Graham's list scheduling algorithm to schedule the tasks in T

Figure 5-18 illustrates the Coffman-Graham scheduling algorithm.

Theorem 5.12. If ω is the length of a schedule produced by the Coffman-Graham algorithm and ω_0 is the length of an optimal schedule, then $w/w_0 \leq 2 - 2/p$, where p is the number of processors and $p \geq 2$ (see Lam and Sethi 1977).

Corollary 5.1. The Coffman-Graham algorithm generates an optimal schedule if the number of processors is two (see Lam and Sethi 1977).

5.3.4 Nondeterministic Models

In a **nondeterministic model**, the execution time of a task is represented by a random variable, making the scheduling problem more difficult. This subsection summarizes mathematics developed by Robinson (1979) that allow an estimate of the execution time of parallel programs with "simple" task graphs on UMA multiprocessors.

We must define a few more terms. Tasks with no predecessors are called **initial tasks**. A set of tasks is **independent** if, for every pair of tasks T_i and

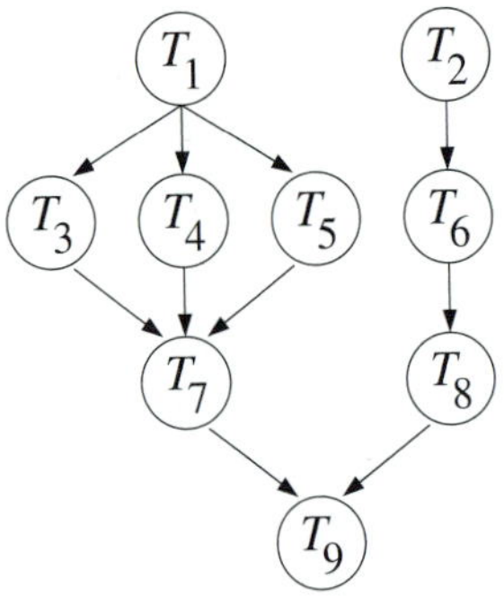

Step 1 of algorithm:
Task T_9 is the only task with no immediate successor. Assign 1 to $\alpha(T_9)$.

Step 2 of algorithm:
$i = 2$. $R = \{T_7, T_8\}$. $N(T_7) = \{1\}$ and $N(T_8) = \{1\}$, trying for lexicographically smallest. Arbitrarily choose task T_7 and assign 2 to $\alpha(T_7)$.

$i = 3$. $R = \{T_3, T_4, T_5, T_8\}$. $N(T_3) = \{2\}$, $N(T_4) = \{2\}$, $N(T_5) = \{2\}$, and $N(T_8) = \{1\}$. Task T_8 is lexicographically smallest. Choose it and assign 3 to $\alpha(T_8)$.

$i = 4$. $R = \{T_3, T_4, T_5, T_6\}$. $N(T_3) = \{2\}$, $N(T_4) = \{2\}$, $N(T_5) = \{2\}$, and $N(T_6) = \{3\}$. Tasks T_3, T_4, and T_5 all tie for lexicographically smallest. Arbitrarily choose T_4 and assign 4 to $\alpha(T_4)$.

$i = 5$. $R = \{T_3, T_5, T_6\}$. $N(T_3) = \{2\}$, $N(T_5) = \{2\}$, and $N(T_6) = \{3\}$. Tasks T_3 and T_5 tie for lexicographically smallest. Arbitrarily choose task T_5 and assign 5 to $\alpha(T_5)$.

$i = 6$. $R = \{T_3, T_6\}$. $N(T_3) = \{2\}$ and $N(T_6) = \{3\}$. Set $N(T_3)$ is lexicographically smaller; assign 6 to $\alpha(T_3)$.

$i = 7$. $R = \{T_1, T_6\}$. $N(T_1) = \{6, 5, 4\}$ and $N(T_6) = \{3\}$. Set $N(T_6)$ is lexicographically smaller; assign 7 to $\alpha(T_6)$.

$i = 8$. $R = \{T_1, T_2\}$. $N(T_1) = \{6, 5, 4\}$ and $N(T_2) = \{7\}$. Set $N(T_1)$ is lexicographically smaller; assign 8 to $\alpha(T_1)$.

$i = 9$. $R = \{T_2\}$. Choose task T_2 and assign 9 to $\alpha(T_2)$.

Step 3 of algorithm:
$L = \{T_2, T_1, T_6, T_3, T_5, T_4, T_8, T_7, T_9\}$.

Step 4 of algorithm:
Schedule is result of applying Graham's list-scheduling algorithm to task graph T and list L.

FIGURE 5-18   Example of the Coffman-Graham scheduling algorithm. The Gantt chart is the result of applying the Coffman-Graham algorithm to the task graph. All tasks take unit time to execute.

T_j in the set, neither is a predecessor of the other. The **width** of a task graph is the size of the maximal set of independent tasks.

A **chain** is a totally ordered task graph. The **length** of a chain is the number of tasks in the chain. The **level** of a task T in a task graph G is the maximum chain length in G from an initial task to T. The **depth** of a task graph G is the maximum level of any task in G.

> **Definition 5.5.** Given a task graph G, let $C_1, C_2, \ldots, C_m$ be all the chains from initial to final tasks in G. For every chain C_i consisting of tasks $T_{i_1}, T_{i_2}, \ldots, T_{i_j}$, let X_i be the expression $x_{i_1}, x_{i_2}, \ldots, x_{i_j}$, where $x_1, x_2, \ldots, x_n$ are polynomial variables. Then G is a **simple task graph** if the polynomial $X_1 + X_2 + \cdots + X_m$ can be factored so that every variable appears exactly once (see Robinson 1979).

Figure 5-19 illustrates simple and nonsimple task graphs. Robinson has observed that the set of simple task graphs corresponds exactly to the set of task graphs that can be generated by parallel languages whose only concurrent programming construct is a `cobegin...coend` statement, or its equivalent.

> **Theorem 5.13.** Given a simple task graph G, if the number of processors exceeds the width of G, the tasks are independent, the jdepth of G is L, and the execution time of all m_j tasks on level j is a random variable with mean μ_j and standard deviation σ_j, then the expected time to execute task graph G falls in the range
>
> $$\sum_{1 \le j \le L} \mu_j \le E(t_G) \le \sum_{1 \le j \le L} \left(\mu_j + \frac{m_j - 1}{\sqrt{2m_j - 1}} \sigma_j \right)$$

(see Robinson 1979).

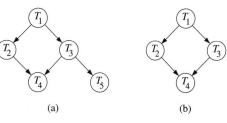

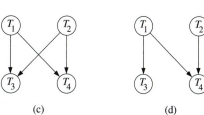

FIGURE 5-19   Simple and nonsimple task graphs. (a) Simple task graph: $x_1 x_2 + x_1 x_3 x_4 + x_1 x_3 x_5 = x_1[x_2 + x_3(x_4 + x_5)]$. (b) Simple task graph: $x_1 x_2 x_4 + x_1 x_3 x_4 = x_1(x_2 + x_3)x_4$. (c) Simple task graph: $x_1 x_3 + x_1 x_4 + x_2 x_3 + x_2 x_4 = (x_1 + x_2)(x_3 + x_4)$. (d) Nonsimple task graph.

For example, consider the following hypothetical parallel algorithm to sort $n = pk$ values by using p processors. The partitioned algorithm has two phases. In the first phase, each p processor sorts $k = n/p$ values. After all the processors snchronize, each processor merges $k = n/p$ values, completing the sort. Suppose that the sort used in the first phase is the best-known sequential sort, with an expected execution time of $3n \log n + 200$ and a standard deviation of $2\sqrt{n}$ to sort n values. Furthermore, suppose that the merge algorithm merges n values with an expected execution time of $4n \log n + 100$ and a standard deviation of $\sqrt{n}$. According to the theorem,

$$E(t_G) \geq 3\frac{n}{p} \log \frac{n}{p} + 200 + 4\frac{n}{p} \log \frac{n}{p} + 100$$

$$\geq 7\frac{n}{p} \log \frac{n}{p} + 300$$

$$E(t_G) \leq 7\frac{n}{p} \log \frac{n}{p} + 300 + \frac{(p-1)3\sqrt{n}}{\sqrt{2p-1}}$$

The expected speedup can be computed by dividing the expected execution time of the sequential algorithm by the expected execution time of the parallel algorithm. Since the sorting algorithm used in the first phase is the fastest known sequential sort, the expected execution time of the sequential algorithm is $3n \log n + 200$. The expected execution time of the parallel algorithm is not known exactly; it falls within a range. Figure 5-20 graphs the expected speedup of the parallel algorithm for two list sizes, 100 and 1000.

Note that Robinson's result does not take into account factors that increase the execution time of a parallel algorithm, such as process creation time, contention for shared variables, and contention for the ready list.

FIGURE 5-20 Expected speedup of hypothetical parallel sort algorithm. Note that for each problem size the predicted speedup is a range between two lines.

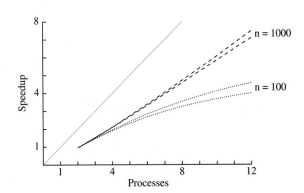

5.4   DEADLOCK

A set of active concurrent processes is said to be **deadlocked** if each holds nonpreemptible resources that must be acquired by some other process in order to proceed. The potential for deadlock exists whenever multiple processes share resources in an unsupervised way. Hence deadlock can exist in multiprogrammed operating systems as well as in multiprocessors and multicomputers.

As an illustration of deadlock, consider the two processes executing in Fig. 5-21. Each process attempts to perform a `lock` operation on two resources. Note that `lock` and `unlock` correspond to `P` and `V` operations on binary semaphores. Process 1 locks `A` while process 2 locks `B`. Process 1 is blocked when it tries to lock `B`; likewise, process 2 is blocked when it tries to lock `A`. Neither process can proceed. If neither of the processes can be made to "back up" and yield its semaphore, the two processes will remain deadlocked indefinitely.

The previous example occurs in the context of a multiprocessor, but deadlock can also occur on a multicomputer as well. We will describe one common type, called **buffer deadlock**. Consider a multicomputer in which processors communicate asynchronously. In other words, a processor sending a message to another processor does not block until there is an attempt to read the message. Instead, when a processor sends a message to another processor, the contents of the message are stored in a system buffer until the receiving processor reads the message. Suppose so many processors are sending data to processor 0 that its system buffer fills up. Further attempts to send data are blocked until processor 0 reads one or more messages, making room in the system buffer. Let processor i be one of the processors unable to send its message to processor 0. If processor 0 attempts to read the message sent by processor i, it will block until the data appears in the system buffer. We have already seen that processor i is blocked until processor 0 removes one or more messages from the system buffer. The two processors are deadlocked. (See Fig. 5-22).

Four conditions are necessary for a deadlock to exist (Coffman and Denning 1973):

	Process 1	Process 2
	.	.
	.	.
	.	.
	lock (A)	lock (B)
	.	.
	.	.
	.	.
	lock (B)	lock (A)

FIGURE 5-21   Illustration of deadlock. As long as each process has exclusive access to a resource desired by the other, neither process can proceed.

FIGURE 5-22   Buffer deadlock can occur on a multicomputer, when a process waits for a message than can never arrive because the system message buffer is already full. In this example, Processor i is blocked trying to write message X to Processor 0, because the message buffer in Processor 0 is full. Processor 0 cannot read message X, which has not yet arrived.

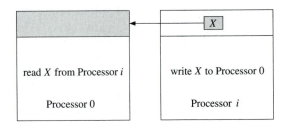

1 Mutual exclusion: each process has exclusive use of its resources

2 Nonpreemption: a process never releases resources it holds until it is through using them

3 Resource waiting: each process holds resources while waiting for other processes to release theirs

4 A cycle of waiting processes: each process in the cycle waits for resources that the next process owns and will not relinquish

The problem of deadlock is commonly addressed in one of three ways. One approach is to detect deadlocks when they occur and try to recover from them. Another approach is to avoid deadlocks by using advance information about requests for resources to control allocation, so that the next allocation of a resource will not cause processes to enter a situation in which deadlock may occur.

The third approach is to prevent deadlock by forbidding one of the last three conditions listed above. This can be accomplished in a number of ways. A cycle of waiting processes can be prevented by ordering shared resources and forcing processes to request resources in that order. Deadlock could have been prevented in the example of Fig. 5-21 if each process had attempted to lock A before locking B. Deadlock can also be prevented by requiring processes to acquire all their resources at once. The second approach often leads to underutilization of resources, however, since it may require processes to retain possession of resources long before and after the resources are being used.

5.5 SUMMARY

In this chapter we have considered some aspects of the problem of matching parallel algorithms to parallel architectures. The fundamental step in designing an algorithm for a processor array or a multicomputer often is determining how to distribute the data structures among the memories of the individual processors. After this step, deciding which processors perform which operations is easy; each processor performs those computations that modify locally stored variables. For this reason we concentrated on the mapping problem, the problem of embedding a graph representing the interaction of data clusters into a graph representing the topology of the underlying architecture.

We also looked at the problem of static scheduling of processes on UMA multiprocessors. Scheduling is determining when and where (on which processor) a process executes. Most operating systems on UMA multiprocessors dynamically schedule parallel processors. In other words, instead of statically mapping processes to processors, all processors share a common ready list. Nevertheless, static scheduling can be beneficial. First, static scheduling sometimes results in faster execution times than dynamic scheduling. Second, program development tools can use static scheduling to predict the speedup of parallel programs. We studied Graham's list-scheduling heuristic for assigning tasks to processors, and we also looked at the Coffman-Graham algorithm for scheduling unit-time tasks.

We briefly considered nondeterministic scheduling models, which are used when the execution time of a task is not a constant, but a random variable.

We concluded the chapter by examining the problem of deadlock, and how it can occur on both multiprocessors and multicomputers.

5.6 BIBLIOGRAPHIC NOTES

The textbook by Leighton (1992) is a rich source of information on known results in the area of graph embedding. The text by Lakshmivarahan and Dhall (1990) has a section on embedding.

Graph embedding can be used to understand the computational equivalence between parallel architectures (Aleliunas and Rosenburger 1982; Bettayeb et al. 1988; Bhatt et al. 1986; Hong et al. 1983; Kosaraju and Atallah 1988; Rosenburg 1979).

Some papers have demonstrated how to use graph emedding to map one architecture into another architecture of the same topology, but smaller size (Atallah 1988; Berman and Snyder 1987; Ellis 1991; Fishburn and Finkel 1982; Gupta and Hambrusch 1992; Kosaraju and Attallah 1988; Sang and Sudborough 1990). Others show how to embed one architecture into another architecture of different topology (Bokhari 1988; Choi and Narahari 1991; Gupta and Hambrusch 1991; Li and King 1988; Manoharan and Thanisch 1991; Ullman and Narahari 1990).

A number of researchers have explored the embedding of grids into hypercubes (Bettayeb et al. 1988; Chan and Chin 1988; Greenberg 1987; Ho and Johnsson 1987; Saad and Schultz 1988; Scott and Brandenberg 1988). Chan (1991) has proven that there exists an embedding with dilation at most 2 of a 2-dimensional grid into the smallest hypercube with at least as many nodes as the grid. Wu (1985) considers the embedding of trees into hypercubes.

Afrati et al. (1985) proved that the problem of deciding if an arbitrary graph is a subgraph of a hypercube is $\mathcal{NP}$-complete, although Krumme and

Venkataraman (1986) have disputed the correctness of the proof. Cybenko et al. (1986) have proven the same result using a different reduction.

Wagner and Corneil (1990) have proven that given a tree T and an integer k, the problem of determining if T is a subgraph of a k-dimensional cube is $\mathcal{NP}$-complete.

Leighton et al. (1992) present randomized algorithms for embedding dynamically growing binary trees in either butterfly or hypercube networks.

Many problems arising in science and engineering are modeled by irregular meshes that cannot be decomposed into the regular graphs we have discussed in this chapter. To learn more about how irregular meshes are mapped to regular architectures, consult De Keyser and Roose (1991), and Fox et al. (1988).

The two-processor unit time scheduling problem has an interesting history. Fujii et al. (1969) published the first polynomial-time algorithm to solve the problem. Their algorithm had complexity $O(n^4)$. A few years later an $O(n^2)$ algorithm was published by Coffman and Graham (1972). Gabow (1982) presented an asymptotically optimal algorithm with time complexity $O(n+e)$. Vazirani and Vazirani (1985, 1989) demonstrated that the two-processor scheduling problem is in $\mathcal{RNC}$. Finally, Helmbold and Mayr (1987) proved that two-processor unit time scheduling is in $\mathcal{NC}$.

Automatic self-scheduling algorithms have been proposed by Fang et al. (1990) and Polychronopoulos and Kuck (1987).

Other papers on parallel scheduling algorithms include Kashara and Narita (1984) and Simons and Warmuth (1989).

Papers that concern the mapping problem include (Berman 1987; Berman and Snyder 1987; Bokhari 1981, 1988; Hansen and Lih 1992; Heath et al. 1988; Lee and Aggarwal 1987; Li and King 1988; Lo 1988; Melhem and Hwang 1990; Saad and Schultz 1988; Sadayappan and Ercal 1987; Sadayappan et al. 1990; Wolfstahl 1989).

Madala and Sinclair (1991) have shown a way to improve upon Robinson's bounds if information is available about the nature of the task time distribution. Other work in the area of performance analysis of parallel algorithms includes Dubois and Briggs (1982), Kruskal and Weiss (1984), Kung (1976), and Weide (1981).

Some authors have used queuing models to study the performance of interconnection networks or parallel computers (Baccelli and Liu 1990; Bambos and Walrand 1991; Bodnar and Liu 1989; Fromm et al. 1983; Harrison and Patel 1990; Thomasian and Bay 1986; Towsley 1986).

Elmagarmid (1986), Isloor and Marsland (1980), and Singhal (1989) have surveyed deadlock detection algorithms for distributed systems.

5.7 PROBLEMS

5-1 Given graphs G and G' of Fig. 5-3, construct an embedding of G into G' that has dilation 2.

5-2   Show that a 2-D mesh with an odd number of rows, an odd number of columns, and no wraparound connections, does not contain a Hamiltonian cycle.

5-3   Devise rules for embedding a ring into a three-dimensional mesh with dilation 1.

5-4   Under what conditions can a 2-D mesh be embedded with dilation 1 in a three-dimensional mesh containing the same number of vertices?

5-5   Prove that the total number of mesh points k or fewer jumps away from an arbitrary point in a 2-D mesh is $2k^2 + 2k + 1$. (Ignore the case where the point is less than k jumps from the edge of the mesh.)

5-6   Prove that $2^{k+1} - 1 > 2k^2 + 2k + 1$ for all $k > 4$.

5-7   Embed a complete binary tree with 31 nodes in a 2-D mesh, or prove no such embedding exists.

5-8   Prove or disprove: If G is a Gray code, then G^{-1} is a Gray code as well.

5-9   Show two different 4-bit Gray codes and their inverses.

5-10   Using the Gray code given in the text, show how to embed a $4 \times 4 \times 4$ mesh into a 64-node hypercube.

5-11   Given $n = 2^{k/2}$ for a positive even integer k, write a function that maps elements of an $n \times n$ mesh with wraparound connections into nodes of a k-dimensional hypercube so that as many mesh connections as possible map directly onto connections in the hypercube.

5-12   Prove that a j-dimensional mesh cannot be embedded with dilation 1 in a k-dimensional hypercube if $j > k$.

5-13*   Prove that the smallest hypercube containing a dilation-1 embedding of an $l_1 \times l_2 \times \cdots \times l_k$ mesh has dimension $d_1 + d_2 + \cdots + d_k$, where $d_i = \lceil \log l_i \rceil$ for $1 \le i \le k$. Assume that the mesh does not contain wraparound connections.

5-14   Prove that a hexagonal mesh (Fig. 5-23) cannot be embedded in a hypercube with dilation 1.

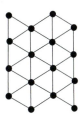

FIGURE 5-23   A hexagonal mesh (see Prob. 5.14).

5-15   Map nodes of a complete binary tree with four levels (Fig. 3-2) to nodes of a four-dimensional hypercube (Fig. 3-6) so that as many tree edges as possible map onto hypercube edges.

5-16   Prove that a complete binary tree with height n can be embedded with dilation 1 in a hypercube with dimension $2n$.

5-17*   Prove that a complete binary tree with height n can be embedded with dilation 1 in an $(n + 2)$-dimensional hypercube.

5-18*   Prove that the problem of embedding an arbitrary graph into a fixed-size hypercube with dilation 1 is $\mathcal{NP}$-complete. (**Hint**: Transformation from 3-partition.)

5-19   Prove that a dilation-1 embedding of a binomial tree of depth n in a shuffle-exchange network with 2^n nodes does not exist.

5-20*   Prove that there is an embedding with dilation 2 of a binomial tree of depth n in a shuffle-exchange network with 2^n nodes.

5-21   Given a task graph and an arbitrarily large number of processors, what is a lower bound on the length of an optimal schedule?

5-22   Devise a Gantt chart showing a two-processor schedule for the task graph of Fig. 5-15 that requires 9 units of time to execute.

5-23   What is the relationship between utilization and efficiency?

5-24   Prove that reducing the execution time of each individual task to 1 does not change the complexity of the scheduling problem.

5-25   Prove that there is a polynomial time-scheduling algorithm if the task graph is a forest (each node has at most one predecessor).

5-26   Give an example (other than one appearing in this book) where Graham's list-scheduling algorithm does not generate an optimum schedule.

5-27   Give an example where the Coffman-Graham algorithm does not generate an optimum schedule.

5-28   Generalize the Coffman-Graham algorithm to handle task graphs in which tasks can have arbitrary integer execution times.

5-29   Describe a solution to the buffer-deadlock problem illustrated in Fig. 5-22.

5-30   Write a C-Linda program that is certain to exhibit deadlock.

5-31   Write a C-Linda program that may or may not exhibit deadlock, depending upon the execution rate of the parallel processes.

5-32   Write an occam program that is certain to exhibit deadlock.

5-33   Write an occam program that may or may not exhibit deadlock, depending upon the execution rate of the parallel processes.

6

ELEMENTARY
PARALLEL
ALGORITHMS

How simple and frugal a thing is happiness: a glass of wine, a roast chestnut, a wretched little brazier, the sound of the sea.

Nikos Kazantzakis, *Zorba the Greek*, Chap. 7

In this chapter we will develop parallel algorithms to solve three simple problems. The first problem is to perform a reduction operation, the second problem is to compute the prefix sums of a list of numbers, and the third problem is to broadcast a value from one processor in a parallel computer to all other processors. In the course of developing parallel algorithms to solve these problems, we will discover some valuable design strategies that we can put to good use when considering more complex problems.

The chapter has four sections. In Section 6.1 we refine our classification of MIMD algorithms, developing a terminology to help us describe the algorithms we design. Section 6.2 covers parallel algorithms used to implement reductions. Sections 6.3 and 6.4 describe parallel algorithms for hypercube multicomputers. Section 6.3 compares two parallel broadcast algorithms, and Section 6.4 presents a parallel prefix sums algorithm.

6.1 CLASSIFYING MIMD ALGORITHMS

In Chap. 1 we made a distinction between control-parallel algorithms and data-parallel algorithms, and described pipelined algorithms as a subclass of control-parallel algorithms. In this section we discuss two ways to implement data-parallel algorithms on MIMD computers, and introduce control-parallel algorithms that are not pipelined.

We have defined data parallelism as using multiple functional units (or processes) to apply the same operation simultaneously to a data set. If the number of functional units is equal to the size of the data set, it makes sense to assign one datum to each functional unit. However, in practice there are usually far more data items than functional units. We can distinguish data-parallel algorithms according to how the functional units divide the data items among themselves.

In a **prescheduled** data-parallel algorithm, the number of data items per functional unit is determined before any of the data items are processed. Prescheduling is commonly used when the time needed to process each data item is identical, or when the ratio of data items to functional units is high.

In a **self-scheduled** data-parallel algorithm, data items are not assigned to functional units until run time. In a self-scheduled algorithm a global list of work to be done is kept, and when a functional unit is without work, another task (or small set of tasks) is removed from the list and assigned. Processes schedule themselves as the program executes, hence the name self-scheduled.

Here is an example to illustrate the difference between prescheduling and self-scheduling. Imagine a single person managing an office of insurance claims adjusters. Every morning the manager begins with a room full of claims adjustors and a stack of claims. The rules are that everybody gets to go home as soon as the last claim is handled, but nobody can leave until the last adjustor finishes. Once the manager has assigned a claim to somebody, it cannot be reassigned to somebody else.

If every claims adjustor works at the same speed, and every claim takes the same amount of time to be processed, then it makes sense to divide the stack of claims by the number of adjustors, and give everybody the same amount of work at the beginning of the day. This method is analogous to prescheduling.

However, if the number of claims per adjustor is not too large and the time needed to process a claim varies, then assigning everybody the same amount of work could lead to a variance in the time it takes adjustors to finish their work. Since the manager cannot reassign work once it is handed out, the early birds must sit idle until the last adjustor has finished. Obviously, this is not an efficient use of the available resources. It makes more sense to have the adjustors come up to the manager's desk when they need work, and receive one claim at a time. The advantage of this method is that when the manager runs out of claims, no adjustor can have more than one claim left to process, which balances the workload. The disadvantage is that the adjustors spend time fetching claims from the manager's desk, and they may actually have to wait in line while the manager hands claims to other adjustors. This method is analogous to self-scheduling.

Control parallelism is achieved through the simultaneous application of different operations to different data elements. The flow of data among these processes can be arbitrarily complex. If the data-flow graph forms a simple directed path, then we say the algorithm is pipelined. We will use the term **asynchronous algorithm** to refer to any control-parallel algorithm that is not pipelined.

6.2 REDUCTION

In this section we consider the problem of performing a reduction operation on a set of n values, where n is much larger than p, the number of available processors. How do we begin?

When writing a parallel program from scratch, it is always a good idea to look for an existing parallel algorithm that can be adopted. Most published parallel algorithms are based upon a PRAM model of parallel computation. When is it appropriate to implement a PRAM-style algorithm on a real parallel computer?

> **Design Strategy 1** If a cost optimal CREW PRAM algorithm exists, and the way the PRAM processors interact through shared variables maps onto the target architecture, a PRAM algorithm is a reasonable starting point.

Our goal is to develop a parallel algorithm with as little overhead as possible —that is, a parallel algorithm that introduces the minimum amount of extra operations compared to the best sequential algorithm. In Chap. 2 we introduced the idea of cost optimality. The total number of operations performed by a cost-optimal PRAM algorithm is in the same complexity class as an optimal sequential algorithm. If the proportionality constants of the cost-optimal PRAM algorithm and the fastest sequential algorithm are about the same, we may be able to use the PRAM algorithm as a basis for our design.

In the remainder of Sec. 6.2 we assume that summation is the reduction operation being performed.

We saw in Chap. 2 that a cost-optimal PRAM algorithm for global sum exists: $n/\log n$ processors can add n numbers in $\Theta(\log n)$ time. We can use the same principle to develop good parallel algorithms for real SIMD and MIMD computers, even if $p < n/\log n$.

We allocate $\lfloor n/p \rfloor$ or $\lceil n/p \rceil$ values to each processor. In the first phase of the parallel algorithm each processor adds its set of values, resulting in p partial sums. In the second phase of the parallel algorithm we combine the p partial sums into a global sum.

It is important to check to make sure that the constant of proportionality associated with the cost of the PRAM algorithm is not significantly higher than the constant of proportionality associated with an optimal sequential algorithm. In other words, we have to make sure that the total number of operations performed by all the processors executing the PRAM algorithm is about the same as the total number of operations performed by a single processor executing the best sequential algorithm. This is certainly true here, so we can proceed with confidence.

6.2.1 Hypercube SIMD Model

If the PRAM processor interaction pattern forms a graph that embeds with dilation 1 in a target SIMD architecture, then there is a natural translation from the PRAM algorithm to the SIMD algorithm. The processors in the PRAM summation algorithm combine values in a binomial tree pattern. In Chap. 5 we saw how to embed a binomial tree in a hypercube. The hypercube processor array version follows directly from the PRAM algorithm. The only signficant difference is that the hypercube processor array model has no shared memory; processors interact by passing data. The resulting algorithm appears in Fig. 6-1. Figure 6-2 illustrates this algorithm.

To compute the worst-case time complexity of this algorithm, we determine the number of computation steps and the number of communication steps. Each processing element adds at most $\lceil n/p \rceil$ values to find its local sum. Processor 0, which iterates the second inner `for` loop more than any other processor, performs $\log p$ communication steps and $\log p$ addition steps. The complexity of finding the sum of n values is $\Theta(n/p + \log p)$ using the hypercube processor array model with p processors.

What if we want every processing element to have a copy of the global sum? One way to accomplish this would be to add a broadcast phase to the end of the algorithm we have already developed. Once processing element 0 has the global sum, the value can be transmitted to the other processors in $\log p$ communication steps by reversing the direction of the edges in the binomial tree illustrated in Fig. 6-2.

A second algorithm that yields the global sum on every processing element is illustrated in Fig. 6-3. In this algorithm each processing element swaps values across every dimension of the hypercube. After $\log n$ swap-and-accumulate steps, every processing element has the global sum, assuming that the values being added are truly associative.

6.2.2 Shuffle-Exchange SIMD Model

If the PRAM processor interaction pattern does not form a graph that embeds in the target SIMD architecture, then the translation is not straightforward, but may still have an efficient SIMD algorithm.

For example, consider implementing the summation algorithm on the shuffle-exchange SIMD model. There is no dilation-1 embedding of a binomial tree in a shuffle-exchange network. We must think about the PRAM algorithm at a higher level. The key to the efficiency of this algorithm is that if the sums are combined in pairs, then a logarithmic number of combining steps can find

SUMMATION (HYPERCUBE SIMD):

Parameter n {Number of elements to add}
       p {Number of processing elements}
Global j
Local $local.set.size,\ local.value[1...\lceil n/p \rceil],\ sum,\ tmp$
begin
  for all P_i, where $0 \leq i \leq p - 1$ do
    if $i < (n$ modulo $p)$ then
      $local.set.size \leftarrow \lceil n/p \rceil$
    else
      $local.set.size \leftarrow \lfloor n/p \rfloor$
    endif
    $sum \leftarrow 0$
  endfor
  for $j \leftarrow 1$ to $\lceil n/p \rceil$ do
    for all P_i, where $0 \leq i \leq p - 1$ do
      if $local.set.size \geq j$ then
        $sum \leftarrow sum + local.value[j]$
      endif
    endfor
  endfor
  for $j \leftarrow \log p - 1$ downto 0 do
    for all P_i, where $0 \leq i \leq p - 1$ do
      if $i < 2^j$ then
        $tmp \Leftarrow [i + 2^j]sum$
        $sum \leftarrow sum + tmp$
      endif
    endfor
  endfor
end

FIGURE 6-1   Algorithm for the hypercube SIMD model to sum n values. Upon completion of the algorithm processor 0's value of *sum* is the global sum.

the grand total. Two data routings—a shuffle followed by an exchange—on the shuffle-exchange model are sufficient to bring together two subtotals. After $\log p$ shuffle-exchange steps, processor 0 has the grand total. The algorithm appears in Fig. 6-4; Fig. 6-5 is an illustration of the algorithm's execution.

At the termination of this algorithm, the value of $[0]sum$ is the sum. (Do any other variables contain the sum?) Figure 6-5 illustrates the action of this algorithm as it adds 16 values.

Every processing element spends $\Theta(n/p)$ time computing its local sum. Since there are $\log p$ iterations of the shuffle-exchange-add loop, and every iteration takes constant time, the parallel algorithm has complexity $\Theta(n/p + \log p)$.

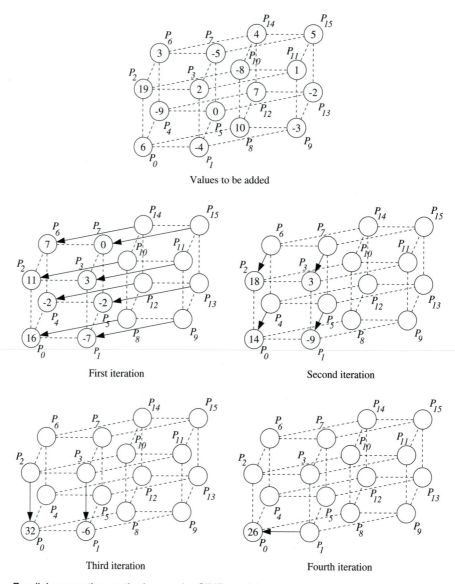

FIGURE 6-2   Parallel summation on the hypercube SIMD model.

6.2.3 2-D Mesh SIMD Model

In the previous example the PRAM processor interaction pattern did not form a graph that embedded in the target machine's processor organization graph, but there was still a parallel algorithm that performed only $\Theta(\log p)$ combining steps. How do we know when it is hopeless to search for a clever transformation

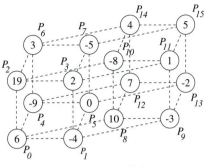

Values to be added

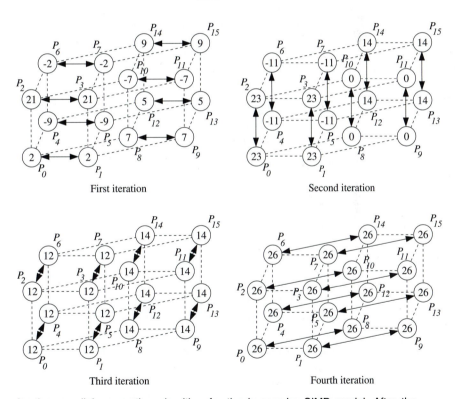

First iteration

Second iteration

Third iteration

Fourth iteration

FIGURE 6-3   Another parallel summation algorithm for the hypercube SIMD model. After the processing elements have found the sum of their local values, they perform $\log p$ swap-and-accumulate steps, one for each dimension of the hypercube.

SUMMATION (SHUFFLE-EXCHANGE SIMD):

```
Parameter n   {Number of elements to add}
          p   {Number of processing elements}
Global    j
Local     local.set.size, local.value[1...⌈ n/p⌉], sum, tmp
begin
  for all Pᵢ, where 0 ≤ i ≤ p − 1 do
    if i < (n modulo p) then
      local.set.size ← ⌈ n/p ⌉
    else
      local.set.size ← ⌊ n/p ⌋
    endif
    sum ← 0
  endfor
  for j ← 1 to ⌈ n/p ⌉ do
    for all Pᵢ, where 0 ≤ i ≤ p − 1 do
      if local.set.size ≥ j then
        sum ← sum + local.value[j]
      endif
    endfor
  endfor
  for j ← 0 to log p − 1 do
    for all Pᵢ, where 0 ≤ i ≤ p − 1 do
      shuffle(sum) ⇐ sum
      exchange(tmp) ⇐ sum
      sum ← sum + tmp
    endfor
  endfor
end
```

FIGURE 6-4   Summation algorithm for the shuffle-exchange processor array model.

of the PRAM algorithm that matches the topology of the processors? One way to avoid a fruitless search is to establish a lower bound on the complexity of any parallel algorithm used to solve the problem on a particular topology. Once the lower bound is established, there is no reason to search for a solution of lower complexity.

For example, consider the problem of finding the sum of n values on a processor array organized as a 2-D mesh. We saw in the last chapter that no dilation-1 embedding exists for a balanced binary tree or a binomial tree in a mesh. On the other hand, even though a dilation-1 embedding of a tree of this type in a shuffle-exchange network does not exist, it is possible to find the sum with only log p shuffle-exchange-add steps. How do we know we cannot pull off a similar feat on a 2-D mesh?

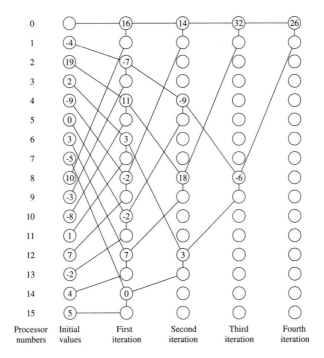

FIGURE 6-5 Finding sum of 16 values on the shuffle-exchange SIMD model.

In order to find the sum of n values spread evenly among p processors organized in a $\sqrt{p} \times \sqrt{p}$ mesh, at least one of the processors in the mesh must eventually contain the grand total. No matter which processor that is, the total number of communication steps to get the subtotals from the corner processors must be at least $2(\sqrt{p} - 1)$, assuming that during any time unit only communications in a single direction are allowed. Since the algorithm has at least $2(\sqrt{p} - 1)$ communication steps, the time complexity of the parallel algorithm is at least $\Theta(n/p + \sqrt{p})$. There is no point looking for a parallel algorithm for a model that requires $\Theta(\log p)$ communication steps.

An optimal parallel algorithm to find the sum is presented in Fig. 6-6. Assume that $n = l^2$. The algorithm finds local subtotals, sums all the rows in column 1, then column 1. When the algorithm completes, element $[1, 1]sum$ contains the grand total. The pseudocode for this algorithm appears in Fig. 6-6; execution of the algorithm is illustrated in Fig. 6-7.

6.2.4 UMA Multiprocessor Model

As our final example, let us consider how to implement the sum-finding algorithm on a UMA multiprocessor. Like the PRAM model, the machine has shared memory, so data is easily accessed. Unlike the PRAM model, the pro-

SUMMATION (2-D MESH SIMD):

```
Parameter    l  {Mesh has size l × l}
Global       i
Local        tmp, sum
begin
   {Each processor finds sum of its local values — code not shown}

   for i ← l − 1 downto 1 do
      for all Pj,i, where 1 ≤ j ≤ l do
         {Processing elements in column i active}
         tmp  ⇐ east(sum)
         sum  ← sum + tmp
      endfor
   endfor
   for i ← l − 1 downto 1 do
      for all Pi,1 do
         {Only a single processing element active}
         tmp  ⇐ south(sum)
         sum  ← sum + tmp
      endfor
   endfor
end
```

FIGURE 6-6 Parallel summation on a processor array organized as a 2-D mesh. Upon termination of algorithm, variable [1,1]*sum* contains the global sum.

cessors execute instructions asynchronously. For that reason we must ensure that no processor accesses a variable containing a partial sum until that variable has been set.

In the pseudocode algorithm in Fig. 6-8, each element of array *flags* begins with the value 0. When the value is set to 1, the corresponding element of array *mono* has a partial sum in it.

Let us determine the worst-case time complexity of this parallel algorithm. First, how long does it take to create the processes? If the initial process creates $p - 1$ other processes all by itself, the time complexity of the process creation is $\Theta(p)$. In practice we do not count this cost, since processes are created only once, at the beginning of the program, and most algorithms we analyze form subroutines of larger applications.

Sequentially initializing array *flags* has time complexity $\Theta(p)$.

Each process finds the sum of n/p values. If we make the assumption that memory bank conflicts do not increase the complexity by more than a constant factor, the complexity of this section of code is $\Theta(n/p)$.

The **while** loop executes $\log p$ times. Each iteration of the **while** loop has time complexity $\Theta(1)$. The total complexity of **while** loop is $\Theta(\log p)$.

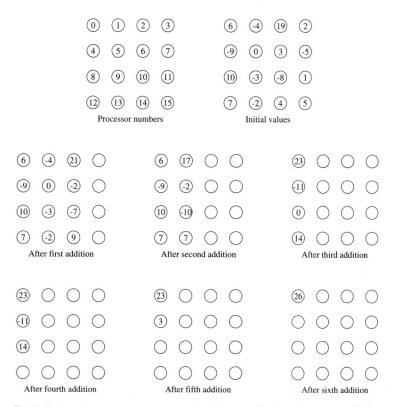

FIGURE 6-7   Finding sum of 16 values on a processor array organized as a 2-D mesh.

Synchronization among all the processes occurs at the final endfor. If synchronization is done via a single global semaphore, then each processor must have exclusive access to the semaphore, and the complexity of synchronization is $\Theta(p)$. The overall complexity of the algorithm is

$$\Theta\left(p + \frac{n}{p} + \log p + p\right) = \Theta\left(\frac{n}{p} + p\right)$$

Since the time complexity of the parallel algorithm is $\Theta(p + n/p)$, why bother with a complicated fan-in-style parallel addition? It is simpler to compute the global sum from the local sums by having each process enter a critical section where its local sum is added to the global sum. The resulting algorithm, presented in Fig. 6-9, still has time complexity $\Theta(p + n/p)$.

We have implemented both algorithms on the Sequent Balance™ (a UMA multiprocessor) using Sequent C. Figure 6-10 compares the execution times of the two reduction steps as a function of the number of active processes. (This comparison does not count the time needed to compute the local sums.) The original fan-in-style algorithm is uniformly superior to the criti-

SUMMATION (UMA MULTIPROCESSOR, VERSION 1):

```
Global    a[0...(n − 1)]          {Values to be added}
          p                       {Number of processes, a power of 2}
          flags[0...(p − 1)]      {Set to 1 when partial sum available}
          partial[0...(p − 1)]    {Contains partial sum}
          global.sum              {Result stored here}

Local     local.sum
begin
  for k ← 0 to p − 1 do
    flags[k] ← 0
  endfor
  for all Pᵢ where 0 ≤ i < p do
    local.sum ← 0
    for j ← i to n − 1 step p do
      local.sum ← local.sum + a[j]
    endfor
    j ← p
    while j > 0 do
      if i ≥ j/2
        partial[i] ← local.sum
        flags[i] ← 1
        break
      else
        while (flags[i + j/2] = 0) do endwhile; { spin }
        local.sum ← local.sum + partial[i + j/2]
      endif
      j ← j / 2
    endwhile
    if i = 0
      global.sum ← local.sum
    endif
  endfor
end
```

FIGURE 6-8   UMA multiprocessor summation program that uses fan-in strategy to compute global sum from subtotals.

cal section-style algorithm. Although the two sum-finding algorithms have the same complexity, the constant of proportionality asssociated with the $\Theta(p)$ term is smaller in the first program.

The moral is simple: It pays to adopt the PRAM algorithm when the constant of proportionality associated with its cost is comparable to that of the best sequential algorithm.

Design Strategy 2 Look for a data-parallel algorithm before considering a control-parallel algorithm.

SUMMATION (UMA MULTIPROCESSOR, VERSION 2):
Global $a[0...(n-1)]$ {Elements to be added}
          $global.sum$ {Result stored here}

Local $local.sum$ {Sum of processor's share of values}
         j {Processor's private loop index}
begin
  $global...sum \leftarrow 0$
  for all P_i, where $0 \leq i \leq p-1$ do
    $local.sum \leftarrow 0$
    for $j \leftarrow i$ to $n-1$ step p do
      $local.sum \leftarrow local.sum + a[j]$
    endfor
    lock ($global.sum$)
    $global.sum \leftarrow global.sum + local.sum$
    unlock ($global.sum$)
  endfor
end

FIGURE 6-9   UMA MIMD summation program in which each process enters a critical section to adds its subtotal to the variable accumulating the global sum.

The only parallelism we can exploit on a SIMD computer is data parallelism. On MIMD computers, however, we can look for ways to exploit both data parallelism and control parallelism. Data-parallel algorithms are more common, easier to design and debug, and better able to scale to large numbers of processors than control-parallel algorithms. For this reason a data-parallel solution should be sought first, and a control-parallel implementation considered a last resort.

When we write in data-parallel style on a MIMD machine, the result is a **SPMD (Single Program Multiple Data)** program. In general, SPMD programs are easier to write and debug than arbitrary MIMD programs.

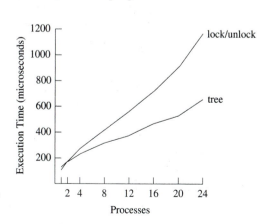

FIGURE 6-10   Comparison of the execution times of the reduction phases of two sum-finding algorithms, implemented on the Sequent Balance. (Data courtesy Bradley K. Seevers.)

Almost every problem we will discuss in this book has a natural solution obtained via a data-parallel algorithm.

6.3 BROADCAST

The eventual size of the application must be considered during the design process. Some parallel algorithms that execute well on test data sets do not scale well when applied to the application data set. Sooner or later one of the machine's resources—CPU speed, communication speed, memory size, etc.—will become strained, limiting the speed at which the system can solve the problem. Superior parallel algorithms make the best use of the available resources to maximize the performance of the system.

Consider the problem of one processor broadcasting a list of values to all other processors on a hypercube multicomputer. The execution time of the implemented algorithm has two primary components: the time needed to initiate the messages and the time needed to perform the data transfers. Message startup time is called **message-passing overhead** or **message latency**.

If the amount of data to be broadcast is small, the message-passing overhead time dominates the data-transfer time, and the best algorithm is the one that minimizes the number of communications performed by any processor. Clearly, at least $\log p$ communications are required. The binomial tree is a suitable broadcast pattern because there is a dilation-1 embedding of a binomial tree into a hypercube, and the resulting algorithm requires only $\log p$ communication steps (see Figs. 6-11 and 6-12).

However, if the amount of data to be broadcast is large, the data-transfer time dominates the message-passing overhead. Under these circumstances the binomial tree-based algorithm has a serious weakness—at any one time no more than $p/2$ out of $p \log p$ communication links are in use. If the time needed to pass the message from one processor to another is M, then the broadcast algorithm requires time $M \log p$.

Johnsson and Ho (1989) have designed a broadcast algorithm that executes up to $\log p$ times faster than the binomial-tree algorithm.

Their algorithm relies upon the fact that every hypercube contains $\log p$ edge-disjoint spanning trees with the same root node. The algorithm breaks the message into $\log p$ parts and broadcasts each part to the other nodes through a

FIGURE 6-11   Hypercube broadcast algorithm based on binomial tree communication pattern. Message elements ABC are sent together, to avoid repeated message startup costs.

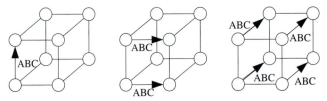

HYPERCUBE.BROADCAST (*id*, *source*, *value*):

Parameter	*p*	{Number of processors}
Value	*id*	{Processor's ID number}
	source	{ID of source processor}
Reference	*value*	{Value to be broadcast}
Local	*i*	{Loop iteration}
	partner	{Partner processor}
	position	{Position in broadcast tree}

{This procedure is called from inside a for all statement}
begin
    position ← *id* ⊗ *source*
    for *i* ← 0 to log *p* − 1 do
     if *position* < 2^i then
       partner ← *id* ⊗ 2^i
       [*partner*]*value* ⇐ *value*
     endif
    endfor
end

FIGURE 6-12 Pseudocode for hypercube broadcast algorithm based on binomial tree communication pattern.

different binomial spanning tree (Fig. 6-13). Because the spanning trees have no edges in common, all data flows concurrently, and the entire algorithm executes approximately in time $M \log p / \log p = M$.

Design Strategy 3 As problem size grows, use the algorithm that makes best use of the available resources.

In the case of broadcasting large data sets on a hypercube multicomputer, the most constrained resource is the network capacity. Johnsson and Ho's algorithm makes better use of this resource than the binomial tree broadcast algorithm and, as a result, achieves higher performance.

FIGURE 6-13 Johnsson and Ho's (1989) hypercube broadcast algorithm makes better use of the available communication links to improve performance when the message is long.

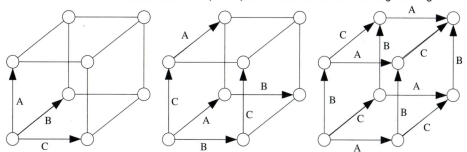

6.4   PREFIX SUMS

In this section we will develop a parallel prefix-sums algorithm suitable for implementation on hypercube multicomputers.

Recall the definition of prefix sums: given an associative operation $\oplus$ and an array A containing n elements, the **prefix-sums** problem is to compute the n quantities:

$A[0]$
$A[0] \oplus A[1]$
$A[0] \oplus A[1] \oplus A[2]$
$\ldots$
$A[0] \oplus A[1] \oplus A[2] \oplus \ldots \oplus A[n-1]$

In Sec. 2.3 we developed a cost optimal PRAM algorithm to solve this problem. The cost optimal algorithm requires $\lceil n/\log n \rceil$ processors to solve the problem in $\Theta(\log n)$ time. In order to achieve cost optimality, each processor uses the best sequential algorithm to manipulate its own set of $\log n$ elements of A. Even though the number of processors available on a multicomputer is likely to be far less than $n/\log n$, we can use the same strategy to design an efficient multicomputer algorithm.

> **Design Strategy 4** Let each processor perform the most efficient sequential algorithm on its share of the data.

Let's use this strategy to develop efficient prefix-sums algorithms for mesh-connected and hypercube multicomputers. We assume the multicomputer has p processors and array A has n elements, where n is an integer multiple of p. Let χ be the time needed to perform operation $\oplus$, λ be the time needed for one processor to initiate a message to another processor, and β be the message transmission time per value. For example, sending a k-element from one processor to another requires time $\lambda + k\beta$.

We follow the same three steps as the cost-optimal PRAM algorithm (see Fig. 6-14). When the algorithm begins execution, the n elements of A are distributed evenly among the local memories of the p processors. During step one each processor finds the sum of its n/p elements. In step two the processors cooperate to find the p prefix sums of the their local sums. During step three each processor computes the prefix sums of its n/p values, adding to each result the sum of the values held in lower-numbered processors.

The computation time of steps one and three is independent of the topology of the multicomputer. During step one each processor finds the sum of n/p values in $(n/p - 1)\chi$ time units. During step three processor 0 computes the prefix sums of its n/p values in $(n/p - 1)\chi$ time units. Processors 1 through $p - 1$ must add the sum of the lower-numbered processors' values to the first element on its list before computing the prefix sums. These processors perform step three in $(n/p)\chi$ time units.

	Processor 0	Processor 1	Processor 2	Processor 3
(a)	3 2 7 6	0 5 4 8	2 0 1 5	2 3 8 6
(b)	18	17	8	19
(c)	18 35 43 62	18 35 43 62	18 35 43 62	18 35 43 62
(d)	3 5 12 18	18 23 27 35	37 37 38 43	45 48 56 62

FIGURE 6-14 Computing prefix sums of 16 values on a four-processor multicomputer. (a) Each processor is allocated its share of the values. (b) In step one each processor finds the sum of its local elements. (c) In step two the prefix sums of the local sums are computed and distributed to all processors. (d) In step three each processor computes the prefix sums of its own elements and adds to each result the sum of the values held in lower-numbered processors.

The communication time required by step two depends upon the multicomputer's topology. First let us consider implementing the parallel prefix-sums algorithm on a hypercube. The memory-access pattern of the PRAM algorithm, illustrated in Chap. 2, Fig. 2-10, does not directly translate into a communication pattern having a dilation-1 embedding in a hypercube. For this reason we should look for a better method of computing the prefix sums.

Finding prefix sums is similar to performing a reduction, except, for each element in the list, we are only interested in values from prior elements. We can modify the hypercube reduction algorithm shown in Fig. 6-3 to perform prefix sums. As in the reduction algorithm, every processor swaps values across each dimension of the hypercube. However, the processor maintains two variables containing totals. The first variable contains the total of all values received. The second variable contains the total of all values received from smaller-numbered processors. At the end of $\log p$ swap-and-add steps, the second variable associated with each processor contains the prefix sum for that processor. Figure 6-15 illustrates the algorithm for a four-processor system.

Let's analyze the total time required by step two of the algorithm. Step two has $\log p$ phases. During each phase a processor performs the $\oplus$ operation, at most, two times, so the computation time required by step two is no more than $2\chi \log p$. During each phase a processor sends one value to a neighboring processor and receives one value from that processor. The total communication time of step two is $2(\lambda + \beta) \log p$. Summing the computation and the communication time yields a total execution time of $2(\chi + \lambda + \beta) \log p$ for step two of the algorithm.

We can estimate the total execution time of the prefix-sums algorithm used on the hypercube multicomputer by combining our expressions for the algo-

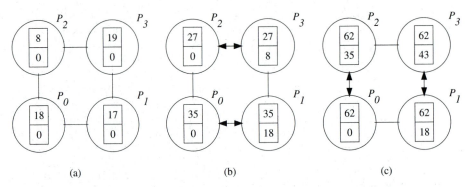

FIGURE 6-15 Computing prefix sums of four local sums on a four-processor multicomputer. This is step (b) of the hypercube prefix sums algorithm illustrated in Fig. 6-14. (a) Every processor has two variables. Upper variable accumulates global sum. Lower variable accumulates prefix sum. The upper variable is initialized to the processor's local value. The lower variable is initially zero. (b) Swap value of upper variable across dimension 0 of hypercube. Every processor adds this value to the value of its upper variable. Higher-numbered processor adds lower-numbered processor's value to the value of its lower variable. (c) Swap value of upper variable across dimension 1 of hypercube. Every processor adds this value to the value of its upper variable. Higher-numbered processor adds lower-numbered processor's value to the value of its lower variable.

rithm's three phases,

$$\left(2\frac{n}{p} + 2\log p - 1\right)\chi + 2\log p\,(\lambda + \beta)$$

The estimated sequential time is $(n-1)\chi$. From these two expressions we can derive an estimate of the speedup:

$$\frac{(n-1)\chi}{\left(2\frac{n}{p} + 2\log p - 1\right)\chi + 2\log (\lambda + \beta)}$$

Note that

$$\lim_{n\to\infty}\frac{(n-1)\chi}{\left(2\frac{n}{p} + 2\log p - 1\right)\chi + 2\log p\,(\lambda + \beta)} \le \lim_{n\to\infty}\frac{n}{\frac{2n}{p}} = \frac{p}{2}$$

In other words, the efficiency of this algorithm cannot exceed 50%, no matter how large the problem size or how small the message latency.

Figure 6-16 compares the predicted speedup with the speedup actually achieved by this algorithm on the nCUBE 3200™, where the associative operator is integer addition, $\chi = 414$ nanoseconds, $\lambda = 363$ microseconds, and $\beta = 4.5$ microseconds.

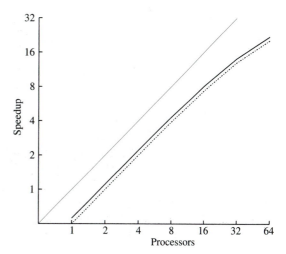

FIGURE 6-16 Predicted speedup (dotted line) and actual speedup (solid line) of parallel prefix sums algorithm implemented on an nCUBE 3200 hypercube multicomputer, where $n =$ 65,536. (Performance data provided by Bradley K. Seevers.)

6.5 SUMMARY

We began the chapter by refining our categorization of MIMD algorithms. We distinguished between prescheduled data-parallel algorithms, in which the number of data items per functional unit is determined before any of the data items are processed, and self-scheduled data-parallel algorithms, in which processes needing work access a global list of work to be done. In the case of control-parallel algorithms, we distinguished between pipelined algorithms, in which data is passed from one process to the next in a simple, directed path, and asynchronous algorithms, in which the flow of data among processes is more complex.

Reduction, broadcast, and prefix sums are three operations that appear in many algorithms. In this chapter we have explored methods of efficiently implementing reductions on several SIMD models. We have also examined hypercube multicomputer algorithms to perform broadcast and prefix sums. In the course of developing these algorithms we have noted four parallel algorithm design strategies:

1 If a cost optimal CREW PRAM algorithm exists, and the way the PRAM processors interact through shared variables maps onto the target architecture, a PRAM algorithm is a reasonable starting point.

2 Look for a data-parallel algorithm before considering a control-parallel algorithm.

3 As problem size grows, use the algorithm that makes best use of the available resources.

4 Let each processor perform the most efficient sequential algorithm on its share of the data.

6.6 BIBLIOGRAPHIC NOTES

The design and analysis of algorithms for MIMD computers are discussed by Baudet (1978a, 1978b), Jones and Gehringer (1980), Kung (1976, 1980), Oleinick (1982), Raskin (1978), and Robinson (1977).

Agerwala and Lint (1978), Lint and Agerwala (1981), and Irani and Chen (1982) have discussed the importance of communications issues in the design of parallel algorithms. Nassimi and Sahni (1980a) present an algorithm for routing data on mesh-connected SIMD models. Their algorithm is optimal for any data routing that can be specified in terms of permutating and complementing the address bits of a processing element. Examples of such data routings include matrix transpose, bit reversal, vector reversal, and perfect shuffle. Raghavendra and Prasanna Kumar (1986) present optimal algorithms for performing a wide variety of permutations on a 2-D mesh with wraparound connections.

Saad and Schultz (1989) proposed broadcast algorithms for multicomputers with a 2-D mesh topology. Simmen (1991) disputes a claim made by Saad and Schultz and proposes an alternative algorithm. Bermond et al. (1992) go beyond these results and give an asymptotically optimal broadcast algorithm for 2-D meshes with wraparound connections and parallel monodirectional links.

6.7 PROBLEMS

6-1 Explain why a PRAM algorithm must be cost optimal in order for it to be a realistic candidate for implementation on a real parallel computer.

6-2 Under what circumstances would the second hypercube SIMD summation algorithm result in different processing elements getting different values of the sum?

6-3 Take another look at the sum-finding algorithm for the shuffle-exchange processor array model. Which processing elements contain the sum when the algorithm terminates?

6-4 Write an $\Theta(p)$ parallel algorithm to simulate a shuffle operation on a one-dimensional mesh of $p = 2^k$ processors.

6-5 Write an algorithm to add $n^{3/2}$ values in $\Theta(\sqrt{n})$ time on a processor array with n processing elements organized in a $\sqrt{n} \times \sqrt{n}$ mesh. Assume each processing element initially contains $\sqrt{n}$ values.

6-6 Design an $\Theta(\sqrt{n})$ algorithm for finding the sum of n integers on a $\sqrt{n} \times \sqrt{n}$ mesh with the property that, at the end of the computation, every processing element contains the sum.

6-7 What is a lower bound on the complexity of a parallel algorithm to find the sum of $n = l^3$ integers on a processor array that is organized as a three-dimensional mesh? Assume that initial values are distributed evenly among the processing elements.

6-8 Answer the previous question, changing the model to a 2-D mesh.

6-9 In the first UMA MIMD algorithm to find sums, why do we sequentially initialize array *flags*? In other words, why not do this step in parallel?

6-10 Modify the UMA multiprocessor algorithm illustrated in Fig. 6-8 so that it will work correctly even if p is not a power of 2.

6-11 Illustrate how the two broadcast algorithms described in Sec. 6.3 would work on a 4-dimensional hypercube.

6-12 What is the average number of communication links in use during Johnsson and Ho's one-to-all broadcast algorithm on the hypercube?

6-13 Another broadcast algorithm, not discussed in this book, would have a binomial tree communication pattern, but would pipeline the broadcast of ABC (see Fig. 6-17). Assume that the messages are so long that the time needed to transfer the message dominates the message startup time. Analyze the communication time of this algorithm and compare it with that of Johnsson and Ho's algorithm.

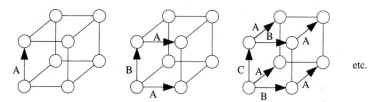

FIGURE 6-17   Illustration for Problem 6-13.

6-14 Experimental measurements on the Gadzooks hypercube multicomputer reveal a message latency of 50 μsec and a message transfer rate of 100 Mbytes/sec. Plot the estimated time needed for the two broadcast algorithms described in Sec. 6.3 to broadcast k bytes on a 1024-processor system, where 1 Kbyte $\leq k \leq$ 1 Mbyte. (Use a log-log scale to plot your graph.)

7

MATRIX
MULTIPLICATION

Only through art can we get outside of ourselves and know another's view of the universe which is not the same as ours and see landscapes which would otherwise have remained unknown to us like the landscapes of the moon. Thanks to art, instead of seeing a single world, our own, we see it multiply until we have before us as many worlds as there are original artists.... And many centuries after their core, whether we call it Rembrandt or Vermeer, is extinguished, they continue to send us their special rays.

Marcel Proust, *The Maxims of Marcel Proust*

Matrix multiplication is a fundamental component of many numerical and non-numerical algorithms. This chapter examines several parallel algorithms used to perform matrix multiplication. In Sec. 7.1 we review the standard sequential matrix multiplication algorithm. Section 7.2 begins with Gentleman's proof that matrix multiplication on the 2-D mesh-connected SIMD model has complexity $\Omega(n)$, and continues with the description of an optimal matrix multiplication algorithm for this model. Matrix multiplication can be done in logarithmic time on the hypercube SIMD and shuffle-exchange SIMD models. So, Sec. 7.2 concludes with a presentation of Dekel et al.'s $\Theta(\log n)$ matrix multiplication algorithm for the hypercube SIMD model. Section 7.3 discusses matrix multiplication on multiprocessors. Three straightforward methods can parallelize the sequential algorithm on this model. We use the design strategy of maximizing grain size to select the most suitable alternative. None of the straightforward algorithms is suitable for the loosely coupled multiprocessor model, since these algorithms require processors to fetch too many nonlocal operands per operation. Thus, another parallel algorithm, based on block-matrix multiplication, is developed for this model. Finally, we develop two parallel matrix multiplication algorithms for hypercube multicomputers in Sec. 7.4.

7.1 SEQUENTIAL MATRIX MULTIPLICATION

The product of an $l \times m$ matrix $\mathbf{A}$ and an $m \times n$ matrix $\mathbf{B}$ is an $l \times n$ matrix $\mathbf{C}$ whose elements are defined by

$$c_{i,j} = \sum_{k=0}^{m-1} a_{i,k} b_{k,j}$$

A sequential algorithm implementing matrix multiplication appears in Fig. 7-1. The algorithm requires $l \times m \times n$ additions and the same number of multiplications. The time complexity of multiplying two $n \times n$ matrices using this sequential algorithm is clearly $\Theta(n^3)$. Sequential matrix multiplication algorithms with a lower time complexity have been developed, such as Strassen's algorithm, but every algorithm developed in this chapter is a parallelization of the straightforward algorithm.

FIGURE 7-1   Sequential matrix multiplication algorithm.

MATRIX MULTIPLICATION (SISD):

```
Global    a[0 ... (l − 1)][0 ... (m − 1)],    {Matrices to be multiplied}
          b[0 ... (m − 1)][0 ... (n − 1)]

          c[0 ... (l − 1)][0 ... (n − 1)]     {Product matrix}
          t                                    {Accumulates dot product}
          i, j, k
begin
  for i ← 0 to l − 1 do
    for j ← 0 to n − 1 do
      t ← 0
      for k ← 0 to m − 1 do
        t ← t + a[i][k] × b[k][j]
      endfor
      c[i][j] ← t
    endfor
  endfor
end
```

7.2   ALGORITHMS FOR PROCESSOR ARRAYS

7.2.1   Matrix Multiplication on the 2-D Mesh SIMD Model

A Lower Bound   Gentleman (1978) has shown that multiplication of two $n \times n$ matrices on the 2-D mesh SIMD model requires $\Theta(n)$ data routing steps.

Definition 7.1. Given a data item originally available at a single processor in some model of parallel computation, let the function $\sigma(k)$ be the maximum number of processors to which the data can be transmitted in k or fewer data routing steps.

For example, in the 2-D mesh SIMD model $\sigma(0) = 1$, $\sigma(1) = 5$, $\sigma(2) = 13$, and in general $\sigma(k) = 2k^2 + 2k + 1$.

Lemma 7.1. Suppose that two $n \times n$ matrices **A** and **B** are to be multiplied, and assume that every element of **A** and **B** is stored exactly once and that no processing element contains more than one element of either matrix. If we ignore any data broadcasting facility, multiplying **A** and **B** to produce the $n \times n$ matrix **C** requires at least s data routing steps, where $\sigma(2s) \geq n^2$. (See Gentleman 1978.)

Proof. Consider an arbitrary element $c_{i,j}$ of the product matrix. This element is the inner product of row i of matrix **A** and column j of matrix **B**. There must be a path from the processors where each of these elements is stored, to the processor where the result $c_{i,j}$ is stored. Let s denote the length of the longest such path (Fig. 7-2a). In other words, the creation of matrix product **C** takes at least s data routing steps.

Note that these paths also can be used to define a set of paths of length at most $2s$ from any element $b_{u,v}$ to every element $a_{i,j}$, where $1 \leq i, j \leq n$. This is because there is a path of length at most s from $b_{u,v}$ to the processor where $c_{i,v}$ is found, and there is also a path of length at most s from $a_{i,j}$ to $c_{i,v}$ (Fig. 7-2b). Hence there is a path of length at most $2s$ from any element $b_{u,v}$ to every element $a_{i,j}$. Similarly these paths define a set of paths of length at most $2s$ from any element $a_{u,v}$ to every element $b_{i,j}$, where $1 \leq i, j \leq n$.

FIGURE 7-2   Gentleman's proof. (a) No path to $c_{i,j}$ has length more than s. (b) Element $b_{u,v}$ cannot be more than $2s$ data routings from element $a_{i,j}$.

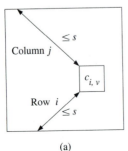
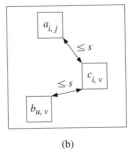

(a)   (b)

The n^2 elements of **A** are stored in unique processors. Since there exist paths of length at most $2s$ from the processor storing $b_{u,v}$ to the processors storing the elements of **A**, it follows from the definition of σ that $\sigma(2s) \geq n^2$.

Theorem 7.1. Matrix multiplication on the 2-D mesh SIMD model requires $\Omega(n)$, or for large values of n, approximately $s \geq 0.35n$, data routing steps (Gentleman 1978).

Proof. From the previous lemma we have $\sigma(2s) \geq n^2$. On the 2-D mesh SIMD model $\sigma(s) = 2s^2 + 2s + 1$. Hence $\sigma(2s) = 2(2s)^2 + 2(2s) + 1$. Combining the two yields

$$8s^2 + 4s + 1 \geq n^2$$

$$\Rightarrow \quad s^2 + \frac{s}{2} + \frac{1}{8} \geq \frac{n^2}{8}$$

$$\Rightarrow \left(s + \frac{1}{4}\right)^2 + \frac{1}{16} \geq \frac{n^2}{8}$$

$$\Rightarrow \quad s \geq \frac{\sqrt{2n^2 - 1}}{4} - \frac{1}{4}$$

When n is large, $\sqrt{2n^2 - 1}/4 - 1/4$ is approximately $0.35n$.

An Optimal Algorithm   Given a 2-D mesh SIMD model with wraparound connections, it is easy to devise an algorithm that uses n^2 processors to multiply two $n \times n$ arrays in $\Theta(n)$ time.

Since n^3 multiplications are required (assuming we are using the straight-forward algorithm), the only way that n^2 processing elements can complete the multiplication in $\Theta(n)$ time is for $\Theta(n^2)$ processing elements to be contributing toward the result at every step. Examine the initial allocation of matrix elements to processing elements, illustrated in Fig. 7-3a. The processing element located at row i, column j in the mesh contains $a_{i,j}$ and $b_{i,j}$. Note that in this original state only n processing elements contain a pair of scalars suitable for multiplication. However, it is possible to stagger matrices **A** and **B** so that every processor has a pair of scalars that need to be multiplied (Fig. 7-3b and 7-3c). Furthermore, an upward rotation of the elements in **B** and a leftward rotation of the elements in **A** present each processing element with a new pair of values to be multiplied.

Let's look at the actions of a single processing element. Examine Fig. 7-4. After matrices **A** and **B** have been staggered, processing element $P(1, 2)$ performs the multiplications and additions that form the dot product $c_{1,2}$.

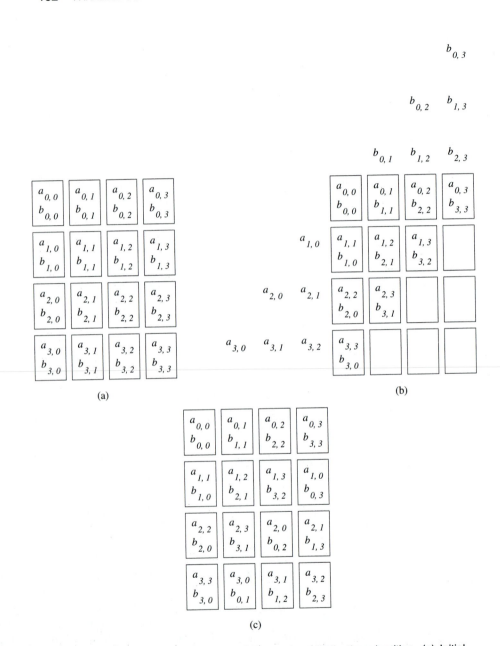

FIGURE 7-3   Matrix alignment phase of 2-D mesh SIMD matrix multiplication algorithm. (a) Initial distribution of matrices **A** and **B** to the processors. Processor $P(i,j)$ contains $a_{i,j}$ and $b_{i,j}$. The matrix multiplication algorithm multiplies all scalar pairs $(a_{i,k}, b_{k,j})$. Note that in this distribution only processors $P(0,0)$, $P(1,1)$, $P(2,2)$, and $P(3,3)$ contain such pairs. (b) The parallel algorithm staggers each row i of matrix **A** to the left by i column positions. It staggers each column i of matrix **B** upward by i row positions. (c) Same as part (b), after wraparound. Now each processor $P(i,j)$ has a pair of elements to multiply.

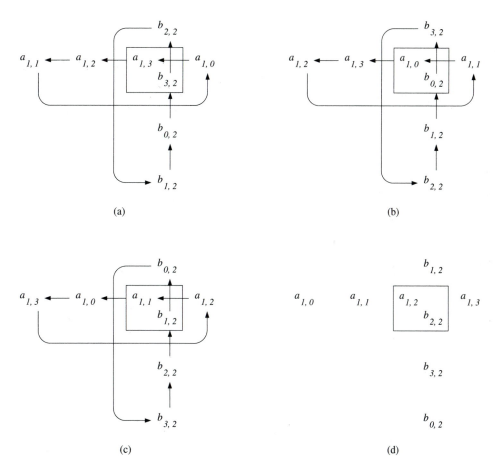

FIGURE 7-4   2-D mesh SIMD matrix multiplication algorithm from the point of view of Processor $P(1,2)$. The matrices have already been staggered. (a) First scalar multiplication step. (b) Second scalar multiplication step occurs after elements of **A** are cycled to the left and elements of **B** are cycled upward. (c) Third scalar multiplication step occurs after second cycle step. (d) Fourth scalar multiplication step occurs after third cycle step. At this point processor $P(1,2)$ has computed the dot product $c_{1,2}$.

The first phase of the parallel algorithm staggers the two matrices. The second phase computes all the products $a_{i,k} \times b_{k,j}$ and accumulates the sums. When phase 2 is complete, $C(i, j) = \sum_{k=1}^{n} A(i, k) \times B(k, j)$. The parallel algorithm appears in Fig. 7-5.

7.2.2   Matrix Multiplication on the Hypercube SIMD Model

Theorem 7.2. Given the hypercube SIMD model with $n^3 = 2^{3q}$ processors, two $n \times n$ matrices can be multiplied in $\Theta(\log n)$ time. (Dekel et al. 1978).

MATRIX MULTIPLICATION (2-D MESH SIMD):

Global n {Dimension of matrices}

         k

Local a, b, c

```
begin
  {Stagger matrices}
  for k ← 1 to n − 1 do
    for all P(i, j) where 1 ≤ i, j ≤ n do
      if i > k then
        a ⇐ east(a)
      endif
      if j > k then
        b ⇐ south(b)
      endif
    endfor
  endfor
  {Compute dot products}
  for all P(i, j) where 1 ≤ i, j ≤ n do
    c ← a × b
  endfor
  for k ← 1 to n − 1 do
    for all P(i, j) where 1 ≤ i, j ≤ n do
      a ⇐ east(a)
      b ⇐ south(b)
      c ← c + a × b
    endfor
  endfor
end
```

FIGURE 7-5   Implementation of parallel matrix multiplication algorithm on the 2-D mesh SIMD model.

Proof. The key to the algorithm of Dekel et al. (1981) is the data routing strategy; $5q = 5 \log n$ routing steps are sufficient to broadcast the initial values through the processor array and to combine the results.

The processing elements should be thought of as filling an $n \times n \times n$ lattice. Processor $P(x)$, where $0 \le x \le 2^{3q} - 1$, has local memory locations a, b, c, s, and t.

When the parallel algorithm begins execution, matrix elements $a_{i,j}$ and $b_{i,j}$, for $0 \le i, j \le n-1$, are stored in variables a and b of processor $P(2^q i + j)$ (see Fig. 7-6). After the parallel algorithm is complete, matrix elements $c_{i,j}$, for $0 \le i, j \le n - 1$, should be stored in variable c of processor $P(2^q i + j)$.

The algorithm has three distinct phases. During the first phase the $a_{i,j}$ and $b_{i,j}$ must be broadcast to the rest of the processors. After this for loop,

$$\left.\begin{array}{l}[2^{2q}k + 2^q i + j]\,a = a_{i,j} \\ [2^{2q}k + 2^q i + j]\,b = b_{i,j}\end{array}\right\} \text{ for } 0 \le k \le n - 1$$

Local Variables

	a	b
$P(0)$	$a_{0,0}$	$b_{0,0}$
$P(1)$	$a_{0,1}$	$b_{0,1}$
$P(2)$	$a_{1,0}$	$b_{1,0}$
$P(3)$	$a_{1,1}$	$b_{1,1}$
$P(4)$		
$P(5)$		
$P(6)$		
$P(7)$		

FIGURE 7-6 Initial allocation of matrix elements to processing elements on hypercube SIMD model, where $n = 2$, $q = 1$, and $p = 8$.

After the second for loop,

$$[2^{2q}k + 2^q i + j]a = a_{i,k} \quad \text{for } 0 \le j \le n - 1$$

After the third for loop,

$$[2^{2q}k + 2^q i + j]b = b_{k,j} \quad \text{for } 0 \le i \le n - 1$$

There are n^3 multiplications to be performed and n^3 processing elements available. Because of the broadcasting done in the first phase, all multiplications $a_{i,k}b_{k,j}$ can be done simultaneously during phase 2. The third phase of the algorithm routes and sums the products.

Two new functions, BIT and BIT.COMPLEMENT, are used by this algorithm. Function BIT, passed integer arguments m and l, returns the value of the lth bit in the binary representation of m. Function BIT.COMPLEMENT, passed integer arguments m and l, returns the value of the integer formed by complementing the value of bit l in the binary representation of m. These functions are illustrated in Fig. 7-7.

The parallel algorithm appears in Fig. 7-8.

Figure 7-9 illustrates the operation of this algorithm as it multiplies a pair of 2×2 matrices on an eight-processor hypercube SIMD machine.

The first for loop requires $2q$ data-routing steps. The last three for loops require q data-routing steps each. Hence a total of $5q$ data-routing steps are sufficient to multiply two matrices on the hypercube SIMD model. The algorithm also uses one multiplication step and q addition steps. Clearly, the complexity

FIGURE 7-7 Functions BIT and BIT.COMPLEMENT.

```
BIT(9, 0) = 1     BIT.COMPLEMENT(9, 0) = 8
BIT(9, 1) = 0     BIT.COMPLEMENT(9, 1) = 11
BIT(9, 3) = 1     BIT.COMPLEMENT(9, 3) = 1
BIT(9, 4) = 0     BIT.COMPLEMENT(9, 4) = 25
BIT(9, 5) = 0     BIT.COMPLEMENT(9, 5) = 41
```

MATRIX MULTIPLICATION (Hypercube SIMD):

Parameter q { Matrix size is $2^q \times 2^q$ }
Global l
Local a, b, c, s, t
begin
  {Phase 1: Broadcast matrices **A** and **B**}
  for $l \leftarrow 3q - 1$ downto $2q$ do
    for all P_m, where BIT$(m, l) = 1$ do
      $t \leftarrow$ BIT.COMPLEMENT(m, l)
      $a \Leftarrow [t]a$
      $b \Leftarrow [t]b$
    endfor
  endfor
  for $l \leftarrow q - 1$ downto 0 do
    for all P_m, where BIT$(m, l) \neq$ BIT$(m, 2q + l)$ do
      $t \leftarrow$ BIT.COMPLEMENT(m, l)
      $a \Leftarrow [t]a$
    endfor
  endfor
  for $l \leftarrow 2q - 1$ downto q do
    for all P_m, where BIT$(m, l) \neq$ BIT$(m, q + l)$ do
      $t \leftarrow$ BIT.COMPLEMENT(m, l)
      $b \Leftarrow [t]b$
    endfor
  endfor
  {Phase 2: Do the multiplications in parallel}
  for all P_m do
    $c \leftarrow a \times b$
  endfor
  {Phase 3: Sum the products}
  for $l \leftarrow 2q$ to $3q - 1$ do
    for all P_m do
      $t \leftarrow$ BIT.COMPLEMENT(m, l)
      $s \Leftarrow [t]c$
      $c \leftarrow c + s$
    endfor
  endfor
end

FIGURE 7-8 Matrix multiplication on the hypercube SIMD model.

of matrix multiplication on the hypercube SIMD model is $\Theta(q) = \Theta(\log n)$, given n^3 processing elements.

7.2.3 Matrix Multiplication on the Shuffle-exchange SIMD Model

Theorem 7.3. Given $n^3 = 2^{3q}$ processors on the shuffle-exchange SIMD model, two $n \times n$ matrices can be multiplied in $\Theta(\log n)$ time (Dekel et al. 1981).

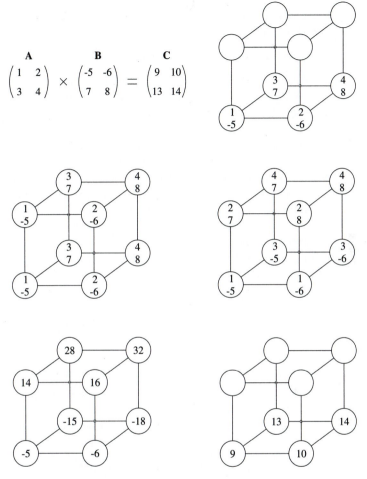

FIGURE 7-9   Matrix multiplication on the hypercube SIMD model. (Quinn and Deo 1984). Copyright ©1986 Association for Computing Machinery. Reprinted by permission.

The algorithm for the shuffle-exchange model simulates the routes followed in the algorithm presented for the hypercube SIMD model. In $13 \log n$ steps the shuffle-exchange SIMD model can perform the same routings done by the hypercube SIMD model in $5 \log n$ steps. Hence matrix multiplication on the shuffle-exchange SIMD model has complexity $\Theta(\log n)$, given $n^3 = 2^{3q}$ processing elements.

7.3 ALGORITHMS FOR MULTIPROCESSORS

Matrix multiplication presents all sorts of opportunities for parallelization on multiprocessors. In the sequential algorithm at the beginning of this chapter, three for loops could be parallelized. That brings up an interesting question:

When there are a number of nested loops, all suitable for parallelization, which loop should be made parallel?

Design Strategy 5 If load balancing is not a problem, maximize grain size.

Grain size is the amount of work performed between processor interactions. Since our goal is to minimize the overhead incurred through parallelization, we ought to maximize grain size, whenever possible.

In the case of matrix multiplication, we can parallelize the j loop or the i loop without causing problems because the only data dependencies are inside the innermost for loop. If we parallelize the j loop, the parallel algorithm executes n synchronizations (one per iteration of the i loop), and the grain size of the parallel code is $O(n^2/p)$. If we parallelize the i loop, the parallel algorithm executes only one synchronization, and the grain size of the parallel code is $\Theta(n^3/p)$. On most UMA multiprocessors the parallelized loop i version will execute faster.

A parallel matrix multiplication algorithm for the UMA multiprocessor model is illustrated in Fig. 7-10. The variables i, j, k, and t represent scalars local to each process.

What is the complexity of this algorithm? Each process calculates n/p rows of matrix **C**; the time needed to calculate a single row is $\Theta(n^2)$. The processes

FIGURE 7-10 Matrix multiplication algorithm written for a UMA multiprocessor.

MATRIX MULTIPLICATION (UMA MULTIPROCESSOR):

```
Global   n                              {Dimension of matrices}
         a[0 ... (n − 1)][0 ... (n − 1)]   {First factor matrix}
         b[0 ... (n − 1)][0 ... (n − 1)]   {Second factor matrix}
         c[0 ... (n − 1)][0 ... (n − 1)]   {Product matrix}
Local    i, j, k                        {Loop indices}
         t                              {Accumulates subtotal}

begin
    for all Pₘ, where 1 ≤ m ≤ p do
      for i ← m to n step p do
        for j ← i to n do
          t ← 0
          for k ← 1 to n do
            t ← t + a[i][k] × b[k][j]
          endfor
          c[i][j] ← t
        endfor
      endfor
    endfor
end
```

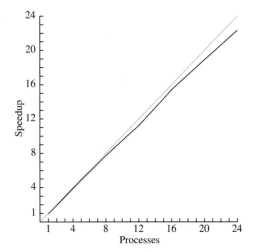

FIGURE 7-11 Speedup of parallel matrix multiplication algorithm on lightly loaded Sequent Symmetry. The algorithm is multiplying two 256×256 floating-point matrices.

synchronize exactly once; synchronization overhead, then, is $\Theta(p)$. Hence the complexity of this parallel algorithm is $\Theta(n^3/p + p)$. Note that since there are only n rows, at most n processes may execute this algorithm. If we ignore memory contention, we can expect speedup to be nearly linear. Figure 7-11 plots the speedup achieved by a lightly loaded Sequent Symmetry multiplying a pair of 256×256 matrices containing floating-point numbers.

Is it realistic to ignore memory access times? Yes, it is often possible to do so on UMA multiprocessors, where every global memory cell is an equal distance from every processor. But it is dangerous to ignore memory access times on loosely coupled multiprocessors, where some matrix elements may be much easier to access than others. Recall that on loosely coupled multiprocessors it is important to keep local as many memory references as possible. The algorithm illustrated in Fig. 7-10 does not do this well. Indeed, not only must a typical process access n/p rows of **A**, but also it must access every element of **B** n/p times! Only a single addition and a single multiplication occur for every element of **B** fetched. This is not a good ratio. Implementation of this algorithm on a BBN TC2000 would yield poor speedup.

Another method must be found to partition the problem. One attractive method is to take advantage of **block matrix multiplication**. Assume that **A** and **B** are both $n \times n$ matrices, where $n = 2k$. Then **A** and **B** can be thought of as conglomerates of four smaller matrices, each of size $k \times k$:

$$\mathbf{A} = \begin{pmatrix} A_{11} & A_{12} \\ A_{21} & A_{22} \end{pmatrix} \qquad \mathbf{B} = \begin{pmatrix} B_{11} & B_{12} \\ B_{21} & B_{22} \end{pmatrix}$$

Given this partitioning of **A** and **B** into blocks, **C** is defined as follows:

$$\mathbf{C} = \begin{pmatrix} C_{11} & C_{12} \\ C_{21} & C_{22} \end{pmatrix} = \begin{pmatrix} A_{11}B_{11} + A_{12}B_{21} & A_{11}B_{12} + A_{12}B_{22} \\ A_{21}B_{11} + A_{22}B_{21} & A_{21}B_{12} + A_{22}B_{22} \end{pmatrix}$$

If we assign processes to do the block matrix multiplications, then the number of multiplications and additions per matrix-element fetch increases. For example, assume that there are $p = (n/k)^2$ processes. Then the matrix multiplication is performed by dividing $\mathbf{A}$ and $\mathbf{B}$ into p blocks of size $k \times k$. Each block multiplication requires $2k^2$ memory fetches, k^3 additions, and k^3 multiplications. The number of arithmetic operations per memory access has risen from 2, in the previous algorithm, to $k = n/\sqrt{p}$, in the new algorithm, a significant improvement. An example of this block matrix approach to parallel matrix multiplication is shown in Fig. 7-12.

Ostlund, Hibbard, and Whiteside (1982) have implemented this matrix multiplication algorithm on Cm* for various matrix sizes. The results of their experiment are shown in Fig. 7-13.

Design Strategy 6 Reduce average memory latency time by increasing locality.

The block matrix multiplication algorithm performs better on the NUMA multiprocessor because it increases the number of computations performed per nonlocal memory fetch. For similar reasons, a careful choice of block sizes to maximize the cache hit-rate can yield a sequential block-oriented matrix multiplication algorithm that executes faster than the traditional algorithm illustrated in Fig. 7-1.

FIGURE 7-12   Block-matrix approach to parallel-matrix multiplication.

$$
\mathbf{A} \qquad \mathbf{B} \qquad \mathbf{C}
$$

$$
\begin{pmatrix} 1 & 0 & 2 & 3 \\ 4 & -1 & 1 & 5 \\ -2 & -3 & -4 & 2 \\ -1 & 2 & 0 & 0 \end{pmatrix}
\begin{pmatrix} -1 & 1 & 2 & -3 \\ -5 & -4 & 2 & -2 \\ 3 & -1 & 0 & 2 \\ 1 & 0 & 4 & 5 \end{pmatrix}
=
\begin{pmatrix} 8 & -1 & 14 & 16 \\ 9 & 7 & 26 & 17 \\ 7 & 14 & -2 & 14 \\ -9 & -9 & 2 & -1 \end{pmatrix}
$$

STEP 1: Compute $C_{i,j} = A_{i,1} B_{1,j}$

$$
\begin{pmatrix} 1 & 0 \\ 4 & -1 \end{pmatrix}\begin{pmatrix} -1 & 1 \\ -5 & -4 \end{pmatrix} \begin{pmatrix} 1 & 0 \\ 4 & -1 \end{pmatrix}\begin{pmatrix} 2 & -3 \\ 2 & -2 \end{pmatrix}
$$
$$
\begin{pmatrix} -2 & -3 \\ -1 & 2 \end{pmatrix}\begin{pmatrix} -1 & 1 \\ -5 & -4 \end{pmatrix} \begin{pmatrix} -2 & -3 \\ -1 & 2 \end{pmatrix}\begin{pmatrix} 2 & -3 \\ 2 & -2 \end{pmatrix}
=
\begin{pmatrix} -1 & 1 & 2 & -3 \\ 1 & 8 & 6 & -10 \\ 17 & 10 & -10 & 12 \\ -9 & -9 & 2 & -1 \end{pmatrix}
$$

STEP 2: Compute $C_{i,j} = C_{i,j} + A_{i,2} B_{2,j}$

$$
\begin{pmatrix} 2 & 3 \\ 1 & 5 \end{pmatrix}\begin{pmatrix} 3 & -1 \\ 1 & 0 \end{pmatrix} \begin{pmatrix} 2 & 3 \\ 1 & 5 \end{pmatrix}\begin{pmatrix} 0 & 2 \\ 4 & 5 \end{pmatrix}
$$
$$
\begin{pmatrix} -4 & 2 \\ 0 & 0 \end{pmatrix}\begin{pmatrix} 3 & -1 \\ 1 & 0 \end{pmatrix} \begin{pmatrix} -4 & 2 \\ 0 & 0 \end{pmatrix}\begin{pmatrix} 0 & 2 \\ 4 & 5 \end{pmatrix}
=
\begin{pmatrix} 8 & -1 & 14 & 16 \\ 9 & 7 & 26 & 17 \\ 7 & 14 & -2 & 14 \\ -9 & -9 & 2 & -1 \end{pmatrix}
$$

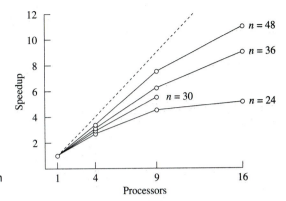

FIGURE 7-13   Speedup of matrix multiplication algorithm on Cm*.

7.4 ALGORITHMS FOR MULTICOMPUTERS

7.4.1 Row-Column-Oriented Algorithm

Let's consider how we can parallelize the standard sequential matrix multiplication algorithm. Multiplying two $n \times n$ matrices **A** and **B** involves the computation of n^2 dot products. Each dot product operation is between a row of **A** and a column of **B**. Given that at any moment in time every matrix element must be stored in the local memory of exactly one processor, it is natural to partition **A** into rows and **B** into columns. Assume that n is a power of two and we are executing the algorithm on an n-processor hypercube.

The triply nested for loop of the serial algorithm is shown in Fig. 7-14a. To maximize grain size we want to parallelize the outmost for loop. A straightforward parallelization of the outer loop would demand that all parallel processes first access column 0 of b, then column 1 of b, etc. This results in a sequence of broadcast steps, each having complexity $\Theta(\log n)$ on a n-processor hypercube.

Contention for shared resources can dramatically lower the performance of a parallel algorithm. In the case of a multiprocessor, too much contention for the same memory bank is called a **hot spot**. On a multicomputer, the processor that controls the variable must broadcast its value to the other processors. If the order in which the processors access the data items is unimportant, we can rewrite the parallel algorithm to eliminate the contention.

> **Design Strategy 7** Eliminate contention for shared resources by changing temporal order of data accesses.

Let's apply this strategy to the matrix multiplication problem. If we change the order in which the algorithm computes the elements of each row of c (Fig. 7-14b), then it is only one more jump to reach an efficient parallel algorithm (Fig. 7-14c).

In this solution, the processes are organized as a ring. After each process has used its current column of b, it fetches the next column of b from its successor

(a) Original sequential code segment:

```
for i ← 0 to n − 1 do
  for j ← 0 to n − 1 do
    t ← 0
    for k ← 0 to n − 1 do
      t ← t + a[i][k] × b[k][j]
    endfor
    c[i][j] ← t
  endfor
endfor
```

(b) After changing the access order:

```
for i ← 0 to n − 1 do
  for j ← i to i + n − 1 do
    m ← j modulo n
    t ← 0
    for k ← 0 to n − 1 do
      t ← t + a[i][k] × b[k][m]
    endfor
    c[i][m] ← t
  endfor
endfor
```

(c) After parallelization:

```
for all Pᵢ, where 0 ≤ i < n do
  for j ← i to i + n − 1 do
    t ← 0
    for k ← 0 to n − 1 do
      t ← t + a[k] × b[k]
    endfor
    c[(j) modulo n] ← t
    b[0...(n − 1)] ⇐ successor(b[0...(n − 1)])
  endfor
endfor
```

FIGURE 7-14 Transforming the sequential matrix multiplication algorithm makes it more suitable for efficient parallelization on a multicomputer.

on the ring. Because we can embed a ring in a hypercube with dilation 1 using Gray codes, each message can be sent in time $\Theta(1)$, compared to the $\Theta(\log n)$ time needed to perform each broadcast.

Now let's generalize our solution. Suppose we are multiplying an $l \times m$ and an $m \times n$ matrix on p processors, where $p < l$ and $p < n$. Assume l and n are integer multiples of p. Each processor begins with a contiguous set of l/p rows of **A** and a contiguous set of n/p columns of **B** and multiplies the $(l/p) \times m$ submatrix of **A** with the $m \times (n/p)$ submatrix of **B**, producing a $(l/p) \times (n/p)$

submatrix of the product matrix (see Fig. 7-15). Then every processor passes its piece of **B** to its successor processor. Again each processor multiplies its piece of **A** with its piece of **B** (Fig. 7-15b). After p iterations, each processor has multiplied its piece of **A** with every piece of **B**, building a $(l/p) \times n$ section of the product matrix.

How many computations and communications are performed by the processors? We will let the number of multiplications serve as the measure of computational effort. During every iteration each processor multiplies an $(l/p) \times m$ matrix by an $m \times (n/p)$ matrix, passes the $m \times (n/p)$ matrix to its ring successor, and receives an $m \times (n/p)$ matrix from its ring predecessor. Hence, every iteration requires $(l/p)m(n/p)$ computational steps. Making the standard assumption that sending or receiving a message has message latency λ plus message transmission time β times the number of values sent, every iteration has communication time $2(\lambda + m(n/p)\beta)$. Over p iterations, the total number of computational steps is $(l/p)m(n/p)p = lmn/p$ and the total communication time is $2(p\lambda + mn\beta)$.

This algorithm achieves reasonable performance on hypercube multicomputers. Figure 7-16 illustrates the speedup achieved by a parallel implementation of the algorithm on the nCUBE 3200.

As the number of processors increases, a scrutiny of this algorithm's performance reveals two related deficiencies that point us to an improved algorithm. First, notice that the communication time increases linearly with the number of processors. Second, notice that the number of computations performed per iteration is inversely proportional to the number of processors used.

7.4.2 Block-Oriented Algorithm

To improve the efficiency of the multicomputer-targeted matrix multiplication algorithm, we want to maximize the number of multiplications performed per iteration. This is done by keeping the submatrices as square as possible.

Once again we are to multiply an $l \times m$ matrix **A** by an $m \times n$ matrix **B**. Assume that l, m, and n are integer multiples of $\sqrt{p}$, where p is an even power of 2. We organize the processors as a two-dimensional mesh with wraparound connections, and give each processor a $(l/\sqrt{p}) \times (m/\sqrt{p})$ subsection of **A** and a $(m/\sqrt{p}) \times (n/\sqrt{p})$ subsection of **B**.

Having chosen this data allocation, a new matrix multiplication algorithm is a corollary of two results shown earlier this chapter. Recall that block matrix multiplication is performed analogously to scalar matrix multiplication; each occurrence of scalar multiplication is replaced by an occurrence of matrix multiplication. Also recall that we have found an efficient algorithm to multiply matrices on a two-dimensional mesh of processing elements. We use the same staggering technique to position the blocks of **A** and **B**, so that every processor multiplies two submatrices every iteration.

It is easy to show that every processor performs an equal number of multiplications. To determine the communication time required, we take into account

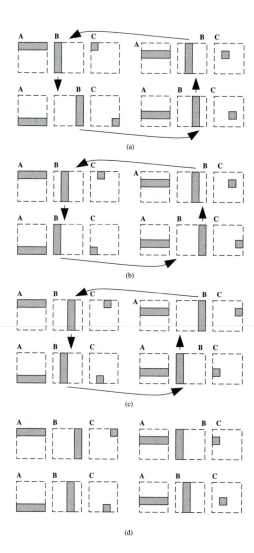

FIGURE 7-15 First hypercube matrix multiplication algorithm. Matrix A is divided into *p* groups of contiguous rows; matrix B is divided into *p* groups of contiguous columns. The processors are organized as a ring. Each processor has one piece of A and one piece of B. (a) First step of parallel algorithm, assuming four processors. Each processor multiplies its A submatrix with its B submatrix, yielding a portion of C. Each processor passes its portion of B to its predecessor on the ring of processors. (b) In step two, processors multiply matrices and pass elements of B. (c) Step three. (d) In step four there is no need to pass elements of B, unless we need to get them back to their starting place. When the algorithm is complete, each processor has computed a portion of C correspondng to the rows of A it controls.

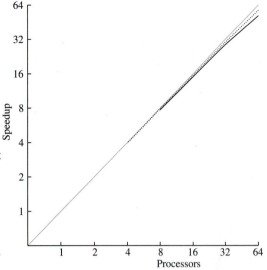

FIGURE 7-16   Scaled speedup of two hypercube multicomputer matrix multiplication algorithms on nCUBE 3200. Both algorithms are multiplying a pair of 256 × 256 matrices containing floating point numbers. The solid line corresponds to the first algorithm, and the dashed line corresponds to the second, block-oriented algorithm.

that for each of $\sqrt{p} - 1$ iterations, every processor sends and receives a portion of matrix **A** and a portion of matrix **B**. In addition, both the staggering and unstaggering of matrices **A** and **B** require $\sqrt{p}/2 - 1$ iterations in which portions of **A** and **B** are sent and received. Unlike the SIMD algorithm, which requires $\sqrt{p} - 1$ iterations for the staggering and unstaggering steps, this MIMD algorithm requires $\sqrt{p}/2$ iterations, because some processing elements can move blocks of **A** to the right while other processing elements move blocks of **A** to the left, and some processing elements can move blocks of **B** down while other processing elements move blocks of **B** up. No block begins more than $\sqrt{p}/2$ moves away from its staggered position. Hence the total communication time is

$$(2\sqrt{p} - 1)(2(\lambda + (l/\sqrt{p})(m/\sqrt{p})\beta + \lambda + (m/\sqrt{p})(n/\sqrt{p})\beta))$$

$$= \quad 2(2\sqrt{p} - 1)(\lambda + [(m/\sqrt{p})((l/\sqrt{p}) + (n/\sqrt{p}))]\beta)$$

Figure 7-16 illustrates the speedup achieved by the second hypercube matrix multiplication algorithm.

Both the block-oriented algorithm and the row-column-oriented algorithms require the same number of computation steps. When does the second algorithm require less communication time? Assume that we are multiplying two $n \times n$ matrices, where n is an integer multiple of p.

$$2p\lambda + 2n^2\beta > (2\sqrt{p} - 1)2(\lambda + (n/\sqrt{p})(2n/\sqrt{p})\beta)$$

$$\Rightarrow \quad p\lambda + n^2\beta > (2\sqrt{p} - 1)(\lambda + (2n^2/p)\beta)$$

$$\Rightarrow \quad p\lambda + n^2\beta > (2\sqrt{p} - 1)\lambda + (4n^2/\sqrt{p} - 2n^2/p)\beta$$

It is easy to determine that $p \geq 2\sqrt{p} - 1$ for all $p \geq 1$ and $n^2 \geq (4n^2/\sqrt{p} - 2n^2/p)$ for all $p \geq 16$. (Recall our analysis assumes p must be an even power of 2.) It follows that the block-oriented matrix multiplication algorithm is uniformly superior to the row-column-oriented algorithm when the number of processors is an even power of 2 greater than or equal to 16.

7.5   SUMMARY

Gentleman (1978) has shown that multiplying two $n \times n$ matrices on the 2-D mesh SIMD model has complexity $\Omega(n)$, and we have derived a matrix multiplication algorithm for the 2-D mesh SIMD model that achieves this lower bound. Dekel et al. (1981) have devised efficient routing algorithms allowing $n^3 = 2^{3q}$ processing elements on either a hypercube SIMD or a shuffle-exchange SIMD model to multiply two $n \times n$ matrices in $\Theta(\log n)$ time.

Matrix multiplication provides many different opportunities for parallelization on UMA multiprocessors. Developing an efficient matrix multiplication algorithm for the NUMA multiprocessor model is complicated by the nonhomogeneous memory structure. Reshaping the algorithm to use block matrix multiplication increases the ratio of arithmetic operations to nonlocal memory accesses and leads to a more efficient algorithm. Examining parallel algorithms for the hypercube multicomputer model, we found that the algorithm based upon a block decomposition of the matrices scaled better than the algorithm based upon a row-column decomposition.

Our study of matrix multiplication on MIMD computers yielded three more parallel algorithm design strategies:

5 If load balancing is not a problem, maximize grain size.

6 Reduce average memory latency time by increasing locality.

7 Eliminate contention for shared resources by changing temporal order of data accesses.

7.6   BIBLIOGRAPHIC NOTES

All the matrix multiplication algorithms presented in this chapter are parallelizations of the most common sequential algorithm. Multicomputer matrix multiplication algorithms using the row-column decomposition have been published in many places, including Organick (1985). A parallelization of Strassen's algorithm appears in Chandra (1976).

Ramakrishnan and Varman (1984) have designed an optimal algorithm for performing matrix multiplication on the one-dimensional mesh-connected SIMD model.

The block-oriented matrix multiplication algorithm described in this chapter has been published by various authors, including Berntsen (1989).

Hwang and Cheng (1982) have designed a VLSI block matrix multiplication algorithm that illustrates how matrices can be multiplied when there are far fewer processing elements than matrix elements. VLSI algorithms used to perform matrix multiplication or related algorithms have also been published by Horowitz (1979), Kulkarni and Yen (1982), Leiserson (1983), and Ullman (1984).

7.7 PROBLEMS

7-1 Write an $\Theta(\log n)$ matrix multiplication algorithm for the CREW PRAM model. Assume that $n = 2^k$, where k is a positive integer.

7-2 What is $\sigma(k)$ for the hypercube SIMD model?

7-3 Gentleman's theorem assumes that every element of **A** and **B** is stored exactly once in the parallel computer and that no processing element contains more than one element of either matrix. Are these assumptions realistic? Explain.

7-4 Add a postamble to the 2-D mesh SIMD matrix multiplication algorithm that unstaggers matrices **A** and **B** so that at the end of the algorithm $A(i, j) = a_{i,j}$, $B(i, j) = b_{i,j}$, and $C(i, j) = c_{i,j}$.

7-5 Write a parallel algorithm that multiplies two $n \times n$ matrices in time $\Theta(n)$ on the 2-D mesh SIMD model with no wraparound connections. Processing element $P(i, j)$ has local variables $A(i, j)$, $B(i, j)$, and $C(i, j)$. When the algorithm begins execution, $A(i, j) = a_{i,j}$ and $B(i, j) = b_{i,j}$. After $\Theta(n)$ steps, $C(i, j) = c_{i,j}$. No processing element should use more than a constant number of variables.

7-6 Write a parallel algorithm that transposes an $n \times n$ matrix in time $\Theta(n)$ on the 2-D mesh SIMD model with wraparound connections. Processing element $P(i, j)$ has local variables $A(i, j)$ and $T(i, j)$, where $1 \leq i, j \leq n$. When the algorithm begins execution, $A(i, j) = a_{i,j}$. After $\Theta(n)$ steps, $T(i, j) = a_{j,i}$. No processing element should use more than a constant number of variables.

7-7 Repeat the previous exercise with all assumptions identical, except that the model does not have wraparound connections.

7-8 Determine the processor efficiency of the hypercube SIMD matrix multiplication algorithm as a function of the matrix dimension n.

7-9 If $p \leq n$ processors are available for matrix multiplication on a UMA multiprocessor, what would be the complexity of the algorithm resulting from parallelizing the middle *for* loop of the sequential algorithm? Would you expect this algorithm to achieve better or worse speedup than the algorithm presented in this book? Why?

7-10 The block-oriented hypercube matrix multiplication algorithm has been outlined for use when the number of processors is an even power of 2. Describe how to modify the algorithm so that it may execute on a hypercube of odd dimension.

8

THE FAST
FOURIER
TRANSFORM

The meeting of two personalities is like the contact of two chemical substances; if there is any reaction, both are transformed.

Carl Gustav Jung, *Modern Man in Search of a Soul*

The discrete Fourier transform has many applications in science and engineering. For example, it is frequently used in digital signal processing. A straightforward implementation of the discrete Fourier transform has time complexity $\Theta(n^2)$. The fast Fourier transform is an $\Theta(n \log n)$ algorithm to perform the discrete Fourier transform, and it can be parallelized easily.

Section 8.1 summarizes what the discrete Fourier transform does in the context of one important application area—speech recognition. Section 8.2 is a formal presentation of the discrete Fourier transform and the inverse discrete Fourier transform. In Sec. 8.3 we present the fast Fourier transform algorithm and describe how to implement it on a hypercube multicomputer.

This chapter relies upon an understanding of complex numbers. Readers needing a refresher course in complex numbers will find a brief presentation in Appendix B.

8.1 INTRODUCTION

Fourier analysis studies the representation of continuous functions by a potentially infinite series of sinusoidal (sine and cosine) functions. We can view the discrete Fourier transform as a function that maps a sequence over time $\{f(k)\}$ to another sequence over frequency $\{F(j)\}$. The sequence $\{f(k)\}$ represents a sampling of a signal's distribution as a function of time. The sequence $\{F(j)\}$ represents a distribution of Fourier coefficients as a function of frequency. We can use $\{F(j)\}$ to compute the sinusoidal components of the sampled signal.

Figure 8-1 illustrates this process. We begin, in Fig. 8-1a, with a plot of $\{f(k)\}$, 16 samples of signal strength between time 0 and time 2π. Figure 8-1b is the plot of $\{F(j)\}$, a sequence of 16 complex numbers representing the frequency distribution. From the nonzero elements of $\{F(j)\}$ we can determine the frequency of the terms generating the signal, where **frequency** means the number of complete cycles the wave completes between time 0 and time 2π. Nonzero real components correspond to cosine functions; nonzero imaginary components correspond to sine function. From Fig. 8-1b we see that there are nonzero real components with frequency 2 and 5 and nonzero imaginary components with frequency 1 and 2. Hence the function generating the signal is of the form

$$s_1 \sin x + c_2 \cos(2x) + s_2 \sin(2x) + c_5 \cos(5x)$$

For each frequency, divide the amplitude shown in the left half of Fig. 8-1b by 8 (half of 16) to determine the coefficients of the various sinusoidal components. The frequency 1 component is $16i$. Dividing 16 by 8 yields a coefficient of 2 for the function $\sin x$. The frequency 2 component is $-8 - 16i$. Dividing -8 by 8 yields a coefficient of -1 for the function $\cos(2x)$, just as the coefficient for the function $\sin(2x)$ is -2. We use the same method to calculate that 0.5 is the coefficient of the function $\cos(5x)$. The four terms generating the signal are

$$2 \sin x - \cos(2x) - 2 \sin(2x) + 0.5 \cos(5x)$$

In Fig. 8-1c we plot the four sinusoidal components and their sum, a continuous function, and in Fig. 8-1d we plot the continuous function against the sampled data points.

The discrete Fourier transform has many applications in science and engineering. In this section we describe one such application—speech recognition by computer.

Most speech analysis has been done by studying the spectral parameters of the speech signal.

Decomposing complex speech signals into periodically recurrent sinusoidal components is the central activity of signal processing work, and is justified by (1) sinusoids being "natural signals" of linear physical (electronic) systems; (2) resonances being prominent cues to articulation configurations; (3) voice sounds being composed out of harmonics of the voice fundamental frequency; and (4) the ear appearing to do some form of spectral analysis. Also, sinusoids (and some other exponential signals) can be added ("superimposed") in linear systems without interfering with each other; thus the sinusoidal parts that we decompose the signal input into for frequency analysis act as independent, "orthogonal signals" (Lea 1980).

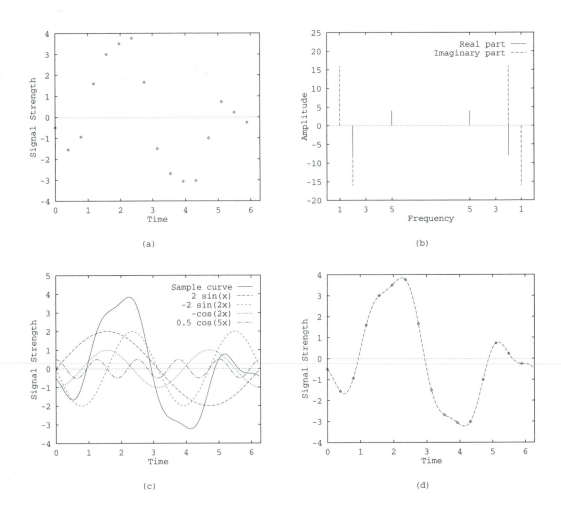

FIGURE 8-1   Example of the discrete Fourier transform. (a) A set of 16 data points representing samples of signal strength in the time interval 0 to (but not through) 2π. (b) The discrete Fourier transform yields the amplitudes and frequencies of the constituent sine and cosine functions. (c) A plot of the four constituent functions and their sum, a continuous function. (d) A plot of the continuous function and the original 16 samples.

The discrete Fourier transform can be used to transform digitized samples of human speech into two-dimensional plots (see Fig. 8-2). The graph shows detected frequencies as a function of time. Each narrow vertical strip shows the amplitudes of the detected frequencies as shades of gray. As the person talks, the speech signal changes, and so do the frequencies that make up the signal. Plots such as this can be used as inputs to speech recognition systems, which attempt to determine spoken phonemes through pattern recognition.

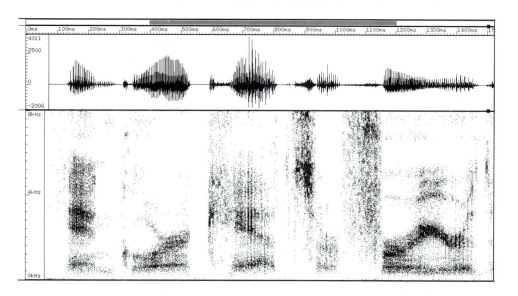

FIGURE 8-2   Discrete Fourier transform of the waveform corresponding to "Angorra cats are furrier...." The upper portion plots the strength of the input signal as a function of time. The lower portion plots frequency and amplitude as a function of time. Each narrow vertical strip represents the discrete Fourier transform of the waveform using a moving 10 ms window within a 3 ms increment. The darker the plot at some vertical position, the higher the amplitude at that frequency. (Figure courtesy Ron Cole and Yeshwant Muthusamy of the Oregon Graduate Institute of Science and Technology.)

8.2 THE DISCRETE FOURIER TRANSFORM

Given an n element vector x, the **discrete Fourier transform (DFT)** is the matrix-vector product $F_n x$, where $f(i, j) = \omega_n^{ij}$ for $0 \leq i, j < n$.

For example, to compute the discrete Fourier transform of the vector $(2, 3)$, we need to know ω_2, the second primitive root of unity, which is -1. The discrete Fourier transform of $(2, 3)$ is

$$\begin{pmatrix} \omega_2^{0 \times 0} & \omega_2^{0 \times 1} \\ \omega_2^{1 \times 0} & \omega_2^{1 \times 1} \end{pmatrix} \begin{pmatrix} x_0 \\ x_1 \end{pmatrix} = \begin{pmatrix} 1 & 1 \\ 1 & -1 \end{pmatrix} \begin{pmatrix} 2 \\ 3 \end{pmatrix} = \begin{pmatrix} 5 \\ -1 \end{pmatrix}$$

Now let's compute the discrete Fourier transform of the vector $(1, 2, 4, 3)$. We will need to use the fourth primitive root of unity, which is i.

$$\begin{pmatrix} \omega_4^0 & \omega_4^0 & \omega_4^0 & \omega_4^0 \\ \omega_4^0 & \omega_4^1 & \omega_4^2 & \omega_4^3 \\ \omega_4^0 & \omega_4^2 & \omega_4^0 & \omega_4^2 \\ \omega_4^0 & \omega_4^3 & \omega_4^2 & \omega_4^1 \end{pmatrix} \begin{pmatrix} x_0 \\ x_1 \\ x_2 \\ x_3 \end{pmatrix} = \begin{pmatrix} 1 & 1 & 1 & 1 \\ 1 & i & -1 & -i \\ 1 & -1 & 1 & -1 \\ 1 & -i & -1 & i \end{pmatrix} \begin{pmatrix} 1 \\ 2 \\ 4 \\ 3 \end{pmatrix} = \begin{pmatrix} 10 \\ -3 - i \\ 0 \\ -3 + i \end{pmatrix}$$

$$\begin{pmatrix} 1 & 1 & 1 & 1 & 1 & 1 & 1 & 1 \\ 1 & \omega^1 & \omega^2 & \omega^3 & \omega^4 & \omega^5 & \omega^6 & \omega^7 \\ 1 & \omega^2 & \omega^4 & \omega^6 & 1 & \omega^2 & \omega^4 & \omega^6 \\ 1 & \omega^3 & \omega^6 & \omega^1 & \omega^4 & \omega^7 & \omega^2 & \omega^5 \\ 1 & \omega^4 & 1 & \omega^4 & 1 & \omega^4 & 1 & \omega^4 \\ 1 & \omega^5 & \omega^2 & \omega^7 & \omega^4 & \omega^1 & \omega^6 & \omega^3 \\ 1 & \omega^6 & \omega^4 & \omega^2 & 1 & \omega^6 & \omega^4 & \omega^2 \\ 1 & \omega^7 & \omega^6 & \omega^5 & \omega^4 & \omega^3 & \omega^2 & \omega^1 \end{pmatrix}$$

FIGURE 8-3   Matrix F_8, containing powers of the primitive eighth root of unity. This matrix is used to compute the discrete Fourier transform of vectors containing eight elements.

To get a better feel for the pattern of the exponents in the F matrix, look at Fig. 8-3, which presents F_8.

Let's put the discrete Fourier transform to use by returning to the example presented in Sec. 8.1. We have a vector of 16 complex numbers representing signal strength in the time interval 0 to 2π. To simplify the presentation we show each number to only 3 digits of accuracy:

$$(-5.00, -1.55, -0.939, 1.60, 3.00, 3.51, 3.77, 1.66,$$

$$-1.50, -2.70, -3.06, -3.02, -1.00, 0.736, 0.232, -0.250)$$

The discrete Fourier transform of this vector is

$$(0, 16i, -8 - 16i, 0, 0, 4, 0, 0, 0, 0, 0, 4, 0, 0, -8 + 16i, -16i)$$

To determine the coefficients of the sine and cosine functions making up this signal, we examine the nonzero elements in the first half of the transformed sequence. (The terms at positions 9 through 15 are a reflection of the terms in positions 1 through 7, with the signs of the imaginary parts reversed.) If we begin counting at 0, the real portion of term k is 8 times the coefficient of the function $\cos(kx)$, and the imaginary portion of term k is 8 times the coefficient of the function $\sin(kx)$. (Eight is half the length of the transformed sequence.) Thus the combination of sine and cosine functions making up the curve is

$$2\sin(x) - \cos(2x) - 2\sin(2x) + 0.5\cos(5x)$$

8.2.1   Inverse Discrete Fourier Transform

Given an n element vector x, the **inverse discrete Fourier transform** is $1/n$th the matrix-vector product $F_n^{-1}x$, where $f^{-1}(ij) = \omega_n^{-ij}$ for $0 \le i, j < n$ and ω_n is the primitive nth root of unity.

For example, the inverse discrete Fourier transform of the vector $(10, -3-i, 0, -3+i)$ is

$$\frac{1}{4}\begin{pmatrix} \omega_4^0 & \omega_4^0 & \omega_4^0 & \omega_4^0 \\ \omega_4^0 & \omega_4^{-1} & \omega_4^{-2} & \omega_4^{-3} \\ \omega_4^0 & \omega_4^{-2} & \omega_4^0 & \omega_4^{-2} \\ \omega_4^0 & \omega_4^{-3} & \omega_4^{-2} & \omega_4^{-1} \end{pmatrix}\begin{pmatrix} x_0 \\ x_1 \\ x_2 \\ x_3 \end{pmatrix} = \frac{1}{4}\begin{pmatrix} 1 & 1 & 1 & 1 \\ 1 & -i & -1 & i \\ 1 & -1 & 1 & -1 \\ 1 & i & -1 & -i \end{pmatrix}\begin{pmatrix} 10 \\ -3-i \\ 0 \\ -3+i \end{pmatrix}$$

$$= \frac{1}{4}\begin{pmatrix} 4 \\ 8 \\ 16 \\ 12 \end{pmatrix} = \begin{pmatrix} 1 \\ 2 \\ 4 \\ 3 \end{pmatrix}$$

8.2.2 Sample Application: Polynomial Multiplication

The discrete Fourier transform evaluates a polynomial at the n complex nth roots of unity. Let $f(x) = a_{n-1}x^{n-1} + a_{n-2}x^{n-2} + \ldots + a_1x + a_0$ be a polynomial of degree $n-1$, and let ω be the primitive nth root of unity. Then

$$\begin{pmatrix} f(\omega^0) \\ f(\omega^1) \\ \ldots \\ f(\omega^{n-1}) \end{pmatrix} = F\begin{pmatrix} a_0 \\ a_1 \\ \ldots \\ a_{n-1} \end{pmatrix}$$

because $f(\omega^i) = a_0 + a_1\omega^i + a_2\omega^{2i} + \ldots a_{n-1}\omega^{(n-1)i}$ for $0 \leq i < n$.

The inverse discrete Fourier transform takes the values of a polynomial at the n complex nth roots of unity and produces the polynomial's coefficients.

Suppose we want to multiply two polynomials

$$p(x) = \sum_{i=0}^{n-1} a_i x^i \quad \text{and} \quad q(x) = \sum_{i=0}^{n-1} b_i x^i$$

The product of these two polynomials of degree $n-1$ is the $(2n-2)$ degree polynomial

$$p(x)q(x) = \sum_{i=0}^{2n-2} \sum_{j=0}^{i} a_j b_{i-j} x^i$$

We can compute the coefficients of the resulting polynomial $p(x)q(x)$ by convoluting the coefficient vectors of the original polynomials.

For example, to multiply the two polynomials

$$p(x) = 2x^3 - 4x^2 + 5x - 1$$

$$q(x) = x^3 + 2x^2 + 3x + 2$$

yielding

$$r(x) = a_6 x^6 + a_5 x^5 + \cdots + a_1 x + a_0$$

we convolute the coefficient vectors:

$$a_6 = 2 \times 1 = 2$$

$$a_5 = 2 \times 2 + (-4) \times 1 = 0$$

$$a_4 = 2 \times 3 + (-4) \times 2 + 5 \times 1 = 3$$

$$a_3 = 2 \times 2 + (-4) \times 3 + 5 \times 2 + (-1) \times 1 = 1$$

$$a_2 = (-4) \times 2 + 5 \times 3 + (-1) \times 2 = 5$$

$$a_1 = 5 \times 2 + (-1) \times 3 = 7$$

$$a_0 = (-1) \times 2 = -2$$

resulting in

$$f(x) = 2x^6 + 3x^4 + x^3 + 5x^2 + 7x - 2$$

Another way to multiply two polynomials of degree $n-1$ is to evaluate them at the n complex nth roots of unity, perform an element-wise multiplication of the polynomials' values at these locations, and then interpolate the results to produce the coefficients of the product polynomial. Let's apply this method to the previous example.

First we perform the discrete Fourier transform on the coefficients of $p(x)$. We list the coefficients' order from low to high. Since the polynomial has degree 3, the last four coefficients are 0. To simplify the figure, we only show two digits beyond the decimal point.

$$\begin{pmatrix} 1 & 1 & 1 & 1 & 1 & 1 & 1 & 1 \\ 1 & \omega^1 & \omega^2 & \omega^3 & \omega^4 & \omega^5 & \omega^6 & \omega^7 \\ 1 & \omega^2 & \omega^4 & \omega^6 & 1 & \omega^2 & \omega^4 & \omega^6 \\ 1 & \omega^3 & \omega^6 & \omega^1 & \omega^4 & \omega^7 & \omega^2 & \omega^5 \\ 1 & \omega^4 & 1 & \omega^4 & 1 & \omega^4 & 1 & \omega^4 \\ 1 & \omega^5 & \omega^2 & \omega^7 & \omega^4 & \omega^1 & \omega^6 & \omega^3 \\ 1 & \omega^6 & \omega^4 & \omega^2 & 1 & \omega^6 & \omega^4 & \omega^2 \\ 1 & \omega^7 & \omega^6 & \omega^5 & \omega^4 & \omega^3 & \omega^2 & \omega^1 \end{pmatrix} \begin{pmatrix} -1 \\ 5 \\ -4 \\ 2 \\ 0 \\ 0 \\ 0 \\ 0 \end{pmatrix} = \begin{pmatrix} 2 \\ 1.12 + .95i \\ 3 + 3i \\ -3.12 + 8.95i \\ -12 \\ -3.12 - 8.95i \\ 3 - 3i \\ 1.12 - .95i \end{pmatrix}$$

Next we perform the discrete Fourier transform on the coefficients of $q(x)$. Again, we are only showing two digits beyond the decimal point.

$$\begin{pmatrix} 1 & 1 & 1 & 1 & 1 & 1 & 1 & 1 \\ 1 & \omega^1 & \omega^2 & \omega^3 & \omega^4 & \omega^5 & \omega^6 & \omega^7 \\ 1 & \omega^2 & \omega^4 & \omega^6 & 1 & \omega^2 & \omega^4 & \omega^6 \\ 1 & \omega^3 & \omega^6 & \omega^1 & \omega^4 & \omega^7 & \omega^2 & \omega^5 \\ 1 & \omega^4 & 1 & \omega^4 & 1 & \omega^4 & 1 & \omega^4 \\ 1 & \omega^5 & \omega^2 & \omega^7 & \omega^4 & \omega^1 & \omega^6 & \omega^3 \\ 1 & \omega^6 & \omega^4 & \omega^2 & 1 & \omega^6 & \omega^4 & \omega^2 \\ 1 & \omega^7 & \omega^6 & \omega^5 & \omega^4 & \omega^3 & \omega^2 & \omega^1 \end{pmatrix} \begin{pmatrix} 2 \\ 3 \\ 2 \\ 1 \\ 0 \\ 0 \\ 0 \\ 0 \end{pmatrix} = \begin{pmatrix} 8 \\ 3.41 + 4.83i \\ 2i \\ .59 + .83i \\ 0 \\ .59 - .83i \\ -2i \\ 3.41 - 4.83i \end{pmatrix}$$

Now we perform an element-wise multiplication of the two polynomials at these eight points.

$$\begin{pmatrix} 2 \\ 1.12 + .95i \\ 3 + 3i \\ -3.12 + 8.95i \\ -12 \\ -3.12 - 8.95i \\ 3 - 3i \\ 1.12 - .95i \end{pmatrix} \begin{pmatrix} 8 \\ 3.41 + 4.83i \\ 2i \\ .59 + .83i \\ 0 \\ .59 - .83i \\ -2i \\ 3.41 - 4.83i \end{pmatrix} = \begin{pmatrix} 16 \\ -.76 + 8.66i \\ -6 + 6i \\ -9.25 + 2.66i \\ 0 \\ -9.25 - 2.66i \\ -6 - 6i \\ -.76 - 8.66i \end{pmatrix}$$

In the final step we perform the inverse discrete Fourier transform on the product vector:

$$\frac{1}{8} \begin{pmatrix} 1 & 1 & 1 & 1 & 1 & 1 & 1 & 1 \\ 1 & \omega^7 & \omega^6 & \omega^5 & \omega^4 & \omega^3 & \omega^2 & \omega^1 \\ 1 & \omega^6 & \omega^4 & \omega^2 & 1 & \omega^6 & \omega^4 & \omega^2 \\ 1 & \omega^5 & \omega^2 & \omega^7 & \omega^4 & \omega^1 & \omega^6 & \omega^3 \\ 1 & \omega^4 & 1 & \omega^4 & 1 & \omega^4 & 1 & \omega^4 \\ 1 & \omega^3 & \omega^6 & \omega^1 & \omega^4 & \omega^7 & \omega^2 & \omega^5 \\ 1 & \omega^2 & \omega^4 & \omega^6 & 1 & \omega^2 & \omega^4 & \omega^6 \\ 1 & \omega^1 & \omega^2 & \omega^3 & \omega^4 & \omega^5 & \omega^6 & \omega^7 \end{pmatrix} \begin{pmatrix} 16 \\ -.76 + 8.66i \\ -6 + 6i \\ -9.25 + 2.66i \\ 0 \\ -9.25 - 2.66i \\ -6 - 6i \\ -.76 - 8.66i \end{pmatrix} = \begin{pmatrix} -2 \\ 7 \\ 5 \\ 1 \\ 3 \\ 0 \\ 2 \\ 0 \end{pmatrix}$$

The vector produced by the inverse discrete Fourier transform contains the coefficients of the product polynomial in order from low to high. In other words,

$$r(x) = 2x^6 + 3x^4 + x^3 + 5x^2 + 7x - 2$$

8.3 THE FAST FOURIER TRANSFORM

At the end of Sec. 8.2 we demonstrated how we can use the discrete Fourier transform and inverse discrete Fourier transform to multiply two polynomials. Why would we use this complicated algorithm to perform convolutions or multiply polynomials, when it can be done directly in time $\Theta(n^2)$? Because we do not have to perform the discrete Fourier transform and inverse discrete Fourier transform using matrix-vector multiplication. An algorithm with time complexity $\Theta(n \log n)$ exists, and it is amenable to parallelization. The improved algorithm is called the **fast Fourier transform** (**FFT**).

The fast Fourier transform uses a divide-and-conquer strategy to evaluate a polynomial of degree n at the n complex nth roots of unity. To evaluate $f(x)$, a polynomial of degree n where n is a power of 2, the algorithm defines two new polynomials of degree $n/2$:

$$f^{[0]}(x) = a_0 + a_2x + a_4x^2 + \cdots + a_{n-2}x^{n/2-1}$$

$$f^{[1]}(x) = a_1 + a_3x + a_5x^2 + \cdots + a_{n-1}x^{n/2-1}$$

Function $f^{[0]}(x)$ contains the elements of $f(x)$ associated with the even powers of x, while function $f^{[1]}(x)$ contains the elements associated with the odd powers of x.

Note that $f(x) = f^{[0]}(x^2) + xf^{[1]}(x^2)$, so the problem of evaluating $f(x)$ at the points $\omega_n^0, \omega_n^1, \ldots, \omega_n^{n-1}$ reduces to evaluating $f^{[0]}$ and $f^{[1]}$ at $(\omega_n^0)^2, (\omega_n^1)^2, \ldots, (\omega_n^{n-1})^2$, and then computing $f(x) = f^{[0]}(x^2) + xf^{[1]}(x^2)$.

Halving lemma. If n is an even positive number, then the squares of the n complex nth roots of unity are identical to the $n/2$ complex $(n/2)$th roots of unity.

Proof. The proof of the halving lemma appears in Appendix B.

By the halving lemma, we know that the set of points $(\omega_n^0)^2, (\omega_n^1)^2, \ldots, (\omega_n^{n-1})^2$ consists of only $n/2$ unique values. In other words, to evaluate the polynomial $f(x)$ at the n complex nth roots of unity we need only evaluate the polynomials $f^{[0]}(x)$ and $f^{[1]}(x)$ at the $n/2$ complex $(n/2)$th roots of unity.

A recursive implementation of the fast Fourier transform algorithm appears in Fig. 8-4. The analysis of the algorithm is straightforward. Let $T(n)$ denote the time needed to perform the fast Fourier transform on a polynomial of degree n, where n is a power of 2.

$$T(n) = 2T\left(\frac{n}{2}\right) + \Theta(n)$$

$$= \Theta(n \log n)$$

A carefully written iterative version of the FFT algorithm eliminates the second evaluation of $\omega_n^k y^{[1]}[k]$ every iteration of the for loop and requires fewer index computations. The resulting algorithm, adopted from Cormen et al. (1990) and presented in Fig. 8-5, is the basis for our parallel algorithm.

Figure 8-6 illustrates how the FFT algorithm combines the elements of the original sequence. The dataflow pattern ought to look familiar; it is identical to a butterfly network. For this reason a multicomputer with either a butterfly or hypercube processor organization is ideally suited to execute the FFT algorithm.

RECURSIVE.FFT (a, n)

Parameter	n	{Number of elements in a}
	$a[0...(n-1)]$	{Coefficients of polynomial to be evaluated}
Local	ω_n	{Primitive nth root of unity}
	ω	{Evaluate polynomial here}
	$a^{[0]}$	{Even-numbered coefficients}
	$a^{[1]}$	{Odd-numbered coefficients}
	y	{Result of transform}
	$y^{[0]}$	{Result of FFT of $a^{[0]}$}
	$y^{[1]}$	{Result of FFT of $a^{[1]}$}

```
begin
  if n = 1 then return a
  else
    ωₙ ← e^{2π i/n}
    ω ← 1
    a^{[0]} ← (a[0], a[2], ..., a[n-2])
    a^{[1]} ← (a[1], a[3], ..., a[n-1])
    y^{[0]} ← RECURSIVE.FFT (a^{[0]})
    y^{[1]} ← RECURSIVE.FFT (a^{[1]})
    for k ← 0 to n/2 - 1 do
      y[k] ← y^{[0]}[k] + ω y^{[1]}[k]
      y[k+n/2] ← y^{[0]}[k] - ω y^{[1]}[k]
      ω ← ω × ωₙ
    endfor
    return y
  endif
end
```

FIGURE 8-4   Recursive sequential implementation of the fast Fourier transform algorithm (adapted from Cormen et al. 1990).

8.3.1 Implementation on a Hypercube Multicomputer

Let's use the efficient iterative algorithm as a starting point for writing a parallel FFT algorithm suitable for implementation on a hypercube multicomputer. We will assume that each of the p processors begins the algorithm with a contiguous group of coefficients. For example, if $n = 16$ and $p = 4$, processor 0 has coefficients a_0, a_1, a_2, and a_3; processor 1 has coefficients a_4, a_5, a_6, and a_7, and so on. We also assume that at the end of the computation each processor will contain a contiguous group of output values corresponding to its set of input coefficients. In other words, the processor starting the computation with $a_i, a_{i+1}, \ldots, a_j$ must end the computation with $y_i, y_{i+1}, \ldots, y_j$.

We can draw a diagram that indicates the flow of data between the processors, to help us understand when we must insert message-passing calls into our parallel algorithm. When message passing is required, the diagram will also help us determine the communication pattern. Figure 8-7 is a communication

ITERATIVE.FFT (a, n)

Parameter	n	{Number of elements in a}
	$a[0...(n-1)]$	{Coefficients of polynomial to be evaluated}
Local	$A[0...(n-1)]$	{Coefficients in bit reverse order}
	j	{Iterates through lower half of butterfly}
	k	{Iterates through indices with same relative} {position}
	m	{Current butterfly width}
	s	{Iteration number}
	t, u	{Temporaries}
	ω	{Evaluate polynomial here}
	ω_m	{Primitive mth root of unity}

```
begin
    REVERSE.INDEX.BITS.AND.COPY (a, A)
    for s ← 1 to log(n) do
        m ← 2^s
        ω_m ← e^{2π i/m}
        ω ← 1
        for j ← 0 to m/2 − 1 do
            for k ← j to n − 1 step m do
                t ← ω × A[k + m/2]
                u ← A[k]
                A[k] ← u + t
                A[k + m/2] ← u − t
            endfor
            ω ← ω × ω_m
        endfor
    endfor
end
```

FIGURE 8-5 Iterative sequential implementation of the FFT algorithm (adapted from Cormen et al. 1990).

pattern for the FFT computation where $n = 16$ and $p = 4$. The original step in which the algorithm permutes the a_i's requires an irregular communication. Every processor must send values to every other processor, and the individual coefficients are scattered. In this situation we should call a routing library function that implements random write.

Once the processors have permuted the values of the a_i's, then each processor can perform $\log n - \log p$ iterations of the FFT without communicating with another processor. During each of the final $\log p$ iterations, each processor must send a copy of all its partially computed results to one other processor and receive partially computed results from that processor as well. In the first such swap every processor trades values with the processor whose number is different in the least significant bit. In the next step the swaps are between

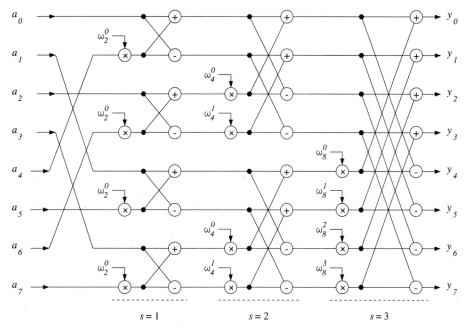

FIGURE 8-6 This diagram illustrates how the FFT algorithm manipulates a set of input coefficients $a_0, a_1, \ldots, a_{n-1}$ with complex roots of unity ($\omega_2^0, \omega_4^0, \omega_4^1$, etc.), to generate the output sequence $y_0, y_2, \ldots, y_{n-1}$. (Courtesy Cormen et al. 1990.)

processors whose numbers differ in the second least significant bit. In the last such swap, processors whose numbers differ in the most significant bit trade values. In other words, to perform the FFT every processor will, at some point, swap values across every dimension of the hypercube.

With these processor communication requirements in mind, we construct the parallel algorithm. Every processor will control two arrays of complex values. The first array, a, contains a contiguous group of input coefficients. The second array, y, holds intermediate values. At the end of the computation, array y contains a contiguous group of transformed values. The parallel algorithm has three phases. In the first phase the processors permute the a's. Each processor must compute, for each element of a, its destination in the form of (processor number, index in y), and send its value of a there. In the second phase the processors perform the first $\log n - \log p$ iterations of the FFT by performing the required multiplications, additions, and subtractions on complex numbers. No message passing is required. In the third phase the processors perform the final $\log p$ iterations of the FFT by swapping y's and performing the requisite multiplications, additions, and subtractions.

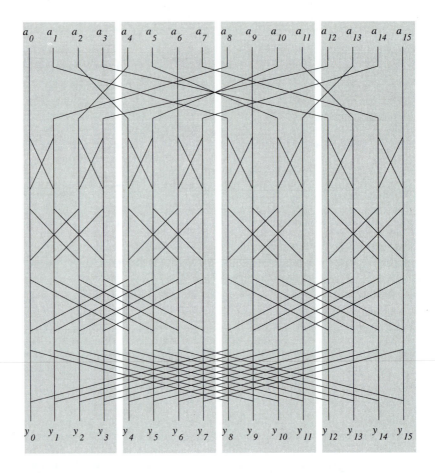

FIGURE 8-7 Imagine we want to implement an *n*-element FFT on a *p*-processor hypercube multicomputer so that at the beginning of the computation every processor contains a contiguous set of input elements, and at the end of the computation every processor contains a contiguous set of output elements. The permutation of the input elements requires a random-write operation, the first $\log n - \log p$ iterations of the FFT require no interprocessor communication, and the last $\log p$ iterations require that every processor swap copies of its values with a processor adjacent across some dimension of the hypercube. This figure illustrates the case where $n = 16$ and $p = 4$.

The parallel algorithm appears in Figs. 8-8a and 8-8b. Figure 8-9 displays the performance of the parallel algorithm transforming a 4096-element sequence on a 64-processor nCUBE 3200. The solid curve is the speedup achieved if the permutation time of the input values is included. The dashed curve is the speedup achieved if the permutation time is not taken into account. As we can see, the speedup is significantly higher when the permutation time is not counted.

FAST FOURIER TRANSFORM (a, y) (HYPERCUBE MULTICOMPUTER):

Global	n	{Number of sample points}
	p	{Number of processors}
Local	$a[0...(n/p - 1)]$	{Input elements}
	pos	{power}
	$t[0...(n/p - 1)]$	{Temporary values}
	$u[0...(n/p - 1)]$	{Temporary values}
	$y[0...(n/p - 1)]$	{Output elements}
	ω_m	{Complex mth root of unity}
	ω	{Power of complex mth root of unity}

{Permute input elements}
for all P_i, where $0 \leq i < p$ do
  for $k \leftarrow 0$ to $n/p - 1$ do
    $id \leftarrow i \times (n/p) + k$
    $dest.processor \leftarrow$ REVERSE$(id)/(n/p)$
    $dest.offset \leftarrow$ REVERSE(id) modulo (n/p)
    $[dest.processor]y[dest.offset] \Leftarrow a[k]$
  endfor
endfor

{Perform iterations not requiring interprocessor communication}
for $s \leftarrow 1$ to $\log(n/p)$ do
  $m \leftarrow 2^s$
  $\omega_m \leftarrow e^{2\pi\ i/m}$
  for all P_i, where $0 \leq i < p$ do
    $\omega \leftarrow 1$
    for $j \leftarrow 0$ to $m/2 - 1$ do
      for $k \leftarrow j$ to $n/p - 1$ step m do
        $q \leftarrow \omega \times y[k + m/2]$
        $r \leftarrow y[k]$
        $y[k] \leftarrow r + q$
        $y[k + m/2] \leftarrow r - q$
      endfor
      $\omega \leftarrow \omega \times \omega_m$
    endfor
  endfor
endfor

FIGURE 8-8a A parallel FFT algorithm suitable for implementation on a hypercube multicomputer (part 1 of 2).

8.4 SUMMARY

The discrete Fourier transform plays an important role in many scientific and engineering applications. The fast Fourier transform algorithm is interesting for two reasons. First, it is an $\Theta(n \log n)$ implementation of the discrete Fourier transform, in contrast to a naïve implementation, which has time complexity

{Perform iterations requiring interprocessor communication}
for $s \leftarrow 1$ to $\log(p)$ do
  $m \leftarrow 2^{s + \log(n/p)}$
  $\omega_m \leftarrow e^{2\pi/m}$
  for all P_i, where $0 \le i < p$ do
    if $i / 2^{s-1}$ is odd then
      $pos \leftarrow (i \times (n/p))$ modulo $m/2$
      $\omega \leftarrow e^{2(pos)\pi/m}$
      for $i \leftarrow 0$ to $n/p - 1$ do
        $t[i] \leftarrow \omega \times y[i]$
        $\omega \leftarrow \omega \times \omega_m$
      endfor
    endif
    $shift \leftarrow 2^{s-1}$
    $partner \leftarrow k \otimes shift$ {Exclusive or}
    if $i / 2^{s-1}$ is odd then
      $[partner]u \Leftarrow t$
    else
      $[partner]u \Leftarrow y$
    endif
  endfor
  for all P_i, where $0 \le i < p$ do
    if $i / 2^{s-1}$ is odd then
      for $i \leftarrow 0$ to $n/p - 1$ do
        $y[i] \leftarrow u[i] - t[i]$
      endfor
    else
      for $i \leftarrow 0$ to $n/p - 1$ do
        $y[i] \leftarrow y[i] + u[i]$
      endfor
    endif
  endfor
endfor

FIGURE 8-8b   A parallel FFT algorithm suitable for implementation on a hypercube multicomputer (part 2 of 2).

$\Theta(n^2)$. Second, the fast Fourier transform is amenable to parallelization on computers supporting the appropriate data-access patterns.

In this chapter we have presented the discrete Fourier transform algorithm and shown how a set of discrete data samples can be modeled by a continuous function, which is the sum of sine and cosine functions. We have described the inverse discrete Fourier transform and have shown how the discrete Fourier transform and inverse discrete Fourier transform can be used to multiply polynomials. We have developed recursive and iterative versions of the fast Fourier

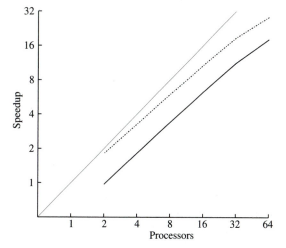

FIGURE 8-9   Speedup achieved by the parallel FFT algorithm on a 64-processor nCUBE 3200 hypercube multicomputer, when the input sequence has 4096 elements. The solid speedup curve takes into account time spent permuting the input values; the dashed speedup curve assumes values are input in bit-reverse order.

transform algorithm, and we have demonstrated one way to implement the fast Fourier transform on a hypercube multicomputer.

8.5 BIBLIOGRAPHIC NOTES

Introductions in computer science texts to the sequential fast Fourier transform algorithm include Aho, Hopcroft, and Ullman (1974); Baase (1978); Cormen et al. (1990); and Horowitz and Sahni (1978). Another presentation of the parallel fast Fourier transform is Leighton (1992).

Early papers describing parallel FFT algorithms include Bergland (1972); Brigham (1973); Chow, Vranesic, and Yen (1983); Corinthios and Smith (1975); Cyre and Lipovski [1972]; Dere and Sakrison (1970); Flanders (1982); Jesshope (1980); Kulkarni and Yen (1982); Lambiotte and Korn (1979); Parker (1980); Pease (1968, 1977); Preparata and Vuillemin (1981); Ramamoorthy and Chang (1971); Redinbo (1979); Stone (1971); Thompson (1983a, 1983b); Wold and Despain (1984); and Zhang and Yun (1984).

Brass and Pawley (1986) discuss the implementation of two- and three-dimensional FFT algorithms on SIMD computers and provide timings for their algorithms on the ICL Distributed Array Processor. Norton and Silberger (1987) explore the performance that might be possible from FFT programs written in a high-level language. Swarztrauber (1987) presents multiprocessor FFT algorithms for both hypercube multicomputers and vector multiprocessors. Chamberlain (1988) describes the implementation of a parallel FFT algorithm on a 64–processor Intel iPSC. Averbuch et al. (1990) document the performance of a parallel FFT algorithm on a custom MIMD machine. Huang and Paker (1991) present a parallel FFT algorithm suitable for MIMD computers and timings for transputer networks of various sizes.

8.6 PROBLEMS

8-1   Represent each of the following complex numbers in the form $re^{i\theta}$.

  a 1

  b i

  c $4 + 3i$

  d $-2 - 5i$

  e $2 - i$

8-2   For each value of n in the range $2, \ldots, 5$, represent the principal nth root of unity as $x + iy$ and $re^{i\theta}$.

8-3   For each vector below, show the result of applying the discrete Fourier transform to it.

  a $(7, 11)$

  b $(13, 17, 19, 23)$

  c $(2, 1, 3, 7, 5, 4, 0, 6)$

8-4   For each vector below, show the result of applying the inverse discrete Fourier transform to it.

  a $(7, 11)$

  b $(13, 17, 19, 23)$

  c $(2, 1, 3, 7, 5, 4, 0, 6)$

8-5   Devise a parallel FFT algorithm suitable for implementation on a UMA multi-processor.

8-6   Write a sequential algorithm to perform the inverse FFT. Given $n = 2^k$, the algorithm should expect the input elements in order $y_0, y_1, \ldots, y_{n-1}$ and produce the output elements in order $a_0, a_1, \ldots, a_{n-1}$.

8-7   Write a parallel version of the inverse FFT algorithm suitable for implementation on a hypercube multicomputer.

8-8   Write a parallel version of the inverse FFT algorithm suitable for implementation on a UMA multiprocessor.

8-9   You can organize the computation of the FFT so that no permutation step is necessary at the beginning of the algorithm. With this algorithm the output elements are in bit-reverse order (see Fig. 8-9). Write a sequential version of this FFT algorithm.

8-10   Parallelize the sequential algorithm you designed in the previous example.

8-11   You can implement an inverse FFT algorithm that assumes its inputs are in bit-reverse order (see Fig. 8-10). Write a sequential version of such an inverse FFT algorithm.

8-12   Parallelize the sequential algorithm you designed in the previous example.

8-13   One application of the discrete Fourier transform is to filter noise from an input signal. Figure 8-11 displays a noisy signal. The curve represents signal strength, and the spikes represent noise. Noise introduces high-frequency components into the continuous function modeling the data points. We can filter out noise by eliminating the high-frequency components.

Figure 8-12 illustrates a three-step process to remove noise from a signal. In the first step the FFT algorithm transforms the input signal into its spectral decomposition. In the second step a filtering algorithm eliminates the high-

Fast Fourier Transform   Inverse Fast Fourier Transform

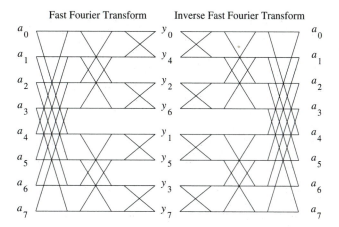

FIGURE 8-10   With no permutation step at the beginning of the FFT algorithm, the output elements $y_0, \ldots, y_7$ are in bit-reverse order.

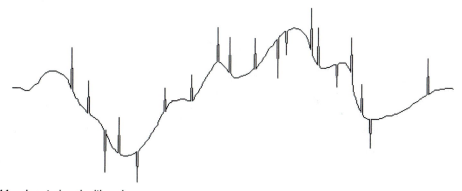

FIGURE 8-11   Input signal with noise.

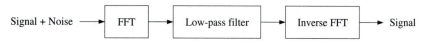

Signal + Noise ⟶ FFT ⟶ Low-pass filter ⟶ Inverse FFT ⟶ Signal

FIGURE 8-12   A three-step process to remove noise from a signal: FFT, low-pass filter, and inverse FFT.

frequency components of the spectal decomposition. In the third step the inverse FFT algorithm transforms the remaining frequency information into a signal (see Fig. 8-13).

Write an algorithm to filter high-frequency noise from an input sample of 512 data points. The filtering program should not modify the amplitude of spectral components with frequency less than or equal to 20. Spectral components with

FIGURE 8-13   Input signal of Fig. 8-11 after filtering.

frequency greater than or equal to 30 should be eliminated. For a component with frequency x, where $20 < x < 30$, the program should multiply its amplitude by $(1 - (x - 20)/10)$.

8-14   Suppose you want to implement a parallel version of the three-stage signal filtering algorithm illustrated in Fig. 8-12, and suppose the target machine is a hypercube multicomputer. Describe how you would map the tasks to the processors. Justify your design.

9

SOLVING
LINEAR
SYSTEMS

Concern for man himself and his fate must always form the chief interest of all technical endeavors, concern for the great unsolved problems of the organization of labor and the distribution of goods—in order that the creations of our mind shall be a blessing and not a curse to mankind. Never forget this in the midst of your diagrams and equations.

Albert Einstein, Address at the California Institute of Technology, 1931

This chapter surveys the parallelization of algorithms used to solve systems of linear equations. Many scientific and engineering problems can take the form of a system of linear equations. Because systems in realistic problems are often quite large, there is good reason to solve these systems efficiently on parallel computers. In Sec. 9.1 we present two examples and introduce the terminology used in the remainder of the chapter. Sections 9.2 through 9.4 cover direct methods for solving linear systems. In Sec. 9.2 we explore how to parallelize the back substitution algorithm used for solving upper triangular systems. Section 9.3 describes odd-even reduction, a parallel algorithm to solve tridiagonal systems. Parallelization of the well-known gaussian elimination algorithm is discussed in Sec. 9.4.

Sections 9.5 through 9.9 cover indirect, or iterative, methods. In Sec. 9.5 we describe the inherently parallel Jacobi algorithm. Section 9.6 discusses ways to parallelize the Gauss-Seidel algorithm, which exhibits faster convergence to a solution than the Jacobi algorithm. Jacobi overrelaxation and successive overrelaxation, variants of the previous two algorithms, are summarized in

Sec. 9.7. Section 9.8 describes multigrid methods, which are often used for the numerical solution of partial differential equations. Finally, Sec. 9.9 covers the parallelization of the conjugate gradient method, a fast converging algorithm that can be used to solve systems of linear equations having certain properties.

9.1   TERMINOLOGY

This section defines some important terms and illustrates how problems can be expressed as systems of linear equations. If you have a good background in numerical linear algebra, you may wish to skip to Sec. 9.2.

Definition 9.1. A **linear equation** in the n variables $x_1, x_2, x_3, \ldots, x_n$ is an equation that can be expressed as

$$a_1x_1 + a_2x_2 + a_3x_3 + \ldots a_nx_n = b \tag{9.1}$$

where $a_1, a_2, a_3, \ldots, a_n$, and b are constants.

Definition 9.2. A finite set of linear equations in the variables $x_1, x_2, x_3, \ldots, x_n$ is called a **system of linear equations** or a **linear system**. A set of numbers $s_1, s_2, \ldots, s_n$ is a **solution** to a system of linear equations if and only if making the substitutions $x_1 = s_1, x_2 = s_2, x_3 = s_3, \ldots, x_n = s_n$ satisfies every equation in the linear system.

A system of n linear equations in n variables

$$
\begin{array}{llllll}
a_{11}x_1 & +a_{12}x_2 & +a_{13}x_3 & \ldots & +a_{1n}x_n & = b_1 \\
a_{21}x_1 & +a_{22}x_2 & +a_{23}x_3 & \ldots & +a_{2n}x_n & = b_2 \\
a_{31}x_1 & +a_{32}x_2 & +a_{33}x_3 & \ldots & +a_{3n}x_n & = b_3 \\
\ldots & \ldots & \ldots & \ldots & \ldots & \ldots \\
a_{n1}x_1 & +a_{n2}x_2 & +a_{n3}x_3 & \ldots & +a_{nn}x_n & = b_n
\end{array}
\tag{9.2}
$$

is usually expressed as $\mathbf{Ax} = \mathbf{b}$, where $\mathbf{A}$ is an $n \times n$ matrix containing the $a_{i,j}$s and $\mathbf{x}$ and $\mathbf{b}$ are n-element vectors storing x_is and b_is, respectively. The location and value of the nonzero elements of matrix $\mathbf{A}$ determine how difficult it is to solve for $\mathbf{x}$. In the most general case, a sequential algorithm having time complexity $O(n^3)$ can solve a system of linear equations.

Here is a problem that generates a linear system with no special form. (The example is taken from Halliday and Resnick [1974].) Consider the elementary circuit shown in Fig. 9-1. Two batteries supply electromotive force E_1 and E_2 to the circuit. Three resistors provide resistance R_1, R_2, and R_3 to the current. Given these values, we want to compute the three currents i_1, i_2, and i_3.

By applying physical laws we can express the problem as three equations, involving the three unknown values i_1, i_2, and i_3:

$$
\begin{array}{rcr}
i_1 \quad -i_2 \quad +i_3 & = & 0 \\
-R_1i_1 \qquad +R_3i_3 & = & -E_1 \\
-R_2i_2 \quad -R_3i_3 & = & E_2
\end{array}
\tag{9.3}
$$

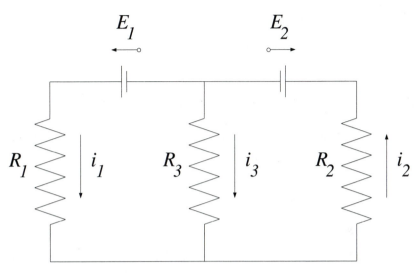

FIGURE 9-1   An elementary circuit with two batteries and three resistors. (Drawing adapted from figure in Halliday and Resnick [1974].)

Linear systems with zeroes in the right places can be solved faster than linear systems of arbitrary form. Examples include triangular, tridiagonal, and positive definite systems.

Definition 9.3. An $n \times n$ matrix **A** is **upper triangular** if

$$i > j \Rightarrow a_{ij} = 0$$

Definition 9.4. An $n \times n$ matrix **A** is **lower triangular** if

$$i < j \Rightarrow a_{ij} = 0$$

Upper triangular and lower triangular systems are solvable in $O(n^2)$ time on sequential computers.

Definition 9.5. An $n \times n$ matrix **A** is **tridiagonal** if and only if

$$|i - j| > 1 \Rightarrow a_{ij} = 0$$

A linear system $\mathbf{Ax} = \mathbf{b}$ is called tridiagonal if coefficient matrix **A** is tridiagonal. Sequential algorithms with time complexity $\Theta(n)$ exist to solve tridiagonal systems.

Let's see how a tridiagonal linear system can be used to solve problems. Suppose we want to determine the steady-state temperature distribution in a

FIGURE 9-2   An insulated rod with fixed end temperatures T_1 and T_2. We want to know the temperatures at points x_1, x_2, x_3, x_4, which divide the bar into five segments of equal length.

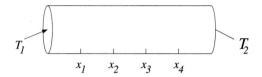

rod of conducting material (Fig. 9-2). We assume the rod has a uniform cross section, so that all points in a cross section have equal temperature. This enables us to describe temperature as a function of distance from one end of the rod. We assume the temperatures T_1 and T_2 at the ends of the rod are fixed through exposure to a constant heat source. Finally, we assume that the rod is swathed in insulating material. In other words, no heat escapes from the sides of the rod—all heat transfer is at the ends.

Finding the steady-state temperature at four evenly spaced points x_1, x_2, x_3, and x_4 can be expressed as a system of linear equations:

$$
\begin{array}{rrrrl}
x_1 & -0.5x_2 & & & = 0.5T_1 \\
-0.5x_1 & +x_2 & -0.5x_3 & & = 0 \\
& -0.5x_2 & +x_3 & -0.5x_4 & = 0 \\
& & -0.5x_3 & +x_4 & = 0.5T_2
\end{array}
\tag{9.4}
$$

Here are three more definitions that we will use later in this chapter.

Definition 9.6. An $n \times n$ matrix **A** is **diagonally dominant** if $|a_{i,i}| > \Sigma_{j \neq i}|a_{i,j}|$ for $1 \leq i \leq n$.

Definition 9.7. An $n \times n$ matrix **A** is **symmetric** if $a_{ij} = a_{ji}$ for $1 \leq i, j \leq n$.

Definition 9.8. An $n \times n$ matrix **A** is **positive definite** if it is symmetric, diagonally dominant, and $a_{ii} > 0$ for $1 \leq i \leq n$.

9.2 BACK SUBSTITUTION

In this section we describe the parallelization of an algorithm used to solve the linear system $\mathbf{Ax} = \mathbf{b}$ where **A** is upper triangular.

Given a system of linear equations $\mathbf{Ax} = \mathbf{b}$, where **A** is an upper triangular $n \times n$ matrix, the back substitution algorithm solves the linear system in time $\Theta(n^2)$. Let's view the algorithm by using a simple example. Suppose we want to solve the system

$$
\begin{array}{rrrrl}
1x_1 & +1x_2 & -1x_3 & +4x_4 & = 8 \\
& -2x_2 & -3x_3 & +1x_4 & = 5 \\
& & 2x_3 & -3x_4 & = 0 \\
& & & 2x_4 & = 4
\end{array}
\tag{9.5}
$$

We can solve the last equation directly, since it has only a single unknown. After we have determined that $x_4 = 2$, we can simplify the other equations by removing their x_4 terms and adjusting the value of their **b** terms:

$$
\begin{aligned}
1x_1 +1x_2 -1x_3 \quad\;\;\;\; &= 0 \\
-2x_2 -3x_3 \quad\;\;\;\; &= 3 \\
2x_3 \quad\;\;\;\; &= 6 \\
2x_4 &= 4
\end{aligned}
\tag{9.6}
$$

Now the third equation has only a single unknown, and a simple division yields $x_3 = 3$. Again, we use this information to simplify the two equations above it:

$$
\begin{aligned}
1x_1 +1x_2 \quad\quad\;\;\;\; &= 3 \\
-2x_2 \quad\quad\;\;\;\; &= 12 \\
2x_3 \quad\;\; &= 6 \\
2x_4 &= 4
\end{aligned}
\tag{9.7}
$$

We have simplified the second equation to contain only a single unknown, and dividing b_2 by a_{22} yields $x_2 = -6$. After subtracting $x_2 \times a_{12}$ from b_1 we have

$$
\begin{aligned}
1x_1 \quad\quad\quad\;\;\;\; &= 9 \\
-2x_2 \quad\quad\;\;\;\; &= 12 \\
2x_3 \quad\;\; &= 6 \\
2x_4 &= 4
\end{aligned}
\tag{9.8}
$$

and it is easy to see that $x_1 = 9$.

A sequential algorithm to perform back substitution appears in Fig. 9-3. The time complexity of this algorithm is $\Theta(n^2)$.

How amenable to parallelization is the back substitution algorithm? It is often difficult to determine the inherent parallelism of an algorithm from a simple examination of the code. Sometimes construction of a task graph can make the parallelism (or lack of parallelism) apparent. The task graph has these properties:

BACK.SUBSTITUTION (SISD):

	Global	n	{Size of system}
		$a[1...n][1...n]$	{Elements of A}
		$b[1...n]$	{Elements of b}
		$x[1...n]$	{Elements of x}
		i	{Column index}
		j	{Row index}

```
1.  begin
2.     for i ← n downto 1 do
3.        x[i] ← b[i] / a[i][i]
4.        for j ← 1 to i − 1 do
5.           b[j] ← b[j] − x[i] × a[j][i]
6.           a[j][i] ← 0        {This line is optional}
7.        endfor
8.     endfor
9.  end
```

FIGURE 9-3 Sequential back substitution algorithm. Given an upper triangular system of size n, the algorithm has time complexity $\Theta(n^2)$.

1. It contains one vertex for every time a variable is assigned a value.

2. It contains one vertex for every variable that is accessed but never assigned a value.

3. It contains one edge for every use-def dependency between a variable referenced on the right-hand side of an assignment statement and a variable assigned a value on the left-hand side. The edge is directed toward the variable assigned a value.

We have used these rules to construct a task graph for the back substitution algorithm applied to an upper triangular system of size 4 (see Fig. 9-4). Note that there are multiple vertices corresponding to each variable $b[i]$, since the algorithm repeatedly updates these variables.

Once the task graph has been constructed, we label each vertex according to the following rules:

1. If no edges enter a vertex, the vertex has label 0.

2. If the vertex has at least one incoming edge, its label is equal to 1 plus the maximum label of any vertex associated with an incoming edge.

The labels inside the vertices in Fig. 9-4 have been assigned using these rules. The labels represent the depth of each part of the computation in the task graph. We have used bold arcs to indicate one of the critical paths of the task graph. It is evident from the critical path that the elements of x must be computed one at a time.

With this knowledge, it is clear our only alternative is to parallelize the inner for loop. The parallel algorithm, designed for a UMA multiprocessor, appears in Fig. 9-5. The grain size is small; even in the first iteration there are only $n - 1$ multiplications and $n - 1$ subtractions. As the algorithm progresses, the

FIGURE 9-4   Task graph for the sequential back substitution algorithm solving an upper triangular system of size 4. Elements of vector b are updated, so the graph shows one vertex for each value of each element. The label inside each vertex indicates the depth of the task in the graph. A critical path is highlighted.

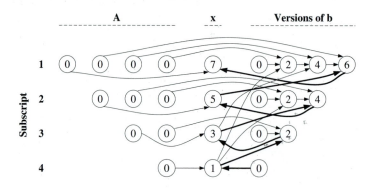

BACK.SUBSTITUTION (UMA MULTIPROCESSOR):

```
Global    n               {Size of system}
          p               {Number of processes}
          a[1...n][1...n]  {Elements of A}
          b[1...n]         {Elements of b}
          x[1...n]         {Elements of x}
          i               {Column index}
Local     j               {Process identifier}
          k               {Row index}

begin
  for i ← n downto 2 do
    x[i] ← b[i] / a[i][i]
    forall Pⱼ where 1 ≤ j ≤ p do
      for k ← j to i − 1 step p do
        b[k] ← b[k] − x[i] × a[k][i]
        a[k][i] ← 0        {This line is optional}
      endfor
    endforall
  endfor
end
```

FIGURE 9-5   Parallel version of back substitution algorithm suitable for implementation on a UMA multiprocessor.

number decreases linearly to 1 multiplication and 1 subtraction. For this reason we cannot expect this algorithm to achieve high speedup.

Figure 9-6 illustrates the speedup achieved by our parallel back substitution algorithm on a lightly loaded Sequent Symmetry UMA multiprocessor. Note the Amdahl effect: speedup on any fixed number of processors increases with the problem size.

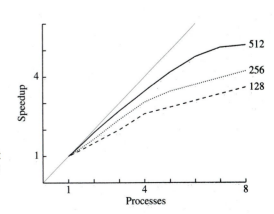

FIGURE 9-6   Speedup achieved on Sequent Symmetry by the parallel back substitution algorithm solving triangular systems of various sizes.

9.3 ODD-EVEN REDUCTION

In this section we explore two algorithms for solving tridiagonal systems of linear equations. The first is a straightforward algorithm, suitable for execution on a serial computer, but is unsuitable for parallelization. The second algorithm, called odd-even reduction or cyclic reduction, has a higher constant of proportionality, but can be parallelized.

We begin by developing the straightforward sequential algorithm. Consider the following tridiagonal linear system:

$$
\begin{array}{rrrr}
16x_1 & +4x_2 & & = 8 \\
4x_1 & +11x_2 & -5x_3 & = 7 \\
& 2x_2 & +14x_3 & -6x_4 = 13 \\
& & 5x_3 & +18x_4 = 24
\end{array}
\tag{9.9}
$$

Unlike the upper triangular system we encountered in the last section, the tridiagonal system generally does not contain any equations with exactly one variable. For this reason we must combine equations to determine the values of the variables.

We may perform three operations on a system of linear equations without changing the value of the solution (Anton 1981):

1. Multiply every term of an equation by a nonzero constant
2. Interchange two equations
3. Add a multiple of one equation to another equation

First we eliminate x_1 from the second equation by subtracting 1/4 times the first equation from the second equation:

$$
\begin{array}{rrrr}
16x_1 & +4x_2 & & = 8 \\
& 10x_2 & -5x_3 & = 5 \\
& 2x_2 & +14x_3 & -6x_4 = 13 \\
& & 5x_3 & +18x_4 = 24
\end{array}
\tag{9.10}
$$

Next we eliminate x_2 from the third equation by subtracting 1/5 times the second equation from the third equation:

$$
\begin{array}{rrrr}
16x_1 & +4x_2 & & = 8 \\
& 10x_2 & -5x_3 & = 5 \\
& & 15x_3 & -6x_4 = 12 \\
& & 5x_3 & +18x_4 = 24
\end{array}
\tag{9.11}
$$

Finally, we remove x_3 from the fourth equation by subtracting 1/3 times the third equation from the fourth equation:

$$
\begin{array}{rrrr}
16x_1 & +4x_2 & & = 8 \\
& 10x_2 & -5x_3 & = 5 \\
& & 15x_3 & -6x_4 = 12 \\
& & & 20x_4 = 20
\end{array}
\tag{9.12}
$$

Here the last equation has a single unknown, and we can solve for x_4 directly. Once x_4 is known, it is easy to solve for x_3. The algorithm continues in this fashion until the values for the rest of the variables have been determined.

Let's consider the form of the equations in the tridiagonal system. Except for the first and last equations, each equation has three variables in it.

$$g_1 x_1 + h_1 x_2 = b_1$$

$$f_i x_{i-1} + g_i x_i + h_i x_{i+1} = b_i \qquad 2 \le i \le n-1$$

$$f_n x_{n-1} + g_n x_n = b_n \qquad\qquad (9.13)$$

A sequential algorithm to solve a tridiagonal system of equations appears in Fig. 9-7. The algorithm has two for loops, each performing $n-1$ iterations (assuming the size of the linear system is n). The steps within each for loop require constant time. Hence the complexity of the sequential algorithm to solve a tridiagonal system of linear equations is $\Theta(n)$.

FIGURE 9-7 Sequential algorithm to solve a system of tridiagonal equations. The algorithm performs $9n - 8$ floating-point operations, assuming the expression $f[i + 1]/g[i]$ is evaluated only once per iteration of the first for loop.

TRIDIAGONAL.SYSTEM.SOLVER (SISD):

{This algorithm solves the set of equations
  $g_1\ x_1\ +\ h_1\ x_2\ =\ b_1$
  $f_i\ x_{i-1}\ +\ g_i\ x_i\ +\ h_i\ x_{i+1}\ =\ b_i$ for $1 < i < n$
  $f_n\ x_{n-1}\ +\ g_n\ x_n\ =\ b_n$
}

```
    Global    n                                 {Size of tridiagonal system}
              f[2...n], g[1...n], h[1...(n − 1)]  {Coefficients of x}
              b[1...n]                           {Constant vector}
              x[1...n]                           { Solution vector }
  begin
    for i ← 1 to n − 1 do
      g[i + 1] ← g[i + 1] − (f[i + 1]/g[i]) × h[i]
      b[i + 1] ← b[i + 1] − (f[i + 1]/g[i]) × b[i]
    endfor
    for i ← n downto 2 do
      x[i] ← b[i] / g[i]
      b[i − 1] ← b[i − 1] − x[i] × h[i − 1]
    endfor
    x[1] ← b[1] / g[1]
  end
```

FIGURE 9-8   Data flow diagram illustrating data dependencies in the first loop of the tridiagonal-system solver of Fig. 9-7, for a system of size 4. The number inside each vertex is the length of the longest path preceding the vertex. The overlapping circles represent instances where the new value of a variable is computed from an expression containing its previous value.

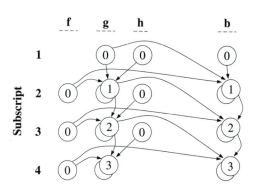

We can determine if an algorithm can be parallelized by exploring its data dependencies. Figure 9-8 is a data-flow diagram for the first loop of the algorithm solving a system of size 4. The overlapping circles represent instances where the new value of a variable is computed from an expression containing its previous value. The data flow diagram makes clear that this particular algorithm is not amenable to parallelization.

To achieve some parallelism, we must take another problem solving approach. First, we want to represent all n equations the same way. We can do this by introducing pseudovariables x_0 and x_{n+2}, both having value 0. Now we are able to write

$$f_i x_{i-1} + g_i x_i + h_i x_{i+1} = b_i \qquad 1 \le i \le n \tag{9.14}$$

Rewriting equation 9.14 to solve for x_i we get

$$x_i = (b_i - f_i x_{i-1} - h_i x_{i+1})/g_i \qquad 1 \le i \le n \tag{9.15}$$

If we introduce two more pseudovariables x_{-1} and x_{n+2}, both having value 0, we can use equation 9.15 to substitute for x_{i-1} and x_{i+1} in equation 9.14:

$$f_i \left(\frac{b_{i-1} - f_{i-1}x_{i-2} - h_{i-1}x_i}{g_{i-1}} \right) + g_i x_i +$$

$$h_i \left(\frac{b_{i+1} - f_{i+1}x_i - h_{i+1}x_{i+2}}{g_{i+1}} \right) = b_i \qquad 1 \le i \le n \tag{9.16}$$

To simplify this equation we define

$$\begin{aligned} \gamma_i &= f_i/g_{i-1} \quad 1 \le i \le n \\ \delta_i &= h_i/g_{i+1} \quad 1 \le i \le n \end{aligned} \tag{9.17}$$

Now we can rewrite it as

$$\gamma_i f_{i-1} x_{i-2} + (g_i - \gamma_i h_{i-1} - \delta_i f_{i+1})x_i - \delta_i h_{i+1} x_{i+2} =$$

$$b_i + \gamma_i h_{i-1} + \delta_i h_{i+1} \qquad 1 \le i \le n \tag{9.18}$$

By this transformation we have expressed the value of x_i in terms of x_{i-2} and x_{i+2}. Taken as a whole, the equations for x_2, x_4, x_6, ... , x_n form a tridiagonal system with $n/2$ variables. Applying this technique recursively yields a divide-and-conquer algorithm, called **odd-even reduction** or **cyclic reduction**, to solve a tridiagonal system of linear equations. The odd-even reduction algorithm was first published by Hockney (1965).

Figure 9-9 illustrates the odd-even reduction algorithm for a system of size 8. In the first step the coefficients of x_1, x_3, x_5, and x_7 are eliminated; the remaining system is tridiagonal and has only the variables with even indices. In the second step the coefficients of x_2 and x_6 are eliminated. In step three x_4 is eliminated, and we are left with a single equation in a single unknown. Once the value of x_8 is known, the value of x_4 can be found. With the values of x_8 and x_4 computed, the algorithm can determine the values of x_2 and x_6, and once x_2, x_4, x_6, and x_8 are known, the algorithm finds values for x_1, x_3, x_5, and x_7.

The odd-even reduction algorithm appears in pseudocode in Fig. 9-10. The time complexity of odd-even reduction is $\Theta(n)$, the same as that of the sequential algorithm presented earlier. However, odd-even reduction is much more amenable to parallelization, as shown in Fig. 9-9, as all three inner for loops can be executed in parallel. We have implemented a parallel odd-even reduction algorithm on the Sequent Symmetry system and measured its performance solving a tridiagonal system of size 65,536. The parallelizability and speedup of this algorithm are shown in Fig. 9-11.

FIGURE 9-9   This diagram illustrates how the odd-even reduction algorithm eliminates variables in a tridiagonal system of size 8. In the first step variables x_1, x_3, x_5, and x_7 are eliminated. In the second step variables x_2 and x_6 are eliminated. In step three variable x_4 is eliminated. Here the equation has a single variable—x_8—whose value can be computed directly. Once the value of x_8 is known, the algorithm solves for x_4. Given values for x_8 and x_4, the algorithm computes the values of x_2 and x_6, and so on.

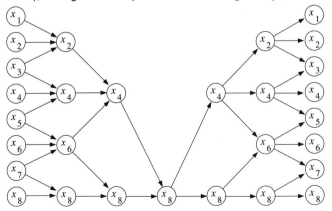

ODD.EVEN.REDUCTION (SISD):

{This algorithm solves a system of tridiagonal equations}

Global	n	{Number of equations in linear system}
	$f[1...n], \; g[1...n], \; h[1...n]$	{Coefficients of the tridiagonal equations}
	$b[1...n]$	{Constant vector}
	$new.f[1...n], \; new.g[1...n],$	{Newly computed coefficients}
	$new.h[1...n], \; new.b[1...n]$	
	$x[1...n]$	{Solution vector}
	d	{Distance between terms being combined}
	$\gamma[1..n], \; \delta[1..n]$	{Temporaries}

```
begin
  for i ← 0 to log n − 1 do
    d ← 2^i
    for j ← 2 × i + 1 to n − 1 step 2 × d do
      γ[j] ← f[j] /g[j − d]
      δ[j] ← h[j]/g[j + d]
      new.f[j] ← −γ[j] × f[j − d]
      new.g[j] ← − δ[j] × f[j + d] − γ[j] × h[j − i]
      new.h[j] ← δ[j] × h[j + d]
      new.b[j] ← b[j] + γ[j] × b[j − d] + δ[j] × b[j + d]
    endfor
    γ[n] ← f[n] /g[n − d]
    f[n] ← −γ[j] × f[n − d]
    g[n] ← g[n] − γ[n] × h[n − d]
    b[n] ← b[n] + γ[n] × b[n − d]
    for j ← 2 × i + 1 to n − 1 step 2 × d do
      f[j] ← new.f[j], g[j] ← new.g[j], h[j] ← new.h[j], b[j] ← new.b[j]
    endfor
  endfor
  x[n] ← b[n] / g[n]
  for i ← log n − 1 downto 0 step −1 do
    d ← 2^i
    x[d] ← (b[d] − h[d] × x[2 × d])/g[d]
    for j ← 3 × d to n step 2 × d
      x[j] ← (b[j] − f[j] × x[j − d] − h[j] × x[j + d])/g[j]
    endfor
  endfor
end
```

FIGURE 9-10 Sequential implementation of the odd-even reduction algorithm to solve a tridiagonal system of linear equations.

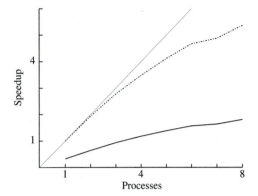

FIGURE 9-11   Speedup (solid line) and parallelizability (dotted line) of parallel odd-even reduction on Sequent Symmetry on a tridiagonal system of size 65,636.

As Fig. 9-11 makes clear, although the algorithm is easily parallelizable, its speedup is poor. Let's explore the reasons for this.

The total number of floating-point operations performed by the sequential algorithm of Fig. 9-7 is

$$\sum_{i=1}^{n-1} 6 + \sum_{i=2}^{n} 3 + 1 = 9n - 8 \tag{9.19}$$

The total number of floating-point operations performed by the odd-even reduction algorithm is

$$\sum_{i=1}^{\log n - 1} \left(\left(\sum_{j=1}^{n/2^i - 1} 13 \right) + 7 \right) + 1 + \sum_{i=1}^{\log n - 1} \left(\left(\sum_{j=1}^{n/2^i - 1} 5 \right) + 3 \right) =$$

$$13\left(n - 2 - (\log n - 1)\right) + 7(\log n - 1) + 1 + 5(n - 2 - (\log n - 1)) \tag{9.20}$$

$$+3(\log n - 1) = 18n - 8\log n - 27$$

Taking the ratio of equations 9.19 and 9.20

$$\lim_{n \to \infty} \left(\frac{9n - 8}{18n - 8\log n - 27} \right) = \frac{1}{2} \tag{9.21}$$

We should not expect a parallel implementation of odd-even reduction to exhibit an efficiency greater than 50 percent.

9.4 GAUSSIAN ELIMINATION

In this section we describe the parallelization of gaussian elimination, a well-known algorithm for solving the linear system $\mathbf{Ax} = \mathbf{b}$ when the matrix $\mathbf{A}$ has nonzero elements in arbitrary locations. Gaussian elimination reduces $\mathbf{Ax} = \mathbf{b}$

to an upper triangular system $\mathbf{Tx} = \mathbf{c}$, at which point back substitution can be performed to solve for $\mathbf{x}$.

Recall that we can replace any row of a linear system by the sum of that row and a nonzero multiple of any row of the system. We used this technique in Sec. 9.3 to eliminate nonzero elements from below the main diagonal in tridiagonal systems. Gaussian elimination uses the same technique.

Figure 9-12 illustrates one iteration of the algorithm. All nonzero elements below the diagonal and to the left of column i have already been eliminated. In step i the nonzero elements below the diagonal in column i are eliminated by replacing each row j, where $i + 1 \le j \le n$, with the sum of row j and $-a_{j,i}/a_{i,i}$ times row i. After $n - 1$ such iterations, the linear system is upper triangular.

In the straightforward gaussian elimination algorithm just described, row i is the **pivot row**, i.e., the row used to drive to zero all nonzero elements below the diagonal in column i. This approach does not exhibit good numerical stability on digital computers. However, a simple variant, called **gaussian elimination with partial pivoting**, does produce reliable results. In step i of gaussian elimination with partial pivoting, rows i through n are searched for the row whose column i element has the largest absolute value. This row is swapped (pivoted) with row i. Here the algorithm uses multiples of the pivot row, now stored as row i, to reduce to zero all nonzero elements of column i in rows $i + 1$ though n.

A sequential gaussian elimination algorithm appears in Fig. 9-13. Rather than actually swapping the pivot row and row i in each iteration, the algorithm makes use of indirection. Array element $pivot[i]$ contains the iteration number in which row i was used as the pivot row. Another array is introduced to make it easy to determine if a particular row has been used as a pivot row; array element $marked[i]$ is set to 1 when row i is chosen as a pivot row.

Let's determine how well-suited gaussian elimination is to parallelization. First, we count every arithmetic operation and comparison involving floating-

FIGURE 9-12   During iteration i of the gaussian elimination algorithm, all elements in column i for each row j below row i are driven to 0 by subtracting a multiple of row i from row j.

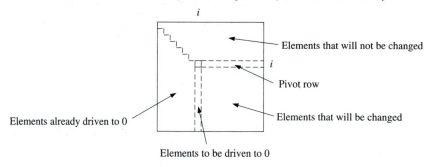

GAUSSIAN.ELIMINATION (SISD):

Global n {Size of linear system}
          $a[1...n][1...n]$ {Coefficients of equations}
          $b[1...n]$ {Right-hand sides of equations}
          $marked[1...n]$ {Indicates which rows have been pivot rows}
          $pivot[1...n]$ {Indicates iteration each row was used as pivot}
          $picked$ {Row picked as pivot row}

```
begin
  for i ← 1 to n do
    marked[i] ← 0
  endfor
  for i ← 1 to n − 1 do
    tmp ← 0
    for j ← i to n do
      if marked[j] = 0 and |a[j][i]| > tmp then
        tmp ← |a[j][i]|
        picked ← j
      endif
    endfor
    marked[picked] ← 1
    pivot[picked] ← i
    for j ← 1 to n do
      if marked[j] = 0 then
        tmp ← a[j][i] / a[picked][i]
        for k ← i + 1 to n do
          a[j][k] ← a[j][k] − a[picked][k] × tmp
        endfor
        b[j] ← b[j] − b[k] × tmp
      endif
    endfor
  endfor
  for i ← 1 to n do
    if marked[i] = 0 then
      pivot[i] ← N
      break
    endif
  endfor
end
```

FIGURE 9-13   Sequential gaussian elimination algorithm with partial pivoting. The algorithm assumes the linear system is nonsingular, i.e., has a solution.

point numbers in the algorithm of Fig. 9-13. The algorithm has $n - 1$ iterations, where the iteration number i varies from 1 to $n - 1$. During iteration i there are $n - i$ comparison steps to determine the pivot row. Once the pivot row is known, the algorithm must reduce $n - i$ rows, where each row-reduction step requires $2(n - i)$ floating-point operations to modify the coefficients of $\mathbf{A}$, and two more floating-point operations to modify the row's entry in $\mathbf{b}$. Hence the total number of floating-point operations and comparisons is

$$\sum_{i=1}^{n-1} \left((n - i + 1) + \sum_{j=i+1}^{n} \left(1 + \sum_{k=i+1}^{n+1} 2 \right) \right) =$$

$$\sum_{i=1}^{n-1} \left((n - i + 1) + \sum_{j=i+1}^{n} (2n - 2i + 3) \right) = \tag{9.22}$$

$$\sum_{i=1}^{n-1} \left(2n^2 + 4n + 1 + 2i^2 - 4i(n + 1) \right) =$$

$$\frac{2n^3 + 3n^2 - 2n - 3}{3}$$

Most of these operations occur inside the innermost for loop. A study of the algorithm's data dependencies reveals that both the innermost for loop indexed by k and the middle for loop indexed by j can be executed in parallel. In other words, once the pivot row has been found, the modifications to all unmarked rows may occur simultaneously. Within each row, once the multiplier $a[j][i]/a[picked][i]$ has been computed, modifications to elements $i+1$ through n of each row may occur simultaneously. Since most of the operations counted in the last equation occur inside these for loops, the algorithm seems to be well-suited to parallelization.

Let's consider the implementation of gaussian elimination on a multicomputer. Assume n is a multiple of p. How should we distribute the elements of matrices a and b to the memories of the individual processors? If we examine the data flow of the algorithm for iteration i (Fig. 9-14), we see that determining the pivot row $picked$ requires that data items in column i be compared, while determining the new value of a particular element $a[j][k]$ requires three values besides the current value of $a[j][k]$. These values are $a[j][i]$, $a[picked][i]$, and $a[picked][k]$.

Clearly the data distribution determines the points in the algorithm where communication is required. Suppose we assign to each processor a contiguous group of rows of a and the associated elements of b (Fig. 9-15). Given this distribution of data, the processors must interact in order to determine the pivot row. Once the pivot row has been determined, the processor owning the pivot row must broadcast its elements to the other processors, so that they

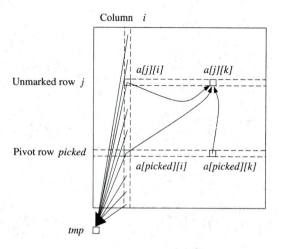

FIGURE 9-14   Data dependencies during a single iteration of the gaussian elimination algorithm. During iteration i the column i element of every unmarked row must be examined to determine the identity of the pivot row *picked*. Once the pivot row has been identified, every element $a[j][k]$ of every unmarked row j must be modified, which requires accessing $a[j][i]$, $a[picked][i]$, and $a[picked][k]$.

FIGURE 9-15   A row-oriented decomposition of the data for the multicomputer-targeted gaussian elimination algorithm. In this example $n = 16$ and $p = 4$.

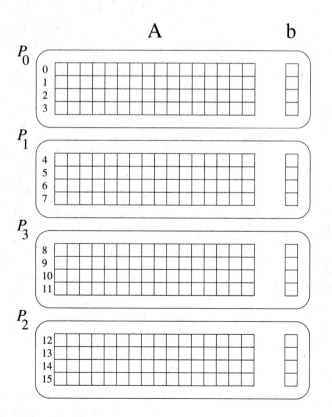

ROW.ORIENTED.GAUSSIAN.ELIMINATION (HYPERCUBE

MULTICOMPUTER):

Local	n	{Size of linear system}
	$a[1...n/p][1...n]$	{Coefficients of equations}
	$b[1...n/p]$	{Right-hand sides of equations}
	$marked[1...n/p]$	{Indicates which rows have been pivot rows}
	$pivot[1...n/p]$	{Indicates iteration each row was used as pivot}
	$picked$	{Row picked as pivot row}
	$magnitude$	{Pivot value}
	$winner$	{Processor controlling pivot row}
	i, j	

begin
  for all P_{id}, where $1 \leq id \leq p$ do

    {Initially no rows have been used as pivot rows}
    for $i \leftarrow 1$ to n/p do
      $marked[i] \leftarrow 0$
    endfor
    for $i \leftarrow 1$ to $n-1$ do

      {Each processor finds candidate for pivot row}
      $magnitude \leftarrow 0$
      for $j \leftarrow i$ to n/p do
        if $marked[j] = 0$ and $|a[j][i]| > magnitude$ then
          $magnitude \leftarrow |a[j][i]|$
          $picked \leftarrow j$
        endif
      endfor
      $winner \leftarrow id$
      {Tournament reduction determines globally best pivot row}
      MAX.TOURNAMENT $(id, magnitude, winner)$
      if $id = winner$ then $marked[picked] \leftarrow 1$ $pivot[picked] \leftarrow i$
        for $j \leftarrow i+1$ to n do
          $tmp.vector[j] \leftarrow a[picked][j]$
          $tmp.vector[n+1] \leftarrow b[picked]$
        endfor
      endif

FIGURE 9-16   Part one of a parallel gaussian elimination algorithm for a hypercube multicomputer, assuming a row-oriented decomposition of the coefficient matrix.

{Processor owning pivot row broadcasts it to other processors}
HYPERCUBE.BROADCAST $(id, winner, tmp.vector[(i+1)..(n+1)])$

{Processors eliminate column i values in their unmarked rows}
for $j \leftarrow 1$ to n/p do
  if marked[j] $= 0$ then
    $tmp \leftarrow a[j][i] / tmp.vector[i]$
    for $k \leftarrow i+1$ to n do
      $a[j][k] \leftarrow a[j][k] - tmp.vector[k] \times tmp$
    endfor
    $b[j] \leftarrow b[j] - tmp.vector[n+1] \times tmp$
  endif
  endfor
endfor

{Locate row never used as a pivot row}
for $i \leftarrow 1$ to n/p do
  if $marked[i] = 0$ then
    $pivot[i] \leftarrow n$
    break
  endif
  endfor
  endfor
end

FIGURE 9-17   Part two of parallel gaussian elimination algorithm for a hypercube multicomputer, assuming a row-oriented decomposition of the coefficient matrix.

can update the values of the umarked rows they control. Pseudocode for this algorithm appears in Figs. 9-16 and 9-17.

We call the processor interaction to determine the pivot row a **tournament**, because we are interested in the identity of the pivot row (the winner) more than the magnitude of the value stored at column i in the pivot row (the score). If we are interested in the identity of the processor with the largest value, we call the interaction a **max-tournament**. If we are interested in the identity of the processor with the smallest value, we call the interaction a **min-tournament**. We can implement a tournament algorithm as a simple variant of the reduction algorithm. Figure 9-18 illustrates max-tournament for a hypercube. At each step of the algorithm, two variables are maintained. Variable $value$ contains the largest value encountered so far, and variable $winner$ contains the number of the processor submitting that value. Although the pseudocode expresses the exchange of these values as two message-passing steps, a real implementation would undoubtedly combine these values into a single structure that could be passed all at once.

A different distribution of data structures results in a different multicomputer algorithm. For example, if we assign to each processor an *interleaved* group

MAX.TOURNAMENT (id, $value$, $winner$)
    Reference id, $value$, $winner$

{This procedure is called from inside a for all statement}
begin
    for $i \leftarrow 0$ to $\log p - 1$ do
        $partner \leftarrow id \otimes 2^i$
        $[partner]tmp.value \Leftarrow value$
        $[partner]tmp.winner \Leftarrow winner$
        if $tmp.value > value$ then
            $value \leftarrow tmp.value$
            $winner \leftarrow tmp.winner$
        endif
    endfor
end

FIGURE 9-18   Pseudocode implementing the max-tournament procedure, which computes the identity of the processor with the largest value.

of columns of a and a copy of b, then the processors do not need to interact to determine the pivot row. Instead, during iteration i the processor controlling column i examines the elements corresponding to unmarked rows and finds the element with the largest magnitude. No tournament is necessary. This processor then broadcasts elements of column i and the identity of the pivot row to the other processors.

Recall that the grain size of a parallel computation is the amount of work performed per processor interaction. The strategy of maximizing grain size, which we have already discussed in the context of multiprocessors, is also important when designing algorithms for multicomputers. (see Design Strategy 5 in Chap. 7.)

On a multicomputer in which message latency is relatively high, maximizing grain size means minimizing the number of messages sent. In particular, if the messages are small, it makes sense to combine messages heading for the same destination processor in order to reduce message passing overhead.

For example, in the row-oriented version of parallel gaussian elimination, the processor controlling the pivot row must make elements $i + 1$ through n of that row available to all the processors executing the for loop. Rather than broadcast these values one at a time, it makes more sense to broadcast the entire set of $n - i$ row elements.

Likewise, the column-oriented, parallel gaussian-elimination algorithm should be implemented so that during iteration i the processor controlling column i combines the elements of column i and the variable containing the identity of the pivot row into a single message.

Comparing the row-oriented versus the column-oriented implementations of gaussian elimination, we see that there is a communication-computation trade-

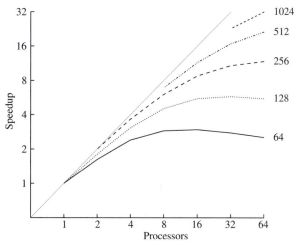

FIGURE 9-19   Scaled speedup achieved by a row-oriented parallel implementation of gaussian elimination on a 64–processor nCUBE 3200, for linear systems of various sizes.

off. In the row-oriented algorithm, processors work together to determine the pivot row. Given a system of size n and p processors, no processor need examine more than n/p values. However, once a processor has determined its local maximum, it must communicate with other processors in order to determine the global maximum. In iteration i of the column-oriented algorithm one processor must perform $n - i$ comparisons, but no communication is required. Both algorithms require a broadcast step after the pivot row has been found. In the case of the row-oriented algorithm a single row is broadcast. In the case of the column-oriented algorithm a single column is broadcast.

For any fixed p, as $n \to \infty$, the time required by the row-oriented algorithm to find the pivot row must be less than that required by the column-oriented algorithm. For this reason, we have chosen to implement the row-oriented algorithm. Figure 9-19 illustrates the scaled speedup achieved by a row-oriented parallel implementation of gaussian elimination on a 64–processor nCUBE 3200, for linear systems of various sizes.

9.5 THE JACOBI ALGORITHM

In the remaining sections of this chapter we will examine iterative methods for solving systems of linear equations. Iterative algorithms are frequently used to solve the large, sparse linear systems generated when working with partial differential equations, using discrete methods. Iterative methods have two advantages over direct methods. First, "while these methods do not formally yield [a solution] in a finite number of steps, one can terminate such a procedure after a finite number of iterations when it has produced a sufficiently good approximate answer." Second, "most iterative schemes possess the attractive feature that they require arithmetic operations only on the nonzero entries of the [coefficient] matrix **A**" (Allen et al. 1988).

Most of the iterative algorithms described in this chapter have the property that, if they converge, then they converge upon a correct solution. However, on some inputs the algorithms may never converge. A discussion of the conditions under which these algorithms converge upon a solution is beyond the scope of this book; see Bertsekas and Tsitsiklis (1989) for a mathematical treatment of this important topic.

The first iterative algorithm to be considered is the Jacobi algorithm. We make the standard assumption that we want to solve the linear system $\mathbf{Ax} = \mathbf{b}$ to determine the value of an unknown vector **x**. Note that

$$x_i = \frac{1}{a_{i,i}}\left[b_i - \sum_{j \neq i} a_{i,j} x_j \right] \tag{9.23}$$

If we knew every value of x_j, where $j \neq i$, we could compute x_i directly. Of course, we do not know these values—they are what we are trying to determine—but if we had an estimate for every such value of x_j, we could come up with an estimate for x_i. The Jacobi algorithm relies upon estimates for every element of vector **x** to come up with a new estimate for **x**. It uses values computed for each variable x_i during iteration t to generate new values during iteration $t + 1$:

$$x_i(t+1) \frac{1}{a_{i,i}}\left(b_i - \sum_{j \neq i} a_{i,j} x_j(t) \right) \tag{9.24}$$

A pseudocode version of the sequential Jacobi algorithm appears in Fig. 9-20.

The Jacobi algorithm is amenable to parallelization because the computation of each element of **x** may proceed simultaneously. The new estimate of **x** is computed from the old estimate of **x** and the value of **A** and **b**.

Let us consider how to implement a parallel Jacobi algorithm on a multicomputer. As in the case of gaussian elimination, the data decomposition determines where in the algorithm communication is required. Suppose each processor is responsible for a contiguous set of rows of **A**, as well as the corresponding elements of **b**. With this data decomposition, processor interaction occurs at two places during every iteration of the do...while loop. First, every processor must have a copy of the entire vector **x** computed during the previous iteration. Hence every processor must broadcast its elements of **x** to all other processors. Second, although each processor may compute a local value of *diff* based upon the change in values of its own elements of **x**, these local values must be combined to yield a global value of *diff*. Hence a max-reduction operation is necessary. At the end of the max-reduction step, every processor will have the same value for *diff*, which will cause all processors to exit the do...while loop on the same iteration.

JACOBI.ALGORITHM.1 (SISD):

Input	n	{Size of linear system}
	ϵ	{Convergence criterion}
	$a[1...n][1...n]$	{Coefficients of linear equations}
	$b[1...n]$	{Constants associated with equations}
Output	$x[1...n]$	{Old estimate of solution vector}
Global	$newx[1...n]$	{New estimate of solution vector}
	$diff$	{Maximum change of any element of solution}
	i, j	{Loop indices}

begin

    {Estimate values of elements of x}
    for $i \leftarrow 1$ to n do
      $x[i] \leftarrow b[i]/a[i][i]$
    endfor

    {Refine estimates of x until values converge}
    do
      $diff \leftarrow 0$
      for $i \leftarrow 1$ to n do
        $newx[i] \leftarrow b[i]$
        for $j \leftarrow 1$ to n do
          if $j \neq i$ then
            $newx[i] \leftarrow newx[i] - a[i][j] \times x[j]$
          endif
        endfor
        $newx[i] \leftarrow newx[i] / a[i][i]$
      endfor
      for $i \leftarrow 1$ to n do
        $diff \leftarrow \max(diff, |x[i] - newx[i]|)$
        $x[i] \leftarrow newx[i]$
      endfor
    while $diff > \epsilon$
end

FIGURE 9-20   Sequential implementation of the Jacobi algorithm.

Figure 9-21 illustrates the parallelizability of the parallel Jacobi algorithm on the nCUBE 3200, for a linear system of size 128.

9.5.1 Sparse Linear Systems

As we discussed earlier, the discretization of partial differential equations often results in sparse linear systems. For example, consider the two-dimensional steady state temperature distribution problem illustrated in Fig. 9-22. A thin

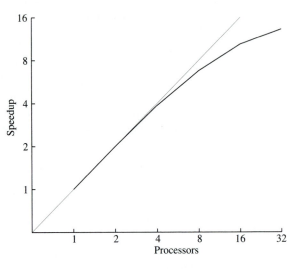

FIGURE 9-21   Parallelizability of the parallel Jacobi algorithm solving a dense 128×128 linear system on the nCUBE 3200 multicomputer.

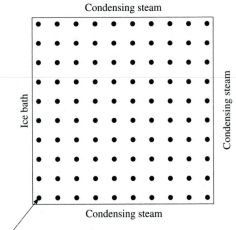

FIGURE 9-22   Two-dimensional steady state temperature distribution problem.

One of 100 points where temperature is to be determined

steel plate is surrounded on three sides by a condensing steam bath (temperature $100°$ C). The fourth side touches an ice bath (temperature $0°$ C). An insulating blanket covers the top and the bottom of the plate. We must find the steady-state temperature distribution at 100 evenly spaced points forming a 10×10 mesh in the plate.

This is an example of a linear second-order partial differential equation. When the steady state temperature distribution has been found, a set of difference equations relates the values of variables on neighboring mesh points:

$$x_{i,j} = \frac{x_{i-1,j} + x_{i,j-1} + x_{i+1,j} + x_{i,j+1}}{4} \tag{9.25}$$

Here the subscripts i and j refer to the coordinates of the mesh points.

We could construct matrix **A** and vector **b** and use the Jacobi algorithm already described to solve for **x**. Because vector **x** has 100 elements, matrix **A** would have size 100×100 and vector **b** would have size 100. This approach is inefficient, because matrix **A** is sparse, with only five nonzero elements per row. With only a constant number of nonzero elements in each row, we waste time executing an $\Theta(n)$ for loop to compute the new value of each element of **x**.

A better approach is constructing a version of the Jacobi algorithm using the previous equation, which performs the same computations more efficiently. In this procedure the values at all the mesh points are simultaneously updated, according to the formula

$$x'_{i,j} = \frac{x_{i-1,j} + x_{i,j-1} + x_{i+1,j} + x_{i,j+1}}{4} \qquad (9.26)$$

The values on the right-hand side of the equation are the old values of the variables; the value on the left-hand side represents the new approximation.

A sequential algorithm to solve the two-dimensional steady state temperature distribution problem appears in Fig. 9-23. Let's consider how to develop a parallel version of this algorithm suitable for implementation on a hypercube multicomputer. Each processor will be responsible for a subset of the elements of the two-dimensional matrix x and the corresponding elements of matrix *newx*. Notice that computing the value of an element of *newx* requires only the values of the four neighboring elements of x. If each processor is assigned a rectangular region of x and *newx*, then computing elements of *newx* on the interior of the rectangle can be performed using locally available values of x. Computing elements of *newx* on the edge of the rectangle require values stored in the memories of other processors. If we assign regions to processors so that neighboring processors control neighboring regions, then nearest neighbor communications are sufficient to implement the parallel algorithm.

If every processor is responsible for a contiguous set of rows or a contiguous set of columns of x and *newx*, then the interprocessor communication pattern for computing *newx* forms a one-dimensional array. If every processor is responsible for a block of elements, the communication pattern forms a two-dimensional array. Both communication patterns map into hypercubes, as we learned in Chap. 5. But which allocation of data to processors results in the faster algorithm?

Suppose we want to map an $n \times n$ mesh onto p processors. To simplify the analysis, assume n is a multiple of both p and $\sqrt{p}$. Consider first the row-oriented data distribution scheme illustrated in Fig. 9-24a. Every processor manages a submesh of size $(n/p) \times n$. During each iteration every interior processor must send n values to both its neighbors and receive n values from these neighbors. If λ is the message latency and β is the time needed to transmit a single value, then the total time spent each iteration communicating values is

$$4(\lambda + n\beta) \qquad (9.27)$$

JACOBI.ALGORITHM.2 (SISD):

Parameter	n	{Number of points in each dimension}
	ϵ	{Convergence criterion}
	$north[1...n]$, $south[1...n]$,	
	$east[1...n]$, $west[1...n]$	{Boundary conditions}
Global	$x[0...(n+1)][0...(n+1)]$	{Solution}
	$newx[0...n+1][0...n+1]$	{New estimate of solution}
	$diff$	{Maximum change}
	i, j	{Loop indices}

```
begin
  {Boundary conditions}
  for i ← 1 to n do
    x[0][i] ← north[i]
    x[n + 1][i] ← south[i]
    x[i][0] ← west[i]
    x[i][n + 1] ← east[i]
  endfor
  {Initialize values of elements of x}
  for i ← 1 to n do
    x[i] ← 50
  endfor
  {Refine estimates of x until values converge}
  do
    diff ← 0
    for i ← 1 to n do
      for j ← 1 to n do
        newx[i][j] ← (x[i − 1][j] + x[i][j − 1] + x[i + 1][j] + x[i][j + 1])/4
      endfor
    endfor
    for i ← 1 to n do
      for j ← 1 to n do
        diff ← max( diff,|newx[i][j] − x[i][j]|)
        x[i][j] ← newx[i][j]
      endfor
    endfor
  while  diff > ϵ
end
```

FIGURE 9-23   Sequential version of the Jacobi algorithm to solve the two-dimensional steady state temperature distribution problem.

FIGURE 9-24   Possible data distributions for solving the two-dimensional steady-state temperature distribution problem on a multicomputer. (a) Illustration of a 16×16 mesh mapped onto 4 processors in a row-oriented fashion. Each processor manages an $(n/p) \times n$ region. Shaded elements must be transmitted to neighboring processor. (b) Illustration of a 16×16 mesh mapped onto 16 processors in a block-oriented fashion. Each processor manages a region of size $(n/\sqrt{p}) \times (n/\sqrt{p})$. Shaded elements must be transmitted to neighboring processor(s).

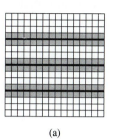

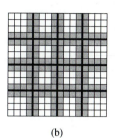

(a)   (b)

Now consider the block-oriented data distribution scheme illustrated in Fig. 9-24b. Every processor manages a submesh of size $(n/\sqrt{p}) \times (n/\sqrt{p})$. During each iteration every interior processor must send $n/\sqrt{p}$ values to all four neighbors and receive $n/\sqrt{p}$ values from these neighbors. The total time spent communicating values in each iteration is

$$8\left(\lambda + \frac{n}{\sqrt{p}}\beta\right) \qquad (9.28)$$

Let's determine when the block-oriented approach is superior to the row-oriented approach.

$$8\left(\lambda + n\beta/\sqrt{p}\right) < 4(\lambda + n\beta) \Rightarrow$$

$$\lambda < \left(1 - 2/\sqrt{p}\right)n\beta \Rightarrow \qquad (9.29)$$

$$n > \frac{\lambda}{\left(1 - 2/\sqrt{p}\right)\beta}$$

For example, suppose we are implementing a parallel version of the algorithm in Fig. 9-23 on a 64–processor multicomputer for which $\lambda = 50\beta$. The block-oriented algorithm is superior to the row-oriented algorithm when

$$n > \frac{50}{\left(1 - \frac{2}{8}\right)1} \approx 66 \qquad (9.30)$$

We assume in our analysis that n is a multiple of p, so we conclude that the row-oriented algorithm is slightly superior to the block-oriented algorithm when $n = 64$, but the block-oriented algorithm is superior for $n = 128, 192, 256, \ldots$.

Until now we have concentrated on the interprocessor communication necessary to compute the value of *newx*. Interprocessor communication is also required to compute the global value of *diff*. On a hypercube multicomputer this reduction step has time complexity $\Theta(\log p)$. In the parallelization of the first Jacobi algorithm for dense linear systems, every iteration already has communication time complexity $\Theta(\log p)$, and the reduction step does not increase the communication complexity of the algorithm. The second Jacobi algorithm relies upon neighbor communications to give each processor the values of x it requires to compute *newx*. In this algorithm the introduction of an $\Theta(\log p)$ communication step would be detrimental to the execution time of the parallel algorithm. We dodge the problem by modifying the algorithm so that the global value of *diff* is updated only once per k iterations, where k is some integer ≥ 1. The best value of k is a function of the architecture and the problem type. If k is too small, time is wasted finding the global value of *diff* when further iterations are necessary. If k is too large, time is wasted performing further iterations when the values of x have already converged on a solution.

9.6   THE GAUSS-SEIDEL ALGORITHM

The Jacobi algorithm attempts to solve the system of equations $\mathbf{Ax} = \mathbf{b}$ through repeated applications of the assignment

$$x_i(t+1)\frac{1}{a_{i,i}}\left(b_i - \sum_{j \neq i} a_{i,j}x_j(t)\right) \tag{9.31}$$

where $x_i(k)$ is the value of x_i computed during iteration k. The Gauss-Seidel algorithm attempts to increase the rate at which the values of $\mathbf{x}$ converge upon a solution by always using the most recently computed value for each element x_i. For example, the following equation illustrates how new values of x_i are computed when the evaluation order is $x_1, x_2, \ldots, x_n$:

$$x_i(t+1)\frac{1}{a_{i,i}}\left(b_i - \sum_{j<i} a_{i,j}x_j(t+1) - \sum_{j>i} a_{i,j}x_j(t)\right) \tag{9.32}$$

Other evaluation orders are also possible. For example, the variables could be updated in the order $x_n, x_{n-1}, \ldots, x_1$. The Gauss-Seidel algorithm can produce different results on the same input if the variable evaluation order is changed.

Let us consider the parallelism inherent in the Gauss-Seidel algorithm. First we consider the case where matrix $\mathbf{A}$ is dense. Assume without loss of generality that the variable evaluation order is $x_1, x_2, \ldots, x_n$. If matrix $\mathbf{A}$ is dense, then the algorithm has a significant sequential component, because the value of $x_i(t+1)$ must be determined before finishing the computation of $x_{i+1}(t+1)$, for all $1 \leq i < n$.

If matrix $\mathbf{A}$ is sparse, then the Gauss-Seidel algorithm is more amenable to parallelization. Consider the solution of the two-dimensional heat equation

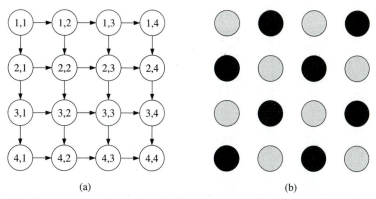

(a)   (b)

FIGURE 9-25   (a) Data dependencies in a single iteration of the Gauss-Seidel algorithm. (b) Two colors are sufficient to label every vertex of the data dependency graph so that each pair of adjacent vertices has one vertex of each color. This is usually called a "red-black" coloring scheme. All vertices having the same color may be updated simultaneously in the parallel Gauss-Seidel algorithm.

seen in Sec. 9.5. The values at all the mesh points are updated according to the formula

$$x_{i,j}(t+1) = \frac{x_{i-1,j}(t+1) + x_{i,j-1}(t+1) + x_{i+1,j}(t) + x_{i,j+1}(t)}{4}$$

Figure 9-25a illustrates the data dependencies for a 4×4 mesh of variables. The new value of $x_{1,1}$ must be computed first. Once the parallel algorithm has computed $x_{1,1}$, it may compute $x_{1,2}$ and $x_{2,1}$ in parallel. With newly computed values of $x_{1,2}$ and $x_{2,1}$, the parallel algorithm may simultaneously compute $x_{1,3}$, $x_{2,2}$, and $x_{3,1}$. At the same time it may compute the next iteration's value for $x_{1,1}$.

Continuing in this fashion, the parallel algorithm in the next step can compute $x_{1,4}$, $x_{2,3}$, $x_{3,2}$, $x_{4,1}$, $x_{1,2}$, and $x_{2,1}$. Concluding this argument, the set of variables is divided into two sets. Each set represents a group of variables that may be updated simultaneously. Figure 9-25b illustrates the partitioning of the variables into these two sets, is called a **red-black coloring** of the data dependency graph.

9.7 JACOBI OVERRELAXATION AND SUCCESSIVE OVERRELAXATION

Jacobi overrelaxation is a variant of the Jacobi algorithm that computes the new value of each x_i through a combination of the old value of x_i and the new value of x_i computed by using the standard Jacobi algorithm. Jacobi overrelaxation replaces the update operation shown in equation 9.24 with

$$x_i(t+1) = (1-\gamma)x_i(t) + \frac{\gamma}{a_{i,i}}\left(b_i - \sum_{j \neq i} a_{i,j}x_j(t)\right) \qquad (9.33)$$

Successive overrelaxation (SOR) is a variant of the Gauss-Seidel algorithm that computes the new value of each x_i through a combination of the old value of x_i and the new value of x_i, computed by using the standard Gauss-Seidel algorithm. Successive overrelaxation replaces the update operation shown in equation 9.33 with

$$x_i(t+1) = (1-\gamma)x_i(t) + \frac{\gamma}{a_{i,i}}\left(b_i - \sum_{j<i}a_{i,j}x_j(t+1) - \sum_{j>i}a_{i,j}x_j(t)\right) \quad (9.34)$$

When γ is chosen properly, Jacobi overrelaxation and SOR can converge to a solution much faster than the Jacobi and Gauss-Seidel algorithms, respectively.

9.8   MULTIGRID METHODS

Multigrid methods form a class of iterative algorithms used for the numerical solution of partial differential equations. The motivation for multigrid methods springs from two observations:

1. Iterative algorithms converge to solutions faster on coarser grids than on finer grids

2. Iterative algorithms converge quicker if the initial approximations of the values of the variables are good

A multigrid method finds a discrete solution to a partial differential equation by iterating between finer and coarser grids, using the values computed at the previous set of grid points to generate initial estimates for the values at the new set of grid points (see Fig. 9-26). In this section we describe the computations performed by multigrid methods and the communications necessary to implement these computations on a multicomputer.

To simplify the discussion, we consider the execution of multigrid methods on two-dimensional grids. Suppose the finest grid, G^0, has dimension $n \times n$, where n is a power of 2. We denote coarser grids by G^i, where $1 \le i < \log n$. With every grid point (i, j) in grid G^k there is an associated variable $x_{i,j}^k$. Multigrid algorithms perform three kinds of computations:

1. *Relaxation:* Compute the values of all $x_{i,j}^k$ on grid G^k. This computation is performed using the Jacobi, Gauss-Seidel, Jacobi overrelaxation, SOR, or another iterative algorithm.

2. *Interpolation:* Compute values of finer grid variables on grid G^{k-1} as a function of coarser grid variables on grid G^k. One interpolation algorithm computes the value of $x_{i,j}^{k-1}$ to be the average of the values on G^k closest to location (i, j). For example, using this interpolation scheme, $x_{3,5}^0$ would be assigned the average of $x_{2,4}^1$, $x_{4,4}^1$, $x_{2,6}^1$, and $x_{4,6}^1$.

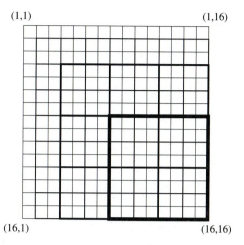

(1,1)   (1,16)

(16,1)   (16,16)

FIGURE 9-26   Illustration of grids used in the multigrid algorithm. The finest (16 × 16) grid is G^0. G^1 is the 8 × 8 grid, G^2 is the 4 × 4 grid, and G^3 is the 2 × 2 grid.

3. *Projection:* Compute values of coarser grid variables on grid G^k as a function of finer grid variables on grid G^{k-1}. A simple projection algorithm, called *injection*, assigns $x_{i,j}^{k-1}$ to $x_{i,j}^k$. For example, using this interpolation scheme $x_{4,4}^2$ would be assigned the value of $x_{4,4}^1$.

We have described the communication requirements of relaxation algorithms in previous sections. Here we focus on the communications required to support interpolation and projection on two-dimensional meshes and hypercubes.

Suppose we map the finest grid G^0 onto an $n \times n$ mesh of processors. Performing relaxation on G^0 requires only nearest neighbor communications. However, the processors that must communicate in order to perform relaxation on the coarser grids G^1, G^2, ..., $G^{\log n}$ are no longer adjacent. Communicating processors are distance two apart when performing relaxation on G^1, distance four apart when performing relaxation on G^2, and so on. Depending upon the hardware of the target architecture, this communication may or may not have a significant impact on the performance of the algorithm.

Now let's consider mapping grids G^0 through $G^{\log n-1}$ onto a hypercube. As we saw in Chap. 5, it is possible to embed a two-dimensional mesh into a hypercube using a binary Gray code. Thus we can map the points of grid G^0 into the nodes of the hypercube so that every pair of neighboring mesh vertices are mapped to neighboring hypercube nodes. However, it is not possible to find a mapping so that this property is preserved for every grid, G^0 through $G^{\log n-1}$, because there are not enough connections. In the worst case, a node has $4 \log n - 2$ neighbors in the $n \times n$ multigrid mesh, while it has only $2 \log n$ neighbors in a hypercube of dimension n^2. For example, consider the 8 × 8 multigrid mesh illustrated in Fig. 9-27. Node 18 has 10 neighbors. Since every node in a 64–node hypercube has only six neighbors, the mesh can't be embedded in the hypercube with dilation 1.

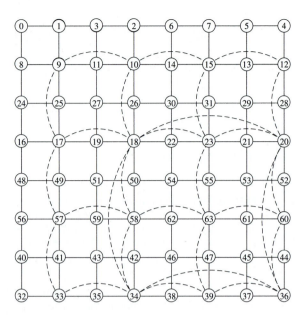

FIGURE 9-27 Mapping a two-dimensional multigrid into a hypercube ensuring that neighboring processors in G^0 are mapped to neighboring nodes in the hypercube, and neighboring processors in G^1 and G^2 are mapped to nodes distance 2 apart in the hypercube.

For this reason we embed the multigrid mesh in the hypercube so that neighboring nodes in G^0 are neighboring nodes in the hypercube and neighboring nodes in G^1 through $G^{\log n}$ are distance 2 away in the hypercube. Using the technique first described in Chap. 5, we divide the processor number into two fields, one representing the row and the other representing the column. We use a Gray code to map adjacent row and column elements to adjacent hypercube nodes.

9.9 CONJUGATE GRADIENT

In this section we describe the conjugate gradient method, used to increase the convergence rate of solutions to linear systems in which the coefficient matrix is positive definite.

An iteration of the conjugate gradient method is of the form

$$x(t) = x(t - 1) + s(t)d(t) \qquad (9.35)$$

The new value of vector $\mathbf{x}$ is a function of the old value of vector $\mathbf{x}$, a scalar step size s, and a direction vector $\mathbf{d}$.

The values of $\mathbf{x}$ are guaranteed to converge in, at most, n iterations. Before iteration 1, values of $\mathbf{x}(0)$, $\mathbf{d}(0)$ and $\mathbf{g}(0)$ must be set. In our implementation of the algorithm $\mathbf{x}(0)$ and $\mathbf{d}(0)$, both are initialized to the zero vector and $\mathbf{g}(0)$ is initialized to $-\mathbf{b}$. Every iteration t calculates $\mathbf{x}(t)$ in four steps.

Step 1: Compute the gradient

$$g(t) = Ax(t-1) - b$$

Step 2: Compute the direction vector

$$d(t) = -g(t) + \frac{g(t)^T g(t)}{g(t-1)^T g(t-1)} d(t-1)$$

where $\mathbf{g}(t)^T \mathbf{g}(t)$ represents the inner product of the transpose of vector $\mathbf{g}(t)$ and vector $\mathbf{g}(t)$.

Step 3: Compute the step size

$$s(t) = -\frac{d(t)^T g(t)}{d(t)^T A d(t)}$$

Step 4: Compute the new approximation of $\mathbf{x}$:

$$x(t) = x(t-1) + s(t)d(t)$$

The conjugate gradient algorithm converges upon a solution after at most n iterations (Bertsekas and Tsitsiklis 1989).

A pseudocode implementation of the conjugate gradient method appears in Fig. 9-28. The program calls subroutines INNER.PRODUCT and MATRIX.VECTOR.PRODUCT, detailed in Fig. 9-29.

Let's consider the parallel implementation of the conjugate gradient algorithm on a distributed memory architecture. Assume each processor has in its local memory one or more rows of a, as well as the corresponding elements of vectors b, d, and g. Given this data decomposition, the only interprocessor communications occur within functions INNER.PRODUCT and MATRIX.VECTOR.PRODUCT.

Inside the parallel version of function INNER.PRODUCT, every processor computes the sum of its local products. When a processor has computed its subtotal, it performs a sum reduction with the other processors to determine the inner product. The parallel version of the function has communication time complexity $\Theta(n/p + \log p)$, where n is the size of the linear system and p is the number of processors.

Function MATRIX.VECTOR.PRODUCT requires each processor to have access to every other processor's portion of vector b at some point during the computation. One way to do this is to fan-in the processors' components of b to the memory of a single processor, then have that processor broadcast the entire array b to the other processors. This strategy results in a communication time complexity of $\Theta(n \log p)$.

CONJUGATE.GRADIENT (SISD):

Parameter	n	{Size of linear system}
	ϵ	{Convergence criterion}
Input	$a[1...n][1...n]$	{Coefficients of linear system}
	$b[1...n]$	{Right-hand side of equations}
Output	$x[1...n]$	{Solution vector}
Global	$d[1...n]$	{Direction vector}
	$g[1...n]$	{Gradient vector}
	i	{Vector element being manipulated}
	$iteration$	{Iteration number}
	s	{Step size}
	$denom1, \ denom2,$	{Temporary variables}
	$num1, \ num2, \ tmpvec[1...n]$	

```
begin
  for i ← 1 to n do
    d[i] ← 0
    x[i] ← 0
    g[i] ← −b[i]
  endfor
  for iteration ← 1 to n do
    denom1 ← INNER.PRODUCT (g[1...n], g[1...n])
    g[1...n] ← MATRIX.VECTOR.PRODUCT (a[1...n][1...n], x[1...n])
    for i ← 1 to n do
      g[i] ← g[i] − b[i]
    endfor
    num1 ← INNER.PRODUCT (g[1...n], g[1...n])
    if num1 < ϵ break endif
    for i ← 1 to n do
      d[i] ← −g[i] + (numerator/denominator) × d[i]
    endfor
    num2 ← INNER.PRODUCT (d[1...n], g[1...n])
      tmpvec[1...n]  ← MATRIX.VECTOR.PRODUCT (a[1...n][1...n],
d[1...n])
    denom2 ← INNER.PRODUCT (d[1...n], tmpvec[1...n])
    s ← −num2 / denom2
    for i ← 1 to n do
      x[i] ← x[i] + s × d[i]
    endfor
  endfor
end
```

FIGURE 9-28   Serial version of the conjugate gradient algorithm.

INNER.PRODUCT $(a[1...n], b[1...n])$:
    Value $a[1...n], b[1...n]$
    Local $i, result$
begin
  $result \leftarrow 0$
  for $i \leftarrow 1$ to n do
   $result \leftarrow result + a[i] \times b[i]$
  endfor
  return $result$
end

MATRIX.VECTOR.PRODUCT $(a[1...n][1...n], b[1...n])$:
    Value $a[1...n][1...n], b[1...n]$
    Local $i, j, result[1...n]$
begin
  for $i \leftarrow 1$ to n do
   $result[i] \leftarrow 0$
   for $j \leftarrow 1$ to n do
    $result[i] \leftarrow result[i] + a[i][j] \times b[j]$
   endfor
  endfor
  return $result[1...n]$
end

FIGURE 9-29 Functions called as subroutines by program CONJUGATE.GRADIENT (see Fig. 9-28). Function INNER.PRODUCT returns a scalar value representing the inner product (dot product) of two vectors. Function MATRIX.VECTOR.PRODUCT returns a vector representing the product of a matrix and a vector.

9.10 SUMMARY

Many problems in science and engineering can be expressed as systems of linear equations. In this chapter we surveyed several sequential algorithms used to solve systems of linear equations, and we considered how to implement parallel versions of these algorithms on both shared memory and distributed memory systems.

We began with an examination of the back substitution algorithm to solve upper triangular systems. Next we considered the odd-even reduction algorithm for solving tridiagonal systems. Then we looked at the well-known gaussian elimination algorithm for solving arbitrary linear systems. All these algorithms are direct—the number of steps performed by the algorithm is independent of the particular system's coefficient values.

The last portion of the chapter discussed iterative algorithms for solving linear systems. The execution time of these algorithms is a function of the co-efficients of the system being solved. Iterative algorithms are frequently used to solve large, sparse systems arising from the solution of partial differential equations. We examined two versions of the Jacobi algorithm. The first is suitable for solving arbitrary systems; the second is useful when variables have a structured relationship to each other, as in the solution to the two-dimensional heat equation. We also looked at the Gauss-Seidel algorithm, which can exhibit faster convergence than the Jacobi algorithm, as well as variants of these algorithms, Jacobi overrelaxation and successive overrelaxation. Multigrid methods, which further accelerate convergence upon a solution, were also discussed. Finally, we discussed the parallelizability of the conjugate gradient algorithm, an iterative algorithm that can converge rapidly onto a solution when the system is positive definite.

9.11 BIBLIOGRAPHIC NOTES

Bertsekas and Tsitsiklis (1989) are the primary source for this chapter. They discuss algorithms to solve nonlinear problems, shortest path problems, network flow problems, and many other topics. Other books that describe parallel numerical algorithms include Dongarra et al. (1991); Fox et al. (1988); Hockney and Jesshope (1981); Hord (1990), Kowalik (1985); and Schendel (1984). Sameh (1977) and Heller (1978) have surveyed parallel numerical algorithms.

Romine and Ortega (1988) have demonstrated that a triangular system solver can be implemented efficiently on a multicomputer "if the machine is able to accomplish fan-in communication reasonably efficiently."

Odd-even reduction (also called cyclic reduction) can be used to solve first-order recurrence relations. The algorithm was introduced by Kogge and Stone (1973).

Many articles describe parallel algorithms for solving tridiagonal linear systems. A sampling includes Kim and Lee (1990); Krechel et al. (1990); Lin and Chung (1990); Piskoulisjki (1992); Reale (1990); Sun et al. [1992]; and van der Vorst (1987a, 1987b).

Bini (1984) presents a parallel algorithm for solving certain Toeplitz linear systems.

Articles on the solution of banded linear systems include Bar-On (1987) and Oyama et al. (1990).

Gallivan et al. (1990) have surveyed parallel algorithms for dense linear algebra computations.

References in the literature to parallel algorithms for solving dense linear systems using gaussian elimination or LU decomposition include Bader and Gehrke (1991); Bampis et al. (1991); Bjorstad (1987); Boreddy and Paulraj (1990); Chu and George (1987); Cosnard et al. (1988); Dongarra (1984); Dongarra and Johnsson (1987); Dongarra and Sameh (1984); Geist and Heath (1986); Marrakchi and Robert (1989); Ortega (1988); Ortega and Romine (1988); Parkinson and Wunderlich (1984); and Yu and Wang (1990).

Sameh and Kuck (1978) and Cosnard and Robert (1986) present parallel algorithms for QR factorization.

Heath et al. (1991) have surveyed parallel algorithms for sparse linear systems. Aykanat et al. (1988) have examined iterative algorithms for solving large sparse systems on hypercube multicomputers. Alaghband and Jordan (1989) have studied sparse gaussian elimination on UMA multiprocessors.

Dimitriadis and Karplus (1990) describe the solution of ordinary differential equations on multiprocessors.

Ortega and Voigt (1985) survey the literature regarding the solution of partial differential equations on vector and parallel computers.

Gropp (1987) and Patrick et al. (1987) have studied the effect of data distribution on the performance of parallel algorithms used to solve partial differential equations. Other papers describing parallel implementation of the SOR algorithm include Bonomo and Dyksen (1989); Evans (1984); and Missirlis (1987); Robert and Trystram (1988) present results that improve upon the work of Missirlis (1987).

Fox and Otto (1984); Reed et al. (1987); and Vrsalovic et al. (1985) explore how the performance of MIMD computers solving partial differential equations is influenced by the interaction between the discretization stencil and the data partitioning.

References to parallel multigrid algorithms include Alef (1991); Chan and Saad (1986); Hoppe and Mühlenbein (1986); Ribbens (1989); and Yadlin and Caughey (1991).

Parallel conjugate gradient algorithms are discussed in Chronopoulos and Gear (1989); Decker et al. (1992); di Brozolo and Robert (1989); Meurant (1987), and O'Leary (1987).

Üresin and Dubois (1990) provide sufficient conditions for the convergence of asynchronous itertive algorithms. Dubois and Briggs (1991) develop a model to estimate the effects of hardware and software contention on the efficiency of asynchronous algorithms.

9.12 PROBLEMS

9-1 Is the linear system that is a result of the problem illustrated in Fig. 9-1 tridiagonal?

9-2 Is the tridiagonal linear system that is a result of the problem illustrated in Fig. 9-2 diagonally dominant? Is it positive definite?

9-3 Why is line 6 of the back substitution algorithm,

$$a[j][i] \leftarrow 0$$

not needed?

9-4 Forward substitution is an analog to the back substitution algorithm. It is used to solve lower triangular systems. Write a sequential forward substitution algorithm in pseudocode.

9-5 Prove that it is possible to implement the odd-even reduction algorithm in $\Theta(n)$ time using $\Theta(n/\log p)$ processors on the CREW PRAM.

9-6* Devise an algorithm implementing gaussian elimination without pivoting on the 2-D mesh SIMD model. Analyze the time complexity of the parallel algorithm.

9-7   Show that a lower bound on the complexity of performing gaussian elimination with row pivoting on the 2-D mesh SIMD model is $\Omega(n^{4/3})$ (Bertsekas and Tsitsiklis 1989).

9-8   Describe a way to reduce the communication overhead of the row-broadcast step of the parallel gaussian elimination algorithm by overlapping some of the communication with computation.

9-9   If a column-oriented gaussian elimination algorithm is implemented, the columns should be interleaved among the processors. In other words, given n columns and p processors, column i should be assigned to processor (i modulo p), for $0 \leq i \leq n - 1$. Why is an interleaved, rather than a contiguous, allocation of columns to processors important for high efficiency?

9-10   Write a multicomputer-targeted gaussian elimination algorithm in which columns of the coefficient matrix **A** are mapped to processors.

9-11   Write a parallel program implementing the more general version of the Jacobi algorithm capable of solving arbitrary linear systems.

9-12   Write a parallel program implementing a version of the Jacobi algorithm capable of solving the two-dimensional heat equation.

9-13   The analysis of the row-oriented versus block-oriented versions of the parallel Jacobi algorithm for the two-dimensional heat equation assumes that sending and receiving messages cannot occur simultaneously. Do the analysis again, assuming that message sends and receives happen simultaneously.

9-14   Write two parallel programs implementing parallel Gauss-Seidel algorithms for UMA multiprocessors. In the first algorithm processes should synchronize when they exchange the values of boundary variables. The synchronization ensures that each process is getting the current value. The second algorithm should be asynchronous. When a process needs the value of a boundary variable updated by another process, it grabs the value currently in that location. Compare the performance of these two parallel programs.

9-15*   Prove that the multigrid-into-hypercube embedding described in this book has the property that neighboring nodes in G^0 are neighboring nodes in the hypercube and neighboring nodes in G^1 through $G^{\log n}$ are distance two away in the hypercube.

9-16   Write a parallel program implementing a simple multigrid algorithm that uses relaxation and interpolation, but not projection. Your algorithm should begin by performing relaxation on the coarsest grid until the values converge, then interpolating these values onto the next finer grid and perform relaxation on that grid. The algorithm should repeat this process until it has performed relaxation on the finest grid.

9-17   Write a parallel program implementing the conjugate gradient algorithm. Test your algorithm on a positive definite system and on a linear system that is not positive definite. What happens in each case?

10

SORTING

Had I been present at the creation, I would have given some useful hints for the better ordering of the universe.

Reaction of Alfonso X to a description of the intricasies of the Ptolemaic system

Sorting is one of the most common activities performed on serial computers. Many algorithms incorporate a sort so that information may be accessed efficiently later. Sorting has additional importance to designers of parallel algorithms; it is frequently used to perform general data permutations on distributed memory computers. These data-movement operations can be used to solve problems in graph theory, computational geometry, and image processing in optimal or near optimal time.

Much work has been done developing parallel sorting algorithms, and we can do little more than explore the basics in this chapter. We will examine a variety of sorting algorithms for processor arrays, multiprocessors, and multicomputers. All these algorithms are **internal sorts**—that is, they sort tables small enough to fit entirely in primary memory. In addition, all the algorithms described in this chapter sort by comparing pairs of elements.

A nonstandard CRCW PRAM can sort n elements in constant time (if the time needed to spawn n^2 processors is not counted). We describe a constant-time enumeration-sort algorithm in Sec. 10.1. In Sec. 10.2 we explore the lower bounds of sorting on more practical parallel architectures. Section 10.3 describes odd-even transposition sort, an optimal algorithm for processor arrays organized as a one-dimensional mesh. The much-cited bitonic merge sort algorithm is the subject of Sec. 10.4. We explore the implementation of bitonic merge sort for a variety of processor organizations. In Sec. 10.5 we discuss several quicksort-based parallel algorithms suitable for implementation on MIMD computers. Section 10.6 describes random read and random write and explains how we can use sorting to implement these general data-routing strategies.

10.1 ENUMERATION SORT

Assume that we are given a table of n elements, denoted $a_0, a_1, \ldots, a_{n-1}$, on which a linear order has been defined. Thus for any two elements a_i and a_j, exactly one of the following cases must be true: $a_i < a_j$, $a_i = a_j$, or $a_i > a_j$. The goal of sorting is to find a permutation $(\pi_0, \pi_1, \ldots, \pi_{n-1})$ such that $a_{\pi_0} \le a_{\pi_1} \le \cdots a_{\pi_{n-1}}$.

An **enumeration sort** computes the final position of each element in the sorted list by comparing it with the other elements and counting the number of elements having smaller value (Knuth 1973). If j elements have smaller value than a_i, then $\pi_j = i$; i.e., element a_i is the $(j+1)$ element on the sorted list, following $a_{\pi_0}, \ldots, a_{\pi_{j-1}}$.

If two or more elements have the same value, we must amend the algorithm slightly. If, for each element in the unsorted list, the algorithm counts the number of elements having smaller value or the same value and smaller index in the unsorted list, the algorithm will produce a unique count for each list element.

Muller and Preparata (1975) have shown that a nonstandard PRAM model can perform an enumeration sort in logarithmic time. In fact, the algorithm requires $\Theta(\log n)$ time to spawn n^2 processors and $\Theta(1)$ time to perform an the sort. If the sort is simply a subroutine to a more general algorithm that requires at least n^2 active processors, then it is fair to disregard the processor spawning time and consider that the sort has constant time complexity.

Imagine a CRCW PRAM model in which, if multiple processors simultaneously write values to a single memory location, the sum of the values is assigned to that location. This model is not as radical as we might think—its conflict resolution mechanism is similar to the fetch-and-add mechanism of the New York University Ultracomputer (Almasi and Gottlieb 1989).

Given n^2 processors, this CRCW PRAM model can compare every pair of elements and compute each element's list position in constant time. Once the machine has computed each element's position, one more step is sufficient to move the element to its sorted location. See Fig. 10-1.

Unfortunately, even if we make the assumptions described earlier and call this a constant-time algorithm, it is not cost optimal. It performs $\Theta(n^2)$ comparisons, whereas a good sequential algorithm can sort a list of n elements with only $\Theta(n \log n)$ comparisons. In addition, the algorithm relies upon a powerful PRAM model. Moving to the CREW PRAM model, for example, would lead to further increases in the cost of the parallel algorithm. Hence we must look elsewhere for a parallel algorithm suitable for implementation on an actual parallel computer.

ENUMERATION SORT (SPECIAL CRCW PRAM):

Parameter	n	{Number of elements}
Global	$a[0...(n-1)]$	{Elements to be sorted}
	$position[0...(n-1)]$	{Sorted positions}
	$sorted[0...(n-1)]$	{Contains sorted elements}

```
begin
   spawn (P_{i,j}, for all 0 ≤ i, j < n)

   for all P_{i,j}, where 0 ≤ i, j < n do
      position[i] ← 0
      if a[i] < a[j] or (a[i] = a[j] and i < j) then
         position[i] ← 1
      endif
   endfor
   for all P_{i,0}, where 0 ≤ i < n do
      sorted[position[i]] ← a[i]
   endfor
end
```

FIGURE 10-1 A set of n elements can be sorted in $\Theta(\log n)$ time with n^2 processors, given a CRCW PRAM model in where simultaneous writes to the same memory location cause the sum of the values to be assigned. If the time needed to spawn the processors is not counted, the algorithm executes in constant time.

10.2 LOWER BOUNDS ON PARALLEL SORTING

Section 10.1 has demonstrated that sorting can be performed in constant time, given enough processors and a model of parallel computation powerful enough. What are the lower bounds for sorting on more reasonable models of parallel computation? In this section we derive lower bounds for sorting on one- and two-dimensional meshes and the shuffle-exchange network.

Theorem 10.1. Assume that n elements are to be sorted on a processor array organized as a one-dimensional mesh. Also assume that before and after the sort the elements are to be distributed evenly, one element per processor. Then a lower bound on the time complexity of any sorting algorithm is $\Theta(n)$.

Proof. The bisection width of a one-dimensional mesh network with n nodes is 1. Suppose the sorted positions of all elements originally on one side of the bisection are on the other side of the bisection, and vice versa. Then all n elements must pass through one link to reach the other side. Since a link can only carry one element at a time, the number of time steps needed to swap elements across the bisection is at least n. Hence a lower bound on the complexity of any sort on the one-dimensional mesh network executing under the given constraints is $\Theta(n)$.

Theorem 10.2. Assume that n elements are to be sorted on a processor array organized as a two-dimensional mesh. Also assume that before and after the sort the elements are distributed evenly, one element per processor. Then a lower bound on the time complexity of any sorting algorithm is $\Theta(\sqrt{n})$.

Proof. The bisection width of a two-dimensional mesh network with n nodes is less than or equal to $\lceil \sqrt{n} \rceil$. Suppose the sorted positions of all elements originally on one side of the bisection are on the other side of the bisection, and vice versa. Then all n elements must pass through one of no more than $\lceil \sqrt{n} \rceil$ links to reach the other side. Since a link can only carry one element at a time, the number of steps needed to swap elements across the bisection is at least $n/\lceil \sqrt{n} \rceil$. Hence a lower bound on the complexity of any sort on a processor array organized as a two-dimensional mesh and executing under the given constraints is $\Theta(n/\lceil \sqrt{n} \rceil) = \Theta(\sqrt{n})$.

Theorem 10.3. Assume that $n = 2^k$ elements are to be sorted on a processor array organized as a shuffle-exchange network. Also assume that before and after the sort the elements are distributed evenly, one element per processor. A lower bound on any sorting algorithm is $\Theta(\log n)$.

Proof. Suppose the sorted position of an element originally at node 0 is node $n - 1$. Moving that element from node 0 to node $n - 1$ demands at least $\log n$ exchange operations and at least $\log n - 1$ shuffle operations. For this reason a lower bound on any shuffle-exchange-based sorting algorithm executing under the given constraints is $\Theta(\log n)$.

10.3   ODD-EVEN TRANSPOSITION SORT

The odd-even transposition sort is designed for the processor array model in which the processing elements are organized into a one-dimensional mesh. Assume that $A = (a_0, a_1, \ldots, a_{n-1})$ is the set of n elements to be sorted. Each of the n processing elements contains two local variables: a, a unique element of array A, and t, a variable containing a value retrieved from a neighboring processing element.

The algorithm performs $n/2$ iterations, and each iteration has two phases. In the first phase, called **odd-even exchange**, the value of a in every odd-numbered processor (except processor $n - 1$) is compared with the value of a stored in the successor processor. The values are exchanged, if necessary, so that the lower-numbered processor contains the smaller value. In the second phase, called **even-odd exchange**, the value of a in every even-numbered processor is compared with the value of a in the successor processor. As in the first phase, the values are exchanged, if necessary, so that the lower-numbered processor contains the smaller value. After $n/2$ iterations the values must be sorted. Fig. 10-2 contains the odd-even transposition sort algorithm. An example of this algorithm's execution appears in Fig. 10-3.

Theorem 10.4. The complexity of sorting n elements on a one-dimensional mesh processor array with n processors using odd-even transposition sort is $\Theta(n)$. (See Habermann 1972.)

ODD-EVEN TRANSPOSITION SORT (ONE-DIMENSIONAL MESH PROCESSOR ARRAY):

Parameter n
Global i
Local a {Element to be sorted}
  t {Element taken from adjacent processor}
begin
  for $i \leftarrow 1$ to $n/2$ do
    for all P_j, where $0 \leq j \leq n - 1$ do
      if $j < n - 1$ and odd(j) then

        {Odd-even exchange}
        $t \Leftarrow successor(a)$ {Get value from successor}
        $successor(a) \Leftarrow max(a, t)$ {Give away larger value}
        $a \leftarrow min(a,t)$ {Keep smaller value}
      endif
      if even(j) then

        {Even-odd exchange}
        $t \Leftarrow successor(a)$ {Get value from successor}
        $successor(a) \Leftarrow max(a,t)$ {Give away larger value}
        $a \leftarrow min(a,t)$ {Keep smaller value}
      endif
    endfor
  endfor
end

FIGURE 10-2   Odd-even transposition sort algorithm for the one-dimensional mesh processor array model.

FIGURE 10-3   Odd-even transposition sort of eight values on the one-dimensional mesh processor array model.

Indices:	0	1	2	3	4	5	6	7
Initial values:	G	H	F	D	E	C	B	A
After odd-even exchange:	G	F <H	D <E	B <C	A
After even-odd exchange:	F <G	D <H	B <E	A <C
After odd-even exchange:	F	D <G	B <H	A <E	C
After even-odd exchange:	D <F	B <G	A <H	C <E
After odd-even exchange:	D	B <F	A <G	C <H	E
After even-odd exchange:	B <D	A <F	C <G	E <H
After odd-even exchange:	B	A <D	C <F	E <G	H
After even-odd exchange:	A <B	C <D	E <F	G <H

Proof. The proof is based upon the fact that after i iterations of the outer `for` loop, no element can be farther than $n - 2i$ positions away from its final, sorted position. Hence $n/2$ iterations are sufficient to sort the elements, and the time complexity of the parallel algorithm is $\Theta(n)$, given n processing elements.

In Sec. 10.2 we derived a lower bound of $\Theta(n)$ for sorting n elements on the one-dimensional mesh processor array model. Hence odd-even transposition sort is an optimal parallel algorithm for this model.

10.4 BITONIC MERGE

In 1968 Batcher introduced a parallel-sorting algorithm with time complexity $\Theta(\log^2 n)$ (Batcher 1968). This algorithm, called **bitonic merge**, is the basis for polylogarithmic time-sorting algorithms on several models of parallel computation. The fundamental operation is called **compare-exchange**: two numbers are routed into a **comparator**, where they are exchanged, if necessary, so that they are in the proper order (Fig. 10-4).

> **Definition 10.1.** A **bitonic sequence** is a sequence of values $a_0, \ldots, a_{n-1}$, with the property that (1) there exists an index i, where $0 \le i \le n - 1$, such that a_0 through a_i is monotonically increasing and a_i through a_{n-1} is monotonically decreasing, or (2) there exists a cyclic shift of indices so that the first condition is satisfied.

If you look at a graph of a bitonic sequence, it contains at most one "peak" and one "valley" (see Fig. 10-5). Remember that the sequence "wraps around" from the last element to the first.

FIGURE 10-4   Two comparators. (a) Low-to-high comparator. (b) High-to-low comparator.

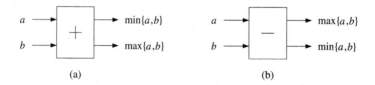

(a)   (b)

FIGURE 10-5   The first three sequences are bitonic sequences; the last sequence is not.

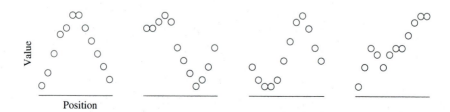

A single compare-exchange step can split a single bitonic sequence into two bitonic sequences, as Lemma 10.1 states.

Lemma 10.1. If n is even, then $n/2$ comparators are sufficient to transform a bitonic sequence of n values,

$$a_0, a_1, a_2, \ldots, a_{n-2}, a_{n-1}$$

into two bitonic sequences of $n/2$ values,

$$\min(a_0, a_{n/2}), \min(a_1, a_{n/2+1}), \ldots, \min(a_{n/2-1}, a_{n-1})$$

and

$$\max(a_0, a_{n/2}), \max(a_1, a_{n/2+1}), \ldots, \max(a_{n/2-1}, a_{n-1})$$

such that no value in the first sequence is greater than any value in the second sequence.

Informal proof. Figure 10-6a contains a generic bitonic sequence before it is split in half. By definition, the sequence contains at most one peak and one valley. We will use $n/2$ comparators to compare every element in the first half of the sequence with the corresponding element in the second half of the sequence. Figure 10-6b

FIGURE 10-6 First part of informal proof of Lemma 10.1. (a) Original bitonic sequence. (b) First half of sequence overlayed on second half of sequence. (c) Minimum values. (d) Maximum values. (e) Transformed sequence.

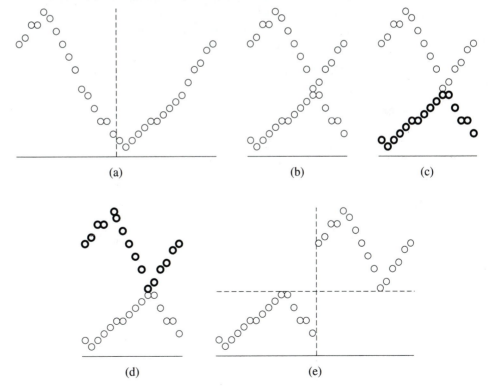

(a)   (b)   (c)

(d)   (e)

shows the two halves overlayed. Figure 10-6c highlights the first half of the trans-formed sequence containing the minimum values emitted by the comparators. The sequence is bitonic, because it contains the valley from the original sequence, plus, at most, one newly introduced peak. Figure 10-6d highlights the second half of the transformed sequence that contains the maximum values emitted by the comparators. The sequence is bitonic, because it contains the peak from the original sequence, plus, at most, one newly introduced valley. Figure 10-6e illustrates the transformed sequence.

We use proof by contradiction to demonstrate that no value in the first half of the final sequence is greater than any value in the second half of the final sequence. If a value in the first half of the final sequence is greater than a value in the second half, then the minimum value returned by one comparator is greater than the maximum value returned by another comparator (Fig. 10-7a). However, if this is true, then the original, nonoverlapped sequence would contain two peaks and two valleys (Fig. 10-7b). In other words, it would not be bitonic. Hence our initial assumption must be false, and no value in the first half of the final sequence is greater than any value in the second half.

We leave a more formal proof to the reader, as Prob. 10.11.

Given a bitonic sequence, a single compare-exchange step divides the sequence into two bitonic sequences half its length (Fig. 10-8). Applying this step recursively yields a sorted sequence. In other words, given a bitonic sequence of length $n = 2^k$, where $k > 0$, then k compare-exchange steps are sufficient to yield a sorted sequence (Fig. 10-9). Figure 10-10 illustrates in detail how a bitonic sequence of length 16 is sorted in four compare-exchange steps.

Theorem 10.5. A list of $n = 2^k$ unsorted elements can be sorted by using a network of $2^{k-2}k(k+1)$ comparators in time $\Theta(\log^2 n)$. (See Batcher 1968.)

Proof. Bitonic merge takes a bitonic sequence and transforms it into a sorted list that can be thought of as half a bitonic sequence of twice the length. If a bitonic sequence of length 2^m is sorted into ascending order, while an adjacent sequence of length 2^m is sorted into descending order, then after m compare-exchange steps the combined

FIGURE 10-7   Second part of informal proof of Lemma 10.1. (a) Suppose the jth element of the first half of the final sequence is greater than the kth element of the last half of the final sequence. (b) If that is true, the original sequence could not be a bitonic sequence.

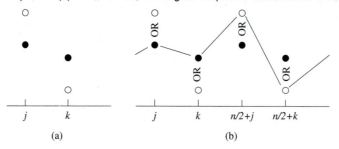

(a)   (b)

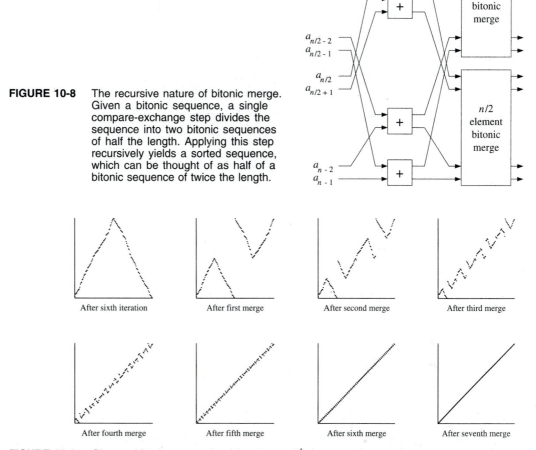

FIGURE 10-8   The recursive nature of bitonic merge. Given a bitonic sequence, a single compare-exchange step divides the sequence into two bitonic sequences of half the length. Applying this step recursively yields a sorted sequence, which can be thought of as half of a bitonic sequence of twice the length.

| After sixth iteration | After first merge | After second merge | After third merge |

| After fourth merge | After fifth merge | After sixth merge | After seventh merge |

FIGURE 10-9   Given a bitonic sequence of length $n = 2^k$, $\log n$ compare-exchange steps transform it into a sorted sequence. In this example seven compare-exchange steps transform a bitonic sequence of length 128 into a sorted sequence of length 128.

sequence of length 2^{m+1} is a bitonic sequence. A list of n elements to be sorted can be viewed as a set of n unsorted sequences of length 1 or as $n/2$ bitonic sequences of length 2. Hence we can sort any sequence of elements by successively merging larger and larger bitonic sequences. Given $n = 2^k$ unsorted elements, a network with $k(k + 1)/2$ levels suffices. Each level contains $n/2 = 2^{k-1}$ comparators. Hence the total number of comparators is $2^{k-2}k(k + 1)$. The parallel execution of each level requires constant time. Note that $k(k+1)/2 = \log n(\log n+1)/2$. Hence the algorithm has complexity $\Theta(\log^2 n)$.

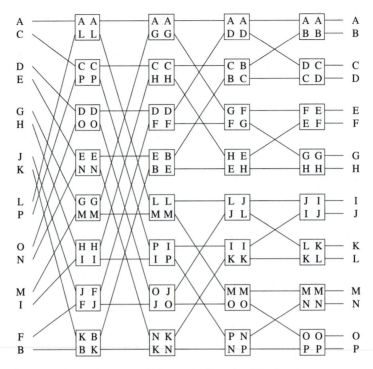

FIGURE 10-10   Sorting a bitonic sequence of length 16 by using bitonic merge.

The graphs in Fig. 10-11 illustrate how a series of bitonic merges sorts a list. Each graph represents a list at some stage of the sort. Unsorted elements form a "cloud" (see the first graph). The sorted elements form a diagonal line (see the final graph). The intermediate graphs show the form of the list after each of $\log n$ iterations. In this case $n = 128$ and $\log n = 7$. Figure 10-9 illustrates what happens on the seventh, and final, iteration. The entire set of n elements has been transformed into a single bitonic sequence, and $\log n$ bitonic merges of shorter and shorter bitonic sequences are enough to complete the sort.

Figure 10-12 shows in detail how a bitonic merge sorts a list of eight elements. The boxes marked with a plus represent comparators that put the smaller value above the larger value. The boxes marked with a minus are comparators that put the larger value above the smaller value.

10.4.1   Bitonic Merge on the Shuffle-Exchange Network

Theorem 10.6. A list of $n = 2^k$ unsorted elements can be sorted in time $\Theta(\log^2 n)$ with a network of $2^{k-1}\left[k(k-1)+1\right]$ comparators using the shuffle-exchange interconnection scheme exclusively. (See Stone 1971.)

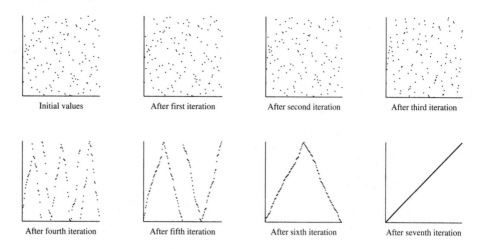

Initial values   After first iteration   After second iteration   After third iteration

After fourth iteration   After fifth iteration   After sixth iteration   After seventh iteration

FIGURE 10-11 Iterations of bitonic mergesort. The list has 128 elements; hence the sort requires $\log 128 = 7$ iterations. Iteration i has i compare-exchange steps, for $1 \le i \le 7$.

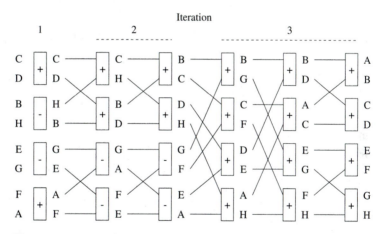

FIGURE 10-12 Bitonic merge-sort of an unsorted list of eight elements.

Stone realized that Batcher's bitonic sorter always compares elements with indices that differ by exactly one bit in their binary representations. Recall that the perfect shuffle routes the element at position i to the position found, by cyclically rotating the binary representation of i one bit to the left. Hence two indices with binary representations differing by exactly one bit can be routed to the same comparator by performing a suitable number of shuffles. Figure 10-13 shows how bitonic merge can be implemented by using the shuffle-exchange interconnection scheme exclusively. Contrast this figure with Fig. 10-10, where the connections between comparators vary from stage to stage. An entire sort

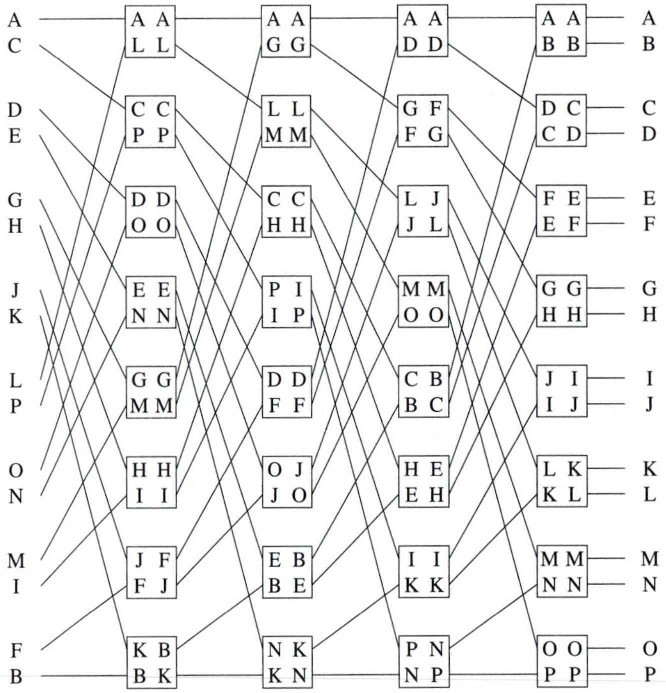

FIGURE 10-13 Sorting a bitonic sequence of length 16 by using Stone's perfect shuffle.

can be accomplished with the shuffle-exchange interconnection. A sort of eight elements appears in Fig. 10-14. Both algorithms require k bitonic merges to sort 2^k elements, but while the ith merge of Batcher's algorithm requires i steps, for a total of $k(k + 1)/2$ steps, the second through kth iterations of Stone's algorithm require k steps, for a total of $k(k - 1) + 1$ steps. For a sort of eight elements there is one extra step in iteration 2, corresponding to the vertical tier of blank boxes in Fig. 10-14. The blank boxes do not perform a compare-exchange operation; they output the values in the same order as they were input. These boxes are used when a number of shuffles are required before the elements to be compared are routed into the same comparator. Note that since the connections between the comparators are the same from step to step, only a single tier of comparators is required (see Fig. 10-15).

A parallel algorithm implementing Batcher's bitonic merge-sort algorithm on the shuffle-exchange processor array model appears in Fig. 10-16. The only tricky part of the algorithm is determining if a pair of elements being compared should be be sorted low to high or high to low. Stone's algorithm uses a mask vector M to indicate the kind of sort to be done by a particular processing element. A value of 0 corresponds to a plus comparator; a value of 1 corresponds to a minus comparator.

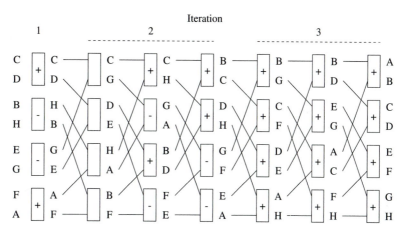

Iteration

FIGURE 10-14   Bitonic merge-sort of an unsorted list of eight elements, by using Stone's perfect shuffle interconnection.

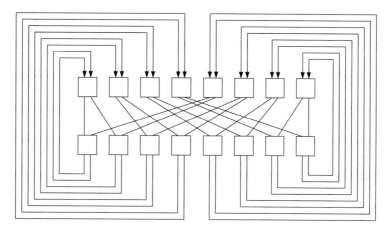

FIGURE 10-15   Sorting machine based upon perfect shuffle connection (Sedgewick 1983).

This algorithm requires $\log n(\log n + 1)/2$ compare-exchange steps, $\log n(\log n - 1)$ shuffle steps of the vector $\mathbf{A}$, and $2 \log n - 1$ shuffles of the vectors $\mathbf{M}$ and $\mathbf{R}$. The time complexity of this algorithm is $\Theta(\log^2 n)$ with n processors.

10.4.2 Bitonic Merge on the Two-Dimensional Mesh Network

Theorem 10.7. An algorithm exists to sort $n = m^2 = 2^k$ elements on the two-dimensional mesh processor array model in time $\Theta(\sqrt{n})$. (See Thompson and Kung 1977.)

BITONIC MERGE SORT (SHUFFLE-EXCHANGE PROCESSOR ARRAY):

Parameter	n	{Size of array}
Global	j, k	
Local	a	{Element to be sorted}
	m	{Mask bit that indicates kind of comparison to perform}
	r	{Bit used to compute mask bit}

begin
  {Compute initial value of the mask M}
  for all P_i where $0 \le i \le n - 1$ do
    $r \leftarrow i$ modulo 2
    $m \leftarrow r$
  endfor
  for $k \leftarrow 1$ to $\log n$ do
    for all P_i where $0 \le i \le n - 1$ do
      $m \leftarrow m \oplus r$ {Exclusive OR}
      $shuffle(m) \Leftarrow m$
    endfor
  endfor

  {Now do the sort}
  COMPARE-EXCHANGE (a, m)
  for $k \leftarrow 1$ to $\log n - 1$ do
    for all P_i where $0 \le i \le n - 1$ do
      $shuffle(r) \Leftarrow r$
      $m \leftarrow m \oplus r$ {Exclusive OR}
      for $j \leftarrow 1$ to $\log n - k - 1$ do
        $shuffle(a) \Leftarrow a$
        $shuffle(m) \Leftarrow m$
      endfor
    endfor
    for $j \leftarrow \log n - k$ to $\log n$ do
      for all P_i where $0 \le i \le n - 1$ do
        $shuffle(a) \Leftarrow a$
        $shuffle(m) \Leftarrow m$
      endfor
      COMPARE-EXCHANGE (a, m)
    endfor
  endfor
end

FIGURE 10-16   Implementation of bitonic merge-sort algorithm on the shuffle-exchange SIMD model.

COMPARE-EXCHANGE (a, m):

Reference a {Element of list to be sorted}

m {Mask bit indicating sort order}

t {Value retrieved from successor processor element}

```
begin
  for all P_i where 0 ≤ i ≤ n − 1 do
  if even(i) then
      t ⇐ exchange(a)
      if m = 0 then                    {Sort low to high}
        exchange(a) ⇐ max(a,t)
        a ← min(a, t)
      else                             {Sort high to low}
        exchange(a) ⇐ min(a,t)
        a ← max(a, t)
      endif
    endif
  endfor
end
```

FIGURE 10-17   Compare-exchange routine called by bitonic merge sort algorithm for shuffle-exchange processor array. The even-numbered processing elements assume the role of comparators.

Summary The algorithm is an adaptation of Batcher's bitonic merge to the mesh. Given $n = 2^k$ elements, bitonic merge-sort consists of k iterations, where each iteration i has i compare-exchange steps. Each compare-exchange requires two data routings: the first routing brings together the elements to be compared, and the second routing redistributes them. Figure 10-18 illustrates a network based on bitonic merge that sorts 16 elements (Knuth 1973). Each row represents the position of an element.

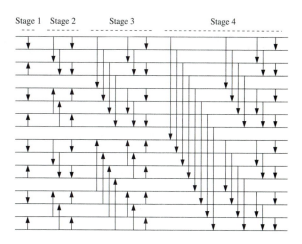

FIGURE 10-18   A sorting network based on bitonic merge. (Knuth 1973.)

Arrows represent compare-exchanges. To perform a compare-exchange, the element at the position marked by the tail of the arrow is routed to the position marked by the arrowhead. After the two elements are compared, the smaller is routed back to the tail position.

Note that elements in positions that differ in their least significant bit are compared every iteration, while elements in positions that differ in their most significant bit are compared only on the last iteration. An efficient implementation of bitonic merge on the two-dimensional mesh processor array model must have the property that, if bit i is less significant than bit j, a compare-exchange on bit i cannot require more data routings than a compare-exchange on bit j. One way to satisfy this condition is to use a "shuffled row-major" addressing scheme, illustrated for a 4×4 mesh in Fig. 10-19a. The advantage of this scheme is that "shuffling" operations occur on square subsections of the mesh, reducing the number of routing operations.

The direction of routing necessary at each compare-exchange step depends upon the index of the particular processor. Figure 10-20 illustrates the bitonic merge sort of 16 elements on a 4×4 mesh. In general, to sort $n = m^2 = 2^k$ elements by using this algorithm requires $\log n$ phases. The total number of routing steps performed is

$$\sum_{i=1}^{\log n} \sum_{j=1}^{i} 2^{\lfloor (j-1)/2 \rfloor}$$

which is $\Theta(\sqrt{n})$. The total number of comparison steps is

$$\sum_{i=1}^{\log n} i$$

which is $\Theta(\log^2 n)$. Thus the worst-case time complexity of bitonic merge on the two-dimensional mesh processor array model is $\Theta(\sqrt{n})$, making it an optimal algorithm for this model.

The function mapping that lists elements into the mesh-connected network is the **index function**. The bitonic merge algorithm sorts the list based on the

FIGURE 10-19   Three index functions mapping list elements into a two-dimensional mesh. (a) Shuffled row-major order. (b) Row-major order. (c) Snakelike row-major order.

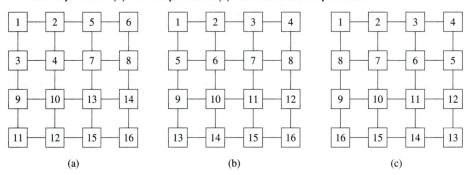

(a)   (b)   (c)

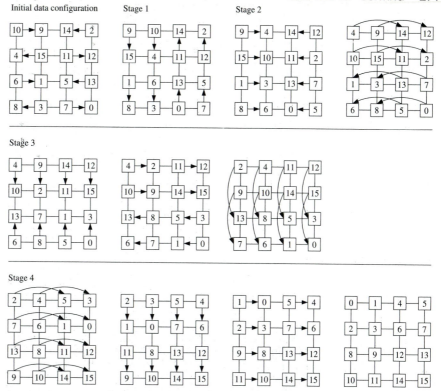

FIGURE 10-20   Sorting values into shuffled row-major order on the two-dimensional mesh processor array model. (Thompson and Kung (1977). Copyright ©1986 Association for Computing Machinery. Reprinted by permission.)

shuffled-row order. What if the sorted list must be arranged in the mesh in row order (Fig. 10-19b) or snakelike order (Fig. 10-19c)? Theorem 10.8 shows that if each processing element has enough memory, the sorted list can be quickly rearranged to the desired order.

Theorem 10.8. If $n = m^2$ elements have already been sorted with respect to some index function, and if each processing element can store m elements, then the n elements can be sorted with respect to any other index function in $\Theta(\sqrt{n})$ time. (See Thompson and Kung [1977].)

10.4.3 Bitonic Merge on the Hypercube Network

Bitonic merge always compares elements whose indices differ in exactly one bit. Since processors in the hypercube processor array model are connected if their indices differ in exactly one bit, it is easy to implement bitonic merge on this model. Processors replace comparators. Instead of routing pairs of elements to comparators, processors route data to adjacent processors, where the elements

BITONIC MERGE SORT (HYPERCUBE PROCESSOR ARRAY):

Global d {Distance between elements being compared}
Local a {One of the elements to be sorted}
        t {Element retrieved from adjacent processor}

```
begin
  for i ← 0 to m − 1 do
    for j ← i downto 0 do
      d ← 2^j
      for all P_k where 0 ≤ k ≤ 2^m − 1 do
        if k mod 2d < d then
          t ⇐ [k + d]a {Get value from adjacent processor}
          if k mod 2^{i+2} < 2^{i+1} then
            [k + d]a ⇐ max (t, a)   {Sort low to high...}
            a ← min (t, a)
          else
            [k + d]a ⇐ min (t, a)      {...or sort high to low}
            a ← max (t, a)
          endif
        endif
      endfor
    endfor
  endfor
end
```

FIGURE 10-21   Implementation of the bitonic merge-sort algorithm on the hypercube processor array model.

are compared. Assume n elements are to be sorted, where $n = 2^m$ for some positive integer m. The parallel algorithm appears in Fig. 10-21.

Clearly the complexity of the parallel for all statement is $\Theta(1)$. Hence the complexity of this parallel algorithm is $\Theta(m^2) = \Theta(\log^2 n)$, given $n = 2^m$ processors.

10.5 QUICKSORT-BASED ALGORITHMS

In Sec. 10.5 we will develop three parallel-sorting algorithms suitable for implementation on MIMD computers. Developing parallel algorithms is easiest when a cost optimal PRAM algorithm exists, in which the processor interactions match the underlying architecture. Unfortunately, we do not have that luxury when it comes to sorting. The cost-optimal PRAM-sorting algorithm of Leighton has time complexity $\Theta(\log n)$ with n processing elements, but its enormous constant of proportionality makes it impractical to use (Leighton 1984). Bitonic merge-sort has cost $\Theta(n \log^2 n)$, which is higher than the cost of the best sequential-sorting algorithms. For this reason we turn to the best general-purpose sequential sorting algorithm—quicksort—as the basis for our parallel algorithms.

10.5.1   Parallel Quicksort

Quicksort is a sorting algorithm commonly used on serial computers. Its popularity is due to its asymptotically optimal average-case behavior of $\Theta(n \log n)$ (Baase 1978).

Quicksort is a recursive algorithm that repeatedly divides an unsorted sublist into two smaller sublists and a supposed median value. One of the smaller sublists contains values less than or equal to the median value; the other sublist contains values greater than the median. The median value, located between the two smaller sublists, is in its correctly sorted position, since all the values to the left are less than or equal to the median value, and all the values to the right are greater than the median value. Given an initially unsorted list, then, the quicksort algorithm chooses one element as the supposed median (e.g., the first element). After a single partitioning step, the list is divided into two sublists, and the algorithm recursively partitions each of the sublists. Quicksort is an example of an algorithm that uses the divide-and-conquer approach. Once a list has been partitioned, the two unsorted sublists form independent problems that can be solved simultaneously.

Consider the following parallel quicksort algorithm. A number of identical processes, one per processor, execute the parallel algorithm. The elements to be sorted are stored in an array in global memory. A stack in global memory stores the indices of subarrays that are still unsorted. When a process is without work, it attempts to pop the indices for an unsorted subarray off the global stack. If it is successful, the processor partitions the subarray, based on a supposed median element, into two smaller arrays, containing elements less than or equal to the supposed median value or greater than the supposed median value, respectively. After the partitioning step, identical to the partitioning step performed by the serial quicksort algorithm, the process pushes the indices for one subarray onto the global stack of unsorted subarrays and repeats the partitioning process on the other subarray. Figure 10-22 illustrates this parallel algorithm.

What speedup can be expected from this parallel quicksort algorithm? Note that it takes $k-1$ comparisons to partition a subarray containing k elements. The expected speedup is computed by assuming that one comparison takes one unit of time and finds the ratio of the expected number of comparisons performed by the sequential algorithm to the expected time required by the parallel algorithm. To simplify the analysis, assume that $n = 2^k - 1$ and $p = 2^m$, where $m < k$. Also assume that the supposed median is always the true median, so that each partitioning step always divides an unsorted subarray into two subarrays of equal size.

With these assumptions the number of comparisons made by the sequential algorithm can be determined by solving the following recurrence relation:

$$T(n) = \begin{cases} n - 1 + 2T((n-1)/2) & \text{for } n = 7, 15, 31, \ldots \\ 2 & \text{for } n = 3 \end{cases}$$

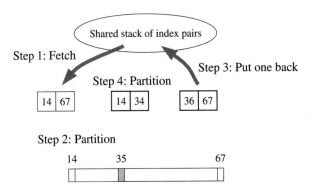

FIGURE 10-22 Illustration of a parallel quicksort algorithm for UMA multiprocessors. A process fetches the indices of an unsorted subarray from a shared stack of index pairs. The process uses the quicksort partitioning step to divide the interval into two subintervals and a median. The process puts the indices of one unsorted subinterval back on the stack and keeps the other index pair, repeating the partitioning step.

	Comparisons	Processors	Time
	$n-1$	1	$n-1$
	$n-3$	2	$(n-3)/2$
	$n-7$	4	$(n-7)/4$

FIGURE 10-23 A view of the beginning of parallel quicksort, when the the number of unsorted intervals is less than or equal to the number of processes. The analysis assumes $n = 2^k - 1$ and every partitioning step divides an interval exactly in half.

The solution to this recurrence relation is

$$T(n) = (n + 1)\log(n + 1) - 2n$$

The parallel algorithm has two phases. First, there are more processes to be sorted than arrays (see Fig. 10-23). For example, when the algorithm begins execution there is only a single unsorted array. All but one of the processes must wait while a single process partitions that array. This iteration, then, requires $n-1$ time units to perform $n-1$ comparisons. If we assume $p \geq 2$, two processes can partition the two resulting subarrays in $(n-1)/2-1 = (n-3)/2$ time units, performing $n - 3$ comparisons. Similarly, if $p \geq 4$, the third iteration requires time at least $[(n - 1)/2 - 1]/2 - 1 = (n - 7)/4$ to perform $n - 7$ comparisons. For the first $\log p$ iterations, there are at least as many processes as partitions, and the time required by this phase of the parallel quicksort algorithm is

$$T_1(n, p) = 2(n + 1)(1 - 1/p) - \log p$$

The number of comparisons performed is

$$C_1(n, p) = (n + 1) \log p - 2(p - 1)$$

In the second phase of the parallel algorithm there are more subarrays to be sorted than processes. All the processes are active. If we assume that every process performs an equal share of the comparisons, then the time required is simply the number of comparisons performed divided by p. Hence

$$C_2(n, p) = T(n) - C_1(n, p)$$

$$T_2(n, p) = \frac{C_2(n, p)}{p}$$

The estimated speedup achievable by the parallel quicksort algorithm is the sequential time divided by the parallel time:

$$\text{Speedup} = \frac{T(n)}{T_1(n, p) + T_2(n, p)}$$

For example, the best speedup we could expect with $n = 65,535$ and $p = 16$ is approximately 5.6. Why is speedup so low? The problem with quicksort is its divide-and-conquer nature. Until the first subarray is partitioned, there are no more partitionings to do. Even after the first partitioning step is complete, there are only two subarrays to work with. Hence many processes are idle at the beginning of the parallel algorithm's execution, waiting for work.

Figure 10-24 contains pseudocode for a UMA multiprocessor-oriented parallel quicksort algorithm, which uses the strategy we have discussed. Function INITIALIZE.STACK initializes the shared stack containing the indices of unsorted subarrays. When a process calls function STACK.DELETE, it receives the indices of an unsorted subarray if the stack contains indices; otherwise, the "low" index is greater than the "high" index, meaning there is no useful work to do at this point. Function STACK.INSERT adds the indices of an unsorted subarray to the stack. Since all these functions access the same shared data structure, their execution must be mutually exclusive. Function ADD.TO.SORTED increases the count of elements that are in their correct positions and execution of this function, too, must be mutually exclusive. We use monitors to implement these functions.

As the pseudocode algorithm shows, we use the familiar strategy of switching from quicksort to insertion sort when the size of the array to be partitioned falls below a predetermined threshold (Sedgewick 1988).

Figure 10-25 compares the predicted speedup with the actual speedup achieved by a Sequent C implementation of the algorithm sorting 65,535 integers on a lightly loaded Symmetry multiprocessor. The correlation is reasonably good, considering the analysis made the simplifying assumption that each partitioning step always divides an unsorted subarray into two subarrays of equal size.

QUICKSORT (UMA MULTIPROCESSOR):

Global n {Size of array of unsorted elements}
               $a[0...(n-1)]$ {Array of elements to be sorted}
               $sorted$ {Number of elements in sorted position}
               $min.partition$ {Smallest subarray that is partitioned rather than sorted directly}

Local $bounds$ {Indices of unsorted subarray}
               $median$ {Final position in subarray of partitioning key}

begin
  $sorted \leftarrow 0$
  INITIALIZE.STACK()

  for all P_i, where $0 \leq i < p$ do
    while ($sorted < n$) do
      $bounds \leftarrow$ STACK.DELETE()

      while ($bounds.low < bounds.high$) do
        if ($bounds.high - bounds.low < min.partition$) then
          INSERTION.SORT ($a, bounds.low, bounds.high$)
          ADD.TO.SORTED ($bounds.high - bounds.low + 1$)
          exit while
        else
          $median \leftarrow$ PARTITION ($bounds.low, bounds.high$)
          STACK.INSERT ($median + 1, bounds.high$)
          $bounds.high \leftarrow median - 1$

          if $bounds.low = bounds.high$ then
            ADD.TO.SORTED (2)
          else
            ADD.TO.SORTED (1)
          endif
        endif
      endwhile
    endwhile
  endfor
end

FIGURE 10-24   Multiprocessor-oriented parallel quicksort algorithm. A shared stack contains the indices of unsorted subarrays. Processes must execute functions STACK.DELETE(), ADD.TO.SORTED(), and STACK.INSERT() inside critical sections to ensure mutual exclusion.

10.5.2 Hyperquicksort

We have seen that the speedup achieved through the parallel quicksort algorithm is constrained by the time taken to perform the initial partitioning steps, when not all processors are active. A number of parallel algorithms have

FIGURE 10-25 Predicted speedup (dashed line) and actual speedup (solid line) of parallel quicksort algorithm. Actual speedup data collected on a lightly loaded 20-processor Sequent Symmetry running the PTX operating system.

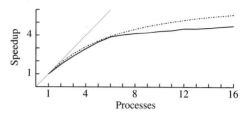

been developed to put all processors to work immediately. Here we describe one such algorithm, hyperquicksort, suitable for implementation on hypercube multicomputers.

Given a list of values initially distributed evenly among the processors of a multicomputer, we define the list to be sorted when (1) every processor's list of values is sorted, and (2) the value of the last element on P_i's list is less than or equal to the value of the first element on P_{i+1}'s list, for $0 \le i \le p - 2$. Note that the sorted values need not be distributed evenly among the processors.

To develop an efficient algorithm, we apply the strategy of letting each processor solve a subproblem using the most efficient sequential algorithm, then using a communication-efficient parallel algorithm to generate the final solution from the partial solutions.

In the first phase of hyperquicksort each processor uses quicksort to sort its local list of values. At this point every processor has a sorted list of values, satisfying condition (1) of the sortedness requirement, but not condition (2). Hyperquicksort is a recursive algorithm that uses a divide-and-conquer approach to fulfill the second condition. During each step of the second phase of the algorithm, a hypercube is split into two subcubes. Each processor sends values to its partner in the other subcube, then each processor merges the values it keeps with the values it receives. The effect of this split-and-merge operation is to divide a hypercube of sorted values into two hypercubes so that each processor has a sorted list of values, and the largest value in the lower hypercube is less than the smallest value in the upper hypercube. After d such split-and-merge steps, the original 2^d processor hypercube has been divided into 2^d single-processor hypercubes, and condition (2) is satisfied. The algorithm is illustrated in Fig. 10-26.

The split-and-merge step divides a d-dimensional hypercube into two hypercubes of dimension $d - 1$. Recall that each processor's values are sorted. A designated processor in the d-dimensional hypercube broadcasts its median value to the $2^d - 1$ other processors in the hypercube. Every processor uses this splitter value to divide its list into two portions: those less than or equal to the splitter and those greater than the splitter. Every processor P_i in the lower half of the hypercube sends the upper portion of its sorted list—those values greater than the splitter—to its partner in the upper half, processor $P_i \otimes 2^{d-1}$ (where $\otimes$ denotes the bit-wise "exclusive or" operation). Every processor P_i in the upper half of the hypercube sends the lower portion of its sorted list—those values

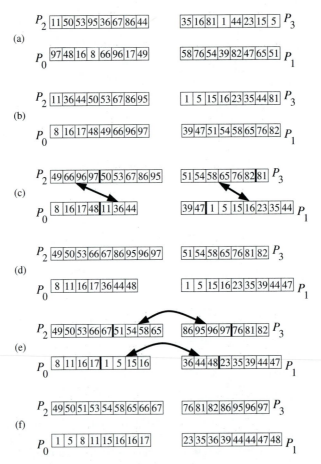

FIGURE 10-26 Illustration of the hyperquicksort algorithm. In this example 32 elements are being sorted on a two-dimensional hypercube. (a) Initially, each processor has eight elements. (b) Each processor performs sequential quicksort on its own list. Processor 0 broadcasts its median value, 48, to the other processors. (c) Processors in the lower half of the hypercube send values greater than 48 to processors in the upper half of the hypercube. The processors in the upper half send values less than or equal to 48. (d) Each processor merges the elements it kept with the elements it received. Processor 0 broadcasts its median value to processor 1, and processor 2 broadcasts its median value to processor 3. (e) Processors swap values across another hypercube dimension. (f) Each processor merges the elements it kept with the elements it received. At this point the list is sorted.

less than or equal to the splitter—to its partner in the lower half, processor $P_i \otimes 2^{d-1}$. Each processor merges the list it receives with the list it keeps to form a new sorted list. Here, all values less than or equal to the splitter are in lower $(d-1)$-dimensional hypercube, and all values greater than the splitter are in the upper $(d-1)$-dimensional hypercube. Figure 10-27 presents the hyperquicksort algorithm in pseudocode.

HYPERQUICKSORT (HYPERCUBE MULTICOMPUTER):

Global	n	{Initial number of elements per processor}
	d	{Dimension of hypercube}
	i	{Dimension number of current hypercube}
Local	*logical.num*	{Unique processor number}
	partner	{Processor's partner in the exchange}
	root	{Root processor of current hypercube}
	splitter	{Median of root processor's sorted list}

begin
   for all P_j, where $0 \leq j < 2^d$ do
     Sort n values using sequential quicksort algorithm
     if $d > 0$ then
       for $i \leftarrow d$ downto 1 do
         root $\leftarrow$ root of the binary i-cube containing processor *logical_num*
         if *logical.num* = *root* then
          splitter $\leftarrow$ median of the sorted list held by processor *logical_num*
         endif
         Processor *root* broadcasts *splitter* to other processors in binary i-cube
         Use *splitter* to partition sorted values into low list, high list
         partner $\leftarrow$ *logical_num* $\otimes$ $2^{(i-1)}$ { Bitwise exclusive "or" }
         if *logical.num* > *partner* then
          Send low list to processor *partner*
          Receive another high list from processor *partner*
         else {*logical.num* < *partner*}
          Send high list to processor *partner*
          Receive another low list from processor *partner*
         endif
         Merge two lists into a single sorted list of values
       endfor
     endif
   endfor
end

FIGURE 10-27   Pseudocode version of hyperquicksort algorithm.

    Suppose at the start of the algorithm each processor has n values. The expected time complexity of the initial quicksort step is $\Theta(n \log n)$. Assuming that each processor keeps $n/2$ values and transmits $n/2$ values in every split-and-merge step, the expected number of comparisons needed to merge the two lists into a single ordered list is $\Theta(n)$. Since the split-and-merge operation is executed for hypercubes of dimension $d, d-1, \ldots, 1$, the expected number of comparisons performed over the split-and-merge phase of the algorithm is $\Theta(nd)$, and the expected number of comparisons performed during the entire algorithm is $\Theta(n(\log n + d))$.

    Let λ denote message latency and β denote the the time needed to transmit a value from one processor to an adjacent processor. Given a d-dimensional cube, broadcasting the splitter value requires communication time $d(\lambda + \beta)$.

Assuming each processor passes half its values, the time needed to send $n/2$ sorted values and receive $n/2$ sorted values from the partner processor is $2\lambda + n\beta$. The expected communication time for the split-and-merge phase is $\sum_{i=1}^{d}(i(\lambda + \beta) + 2\lambda + n\beta) = d(d + 1)(\lambda + \beta)/2 + d(2\lambda + n\beta)$. Since the original quicksort phase requires no interprocessor communications, this value is the expected communication time of the entire hyperquicksort algorithm.

If we know the computation speed, message initiation time, and communication speed of a particular hypercube architecture, we can use this analysis to predict the speedup achievable by the hyperquicksort algorithm. For example, sequential quicksort implemented in C on the NCUBE 3200 requires about 12.2 microseconds per comparison, while $\lambda = 500$ microseconds and $\beta = 11$ microseconds (Quinn 1989).

Figure 10-28 compares the predicted and actual speedup of the hyperquicksort algorithm sorting 16,384 integers on an nCUBE 3200 hypercube multicomputer (Quinn 1989). The predicted speedup is somewhat optimistic. Because the median of a single processor's list is almost certainly not the median of the entire set of values, it is likely that, at the end of the hyperquicksort algorithm, some processors will contain more values than others. This uneven distribution affects the execution time, because processors with more values must spend more time merging. It also affects the communication complexity, because communication time is a function of message length.

One way to make the final distribution of values more balanced is to modify the step that selects the splitter. Rather than let a single processor choose its

FIGURE 10-28 Predicted speedup (dashed line) and actual speedup (solid line) of hyperquicksort algorithm sorting 16,384 integers on an nCUBE 3200 hypercube multicomputer (Quinn 1989).

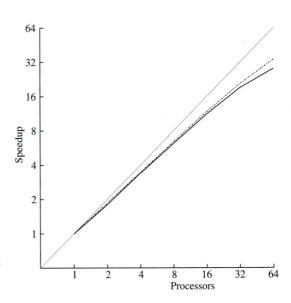

median to be the splitter for a d-dimensional hypercube, calculate the splitter as the mean of all 2^d processors' median values. Implementing this modification means introducing a fan-in step before the broadcast step every time the split-and-merge is performed, doubling the communication time. We call this algorithm *modified hyperquicksort*.

Quinn (1989) implemented the modified hyperquicksort algorithm and discovered that for lists of this size, hyperquicksort slightly outperforms modified hyperquicksort. The modified hyperquicksort algorithm does a better job balancing the number of elements managed by each processor, reducing the variance in the time the processors spend merging their lists. However, this time savings is wiped out by the increase in time spent passing messages to compute the new splitter value.

10.5.3   Parallel Sorting by Regular Sampling

The following algorithm, developed by Li et al. (1992), has been shown effective for a wide variety of MIMD architectures. Li et al. call their algorithm "parallel sorting by regular sampling;" henceforth we shall refer to it as the PSRS algorithm.

The PSRS algorithm has four phases (Fig. 10-29). Assume the list has n elements. In phase one each of the p processors uses the sequential quicksort algorithm to sort a contiguous set of no more than $\lceil n/p \rceil$ elements. The n elements now form p independent lists of size no more than $\lceil n/p \rceil$. Each processor selects data items at local indices 1, $(n/p^2) + 1$, $(2n/p^2) + 1$, $\dots$, $(p-1)(n/p^2) + 1$ as a regular sample of its locally sorted block.

In the second phase of the algorithm one processor gathers and sorts the local regular samples. It selects $p - 1$ pivot values from the sorted list of regular samples. The pivot values are at indices $p + \lfloor p/2 \rfloor$, $2p + \lfloor p/2 \rfloor$, $\dots$, $(p-1)p + \lfloor p/2 \rfloor$ in the sorted list of regular samples. At this point each processor partitions its sorted sublist into p disjoint pieces, using the pivot values as separators between the pieces.

In the third phase of the algorithm each processor i keeps its ith partition and assigns the jth partition to processor j. In other words, each processor keeps one partition and reassigns $p - 1$ other partitions to other processors.

During the fourth phase of the algorithm each processor merges its p partitions into a single list. The values on this list are disjoint from the values on the lists of the other processors. The concatenation of the processor's individual lists forms the final sorted list.

To simplify the following analysis of the PSRS algorithm, we assume that p processors sort n distinct elements, where p is even, $n = p^2 k$ and k is a positive integer. For a more rigorous analysis, see Li et al. (1992).

Definition 10.2. Let $X = \{X_1, \dots, X_n\}$ denote the list of n elements to be sorted.

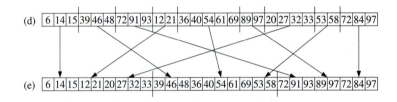

(a) | 15 46 48 93 39 6 72 91 14 36 69 40 89 61 97 12 21 54 53 97 84 58 32 27 33 72 20 |

(b) | 6 14 15 39 46 48 72 91 93 12 21 36 40 54 61 69 89 97 20 27 32 33 53 58 72 84 97 |

(c) Regular samples: 6 39 72   12 40 69   20 33 72

Sorted regular samples: 6 12 20 33 39 40 69 72 72

Pivots: 33 69

(d) | 6 14 15 39 46 48 72 91 93 12 21 36 40 54 61 69 89 97 20 27 32 33 53 58 72 84 97 |

(e) | 6 14 15 12 21 20 27 32 33 39 46 48 36 40 54 61 69 53 58 72 91 93 89 97 72 84 97 |

(f) | 6 12 14 15 20 21 27 32 33 36 39 40 46 48 53 54 58 61 69 72 72 84 89 91 93 97 97 |

FIGURE 10-29 This example illustrates how three processors would sort 27 elements using the PSRS algorithm. (a) Original unsorted list of 27 elements. (b) Each processor sorts its share of the list (nine elements) using sequential quicksort algorithm. (c) Select regular samples from each sorted sublist (first, fourth, and seventh elements). One processor sorts these elements using sequential quicksort. Choose pivot elements (fourth and seventh elements). (d) Use pivots computed in step (c) to divide each sorted sublist into three parts. (e) Copy sorted sublists into new array so that elements having the same relation to the pivots are placed together. (f) Each processor merges its sorted sublists.

Definition 10.3. Let $Y = \{Y_1, Y_2, \ldots, Y_{p^2}\}$ denote the sorted set of p^2 regular samples selected from the p sorted sublists of X.

Definition 10.4. Let $N(cond)$ denote the number of elements of X which satisfy a certain boolean condition $cond$.

For example, $N(\leq Y_2)$ is the number of elements of X less than or equal to Y_2, the second regular sample selected from the sorted sublists of X.

First we establish a lower bound on the number of elements in X less than or equal to certain elements of the sample set Y.

Lemma 10.2. For $1 \leq i \leq p$

$$N(\leq Y_{(i-1)p+p/2}) \geq \begin{cases} \frac{p}{2}, & \text{if } i = 1 \\ \frac{n}{p^2}((i-1)p - \frac{p}{2}) + p, & \text{if } i > 1 \end{cases}$$

Proof. When $i = 1$, $Y_{(i-1)p+p/2}$ is $Y_{p/2}$. Since the elements of Y are sorted, there are $p/2$ elements of Y less than or equal to $Y_{p/2}$. The elements of Y are selected from X. Hence there are at least $p/2$ elements of X less than or equal to $Y_{p/2}$.

Each element of Y represents a set of n/p^2 elements of X with equal or greater value. When $i > 1$, the sum $(i - 1)p + p/2$ is greater than p. This means that when we consider the samples Y_1, Y_2, ... , $Y_{(i-1)p+p/2}$, some samples must have come from the same processor. If Y_j and Y_k are from the same processor and $j < k$, then all of the n/p^2 elements of X represented by Y_j must be less than or equal to Y_k. This in turn is less than or equal to $Y_{(i-1)p+p/2}$. For the p samples representing the largest elements of Y associated with each processor, we only know that the samples themselves are less than or equal to $Y_{(i-1)p+p/2}$. Hence the number of elements of X less than or equal to elements of Y is

$$N(\leq Y_{(i-1)p+p/2}) = \frac{n}{p^2}((i - 1)p + \frac{p}{2} - p) + (1)p$$

$$= \frac{n}{p^2}\left((i - 1)p - \frac{p}{2}\right) + p$$

Now we determine an upper bound on the number of elements of X greater than certain elements of the sample set Y.

Lemma 10.3. For $1 \leq i \leq p$

$$N(> Y_{ip+p/2}) \geq \frac{n}{p^2}((p - i)p - \frac{p}{2} + 1) - 1$$

Proof. There are $p^2 - (ip + p/2) = (p - i)p - p/2$ samples greater than $Y_{ip+p/2}$. That means the $(n/p^2)((p - i)p - p/2)$ elements of X associated with these samples are all greater than $Y_{ip+p/2}$. The $n/p^2 - 1$ elements of X immediately following $Y_{ip+p/2}$ are also greater than $Y_{ip+p/2}$. Hence

$$N(> Y_{ip+p/2}) \geq \frac{n}{p^2}((p - i)p - \frac{p}{2}) + (\frac{n}{p^2} - 1)$$

$$\geq \frac{n}{p^2}((p - i)p - \frac{p}{2} + 1) - 1$$

Definition 10.5. Let Φ_i denote the number of X elements merged by processor i in phase four of the PSRS algorithm.

Theorem 10.9. An upper bound on $\max_{1 \leq i \leq p} \Phi_i$ is $2n/p - n/p^2 - p + 1$.

Proof. We begin by deriving upper bounds for Φ_i for each of the three cases $i = 1$, $i = p$, and $1 < i < p$.
Case 1: $i = 1$.

All the X elements merged by processor 1 must be less than or equal to $Y_{p+p/2}$. By Lemma 10.3 we know that

$$N(> Y_{p+p/2}) \geq \frac{n}{p^2}((p - 1)p - \frac{p}{2} + 1) - 1$$

Hence

$$\Phi_1 = N(\leq Y_{p+p/2}) \leq n - \frac{n}{p^2}((p-1)p - \frac{p}{2} + 1) - 1$$

$$\leq \frac{n}{p^2}(p + \frac{p}{2} - 1) + 1$$

Case 2: $i = p$

All the X elements merged by processor p must be greater than $Y_{(p-1)p+p/2}$. By Lemma 10.2 we know that

$$N(\leq Y_{(p-1)p+p/2}) \geq \frac{n}{p^2}((p-1)p - \frac{p}{2}) + p$$

Hence

$$\Phi_p = n - N(\leq Y_{(p-1)p+p/2}) \leq \frac{n}{p^2}(p + \frac{p}{2}) - p$$

Case 3: $1 < i < p$

The number of elements merged by processor i is equal to $n - N(\leq Y_{(i-1)p+p/2})$ $-N(> Y_{ip+p/2})$. Applying Lemmas 10.2 and 10.3:

$$\Phi_i \leq n - \left(\frac{n}{p^2}((i-1)p - \frac{p}{2}) + p \right) - \left(\frac{n}{p^2}((p-i)p - \frac{p}{2} + 1) - 1 \right)$$

$$\leq \frac{n}{p^2}(2p - 1) - p + 1$$

The largest upper bound for Φ_i comes from Case 3. Hence an upper bound on the number of X elements merged by any processor in phase four of the PSRS algorithm is $2n/p - n/p^2 - p + 1$.

Now that we have established an upper bound on the number of elements that any processor may have to merge in phase four of the PSRS algorithm, we can analyze the algorithm's computational complexity.

In phase one each processor performs quicksort on n/p elements. The computational complexity is $O((n/p) \log(n/p)) = O(n/p \log n)$. (Actually, $O(n \log n)$ is the expected time complexity of performing quicksort on a list of n elements; the worst-case time complexity is $O(n^2)$. However, we will assume $O(n \log n)$ complexity in our analysis. If we must use the worst-case complexity in the analysis, we could substitute mergesort or another algorithm with worst-case time complexity $O(n \log n)$.)

In phase two of the algorithm one processor sorts the p^2 elements of Y. This step has complexity $O(p^2 \log p^2) = O(p^2 \log p)$.

In phase three of the algorithm each processor sends portions of its section of X to the other processors. Since each processor has n/p elements, the complexity is $O(n/p)$ (ignoring message-startup times on distributed memory systems).

In the fourth phase of the algorithm each processor merges p sorted sublists. From Theorem 10.9 we know that no processor has more than $2n/p$ elements to merge. The time complexity of the merge phase is $O(n/p \log p)$.

The overall computational complexity of the PSRS algorithm is $O((n/p) \log n + p^2 \log p + n/p \log p)$. If $n \geq p^3$, the first term dominates, and the complexity of the algorithm is $O((n/p) \log n)$, which is cost optimal.

Li et al. (1992) have implemented the PSRS algorithm on a variety of different MIMD architectures. Figure 10-30 illustrates the speedup achieved by the PSRS algorithm on the BBN TC2000, a NUMA multiprocessor. Figure 10-31 presents the speedup achieved on the iPSC/860 multicomputer. The algorithm achieves good speedup on both architectures.

Li et al. (1992) have also measured the relative deviation in size between the largest partition merged in phase four and the average partition size. Their experiments show that if the elements are selected from a uniform random distribution, the largest partition size is usually no more than a few percent larger than n/p, the averge partition size.

Looking back at our three quicksort-based parallel sorting algorithms, we see that hyperquicksort and the PSRS algorithm achieve better speedup and are more scalable than parallel quicksort. Hyperquicksort and the PSRS algorithm reflect better attention to the parallel algorithm design strategies we have developed. In particular, they are data-parallel algorithms, each processor performs the most efficient sequential algorithm on its share of the data, and grain size is maximized.

FIGURE 10-30   Speedup achieved by the PSRS sorting algorithm on the BBN TC200, a NUMA multiprocessor (Li et al. 1992).

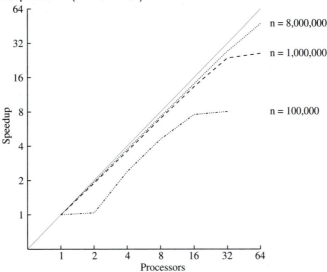

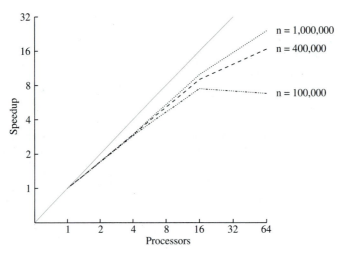

FIGURE 10-31   Speedup achieved by the PSRS sorting algorithm on the Intel iPSC/860 multicomputer (Li et al. 1992).

10.6   RANDOM READ AND RANDOM WRITE

Random read and random write are frequently used data movement operations on distributed-memory computers. Each operation involves two sets of processing elements: the source processors and the destination processors. Source processors send a record containing a key and its associated data. Destination processors receive a record. A processing element may be both a source and a destination.

In a random read operation, each destination processing element specifies the record key it wishes to receive, or else it specifies a null key, meaning it does not wish to receive a record. Several destination-processing elements can specify the same key. In a random write operation, each source-processing element sends a record to a specified destination-processing element, or else it specifies a null address, meaning it does not wish to send a record. Several source-processing elements may specify the same address, in which case the record actually received by the destination processing element is determined by some constant-time commutative, associate, binary operation. For example, the record kept could be the one with the minimum key.

Many portions of parallel algorithms implemented on multicomputers are characterized by no communication or regular communication.

Consider the following code fragment:

```
for i ← 1 to n do
    a[i] ← [i] + c[i]
endfor
```

If arrays a, b, and c are partitioned identically among the processors, the additions can be performed without any communications. Each processor will work on values it controls.

Sometimes communication patterns are regular. Here is an example of a regular communication:

```
for i ← 1 to n do
    a[i] ← min (a[0], a[i])
endfor
```

The processor owning $a[0]$ can broadcast the value to other processors, and they can independently perform the mininum operation on elements of array a they control.

Other algorithms, however, are characterized by irregular patterns of communication that are data dependent. This means they cannot be precomputed at compile time. Consider the following code segment:

```
for i ← 1 to n do
    a[b[i]] ← c[i] + d[i]
endfor
```

The extra level of indirection means that, in general, the processor controlling the variables $c[i]$ and $d[i]$ doesn't own $a[b[i]]$. In this case one way to implement the algorithm is to have each processor compute $c[i] + d[i]$ for its value of i, compute index $b[i]$, then send the sum to the processor controlling $a[b[i]]$. We call this communication pattern **random write**—every processor generates a group of data values destined for arbitrary locations in the multicomputer.

Here is another example of a irregular communication pattern:

```
for i ← 1 to n do
    a[i] ← b[c[i]]
endfor
```

In this case each processor computes index $c[i]$, then must fetch the value stored at location $b[c[i]]$. We call this communication pattern **random read**. Every processor generates a list of addresses in the multicomputer—(processor, offset) pairs—from which values must be retrieved.

What is the best way to implement random write and random read algorithms on a multicomputer? In most cases it doesn't make sense for every processor to generate one message for every data element it needs to store or fetch. The message-passing overhead would be too high. A better strategy is to bundle messages. There are two ways to do this.

One message-bundling strategy binds messages according to their destination processor. Each processor sends a message to each of the other $p-1$ processors.

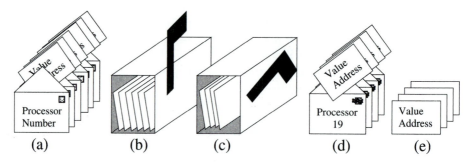

<table>
</table>

(a)	(b)	(c)	(d)	(e)

FIGURE 10-32   A high-level view of random write on a multicomputer, from the processor 19. (a) The processor begins with a list of triples. Each triple contains a value *v*, a processor number *k*, and an address *a*. Value *v* should be written at memory location *a* on processor *k*. One letter is mailed for each triple. For each triple, processor 19 labels the envelope with the processor number and encloses the value/address pair inside. (b) The letters are about to be routed. (c) Letter routing has been completed. (d) Processor 19 now has all the letters addressed to it. (e) For each value/address pair, processor 19 writes the value at the specified address. (Courtesy Hatcher and Quinn [1991].)

This strategy may be sensible if the underlying hardware has circuit-switched routing and there are a large number of data items going to the same destination.

A second message-bundling strategy uses sorting to route packets to the correct processor. Given that every address is in the form of a (processor, offset) pair, a sorting algorithm can route data so that each processor receives those packets with a matching processor number.

Figures 10-32 and 10-33 illustrate the phases of sort-based random write and random read algorithms, respectively.

10.7   SUMMARY

Sorting is an important utility on both serial and parallel computers. It is the foundation of many important parallel algorithms. On distributed-memory models, for example, random read and write are used in sorting.

In this chapter we have seen how a modified CRCW PRAM with *n* processing elements can sort *n* elements in constant time (if processor spawning time is not counted). We have explored lower bounds for sorting on several different processor organizations, and we have seen how odd-even transposition sort is an optimal algorithm for processor arrays organized as a one-dimensional mesh.

Batcher's bitonic merge algorithm, although not directly implementable in VLSI, is the basis for the sorting algorithms used in processor arrays organized as shuffle-exchange networks and hypercubes, as well as multicomputer models. Sorting can be performed in $\Theta(\log^2 n)$ time on the shuffle-exchange and hypercube processor array models, given *n* processing elements. The two-dimensional mesh-processor array model cannot sort *n* elements in polyloga-

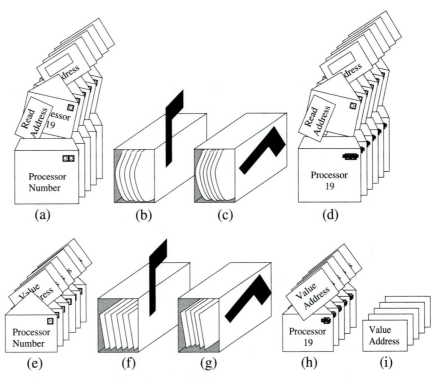

FIGURE 10-33 A high-level view of random read, from the perspective of physical processor 19. (a) Processor 19 begins with a list of quadruples. Each quadruple contains a source processor P_s, a source address A_s, a destination processor P_d, and a destination address P_a. In this figure we are assuming that the processor sending the requests is also the destination processor; hence P_d is 19. The value currently at address A_s on processor P_s must be written at address A_d on processor 19. One letter is mailed for each quadruple. The letter is addressed to processor P_s. Inside the letter are a slip of paper containing A_s and a return envelope addressed to processor 19. Inside the return envelope is another piece of paper containing A_d. (b) Outgoing letters. (c) Incoming letters. (d) Processor 19 examines its mail. These are the requests from other processors for values stored in processor 19's memory. (e) For each request, processor 19 reads the value from the address requested, fills in the blank value field, and stuffs the value/address pair in the return envelope. (f) Outgoing letters. (g) Incoming letters. (h) Processor 19 has received the values it requested. (i) For every value/address pair, processor 19 writes the value at the address indicated. (Courtesy of Hatcher and Quinn [1991].)

rithmic time; the bisection width puts a lower bound of $\Theta(\sqrt{n})$ for sorting on this model.

We looked at three quicksort-based algorithms for sorting on MIMD computers. The first algorithm, parallel quicksort, is targeted for a UMA multiprocessor, because it assumes every processor has fast access to every unsorted element, as well as to a shared stack containing indices of unsorted subarrays.

The analysis of parallel quicksort demonstrates that divide-and-conquer algorithms may achieve unsatisfactory speedup if they do not get all the processors involved in the computation fast enough. The hyperquicksort algorithm demonstrates that sorting may be performed efficiently on multicomputers. Finally, the PSRS algorithm has been applied to a variety of MIMD architectures and has achieved reasonably good speedup on them all. An attribute of the PSRS algorithm is that an upper bound on the amount of work performed by any processor can be derived analytically.

10.8 BIBLIOGRAPHIC NOTES

Parallel sorting algorithms have been the object of much study. In fact, an entire book has been devoted to the topic: *Parallel Sorting Algorithms* (Akl 1985). Two survey articles on parallel sorting are by Lakshmivarahan, Dhall, and Miller (1984); and Bitton et al. (1984). Knuth (1973) also discusses parallel sorting algorithms, including odd-even transposition sort.

Atjai, Komlós, and Szemerédi (1983) describe an algorithm that uses $\Theta(n \log n)$ processors to sort n elements in time $\Theta(\log n)$. Leighton (1984) shows how this algorithm can be used to sort n elements in time $\Theta(\log n)$ by using n processors, which is asymptotically optimal. However, Leighton points out that the constant of proportionality of this algorithm is immense and that unless $n > 10^{100}$, these algorithms would be slower in practice than other parallel sorting algorithms. Other $O(\log n)$ time PRAM sorting algorithms in the literature include Hirschberg (1978); Preparata (1978); and Reischuk (1981). Rajasekaran and Reif (1989) discuss sublogarithmic time randomized parallel sorting algorithms.

In contrast, some papers have described parallel sorting algorithms for constant-valence, fixed connection networks. Batcher's bitonic sorter, already discussed in this chapter, is such a sorter. It uses n processors to sort n elements in time $O(\log n)$. Preparata and Vuillemin (1981) have achieved the same time complexity with the same number of processors using the cube-connected cycles network. Reif and Valient (1987) have devised a randomized $O(\log n)$ algorithm that sorts n elements on an n-node cube-connected cycles network.

Other references to parallel sorting algorithms based on bitonic merge include Baudet and Stevenson (1978); Brock et al. (1981); Flanders (1982); Kumar and Hirschberg (1983); Lorin (1975); Meertens (1979); Nassimi and Sahni (1979, 1982); Perl (1983); Preparata (1978); Preparata and Vuillemin (1981); Rudolph (1984); and Schwartz (1980). In addition to the bitonic merge-sort discussed in this chapter, Thompson and Kung (1977) present another sorting algorithm for the two-dimensional mesh-processor array model, called the s^2-way odd-even merge, which also can sort $n = m^2$ elements in time $\Theta(\sqrt{n})$.

Papers on bitonic merge sort include Bilardi and Nicolau (1986); Brock et al. (1981); Hoey and Leiserson (1980); Kleitman et al. (1981); Knuth (1973); Leighton (1983); Meertens (1979); Schwartz (1980); and Stone (1978).

Early references to odd-even transposition sort include Demuth (1956), Knuth (1973), and Kung (1980). Besides the references cited earlier in the chapter, other implementations of the odd-even transposition sort include Chen et al. (1978a, 1978b); Kramer and van Leeuwen (1982); Kumar and Hirschberg (1983); Lee, Chang, and Wong (1981); and Miranker, Tang, and Wong (1983). Baudet and Stevenson (1978) generalized the algorithm so that each processor sorts a subsequence, rather than a single value.

Thompson and Kung (1977) discuss the row-major, snakelike row-major, and shuffled row-major processor numbering schemes on processor arrays organized as two-dimensional meshes. Nassimi and Sahni (1979) discuss the lower bound for sorting on this model. They also describe algorithms to sort elements into row-major order and snakelike row-major order.

Muller and Preparata (1975) first proposed the idea of sorting by using a tree of processors to augment a mesh-connected processor array. Leighton (1981) derives lower bounds for several computations performed on this model. Other references to sorting algorithms based on treelike networks of processors include Aggarwal (1984), Bentley and Kung (1979), Horowitz and Zorat (1983), Mead and Conway (1980), Stout (1983a), and Tanimoto (1982a, 1982b). Implementing tree machines in VLSI is the subject of papers by Bhatt and Leiserson (1982), Leiserson (1980), Mead and Rem (1979), Ruzzo and Snyder (1981), and Valiant (1981).

Todd (1978) describes how to perform mergesort on a pipeline of processors.

Muller and Preparata (1975) have proposed a parallel enumeration sort. Other implementations of enumeration sorts appear in Hsiao and Snyder (1983); Leighton (1981); Nath, Maheshwari, and Bhatt (1983); and Yasuura, Tagaki, and Yajima (1982).

Other sorting networks are discussed in Armstrong and Rem (1982); Atjai et al. (1983); Carey et al. (1982); Chen et al. (1978a, 1978b); Chin and Fok (1980); Chung et al. (1980a, 1980b); De Bruijn (1984); Dowd et al. (1983); Hong and Sedgewick (1982); Lee et al. (1981); Miranker et al. (1983); Moravec (1979); Mukhopadhyay (1981); Mukhopadhyay and Ichikawa (1972); Tseng and Lee (1984a, 1984b); Winslow and Chow (1981, 1983); and Wong and Ito (1984).

Valiant (1975), Hirschberg (1978), Horowitz and Zorat (1983), Kruskal (1983), Preparata (1978), Reischuk (1981), Shiloach and Vishkin (1981), Borodin and Hopcroft (1985), and Cole (1988) have proposed parallel sorting algorithms for PRAM models.

Alon and Azar (1988) compare the average complexity of deterministic and randomized PRAM sorting algorithms. Auf der Heide and Wigderson (1987) and Azar and Vishkin (1987) prove lower bounds on the complexity of sorting on CRCW PRAM models.

The tree sorter of Bentley and Kung (1979) and the rebound sorter of Chen et al. (1978b) incorporate sorting time into data I/O time.

Chabbar (1980) presents a parallel enumeration sort for the MIMD model. Bilardi and Nicolau (1989) describe a parallel bitonic sort for multiprocessors. Besides the earlier citations, other references for MIMD quicksort algorithms include Chen et al. (1984), Evans and Yousif (1985), Francis and Pannan (1992), Heidelberger (1990), Lorin (1975), Robinson (1977), and Singh et al. (1991).

Various authors have proposed MIMD sorting algorithms that have two phases: a phase in which each processor quicksorts its own subset of the data, followed by a phase in which processes cooperate to merge their sorted subsets. References to such algorithms in the literature include work by Francis and Mathieson (1988); Quinn (1988); Wheat and Evans (1992). Evans and Yousif (1986) proposed a two phase sort in which each processor uses the two-way merge algorithm during the first step to sort its share of the elements.

Winslow and Chow (1983) and Yang et al. (1987) have explored sorting algorithms that rely upon good, initial data partitioning to allocate about the same number of elements to each processor, at which point the processors sort their portion of the elements.

Robinson (1977), Tolub and Wallach (1978), and Varman and Doshi (1992) have described parallel-sorting algorithms for MIMD computers based on merging. Tolub and Wallach (1978) also discuss a parallel bucket sort. Quinn (1988) discusses parallel shell sort.

Loui (1984) derives upper and lower bounds for sorting on distributed computers. References to distributed sorting algorithms include Rotem et al. (1983) and Wegner (1982).

Parallel external sorting algorithms are discussed in Akl and Schmeck (1984); Bonuccelli et al. (1984); Lee et al. (1981); and Yasuura et al. (1982).

10.9 PROBLEMS

10-1   Rewrite the CRCW PRAM enumeration sort algorithm so that it requires only $n(n-1)/2$ processing elements, yet still executes in constant time.

10-2   Use the proof technique of Theorems 10.1 and 10.2 to derive a lower bound for sorting on the shuffle-exchange processor array model.

10-3   Use the proof technique of Theorem 10.3 to derive a lower bound for sorting on the one-dimensional mesh processor array model.

10-4   Use the proof technique of Theorem 10.3 to derive a lower bound for sorting on the two-dimensional mesh processor array model.

10-5   Sorting on the two-dimensional mesh processor array model has complexity $\Omega(\sqrt{n})$. How would the complexity change if the processing elements on the left edge were connected to processing elements on the right edge, and the processing elements on the top edge were connected to processing elements on the bottom edge, giving every processing element four neighbors?

10-6   Derive a lower bound for sorting n elements on the hypercube processor array model with n nodes, where the elements are distributed one-per-node before and after the sort.

10-7   Use odd-even transposition sort to sort these sequences:
(a) 5, 8, 3, 2, 4, 6, 4, 1
(b) 1, 3, 5, 7, 2, 4, 6, 8

10-8 Do you think it is accurate to describe odd-even transposition sort as a parallel bubble sort? Justify your answer.

10-9 Which of the following sequences are bitonic sequences?

    (a) 2, 3

    (b) 8, 1

    (c) 2, 5, 3

    (d) 6, 2, 6, 9, 7

    (e) 3, 3, 4, 5, 2

    (f) 1, 3, 6, 4, 7, 9

    (g) 8, 4, 2, 1, 2, 5, 7, 9

    (h) 1, 9, 7, 3, 2, 5

10-10 Prove or disprove: All sequences containing fewer than four elements are bitonic sequences.

10-11* Prove Lemma 10.1.

10-12 Show how the following 16 values would be sorted by Batcher's bitonic merge algorithm: 7, 9, 10, 2, 3, 6, 16, 1, 14, 5, 15, 8, 4, 11, 13, 12.

10-13 In general the bitonic sort of 2^k numbers requires how many comparison steps, with each step using 2^{k-1} comparators?

10-14 Show how the following 16 values would be sorted by the shuffle-exchange network implementation of bitonic merge-sort: 7, 9, 10, 2, 3, 6, 16, 1, 14, 5, 15, 8, 4, 11, 13, 12.

10-15 How many shuffle-exchange steps does Stone's bitonic sorter require for n values, where $n = 2^k$ and each step uses $n/2$ comparators?

10-16* Given a n-element processor array organized as a j-dimensional mesh, prove that bitonic sort can be performed in time $\Theta(n^{1/j})$, using the j-way shuffled row-major index scheme.

10-17* Prove that the bound in the previous exercise is optimal.

10-18 Why must Stone's perfect-shuffle algorithm carry a mask vector, while the hypercube-based algorithm does not?

10-19 A problem with the parallel quicksort algorithm presented is that too many processes wait too long before getting work to do. Find at least two ways to modify the parallel algorithm so that more processes are busy sooner.

10-20 What is the worst-case time complexity of the parallel quicksort algorithm?

10-21 What is wrong with the following termination condition for the parallel quicksort algorithm? The processes should halt when the stack containing indices of unsorted subarrays is empty.

10-22 Under what conditions, if any, is hyperquicksort cost optimal?

10-23 Predict the performance of the hyperquicksort, modified hyperquicksort, and PSRS algorithms, assuming the elements are already sorted when the algorithm begins execution.

10-24* Theorem 10.9 assumes no two elements of X have the same value. Derive an upper bound on the number of elements of X any processor may have to merge in phase four of the PSRS algorithm, when any value may appear as many as d times.

11

DICTIONARY
OPERATIONS

Expletive deleted.

White House transcripts published 1974

This chapter describes parallel algorithms used to solve the problems of searching an ordered table for the existence of a particular key, inserting keys into an ordered table, and deleting keys. Efficient sequential algorithms have been developed to allow dictionary operations to be performed in logarithmic time relative to the size of the table, an enormous improvement over the linear time needed if keys were kept in an unordered list. Sometimes it is important for multiple processes to perform dictionary operations concurrently. For example, it is probable that a parallel compiler must allow more than one process to access the symbol table simultaneously.

Search algorithms operate on elements, called **keys**, stored in a **table** of finite size. The goal is to organize the table and implement the algorithms so that functions such as inserting keys and their associated data into the table, deleting keys and data from the table, and searching for keys in the table, execute as quickly as possible.

This chapter is divided into two principal sections. Section 11.1 studies the inherent complexity of parallel search algorithms. We find that using multiple processors to perform a single operation is not particularly efficient—speedup is only logarithmic in the number of processors used. Section 11.2 presents two algorithms that perform **batch searching**; that is, they allow a number of searches to proceed concurrently. The first algorithm, developed by Ellis

(1980b), allows concurrent search and insertion on AVL trees. The second algorithm, credited to Manber and Ladner (1982), allows deletions as well, although the AVL property is sacrificed.

11.1 COMPLEXITY OF PARALLEL SEARCH

How quickly can the search for a single key be performed on a parallel computer? It is useful to have a bound on the number of operations required to perform a particular function on a parallel computer, because we then have a standard by which to gauge various proposed algorithms. The CREW PRAM model is frequently used to find this bound.

> **Theorem 11.1.** Given positive integers k, n, and p, where $n = (p+1)^k - 1$, searching for a key in an n-element table while using the CREW PRAM model requires $\leq \lceil \log(n+1)/\log(p+1) \rceil$ comparisons. This bound is tight. (See Kruskal [1982, 1983].)

> **Proof.** We use induction on k to show that $\lceil \log(n+1)/\log(p+1) \rceil$ comparisons are sufficient. *Basis:* Let $k = 1$. Then $n = (p+1)^1 - 1 = p$. Clearly one comparison step is sufficient for p processors to determine whether the key is in the table, and $\lceil \log(p+1)/\log(p+1) \rceil = 1$. *Induction:* Assume true for all tables of size $(p+1)^j - 1$, where $1 \leq j < k$. To search a list of size $(p+1)^k - 1$, during the first comparison processor i, for $1 \leq i \leq p$, compares the key with the table element indexed by $i(p+1)^{k-1}$. After this step, either one of the table elements has matched the key, or else the key lies inside one of the unexamined subsections of the table. All these unexamined subsections have size $(p+1)^{k-1} - 1$. By the induction hypothesis, $k - 1$ comparison steps are sufficient to search any of these subtables (Fig. 11-1).
>
> The second step of the proof is to show that the bound is tight. During the first parallel comparison step, only p elements of the table are compared with the key. There must be one or more contiguous unexamined segments of the table with length at least
>
> $$\left\lceil \frac{n-p}{p+1} \right\rceil \geq \frac{n-p}{p+1} = \frac{n+1}{p+1} - 1$$

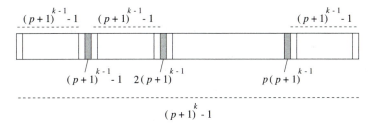

FIGURE 11-1   First induction step for Theorem 11.1.

An inductive argument shows that after k parallel comparison steps there must be one or more contiguous unexamined segments of the table with length at least

$$\frac{n+1}{(p+1)^k} - 1$$

Thus the number of steps required by any parallel algorithm in the worst case is at least the minimum k, satisfying

$$n + 1/(p+1)^k - 1 \leq 0$$

$$\Rightarrow \qquad k \geq \log(n+1)/\log(p+1)$$

$$\Rightarrow \qquad k = \lceil \log(n+1)/\log(p+1) \rceil$$

Using the results of Theorem 11.1, we can calculate the speedup achieved by the parallel algorithm searching an ordered list. Taking the number of comparisons made by the sequential binary search algorithm in the worst case, divided by the least number of comparisons made by the parallel algorithm in the worst case, we find that

$$S = \frac{\lceil \log(n+1) \rceil}{\lceil \log(n+1)/\log(p+1) \rceil} \approx \log(p+1)$$

In other words, the speedup achieved through parallelization is logarithmic in the number of processors used.

What conclusions should we draw from this theorem? Since the CREW PRAM model can require as many as $\lceil \log(n+1)/\log(p+1) \rceil$ comparison steps, it is safe to assume that *any* realistic model of parallel computation will require at least that many comparison steps in the worst case. More realistic models could also have other time-consuming operations, such as data routing and process synchronization. Thus real parallel computers will experience speedup that is no more than logarithmic in the number of processors used, and it is not fruitful to attempt to speed up a single search. We cannot make much improvement on the sequential algorithm, which has logarithmic complexity.

Our strategy for the rest of Chap. 11, then, is to speed up a series of searches. Search algorithms are not used for final results; they are frequently called subalgorithms for larger problems. Thus, it would be useful to develop a method to perform searches, insertions, and deletions in parallel.

11.2 SEARCHING ON MULTIPROCESSORS

A logical way to approach the problem is to store the search tree in a shared memory and assign processors individual requests, making a single processor responsible for responding to a command to insert, delete, or search. This is the strategy behind both the following algorithms.

11.2.1 Ellis's Algorithm

Ellis (1980b) has suggested a parallel algorithm that allows concurrent inserting and searching to take place in AVL trees. Here are some important definitions to aid us in our discussion of this algorithm.

> **Definition 11.1.** The **height** of a rooted tree is the length of the longest path from the root to a leaf node. The "empty tree"—tree without even a root—has height -1. (See Aho, Hopcraft, and Ullman [1974].)

> **Definition 11.2.** An **AVL tree** is a binary tree having the property that for any node v in the tree, the difference in height between the left and right subtrees of node v is no more than 1.

Baer and Schwab (1977) have shown that AVL tree construction is the asymptotically optimal way of keeping binary search trees balanced when searching and inserting are the only operations performed. As keys are added to the AVL tree, two types of rotations are sufficient to keep the tree balanced: single rotation and double rotation. Both rotations occur when the two subtrees of a particular node do not have the same height and the height of the taller subtree increases. These rotations, illustrated in Fig. 11-2, require $O(\log n)$ time.

Sequential Insertion Algorithm   Each node v of an AVL tree has four fields associated with it. $Key(v)$ contains a unique key; $left(v)$ is a pointer to the left subtree and $right(v)$ is a pointer to the right subtree. $Bal(v)$ is an integer whose value is 0 if the left and right subtrees are balanced, whose value is -1 if the left tree is taller than the right subtree, and whose value is $+1$ if the right tree is taller than the left subtree.

The sequential insertion algorithm has three phases. In the first phase the tree is searched to find the appropriate place to attach the new leaf node. During the search a pointer is set to indicate the last node encountered with subtrees of a different height. This node, hereafter referred to as node c, is called the **critical node**. If every node along the search path has balanced subtrees, then the root is the critical node. The first phase ends by inserting the new leaf node.

Phase 2 consists of traversing all the nodes on the path between the newly inserted node v and the critical node c. For each such node w, if $key(v) < key(w)$, then $bal(w)$ is given the value -1; otherwise, $bal(w)$ is given the value $+1$.

Phase 3 modifies the value of $bal(c)$ and rotates the tree if necessary. If $bal(c) = +1$ and v was inserted in the left subtree, or if $bal(c) = -1$ and v was inserted in the right subtree, then $bal(c)$ is changed to 0 and no rotation is necessary. If c is the root node and $bal(c) = 0$, then $bal(c)$ is set to -1 or $+1$, depending upon whether the insertion was into the left or right subtree.

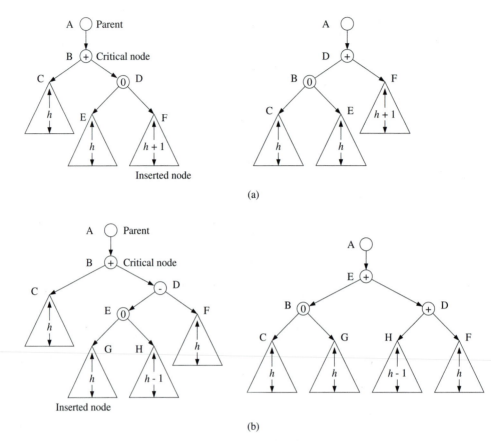

FIGURE 11-2   Rotations to keep AVL tree balanced. (a) Single rotation. (b) Double rotation.

Otherwise v was inserted into the subtree with greater height, and a single or double rotation must be performed.

Parallel Algorithm   The goal of the parallel algorithm is to keep as many search and insertion processes active as possible. It is not possible for each process to ignore the other processes. For example, consider the AVL tree of Fig. 11-3a. Assume that two processes are active: the first is inserting the value 37, and the second is searching for the value 13. After the value 37 is inserted into the tree, a single rotation must be performed to preserve the AVL property. This rotation requires that the values of certain *left* and *right* pointers be changed. The process of changing these pointers is illustrated in Fig. 11-3b and c. (Figure 11-3d is a redrawing of Fig. 11-3c.) Suppose that the process searching for key 13 follows the right child of node 6 and the left child of node 25, when the tree is in the state depicted by Fig. 11-3b. The value 13 would

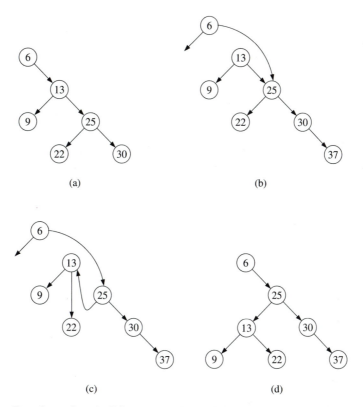

FIGURE 11-3   Transformations in AVL tree as value 37 is added.

not be found, even though it is in the tree. Another contention problem could occur if two processes attempted to rotate subtrees that have nodes in common.

Ellis solves contention problems by adding three lock fields to each node. These lock fields enable search processes to be locked out of a rotating subtree. They also enable an insert process to lock subsequent insert processes out of the entire subtree rooted by the parent of the critical node.

Three lock fields are added to each node of the AVL tree: ρ lock, α lock, and ξ lock. A process performing a search must hold a node's ρ lock before examining the contents of that node. The α locks are set by an insert process to keep other insert processes off the path from the parent of the critical node to the point of insertion. The ξ locks exclude search processes from nodes involved in a rotation. More than one search process can share a single ρ lock, and multiple search processes can hold a node's ρ lock while a single insert process holds node's *alpha* lock. However, α locks and ξ locks may not be shared, and if an insert process holds a node's ξ lock, then no other processes can hold the α lock or the ρ lock.

In the case of a single rotation, the ξ locks of the critical node and its parent must be set. A double rotation requires that the ξ locks be set on the critical node, the parent of the critical node, and the child of the critical node lying along the insertion path. Table 11.1 illustrates what locks are held on an AVL tree at various times during the execution of four processes performing insert or search operations.

During execution of Ellis's algorithm, a process performing an insertion sets α locks as it traverses the tree. The α locks from the parent of the critical node through the place of insertion remain locked during insertion and rotation. This locking strategy excludes other processes from performing insertions along the entire subtree rooted by the parent of the critical node. Hence the number of concurrent insertions is quite limited. (Ellis 1980b) has designed another parallel algorithm requiring that fewer nodes be locked, allowing more insertions to take place concurrently.

TABLE 11-1   EXECUTION OF ELLIS'S ALGORITHM.

	Task		
Insert 51	Search for 46	Insert 25	Search for 17
Lock α 26	Lock ρ 26		
	Unlock ρ 26		
Lock α 34	Lock ρ 34		
Lock α 49	Unlock ρ 34		
	Lock ρ 49		
	Current state illustrated in Fig. 11-4a		
Lock α 66	Unlock ρ 49		
Insert key 51	Terminate		
Lock ξ 26			
Lock ξ 34		Waiting for α 26	
	Current state illustrated in Fig. 11-4b		
Rotate at 34			
Release all locks		Lock α 26	
Terminate		Lock α 20	
		Lock α 23	
		Insert key 25	Lock ρ 26
		Waiting for ξ 26	
	Current state illustrated in Fig. 11-4c		
			Unlock ρ 26
		Lock ξ 26	Lock ρ 20

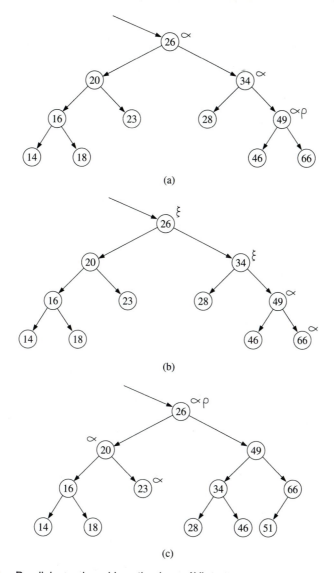

FIGURE 11-4   Parallel search and insertion in an AVL tree.

To summarize, Ellis's algorithm assigns individual processes to search for or insert particular keys. A number of searches and insertions can take place concurrently. The algorithm has three important weaknesses. First, it does not allow deletions to be performed. Second, it suffers from contention for a shared resource—processes performing insertions prevent other insertion processes from accessing entire subtrees. Third, the parallel algorithm has a lot of overhead. Even a search process must lock and unlock every node it examines.

11.2.2   Manber and Ladner's Algorithm

Manber and Ladner (1982) have suggested a parallel searching algorithm for the UMA multiprocessor model that allows deletions but sacrifices the AVL tree property. Manber and Ladner's algorithm does not try to maintain a balanced tree. They hope that the insertions and deletions will be random enough to maintain a reasonably balanced tree. (A study by Eppinger (1983) suggests that this hope is justified only under certain conditions.) In return for this concession, their algorithm is much simpler, because insertion and deletion processes do not have the responsibility of rotating the tree. An interesting feature of this algorithm is the use of maintenance processes to physically delete nodes.

Every node v in the search tree has 10 fields associated with it:

Key(v), according to which the nodes are ordered
Data(v), a pointer to the data associated with the key
Left(v), a pointer to the left subtree of v
Right(v), a pointer to the right subtree of v
Parent(v), a pointer to the parent of v
Garbage(v), set to *true* when the node has been removed from the tree
Redundant(v), set to *true* when the node has a copy in the tree
Copy(v), which when *true* means v is a copy of another node
Userlock(v), a lock that can be set by a delete process
Mlock(v), a lock that can be set by a maintenance process

The root of the tree is a special-purpose node with key ∞. It contains no data and cannot be deleted. This simplifies the parallel algorithms.

There are two reasons why nodes need to be locked. First, a node needs to be locked to ensure that only one process at a time updates its data. Second, nodes need to be locked to make sure that two or more processes cannot attempt to change the shape of the tree at the same place at the same time. These two purposes are not independent; for example, one process cannot be allowed to delete a node while another process is updating it. Thus, one kind of lock, the *userlock*, is used for both purposes.

Every key is associated with a unique node. If the key is in the tree, its associated node contains the key. If the key is not in the tree, its associated node would be the parent of the key node if the key were inserted in the tree. Hence internal nodes are associated with a single key, while leaf nodes may be associated with a number of keys corresponding to a range of values. The basic operations of update, insert, and delete involve a single node. These operations begin by performing a *strong search* (defined later), which finds the node associated with the key and locks the *userlock* of that node. If the *userlock* is already locked, the process performing the operation is blocked until the node is unlocked. Only one basic operation can be performed on a particular node at one time. In contrast to Ellis's algorithm, however, all basic operations can be performed by locking only one node. This provides much more latitude for concurrency. Note that except for the data field, all fields of a node may be examined while the node is locked. This allows a search to work its way through a locked interior node.

Basic User Operations The basic user operations are strong search, weak search, update, insert, and delete. This section describes these operations.

Since searching does not change the tree, its parallel implementation is similar to the sequential algorithm. However, there is one important factor to consider. What happens if the search is performed and the result of the search reported, but another process has modified the tree between the time when the search was terminated and the result was reported? Sometimes this factor is irrelevant to the computation; at other times this factor may be crucial. Therefore we define two different search algorithms.

Weak search returns a result that is not guaranteed to be up-to-date. Weak search should be used whenever possible, because it does not require locking any nodes. Thus the parallel algorithm has no overhead and a process performing a weak search interferes with no other processes.

Strong search looks for a given key and returns the node v associated with that key. To make sure that v will remain the node associated with the key as long as it is needed, the process performs a weak search, then locks v. After node v is locked, however, a check is done to ensure that v is still the node associated with the key. Between the time when v is found and when v is locked, three different events could invalidate the association between the key and v. First, v might have been removed from the tree [that is, $garbage(v)$ set to $true$]. Second, if $key(v)$ is not the key being searched for, another node might have been inserted into the tree that is now the node associated with the key. Third, v might have become a redundant node [that is, $redundant(v)$ set to $true$]. Redundant nodes are created as a side effect of deletions. Thus, when strong search returns a node, that node is guaranteed to be the one associated with the key and is locked. The node is unlocked only after the operation—update, insert, or delete—is completed.

In Manber and Ladner's algorithm deletion is simple, because the deletion process must only logically delete the node. Maintenance processes take care of physically deleting the node. The delete process uses strong search to find the node v associated with the key and lock it. Assuming the key values match, $data(v)$ is set to nil. The delete process puts v on a special maintenance list, the *delete list*, so that a maintenance process can come along later and physically delete the node.

Concurrent insertion begins by performing a strong search for the node v associated with the key. If a node associated with the key is found, it may have been logically deleted [that is, $data(v)$ is nil]. If so, the process adds the new data field, unlocks v, and terminates. If v has not been logically deleted, the process reports that the node already exists, unlocks v, and terminates.

Assuming the key is not in the tree, then v is the leaf node that becomes the parent of the inserted node, and the insertion is performed identically to the sequential algorithm. After the correct child pointer of v has been set to indicate the inserted node, the process unlocks v and terminates.

Maintenance Processes The maintenance processes physically delete nodes from the search tree. Recall that when a node is deleted, its pointer is put on a deletion list. Idle maintenance processes access this list to get pointers to nodes needing deletion.

If node v is to be deleted and v has only one child, the deletion is simple. The pointer from v's parent to v is redirected to v's child, and v is effectively detached from the tree (see Fig. 11-5). (If v is a leaf node, then the pointer from v's parent to v is made nil.)

How soon can node v be reused? Although v is no longer a part of the tree, another process may have accessed v while it was being detached. The purpose of the boolean $garbage(v)$ is to alert such a process that v is no longer a part of the tree. Since $parent(v)$ still points to its parent, an otherwise stranded search process can get back into the tree and continue.

As we have seen, v cannot be reused immediately. Manber and Ladner suggest that the garbage collection algorithm of Kung and Lehman (1980) be used. This algorithm uses three lists of nodes: the passive garbage list, the active garbage list, and the available list. When a maintenance process first removes a node from the tree, the node is put on the passive garbage list. This list grows until a maintenance process is ready to perform garbage collection. Garbage collection begins by copying a group of nodes from the passive garbage list into the active garbage list and noting which processes are active at the time of the copy. When all these processes have terminated, the active garbage list is appended to the available list. Since the only processes that can access nodes on the passive garbage list are those that were active when the copy to the active list was made, the nodes are truly inactive and suitable for reuse once these processes have terminated.

The physical deletion algorithm is more complicated if the node v has two children. Conceptually the deletion is performed in two steps (see Fig. 11-6). First, the node w having the largest key less than $key(v)$ is found (Fig. 11-6a). Node w has, at most, one child (since it cannot have a right child). Hence it is easy to delete w by using the algorithm described earlier (Fig. 11-6b).

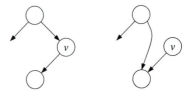

FIGURE 11-5 Deletion of a node with one child.

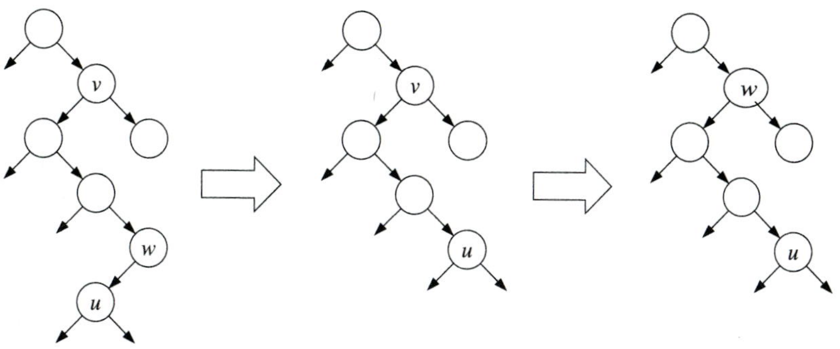

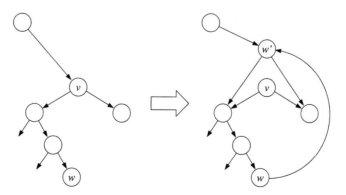

FIGURE 11-6   Conceptual idea of deletion of a node with two children.

The second step is to replace v with w (Fig. 11-6c). Since w is the immediate predecessor of v, the tree remains consistent. However, we must implement the deletion in a slightly different way to ensure that a copy of w is always accessible to a process searching for it.

The algorithm used by Manber and Ladner is illustrated in Fig. 11-7. First, create a copy of w, called w'. Note that $data(w') = data(w)$ and $copy(w') = true$. Second, set $left(w')$ to point to $left(v)$ and $right(w')$ to point to $right(v)$. Third, set $right(w)$ to point to w', and set $redundant(w)$ to $true$. What happens if a process searching for node w is on the way from node u to w when this operation takes place? This process may, for example, want to insert to the right of node w. When the process encounters node w, it will find that $redundant(w) = true$ and will therefore follow $right(w)$ to w', where it will continue to node t. Fourth, remove node v by setting the appropriate child pointer of $parent(v)$ to point to w' and setting $garbage(v)$ to $true$.

Node w cannot be deleted immediately, because there may be processes looking for w along the way from u to w. A method similar to the garbage col-

FIGURE 11-7   Deletion of a node with two children.

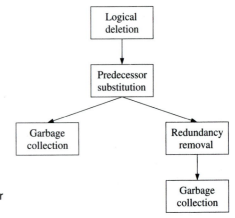

FIGURE 11-8 Phases of the deletion process of Manber and Ladner's algorithm.

lection algorithm solves the problem. We put node w on a *passive redundancy list*. Nodes on the passive redundancy list become available for physical deletion only after all the processes alive at the time of the substitution terminate. Once w is available for physical deletion, the process is straightforward, since w has only a single child. The phases of the deletion process are summarized in Fig. 11-8.

11.3 SUMMARY

It is hard to use processors efficiently if we want to speed up a single search operation. The sequential algorithm has logarithmic complexity, and the speedup achieved by the parallel algorithm can be, at most, logarithmic in the number of processors used. Achieving even this modest speedup is difficult on real parallel computers. Hence the goal should be to perform a series of searches, insertions, and deletions as quickly as possible.

This chapter has described parallel algorithms to implement searching, inserting, and deleting on UMA multiprocessors. Both algorithms associate processes with particular operations to be performed. Locks must be used to keep processes from interfering with each other during critical operations. A primary difference between the two algorithms is that Ellis's algorithm may require locking a number of nodes logarithmic in the size of the tree, whereas Manber and Ladner's algorithm never requires more than a single node to be locked.

Ellis's algorithm allows searching and inserting to take place in AVL trees. A process inserting a key must lock the subtree rooted by the parent of the node to be rotated. Hence the amount of concurrency among inserting processes is limited. Search processes must lock and unlock every node they examine. Although more than one search process can share such a lock, the frequency of the lock-unlock operation adds to the overhead of the parallel algorithm.

Manber and Ladner's algorithm requires that no search, insert, delete, or update process lock more than a single node of the search tree. This greatly improves the efficiency of the parallel algorithm. The delete process simply marks a node for deletion. Separate maintenance processes, which must lock three nodes, perform the physical deletion of nodes from the search tree. The algorithm does not maintain a balanced tree. Manber and Ladner hope that the insertions and deletions will be random enough to keep the tree reasonably balanced. Evidence published after Manber and Ladner's work suggests that this hope is justified only under certain conditions (Eppinger 1983).

Our description of parallel searching has avoided the topic of memory bank conflicts. This important issue is addressed in Probs. 11-10 and 11.11.

11.4 BIBLIOGRAPHIC NOTES

Most books on data structures, including Wirth (1976) and Helman and Veroff (1986), discuss AVL trees.

This chapter does not describe Ellis's second parallel search and insertion algorithm for AVL trees. It can be found in Ellis (1980b). In addition to her work on AVL trees, Ellis (1980a) has described algorithms allowing concurrent search and insertion in 2–3 trees. Code for all Manber and Ladner's procedures described in this chapter appears in Manber and Ladner (1982).

Two early papers discussing concurrent insertion into and balancing of binary search trees are Wong and Chang (1974) and Chang (1974). Work on concurrent access to trees holds interest for designers of data base systems. Kung and Lehman (1980) discuss the concurrent manipulation of binary search trees; Lehman and Yao (1981) describe concurrent algorithms for B* trees. These algorithms have tree rotations require no more than a small, constant number of nodes to be locked.

Baer et al. (1983) investigate a number of algorithms to perform batch searching on processor arrays and UMA multiprocessors. Their paper focuses on the important problem of avoiding memory bank conflicts. Carey and Thompson (1984) have proposed a systolic algorithm for implementing search trees on MIMD computers. Ottman et al. (1982) have designed searching algorithms suitable for implementation in VLSI. Potter (1985) briefly describes the ease of searching on Goodyear's MPP, a 2-D mesh SIMD computer. Ramamoorthy et al. (1978) have proposed a searching machine based upon associative memory.

11.5 PROBLEMS

11-1   Fill in the inductive argument of the second step of the proof of Theorem 11.1 by proving that after k parallel computation steps there must be one or more contiguous, unexamined segments of the table with length at least

$$\frac{n+1}{(p+1)^k} - 1$$

11-2   Given an $n \times n$ 2-D mesh SIMD model containing a sorted list of n^2 items and $n \log n$ items to search for, what is the time needed to complete all $n \log n$ searches?

11-3   Is Ellis's algorithm control parallel or data parallel? Explain your answer.

11-4   In the context of Ellis's algorithm, provide an example showing how two processes performing rotations could contend with each other if the entire subtree rooted by the parent of the node to be rotated were not locked.

11-5   Is Manber and Ladner's algorithm control parallel or data parallel? Explain your answer.

11-6   Provide an example showing why physical deletion of a node with two children cannot be performed as shown in Fig. 11-6.

11-7   Provide an example showing why deleted nodes must be put on both the passive garbage list and the active garbage list before being put on the list of available nodes.

11-8   In the context of Manber and Ladner's algorithm, explain which nodes need to be locked by a maintenance process and why.

11-9   Explain how to implement the update operation of Manber and Ladner's algorithm. An update operation finds a node associated with a specified key and changes the data field of that node to point to a different data item.

11-10   Assume a UMA multiprocessor with four CPUs and four memory banks. Assume a table A of n keys is to be searched, where $a[1] < a[2] < \cdots < a[n]$, and $a[i]$ is stored in memory bank i, modulo 4. Furthermore, make the simplifying assumption that the processors work in lockstep and that every processor fetches and compares an element of A every memory cycle. If two processors P_i and P_j, where $i < j$, try to access the same memory bank in the same cycle, processor P_i gets the value it desires, while P_j must repeat the access attempt on the next cycle. It is helpful to think of the binary search of an array as the traversal of a binary tree. See Fig. 11-9 for an example of a binary tree representing an array of 20 keys. Given all these assumptions, suppose that $n = 20$ and $a[i] = i$ for $1 \le i \le 20$. Suppose processor P_0 is searching for value 13, P_1 is searching for 4, P_2 is searching for 10, and P_3 is searching for 17. Draw a table showing the execution of the batch search for these keys. In particular, indicate which memory bank a processor accesses (or fails to access) each memory cycle.

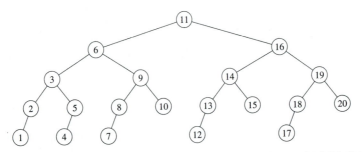

FIGURE 11-9   A binary search of a 20-key table can be viewed as a search of this tree.

11-11   Repeat the previous exercise, with the following modifications. Suppose $n = 31$ and $a[i] = i$ for $1 \le i \le 31$.

12

GRAPH
ALGORITHMS

I learn by going where I have to go.

Theodore Roethke

One way the early use of parallel computers has resembled the early use of sequential computers has been the emphasis on numerical algorithms. However, as the field of parallel algorithms matures, the emphasis can be expected to shift to nonnumerical algorithms because more and more problems being solved on computers are symbolic in nature. This chapter examines a number of parallel algorithms developed to solve problems in graph theory. These problems relate to searching graphs and finding connected components, minimum-cost spanning trees, and shortest paths in graphs.

A review of elementary graph theoretic terminology appears in Appendix A.

PRAM algorithms for searching graphs are covered in Sec. 12.1. Section 12.2 presents three algorithms for finding the connected components of a graph. Sections 12.3 and 12.4 cover the all-pairs shortest path and single-source shortest path algorithms, respectively. In Sec. 12.5 we describe the parallelization of two algorithms to solve the minimum-cost spanning tree problem. The primary references for this chapter are Quinn and Deo (1984) and Quinn and Yoo (1984).

12.1 SEARCHING A GRAPH

Given a CREW PRAM model of computation with p processing elements, Reghbati and Corneil (1978) have determined the number of operations required for three parallel graph-searching algorithms. Recall that depth-first search of an arbitrary graph is most likely inherently sequential, since it is a $\mathcal{P}$-complete problem (Sec. 2.5). Reghbati and Corneil thus consider a parallel variant of depth-first search, called p-depth search (defined later), as well as parallel breadth-depth and parallel breadth-first search.

For these algorithms an adjacency matrix is not a suitable representation of the graph to be searched, since the process of searching through the elements of the matrix to find edges consumes too much processor time. Hence Reghbati and Corneil use adjacency lists to represent the graph.

How quickly can a graph be searched? Initially a master list of vertices still to be searched contains a single vertex. Each processor examines one or more edges emanating from a vertex being searched. If the edge leads to a previously undiscovered vertex, it is added to that processor's partial list, containing vertices to be added to the master list. At certain intervals the partial lists formed by the processors are linked and combined with the master list. Assume that the only operations that consume time are the vertex selection process and the list-linking and combining process. Assume that it takes one of these *active operations* to select a vertex. For the sequential algorithm, only one active operation is required for the lone processor to add a new vertex to the master list. Let n denote the number of vertices, d_i denote the degree of vertex i, and m denote the number of edges in a graph. It is clear, then, that an upper bound for a sequential algorithm to search a graph is

$$T_1 = \sum_{i=1}^{n}(d_i + 1) = 2m + n$$

since vertex i can be added to a partial list only once, and d_i is the maximum number of times that vertex i can be chosen as the vertex from which searching is to be done.

12.1.1 P-Depth Search

In p-depth search, p edges incident upon a selected vertex are simultaneously searched. (In other words, processors are assigned to edges, one processor per edge.) One of the most recently searched vertices is then chosen as the point from which the search is continued. This procedure ends when the master list of vertices having unexplored edges is empty. Figure 12-1b illustrates p-depth search for $p = 2$. Note that if $p = 1$, the result is a depth-first search.

Theorem 12.1. Given $p \geq 2$ processors, an upper bound on the number of active operations required by p-depth search on the CREW PRAM model is

$$\sum_{i=1}^{n}\left\lceil \frac{d_i + 1}{p} \right\rceil (\lceil \log p \rceil + 1)$$

(See Reghbati and Corneil [1978].)

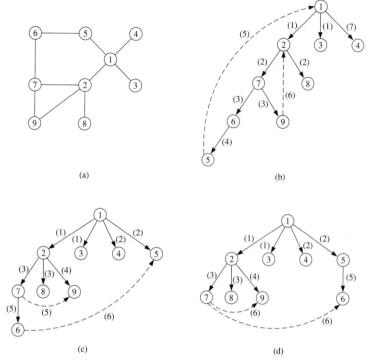

FIGURE 12-1 Parallel algorithms to search graphs. Parenthesized numbers indicate order edges are traversed. (a) Graph to be searched. (b) Two-processor p-depth search. (c) Two-processor parallel breadth-depth search. (d) Two-processor parallel breadth-first search. (Quinn and Deo (1984). Copyright ©1986 Association for Computing Machinery. Reprinted by permission.)

Proof. The new vertices found at each state of the algorithm can be added to the master list of vertices in $\lceil \log p \rceil + 1$ active operations, by linking lists in a treelike manner. The number of times that searching begins at vertex i is $\lceil (d_i + 1)/p \rceil$. Therefore, the number of active operations required for parallel p-depth search is

$$T_p^1 = \sum_{i=1}^{n} \left\lceil \frac{d_i + 1}{p} \right\rceil (\lceil \log p \rceil + 1)$$

$$1 \le \sum_{i=1}^{n} \left(\frac{d_i + 1}{p} + 1 \right) (\lceil \log p \rceil + 1)$$

$$\le \frac{T_1(\lceil \log p \rceil + 1)}{p} + n(\lceil \log p \rceil + 1)$$

Note that in order for p-depth search to require fewer active operations than a sequential search, the term $(\lceil \log p \rceil + 1)/p$ must be less than 1. Hence $p \geq 4$ is a necessary condition for p-depth search to require fewer active operations than a sequential search.

12.1.2 Breadth-Depth Search

A breadth-depth search proceeds by examining all the edges adjacent to a vertex before selecting one of the most recently reached vertices and continuing the search from there. In a parallel breadth-depth search, each processor keeps track of the new vertices it has discovered. Once all the edges from a vertex have been examined, these partial lists are linked and added to the master list. Since this parallel algorithm requires that partial lists link and combine with the master list less often than a p-depth search, the algorithm requires fewer active operations. Figure 12-1c illustrates parallel breadth-depth search.

Theorem 12.2. Given $p \geq 2$ processors, parallel breadth-depth search requires no more than

$$\sum_{i=1}^{n} \left(\left\lceil \frac{d_i}{p} \right\rceil + 1 + \lceil \log p \rceil + 1 \right)$$

active operations on the CREW PRAM model. (See Reghbati and Corneil [1978].)

Proof. It requires $\lceil \log p \rceil + 1$ active operations to link the vertices found during exploration from vertex i. There are $\lceil d_i/p \rceil + 1$ examination steps beginning from vertex i. Hence parallel breadth-depth search has an upper bound of

$$T_p^2 = \sum_{i=1}^{n} \left(\left\lceil \frac{d_i}{p} \right\rceil + 1 + \lceil \log p \rceil + 1 \right)$$

$$\leq \frac{T_1}{p} + n(\lceil \log p \rceil + 3)$$

12.1.3 Breadth-First Search

Parallel breadth-first search requires even fewer link-and-combine steps, because processors examine all vertices at level i of the search tree before moving on to level $i + 1$ (Fig. 12-1d). Thus, there is only one link-and-combine step for each level of the search tree.

Theorem 12.3. Given $p \geq 2$ processors on the CREW PRAM model, the number of active operations required by parallel breadth-first search is

$$T_p^3 = \sum_{i=1}^{n} \left(\left\lceil \frac{d_i}{p} \right\rceil + 1 \right) + L\lceil \log p \rceil$$

where L is the distance of the vertex farthest from the start vertex (Reghbati and Corneil 1978.)

Proof. This is left to the reader.

12.2 CONNECTED COMPONENTS

There are three common approaches to finding the connected components of an undirected graph. The first approach uses some form of search, such as depth-first or breadth-first. The second approach finds the transitive closure of the graph's adjacency matrix. Letting **A** denote the adjacency matrix of the original undirected graph G and **B** denote the transitive closure of **A**, we compute **B** by $\lceil \log n \rceil$ plus-min multiplications of **A**. (A plus-min multiplication is analogous to matrix multiplication, with scalar multiplication replaced by scalar addition and scalar addition replaced by the minimum operation.) The third approach collapses vertices into larger and larger sets of vertices until each set corresponds to a single connected component.

Hirschberg has used the third method to develop a connected components algorithm for processor arrays (Hirschberg 1976; Hirschberg et al. 1979). Although the algorithm is based on the CREW PRAM model of parallel computation, it has been widely studied and merits discussion.

Theorem 12.4. The connected components of an undirected graph can be found in $\Theta(\log^2 n)$ time on the CREW PRAM model with $\Theta(n^2)$ processors (Hirschberg 1976).

Summary of Algorithm. The primary data structure is the adjacency matrix. Instead of computing the transitive closure, however, adjacent vertices are combined into *supervertices*, which are themselves combined until each remaining supervertex represents a connected component of the graph. Like the transitive closure algorithm on the CREW PRAM model, this algorithm has a complexity of $\Theta(\log^2 n)$, but requires only n^2 processors.

Each vertex is always a member of exactly one supervertex, and every supervertex is identified by its lowest-numbered member vertex, the *root*. The parallel algorithm iterates through three stages. In the first, the lowest-numbered neighboring supervertex of each vertex is found. The second stage connects each supervertex root to the root of the lowest-numbered neighboring supervertex. In the third stage all newly connected supervertices are collapsed into larger supervertices. Since the number of supervertices is reduced by a factor of at least 2 in each iteration, $\lceil \log n \rceil$ iterations are sufficient to collapse each connected component into a single supervertex. The operation of this algorithm is illustrated in Fig. 12-2.

Theorem 12.5. The connected components of an undirected graph can be found in $\Theta(\log^2 n)$ time on the CREW PRAM model with $\Theta(n \lceil n / \log n \rceil)$ processors (Hirschberg et al. 1979).

Summary of Algorithm. Hirschberg's original algorithm uses n^2 processors to assign values to the matrix containing the root numbers of neighboring supervertices.

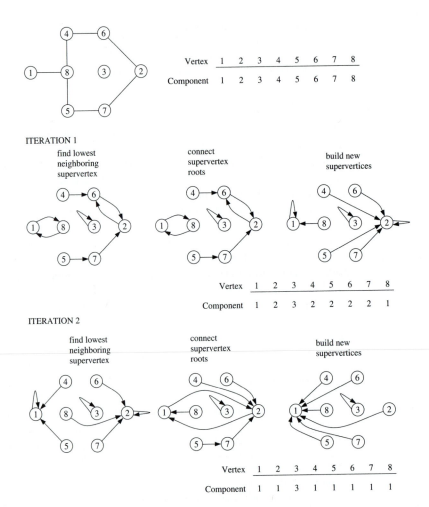

FIGURE 12-2   Hirschberg's connected-component algorithm. (Quinn and Deo (1984). Copyright ©1986 Association for Computing Machinery. Reprinted by permission.)

By applying Brent's theorem it is easy to see that $\lceil n/\log n\rceil$ processors are sufficient to assign n values and find the minimum of n elements, both in $\Theta(\log n)$ time. Each processor can assign values to $\log n$ elements, instead of only one element, without increasing the time complexity of the algorithm. Similarly, in the first phase of minimization, each processor can find the minimum of $\log n$ values, rather than two values, without increasing the complexity of the algorithm. Hirschberg's algorithm thus can be implemented by using $n\lceil n/\log n\rceil$ processors, instead of n^2.

Theorem 12.6. The connected components of an undirected graph can be found in $\Theta(\log^2 n)$ time on the CREW PRAM model with $\Theta(n\lceil n/\log^2 n\rceil)$ processors (Chin et al. 1981; 1982).

Summary of Algorithm. Every vertex is involved during each iteration of Hirschberg's algorithm. Chin et al. noted that by restricting participation in each iteration to a representative vertex of each supervertex (the root) and by removing isolated supervertices from further consideration, the algorithm requires fewer processors.

Nassimi and Sahni (1980b) have adapted Hirschberg's algorithm to the q-dimensional mesh-connected SIMD model. Let us examine their algorithm for the particular case of a two-dimensional processors mesh. At various points in the parallel algorithm the processors execute a random read or a random write, as described in Chap. 10. Procedure RANDOM.READ has two arguments. The first argument denotes the address that receives the data; the second argument denotes the value to be read. For example, after statement

RANDOM.READ *(a, [b]c)*

has executed, the value of local variable a of every unmasked processor is identical to the value of variable c of the processor indexed by the value of local variable b.

Procedure RANDOM.WRITE has two arguments. The first argument denotes the value written; the second argument is the address to which the value is written. For example, when the statement

RANDOM.WRITE *(a, [b]c)*

executes, the value of local variable a of every active processor is written to variable c of the processor indexed by the value of local variable b. If more than one value is written to the same location, then the minimum of these values is the resultant value.

The complexity of performing a random read or a random write on the 2-D mesh SIMD model with p processing elements is $\Theta(p)$.

The algorithm uses a new function called BITS. BITS (i, j, k) returns the value of bits j through k of integer value i, where bit 0 is considered to be the least significant bit. If $j < k$ the function returns 0. For example,

BITS *(17, 3, 1)* = 0   BITS *(10, 3, 2)* = 2
BITS *(16, 4, 4)* = 1   BITS *(15, 2, 3)* = 0

Given a graph G with $n = 2^k$ vertices, the 2-D mesh SIMD algorithm shown in Figs. 12-3 and 12-4 finds the connected components of G. Assume that the maximum degree of any vertex in G is d. Let $adj(i, j)$, where $1 \leq i \leq n$ and $1 \leq j \leq d$, denote the edges of G stored as an adjacency list. If vertex i has $d_i < d$ edges, then $adj(i, j) = \infty$ for $d + i + 1 \leq j \leq d$. This adjacency list is stored in the local memory of processing element $P(i)$. Assume that $p = 2^k$ and that the processing elements are numbered in shuffled row-major order.

CONNECTED COMPONENTS (2-D mesh SIMD):

Parameter	d	{Maximum vertex degree}
	n	{Number of vertices}
Global	e	{Edge being considered}
	iteration	{Iteration number}
Local	*candidate*	{Root of neighboring vertex}
	neighbor[1...d]	{Neighboring vertices}
	r	{Root number}

```
1. begin
      {Initially every node is a tree unto itself}
2.    for all Pᵢ where 1 ≤ i ≤ n do
3.       r ← i
4.    endfor

      {Merge trees}
5.    for iteration ← 0 to ⌈ log n ⌉ − 1 do

         {It is not known whether there is a neighboring tree}
6.       for all Pᵢ where 1 ≤ i ≤ n do
7.          candidate ← ∞
8.       endfor

         {Look for the lowest-numbered neighboring root}
9.       for e ← 1 to d do
10.         for all Pᵢ where 1 ≤ i ≤ n do
11.            FETCH.AND.COMPARE ( neighbor[e], r, candidate)
12.         endfor
13.      endfor
14.      for all Pᵢ where 1 ≤ i ≤ n do
15.         UPDATE.SUPERVERTEX.NUMBERS ( candidate, r)
16.      endfor

         {Collapse supervertices}
17.      REDUCE (r, n)
18.   endfor
19. end
```

FIGURE 12-3   Nassimi and Sahni's adaption of Hirschberg's algorithm for the 2-D mesh SIMD model. This pseudocode program references three subroutines (see Fig. 12-4).

In addition to the edges of vertex i, each processing element $P(i)$ has a local variable r that corresponds to the pointer of the supervertex root in Hirschberg's algorithm, and another local variable tmp, used as temporary storage. Procedure REDUCE corresponds to the third stage of Hirschberg's algorithm, collapsing vertices so that every vertex in a supervertex points to the root.

FETCH.AND.COMPARE $(v, r,$ *candidate*)

      Value v {Neighboring vertex}

                    r {Vertex's current root number}

      Reference   *candidate*   {Lowest-numbered neighboring root}

      Local   *tmp*   {Value fetched from other processor}

   begin

1.   RANDOM.READ $($ *tmp*, $[v]r)$

2.   if $tmp = r$ then

3. $tmp \leftarrow \infty$

4.   endif

5.   *candidate* $\leftarrow$ min(*candidate*, *tmp*)

6. end

UPDATE.SUPERVERTEX.NUMBERS (*candidate*, r)

   Value *candidate*, r

   begin

      {Each supervertex root gets the minimum

          of the root numbers of neighboring supervertices}

1.   RANDOM.WRITE (*candidate*, $[r]r)$

      {Take care of supervertices with no neighbors}

2.   if $r = \infty$ then

3. $r \leftarrow i$

4.   endif

       {Make sure no cycles are formed}

5.   if $r > i$ then

6.   RANDOM.READ $(r, [r]r)$

7.   endif

8. end

REDUCE (r, n):

   Reference r, Value n

1. begin

2.   for $b \leftarrow 1$ to $\log n$ do

3.   for all P_i do

4.   if BITS$(r, \log n - 1, b)$ = BITS$(i, \log n - 1, b)$ then

5.   RANDOM.READ $(r, [r]r)$

6.   endif

7.   endfor

8.   endfor

9. end

FIGURE 12-4   Subroutines called by connected-components algorithm of Fig. 12-3.

Theorem 12.7. The connected components of an undirected graph G with $n = 2^k$ vertices and maximum vertex degree d can be found in time $O(dn \log n)$ on the 2-D mesh SIMD model having n processors (Nassimi and Sahni 1980b).
Complexity Analysis. This is left to the reader.

Theorem 12.8. Suppose the adjacency matrix of an undirected graph G with n vertices is stored in the base of a pyramid SIMD computer of size n^2. Then the connected components of G can be found in time $O(\sqrt{n})$ (Miller and Stout 1987).
Summary of Algorithm. Miller and Stout, like authors previously mentioned, have based their algorithm on the work of Hirschberg. Their innovation is the effective use of the pyramid's topology. As the algorithm progresses, there are fewer and fewer supervertices (min trees) to be combined. When the forest of min trees is to be relabeled, data are moved up the pyramid, where the combining step can be performed on a mesh of appropriate size.

12.3 ALL-PAIRS SHORTEST PATH

A variant of matrix multiplication can be used to solve a number of graph problems, including the all-pairs shortest-path problem. The proof of Theorem 12.9 describes the transformation needed.

Theorem 12.9. Given an n-vertex weighted graph, the all-pairs shortest-path problem can be solved in $\Theta(\log^2 n)$ time on the hypercube SIMD and shuffle-exchange SIMD models, given $n^3 = 2^{3q}$ processors (Dekel et al. 1981).

Proof. Let G be an n-vertex weighted graph. Our goal is to produce an $n \times n$ matrix $\mathbf{A}$ such that $a_{i,j}$ is the length of the shortest path from i to j in G. Let $a_{i,j}^k$ denote the length of the shortest path from i to j with, at most, $k - 1$ intermediate vertices. Since there are no negative weight cycles in G, $a_{i,j} = a_{i,j}^{n-1}$. In this example, $a_{i,i}^1 = 0$, for all i, $1 \le i \le n$, and for all distinct i and j, $a_{i,j}^1$ is the weight of the edge from i to j; if no such edge exists, $a_{i,j}^1 = \infty$. It follows from the principle of combinatorial optimality that $a_{i,j}^k = \min_m \{a_{i,m}^{\lceil k/2 \rceil} + a_{m,j}^{\lceil k/2 \rceil}\}$. Hence $\mathbf{A}^{n-1}$ may be computed from $\mathbf{A}^1$ by repeated plus-min multiplications. By substituting plus for multiply and min for plus, $\lceil \log n \rceil$ matrix multiplications are sufficient to generate the matrices $\mathbf{A}^2, \mathbf{A}^4, \ldots, \mathbf{A}^{n-1}$. Recall that a single matrix multiplication has complexity $O(\log n)$ on the hypercube SIMD and shuffle-exchange SIMD models, given $n^3 = 2^{3q}$ processors. Thus the all-pairs shortest-path problem can be solved in $\Theta(\log^2 n)$ time on the hypercube SIMD and shuffle-exchange SIMD models, given $n^3 = 2^{3q}$ processors.

12.4 SINGLE-SOURCE SHORTEST PATH

In a **single-source shortest-path problem** we must find the shortest path from a specified vertex s, the **source**, to all other vertices in a weighted, directed graph. Let *weight* (u, v) represent the length of the edge from u to v; if no such edge exists, then *weight*$(u, v) = \infty$.

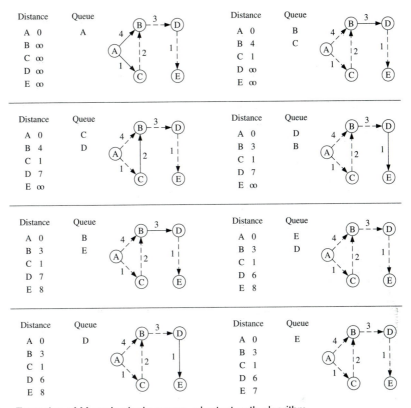

Distance	Queue
A 0	A
B ∞	
C ∞	
D ∞	
E ∞	

Distance	Queue
A 0	B
B 4	C
C 1	
D ∞	
E ∞	

Distance	Queue
A 0	C
B 4	D
C 1	
D 7	
E ∞	

Distance	Queue
A 0	D
B 3	B
C 1	
D 7	
E ∞	

Distance	Queue
A 0	B
B 3	E
C 1	
D 7	
E 8	

Distance	Queue
A 0	E
B 3	D
C 1	
D 6	
E 8	

Distance	Queue
A 0	D
B 3	
C 1	
D 6	
E 8	

Distance	Queue
A 0	E
B 3	
C 1	
D 6	
E 7	

FIGURE 12-5   Execution of Moore's single-source, shortest path algorithm.

A sequential algorithm, developed by Moore (1959), solves this problem (see Fig. 12-5). In Moore's single-source shortest-path algorithm, *distance(v)* is initially assigned the value ∞, for all $v \in V - \{s\}$. The distance from s to itself is, of course, zero. A queue contains vertices from which further searching must be done; initially it contains s. As long as the queue remains nonempty, the vertex u from the head of the queue is removed, and all edges $(u, v) \in E$ are examined. If *distance(u) + weight(u, v) < distance(v)*, a new shorter path to v has been found (through u). In this case *distance(v)* is revised and v is added to the tail of the queue, if it is not already in the queue. The algorithm continues this process until the queue is empty. Moore's algorithm is shown in Fig. 12-5.

Procedure INITIALIZE, called in line 3 of Fig. 12-6, initializes the distance of every nonsource vertex to ∞ and the distance of s to zero. The **for** loop in lines 12 to 20 corresponds to the search for shorter paths to vertices directly reachable from vertex u.

SHORTEST PATH (SISD):

Parameter	n	{Number of vertices in graph}
Global	*distance*	{Element i contains distance from s to i}
	s	{Source vertex}
	weight	{Contains weight of every edge}

```
1. begin
2.   for i ← 1 to n do
3.     INITIALIZE(i)
4.   endfor
5.   insert s into the queue
6.   while the queue is not empty do
7.     SEARCH()
8.   endwhile
9. end
```

SEARCH():

Local	*new.distance*	{Distance to v if pass through u}
	u	{Examined edge leaves this vertex}
	v	{Examined edge enters this vertex}

```
10. begin
11.   dequeue vertex u
12.   for every edge {u, v} in the graph do
13.     new.distance ← distance(u) + weight({u, v})
14.     if new.distance < distance(v) then
15.       distance(v) ← new.distance
16.       if v is not in the queue then
17.         enqueue vertex v
18.       endif
19.     endif
20.   endfor
21. end
```

FIGURE 12-6   Sequential version of Moore's single-source shortest-path algorithm.

This algorithm is amenable to parallelization. There are two methods to consider. The first makes the for loop in lines 12 to 20 parallel. Any given vertex is likely to have several outgoing edges and could all be explored in parallel. The second method is to parallelize the while loop in lines 6 to 8. At any time in the execution of the algorithm, there are probably many vertices in the queue. It should be possible to explore edges from more than one vertex at a time. Which method is better? There are at least two reasons to favor the second method. First, the second method produces larger-grained tasks for the processes to perform, thus, by Design Strategy 5 it would be more likely to produce reasonable speedup. Second, the parallelizability of the first method is limited by the number of edges leaving each vertex. If the graph is relatively sparse, i.e. relatively few edges per vertex, the number of processes that can be used is too constrained.

Consider the following parallel algorithm, based on the second method described. The queue is initialized with the source vertex, then a number of asynchronous processes are created. Each of these processes completes the steps of deleting a vertex from the queue, examining its outgoing edges, and inserting vertices with shorter paths into the queue.

The for loop in lines 2 to 4 of the sequential algorithm is easily transformed to a parallel for loop by using the prescheduling method. The parallel for loop occupies lines 2 to 6 of the parallel algorithm shown in Fig. 12-8. The while loop of lines 6 to 8 of the sequential algorithm must be changed to reflect the existence of a number of asynchronous processes performing the SEARCH procedure in parallel. Clearly it is not appropriate for a process to terminate when it discovers that the queue is empty. (Why?) Hence a more complicated method must be used. In the following algorithm two variables are used together to determine when there is no more work to do. The first variable, *waiting*, is an array that keeps track of processes waiting for work. The second variable, the boolean *halt*, is set to the value *true* only when all the processes are waiting and the queue is empty. Procedure INITIALIZE initializes every entry in array *waiting* to *false*. Lines 6 to 8 of the sequential algorithm become lines 8 to 11 of the parallel algorithm.

How must the SEARCH procedure be modified? Because enqueuing and dequeuing are not atomic operations, the queue must be locked whenever an element is enqueued or dequeued. Second, before a process compares the newly found distance to vertex v, *new.distance*, to the current shortest distance to v, *distance*(v), variable *distance*(v) must be locked. Otherwise, both processes could find themselves trying to update *distance*(v) simultaneously, resulting in the wrong value (see Fig. 12-7). Finally, if a process finds that the queue is empty, it sets its entry in array *waiting* to *true*. If process 1 is waiting, then it checks to see whether every process is waiting. If every process is waiting, the value of *halt* is set to *true*. Notice that the queue must be locked while process 1 checks to see if every process is waiting. The parallel algorithm appears in two parts in Figs. 12-8 and 12-9.

How much speedup can be achieved by this algorithm? Initially, creating more processes decreases the total execution time of the algorithm, because the outgoing edges of several vertices can be examined in parallel. However, since each process demands exclusive control of the queue to insert or delete vertices, maximum speedup is eventually constrained.

Design Strategy 8 Change data structures to reduce the amount of contention for the same shared resource.

There would be no contention between the processes if each process maintained a private list of vertices to be searched, inserting and deleting elements

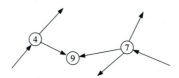

Current value of *distance* (9)	Process 1	Process 2
28	Dequeue vertex 4	Dequeue vertex 7
28	Consider edge (4, 9)	Consider edge (7, 9)
28	*new.distance* ← 22	*new.distance* ← 24
28	*new.distance* < *distance* (9)	*new.distance* < *distance* (9)
28	*distance* (9) ← 22	●
22	●	*distance* (9) ← 24
24	●	●

FIGURE 12-7   If locking is not used, two processes may attempt to update the value of *distance*(v) simultaneously, causing an error.

FIGURE 12-8   Parallel version of Moore's single-source shortest path algorithm, suitable for implementation on a UMA multiprocessor.

SHORTEST PATH (UMA MULTIPROCESSOR):

Parameter n {Number of vertices in graph}
            p {Number of processes}
Global   *distance*   {Element i contains distance from s to vertex i}
            halt   {Set to *true* when it is time for processes to stop}
            s {Source vertex}
            weight   {Contains weight of every edge}

1. begin
2.   for all P_i where $1 \le i \le p$ do
3.   for $j \leftarrow i$ to n step p do
4.   INITIALIZE(j)
5.   endfor
6.   endfor
7.   enqueue s
8.   *halt* ← *false*
9.   for all P_i where $1 \le i \le p$ do
10.   repeat SEARCH (i) until *halt*
11.   endfor
12. end

SEARCH (i):
        Value i {Process number}
        Local $new.distance$ {Distance to v if go through v}
                  u {Vertex edge leaves}
                  v {Vertex edge enters}

1. begin
2.   lock the queue
3.   if the queue is empty then
4. $waiting(i) \leftarrow true$
5.   if $i = 1$ then
6. $halt \leftarrow waiting(2)$ and $waiting(3)$ and ... and $waiting(p)$
7.   endif
8.   unlock the queue
9.   else
10.   dequeue u
11. $waiting(i) \leftarrow false$
12.   unlock the queue
13.   for every edge $\{u, v\}$ in the graph do
14. $new.distance \leftarrow distance(u) + weight(\{u, v\})$
15.   lock ($distance(v)$)
16.   if $new.distance < distance(v)$ then
17. $distance(v) \leftarrow new.distance$
18.   unlock ($distance(v)$)
19.   if v is not in the queue then
20.   lock the queue
21.   if v is not in the queue then
22.   enqueue v
23.   endif
24.   unlock the queue
25.   endif
26.   else unlock ($distance(v)$)
27.   endif
28.   endfor
29.   endif
30. end

FIGURE 12-9   Subroutine SEARCH referenced by UMA multiprocessor-targeted version of Moore's algorithm.

on its own. If the variance in the size of these lists were large, however, then letting each process handle its own list could cause a severe imbalance in the workloads. A middle course is to let each process insert elements into its own private space, then join these lists, so that deletions can occur by letting each of the p processes examine every pth element of the combined list, balancing the work done by each process (Fig. 12-10).

The **linked array** is a data structure designed to allow the joining of various-sized lists so that the inserting and searching of list elements are done in

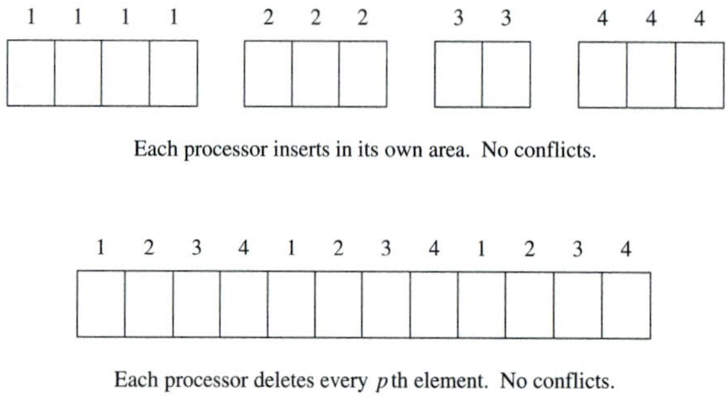

Each processor inserts in its own area. No conflicts.

Each processor deletes every pth element. No conflicts.

FIGURE 12-10   Logical form of linked array.

parallel without contention (Quinn 1983; Quinn and Yoo 1984). Assume that in a single iteration no processor ever inserts more than w elements. The linked array, in that case, contains $p(w + p)$ elements, $w + p$ elements per process. In contiguous group of $w + p$ locations a process may store the names of elements to be searched in the next iteration. If processor i, $1 \le i \le p$, generates the names of e_i elements to be considered in the next iteration, then locations $(i - 1)(w + p) + 1$ through $(i - 1)(w + p) + e_i$ contain these names. Locations $(i - 1)(w + p) + e_i + 1$ through $(i - 1)(w + p) + e_i + p$ contain the values $-i(w + p + 1)$ down to $-[i(w + p) + p]$, respectively.

In the next iteration, when the elements with names in the linked array are to be examined, processor i, $1 \le i \le p$, examines every pth location, beginning with location i. If the value encountered is greater than zero, that is the vertex to be searched. If the value is less than zero, it is a pointer, and the processor immediately jumps to the index indicated (the absolute value). When the pointer has value less than $-p(w + p)$, the search terminates.

Theorem 12.10. Given a set of n elements stored in a linked array and $p \ge 1$ processors, the difference between the greatest number of elements searched by any processor and the least number of elements, is less than or equal to 1 (Quinn 1983).

Proof. This is left to the reader.

Procedure **EXAMINE** in Fig. 12-11 illustrates how a process removes its share of elements from an array containing vertex numbers and pointers.

The space overhead of linked arrays can be high. Unless it can be guaranteed that not all the insertions will be done by a single processor, then the space allocated to the linked array must be approximately p times the space allocated to a simple array. A data-parallel version of Moore's algorithm can be devised to use the linked array. In a single iteration each process has a number of vertices to examine. Every process compiles its own list of vertices to which

EXAMINE (a, i, p, w):

Value	$a[1..p \times (w+p)]$,	{Array containing vertex numbers and pointers}
	i,	{Process number}
	p,	{Number of processes}
	w	{Size of subarray allocated to each process}
Local	j	{Index into a}

```
1. begin
2.    j ← i
3.    while j ≤ p × (w + p) do
4.       if a[j] < 0 then
5.          j ← −a[j]      {Follow pointer}
6.       else
7.          manipulate vertex whose value is a[j]
8.          j ← j + p
9.       endif
10.    endwhile
11. end
```

FIGURE 12-11   Given a linked-array sorting vertex numbers, a process can use procedure EXAMINE to remove its share of the vertex numbers.

shorter paths have been found and builds links to the next process's list. In the next iteration these lists are examined in parallel. Two arrays are used. In any iteration one array is being read while the other array is being written. In the next iteration the roles of the two arrays are reversed.

Quinn and Yoo (1984) have compared the speedup achieved by a linked-array version of Moore's algorithm with the speedup achieved by a sequential deque version of Pape-d'Esopo's algorithm (a variant of Moore's algorithm that uses a double-ended queue, or **deque**) on a UMA multiprocessor. Processes executing this new algorithm must spend time traversing links and synchronizing with each other, adding to the overhead of the algorithm. Thus the slope of the speedup curve is less than that of the asynchronous parallel algorithm that uses the sequential deque. However, the problem of excess contention for a shared data structure is eliminated in this algorithm, and the maximum speedup achieved is higher.

12.5 MINIMUM-COST SPANNING TREE

Determining the minimum-cost spanning forest of a weighted graph is a simple variation of determining connected components. At each iteration the minimum edge, rather than the minimum labeled vertex, is found. Hence, similar complexity results exist for the minimum-cost spanning forest problem. For example, consider Theorem 12.11.

Theorem 12.11. Suppose the weight matrix of a weighted, undirected graph G with n vertices is stored in the base of a pyramid SIMD computer of size n^2. Then the minimum-cost spanning forest of G can be found in time $O(\sqrt{n})$ (Miller and Stout 1986).

If the graph is connected, the minimum-cost spanning forest is a single tree. Efforts to find the minimum-cost spanning tree of a weighted, connected, undirected graph have focused on three classical sequential algorithms: Sollin's (1977) algorithm, the Prim-Dijkstra algorithm (Prim 1957; Dijkstra 1959), and Kruskal's (1956) algorithm. Next we will discuss parallel algorithms based on Sollin's algorithm and Kruskal's algorithm.

12.5.1 Sollin's Algorithm

The most obvious candidate for investigation is a sequential algorithm attributed to Sollin. In this algorithm we start with a forest of n isolated vertices, with every vertex regarded as a tree. In an iteration, the algorithm determines for each tree the smallest edge joining that tree to another tree. All such edges are added to the forest, except that two trees are never joined by more than one edge. (Ties between edges, which would cause a cycle, are resolved arbitrarily.) This process continues until there is only one tree in the forest—the minimum-cost spanning tree. Since the number of trees is reduced by a factor of at least 2 in each iteration, Sollin's algorithm requires at most $\lceil \log n \rceil$ iterations to find the minimum-cost spanning tree. An iteration requires at most $O(n^2)$ comparisons to find the smallest edge incident on each vertex. Thus the sequential algorithm has complexity $O(n^2 \log n)$. Sollin's algorithm is illustrated in Fig. 12-12. Pseudocode for the algorithm appears in Fig. 12-13. Note that this algorithm uses sets to keep track of which vertices are in which trees. The FIND function, passed a vertex v, returns the name of the set (tree) v is in. The procedure UNION, passed two vertices v and w, performs the set union of the sets containing v and w; in other words, it connects the trees containing vertices v and w. Hopcroft and Ullman (1973) showed how these two operations can be performed extremely efficiently. Readers unfamiliar with these two operations can find descriptions in the above-mentioned reference or in a variety of texts on algorithms, including Aho et al. (1974).

How should this algorithm be parallelized for the UMA multiprocessor model? According to Design Strategy 5, parallelization should be done on the outermost loop possible. Unfortunately, we cannot make the while loop parallel, because there are precedence constraints between iterations. Each of the trees existing on iteration i must be joined with the nearest tree before iteration $i + 1$ can begin. Hence parallelization must be done inside the while loop. Lines 7 to 9 can be made parallel through the prescheduling method; each processor is responsible for $1/p$ of the trees. The for loop in lines 10 to 17 can also be made parallel through prescheduling. This is most efficiently

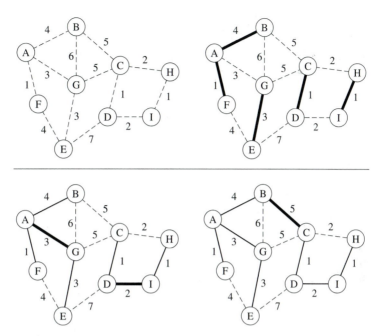

FIGURE 12-12   Sollin's minimum-cost spanning tree algorithm.

done by assigning each processor its fair share of the vertices, then allowing it to examine every outgoing edge from this set.

Parallelizing the loop in lines 18 to 24 is more complicated. The complicating situation is illustrated in Fig. 12-14. Suppose one processor is attempting to connect tree A with its closest neighbor B, while another processor is attempting to connect tree B with its closest neighbor A. Variable $edge[A]$ contains edge $\{v_A, w_A\}$ with length k. Variable $edge[B]$ contains edge $\{v_B, w_B\}$, also with length k. If both processors perform the test in line 20 before either processor performs the UNION operation in line 22, then both edges will be added to T, an error. Therefore, if the loop in lines 18 to 24 is to be made parallel, trees FIND(v) and FIND(w) must be locked before line 20 and unlocked after line 23, since we can allow only one processor at a time to operate in this critical section. Given that only one tree can be locked at a time, we must be careful to avoid deadlock. One way to prevent this is to lock the lower-numbered tree first.

Theorem 12.12. The parallel version of Sollin's algorithm already described has complexity $O(\log n(n^2/p + n/p + n + p))$.

Proof. A series of n UNION and FIND operations has worst-case time complexity $O(n \log^* n)$: the time spent per individual operation amortizes to $O(\log^* n)$, virtually a constant. Hence we make the simplifying assumption that UNION and FIND are constant-time operations. The parallelization of the for loop in lines 7 to 9 has

MINIMUM-COST SPANNING TREE (SISD):

Parameter   *n*   {Number of vertices}
Global   *closest*[] {Distance of closest tree}
            edge[]   {Edge connecting tree with closest tree}
            i
            T   {Minimum-cost spanning tree}
            v, w   {Endpoints of edge under consideration}
            weight[]   {Contains edge weights}

```
1. begin
2.    for i ← 1 to n do
3.       Vertex i is initially in set i
4.    endfor
5.    T ← ∅
6.    while |T| < n − 1 do
7.       for every tree i do
8.          closest[i] ← ∞
9.       endfor
10.      for every edge {v, w} do
11.         if FIND(v) ≠ FIND(w) then
12.            if weight[{v, w}] < closest[FIND(v)] then
13.               closest[FIND(v)] ← weight[{v, w}]
14.               edge[FIND(v)] ← {v, w}
15.            endif
16.         endif
17.      endfor
18.      for every tree i do
19.         (v, w) ← edge[i]
20.         if FIND(v) ≠ FIND(w) then
21.            T ← T ∪ {(v, w)}
22.            UNION(v, w)
23.         endif
24.      endfor
25.   endwhile
26. end
```

FIGURE 12-13   Sequential version of Sollin's minimum-cost spanning tree algorithm.

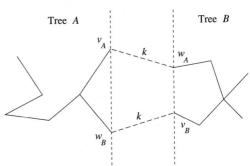

FIGURE 12-14   A complication that arises in the parallelization of Sollin's minimum-cost spanning tree algorithm.

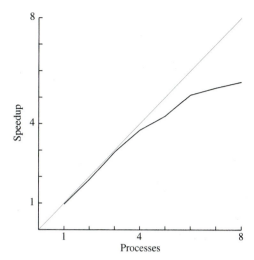

FIGURE 12-15   Speedup of a parallel implementation of Sollin's algorithm on a Sequent Symmetry, given a 350 × 350 grid graph (Barr et al. 1989).

complexity $O(n/p + p)$. The parallelization of the for loop in lines 10 to 17 has complexity $O(n^2/p + p)$. The parallelization of the for loop in lines 18 to 24 has complexity $O((n/p)p + p)$. The factor of p in the last loop occurs because in the worst case, a processor wanting to lock a particular tree A may have to wait for every other processor to lock and unlock A. Remember that the outer while loop executes at most $\lceil \log n \rceil$ times. The overall complexity of the parallel version of Sollin's algorithm, then, is $O(\log n(n^2/p + n/p + n + p))$.

The complexity of this parallel algorithm is minimized when $p = O(\sqrt{n})$. If $p \ll n$, we can expect the parallel algorithm to achieve good speedup.

Barr et al. (1989) have implemented a parallel version of Sollin's algorithm on the Sequent Symmetry. Figure 12-15 illustrates the speedup achieved by their algorithm on a 350 × 350-vertex grid graph (where the vertices and edges form a 2-D mesh without wraparound connections).

12.5.2 Kruskal's Algorithm

In Kruskal's algorithm initially the graph consists of a forest of isolated vertices. The edges are scanned in increasing order of their weights, and every edge that connects two disjoint trees is added to the minimum-cost spanning tree. (In other words, all edges that do not cause cycles with previously selected edges are selected.) The algorithm halts when the graph consists of a single tree, a minimum-cost spanning tree. Figure 12-16 illustrates Kruskal's algorithm.

Lemma 12.1. A UMA multiprocessor with $\lceil \log m \rceil$ processors can remove an element from an m-element heap in constant time (Yoo 1983).

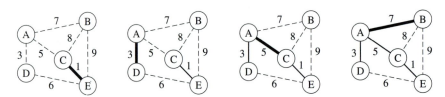

FIGURE 12-16   Kruskal's minimum-cost spanning tree algorithm.

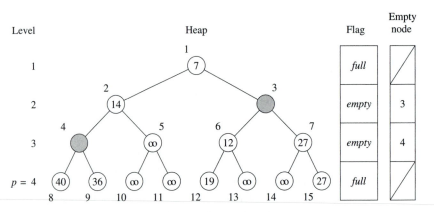

FIGURE 12-17   Yoo's pipelined algorithm to empty heap (Quinn and Deo 1984).

Description of Algorithm. This pipelined algorithm is illustrated in Fig. 12-17. An array is used to implement the heap in the usual way, with the root of the heap being stored in the first element and the left and right children of node i being stored in elements $2i$ and $2i + 1$. The heap is a full binary tree with p levels, p being the number of processors. Some nodes in the bottom level of the tree are assigned the value ∞, if necessary, to fill the tree. During the course of an algorithm's execution, a node is *full* if it contains a value (including ∞). A node is *empty* if its value has been transmitted to its parent and no replacement value has been received from any of its children. The array *flag* indicates what levels contain an empty node; $flag(i) = empty$ if level i has an empty node, otherwise $flag(i) = full$. If $flag(i) = empty$, then $empty\_node(i)$ indicates which node is empty. For all i, where $2 \le i \le p$, processor i is assigned the task of keeping all the nodes at level $i - 1$ full. If $flag(i - 1) = empty$ and $flag(i) = full$, then processor i fills the empty node at level $i - 1$ with the appropriate child at level i. Then $flag(i - 1)$ becomes *full*, and $flag(i)$ becomes *empty*. When a leaf node is emptied, it is filled with an ∞. Eventually the ∞'s fill the tree. Processor 1 empties node 1 whenever it is full and terminates the procedure when node 1 has the value ∞ (i.e., when the heap is empty).

Yoo has also described a parallel method for initializing a heap. The common sequential algorithm is described in Fig. 12-18.

HEAP CONSTRUCTION (SISD):

Parameter	d	{Depth of heap}
Global	k, v, w	{Particular heap elements}
	$key[1...(2^{d+1} - 1)]$	{The heap}
	l	{Level number}

```
1. begin
2.    for l ← d − 1 downto 0 do
3.       for each nonleaf node v at level l do
4.          k ← key[v]
5.          repeat
6.             w ← child of v with the smaller key
7.             if k > key[w] then
8.                key[v] ← key[w]
9.                v ← w
10.            else
11.               exit loop
12.            endif
13.         until v is a leaf node
14.         key[v] ← k
15.      endfor
16.   endfor
17. end
```

FIGURE 12-18 Sequential algorithm for constructing a heap.

The for loop in lines 3 to 15 can be made parallel in a straightforward manner by using prescheduling; each processor makes its share of the nonleaf nodes into heaps at level l. A better method is to allow heap construction to occur at a node once both its children have been made into heaps (Yoo 1983). This method eliminates the requirement that processors synchronize as they reach the end of every level.

Theorem 12.13. The minimum-cost spanning tree of a weighted, undirected, connected graph with m edges can be found in time $O(m)$ on a UMA multiprocessor with $\lceil \log m \rceil$ processors (Yoo 1983).

Summary of Algorithm. The first step is to make a heap out of the edges of the weighted graph, based on their lengths. In the second step, a single process repeatedly removes an edge from the heap and determines whether it is an element of the minimum-cost spanning tree, while the remaining processes repeatedly restore the heap. Recall that the edge is an element of the minimum-cost spanning tree if it connects two unconnected subtrees. Determining whether an edge connects two unconnected subtrees, and if necessary, connecting the subtrees, can be accomplished in virtually constant time by using the efficient FIND and UNION algorithms described earlier. The pipelined processes emptying the heap can provide a new edge in constant time. Since the heap contains m edges, the worst-case time complexity is $O(m)$.

12.6 SUMMARY

Several graph algorithms have been presented in this chapter. Three parallel graph-searching algorithms were defined, and their complexity was analyzed for the CREW PRAM model. Many algorithms appear to solve the connected components problem. Most of these algorithms are related to Hirschberg's algorithm, which uses the vertex-collapsing approach.

Variants of matrix multiplication can be used to solve a variety of graph theoretic problems. We showed how to modify Dekel's parallel matrix multiplication algorithm to solve the all-pairs shortest-path problem (Dekel et al. 1981).

Implementation of a variant of Moore's algorithm to solve the single-source shortest-path problem illustrates two important ideas (Deo et al. 1980). First, contention for a single resource—a queue—severely impairs the speedup achievable by their algorithm on a UMA multiprocessor. Second, implementing halting conditions for asynchronous algorithms is not always a straightforward task. Another single-source shortest-path algorithm, based on the linked array concept, eliminates the resource contention problem. Being data-parallel, rather than asynchronous, the improved algorithm also has a cleaner halting condition. Replacing the queue with the linked array is an example of parallel algorithm Design Strategy 8: Change data structures to reduce the amount of contention for the same shared resource.

We examined parallelizations of two minimum-cost spanning tree algorithms for UMA multiprocessors. Sollin's algorithm has a straightforward parallelization. Kruskal's algorithm also has an efficient parallelization for a small number of processors, because it is possible to pipeline the initialization and the emptying of a heap.

12.7 BIBLIOGRAPHIC NOTES

A more detailed description of graph theoretic terms can be found in numerous texts: Harary (1969); Deo (1974); Reingold et al. (1977). Moitra (1987) and Quinn and Deo (1984) have surveyed parallel graph algorithms.

Reif (1985) proved that the problem of finding a depth-first search tree of a general graph is $\mathcal{P}$-complete. Aggarwall and Anderson (1988) and Aggarwall et al. (1990) published $\mathcal{RNC}$ algorithms for computing depth-first search trees in undirected and directed graphs, respectively. Deterministic algorithms for depth-first search have been described by Aggarwal et al. (1990), Chaudhuri (1990), Goldberg et al. (1988), and Hagerup (1990). Tiwari (1986) has explored the related problem of finding the depth-first spanning tree of a graph with a specified root, given the depth-first spanning tree of the same graph with a different root.

A parallel breadth-first PRAM search algorithm different from the one described in this chapter has been devised by Alton and Eckstein (1979).

Most connected components algorithms in the literature use Hirschberg's approach of collapsing vertices. A number of graph problems are related to the connected components problem, including finding weakly connected components and strongly connected components in a digraph, finding lowest common ancestors, finding articulation points, finding biconnected and k-connected components, and planarity testing. References to connectivity-related algorithms in the literature include Attalah (1983); Attalah and Kosaraju (1982); Belkhale and Banerjee (1992); Cole and Vishkin (1986); Cypher et al. (1990); Eckstein (1979a); Doshi and Varman (1987); Fussell and Thurimella (1988); Fussell et al. (1989); Guibas et al. (1979); Hambrusch (1982, 1983); Han and Wagner (1990); Kanevsky and Ramachandran (1987); Khuller and Schieber (1991); Kosaraju (1979); Levialdi (1972); Levitt and Kautz (1972); Lipton and Valdes (1981); Miller and Reif (1991); Miller and Stout (1985a, 1987); Nassimi and Sahni (1980b); Nath and Maheshwari (1982); Reghbati and Corneil (1978); Reif (1982); Reif and Spirakis (1982); C. Savage (1977, 1981); Savage and Ja'Ja' (1981); Shiloach and Vishkin (1982a); Shyu (1990); Tsin and Chin (1984); Tarjan and Vishkin (1985); van Scoy (1976); Wyllie (1979), and Yang et al. (1990).

Lin and Olariu (1992), Schieber and Vishkin (1988), and Tsin (1986) have presented algorithms to solve the lowest common ancestor problem.

Browning (1980a, 1980b) has designed multicomputer algorithms that use an exponential number of processors to solve the maximum clique, color cost, and traveling salesperson problems.

Dekel and Sahni (1982) have developed an EREW PRAM algorithm to find the maximum matching of a convex bipartite graph.

Determining the minimum-cost spanning forest of a graph can be seen as a simple variation of determining connected components. At each iteration the minimum edge, rather than the minimum labeled vertex, is found. Hence it is not surprising that Chin et al. (1982) have modified Hirschberg's algorithm to solve the minimum-cost spanning tree problem by using the CREW PRAM model. Deo and Yoo (1981) have implemented parallelizations of Kruskal's, Sollin's, and Prim-Dijkstra's minimum-cost spanning tree algorithms on the Denelcor HEP. They report that Cheriton and Tarjan's (1976) minimum-cost spanning tree algorithm, when parallelized, is identical to the parallel version of Sollin's algorithm. Other references to parallel minimum-cost spanning tree algorithms in the literature include Bentley (1980); Atallah (1983); Atallah and Kosaraju (1984); Doshi and Varman (1987); Hambrusch (1982); Hirschberg (1982); Kučera (1982); Levitt and Kautz (1972); Reif (1982); and Savage (1977).

A number of papers describe parallel graph algorithms for hypercube multicomputers. Das et al. (1990a) present a variety algorithms, including algorithms for checking bipartiteness, finding a spanning forest, and determining connected components. Das et al. (1990b) describe two algorithms to solve the minimum-cost spanning forest problem. Sheu et al. (1990) give algorithms for breadth-first search, depth-first search, and maximum matching in a bipartite graph.

Crane (1968) has proposed a parallel single-source shortest-path algorithm for use on an associative processor. Other shortest-path algorithms in the literature and not already described in this chapter include those by Ahuja et al. (1990); Arjomandi (1975); Driscoll et al. (1988); El-Horbaty and Mohamed (1992); Ghosh and Bhattacharjee (1986); Gu and Takaoka (1990); Kučera (1982); Levitt and Kautz (1972); Mateti and Deo (1981); and Price (1982, 1983).

Shiloach and Vishkin (1982b) have developed a parallel algorithm for finding the maximum flow in a directed, weighted graph. Their algorithm is based upon the usual layered network approach. Chen and Feng (1973) and Chen (1975) discuss parallel algorithms for the maximum-capacity path problem.

PRAM algorithms for the maximum independent set problem have been proposed by Goldberg and Spencer (1989) and Karp and Wigderson (1985), and Luby (1986).

Chandrasekharan and Sitharama Iyengar (1988) and Naor et al. (1989) discuss parallel algorithms for chordal graphs.

Parallel algorithms for the stable-marriage problem have been discussed by Hull (1984), Quinn (1985), and Tseng and Lee (1984b).

12.8   PROBLEMS

12-1   Illustrate the search trees resulting from p-depth search, parallel breadth-depth search, and parallel breadth-first search of the graph in Fig. 12-19. Assume the following: $p = 3$, the search begins at vertex 1, and adjacent vertices are always explored in increasing order of the vertex numbers.

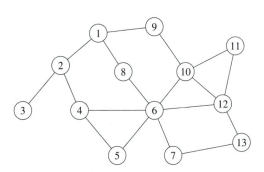

FIGURE 12-19   Undirected graph for Prob. 12-1.

12-2   Prove Theorem 12.3.

12-3   Write an $\Theta(\log^2 n)$ transitive closure algorithm for the CREW PRAM model. Assume that $n = 2^k$, where k is a positive integer.

12-4*   Prove Theorem 12.7.

12-5   Is the parallel all-pairs shortest path algorithm proposed by Dekel et al. (1981) cost optimal?

12-6   In the parallel version of Moore's algorithm for the UMA multiprocessor model, why is it not appropriate for a process to terminate when it discovers that the queue is empty?

12-7   Explain why the queue must be locked when process 1 examines the status of the array *waiting* in the UMA multiprocessor version of Moore's algorithm.

12-8   Explain why the test to see if v is in the queue must be repeated on line 21 of Fig. 12-9. Recode lines 19-25 so that there is no need to repeat the test. Under what circumstances will the new version execute faster than the version shown in this book?

12-9   Prove Theorem 12.10.

12-10*   Use of a linked array is one way to avoid the shared-data structure contention problem encountered by the parallel single-source shortest-path algorithm using a single queue (Deo et al. 1980). Devise a parallel single-source shortest-path algorithm by using another data structure that avoids (or at least reduces) contention.

12-11   Why is the number of trees in Sollin's algorithm reduced by at least a factor of 2 every iteration?

12-12   Give an example of a graph in which Sollin's algorithm requires only a single iteration to produce a minimum-cost spanning tree.

12-13   Give an example of a graph in which Sollin's algorithm requires $\lceil \log n \rceil$ iterations to produce a minimum-cost spanning tree.

12-14   Write a parallel version of Sollin's algorithm for the UMA multiprocessor model.

12-15   Explain how Yoo's parallel heap-emptying algorithm can be modified if $p < \log m$ processors are available.

13

COMBINATORIAL SEARCH

Attempt the end, and never stand to doubt;
Nothing's so hard but search will find it out.

Robert Herrick, "Seek and Find," *Hesperides*

Combinatorial algorithms perform computations on discrete, finite mathematical structures (Reingold et al. 1977). Combinatorial search is the process of finding "one or more optimal or suboptimal solutions in a defined problem space" (Wah et al. 1985), and has been used for such problems as laying out circuits in VLSI to minimize the area dedicated to wires, finding traveling salesperson tours, theorem proving, and game playing.

Chapter 13 surveys the parallelization of divide-and-conquer, branch-and-bound, and alpha-beta search algorithms. Section 13.1 discusses the three kinds of search trees that arise from combinatorial optimization algorithms. Section 13.2 summarizes parallel methods to solve divide-and-conquer problems. Section 13.3 introduces the branch-and-bound algorithm, using the 8–puzzle as an example. The section ends by describing a well-known algorithm to solve the traveling salesperson problem. In Sec. 13.4 we present parallelizations of the branch-and-bound algorithm for multiprocessors and multicomputers. We also show how parallel branch-and-bound algorithms can exhibit anomalous behavior that sometimes results in superlinear speedup. Section 13.5 contains an overview of the sequential alpha-beta algorithm, commonly used to search game trees, and Sec. 13.6 describes methods used to parallelize the alpha-beta search algorithm.

13.1 INTRODUCTION

There are two kinds of combinatorial search problems. An algorithm to solve a **decision problem** must find a solution that satisfies all the constraints. An algorithm that solves an **optimization problem** must also minimize (or maximize) an objective function associated with solutions. All examples of combinatorial search in this chapter are optimization problems.

A search problem can be represented by a tree. The root of the tree represents the initial problem to be solved. The nonterminal nodes are either AND nodes or OR nodes. An AND node represents a problem or subproblem that is solved only when all its children have been solved; an OR node represents a problem or subproblem that is solved when any of its children has been solved. Every nonterminal node in an **AND tree** is an AND node (Fig. 13-1a). The search

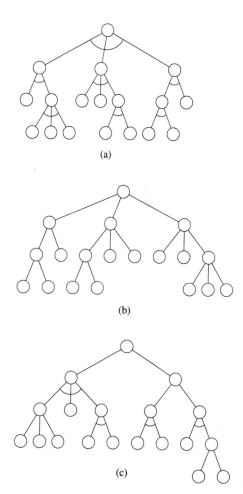

FIGURE 13-1 A search problem can be represented by a tree. (a) An AND tree. (b) An OR tree. (c) An AND/OR tree.

tree corresponding to a divide-and-conquer algorithm is an AND tree, since the solution to a problem is found by combining the solutions to all its subproblems. Every nonterminal node in an **OR tree** is an OR node (Fig. 13-1b). Branch-and-bound algorithms yield OR trees, since the solution to a problem can be found by solving any of its subproblems. An **AND/OR tree** is characterized by the presence of both AND nonterminal nodes and OR nonterminal nodes (Fig. 13-1c). Game trees are examples of AND/OR trees.

13.2 DIVIDE AND CONQUER

Divide and conquer is a problem-solving methodology that involves partitioning a problem into subproblems, solving the subproblems, and then combining those solutions into a solution for the original problem. The methodology is recursive; that is, the subproblems themselves may be solved by the divide-and-conquer technique. The odd-even reduction algorithm in Chap. 9 and the quicksort algorithm of Chap. 10 are examples of the divide-and-conquer technique.

The divide-and-conquer problem solution can be represented by an AND tree, since the solution to any problem represented by an interior node requires the solution of all its subproblems, represented by the children of that node. In other words, every node in the tree must be examined.

Three ways of executing divide-and-conquer algorithms on MIMD computers have been proposed. The first method is to build a tree of processors that corresponds to the search tree. This method has two disadvantages: The root processor can become a bottleneck, since it is the conduit for all input and output; and any particular processor tree, having a fixed interconnection structure, is appropriate for only some divide-and-conquer algorithms. A second method is to use a virtual tree machine that has a robust interconnection network, such as a multicomputer with a hypercubic processor organization. Since the virtual links between problems and subproblems may not be actualized by physical links, we need a good algorithm to map subproblems to processors in order to minimize communication times. The third method suggests using UMA multiprocessors to execute divide-and-conquer algorithms. The shared global memory facilitates access to subproblems by the various processes.

The parallel search of an AND tree can be divided into three phases. In the first phase problems are divided and propagated throughout the parallel computer. For most of the first phase there are fewer tasks than processors, and processors idle until they are given a problem to divide and propagate. In the second phase all the processors stay busy computing. In the third phase there are again fewer tasks than processors, and some processors combine results while other processors idle. Hence the maximum speedup achievable is limited by the propagation and combining overhead.

13.3 BRANCH AND BOUND

Backtrack is a familiar form of exhaustive search. The branch-and-bound method is a variant of backtrack that takes advantage of information about the optimality of partial solutions to avoid considering solutions that cannot be optimal. As an example of the branch-and-bound technique, consider the 8-puzzle (Fig. 13-2), a simplified version of the 15-puzzle invented by Sam Loyd in 1878. The 8-puzzle consists of eight tiles, numbered one through eight, arranged on a 3 × 3 board. Eight locations contain exactly one tile; the ninth location is empty. The object of the puzzle is to repeatedly fill the hole with a tile adjacent to it in the horizontal or vertical direction until the tiles are in row-major order.

Given an initial board position and a mechanism for generating legal moves from any position, it is possible to construct a tree of board positions that can be reached from the initial position. This tree is called the **state space tree** (Fig. 13-3). One way to solve the puzzle is to pursue a breadth-first search of this state space tree until the sorted state is discovered. However, the goal is

1	5	2
4	3	Hole
7	8	6

FIGURE 13-2 The 8-puzzle, a simplified version of the 15-puzzle invented by Sam Loyd in 1878.

FIGURE 13-3 A portion of the state space tree corresponding to the search for a solution to a particular arrangement of the 8-puzzle.

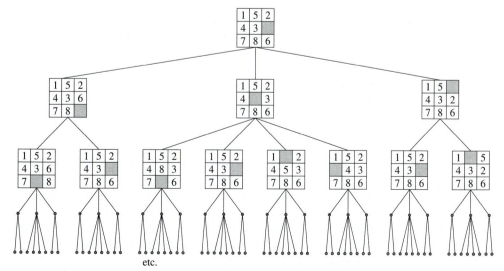

etc.

to examine as few alternative moves as possible. A means for achieving that goal is to associate with each state an estimate of the minimum number of tile moves needed to solve the puzzle, given the moves made so far.

One such function adds the number of tile moves made so far to the Manhattan distance between each out-of-place tile and its correct location. [The Manhattan distance between two tiles with (row, column) coordinates (x_1, y_1) and (x_2, y_2) is $|x_1 - x_2| + |y_1 - y_2|$.] Given such a function, the search can be concentrated on the portions of the state space tree that contain the most promising moves. The search always proceeds from the node having the smallest function value. If two or more nodes have the same value, then the node farthest from the root of the state space tree is examined. If two or more nodes the same distance from the root have the same value, then one node is chosen arbitrarily. The branch-and-bound search of an 8-puzzle appears in Fig. 13-4. Note that the algorithm requires that far fewer nodes be examined than in the breadth-first search.

Now that we have given a concrete example, we will define the branch-and-bound technique. Given an initial problem and some objective function f to be minimized, a branch-and-bound algorithm attempts to solve it directly. If the problem is too large to be solved immediately, it is decomposed into a set of two or more subproblems of smaller size. Every subproblem is characterized by the inclusion of one or more constraints. The decomposition process is repeated until each unexamined subproblem is decomposed, solved, or shown not to be leading to an optimal solution to the original problem.

In the 8-puzzle example, the problem is to put the pieces in order. The objective function f is the number of moves needed to order the pieces. If only a single move is necessary to order the pieces, the algorithm solves the problem directly. Otherwise, it decomposes the problem by generating a number of subproblems, one per legal move.

As we have seen in the case of the 8-puzzle, the decomposition process applied to the original problem may be represented by a rooted tree, called the **state space tree**. The nodes of this tree correspond to the decomposed problems, and the arcs of the tree correspond to the decomposition process. The original problem is the root of the tree. The leaves of the tree are those partial problems that are solved or discarded without further decomposition.

A branch-and-bound tree is distinguished in two important ways from trees representing divide-and-conquer algorithms. First, the tree is an **OR tree** (Fig. 13-1b); the solution to any subproblem is a solution to the original problem. Hence the entire tree need not be searched. In fact, the state space tree representing a branch-and-bound algorithm may be infinite. This is the second important difference between branch-and-bound trees and divide-and-conquer trees.

Recall that the goal of the branch-and-bound technique is to solve the problem by examining a small number of elements in this tree. Assume that a minimum cost solution f^* is desired. A lower bounding function g is calculated for

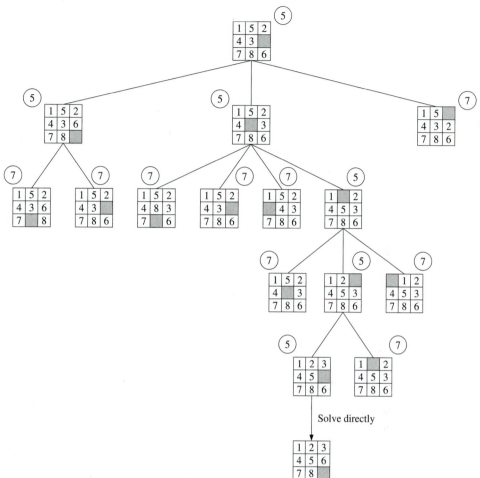

FIGURE 13-4   The branch-and-bound search for a solution to an arrangement of the 8-puzzle identical to that of Fig. 13-3.

each decomposed subproblem as it is created. This lower bound represents the smallest possible cost of a solution to that subproblem, given the subproblem's constraints. On any path from the root to a terminal node, the lower bounds are always nondecreasing. In addition, the lower bound $g(x)$ at every leaf node x representing a feasible solution is identical to the value of the objective function $f(x)$ for that subproblem. Leaf nodes representing infeasible solutions have the value ∞. Figure 13-5 is another example of a state space tree. The values inside the nodes are the lower bounds of the corresponding subproblems. Nodes corresponding to feasible solutions are represented by heavy circles. The best solution to this problem has cost 18; i.e., the value of f^* is 18.

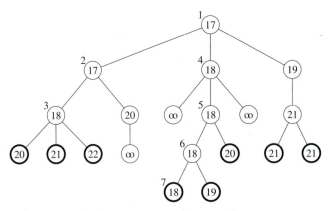

FIGURE 13-5 Another example of a state space tree. The values inside the nodes are the lower bounds of the solutions to the corresponding subproblems. Nodes corresponding to feasible solutions are represented by heavy circles. The best solution to this problem has cost 18. The numbers near the nodes represent the order in which they are examined by the best-first search strategy.

At any point during the execution of a branch-and-bound algorithm there exists a set of problems that have been generated but not yet examined. A search strategy determines the order in which the unexamined subproblems are examined. The best-first (best-bound) search strategy selects the unexamined subproblem with the smallest lower bound. In the case of a tie, the subproblem deepest in the state space tree (i.e., the subproblem with the most constraints) is chosen. Ties unresolved by the deepness heuristic are broken arbitrarily. The numbers near the nodes in Fig. 13-5 indicate the order in which the nodes are examined by the best-first search strategy.

A branch-and-bound algorithm can be characterized by how subproblems are generated, how a particular subproblem is selected as the point to continue the search, how hopeless subproblems are discarded, and how the algorithm terminates. Any of these steps can be performed in parallel.

13.3.1 Traveling Salesperson Problem

The traveling salesperson problem (TSP) can be solved by a branch-and-bound algorithm. The TSP is defined as follows: Given a set of vertices and a non-negative cost $c_{i,j}$ associated with each pair of vertices i and j, find a circuit containing every vertex in the graph so that the cost of the entire tour is minimized. An example of a weighted graph and its traveling salesperson tour are given in Fig. 13-6.

Little et al. (1963) devised a famous branch-and-bound algorithm to solve the traveling salesperson problem. When an unsolvable problem is encountered, it is broken into two subproblems representing tours that must include or exclude a

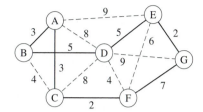

FIGURE 13-6   A weighted graph and its traveling salesperson tour (solid lines).

particular edge. The edge to be used as the added constraint for the subproblems is chosen so that the lower bound on the solution cost of the subproblem, excluding that edge, is maximized. In other words, when a problem is broken into subproblems, the algorithm examines the minimum increase in the tour length, when various edges are excluded, and chooses the edge where exclusion has caused the largest increase in the tour length.

Reduction is used to find a lower bound on the cost of the tour, given the constraints made so far. The reduction algorithm works as follows: For every vertex i in the graph, the length c_i of the shortest edge leading to vertex i is found. If $c_i > 0$, then the lower bound can be increased by c_i, if c_i is subtracted from the length of every edge leading to vertex i. After this step has been performed, the rows can be reduced in a similar fashion. For every vertex i in the graph, the length r_i of the shortest edge leading from vertex i is found. If $r_i > 0$, then the lower bound can be increased by r_i if r_i is subtracted from the length of every edge leading from vertex i. An example of matrix reduction appears in Fig. 13-7.

A problem is broken into subproblems that are easier to solve because the subproblems contain additional constraints. In this algorithm, for example, including an edge reduces the number of edges that must be added to complete the tour, while excluding an edge reduces the number of candidate edges. By driving up the lower bound as quickly as possible, the goal is to limit the number of subproblems (nodes in the state space tree) that must actually be examined. Figure 13-8 contains a high-level description of a best-first branch-and-bound algorithm using the best-first variant of Little et al.'s problem decomposition heuristic.

Figure 13-9 presents the state space tree corresponding to this algorithm's search for the traveling salesperson tour of the graph shown in Fig. 13-7. Each node in the state space tree represents a set of possible tours satisfying constraints specified by the path from the root to that node. The root represents the set of all possible tours. Since reducing the weight matrix of the directed graph results in the value 25 being assigned to the root, a lower bound on the length of any tour is 25. The edge whose exclusion causes the greatest increase in the lower bound is (B,C). Hence the two children of the root represent the alternatives of including or excluding edge (B,C). Every tour explored in the left subtree must contain edge (B,C), but no tour explored in the right subtree

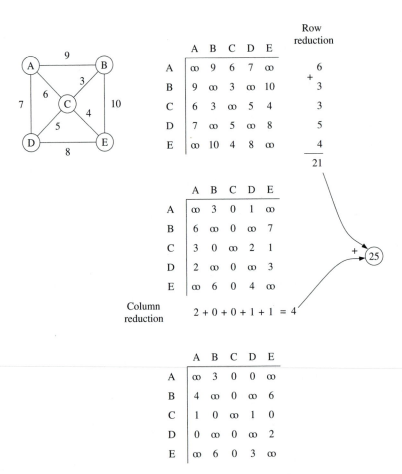

FIGURE 13-7   An example of matrix reduction used by Little et al.'s traveling salesperson algorithm. A lower bound on the length of the traveling salesperson tour of this graph is 25.

may contain edge (B,C). Given its constraint, each child node of the parent can be reduced, and lower bounds on all solutions based on that constraint can be determined. The lower bound of the left child is 31, while the lower bound on the right child is 29. In other words, tours that contain edge (B,C) must have length at least 31, while tours that do not contain edge (B,C) must have length at least 29. Hence the right child is the next node to be explored. Excluding edge (E,C) causes the greatest increase in the lower bound. The value in the right child—32—is a lower bound on all solutions that do not have edge (B,C) or edge (E,C). The value in the left child—31—is a lower bound on all solutions that do not have edge (B,C), but do have edge (E,C).

Since there are two unexplored nodes with the same lower bound (31), we explore the node deeper in the tree. This process continues until a tour is

TRAVELING SALESPERSON (SISD):
  begin
    reduce weight matrix, determining the root's lower bound
    initially only the root is in the state space tree
    {The root represents the set of all possible tours}
    repeat
      select the unexamined node in the state space tree
            with the smallest lower bound
      if the node represents a tour then exit the loop endif
      select the edge whose exclusion increases
            the lower bound the most
      for the two cases representing the inclusion and
            exclusion of the selected edge do
        create a child node with the correct constraint
        find the lower bound for the child node
      endfor
    forever
  end

FIGURE 13-8   A high-level description of a sequential best-first branch-and-bound algorithm to solve the traveling salesperson problem. The algorithm is based on the problem decomposition heuristic devised by Little et al.

FIGURE 13-9   The state space tree corresponding to a best-first branch-and-bound search for a traveling salesperson tour of the graph shown in Fig. 13-7.

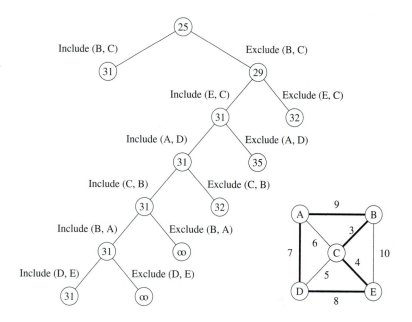

discovered, at which point the algorithm terminates. The tour contains edges (E,C), (A,D), (C,B), (B,A), and (D,E).

13.4   PARALLEL BRANCH-AND-BOUND ALGORITHMS

The first two parts of Sec. 13.4 describe parallelizations of the branch-and-bound algorithm for multiprocessors and multicomputers, respectively. We use as our problem domain the traveling salesperson problem described in Sec. 13.3. All the parallel algorithms described in this section use the branching and bounding heuristics developed by Little et al.

The final part of this section discusses anomalies in parallel branch-and-bound algorithms—conditions under which adding processors may result in slowdown or superlinear speedup.

13.4.1   Multiprocessor Algorithms

Mohan (1983) has developed two parallelizations of the traveling salesperson algorithm presented in Fig. 13-8. The first parallel algorithm involves a parallelization of the for loop; the second parallel algorithm executes the repeat loop in parallel.

As presented before, the for loop has a natural parallelism of 2—each node has only two children. However, by selecting k edges to be considered for inclusion or exclusion, the number of children of each node increases to 2^k, since constraints reflecting all combinations of inclusion and exclusion must be generated. The modified algorithm is shown in Fig. 13-10. Clearly this data-parallel algorithm is appropriate for 2^k processors.

The second algorithm creates a number of processes that asynchronously explore the tree of subproblems until a solution has been found. Each process repeatedly removes the unexplored subproblem with the smallest lower bound from the ordered list of unexplored subproblems. Then it decomposes the problem (unless it can be solved directly), and inserts the two newly created subproblems in their proper places in the ordered list of problems to be examined. A process must have exclusive control of the list in order to insert and delete elements, but the time taken for these tasks is relatively small compared to the time needed to decompose a problem. Thus contention for this list should not be a significant inhibitor of speedup.

The speedup of these two parallel algorithms on Cm* (a NUMA multiprocessor) is contrasted in Fig. 13-11. The first algorithm achieves extremely poor speedup. The additional processors spend most of their time creating nodes that are never explored, because their lower bounds are too high. Mohan's second algorithm achieves, with 16 processors, a speedup of about 8 when solving a 30-vertex TSP. The major obstacle to higher speedup is the number of nonlocal memory references made by the processors.

TRAVELING SALESPERSON (UMA MULTIPROCESSOR):
begin
   reduce weight matrix, determining the root's lower bound
   initially only the root is in the state space tree
   while *true* do
      select the unexamined node in the state space tree
          with the smallest lower bound
      if the node represents a tour then exit the loop endif
      select the k edges whose exclusion increases
          the lower bound the most
      for the 2^k cases representing all inclusion-exclusion
          combinations of the selected edges do
        create a child node with the correct constraints
        find the lower bound for the child node
      endfor
   endwhile
end

FIGURE 13-10   High-level description of a parallel traveling salesperson algorithm developed by Mohan (1983). The algorithm is designed for implementation on a UMA multiprocessor, but it does not achieve good speedup.

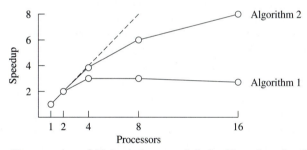

FIGURE 13-11   The speedup of Mohan's two parallel algorithms to solve the traveling salesperson problem with 30 vertices on Cm*.

13.4.2 Multicomputer Algorithms

Quinn (1990) has implemented four variants of an algorithm to solve the traveling salesperson problem on hypercube multicomputers. The algorithm uses distributed priority queues of unexamined subproblems—one queue per processor. The performance of the parallel algorithm depends upon the heuristic the processors use to exchange unexamined subproblems with each other. Major portions of this subsection first appeared in Quinn (1990).

Let $p = 2^d$ denote the number of processors. Assume that the branching factor of the state space tree is k; i.e., assume that each node in the tree has k children. Let N be the minimum number of constraints that must be added to the original problem in order to produce a subproblem that is solvable. In other words, any solution node must have depth $\geq N$ in the state space tree. Let χ be the time needed to examine a subproblem and either solve it or decompose it into k subproblems. Let λ be the time needed to transfer a subproblem from one processor's priority queue to another processor's queue, and assume that both the sender and the receiver processors must devote time λ to the transfer.

The asynchronous branch-and-bound algorithm distributes the unexamined subproblems among the processors. In each of its iterations every processor with a nonempty priority queue removes the unexamined subproblem with the smallest lower bound and either solves the problem directly or divides it into k subproblems. (Note: Although each processor iterates through a sequence of operations, there is no synchronization among processors.) If a processor divides a problem into k subproblems, it puts the subproblems into its priority queue, then uses a heuristic to send m of its unexamined subproblems to neighboring processors, where $m < k$. At the beginning of execution, Processor 0 contains the original problem in its priority queue. Because each processor distributes m subproblems every iteration, $I(p) = \lceil \log_{m+1} p \rceil$ iterations are sufficient to provide every processor with at least one unexamined subproblem.

In order for a solution to be found and guaranteed optimal, two conditions must be met. First, at least one of the solution nodes (and hence all of its ancestors in the state space tree) must be examined. Second, processors must examine all nodes in the state space tree whose lower bounds are less than the cost of the optimal solution. The execution time of the algorithm is determined by whichever event occurs last. The event occuring last is determined by the number of processors and the shape of the state space tree.

To derive an expression for the execution time of the parallel algorithm, we first determine the amount of time needed to examine all of the worthwhile nodes in the state space tree. Assuming that subproblems are exchanged evenly among processors, every iteration requires time $\chi + 2m\lambda$: time χ to decompose or solve a subproblem, time $m\lambda$ to send m subproblems to other processors, and time $m\lambda$ to receive (on average) m subproblems from other processors. If S is the number of worthwhile subproblems in the state space tree, $I(p)$ is the number of iterations before all processors are actively involved, and $G(p)$ is the number of worthwhile subproblems examined in the first $I(p)$ iterations, then $S - G(p)$ worthwhile subproblems remain to be examined after the first $I(p)$ iterations. If the percentage of worthwhile node examinations performed by the p processors after the first $I(p)$ iterations is $E(p)$, the number of additional iterations required to examine all worthwhile subproblems is $\lceil (S - G(p))/(pE(p)) \rceil$. Multiplying the time per iteration by the number of iterations, we see that the amount of time needed to examine all worthwhile subproblems is

$$(\chi + 2m\lambda)\left(I(p) + \left\lceil \frac{S - G(p)}{pE(p)} \right\rceil \right) \qquad (13.1)$$

Second, we determine the amount of time needed for the search to reach a solution node, the length of the critical path. Let M denote the depth of the solution node in the state space tree. Let $T(p)$ denote the number of transfers on the critical path from the root of the state space tree to the solution node. In other words, $T(p)$ is the number of times that subproblems leading to the solution are transferred from one processor's priority queue to another processor's queue. Every transfer incurs a penalty of $\chi/2 + \lambda$. The λ term is the time needed to perform the transfer. The $\chi/2$ term is the expected delay before the subproblem can be evaluated by the destination processor, since the destination processor is likely to be in the middle of decomposing another subproblem when the transfer begins. The total amount of time needed for the search to find a solution is

$$(M + 1)(\chi + 2m\lambda) + T(p)(\chi/2 + \lambda) \tag{13.2}$$

Since the asynchronous algorithm completes when both previously mentioned conditions are met, the execution time of the algorithm is the maximum of the times in expressions 13.1 and 13.2.

Quinn has tested the model by implementing four parallel best-first, branch-and-bound algorithms to solve the traveling salesperson problem. All these algorithms use the reduction heuristic of Little et al. The algorithms have been implemented on a 64-processor nCUBE 3200 hypercube multicomputer.

All four algorithms have been executed on the same set of ten 30-vertex graphs. The edge weights are asymmetrical and randomly chosen from a uniform distribution of integer values ranging from 0 through 99. Every algorithm begins with Processor 0 possessing the original problem, and relies upon successive subproblem decomposition steps to work toward a solution.

During an iteration every processor with a nonempty priority queue removes the unexamined subproblem with the smallest lower bound and either solves the problem directly or divides it into two subproblems. It sends one unexamined subproblem to a neighboring processor and receives (on average) one unexamined subproblem from a neighboring processor. Quinn determined the parameters needed for the analytical model by recording the actions taken by the processors during their solution of the ten 30-vertex problem instances. All these parallel algorithms had the following parameters: $S = 559$, $k = 2$, $m = 1$, $\chi = 125$ msec, and $\lambda = 1$ msec. Values of $G(p)$, $E(p)$, and $T(p)$ varied from algorithm to algorithm.

All four algorithms use the following rule to distribute subproblems among the processors. Let $p = 2^d$ be the number of processors. On iteration i Processor j sends the unexamined subproblem to Processor r, where r is found by inverting bit ($i \bmod d$) of j. With this distribution rule $I(p) = \log_2 p$.

Each algorithm has a unique heuristic for choosing which unexamined subproblem to send to a neighboring processor. Algorithm 1 puts the newly created subproblem with the edge inclusion constraint into the priority queue and sends the subproblem with the edge exclusion constraint. Algorithm 2 puts the newly created subproblem with the smaller lower bound into the priority queue and sends the subproblem with the higher lower bound. Algorithm 3 puts both newly created subproblems on its priority queue, then deletes the second-best

Processors			Alg. 1	Alg. 2	Alg. 3	Alg. 4
1		Actual	1.00	1.00	1.00	1.00
		Predicted	1.00	1.00	1.00	1.00
2		Actual	1.88	1.87	1.89	1.93
		Predicted	1.90	1.90	1.96	1.96
4		Actual	3.52	3.43	3.73	3.65
		Predicted	3.58	3.58	3.85	3.85
8		Actual	5.67	5.43	6.59	6.50
		Predicted	5.76	5.69	7.09	7.09
16		Actual	7.39	6.86	10.20	9.12
		Predicted	7.58	7.00	11.33	10.51
32		Actual	8.07	7.96	12.92	11.50
		Predicted	7.89	7.89	15.20	12.91
64		Actual	7.01	7.34	12.57	12.99
		Predicted	9.05	6.27	13.74	13.10

FIGURE 13-12   Actual and predicted speedups of asynchonrous branch-and-bound algorithms 1, 2, 3, and 4 on nCUBE 3200. Values represent averages over ten 30–vertex instances of the traveling salesperson problem with asymmetrical integer distances.

problem from the priority queue and sends it. Algorithm 4 puts both newly created subproblems on its priority queue, then deletes the best problem from the priority queue and sends it.

The upper entries of Fig. 13-12 indicate the speedup measured on the nCUBE 3200 for each of these four algorithms. The lower, italicized values are the speedups predicted by Quinn's model. Despite the simplifying assumptions, most notably the assumption that all subproblem decompositions require the same amount of time, the model is a reasonably accurate predictor of speedup.

For the solution of a 30-vertex traveling salesperson problem on 64 processors, execution time is dominated by the time needed to examine all worthwhile subproblems. Hence the difference in speedup among the four asynchronous algorithms is a reflection of how well they kept processors busy doing useful work. Figure 13-13 plots the percentage of worthwhile subproblem examinations as a function of distance from Processor 0, the processor given the initial problem, as the algorithms execute on a six-dimensional hypercube. The "distance" between two processors is the length of the shortest path in the hypercube linking them. The significant differences in the curves illustrate how a simple change in the subproblem distribution heuristic can have a dramatic effect on the efficiency of the parallel algorithm, by increasing or decreasing the percentage of time various processors spend examining useful subproblems.

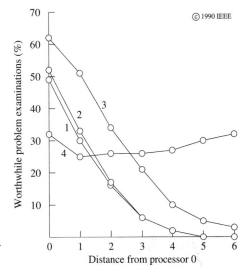

FIGURE 13-13   Percentage of worthwhile subproblem examinations for asynchronous algorithms solving 30-vertex traveling salesperson problem on a 64-processor nCUBE 3200 hypercube multicomputer.

Because the execution times of the asynchronous algorithms on the 30-vertex traveling salesperson problem are dominated by the time needed to solve all worthwhile subproblems, Fig. 13-12 does not validate expression 13.2. To illustrate the precision of this part of the model, we present the performance of Algorithm 4, solving 10 instances of the 20-vertex traveling salesperson problem. For this smaller-sized problem the speedup of Algorithm 4 is constrained by the time needed to traverse the critical path, because: (1) the state space tree has relatively few worthwhile subproblems, and (2) subproblems leading to the solution are frequently transferred from one processor to another. Figure 13-14 contrasts the actual and predicted speedups of this algorithm.

We can use the model to predict the performance of these algorithms on other multicomputers, because changing the value of λ does not affect the values of the other parameters.

To summarize, multicomputer implementations of parallel branch-and-bound algorithms that keep unexamined subproblems in a single priority queue have a

FIGURE 13-14   Actual and predicted speedups for Algorithm 4 solving 20-vertex traveling salesperson problem. Values represent averages over ten problem instances.

Processors	Actual	Predicted
1	1.00	1.00
2	1.63	1.87
4	1.92	2.00
8	1.90	2.01
16	2.04	2.01
32	2.26	2.01
64	2.21	2.04

number of disadvantages. One processor must have a disproportionately large memory, and that processor is involved in every communication. Distributing the unexamined subproblems among the processors balances the memory requirements, reduces the number of communications, and distributes the messages over the network, which can result in a more practical algorithm that actually achieves higher speedup. Whether or not the potential for higher speedup is realized depends upon the effectiveness of the subproblem-distribution heuristic in assigning processors useful work.

13.4.3   Anomalies in Parallel Branch and Bound

In this section we present Lai and Sahni's (1984) analysis of the speedups theoretically achievable by a parallel branch-and-bound algorithm. We must make a few assumptions in order for the analysis to be manageable. Assume that the time needed to examine any node in the tree and decompose it is constant for all nodes in the state space tree. Furthermore, assume that execution of the parallel algorithm consists of a number of "iterations." During each iteration every processor examines a unique subproblem, if one is available, and decomposes it. Given a particular branch-and-bound problem to be solved and a particular lower bounding function g, define $I(p)$ to be the number of iterations required to find a solution node when p processors are used.

The first theorem shows that increasing the number of processors can actually increase the number of iterations required to find a solution.

Theorem 13.1. Given $n_1 < n_2$ and $k > 0$, there exists a state space tree such that $kI(n_1) < I(n_2)$. (See Lai and Sahni [1984].)

Proof. Consider the state space tree shown in Fig. 13-15. All nodes labeled "=" have the same lower bound, which happens to be the value of the least-cost answer node (node A). Nodes labeled ">" have a lower bound greater than the value of the least-cost answer node. When n_1 processors conduct the search, on the first iteration the root node is expanded into $n_1 + 1$ children nodes. The second iteration consists of expanding the n_1 leftmost nodes at level 2 into n_1 nodes at level 3. Of the nodes at level 3, $n_1 - 1$ of them cannot lead to the solution and are discarded. On iteration 3 the remaining node at level 3 and node B are expanded. Since the node at level 3 leads to the solution node, the algorithm terminates. Hence $I(n_1) = 3$.

When n_2 processors conduct the search, the first iteration is the same: The root node is expanded into $n_1 + 1$ children nodes. On the second iteration, however, all $n_1 + 1$ nodes at level 2 are expanded, yielding $n_1 + n_2$ nodes at level 3. Since only n_2 nodes at level 3 can be expanded on iteration 3, it could happen that the n_2 rightmost nodes would be the nodes chosen. If we assume the processors expanded the n_2 rightmost nodes at level 3, n_2 nodes at level 4 would be created, and iterations 4, 5, 6, ..., $3k$ could be devoted to a wild-goose chase, expanding nodes down the right part of the tree. The solution node A would be expanded on iteration $3k + 1$. Hence $I(n_2) = 3k + 1$. Combining the two results yields $kI(n_1) = 3k < 3k + 1 = I(n_2)$.

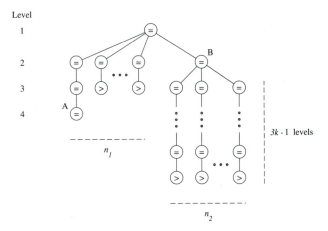

FIGURE 13-15   A state space tree illustrating that increasing the number of processors may actually increase the execution time of a branch-and-bound algorithm.

Because many nodes have a lower bound equal to the value of the least-cost answer node—f^*—we see the anomaly described in the Theorem 13.1. What would happen if $g(x) \neq f^*$, whenever x is not a solution node?

Definition 13.1. A node x is **critical** if $g(x) < f^*$.

Theorem 13.2. If $g(x) \neq f^*$ whenever x is not a solution node, then $I(1) \geq I(n)$ for all $n > 1$. (See Lai and Sahni (1984).)

Proof. By the definition of the best-first branch-and-bound heuristic, only critical nodes and least-cost answer nodes can be expanded. In addition, every critical node must be expanded before any least-cost answer node is expanded. Hence if the number of critical nodes is m, then $I(1) = m$. When $n > 1$, at least one of the nodes expanded each iteration must be a critical node (Prob. 13-5). Hence a least-cost answer node must be examined no later than iteration m. Thus if the number of critical nodes is m, then $I(n) \leq m$. Therefore $I(1) \geq I(n)$ for all $n > 1$.

The following theorem proves that increasing the number of processors can actually cause a disproportionate decrease in the number of iterations required to find a solution node.

Theorem 13.3. Given $n_1 < n_2$ and $k > n_2/n_1$, then there exists a state space tree such that $I(n_1)/I(n_2) \geq k > n_2/n_1$. (See Lai and Sahni [1984].)

Proof. This is left to the reader as Prob. 13-6.

Theorem 13.4. If $g(x) \neq f^*$ whenever x is not a least-cost answer node, then $I(1)/I(n) \leq n$ for $n > 1$. (See Lai and Sahni [1984].)

Proof. Let m be the number of critical nodes. Then $I(1) = m$ (Theorem 13.2). All critical nodes must be expanded before the parallel branch-and-bound algorithm can terminate (Prob. 13-7). Hence $I(n) \geq m/n$, or $I(1)/I(n) \leq n$.

Lai and Sahni have found anomalous behavior in some instances of the 0–1 knapsack problem, but they conclude that anomalous behavior is rarely encountered in practice and that, in general, (1) increasing the number of processors will not increase execution time (assuming the problem is large enough), and (2) superlinear speedup cannot be expected.

13.5 ALPHA-BETA SEARCH

The most successful computer programs to play two-person zero-sum games of perfect information, such as chess, checkers, and go, have been based on exhaustive search algorithms. These algorithms consider series of possible moves and countermoves, evaluate the desirability of the resulting board positions, then work their way back up the tree of moves to determine the best initial move.

Given a trivial game, the **minimax** algorithm can be used to determine the best strategy. Figure 13-16a represents the **game tree** of a hypothetical game, with rules left unstated, played for money. Dotted edges represent moves made by the first player; solid lines represent moves made by the second player. The root of the tree is the initial condition of the game. The leaves of this game tree represent outcomes of the game. Interior nodes represent intermediate conditions. The outcomes are always put in terms of advantage to the first player. Thus positive numbers indicate the amount of money won by the first player, while negative numbers indicate the amount of money lost by the first player. The algorithm assumes that the second player tries to minimize the gain of the first player, while the first player tries to maximize his or her own gain, hence the name of the algorithm. Figure 13-16b is the same tree with the values of the interior nodes filled in. The value of this game to the first player is 2. If the first player plays the minimax strategy, he or she is guaranteed to win at least two dollars.

Stockman (1979) has pointed out that a game tree is an example of an AND/OR tree. The AND nodes represent positions where it is the second player's turn to move. The OR nodes represent positions where it is the first player's turn to move.

Nontrivial games such as chess have game trees that are far too complicated to be evaluated exactly. For example, de Groot has estimated that there may be 38^{84} positions in a chess game tree (de Groot 1965). Thus current chess-playing programs examine moves and countermoves only to a certain depth, then, at that point, estimate the value of the board position to the first player. Of course, evaluation functions are unreliable. If a perfect evaluation function existed, the need for searching would be eliminated (Prob. 13-9). As we have seen, all

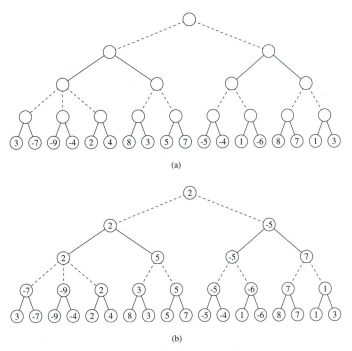

(a)

(b)

FIGURE 13-16 (a) A game tree. Dotted edges represent the moves available to the first player; solid edges represent moves available to the second player. (b) The same tree with the values of the interior nodes filled in.

possible moves and countermoves from a position p to some predetermined lookahead horizon can be represented by a game tree. The minimax value of the game tree can be found by applying the evaluation function to the leaves of the tree (the terminal nodes), then working backward up the tree. If it is the second player's move at a particular nonterminal node in the game tree, the value assigned is the minimum over all its children nodes. If it is the first player's move, the value assigned is the maximum over all its children nodes.

Given a game tree in which every position has b legal moves, it is easy to see that a minimax search of the game tree to depth d examines b^d leaves.

It is generally true that the deeper the search, the better the quality of play. That is why **alpha-beta pruning** has proven to be valuable. Alpha-beta pruning, a form of branch-and-bound algorithm, avoids searching subtrees whose evaluation cannot influence the outcome of the search, i.e., cannot change the choice of move. Hence it allows a deeper search in the same amount of time.

The alpha-beta algorithm, displayed in Fig. 13-17, is called with four arguments: *pos*, the current condition of the game; α and β, the range of values over which the search is to be made; and *depth*, the depth of the search that is

ALPHA.BETA (pos, α, β, $depth$)

Reference	α	{Lower cutoff value}
	β	{Upper cutoff value}
Value	pos	{Position}
	$depth$	{Search depth}
Parameter	$max.c$	{Maximum possible number of moves}
Local	$c[1...max.c]$	{Children of pos in game tree}
	$cutoff$	{Set to TRUE when okay to prune}
	i	{Iterates through legal moves}
	val	{Value returned from search}
	$width$	{Number of legal moves}

```
begin
  if depth ≤ 0 then
    return (EVALUATE (pos))        {Evaluate terminal node}
  endif
  width ← GENERATE.MOVES(pos)
  if width = 0 then
    return (EVALUATE (pos))        {No legal moves}
  endif
  cutoff ← FALSE
  i ← 1
  while i ≤ width and cutoff = FALSE do
    val ← ALPHA.BETA (c[i], α, β, depth-1)
    if pos is MAX-NODE and val > α then
      α ← val
    else if pos is MIN-NODE and val < β then β ← val endif
    endif
    if α > β then
      cutoff ← TRUE
    endif
    i ← i + 1
  endwhile
  if pos is MAX-NODE then return α
  else return β
  endif
end
```

FIGURE 13-17   Sequential alpha-beta algorithm.

to be made. The function returns the minimax value of the position pos. The original board position is a MAX-NODE. Every child of a MAX-NODE is a MIN-NODE. Every child of a MIN-NODE is a MAX-NODE.

To illustrate the workings of the alpha-beta algorithm, consider the game tree in Fig. 13-18. This tree represents the same game as that in Fig. 13-16,

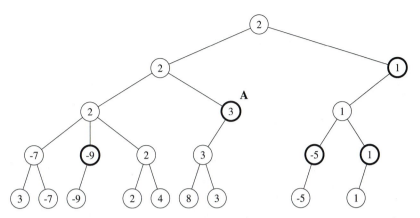

FIGURE 13-18   An illustration of alpha-beta search. The number inside each node is the value of the position. In the case of leaf nodes, an evaluation function computes the value of the position. In the case of interior nodes, the value is computed from the values of its children. Highlighted circles represent nodes in which pruning occurs.

except that nodes not examined by the alpha-beta algorithm are not included. When the algorithm begins execution, $\alpha = -\infty$ and $\beta = \infty$. The algorithm traverses the nodes of the tree in preorder; the values of α and β converge as the search progresses.

The nodes drawn in heavy lines in Fig. 13-18 represent places where pruning occurs. To explore the conditions under which pruning happens let us consider an arbitrary interior node in the search tree. When the search reaches this node, we know that some choice of moves that has already been considered leads to a value of at least α for the player moving first. We also know that correct play on the part of the opponent will ensure that the first player cannot get a value more than β. Hence α and β define a window for the search.

If the interior node *pos* is a MAX-NODE, then it is the first player's move. If *val*, the value of the game tree searched from node *pos* is greater than α, then α is changed to *val*, a better line of play has been found for player one.

Analogously, if the interior node *pos* is a MIN-NODE, then it is the second player's move. If *val*, the value of the game tree searched from node *pos* is less than β, then β is changed to *val*; a better line of play has been found for player two.

However, if at any time the value of α exceeds the value of β, there is no need to search further. It is in the best interests of one of the players to block the line of play leading to node *pos*.

For example, consider the node labeled **A** in Fig. 13-18. The value returned from the search of the first child of **A** is 3, which is greater than 2, the value β. It is not in the second player's interest to allow play to reach this position, since there is another line of play guaranteeing a value no higher than 2. Hence there is no point in continuing the search from this game position.

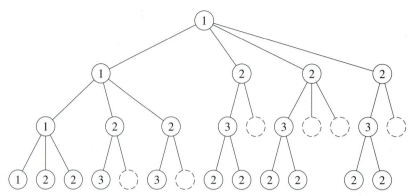

FIGURE 13-19 Alpha-beta pruning of a perfectly ordered game tree. The number inside each node indicates its classification as either type 1, type 2, or type 3. The root of the tree is a type 1 node. The first child of a type 1 node is a type 1 node. All other children of a type 1 node are type 2 nodes. The first child of a type 2 node is a type 3 node; all other children of a type 2 node may be pruned. All children of a type 3 node are type 2 nodes.

To what extent can alpha-beta pruning reduce the number of leaf nodes that must be examined? The algorithm does the most pruning on a **perfectly ordered game tree**, that is, a game tree in which the best move from each position is always searched first (see Fig. 13-19). Assuming a perfectly ordered game tree with a search depth of d and uniform branching factor b, Slagle and Dixon (1969) have shown that the number of leaf nodes examined by the alpha-beta algorithm is

$$Opt(b, d) = b^{\lceil d/2 \rceil} + b^{\lfloor d/2 \rfloor} - 1$$

In other words, in the best case it is possible for the alpha-beta algorithm to examine no more than approximately twice the square root of the number of nodes searched by the minimax algorithm.

> **Definition 13.2.** The **effective branching factor** of an algorithm searching a game tree of depth d is the dth root of the number of leaf nodes evaluated by the algorithm.

Casting Slagle and Dixon's result in terms of this definition, an alpha-beta search reduces the effective branching factor from b to $\sqrt{b}$ when searching a perfectly ordered game tree.

Of course, a perfectly ordered search is not possible in practice. However, experimental evidence indicates that sequential alpha-beta algorithms often search no more than 50 percent more nodes than would be searched if the tree were perfectly ordered. Hence in practice the alpha-beta search algorithm exhibits much higher performance than minimax.

Two common enhancements to the alpha-beta search algorithm are aspiration search and iterative deepening. **Aspiration search** makes an estimate of the value v of the board position at the root of the game tree, figures the probable error e of that estimate, then calls the alpha-beta algorithm figuring the probable error e of that estimate, then calls the alpha-beta algorithm with the initial window $(v - e, v - e)$. If the value of the game tree does indeed fall within this window of values, then the search will complete sooner than if the algorithm had been called with the initial window $(-\infty, \infty)$. If the value of the game tree is less than $v - e$, then the search will return the value $v - e$, and the algorithm must be called again with another window, such as $(-\infty, v - e)$. Similarly, if the value of the game tree is greater than $v + e$, then the search returns the value $v + e$, and another search will have to be done with a modified initial window, such as $(v + e, \infty)$.

Another variant on the standard alpha-beta algorithm is called **iterative deepening**. Each level of a game tree is called a **ply** and corresponds to the moves of one of the players. Iterative deepening is the use of a $(d-1)$-ply search to prepare for a d-ply search. This technique has three advantages (Marsland and Campbell 1982). First, it allows the time spent in a search to be controlled. The search can continue deeper and deeper into the game tree until the time allotted has expired. Second, results of the $(d - 1)$-ply search can be used to improve the ordering of the nodes during the d-ply search, making the node ordering similar to perfect ordering, and allowing the alpha-beta search to execute more quickly. Finally, the value returned from a $(d - 1)$-ply search can be used as the center of the window for a d-ply aspiration search.

13.6   PARALLEL ALPHA-BETA SEARCH

13.6.1   Parallel Move Generation and Position Evaluation

Alpha-beta search has a number of opportunities for parallel execution. One approach is to parallelize move generation and position evaluation. The custom chess machine HITECH™, with 64 processors organized as an 8×8 array, has taken this route. However, the speedup that can be achieved with this approach is limited by the parallelism inherent in these activities. Further improvements in speedup lie in parallelizing the search process.

13.6.2   Parallel Aspiration Search

Another straightforward parallelization of the alpha-beta algorithm is done by performing an aspiration search in parallel. If three processors are available, then each processor can be assigned one of the windows $(-\infty, v - e)$, $(v - e, v + e)$, and $(v + e, \infty)$. Ideally the processor searching $(v - e, v + e)$ will succeed, but all three processors will finish no later than a single processor searching the window $(-\infty, \infty)$. More processors can be accommodated by creating more windows with smaller ranges. Baudet (1978a, 1978b) explored parallel aspiration on the Cm* NUMA multiprocessor.

Work on parallel aspiration for the game of chess has led to two conclusions. First, the maximum expected speedup is typically five or six, regardless of the number of available processors. This is because $Opt(b, d)$ is a lower bound on the cost of alpha-beta search, even when both α and β are initially set equal to the value eventually returned from the search. Second, parallel aspiration search can sometimes lead to superlinear speedup when two or three processors are being used.

13.6.3   Parallel Subtree Evaluation

Many believe that significant speedups can only be achieved by allowing processors to examine independent subtrees in parallel. There are two important overheads to be considered. **Search overhead** refers to the increase in the number of nodes that must be examined owing to the introduction of parallelism. **Communication overhead** refers to the time spent coordinating the processes performing the searching. Search overhead can be reduced at the expense of communication overhead by keeping every processor aware of the current search window. Communication overhead can be reduced at the expense of search overhead by allowing processors to work with outdated search windows.

For example, consider this simple method of performing alpha-beta search in parallel. Split the game tree at the root, and give every processor an equal share of the subtrees. Let every processor perform an alpha-beta search on its subtrees. Each processor begins with the search window $(-\infty, \infty)$, and no processor ever notifies other processors of the changes in its search window. Clearly this algorithm minimizes communication overhead. What is the speedup achievable by this method?

Theorem 13.5. Given a perfectly ordered uniform game tree of depth d and branching factor b, the number of node examinations performed by alpha-beta search in the first branch's subtree is

$$b^{\lceil (d-1)/2 \rceil} + b^{\lfloor (d-1)/2 \rfloor} - 1$$

(See Hyatt et al. [1989].)

Proof. Slagle and Dixon (1969) showed that the minimum number of nodes examined from a type 1 node of depth d is $b^{\lceil (d-1)/2 \rceil} + b^{\lfloor (d-1)/2 \rfloor} - 1$. In a perfectly ordered game tree, the first child of a type 1 node is also a type 1 node, so we simply replace d with $d - 1$ in their expression.

Theorem 13.5 demonstrates that the examination of the first branch of a perfectly ordered game tree takes a disproportionate share of the computation time. For example, consider a 10–ply search of a perfectly ordered tree that has a branching factor of 38 (such as a chess game tree). The minimum number of node examinations is 158,470,335. The minimum number of node examinations in the first branch is 81,320,303. By Amdahl's law it is clear that if only one processor is responsible for searching the first move's subtree, speedup will be less than two.

In addition, because every processor's search must begin with $-\infty$ and ∞ as the values for α and β, respectively, the parallel algorithm will not prune as many subtrees as the sequential algorithm. A complete elimination of communication overhead creates significant search overhead.

Let's look at the other extreme. What must be done to eliminate search overhead completely? We will make the assumption that the game tree is perfectly ordered. Look at Fig. 13-19. If we want to eliminate search overhead, we must ensure the parallel algorithm prunes the same nodes as the sequential algorithm. First consider searching the subtree of a type 1 node. The first child is a type 1 node; the remaining children are type 2 nodes. Searching subtrees rooted by type 2 nodes requires up-to-date values of α and β in order to prune all but the first children of the type 2 nodes. To get up-to-date values, the search of the subtrees rooted by type 2 nodes cannot begin until the search of the subtree rooted by the type 1 node has finished, returning α and β. However, once the values of α and β are known, all type 2 nodes may be searched in parallel without processor interaction.

Next, let's look at the search of a subtree of a type 2 node. Since all but the first child are pruned, there is no parallelism to be exploited.

Finally, consider the search of a subtree of a type 3 node. All its children are type 2 nodes, and these nodes may be searched in parallel without processor interaction.

In practice, search trees are not perfectly ordered, but this exercise has demonstrated that a parallel alpha-beta algorithm can significantly reduce search overhead by delaying the search of some subtrees until more accurate bounds information is available.

13.6.4 Distributed Tree Search

Ferguson and Korf (1988) have developed a parallel tree searching algorithm called Distributed Tree Search (DTS), which, when evaluating game trees, has achieved good speedups. Although the DTS algorithm is suitable for solving a variety of tree search problems, we will describe its use as a tool to perform parallel alpha-beta search.

The DTS algorithm executes by assigning processes to nodes of the search tree. Each process controls one or more physical processors. When the algorithm begins execution, a single process, called the root process, is assigned to the root node of the search tree. It controls the entire set of physical processors performing the search.

When a process is assigned to a nonterminal node, it generates the children of that node by evaluating the legal moves. The process assigns processors to the children nodes based upon the processor allocation strategy. For example, if the search is using a breadth-first processor allocation scheme, one processor is allocated to each child node until there are no more processors to allocate. At this point a new process is created for each child node that is allocated at least one processor. The parent process suspends operation until it receives a message from another process.

When a process is assigned to a terminal node, it returns the value of that node and its set of allocated processors to the parent, then terminates.

The first child process to complete the search of its subtree sends a message with its values of α and β to the parent. It returns its set of processors to the parent and terminates. The parent process wakes up when it receives the message from its child. It reallocates the freed processors to one or more of its active child processes. It may also send one or more of its child processes new values of α and β. The reallocation of processors from quicker processes to slower processes produces efficient load balancing. Notice that in this scheme a child process may be awakened by its parent, which is passing along additional processors. After reallocating processors, parent processes suspend operation until they receive another message. When all child processes have terminated, the parent process returns α, β, and the set of processors to the parent and terminates. When the root process terminates, the algorithm has completed.

Three implementation details improve the performance of the DTS algorithm. First, every blocked process should share a physical processor with one of its child processes. In this way all processors stay busy. Second, when a blocked parent process is awakened, it should have higher priority for execution than processes corresponding to nodes deeper in the search tree. Third, when the search reaches a point where there is only a single processor allocated to a node, the process controlling the processor should execute the standard sequential alpha-beta search algorithm.

Theorem 13.6. Given a uniform game tree with depth d and branching factor b, if the alpha-beta algorithm searches the tree with effective branching factor b^x (where $0.5 \leq x \leq 1$), then DTS with p processors and breadth-first allocation will achieve a speedup of $O(p^x)$.

Proof. The execution time of the sequential algorithm is proportional to the number of leaf nodes it evaluates, or $O((b^x)^d) = O(b^{xd})$. The DTS algorithm with breadth-first allocation distributes processors evenly among the branches of the search tree, until there is one processor per node. This occurs at depth $O(\log_b p)$. The time complexity of this part of the search is also $O(\log_b p)$, since allocations at the same level in the tree occur in parallel. Once the search has reached a point where there is one processor per node, every processor performs the sequential alpha-beta algorithm on the remaining subtree of depth $O(d - \log_b p)$. The time needed for these searches is $O(b^{x(d-\log_b p)})$, since the effective branching factor is b^x. Propagating values back to the root has time complexity $O(\log_b p)$. The overall time complexity of the DTS algorithm is $O(\log_b p + b^{x(d-\log_b p)})$. As the depth d grows, the second term dominates, and the parallel time complexity is $O(b^{x(d-\log_b p)})$. The speedup is the sequential time complexity divided by the parallel time complexity, or

$$O\left(\frac{b^{xd}}{b^{x(d-\log_b p)}}\right) = O\left(b^{xd-x(d-\log_b p)}\right) = O\left(b^{(\log_b p)x}\right) = O(p^x)$$

To test the DTS algorithm, Ferguson and Korf (1988) have implemented the game of Othello. Their node-ordering function results in an effective branching factor of about $b^{.66}$. The program implements parallel alpha-beta search using the DTS algorithm. Ferguson and Korf executed the algorithm on 40 midgame positions using 1, 2, 4, 8, 16, and 32 nodes of an Intel iPSC hypercube multicomputer. They estimated the speedup achieved by the program by dividing the number of node evaluations performed by the sequential algorithm by the number of node evaluations performed per processor by the parallel algorithm. For example, they estimate an average speedup of 10 for 32 processors. Figure 13-20 plots the speedup achieved by their algorithm.

Ferguson and Korf have implemented another processor allocation strategy, called **bound-and-branch**, which corresponds closely to the algorithm described at the end of the last subsection. When the search reaches a type 1 node, all processors are allocated to the leftmost child. After the search returns with cutoff bounds from the subtree rooted by the leftmost child, the processors are assigned to the remaining children nodes in a breadth-first manner. When the search reaches a node having type 2 or 3, cutoff bounds already exist, and the processors are assigned in breadth-first fashion.

Ferguson and Korf have empirically determined that the bound-and-branch strategy achieves higher speedup than the breadth-first allocation strategy, even when the node ordering is not perfect. They have implemented a version of the Othello program that uses iterative deepening and the bound-and-branch

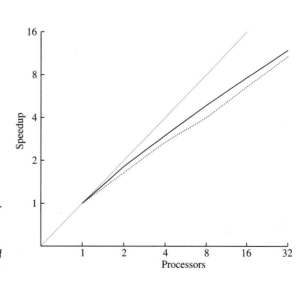

FIGURE 13-20 Speedup achieved by the DTS algorithm for game of Othello on Intel iPSC. Solid line represents bound-and-branch processor allocation strategy; dashed line represents breadth-first strategy (Ferguson and Korf 1988).

processor allocation strategy. The actual speedup achieved by the program is 12 on 32 processors.

13.7 SUMMARY

One way to differentiate between combinatorial search problems is to categorize them by the kind of state space tree they traverse. Divide-and-conquer algorithms traverse AND trees: the solution to a problem or subproblem is found only when the solution to all its children is found. Branch-and-bound algorithms traverse OR trees: the solution to a problem or subproblem can be found by solving any of its children. Game trees contain both AND nonterminal nodes and OR nonterminal nodes.

Parallel combinatorial search algorithms for all these trees have been proposed. The speedup achievable through the parallel search of an AND tree is limited by propagation and combining overhead.

Mohan (1983) has implemented programs to solve the traveling salesperson problem on a NUMA multiprocessor. Quinn (1990) has implemented programs to solve the same problem on hypercube multicomputers. Their work demonstrates the potential for implementing branch-and-bound algorithms on MIMD computers. The fundamental problem faced by designers of parallel branch-and-bound algorithms is keeping the efficiency of the processors high by focusing the search on the nodes the sequential algorithm examines.

Lai and Sahni (1984) have given examples of state space trees for which parallel best-first branch-and-bound algorithms can show anomalous behavior, such as superlinear speedup. Experiments they have performed with the simulated parallel solution of the 0–1 knapsack problem show that anomalous behavior can really occur, albeit rarely.

Alpha-beta search has proven to be an efficient method for evaluating game trees. Several improvements on the standard alpha-beta search have been invented, including aspiration search and iterative deepening. Several methods have been proposed to parallelize alpha-beta search. These methods include parallel move generation and evaluation, parallel aspiration search, and the parallel search of independent subtrees. Only the third method seems to have enough parallelism to scale to massively parallel machines. Minimizing communication overhead can cause an unacceptable amount of search overhead, and vice versa. Ferguson and Korf (1988) have developed the bound-and-branch strategy to keep an acceptable balance while minimizing the two kinds of overhead.

13.8 BIBLIOGRAPHIC NOTES

Ibaraki (1976a, 1976b) has analyzed sequential branch-and-bound algorithms.

Imai et al. (1979) wrote an early paper describing a parallel branch-and-bound algorithm. Wah et al. (1984, 1985) discuss Manip™, a computer specifically designed to execute best-first branch-and-bound algorithms. They also describe parallelism in dynamic programming. Kumar and Kanal (1983) recast branch-and-bound algorithms to encompass AND/OR tree search as well as OR tree search. Other papers on parallel branch-and-bound algorithms include Dehne et al. (1990), Janakiram et al. (1988), Kalé and Saletore (1990), Kumar and Kanal (1984), Li and Wah (1984a, 1984b), Troya and Ortega (1989), and Wah et al. (1990).

Balas et al. (1991) have used a parallel branch-and-bound algorithm to solve a 30,000–city traveling salesperson problem on the Butterfly Plus NUMA multiprocessor.

Deriving results similar to those of Lai and Sahni (1984), Quinn and Deo (1986) describe anomalous behavior of branch-and-bound algorithms.

Knuth and Moore (1975) analyzed the sequential alpha-beta algorithm.

Marsland and Campbell (1982) wrote an early survey paper describing the parallel search of strongly ordered game trees. Their treatment is much more detailed than the one presented in this chapter, and they cover many more interesting variations of parallel alpha-beta search. Parallel alpha-beta search has also been explored by Finkel and Fishburn (1982).

Hyatt et al. (1989) develop the mathematics for predicting the performance of parallel implementation of the principal variation splitting (PVS) algorithm. They also describe an enhancement that improves the performance of the parallel algorithm in most test cases, and they have implemented their parallel PVS algorithm on a Sequent Balance.

Huntbach and Burton (1988) describe the implementation of parallel alpha-beta search on the *virtual tree machine*, a network of processors. Schaeffer (1989) also describes parallel alpha-beta search algorithms on computer networks.

Bhattacharya and Bagchi (1990) describe a parallelization of the SSS* search algorithm. Their work is based on the DTS algorithm described in this chapter.

Newborn (1989) has surveyed the progress in computer chess during the 1980s and briefly describes parallel search techniques.

Felten and Otto (1988) present the results of implementing a parallel chess program on the nCUBE 3200 multicomputer. They report a speedup of up to 100 on a 256–processor system. Their algorithm has many similarities to the DTS algorithm, but it has many other enhancements as well.

Earlier in the chapter we pointed out that the quality of play usually improves as the game tree search is deepened. Nau has shown that this rule of thumb is not true for an infinite class of pathological game trees. However, he adds that "pathology does not occur in games such as chess or checkers" (Nau 1982).

13.9 PROBLEMS

13-1   Explain this statement by Wah et al. (1985): Multiprocessing is generally used to improve the computational efficiency of solving a given problem, *not to extend the solvable problem space of the problem* (their italics).

13-2   Given a divide-and-conquer algorithm whose complexity is described by the recurrence relation

$$T(n) = \Omega(n) + kT\left(\frac{n}{k}\right)$$

$$T(1) = \Omega(1)$$

derive a lower bound on the complexity of a parallel divide-and-conquer algorithm, assuming that the decomposition step [with complexity $\Omega(n)$] cannot be made parallel.

13-3   Using the 8-puzzle as an example, explain why it is likely that a depth-first search of the state space tree would not yield a solution.

13-4   Justify the deepness heuristic used by the best-first search strategy to choose between unexamined subproblems sharing the smallest lower bound.

13-5   In the context of Theorem 13.2, why must at least one critical node be examined every iteration when $p > 1$?

13-6*   Prove Theorem 13.3.

13-7   In the context of Theorem 13.4, why must all critical nodes be expanded before the algorithm can terminate?

13-8   Explain the difficulties faced by an implementor of a parallel best-first branch-and-bound algorithm on a multicomputer. Describe possible solutions to these difficulties.

13-9   If a perfect evaluation function existed, the need for searching would be eliminated. Explain.

13-10   Use the minimax algorithm to evaluate the game tree of Fig. 13-21.

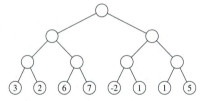

FIGURE 13-21   A game tree.

13-11   Use the alpha-beta algorithm to evaluate the game tree of Fig. 13-21.

13-12   Extend the perfectly ordered game tree of Fig. 13-19 by one level to illustrate how nodes are pruned at level 4. Assume a branching factor of 2.

13-13   Reorganize the game tree of Fig. 13-16a so that it is a perfectly ordered game tree. Indicate which subtrees would be pruned by the alpha-beta algorithm.

13-14   Explain why sequential depth-first search is simply a special case of DTS, when the DTS algorithm is provided only a single processor.

13-15*   Prove this theorem: Given a perfectly ordered game tree, the bound-and-branch allocation strategy causes the parallel DTS algorithm to evaluate the same nodes as the sequential alpha-beta algorithm.

GRAPH
THEORETIC
TERMINOLOGY

This section consolidates the definitions of graph theoretic terms used throughout this book. It also contains brief descriptions of data structures used to represent graphs.

A **graph** $G = (V, E)$ consists of V, a finite set of **vertices**, and E, a finite set of **edges** between pairs of vertices. In an **undirected graph** the edges have no orientation; in a **directed graph** every edge is an ordered pair (u, v) and is said to go **from** u **to** v. See Fig. A-1.

A **weighted graph** has a real number, called the **weight**, assigned to each edge. Depending upon the context, it may be more appropriate to think of the weight of a weighted graph's edge as a length, a time, a probability, or some other attribute.

The number of vertices in a graph is referred to by the letter n, and m denotes the number of edges in a graph.

Four graph representations are common. An unweighted graph can be represented by an $n \times n$ matrix, with one row and one column for each vertex. The element at row i and column j is equal to 1 if and only if there is an edge from vertex i to vertex j; the value is 0 otherwise. This matrix is called an **adjacency matrix**. Weighted graphs can be represented by a **weight matrix**, that

FIGURE A-1　Undirected and directed graphs. Undirected graph G has vertices A,B,C, and D and edges (A,B), (A,C), (A,D) and (B,D). Directed graph G' has vertices H,I,J, and K, and edges (H,I), (H,J), (J,H), and (J,K). Edge (H,J) goes from H to J. Edge (J,H) goes from J to H.

G

G'

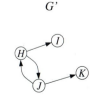

FIGURE A-2 A weighted directed graph and its corresponding weight matrix. Depending upon the algorithm, nonexistent edges may be represented as 0 or as ∞ in the weight matrix. In this example nonexistent edges are represented as 0.

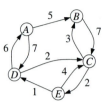

	A	B	C	D	E
A	0	5	0	7	0
B	0	0	7	0	0
C	0	3	0	0	2
D	6	0	2	0	0
E	0	0	4	1	0

is similar to an adjacency matrix, except that the value of the matrix element at row i and column j gives the weight of the edge from vertex i to vertex j. Nonexistent edges may be represented by either 0 or ∞ entries, depending upon the particular problem being solved. Figure A-2 illustrates a weighted directed graph and its weight matrix.

Another representation stores a graph as a list of edges and a cardinal number indicating the number of vertices. A third representation uses adjacency lists—a list, for every vertex, of the edges leaving that vertex. A fourth representation, often used to represent digitized picture input, consists of a two-dimensional boolean matrix. If we label the elements 1 and 0, then the set of vertices consists of the matrix elements having the value 1; the set of edges is the set of all pairs of vertically or horizontally adjacent 1s.

A **path** from v_1 to v_i in a graph $G = (V, E)$ is a sequence of edges (v_1, v_2), (v_2, v_3), $(v_3, v_4), \ldots, (v_{i-2}, v_{i-1}), (v_{i-1}, v_i)$, such that every vertex is in V, every edge is in E, and no two vertices are identical.

A **cycle** in a graph $G = (V, E)$ is a sequence of edges $(v_1, v_2), (v_2, v_3)$, $(v_3, v_4), \ldots, (v_{i-1}, v_i), (v_i, v_1)$, such that every vertex is in V, every edge is in E, and only the first and last vertices in the sequence of edges are identical. A graph without cycles is said to be **acyclic**.

There are two common shortest-path problems. Given a weighted, directed graph $G = (V, E)$, the **all-pairs shortest-path problem** is to find, for every pair of vertices $i, j \in V$, the shortest path from i to j along edges in E. Given a weighted, directed graph $G = (V, E)$ and a vertex $s \in V$, the **single-source shortest-path problem** is to find, for every vertex $i \in V$, the shortest path from s to i along edges in E. Figure A-3 illustrates these two kinds of shortest-path problems.

A **subgraph** of a graph G is a graph with vertices and edges in G.

An undirected graph is **connected** if, for every pair of vertices i and j in G, there is a path from i to j. The **connected component** problem is to find, for some undirected graph G, the minimal set of subgraphs such that every subgraph is connected (Fig. A-4). This problem is also known as the **component labeling** problem, since by the end of the algorithm every component's vertices share a label unique to that component. The **connected 1s** problem is the connected component problem applied to digitized picture input (the fourth graph representation described earlier).

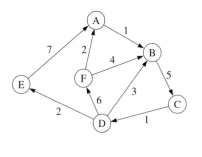

Length of shortest path

	A	B	C	D	E	F
A	0	1	6	7	9	13
B	14	0	5	6	8	12
C	9	4	0	1	3	7
D	8	3	8	0	2	6
E	7	8	13	14	0	20
F	2	3	8	9	11	0

(a)

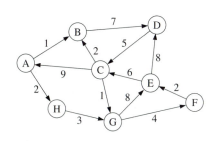

Length of shortest
path from C

A	9
B	2
C	0
D	9
E	7
F	5
G	1
H	11

(b)

FIGURE A-3 Shortest-path problems. (a) All pairs. (b) Single source.

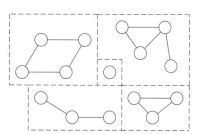

FIGURE A-4 Connected components.

A **tree** is a connected, undirected acyclic graph. A **spanning tree** for a graph *G* is a subgraph that is a tree containing every vertex of *G*. The **weight** of a spanning tree of a weighted graph is the sum of the weights of the tree's edges. Given a weighted, undirected graph *G*, a **minimum-cost spanning tree** of *G* is a spanning tree with the smallest possible weight among all spanning trees of *G* (see Fig. A-5).

In some problems involving trees a particular vertex is designated as the **root**. In these problems the **height** of the tree is the maximum distance from

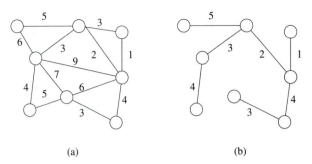

FIGURE A-5   Minimum-cost spanning tree problem. (a) Weighted graph. (b) Minimum-cost spanning tree.

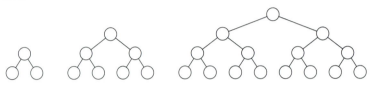

FIGURE A-6   Complete binary trees of height one, two, and three.

the root of the tree to a leaf. Every edge (u, v) in a rooted tree establishes a parent-child relationship between the two vertices. The **parent** is the vertex closer to the root; the **child** is the vertex farther from the root.

A **binary tree** is a rooted tree in which no node has more than two children. A **complete binary tree** is a binary tree of height n having $2^{n+1} - 1$ nodes (of which 2^n are leaves). Figure A-6 illustrates complete binary trees of height one, two, and three.

A **binomial tree** of height 0 is a single node. For all $i > 0$, a binomial tree of height i is a tree formed by connecting the roots of two binomial trees of height $i - 1$ with an edge and designating one of these roots to be the root of the new tree. A binomial tree of height n has 2^n nodes. Figure A-7 illustrates binomial trees of height one through four.

FIGURE A-7   Binomial trees of height one through four.

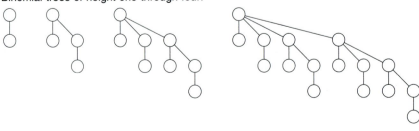

APPENDIX B

REVIEW OF COMPLEX NUMBERS

In this section we review how to perform arithmetic on complex numbers. The material in this section closely follows the presentation of Weaver (1983).

A **complex number** is an ordered pair of real numbers, denoted (x, y). We call x the **real part** of the complex number and y the **imaginary part**. Two complex numbers (x_1, y_1) and (x_2, y_2) are equal if and only if $x_1 = x_2$ and $y_1 = y_2$.

Let $z_1 = (x_1, y_1)$ and $z_2 = (x_2, y_2)$ be two complex numbers. The sum of these complex numbers is

$$z_1 + z_2 = (x_1 + x_2, y_1 + y_2)$$

Let $z_1 = (x_1, y_1)$ and $z_2 = (x_2, y_2)$ be two complex numbers. The product of these complex numbers is

$$z_1 z_2 = (x_1 x_2 - y_1 y_2, x_1 y_2 + y_1 x_2)$$

Addition and multiplication with complex numbers is commutative, associative, and distributive.

Any real number x can be represented as the complex number $(x, 0)$.

Three special complex numbers are the zero element, the unit element, and the imaginary unit element.

The **zero element**, denoted $\mathbf{0}$, is the complex number $(0, 0)$.

The sum of any complex number z and the zero element is z:

$$z + \mathbf{0} = (x, y) + (0, 0) = (x + 0, y + 0) = (x, y) = z$$

The product of any complex number z and the zero element is $\mathbf{0}$:

$$z\mathbf{0} = (x, y)(0, 0) = (x \times 0 - y \times 0, x \times 0 + y \times 0) = (0, 0) = \mathbf{0}$$

371

The **unit element**, denoted **1**, is the complex number $(1, 0)$.

The product of any complex number z and the unit element is z:

$$z \times \mathbf{1} = (x, y)(1, 0) = (x \times 1 - y \times 0, 1 \times y + 0 \times x) = (x, y) = z$$

The **imaginary element**, denoted i, is the complex number $(0, 1)$. The imaginary element is the square root of -1:

$$i^2 = (0, 1)(0, 1) = (0 \times 0 - 1 \times 1, 0 \times 1 + 1 \times 0) = (-1, 0) = -1$$

Theorem B.1. Every complex number $z = (x, y)$ can be represented as $x + iy$.

Proof. The real number $x = (x, 0)$. The product of real number y with the imaginary element i is

$$iy = (0, 1)(y, 0) = (0 \times y - 1 \times 0, 0 \times 0 + y \times 1) = (0, y)$$

Hence

$$x + iy = (x, 0) + (0, y) = (x, y)$$

See Fig. B-1. We have represented the complex number z as $x + iy$, where the horizontal axis corresponds to the real part of z and the vertical axis corresponds to the imaginary part of z.

We can also think of z as a vector having length r and angle θ, where θ is measured counterclockwise from the real axis. Note that

$$x = r \cos \theta$$

$$y = r \sin \theta$$

Using these equations we can write $z = x + iy = r(\cos \theta + i \sin \theta)$.

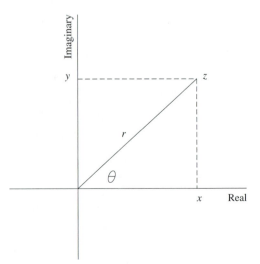

FIGURE B-1   Every complex number z can be represented as an ordered pair of real numbers (x, y), where x is the real part and y is the imaginary part. It can also be represented as a vector having length r and angle θ, where θ is measured counterclockwise from the real axis.

When we study the discrete Fourier transform we want to represent z in exponential form, which we derive here. Using Taylor series we can show

$$\sin\theta = \theta - \frac{\theta^3}{3} + \frac{\theta^5}{5} - \frac{\theta^7}{7} + \ldots$$

$$\cos\theta = 1 - \frac{\theta^2}{2} + \frac{\theta^4}{4} - \frac{\theta^6}{6} + \ldots$$

$$e^{i\theta} = 1 + i\theta - \frac{\theta^2}{2} - \frac{i\theta^3}{3} + \frac{\theta^4}{4} + \frac{i\theta^5}{5} + \ldots$$

$$= (1 - \frac{\theta^2}{2} + \frac{\theta^4}{4} + \ldots) + i(\theta - \frac{\theta^3}{3} + \frac{\theta^5}{5} + \ldots)$$

Combining these equations yields

$$e^{i\theta} = \cos\theta + i\sin\theta$$

and

$$e^{-i\theta} = \cos\theta - i\sin\theta$$

Recall that $z = x + iy = r(\cos\theta + i\sin\theta)$. Hence

$$z = re^{i\theta}$$

is another way to represent a complex number.

One property of the exponential representation of complex numbers is that it simplifies multiplication and division. Let $z_1 = r_1 e^{\theta_1}$ and $z_2 = r_2 e^{\theta_2}$ be two complex numbers. Then

$$z_1 z_2 = r_1 e^{\theta_1} r_2 e^{\theta_2} = r_1 r_2 e^{\theta_1 + \theta_2}$$

$$z_1 / z_2 = (r_1 e^{\theta_1})/(r_2 e^{\theta_2}) = (r_1 / r_2) e^{\theta_1 - \theta_2}$$

A **complex nth root of unity** is a complex number ω such that $\omega^n = 1$, the unit element.

There are exactly n complex nth roots of unity, represented by $e^{2\pi i k/n}$ for $k = 1, 2, \ldots, n - 1$.

The complex number $e^{2\pi i/n}$, denoted ω_n, is the **principal nth root of unity**.

Figure B-2 illustrates the principal eighth root of unity and its powers, the other complex eighth roots of unity.

Lemma B.1. (Cancellation lemma) For any integers $n \geq 0, k \geq 0$, and $d > 0$, $\omega_{dn}^{dk} = \omega_n^k$.

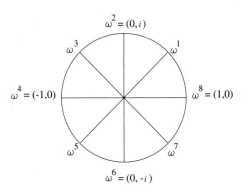

FIGURE B-2 The principal eighth root of unity and its powers.

Proof.

$$\omega_{dn}^{dk} = \left(e^{2\pi i/dn}\right)^{dk} = \left(e^{2\pi i/n}\right)^{k} = \omega_n^k$$

Corollary B.1. For any even integer $n > 0$, $\omega_n^{n/2} = \omega_2 = -1$.

Proof.

$$\omega_n^{n/2} = \omega_{(n/2)2}^{(n/2)1} = \omega_2^1 = \omega_2 = -1$$

Lemma B.2. (Halving lemma) If n is an even positive number, then the squares of the n complex nth roots of unity are identical to the $n/2$ complex $(n/2)$th roots of unity.

Proof. By the cancellation lemma we know that if k is nonnegative then $(\omega_n^k)^2 = \omega_{n/2}^k$. If we square all of the complex nth roots of unity, we get every $(n/2)$th root of unity twice, because

$$(\omega_n^{k+n/2})^2 = \omega_n^{2k+n} = \omega_n^{2k}\omega_n^n = \omega_n^{2k} = (\omega_n^k)^2$$

APPENDIX C

PARALLEL ALGORITHM DESIGN STRATEGIES

The following list contains each parallel algorithm design strategy and the page number on which it appears:

1. If a cost optimal CREW PRAM algorithm exists, and the way the PRAM processors interact through shared variables maps onto the target architecture, a PRAM algorithm is a reasonable starting point (p. 159).

2. Look for a data-parallel algorithm before considering a control-parallel algorithm (p. 168).

3. As problem size grows, use the algorithm that makes best use of the available resources (p. 171).

4. Let each processor perform the most efficient sequential algorithm on its share of the data (p. 172).

5. If load balancing is not a problem, maximize grain size (p. 188).

6. Reduce average memory latency time by increasing locality (p. 190).

7. Eliminate contention for shared resources by changing temporal order of data accesses (p. 191).

8. Change data structures to reduce the amount of contention for the same shared resource (p. 321).

GLOSSARY

Acyclic   Refers to a graph without any cycles.

Adjacency Matrix   A boolean matrix that indicates if there is an edge from i to j for each pair of vertices i and j in a graph.

All-Pairs Shortest-Path Problem   Given a weighted graph, find the shortest path between every pair of vertices.

Alpha-Beta Pruning   An algorithm used to determine the minimax value of a game tree. Alpha-beta pruning prevents the search of subtrees whose evaluation cannot influence the outcome of the search.

Amdahl Effect   (1) As the problem size increases, the fraction f of inherently sequential operations decreases, making the problem more amenable to parallelization, (2) For any fixed number of processors, speedup is usually an increasing function of problem size.

Amdahl's Law   If f is the fraction of operations in a computation that must be performed sequentially, the maximum speedup that can be achieved with p processors is $\leq 1/(f + (1 - f)/p)$.

AND Tree   A search tree with nonterminal nodes that are all AND nodes.

AND/OR Tree   A search tree with both AND and OR nonterminal nodes.

Applicative Language   A language that performs all computations by applying functions to values.

ARBITRARY PRAM   CRCW PRAM with the attribute that if multiple processors simultaneously write to the same global register, one of the competing processors is arbitrarily chosen the "winner," and its value is written into the register.

Aspiration Search   Enhancement to alpha-beta algorithm that attempts to reduce the number of positions evaluated by beginning the search with an alpha-beta "window" smaller than $(-\infty, \infty)$.

Asynchronous Algorithm   A control-parallel algorithm that is not pipelined.

376

AVL Tree   Binary tree having the property that, for any node v in the tree, the difference in height between the left and right subtrees of node v is no more than 1.

Bandwidth   (1) Data transfer rate; (2) the value $1 + 2k$, where k is the largest number of columns from the main diagonal any nonzero element of a matrix can be.

Bank   Unit of interleaved memory, allowing only a single read or write at a time. Also called a **module**.

Barrier   A synchronization point. No process may continue execution beyond the barrier until all processes have reached the barrier.

Batch Search   A concurrent search for a number of keys.

Binary n-Cube   Hypercube.

Binary Tree   A rooted tree in which no node has more than two children.

Binary Tree Network   A network in which the nodes are arranged as a complete binary tree.

Binomial Tree   A recursively defined tree with 2^k nodes and depth k.

Bisection Bandwidth   Bisection width of processor organization multiplied by link bandwidth.

Bisection Width   The minimum number of edges that must be removed in order to divide a network into two halves of identical size (within one).

Bitonic Merge   A parallel algorithm to merge two bitonic sequences of length 2^k into a single bitonic sequence of length 2^{k+1} in $k + 1$ steps.

Bitonic Sequence   A sequence of numbers $a_0, a_1, \ldots, a_{n-1}$ with the property that (1) there exists an index i, $0 \le i \le n - 1$, such that a_0 through a_i are monotonically increasing and a_i through a_{n-1} are monotonically decreasing, or (2) there exists a cyclic shift of indices so that condition 1 is satisfied.

Block Matrix Multiplication   Algorithm analogous to standard matrix multiplication, where matrices replace scalars, standard matrix multiplication replaces scalar multiplication, and matrix addition replaces scalar addition.

Bound and Branch   Processor allocation strategy for parallel alpha-beta search.

Branch and Bound   Algorithm for searching OR trees with the goal of finding an optimal solution while minimizing the total number of nodes examined.

Brent's Theorem   Given A, a parallel algorithm with computation time t, if parallel algorithm A performs m computational operations, then p processors can execute algorithm A in time $t + (m - t)/p$.

Broadcast   When one processor sends a value or set of values to all other processors.

Buffer Deadlock   A kind of deadlock that can occur in multicomputers when message buffers fill up.

Busy-Waiting   Using processor cycles to test a variable until it assumes a desired value. Also called **spinning**.

Butterfly Network   A processor organization containing $(k + 1)2^k$ nodes, divided into 2^k columns and $k + 1$ rows, or ranks in which edges form "butterfly" patterns.

Cache Memory   Small, fast memory unit used as a buffer between a processor and primary memory.

Centralized Load Balancing Algorithm   Load balancing algorithm that makes a global decision about the reallocation of work to processors.

Chain   A totally ordered task graph.

Chaining   Method of increasing concurrency by connecting the output of one or more pipelines to the input of another pipeline.

Channel   (1) I/O processor, (2) In the programming language occam, a point-to-point, synchronous communication link from one process to another process.

Child   The vertex u or v farther from the root, given an edge (u,v) establishing a parent-child relationship between two vertices in a rooted tree.

Circuit-Switched Message Routing   Message-passing scheme in which a circuit is set up from the source processor to the destination processor, and the message flows in a pipelined fashion through the intermediate processors. None of the intermediate processors stores the message.

COMMON PRAM   CRCW PRAM with the restriction that if multiple processors simultaneously write to the same global register, they must be writing the same value.

Communication Overhead   In a parallel game-tree search, the time spent coordinating the processes performing the searching.

Comparator   A device that performs the compare-exchange operation in bitonic merge.

Compare-Exchange   Fundamental operation of bitonic merge algorithm. Two numbers are brought together, compared, then exchanged, if necessary, so that they are in the proper order.

Complete Binary Tree   A binary tree of height n having $2^{n+1} - 1$ nodes (of which 2^n are leaves).

Complex nth Root of Unity   A complex number ω such that $\omega^n = 1$.

Complex Number   Ordered pair of real numbers. First element is real part; second element is imaginary part.

Complexity   Measure of time or space used by an algorithm. Without adjective, refers to time complexity.

Component Labeling Problem   Given an undirected graph G, find the minimal set of subgraphs such that every subgraph is connected. Also known as the **connected component problem**.

Connected   Given undirected graph G, the property that for every pair of vertices i and j in G, there is a path from i to j in G.

Connected 1s Problem   Connected component problem applied to digitized picture input, where each pixel is a bit.

Connected Component Problem   Given an undirected graph G, find the minimal set of subgraphs such that every subgraph is connected. Also known as the **component labeling problem**.

Control Parallelism   Parallelism achieved through the simultaneous application of different operations to different data elements.

Copy-Back Cache   Caching policy in which values in modified cache block are not copied to system memory until cache block is swapped out or another processor tries to access a data item in that block.

Cost   Product of the time complexity of an algorithm and the maximum number of processors used.

Cost Optimal   Parallel algorithm for which the cost is in the same complexity class as an optimal sequential algorithm.

CRCW PRAM   Concurrent read, concurrent write PRAM.

CREW PRAM   Concurrent read, exclusive write PRAM.

Critical Node   The root of a subtree about which a rebalancing will take place when a node is inserted into an AVL tree.

Critical Section   A sequence of operations that must appear to be executed as an atomic operation.

Cube-Connected Cycles Network   A butterfly network whose lowest and highest ranks have been combined into a single rank.

Cube-Connected Network   Hypercube.

Cubical   Describes a graph that can be embedded into a hypercube with dilation 1.

Cycle   Same as path, except the first and last vertices are identical.

Cyclic Reduction   Recursive algorithm used to solve tridiagonal linear systems. Also called **odd-even reduction**.

Data-Flow   An architecture in which the sequence of instruction execution depends not on a program counter, but on the availability of data.

Data-Flow Analysis   Process of finding the data dependencies among instructions.

Data-Flow Graph   (1) Machine language for a data-flow computer; (2) result of data flow analysis.

Data Parallelism   The use of multiple functional units to apply the same operation simultaneously to elements of a data set.

Data Stream   Sequence of data manipulated by an instruction stream.

de Bruijn Network   A network with $n = 2^k$ nodes labeled $0, 1, \ldots, n - 1$. Two edges leave each node. From node i one edge leads to node ($2i$ modulo n); the other edge leads to node ($2i$ modulo n) $+1$.

Deadlock   A situation in which a set of active concurrent processes cannot proceed because each holds nonpreemptible resources that must be acquired by some other process.

Decision Problem   A problem with a solution (if any) that is found by satisfying a set of constraints.

Depth   Maximum level of any task in a task graph.

Deque   A double-ended queue; i.e., a list of elements on which insertions and deletions can be performed at both the front and the rear.

Deterministic Model   A task model in which precedence relations between tasks and the execution time needed by each task are fixed and known before the schedule is devised.

DFT   Discrete Fourier transform.

Diagonally Dominant   Refers to a matrix in which the magnitude of each diagonal element is greater than the sums of the magnitudes of the other matrix elements in the same row.

Diameter   The largest distance between any two nodes in a network.

Dilation $\max\{dist[\phi(u),\phi(v)]|(u, v) \in E\}$, given ϕ, a function that embeds graph $G = (V,E)$ into graph $G' = (V', E')$, and where $dist[a, b]$ is the distance between vertices a and b in G'.

Directed Graph   Graph with ordered edges.

Discrete Fourier Transform   The matrix-vector product $F_n x$, where x is an n-element vector, $\omega_n = e^{2\pi i/n}$, and $f(i, j) = \omega_n^{ij}$ for $0 \le i, j < n$.

Divide and Conquer   A problem-solving methodology that involves partitioning a problem into subproblems, solving the subproblems, then combining the subproblem solutions into a solution for the original problem.

Dynamic Decomposition   A task-allocation policy that assumes tasks are generated at execution time.

Dynamic Scheduling   see Self-scheduled.

Edge   Component of a graph. An edge is a pair of vertices. If the edge is directed, the pair is ordered; if the edge is undirected, the pair has no order.

Effective Branching Factor   Given an algorithm searching a game tree of depth d, the dth root of the number of leaf nodes evaluated by the algorithm.

Efficiency   Ratio of speedup to number of processors used.

Embedding   A function mapping V to V', given two graphs $G = (V, E)$ and $G' = (V', E')$.

Enumeration Sort   A sort that finds the position of each element by determining the number of elements that precede it in the ordered list.

EREW PRAM   Exclusive read, exclusive write PRAM.

Even-Odd Exchange   Phase of odd-even transposition sort.

Exchange   One link type in a shuffle-exchange network. Exchange links connect nodes whose addresses differ in the least significant bit.

Expected Space Complexity   A function $f(n)$ equal to the average amount of space used by an algorithm over all possible inputs of size n.

Expected Time Complexity   A function $f(n)$ equal to the average amount of time required by an algorithm over all possible inputs of size n.

Fact   In the context of logic programming, a fact is a Horn clause with a head but no body.

Fan-in   Algorithm in which a set of values is combined to yield a single result. Same as **reduction**.

Fast Fourier Transform $\Theta(n \log n)$ algorithm for performing the discrete Fourier transform.

FFT   Fast Fourier transform.

Fifth-Generation Computer   A computer system capable of knowledge processing.

Fork   A method of specifying concurrency. Similar to a procedure call, but the calling process continues execution. See **Join**.

Fourier Analysis   Study of representing continuous functions by a potentially infinite series of sinusoidal (sine and cosine) functions.

Frequency   In the context of the discrete Fourier transform, the number of complete cycles a sinusoidal wave completes between time 0 and time 2π.

From   Preposition denoting the originating vertex of an edge in a directed graph.

Front End   Sequential computer component found in processor arrays, as well as some multicomputers.

Fully Distributed Load Balancing Algorithm   Load balancing algorithm in which processors exchange information with neighboring processors and use this information to make local changes in the allocation of work.

Game Tree   State space tree representation of a game position.

Gantt Chart   Diagram used to illustrate a deterministic schedule.

Gaussian Elimination   Algorithm used to solve arbitrary linear systems.

Gaussian Elimination With Partial Pivoting   Variant of gaussian elimination in which rows are interchanged when necessary to bring the largest element into the pivotal position.

Gigabyte 2^{30} bytes.

Gigaflops   Billion floating-point operations per second.

Grain Size   Relative number of operations done between synchronizations in a MIMD algorithm.

Graph   Set consisting of V, a finite set of vertices, and E, a finite set of edges between pairs of vertices.

Graph Coloring Problem   Determine whether vertices of a graph can be colored with c colors so that no two adjacent vertices are assigned the same color.

Gray Code   An encoding G of the integers $0, \ldots, 2^k - 1$ having the following properties: (1) $G(i) = G(j) \Rightarrow i = j$; (2) $G(i)$ and $G(i + 1)$ differ in exactly one bit position, for all i in the range 0 through $n - 2$; (3) $G(2^k - 1)$ and $G(0)$ differ in exactly one bit position.

Height   In graph theory, the length of the longest path from the root of a tree to any of its leaves.

Hot Spot   Memory bank experiencing too much contention from processors.

Hypercube   Boolean k-cube. Every processor has a unique address in the range from 0 to $2^k - 1$. Processors whose addresses differ in exactly 1 bit are connected.

Hypertree   Graph formed by computing the cross-product of a k-ary tree of height d and an upside-down binary tree of height d.

Imaginary Element   The complex number $(0, 1)$, denoted i.

Imaginary Part   Second component of complex number.

Immediate Predecessor   Task at the tail of an edge representing a precedence relation.

Immediate Successor   Task at the head of an edge representing a precedence relation.

Independent   Describes a set of tasks in a task graph such that no task is the predecessor of another.

Index Function   Function mapping lists elements into a mesh-connected network.

Information   Collection of related data objects.

Initial Tasks   Tasks with no predecessors in the task graph.

Instruction Buffering, Instruction Look-Ahead   Prefetching instructions used to prevent the CPU from waiting for an instruction to be fetched.

Instruction Pipelining   Allowing more than one instruction to be in some stage of execution at the same time.

Instruction Stream   Sequence of instructions performed by a CPU.

Interleaved Memory   Memory divided into a number of modules or banks that can be accessed simultaneously.

Internal Sort   Algorithm that orders a table of elements contained entirely in primary memory.

Inverse Discrete Fourier Transform   Function that maps a sequence over frequency to another sequence over time.

Iterative Deepening   Use of a $(d - 1)$-ply search to prepare for a (d)-ply search.

Key   Unique object of a search.

Knapsack problem   Given a finite set of objects, each with a weight and a value, find the subset of these objects having greatest value, while also satisfying the constraint that the total weight of these objects must be no greater than a specified weight limit.

Length   Number of tasks in a chain of a task graph.

Level   Given a task T in a task graph G, refers to the maximum chain length from an initial task in G to T.

Light-Weight Threads   Processes that can be created and destroyed with relatively few instructions.

Linear Equation   An equation of the form $a_1 x_1 + a_2 x_2 + \cdots + a_n x_n = b$, where $x_1, x_2, \ldots, x_n$ are variables and $a_1, a_2, \ldots, a_n$ and b are constants.

Linear System   A finite set of linear equations. Also called a **system of linear equations**.

Linked Array   Data structure designed to allow the joining of various sized lists so that the inserting and deleting of the list elements can be done in parallel without contention.

List Ranking   Suffix sums applied to a list of 0s and 1s when the associative operation is addition.

Load   Given an embedding $\phi : G \to G$", the maximum number of vertices of G that are mapped to a single vertex of G'.

Locality of Reference   The observation that references to memory tend to cluster. Temporal locality refers to the observation that a particular datum or instruction, once referenced, is often referenced again in the near future. Spatial locality refers to the observation that once a particular location is referenced, a nearby location is often referenced in the near future.

Logarithmic Cost Criterion   Cost criterion that assumes the cost of performing an instruction is proportional to the length of the operands. The integer n requires $\lfloor \log n + 1 \rfloor$ bits of memory, hence the name.

Lower Triangular   A matrix with no nonzero elements above the main diagonal.

LU Decomposition   Process of factoring a matrix $\mathbf{A}$ into a product of a lower triangular matrix $\mathbf{L}$ and an upper triangular matrix $\mathbf{U}$.

Max-Tournament   Tournament returning the identity of the processor submitting the maximum value.

Megabyte 2^{20} bytes.

Megaflops   Million floating-point operations per second.

Mesh Network   A processor organization in which the nodes are arranged into a q-dimensional lattice and communication is allowed only between neighboring nodes.

Message Latency   Message startup time. Same as **message-passing overhead**.

Message-Passing Overhead   Message startup time. Same as **message latency**.

Microsecond 10^{-6} seconds.

Millisecond 10^{-3} seconds.

MIMD   Multiple-instruction stream, multiple data stream (category of Flynn's taxonomy). See **Multicomputer** and **Multiprocessor**.

Minimax   Algorithm used to determine the value of a game tree.

Minimum-Cost Spanning Tree   Given graph G, a spanning tree with the smallest possible weight among all spanning trees of G.

Minsky's Conjecture   Speedup achievable by a parallel computer increases as the logarithm of the number of processing elements.

Min-Tournament   Tournament returning the identity of the processor submitting the minimum value.

MISD   Multiple-instruction stream, single data stream (category of Flynn's taxonomy).

Module   Unit of interleaved memory, allowing only a single read or write at a time. Also called a **bank**.

Monitor   A structure consisting of variables representing the state of some resource, procedures to implement operations on that resource, and initialization code.

Multicomputer   A multiple-CPU parallel computer lacking a shared memory.

Multiprocessor   A shared memory multiple-CPU parallel computer.

Multiprogramming   Allowing more than one program to be in some state of execution at the same time.

Mutual Exclusion   Ensuring a shared resource is accessed by only a single process at a time.

Nanosecond 10^{-9} seconds.

$\mathcal{NC}$ Class of problems solvable in polylogarithmic time on a PRAM using a polynomial number of processors.

Necklace   The nodes through which a data item travels by following a sequence of shuffle links in a shuffle-exchange network.

NEWS Grid   A subset of wires in a Connection Machine router that forms a Cartesian mesh.

Nondeterministic Model   A task model in which the execution time of each task is represented by a random variable.

Non-Uniform Memory Access Multiprocessor   A multiprocessor that does not support constant-time memory access. "In most NUMA architectures, memory is organized hierarchically, so that some portions can be read and written more quickly by some processors than by others" (Wilson 1993).

NUMA   Non-Uniform Memory Access.

Odd-Even Exchange   Phase of odd-even transposition sort.

Odd-Even Reduction   Recursive algorithm used to solve tridiagonal linear systems. Also called **cyclic reduction.**

Omega Network   A composition of k shuffle-exchange networks, each of size 2^k.

Optimal Schedule   A schedule that minimizes the total execution time.

Optimization Problem   A problem whose solution involves satisfying a set of constraints and minimizing (or maximizing) an objective function.

OR Tree   A state space tree whose nonterminal nodes are all OR nodes.

Parallel Computation Thesis   The class of problems solvable in time $T(n)^{O(1)}$ by a PRAM is equal to the class of problems sovable in work space $T(n)^{O(1)}$ by a RAM, if $T(n) \geq \log n$.

Parallel Computer   A multiple-processor computer capable of parallel processing.

Parallel Computing   The process of solving problems on parallel computers.

Parallelism   The use of multiple resources to increase concurrency.

Parallelizability   The ratio between the time taken by a parallel computer executing a parallel algorithm on one processor and the time taken by the same parallel computer executing the same parallel algorithm on p processors.

Parallelization   The process of making an algorithm parallel.

Parallel Prefix   See Prefix Sums.

Parallel Processing   Information processing that emphasizes the concurrent manipulation of data elements belonging to one or more processes solving a single problem.

Parent   The vertex u or v closer to the root, given an edge (u, v) establishing a parent-child relationship between two vertices in a rooted tree.

Partial Sum   See Prefix Sums.

Path   A sequence of edges (v_1, v_2), (v_2, v_3), (v_3, v_4), $\ldots$, (v_{i-2}, v_{i-1}), (v_{i-1}, v_i) in a graph $G = (V, E)$ such that every vertex is in V, every edge is in E, and no two vertices are identical.

$\mathcal{P}$**-complete**   Describes a problem to which every other problem in $\mathcal{P}$ can be transformed in polylogarithmic parallel time using a PRAM with a polynomial number of processors.

Perfectly Ordered Game Tree   Game tree in which the best move from each position is always examined first.

Perfect Shuffle   See Shuffle.

Picosecond 10^{-12} seconds.

Pipelined Algorithm   In the context of MIMD models, a pipelined algorithm is the software analog to pipelining in hardware. The algorithm is divided into an ordered set of segments in which the output of each segment is the input of its successor.

Pipelined Computation   Computation that achieves concurrency through the division of the task into a number of stages (segments) that may execute simultaneously, where the output of one stage is the input of the next stage.

Pipelined Vector Processor   Vector computer implemented through the use of pipelined functional units. Examples include the Cray-1 and the Cyber-205.

Pipelining   Increasing concurrency by dividing a computation into a number of steps and allowing a number of tasks to be in various stages of execution at the same time.

Pivot Row   In the context of gaussian elimination, the row used to drive to zero all nonzero elements below the main diagonal in a particular column.

Ply   Level of a game tree.

Pointer Jumping   Parallel algorithm used to collapse linked list in logarithmic time.

Polylogarithmic   The set $\log n^{O(1)}$.

Polylogarithmic Time Complexity   Time complexity that is a polylogarithmic function of the problem size.

Positive Definite   Refers to a matrix that is symmetric, diagonally dominant, and has positive elements on the main diagonal.

PRAM   Model of parallel computation consisting of a control unit, global memory, and an unbounded set of processors, each with its own private memory.

Prefix Sums   Given a set of n values $a_1, a_2, \ldots, a_n$, and an associative operation $\oplus$, the computation of the n quantities $a_1, a_1 \oplus a_2, \ldots, a_1 \oplus a_2 \oplus \ldots \oplus a_n$.

Prescheduled   Describes a data-parallel algorithm in which the number of data items per functional unit is determined before any of the data items are processed.

Principal nth Root of Unity   The complex number $e^{2\pi i/n}$.

PRIORITY PRAM   CRCW PRAM with the attribute that if multiple processors simultaneously write to the same global register, the processor with the lowest index succeeds in writing its value into the register.

Processor Array   Vector computer implemented as a sequential computer connected to a set of identical synchronized processing elements capable of simultaneously performing the same operation on different data.

Pyramid Network   A complete 4-ary rooted tree augmented with additional interprocessor links so that the processors in every tree level form a 2-D mesh network.

RAM   Random access machine.

Random Access Machine   Model of a one-address computer consisting of a memory, a read-only input tape, a write-only output tape, and a program.

Random-Read   A communication step in which processors generate lists of addresses—(processor, offset) pairs—from which values must be retrieved.

Random Uniform Game Tree   A game tree whose terminal node values are randomly chosen from some uniform distribution.

Random-Write   A communication step in which processors generate lists of addresses—(processor, offset) pairs—where values are to be stored.

Rank Row of a butterfly network.

Real Part First component of complex number.

Reasonable A parallel model in which the number of processors with which each can communicate directly is bounded by a constant.

Receiver Initiated Load Balancing Algorithm A load balancing algorithm in which processors with too little work take work from other processors.

Reduction (1) Algorithm in which a set of values is combined via an associative binary operator to yield a single result (same as **fan-in**), (2) in the algorithm for the traveling salesperson problem, (Little et al. 1963), the process of determining the increase in the lower bound as the result of including or excluding an edge.

Root Designated vertex of a tree.

Scalable Algorithm An algorithm in which the level of parallelism increases at least linearly with the problem size.

Scalable Architecture An architecture that continues to yield the same performance per processor, albeit on a larger problem size, as the number of processors increases.

Scaled Efficiency Scaled speedup divided by number of processors used.

Scaled Speedup Ratio between how long a given optimal sequential program would have taken had it been able to run on a single processor of a parallel computer, and the length of time that a parallel program requires, when executing on multiple processors of the same parallel computer.

Scan See Prefix Sums.

Schedule An allocation of tasks to processors.

Search Overhead In a game-tree search, the increase in the number of nodes that must be examined owing to the introduction of parallelism.

Segment Fundamental unit of a pipeline. Also called a **stage**.

Self-Scheduled Describes a data-parallel algorithm in which data items are dynamically scheduled to functional units at run time.

Semi-Distributed Load Balancing Algorithm A load balancing algorithm in which processors are divided into regions. Within each region a centralized algorithm distributes the workload among processors. A higher level scheduling mechanism balances the workload between regions.

Sender Initiated Load Balancing Algorithm A load balancing algorithm in which processors with too much work send work to other processors.

Sequential Algorithm An algorithm designed to run on a sequential computer.

Sequential Computer A computer with an instruction set that includes operations on scalar variables only.

Serial Sequential.

Shape Specifies the way parallel data are organized in C*.

Short Necklace A necklace of length less than k in a shuffle-exchange network containing 2^k nodes.

Shuffle One link type in a shuffle-exchange network. For every node i in a shuffle-exchange network of size $n = 2^k$, the shuffle link leads to node $2i$ modulo $n - 1$, except that the shuffle link from node $n - 1$ goes to node $n - 1$.

Shuffle-Exchange Network Processor organization containing 2^k nodes, labeled, $0, 1, ..., 2^{k-1}$, with two connections per node, called shuffle and exchange.

SIMD Single-instruction stream, multiple-data stream (category of Flynn's taxonomy). See Processor Array.

Simple Task Graph   A task graph with a polynomial representation that can be factored so that every variable appears exactly once.

Single-Source Shortest-Path Problem   Problem of finding the shortest path from a single designated vertex (the source) to all the other vertices in a weighted, directed graph.

SISD   Single-instruction stream, single-data stream (category of Flynn's taxonomy).

Solution   A substitution of values for variables in a linear system such that every equation is satisfied.

SOR   Successive overrelaxation.

Source   In the single-source shortest-path problem, the vertex from which all distances are calculated.

Space   Memory.

Space Complexity   Memory used by an algorithm as a function of problem size.

Spanning Tree   Given a graph G, a tree that includes every vertex in G.

Spatial Locality   The observation that once a particular location is referenced, a nearby location is often referenced in the near future.

Speedup   Ratio between the time needed for the most efficient sequential algorithm to perform a computation and the time needed to perform the same computation on a machine incorporating pipelining and/or parallelism.

Spin Lock   Shared variable used for busy waiting.

Spinning   Describes an active process that continually tests the value of a spin lock, waiting for it to change. Also called **busy waiting**.

SPMD   Single program, multiple data programming style. Programs written in this style are loosely synchronous. Between synchronization points—usually barrier synchronizations on a multiprocessor and communication functions on a multicomputer—processors asynchronously execute the same program but manipulate their own portion of the data.

Spread   Form of broadcast on the Connection Machine that may incorporate a scan operation.

Stage   Fundamental unit of a pipeline. Also called a **segment**.

State Space Tree   Representation of the decomposition of an original problem into subproblems through the addition of constraints.

Store-and-Forward Message Passing   Message routing scheme in which every intermediate processor along the message's path must store the entire message before forwarding it to the next processor down the line.

Strong Search   An algorithm that searches for a given key, locks the node associated with that key, and returns the node.

Subgraph   Given graph G, a graph with vertices and edges in G.

Successive Overrelaxation   A variant of the Gauss-Seidel algorithm that computes the new value of each element of the solution vector through a combination of its old value and the new value generated by the standard Gauss-Seidel algorithm.

Suffix Sums   Given a set of n values $a_1, a_2, \ldots, a_l$ and an associative operator $\oplus$, the computation of the n quantities $a_1 \oplus a_2 \oplus \ldots \oplus a_{n-1} \oplus a_n, \ldots, a_{n-1} \oplus a_n, a_n$.

Supercomputer   A general-purpose computer capable of solving individual problems at extremely high computational speeds, compared with other computers built during the same time.

Superlinear Speedup   Speedup that exceeds the number of processors used.

Symmetric   Refers to a matrix A having the property that $a_{i,j} = a_{j,i}$ for $1 \leq i, j \leq n$.

System of Linear Equations   Finite set of linear equations. Also called a **linear system**.

Table   Finite set of keys.

Task Graph   A directed graph representing a computation. Nodes denote tasks and edges denote precedence constraints between tasks.

Temporal Locality   The observation that a particular datum or instruction, once referenced, is often referenced again in the near future.

Terabyte 2^{40} bytes.

Throughput   Number of results produced per time unit.

Time   See **Time Complexity**.

Time Complexity   Time used by an algorithm as a function of problem size.

To   Preposition denoting the destination vertex of an edge in a directed graph.

Tournament   A variant of reduction with operation minimum or maximum in which the value returned is the identity of a processor submitting the "winning" value (i.e., the result of the reduction).

Traveling Salesperson Problem   Given a weighted graph, find a minimum-weight cycle containing every vertex exactly once.

Tree   Connected, undirected, acyclic graph.

Tridiagonal   Refers to a linear system **A** with the property that $|i - j| > 1 \Rightarrow a_{i,j} = 0$.

TSP   Traveling Salesperson Problem.

Tuple Space   A shared associative memory used by Linda programs.

UMA   Uniform Memory Access.

Uniform Memory Access Multiprocessor   A multiprocessor in which all processors work through a central switching mechanism to reach a shared global memory.

Undirected Graph   A graph with edges that have no orientation.

Uniform Cost Criterion   Assumes every RAM instruction takes one unit of time to execute and every register requires one unit of space.

Unit Element   The complex number $(1, 0)$, denoted **1**.

Upper Triangular   A matrix with no nonzero element below the main diagonal.

Utilization   Parallelizability divided by the number of processors used.

Vector Computer   A computer with an instruction set that includes operations on vectors as well as scalars.

Vertex   Component of a graph. Also called a node.

Virtual Processors   Processing elements in an abstract model of parallel computation supported by some programming languages, such as C*.

Weak Search   A search algorithm that searches for a key and returns the node that contained the key at the time it was examined. Weak search is not guaranteed to provide an up-to-date result.

Weight   (1) Real number assigned to an edge in a weighted graph; (2) sum of the weights of a spanning tree's edges.

Weighted Graph   Graph with a real number assigned to each edge.

Weight Matrix   A matrix indicating, for each pair of vertices i and j, the weight of the edge from vertex i to vertex j.

Width   The size of the maximal set of independent tasks in a task graph.

Worst-Case Space Complexity   A function $f(n)$ equal to the greatest amount of space used by an algorithm over all possible inputs of size n.

Worst-Case Time Complexity   A function $f(n)$ equal to the greatest amount of time spent by an algorithm over all possible inputs of size n.

Write-Through Cache   Caching policy in which every data write is sent directly to system memory, and all copies of the data item in other processors' caches are invalidated.

Zero element   The complex number $(0, 0)$, denoted **0**.

CALL NUMBERS

Call Number	Title
QA76.6.A8	ACM Transactions on Mathematical Software
QA76.7.A281	ACM Transactions on Programming Languages and Systems
QA76.A265	Acta Informatica
QA76.A4	Advances in Computers
Q335.A7	Artificial Intelligence
QA76.N62	BIT
QA76.C539	Communications of the ACM
QA76.C545	Computer
QA76.C55	Computer Journal, The
QA76.C592	Computing Surveys
QA76.6.I161	IEEE Software
TK1.I47	IEEE Spectrum
TK6540.I62	IEEE Transactions on Computers
QA76.58.I44	IEEE Transactions on Parallel and Distributed Systems
TK6540.I62	IEEE Transactions on Pattern Analysis and Machine Intelligence
TK1001.I467	IEEE Transactions on Power Systems
TK6540.I62	IEEE Transactions on Software Engineering
Q350.I5	Information and Control
QA76.I51	Information Processing Letters

Call Number	Title
QA76.5.I564	International Journal of Parallel Programming
QA76.A69	Journal of the ACM
QA76.6.J69	Journal of Algorithms
QA76.J6	Journal of Computer and System Sciences
QA76.5.J73	Journal of Parallel and Distributing Computing
T58.A2.O7	Operations Research
QA76.6.P3491	Parallel Computing
QA267.A27	Proc. of the Annual ACM Symposium on the Theory of Computing
TK7885.A1.S9	Proc. of the Annual Symposium on Foundations of Computer Science
QA76.6.L58741	Proc. of the International Conference on Logic Programming
QA76.6.I52	Proc. of the International Conference on Parallel Processing
QA76.5.S94	Proc. of the Annual International Symposium on Computer Architecture
QA297.S6	SIAM Journal on Computing
QA1.S44	SIAM Review
TJ211.S531	SIGACT News
QA76.S58	Software Practice and Experience

BIBLIOGRAPHY

Ackerman, W. B. 1982. Data flow languages. *Computer*, vol. 14, no. 2, Feb., pp. 15–25.

Adams, G. B., III, D. P. Agrawal, and H. J. Siegel. 1987. A survey and comparison of fault-tolerant multistage interconnection networks. *Computer*, June, pp. 14–27.

Afrati, F., C. H. Papadimitriou, and G. Papageorgiou. 1985. The complexity of cubical graphs. *Information and Control*, vol. 66, pp. 53–60.

Agerwala, T., and B. Lint. 1978. Communication in parallel algorithms for boolean matrix multiplication. In *Proceedings of the 1978 International Conference on Parallel Processing*, IEEE, New York. Aug., pp. 146–153.

Aggarwal, A. 1984. A comparative study of X-tree, pyramid and related machines. *Proceedings of the 25th Annual Symposium on Foundations of Computer Science*, IEEE, New York, Oct., pp. 89–99.

Aggarwal, A., and R. J. Anderson. 1988. A random *NC* algorithm for depth first search. *Combinatorica*, vol. 8, pp. 1–12.

Aggarwal, A., R. J. Anderson, and M. Y. Kao. 1990. Parallel depth-first search in general directed graphs. *SIAM Journal on Computing*, vol. 19, no. 2, Apr., pp. 397–409.

Aho, A., J. Hopcroft, and J. Ullman. 1974. *The Design and Analysis of Computer Algorithms*. Addison-Wesley, Reading, MA.

Ahuja, N., and S. Swamy. 1984. Multiprocessor pyramid architecture for bottom-up image analysis. *IEEE Transactions on Pattern Analysis and Machine Intelligence*, PAMI-6, no. 4, July, pp. 463–474.

Ahuja, R. K., K. Mehlhorn, J. B. Orlin, and R. E. Tarjan. 1990. Faster algorithms for the shortest path problem. *Journal of the ACM*, vol. 37, no. 2, Apr., pp. 215–223.

Ahuja, S., N. Carriero, and D. Gelernter. 1986. Linda and friends. *Computer*, vol. 19, no. 8, Aug., pp. 26–34.

Aigner, M. 1982. Parallel complexity of sorting problems. *Journal of Algorithms*, vol. 3, pp. 79–88.

Ajtai, M., J. Komlós, and E. Szemerédi. 1983. An $O(n \log n)$ sorting network. In *Proceedings of the 15th Annual ACM Symposium on the Theory of Computing*, ACM, New York, May, pp. 1–9.

Akl, S. G. 1982. A constant-time parallel algorithm for computing convex hulls. *BIT*, vol. 22, no. 2, pp. 130–134.

Akl, S. G. 1984a. An optimal algorithm for parallel selection. *Information Processing Letters*, vol. 19, no. 1, pp. 47–50.

Akl, S. G. 1984b. Optimal parallel algorithms for computing convex hulls and for sorting. *Computing*, vol. 33, no. 1, pp. 1–11.

Akl, S. G. 1985. *Parallel Sorting Algorithms*. Academic Press, Orlando, FL.

Akl, S. G. 1989. *The Design and Analysis of Parallel Algorithms*. Prentice Hall, Englewood Cliffs, NJ.

Akl, S. G., D. Barnard, and R. Doran. 1982. Design, analysis, and implementation of a parallel tree search algorithm. *IEEE Transactions on Pattern Analysis and Machine Intelligence*, PAMI-4, Mar., pp. 192–203.

Akl, S. G., and H. Schmeck. 1984. Systolic sorting in a sequential input/output environment. In *Proceedings of the 22d Annual Allerton Conference on Communication, Control, and Computing*, Oct., pp. 946–955.

Alaghband, G., and H. F. Jordan. 1989. Sparse gaussian elimination with controlled fill-in on a shared memory multiprocessor. *IEEE Transactions on Computers*, vol. C-38, no. 11, Nov., pp. 1539–1557.

Alef, M. 1991. Concepts for efficient multigrid implementations on SUPRENUM-like architectures. *Parallel Computing*, vol. 17, pp. 1–16.

Aleliunas, R., and A. L. Rosenberg. 1982. On embedding rectangular grids in square grids. *IEEE Transactions on Computers*, C-31, no. 9, pp. 907–913.

Allan, S. J., and R. R. Oldehoeft. 1985. HEP SISAL: Parallel functional programming. In J. S. Kowalik, ed. *Parallel MIMD Computation: HEP Supercomputer and Its Applications*, MIT Press, Cambridge, pp. 123–150.

Allen, M. B., III, I. Herrera, and G. F. Pinder. 1988. *Numerical Modeling in Science and Engineering*. John Wiley & Sons, New York.

Almasi, G. S., and A. Gottlieb. 1989. *Highly Parallel Computing*. Benjamin/Cummings, Redwood City, CA.

Alon, N., and Y. Azar. 1988. The average complexity of deterministic and randomized parallel comparison-sorting algorithms. *SIAM Journal on Computing*, vol. 17, no. 6, Dec., pp. 1178–1192.

Alt, H., T. Hagerup, K. Mehlhorn, and F. P. Preparata. 1987. Deterministic simulation of idealized parallel computers on more realistic ones. *SIAM Journal on Computing*, vol. 16, no. 5, Oct., pp. 808–835.

Alton, D. A., and D. M. Eckstein. 1979. Parallel breadth-first search of p-sparse graphs. In *Proceedings of the West Coast Conference on Combinatorics, Graph Theory and Computing. Congressus Numerantium*, vol. 26.

Amdahl, G. 1967. Validity of the single processor approach to achieving large scale computing capabilities. In *AFIPS Conference Proceedings*, vol. 30, Apr., Thompson Books, Washington, DC, pp. 483–485.

Anderson, A. J. 1989. *Multiple Processing: A Systems Overview*. Prentice Hall, New York.

Andrews, G. R. 1981. Synchronizing resources. *ACM Transactions on Programming Languages and Systems*, vol. 3, no. 4, Oct., pp. 405–430.

Andrews, G. R. 1982. The distributed programming language SR—Mechanisms, design, and implementation. *Software Practice and Experience*, vol. 12, no. 8, Aug., pp. 719–754.

Andrews, G. R., and F. B. Schneider. 1983. Concepts and notations for concurrent programming. *Computing Surveys*, vol. 15, no. 1, Mar., pp. 3–43.

Angus, I. G., G. C. Fox, J. S. Kim, and D. W. Walker. 1990. *Solving Problems on Concurrent Processors, vol. II, Software for Concurrent Processors.* Prentice Hall, Englewood Cliffs, NJ.

Anton, H. 1981. *Elementary Linear Algebra.* 3d ed. John Wiley & Sons, New York.

Archibald, J., and J. L. Baer. 1986. Cache-coherence protocols: Evaluation using a multiprocessor simulation model. *ACM Transactions on Computer Systems*, vol. 4, no. 4, pp. 273–298.

Arjomandi, E. 1975. A study of parallelism in graph theory. Ph.D. dissertation, University of Toronto, Ontario, Canada.

Armstrong, P., and M. Rem. 1982. A serial sorting machine. *Computers and Electrical Engineering*, vol. 9, no. 1, pp. 53–58.

Atallah, M. J. 1983. Algorithms for VLSI networks of processors. Ph.D. dissertation, The Johns Hopkins University, Baltimore, MD.

Atallah, M. J. 1988. On multidimensional arrays of processors. *IEEE Transactions on Computers*, vol. 37, no. 10, Oct., pp. 1306–1309.

Atallah, M. J., R. Cole, and M. T. Goodrich. 1989. Cascading divide-and-conquer: A technique for designing parallel algorithms. *SIAM Journal on Computing*, vol. 18, no. 3, June, pp. 499–532.

Atallah, M. J., and S. R. Kosaraju. 1984. Graph problems on a mesh-connected processor array. *Journal of the ACM*, vol. 31, no. 3, July, pp. 649–667.

Athas, W. C., and C. L. Seitz. 1988. Multicomputers: Message-passing concurrent computers. *Computer*, Aug., pp. 9–24.

Auf der Heide, F. M., and A. Wigderson. 1987. The complexity of parallel sorting. *SIAM Journal on Computing*, vol. 16, no. 1, Feb., pp. 100–107.

Averbuch, A., E. Gabber, B. Gordissky, and Y. Medan. 1990. A parallel FFT on an MIMD machine. *Parallel Computing*, vol. 15, pp. 61–74.

Aykanat, C., F. Özgüner, F. Ercal, and P. Sadayappan. 1988. Iterative algorithms for solution of large sparse systems of linear equations on hypercubes. *IEEE Transactions on Computers*, vol. 37, no. 12, Dec., pp. 1554–1568.

Azar, Y., and U. Vishkin. 1987. Tight comparison bounds on the complexity of parallel sorting. *SIAM Journal on Computing*, vol. 16, no. 3, June, pp. 458–464.

Baase, S. 1978. *Computer Algorithms: Introduction to Design and Analysis.* Addison-Wesley, Reading, MA.

Babb, R. G., II. 1988. *Programming Parallel Processors.* Addison-Wesley, Reading, MA.

Baccelli, F., and Z. Liu. 1990. On the execution of parallel programs on multiprocessor systems—A queuing theory approach. *Journal of the ACM*, vol. 37, no. 2, Apr., pp. 373–414.

Backus, J. 1978. Can programming be liberated from the von Neumann style? A functional style and its algebra of programs. *Communications of the ACM*, vol. 21, no. 8, Aug., pp. 613–641.

Bader, G., and E. Gehrke. 1991. On the performance of transputer networks for solving linear systems of equations. *Parallel Computing*, vol. 17, pp. 1397–1407.

Baer, J. L. 1980. *Computer Systems Architecture*. Computer Science Press, Potomac, MD.

Baer, J. L. 1982. Techniques to exploit parallelism. In D. J. Evans, ed., *Parallel Processing Systems: An Advanced Course*, Cambridge University Press, Cambridge, pp. 75–99.

Baer, J. L., H. C. Du, and R. E. Ladner. 1983. Binary search in a multiprocessing environment. *IEEE Transactions on Computers*, C-32, no. 7, July, pp. 667–677.

Baer, J. L., and B. Schwab. 1977. A comparison of tree-balancing algorithms. *Communications of the ACM*, vol. 20, no. 5, May, pp. 322–330.

Balas, E., D. Miller, J. Pekny, and P. Toth. 1991. A parallel shortest augmenting path algorithm for the assignment problem. *Journal of the ACM*, vol. 38, no. 4, Oct., pp. 985–1004.

Balzer, R. M. 1971. PORTS—A method for dynamic interprogram communication and job control. In *Proceedings of the AFIPS Spring Joint Computer Conference*, vol. 38, AFIPS Press, Arlington, VA, pp. 485–489.

Bambos, N., and J. Walrand. 1991. On the stability and performance of parallel processing systems. *Journal of the ACM*, vol. 38, no. 2, Apr., pp. 429–452.

Bampis, E., and J. C. Konig. 1991. Impact of communications on the complexity of the Parallel Gaussian Elimination. *Parallel Computing*, vol. 17, pp. 55–61.

Banerjee, U. 1988. *Dependence Analysis for Supercomputing*. Kluwer Academic Publishers, Norwell, MA.

Barnes, G. H., R. M. Brown, M. Kato, D. J. Kuck, D. L. Slotnick, and R. A. Stokes. 1968. The Illiac IV computer. *IEEE Transactions on Computers*, C-27, no. 1, Jan., pp. 84–87.

Bar-On, I. 1987. A practical parallel algorithm for solving band symmetry positive definite systems of linear equations. *ACM Transactions on Mathematical Software*, vol. 13, Dec., pp. 323–332.

Barr, R. S., R. V. Helgaon, and J. L. Kennington. 1989. Minimal spanning trees: An empirical investigation of parallel algorithms. *Parallel Computing*, vol. 12, pp. 45–52.

Batcher, K. E. 1968. Sorting networks and their applications. In *Proceedings of the AFIPS Spring Joint Computer Conference*, vol. 32, AFIPS Press, Reston, VA, pp. 307–314.

Batcher, K. E. 1979. The STARAN Computer. In C. R. Jesshope and R. C. Hockney, eds., *Infotech State of the Art Report: Supercomputers*, vol. 2, Infotech, Maidenhead, England, pp. 33–49.

Batcher, K. E. 1980. Design of massively parallel processor. *IEEE Transactions on Computers*, vol. C-29, no. 9, pp. 836–840.

Baudet, G. M. 1978a. Asynchronous iterative methods for multiprocessors. *Journal of the ACM*, vol. 25, no. 2, Apr., pp. 226–244.

Baudet, G. M. 1978b. The design and analysis of algorithms for asynchronous multiprocessors. Ph.D. dissertation, Carnegie-Mellon University, Pittsburgh, PA.

Baudet, G., and D. Stevenson. 1978. Optimal sorting algorithms for parallel computers. *IEEE Transactions on Computers*, vol. C-27, no. 1, Jan., pp. 84–87.

BBN. 1985. Butterfly™ parallel processor overview. Vers. 1. Tech. rept., BBN Laboratories, Inc., Dec. Cambridge, MA.

Beck, B., and D. Olien. 1989. A parallel-programming process model. *IEEE Software*, May, pp. 63–72.

Belkhale, K. P., and P. Banerjee. 1992. Parallel algorithms for geometric connected component labeling on a hypercube multicomputer. *IEEE Transactions on Computers*, vol. 41, no. 6, June, pp. 699–709.

Bell, G. 1989. The future of high performance computers in science and engineering. *Communications of the ACM*, vol. 32, no. 9, Sept., pp. 1091–1101.

Ben-Ari, M. 1982. *Principles of Concurrent Programming*. Prentice-Hall, Englewood Cliffs, NJ.

Bentley, J. L. 1980. A parallel algorithm for constructing minimum spanning trees. *Journal of Algorithms*, vol. 1, no. 1, Mar., pp. 51–59.

Bentley, J. L., and D. J. Brown. 1980. A general class of recurrence tradeoffs. In *Proceedings of the 21st Annual Symposium on Foundations of Computer Science*, IEEE, New York, Oct., pp. 217–228.

Bentley, J. L. and H. T. Kung. 1979. A tree machine for searching problems. In *Proceedings of the 1979 International Conference on Parallel Processing*, IEEE, New York, Aug., pp. 257–266.

Berg, H. K., W. E. Boebert, W. R. Franta, and T. G. Moher. 1982. *Formal Methods of Program Verification and Specification*. Prentice-Hall, Englewood Cliffs, NJ, Chap. 6.

Bergland, G. D. 1972. A parallel implementation of the Fast Fourier Transform algorithm. *IEEE Transactions on Computers*, vol. C-21, no. 4, Apr., pp. 366–370.

Berliner, H., and C. Ebeling. 1986. The SUPREM architecture: A new intelligent paradigm. *Artificial Intelligence*, vol. 28, pp. 3–8.

Berman, F. 1987. Experience with an automatic solution to the mapping problem In L. Jamieson, D. Gannon, and R. Douglass, eds., *The Characteristics of Parallel Algorithms*, MIT Press, Cambridge, MA, pp. 307–334.

Berman, F., and L. Snyder. 1987. On mapping parallel algorithms into parallel architectures. *Journal of Parallel and Distributed Computing*, vol. 4, pp. 439–458.

Bermond, J. C., P. Michallon, and D. Trystram. 1992. Broadcasting in wraparound meshes with parallel monodirectional links. *Parallel Computing*, vol. 18, pp. 639–648.

Bernhard, R. 1982. Computing at the speed limit. *IEEE Spectrum*, vol. 19, no. 7, pp. 26–31.

Berntsen, J. 1989. Communication efficient matrix multiplication on hypercubes. *Parallel Computing*, vol. 12, pp. 335–342.

Bertsekas, D. P., and J. N. Tsitsiklis. 1989. *Parallel and Distributed Computation: Numerical Methods*. Prentice-Hall, Englewood Cliffs, NJ.

Bettayeb, S., Z. Miller, and I. H. Sudborough. 1988. Embedding grids into hypercubes. In *Proceedings of the 3d Aegean Workshop on Computing*.

Bhatt, S. N., and C. E. Leiserson. 1982. How to assemble tree machines. In *Proceedings of the 14th Annual ACM Symposium on Theory of Computing*, ACM, New York, May, pp. 77–84.

Bhatt, S., F. Chung, T. Leighton, and A. Rosenberg. 1986. Optimal simulations of tree machines. In *Proceedings of the 27th Annual Symposium on Foundations of Computer Science*, IEEE Press, New York, pp. 274–282.

Bhattacharya, S., and A. Bagchi. 1990. Searching game trees in parallel using SSS*. In *Proceedings AAAI-90*, pp. 42–47.

Bhuyan, L. N., Q. Yang, and D. P. Agrawal. 1989. Performance of multiprocessor interconnection networks. *Computer*, Feb., pp. 25–37.

Bilardi, G., and A. Nicolau. 1986. Bitonic sorting with $O(n \log n)$ comparisons. In *Proceedings of the 20th Annual Conference on Information Sciences and Systems*, pp. 336–341.

Bilardi, G., and A. Nicolau. 1989. Adaptive bitonic sorting: An optimal parallel algorithm for shared-memory machines. *SIAM Journal on Computing*, vol. 18, no. 2, Apr., pp. 216–228.

Bilardi, G., M. Pracchi, and F. P. Preparata. 1981. A critique and an appraisal of VLSI models of computation. In H. T. Kung, B. Sproull, and G. Steele, eds. *VLSI Systems and Computations*, Springer-Verlag, New York, pp. 81–88.

Bilardi, G., and F. P. Preparata. 1983. A VLSI optimal architecture for bitonic sorting. In *Proceedings of the 7th Conference on Information Science Systems*, pp. 1–5.

Bilardi, G., and F. P. Preparata. 1984a. A minimum area VLSI architecture for $O(\log n)$ time sorting. In *Proceedings of the 16th Annual ACM Symposium on Theory of Computing*, ACM, New York, May, pp. 64–70.

Bilardi, G., and F. P. Preparata. 1984b. An architecture for bitonic sorting with optimal VLSI performance. *IEEE Transactions on Computers*, vol. C-33, no. 7, July, pp. 646–651.

Bini, D. 1984. Parallel solution of certain Toeplitz linear systems. *SIAM Journal on Computing*, vol. 13, May, pp. 268–276.

Bitton, D., D. J. DeWitt, D. K. Hsaio, and J. Menon. 1984. A taxonomy of parallel sorting. *ACM Computing Surveys*, vol. 16, no. 3, Sept., pp. 287–318.

Bitton-Friedland, D. 1982. Design, analysis and implementation of parallel external sorting algorithms. Ph.D. dissertation, University of Wisconsin-Madison.

Bjørstad, P. E. 1987. A large scale, sparse, secondary storage, direct linear equation solver for structural analysis and its implementation on vector and parallel architectures. *Parallel Computing*, vol. 5, pp. 3–12.

Blelloch, G. E. 1990. *Vector Models for Data-Parallel Computing*. MIT Press, Cambridge.

Blelloch, G. E., and S. Chatterjee. 1990. VCODE: A data-parallel intermediate language. In *Proceedings of the Third Symposium on the Frontiers of Massively Parallel Computation*. IEEE Press, New York.

Bodnar, B. L., and A. C. Liu. 1989. Modeling and performance analysis of single-bus tightly-coupled multiprocessors. *IEEE Transactions on Computers*, vol. 38, no. 3, Mar., pp. 464–470.

Bokhari, S. 1981. On the mapping problem. *IEEE Transactions on Computers*, vol. C-30, no. 3, pp. 207–214.

Bokhari, S. H. 1987. Multiprocessing the Sieve of Eratosthenes. *Computer*, vol. 20, no. 4, Apr., pp. 50–58.

Bokhari, S. H. 1988. Partitioning problems in parallel, pipelined, and distributed computing. *IEEE Transactions on Computers*, vol. 37, no. 1, Jan., pp. 48–57.

Bonomo, J. P., and W. R. Dyksen. 1989. Pipelined iterative methods for shared memory machines. *Parallel Computing*, vol. 11, pp. 187–199.

Bonuccelli, M. A., E. Lodi, and L. Pagli. 1984. External sorting in VLSI. *IEEE Transactions on Computers*, vol. C-33, no. 10, Oct., pp. 931–934.

Boreddy, J., and A. Paulraj. 1990. On the performance of transputer arrays for dense linear systems. *Parallel Computing*, vol. 15, pp. 107–117.

Borodin, A., and J. Hopcroft. 1985. Routing, merging, and sorting on parallel models of computation. *Journal of Computer and System Sciences*, vol. 30, pp. 130–145.

Brass, A., and G. S. Pawley. 1986. Two and three dimensional FFTs on highly parallel computers. *Parallel Computing*, vol. 3, pp. 167–184.

Brent, R. P. 1974. The parallel evaluation of general arithmetic expressions. *Journal of the ACM*, vol. 21, no. 2, pp. 201–206.

Brigham, E. O. 1973. *The Fast Fourier Transform*. Prentice-Hall, Englewood Cliffs, NJ.

Brinch Hansen, P. 1973a. *Operating System Principles*. Prentice-Hall, Englewood Cliffs, NJ.

Brinch Hansen, P. 1973b. Concurrent programming concepts. *ACM Computing Surveys*, vol. 5, no. 4, Dec., pp. 223–245.

Brinch Hansen, P. 1975. The programming language Concurrent Pascal. *IEEE Transactions on Software Engineering*, vol. SE-1, no. 2, June, pp. 199–206.

Brinch Hansen, P. 1977. *The Architecture of Concurrent Programs*. Prentice-Hall, Englewood Cliffs, NJ.

Brinch Hansen, P. 1978. Distributed processes: A concurrent programming concept. *Communications of the ACM*, vol. 21, no. 11, Nov., pp. 934–941.

Brinch Hansen, P. 1981. Edison: A multiprocessor language. *Software Practice and Experience*, vol. 11, no. 4, Apr., pp. 325–361.

Brock, H. K., B. J. Brooks, and F. Sullivan. 1981. Diamond: A sorting method for vector machines. *BIT*, vol. 21, pp. 142–152.

Browning, S. A. 1980a. The tree machine: A highly concurrent computing environment. Ph.D. dissertation, California Institute of Technology, Pasadena, CA.

Browning, S. A. 1980b. Algorithms for the tree machine. In C. Mead and L. Conway, eds., *Introduction to VLSI Systems*, Addison-Wesley, Reading, MA.

Bucher, I. Y., and M. L. Simmons. 1985. Performance assessment of supercomputers. Preprint LA-UR-85-1505, Los Alamos National Laboratory, Los Alamos, NM., M. Ginsberg, ed., North-Holland, Amsterdam.

Burton, F. W., and M. M. Huntbach. 1984. Virtual tree machines. *IEEE Transactions on Computers*, vol. C-33, no. 3, Mar., pp. 278–280.

Carey, M. J., P. M. Hansen, and C. D. Thompson. 1982. RESST: A VLSI implementation of a record-sorting stack. Tech. rept. UCB/CSD 82/102, Computer Science Div., University of California, Berkeley.

Carey, M. J., and C. D. Thompson. 1984. An efficient implementation of search trees on $\lceil \lg N + 1 \rceil$ processors. *IEEE Transactions on Computers*, vol. C-33, no. 11, Nov., pp. 1038–1041.

Carriero, N., and D. Gelernter. 1988. Applications experience with Linda. In *Proceedings of the ACM Symposium on Parallel Programming: Experience with Applications, Languages, and Systems*, pp. 173–187.

Carriero, N., and D. Gelernter. 1989a. Linda in context. *Communications of the ACM*, vol. 32, no. 4, Apr., pp. 444-458.

Carriero, N., and D. Gelernter. 1989b. How to write parallel programs: A guide to the perplexed. *ACM Computing Surveys*, vol. 21, no. 3, Sept., pp. 323–357.

Carriero, N., and D. Gelernter. 1990. *How to Write Parallel Programs: A First Course*. MIT Press, Cambridge.

Carriero, N., D. Gelernter, and J. Leichter. 1986. Distributed data structures in Linda. In *Proceedings of the ACM Symposium on Principles of Programming Languages*.

Chabbar, E. 1980. Contrôle et gestion du parallélisme: tris synchrones et asynchrones. Thesis, Université de Franche-Comté, France.

Chaiken, D., C. Fields, K. Kurihara, and A. Agarwal. 1990. Directory-based cache coherence in large-scale multiprocessors. *Computer*, June, pp. 49–58.

Chamberlain, R. M. 1988. Gray codes, Fast Fourier Transforms and hypercubes. *Parallel Computing*, vol. 6, pp. 225-233.

Chan, M. Y. 1991. Embedding of grids into optimal hypercubes. *SIAM Journal on Computing*, vol. 20, no. 5, Oct., pp. 834–864.

Chan, M. Y., and F. Y. L. Chin. 1988. On embedding rectangular grids into hypercubes. *IEEE Transactions on Computers*, vol. C-37, no. 10, Oct., pp. 1285–1288.

Chan, T. F., and Y. Saad. 1986. Multigrid algorithms on the hypercube multiprocessor. *IEEE Transactions on Computers*, vol. C-35, no. 11, Nov., pp. 969–977.

Chandra, A. K. 1976. Maximal parallelism in matrix multiplication. IBM Tech. rept. RC6193, Thomas J. Watson Research Center, Yorktown Heights, NY.

Chandra, A. K., and L. J. Stockmeyer. 1976. Alternation. In *Proceedings of the 17th Annual Symposium on Foundations of Computer Science*, IEEE, New York, Oct., pp. 98–108.

Chandrasekharan, N., and S. Sitharmama Iyengar. 1988. NC algorithms for recognizing chordal graphs and k trees. *IEEE Transactions on Computers*, vol. C-37, no. 10, Oct., pp. 1178–1183.

Chang, S.-K. 1974. Parallel balancing of binary search trees. *IEEE Transactions on Computers*, vol. C-23, no. 4, Apr., pp. 441–445.

Chang, J., and A. M. Despain. 1985. Semi-intelligent backtracking of Prolog based on a static data dependency analysis. In *Proceedings of the IEEE Symposium on Logic Programming*, Aug., pp. 43–70.

Charlesworth, A. E., and J. L. Gustafson. 1986. Introducing replicated VLSI to supercomputing: the FPS-164/MAX scientific computer. *Computer*, vol. 19, no. 3, Mar., pp. 10-22.

Chatterjee, S., G. E. Blelloch, and A. L. Fisher. 1991. Size and access inference for data-parallel programs. In *Proceedings of the 1991 ACM SIGPLAN Conference on Design and Implementation of Programming Languages*.

Chaudhuri, P. 1990. Finding and updating depth-first spanning trees of acyclic digraphs in parallel. *The Computer Journal*, vol. 33, June, pp. 247–251.

Chazelle, B. M., and L. M. Monier. 1981a. A model of computation for VLSI with related complexity results. In *Proceedings of the 13th Annual ACM Symposium on Theory of Computing*, ACM, New York, May, pp. 318–325.

Chazelle, B. M., and L. M. Monier. 1981b. Optimality in VLSI. In J.P. Gray, ed. *VLSI 81*, Academic Press, London, pp. 269–278.

Chen, A. C., and C. L. Wu. 1984. Optimum solution to dense linear systems of equations. In *Proceedings of the 1984 International Conference on Parallel Processing*, IEEE, New York, Aug., pp. 417–424.

Chen, A. C., and C. L. Wu. 1991. A parallel execution model of logic programs. *IEEE Transactions on Parallel and Distributed Systems*, vol. 2, no. 1, Jan., pp. 79–92.

Chen, I. N. 1975. A new parallel algorithm for network flow problems. In *Parallel Processing, Lecture Notes in Computer Science*, vol. 24, Springer-Verlag, New York, pp. 306–307.

Chen, J., E. L. Dagless, and Y. Guo. 1984. Performance measurements of scheduling strategies and parallel algorithms for a multiprocessor quick sort. *IEE Proceedings, Part E, Computers and Digital Techniques*, vol. 131, Mar., pp. 45–54.

Chen, M. C. 1986. Crystal: A synthesis approach to programming parallel machines. In M. T. Heath, ed., *Hypercube Multiprocessors 1986*, SIAM Press, Philadelphia, pp. 87–107.

Chen, M. C. 1987. Very-high-level parallel programming in Crystal. In M. T. Heath, ed., *Hypercube Multiprocessors 1987*, SIAM Press, Philadelphia, PA, pp. 39–47.

Chen, T. C., K. P. Eswaran, V. Y. Lum, and C. Tung. 1978a. Simplified odd-even sort using multiple shift-register loops. *International Journal of Computer and Information Science*, vol. 7, no. 3, pp. 295–314.

Chen, T. C., V. Y. Lum, and C. Tung. 1978b. The rebound sorter: An efficient sort engine for large files. In *Proceedings of the 4th International Conference on Very Large Data Bases*, pp. 312–318.

Chen, Y. K., and T. Feng. 1973. A parallel algorithm for maximum flow problem. In *Proceedings of the 1973 Computer Conference on Parallel Processing*, Aug., pp. 60.

Cheong, H., and A. V. Veidenbaum. 1990. Compiler-directed cache management in multiprocessors. *Computer*, June, pp. 39–47.

Cheriton, D. R., H. A. Goosen, and P. D. Boyle. 1991. Paradigm: A highly scalable shared-memory multicomputer architecture. *Computer*, Feb., pp. 33–46.

Cheriton, D., and R. E. Tarjan. 1976. Finding minimum spanning trees. *SIAM Journal on Computing*, vol. 5, no. 4, Dec., pp. 724–742.

Chern, M. Y., and T. Murata. 1983a. A fast algorithm for concurrent LU decomposition and matrix inversions. In *Proceedings of the 1983 International Conference on Parallel Processing*, IEEE, New York, Aug., pp. 79–86.

Chern, M. Y., and T. Murata. 1983b. Efficient matrix multiplications on a concurrent data-loading array processor. In *Proceedings of the 1983 International Conference on Parallel Processing*, IEEE, New York, Aug., pp. 90–94.

Cheung, J., S. Dhall, S. Lakshmivarahan, L. Miller, and B. Walker. 1982. A new class of two stage parallel sorting schemes. In *Proceedings of the ACM '82 Conference*, ACM, New York, Oct., pp. 26–29.

Chin, F. I., and K. S. Fok. 1980. Fast sorting algorithms on uniform ladders (multiple shift register loops). *IEEE Transactions on Computers*, vol. C-29, no. 7, July, pp. 618–631.

Chin, F. Y., J. Lam, and I. N. Chen. 1981. Optimal parallel algorithms for the connected component problem. In *Proceedings of the 1981 International Conference on Parallel Processing*, IEEE, New York, Aug., pp. 170–175.

Chin, F. Y., J. Lam, and I. N. Chen. 1982. Efficient parallel algorithms for some graph problems. *Communications of the ACM*, vol. 25, no. 9, Sept., pp. 659–665.

Choi, H. A., and B. Narahari. 1991. Efficient algorithms for mapping and partitioning a class of parallel computers. Tech. rept. GWU-IIST-91-04, George Washington University, Washington, DC.

Chow, P., Z. G. Vranesic, and J. L. Yen. 1983. A pipeline distributed arithmetic PFFT processor. *IEEE Transactions on Computers*, vol. C-32, no. 12, Dec., pp. 1128–1136.

Chronopoulos, A. T., and C. W. Gear. 1989. On the efficient implementation of preconditioned s-step conjugate gradient methods on multiprocessors with memory hierarchy. *Parallel Computing*, vol. 11, pp. 37–53.

Chu, E., and A. George. 1987. Gaussian elimination with partial pivoting and load balancing on a multiprocessor. *Parallel Computing*, vol. 5, pp. 65–74.

Chung, K. M., F. Luccio, and C. K. Wong. 1980a. On the complexity of sorting on magnetic bubble memory systems. *IEEE Transactions on Computers*, vol. C-29, no. 7, July, pp. 553–563.

Chung, K.-M., F. Luccio, and C. K. Wong. 1980b. Magnetic bubble memory structures for efficient sorting and searching. In *Proceedings IFIP Congress: Information Processing*, vol. 80, pp. 439–444.

Church, K. W. 1987. *Phonological Parsing in Speech Recognition*, Kluwer Academic Publishers, Boston, MA.

Cichelli, R. J. 1973. Research progress report in computer chess. *SIGART Newsletter*, vol. 41, Aug., pp. 32–36.

Clocksin, W. F., and C. S. Mellish. 1981. *Programming in Prolog*. Springer-Verlag, New York.

Cocke, J. 1988. The search for performance in scientific processors. *Communications of the ACM*, vol. 31, no. 3, Mar., pp. 250–253.

Coffman, E. G., Jr., and P. J. Denning. 1973. *Operating Systems Theory*. Prentice-Hall, Englewood Cliffs, NJ.

Coffman, E., Jr., and R. Graham. 1972. Optimal scheduling for two processor systems. *Acta Informatica*, vol. 1, pp. 200–213.

Cole, R. 1987. Slowing down sorting networks to obtain faster sorting algorithms. *Journal of the ACM*, vol. 34, Jan., pp. 200–208.

Cole, R. 1988. Parallel merge sort. *SIAM Journal on Computing*, vol. 17, no. 4, Aug., pp. 770–785.

Cole, R., and U. Vishkin. 1986. Approximate and exact parallel scheduling with applications to list, tree, and graph problems. In *Proceedings of the 27th Annual IEEE Symposium on Foundations of Computer Science*, pp. 478–491.

Colmerauer, A., H. Kanoui, R. Pasero, and P. Roussel. 1973. Un système de comunication homme-machine en Français. Rapport, Groupe Intelligence Artificielle, Universite d'Aix Marseille, Luminy, France.

Conery, J. S. 1987. *Parallel Execution of Logic Programs*. Kluwer Academic Publishers, Norwell, MA.

Conery, J. S., and Kibler. D. F. 1981. Parallel interpretation of logic programs. In *Proceedings of the Conference on Functional Programming Languages and Computer Architecture*. ACM Press, Oct., pp. 163–170.

Conway, M. E. 1963. A multiprocessor system design. In *Proceedings AFIPS Fall Joint Computer Conference*, vol. 24, Spartan Books, Baltimore, MD, pp. 139–146.

Cook, S. A. 1974. An observation on time-storage trade-off. *Journal of Computer and System Sciences*, vol. 9, no. 3, pp. 308–316.

Cook, S. A. 1983. The classification of problems which have fast parallel algorithms. In *Proceedings of the 1983 International Foundation of Computation Theory Conference, Lecture Notes in Computer Science*, vol. 158, Springer-Verlag, New York, pp. 78–93.

Cook, S. A. 1985. A taxonomy of problems with fast parallel algorithms. *Information and Control*, vol. 64, pp. 2–22.

Corinthios, M. J., and K. C. Smith. 1975. A parallel radix-4 fast Fourier transform computer. *IEEE Transactions on Computers*, vol. C-24, no. 1, Jan., pp. 80–92.

Cormen, T. H., C. E. Leiserson, and R. L. Rivest. 1990. *Introduction to Algorithms*. MIT Press, Cambridge.

Cosnard, M., M. Marrakchi, and Y. Robert. 1988. Parallel Gaussian elimination on an MIMD computer. *Parallel Computing*, vol. 6, pp. 275–296.

Cosnard, M., and Y. Robert. 1986. Complexity of parallel QR factorization. *Journal of the ACM*, vol. 33, no. 4, Oct., pp. 712–723.

Crane, B. A. 1968. Path finding with associative memory. *IEEE Transactions on Computers*, vol. C-17, no. 7, July, pp. 691–693.

Crane, B. A., M. J. Gilmartin, J. H. Huttenhoff, P. T. Rux, and R. R. Shively. 1972. PEPE computer architecture. *COMPCON 72 Digest*, IEEE, New York, pp. 57–60.

Cybenko, G., D. W. Krumme, and K. N. Venkataraman. 1986. Hypercube embedding is NP-complete. In *Proceedings of the First Conference on Hypercube Multiprocessors*, SIAM Press, Philadelphia, PA, pp. 148–157.

Cypher, R. E., J. L. C. Sanz, and L. Snyder. 1990. Algorithms for image component labeling on SIMD mesh-connected computers. *IEEE Transactions on Computers*, vol. C-39, no. 2, Feb., pp. 276–281.

Cyre, W. R., and G. J. Lipovski. 1972. On generating multipliers for a cellular fast Fourier transform processor. *IEEE Transactions on Computers*, vol. C-21, no. 1, Jan., pp. 83–87.

Das, C. R., J. T. Kreulen, M. J. Thazhuthaveetil, and L. N. Bhuyan. 1990. Dependability modeling for multiprocessors. *Computer*, vol. 23, Oct., pp. 7–19.

Das, S. K., N. Deo, and S. Prasad. 1990a. Parallel graph algorithms for hypercube computers. *Parallel Computing*, vol. 13, pp. 143–158.

Das, S. K., N. Deo, and S. Prasad. 1990b. Two minimum spanning forest algorithms on fixed-size hypercube computers. *Parallel Computing*, vol. 15, pp. 179–187.

Davis, A. L., and R. M. Keller. 1982. Data flow program graphs. *Computer*, vol. 14, no. 2, Feb., pp. 26–41.

De Bruijn, N. G. 1984. Some machines defined by directed graphs. *Theoretical Computer Science*, vol. 32, pp. 309–319.

Decker, I. C., D. M. Falcão, and E. Kaszkurewicz. 1992. Parallel implementation of a power system dynamic simulation methodology using the conjugate gradient method. *IEEE Transactions on Power Systems*, vol. 7, Feb., pp. 458–465.

deGroot, A. D. 1965. *Thought and Choice in Chess*. Mouton, The Hague.

Dehne, F., A. G. Ferreira, and A. Rau-Chaplin. 1990. Parallel branch and bound on fine-grained hypercube multiprocessors. *Parallel Computing*, vol. 15, pp. 201–209.

Dekel, E., D. Nassimi, and S. Sahni. 1981. Parallel matrix and graph algorithms. *SIAM Journal on Computing*, vol. 10, no. 4, Nov., pp. 657–675.

Dekel, E., and S. Sahni. 1982. A parallel matching algorithm for convex bipartite graphs. In *Proceedings of the 1982 International Conference on Parallel Processing*, IEEE, New York, Aug., pp. 178–184.

De Keyser, J., and D. Roose. 1991. A software tool for load balanced adaptive multiple grids on distributed memory computers. In *The Sixth Distributed Memory Computing Conference Proceedings*. IEEE Computer Society Press, Los Alamitos, CA, pp. 122–128.

Deminet, J. 1982. Experience with multiprocessor algorithms. *IEEE Transactions on Computers*, vol. C-31, no. 4, Apr., pp. 278–288.

Demuth, H. B. 1956. Electronic data sorting. Ph.D. dissertation, Stanford University, Stanford, CA.

Dennis, J. B., and E. C. Van Horn. 1966. Programming semantics for multiprogrammed computations. *Communications of the ACM*, vol. 9, no. 3, Mar., pp. 143–155.

Deo, N. 1974. *Graph Theory with Applications to Engineering and Computer Science*. Prentice-Hall, Englewood Cliffs, NJ.

Deo, N., C. Y. Pang, and R. E. Lord. 1980. Two parallel algorithms for shortest path problems. In *Proceedings of the 1980 International Conference on Parallel Processing*, IEEE, New York, Aug., pp. 244–253.

Deo, N., and Y. B. Yoo. 1981. Parallel algorithms for the minimum spanning tree problem. In *Proceedings of the 1981 International Conference on Parallel Processing*, IEEE, New York, Aug., pp. 188–189.

Dere, W. Y., and D. J. Sakrison. 1970. Berkeley array processor. *IEEE Transactions on Computers*, vol. C-19, no. 5, May, pp. 444–447.

Desai, B. C. 1978. The BPU: A staged parallel processing system to solve the zero-one problem. In *Proceedings ICS '78*, Dec., pp. 802–817.

Dijkstra, E. W. 1959. A note on two problems in connexion with graphs. *Numererische Mathematik*, vol. 1, pp. 269–271.

Dijkstra, E. W. 1968a. The structure of the 'THE' multiprogramming system. *Communications of the ACM*, vol. 11, no. 5, May, pp. 341–346.

Dijkstra, E. W. 1968b. Cooperating sequential processes. In F. Genuys, ed., *Programming Languages*, Academic Press, New York.

Dimitriadis, S., and Karplus. W. J. 1990. Multiprocessor implementation of algorithms for ordinary differential equations. *Simulation*, vol. 55, Oct., pp. 236–246.

Dinning, A. 1989. A survey of synchronization methods for parallel computers. *Computer*, July, pp. 66–77.

Dongarra, J. J., and L. Johnsson. 1987. Solving banded systems on a parallel processor. *Parallel Computing*, vol. 5, pp. 219–246.

Dongarra, J. J., and A. H. Sameh. 1984. On some parallel banded system solvers. *Parallel Computing*, vol. 1, pp. 223–235.

Dongarra, J. J., I. S. Duff, D. C. Sorenson, and H. A. van der Vorst. 1991. *Solving Linear Systems on Vector and Shared Memory Computers*. SIAM Press, Philadelphia.

Doshi, K. A., and P. J. Varman. 1987. Optimal graph algorithms on a fixed-size linear array. *IEEE Transactions on Computers*, vol. C-36, no. 4, Apr., pp. 460–470.

Douglas, C. C., and B. F. Smith. 1989. Using symmetries and antisymmetries to analyze a parallel multigrid algorithm: the elliptic boundary value problem case. *SIAM Journal on Numerical Analysis*, vol. 26, Dec., pp. 1439–1461.

Douglass, R. J. 1984. Characterizing the parallelism in rule-based expert systems. Tech. Rept. LA-UR-84-3428, Los Alamos National Laboratory, Los Alamos, NM.

Dowd, M., Y. Perl, L. Rudolph, and M. Saks. 1983. The balanced sort network. In *Proceedings of the Conference on Principles of Distributed Computing*, pp. 161–172.

Dragon, K. M., and J. L. Gustafson. 1989. A low-cost hypercube load-balance algorithm. In *Proceedings of the Fourth Conference on Hypercubes, Concurrent Computers, and Applications*, pp. 583–589.

Driscoll, J. R., H. N. Gabow, R. Shrairman, and R. E. Tarjan. 1988. Relaxed heaps: An alternative to Fibonacci heaps with applications to parallel computation. *Communications of the ACM*, vol. 31, no. 11, Nov., pp. 1343–1354.

Dubois, M., and F. A. Briggs. 1982. Performance of synchronized iterative processes in multiprocessor systems. *IEEE Transactions on Software Engineering*, vol. SE-8, no. 4, July, pp. 419–431.

Dubois, M., and F. A. Briggs. 1991. The run-time efficiency of parallel asynchronous algorithms. *IEEE Transactions on Computers*, vol. C-40, no. 11, Nov., pp. 1260–1266.

Dubois, P. F. 1982. Swimming upstream: Calculating table lookups and piecewise functions. In G. Rodrigue, ed., *Parallel Computations*, Academic Press, New York, pp. 129–151.

Duff, I. S. 1986. Parallel implementation of multifrontal schemes. *Parallel Computing*, vol. 3, pp. 193–204.

Duncan, R. 1990. A survey of parallel computer architectures. *Computer*, Feb., pp. 5–16.

Duncan, R. 1992. Parallel computer architectures. In *Advances in Computers*, vol. 34, Academic Press, Orlando, FL, pp. 113–152.

Dyer, C. R. 1981. A VLSI pyramid machine for hierarchical parallel image processing. In *Proceedings PRIP*, pp. 381–386.

Dyer, C. R. 1982. Pyramid algorithms and machines. In K. Preston and L. Uhr, eds., *Multicomputers and Image Processing Algorithms and Programs*, Academic Press, New York, pp. 409–420.

Dyer, C. R., and A. Rosenfeld. 1981. Parallel image processing by memory augmented cellular automata. *IEEE Transactions on Pattern Analysis and Machine Intelligence*, vol. PAMI-3, pp. 29–41.

Eager, D. L., J. Zahorjan, and E. D. Lazowska. 1989. Speedup versus efficiency in parallel systems. *IEEE Transactions on Computers*, vol. C-38, no. 3, Mar., pp. 408–423.

Eckstein, D. M. 1979. BFS and biconnectivity. Tech. Rept. 79-11, Dept. of Computer Science, Iowa State University of Science and Technology, Ames.

Eckstein, D. M., and D. A. Alton. 1977a. Parallel searching of non-sparse graphs. Tech. rept. 77-02, Dept. of Computer Science, University of Iowa, Iowa City.

Eckstein, D. M., and D. A. Alton. 1977b. Parallel graph processing using depth-first search. In *Proceedings of the Conference on Theoretical Computer Science*, University of Waterloo, Waterloo, Ontario, pp. 21–29.

Eggers, S. J., and R. H. Katz. 1989. The effect of sharing on the cache and bus performance of parallel programs. In *Proceedings of the Third International Conference on Architectural Support for Programming Languages and Operating Systems, ASPLOS III*, pp. 257–270.

Ein-Dor, P. 1985. Grosch's law re-revisited: CPU power and the cost of computation. *Communications of the ACM*, vol. 28, no. 2, Feb., pp. 142–151.

El-Dessouki, O. I., and W. H. Huen. 1980. Distributed enumeration on network computers. *IEEE Transactions on Computers*, vol. C-29, no. 9, Sept., pp. 818–825.

El-Horbaty, E. M., and A. E. H. Mohamed. 1992. A synchronous algorithm for shortest paths on a tree machine. *Parallel Computing*, vol. 18, pp. 103–107.

Ellis, C. 1980a. Concurrent search and insertion in 2-3 trees. *Acta Informatica*, vol. 14, pp. 63–86.

Ellis, C. 1980b. Concurrent search and insertion in AVL trees. *IEEE Transactions on Computers*, vol. C-29, no. 9, Sept., pp. 811–817.

Ellis, J. A. 1991. Embedding rectangular grids into square grids. *IEEE Transactions on Computers*, vol. C-40, no. 1, Jan., pp. 46–52.

Elmagarmid, A. K. 1986. A survey of distributed deadlock detection algorithms. *ACM Sigmod Records*, Sept., pp. 37–45.

Enslow, P. H., ed. 1974. *Multiprocessors and Parallel Processing*. John Wiley & Sons, New York.

Enslow, P. H. 1977. Multiprocessor organization—A survey. *Computing Surveys*, vol. 9, no. 1, Mar., pp. 102–129.

Eppinger, J. L. 1983. An empirical study of insertion and deletion in binary search trees. *Communications of the ACM*, vol. 26, no. 9, Sept., pp. 663–669.

Esfahanian, A. H., and S. L. Hakimi. 1985. Fault-tolerant routing in De Bruijn communication networks. *IEEE Transactions on Computers*, vol. C-34, pp. 777-788.

ETA. 1984. Kuck and Associates to develop advanced preprocessor for ETA[10]. *ETA Systems i/o*, vol. 1, no. 2, Fall, p. 2.

Evans, D. J., ed. 1982. *Parallel Processing Systems*. Cambridge University Press, Cambridge.

Evans, D. J. 1984. Parallel S.O.R. iterative methods. *Parallel Computing*, vol. 1, pp. 3–18.

Evans, D. J., and Y. Yousif. 1985. Analysis of the performance of the parallel quicksort method. *BIT*, vol. 25, pp. 106–112.

Evans, D. J., and N. Y. Yousif. 1986. The parallel neighbour sort and 2-way merge algorithm. *Parallel Computing*, vol. 3, Mar., pp. 85–90.

Evans, D. J. 1990. A parallel sorting-merging algorithm for tightly coupled multiprocessors. *Parallel Computing*, vol. 14, pp. 111-121.

Even, S. 1974. Parallelism in tape-sorting. *Communications of the ACM*, vol. 17, no. 4, Apr., pp. 202–204.

Faber, V., O. M. Lubeck, and A. B., White, Jr. 1986. Superlinear speedup of an efficient sequential algorithm is not possible. *Parallel Computing*, vol. 3, pp. 259–260.

Fagin, B. S., and A. M. Despain. 1990. The performance of parallel Prolog programs. *IEEE Transactions on Computers*, vol. C-39, no. 12, Dec., pp. 1434–1445.

Falk, H. 1976. Reaching for the gigaflop. *IEEE Spectrum*, vol. 13, no. 10, Oct., pp. 64–70.

Fang, Z., P. Tang, P. C. Yew, and C. Q. Zhu. 1990. Dynamic processor self-scheduling for general parallel nested loops. *IEEE Transactions on Computers*, vol. C-39, no. 7, July, pp. 919–929.

Feierbach, G., and D. Stevenson. 1979. The ILLIAC IV. In C. R. Jesshope and R. W. Hockney, eds., *Infotech State of the Art Report: Supercomputers*, vol. 2, Infotech, Maidenhead, England, pp. 77–92.

Feldman, J. A. 1979. High level programming for distributed computing. *Communications of the ACM*, vol. 22, no. 6, June, pp. 353–368.

Feldmann, R., B. Monien, P. Mysliwietz, and O. Vornberger. 1990. Distributed game tree search. In V. Kumar, P. S. Gopalakrishnan,and L. N. Kanal, eds., *Parallel Algorithms for Machine Intelligence and Vision*, Springer-Verlag, New York, pp. 66–101.

Felten, E. W., and S. W. Otto. 1988. A highly parallel chess program. In *Proceedings of the International Conference on Fifth Generation Computer Systems 1988*. ICOT, pp. 1001–1009.

Feng, T.-Y. 1981. A survey of interconnection networks. *Computer*, vol. 14, no. 12, Dec, pp. 12–27.

Ferguson, C., and R. E. Korf. 1988. Distributed Tree Search and its application to alpha-beta pruning. In *Proceedings AAAI-88*, pp. 128–132.

Fich, F. E., P. Ragde, and V. Wigderson. 1988. Relations between concurrent-write models of parallel computation. *SIAM Journal on Computing*, vol. 17, no. 3, June, pp. 606–627.

Finkel, R., and J. Fishburn. 1982. Parallelism in alpha-beta. *Artificial Intelligence*, vol. 19, no. 1, Sept., pp. 89–106.

Fishburn, J. P. 1981. Analysis of speedup in distributed algorithms. Ph.D. dissertation, University of Wisconsin-Madison.

Fishburn, J. P., and R. A. Finkel. 1982. Quotient networks. *IEEE Transactions on Computers*, vol. C-31, no. 4, Apr., pp. 288–295.

Fisher, D. C. 1988. Your favorite parallel algorithms might not be as fast as you think. *IEEE Transactions on Computers*, vol. C-37, no. 2, Feb., pp. 211–213.

Flanders, P. M. 1982. A unified approach to a class of data movements on an array processor. *IEEE Transactions on Computers*, vol. C-31, no. 9, Sept., pp. 809–819.

Flanders, P. M., D. J. Hunt, S. F. Reddaway, and D. Parkinson. 1977. Efficient high speed computing with the Distributed Array Processor. In *High Speed Computer and Algorithm Organisation*. Academic Press, London, pp. 113–128.

Flanders, P. M., and S. F. Reddaway. 1984. Sorting on DAP. In M. Feilmeier, G. Joubert, and U. Schendel, eds., *Parallel Computing*, vol. 83, North-Holland, Amsterdam, pp. 247–252.

Flatt, H. P., and K. Kennedy. 1989. Performance of parallel processors. *Parallel Computing*, vol. 12, pp. 1–20.

Floyd, R. W. 1962. Algorithm 97: Shortest path. *Communications of the ACM*, vol. 5, no. 6, June, p. 345.

Flynn, M. J. 1966. Very high-speed computing systems. *Proceedings of the IEEE*, vol. 54, no. 12, Dec., pp. 1901–1909.

Flynn, M. J. 1972. Some computer organizations and their effectiveness. *IEEE Transactions on Computers*, vol. C-21, no. 9, Sept., pp. 948–960.

Fortune, S., and J. Wyllie. 1978. Parallelism in random access machines. *Proceedings of the 10th Annual ACM Symposium on Theory of Computing*, pp. 114–118.

Foster, C. C. 1976. *Content-Addressable Parallel Processors*. Van Nostrand Reinhold, New York.

Foster, I. T., and S. Taylor. 1988. Flat Parlog: A basis for comparison. *International Journal of Parallel Programming*, vol. 16, no. 2.

Foster, I., and S. Taylor. 1990. *Strand: New Concepts in Parallel Programming*. Prentice Hall, Englewood Cliffs, NJ.

Foster, M. J., and H. T. Kung. 1980. Design of special-purpose VLSI chips—Example and opinions. *Computer*, vol. 13, no. 1, Jan., pp. 26–40.

Fox, G. C. 1988. What have we learnt from using real parallel machines to solve real problems? In *Proceedings of the Third Conference on Hypercube Concurrent Computers and Applications*, ACM Press, New York, pp. 897–955.

Fox, G. C. 1989. 1989—The first year of the parallel supercomputer. In *Proceedings of the Fourth Conference on Hypercubes, Concurrent Computers, and Applications*, pp. 1–37.

406

Fox, G. C., and S. W. Otto. 1984. Algorithms for concurrent processors. *Physics Today*, vol. C-37, May, pp. 50–59.

Fox, G. C., M. A. Johnson, G. A. Syzenga, S. W. Otto, J. K. Salmon, and D. W. Walker. 1988. *Solving Problems on Concurrent Processors*, vol. 1, *General Techniques and Regular Problems*. Prentice Hall, Englewood Cliffs, NJ.

Francis, R. S., and I. D. Mathieson. 1988. A benchmark parallel sort for shared memory multiprocessors. *IEEE Transactions on Computers*, vol. C-37, no. 12, Dec., pp. 1619–1626.

Francis, R. S., and L. J. H. Pannan. 1992. A parallel partition for enhanced parallel QuickSort. *Parallel Computing*, vol. 18, pp. 543–550.

Frenkel, K. A. 1986. Evaluating two massively parallel machines. *Communications of the ACM*, vol. 29, no. 8, Aug., pp. 752–758.

Fritsch, G., W. Kleinoeder, C. U. Linster, and J. Volkert. 1983. EMSY85—The Erlanger multi-processor system for a broad spectrum of applications. In *Proceedings of the 1983 International Conference on Parallel Processing*, IEEE, New York, Aug., pp. 325–330.

Fromm, H. J., U. Hercksen, U. Herzog, K. H. John, R. Klar, and W. Kleinoder. 1983. Experiences with performance measurement and modeling of a processor array. *IEEE Transactions on Computers*, vol. C-32, Jan., pp. 15–31.

Fuller, S. H., and P. N. Oleinick. 1976. Initial measurements of parallel programs in a multi-miniprocessor. In *Proceedings of the 13th IEEE Computer Society International Conference*, IEEE, New York, pp. 358–363.

Fujii, M., T. Kasami, and K. Ninamiya. 1969. Optimal sequencing of two equivalent processors. *SIAM Journal of Applied Mathematics*, vol. 17, pp. 784–789.

Fung, L. 1977. A massively parallel processing computer. In D. J. Kuck, D. H. Lawrie, and A. H. Sameh, eds., *High Speed Computer and Algorithm Organisation*, Academic Press, London, pp. 203–204.

Fussell, D., and R. Thurimella. 1988. Separation pair detection. In *Proceedings of AWOC 88, Lecture Notes In Computer Science 319*, Springer-Verlag, New York, pp. 149–159.

Fussell, D., V. Ramachandran, and R. Thurimella. 1989. Finding triconnected components by local replacements. In *Proceedings of the 16th International Colloquium on Automata, Languages and Programming, Lecture Notes In Computer Science 372*, Springer-Verlag, New York, pp. 379–393.

Gabow, H. 1982. An almost-linear time algorithm for two-processor scheduling. *Journal of the ACM*, vol. 29, no. 3, July, pp. 766–780.

Gajski, D. D., D. A. Padua, D. J. Kuck, and R. H. Kuhn. 1982. A second opinion on data flow machines and languages. *Computer*, Feb., pp. 58–69.

Galil, Z. 1976. Hierarchies of complete problems. *Acta Informatica*, vol. 6, pp. 77–88.

Galil, Z., and W. J. Paul. 1981. An efficient general purpose parallel computer. In *Proceedings of the 13th Annual ACM Symposium on Theory of Computing*, ACM, New York, May, pp. 247–262.

Galil, Z., and W. J. Paul. 1983. An efficient general-purpose parallel computer. *Journal of the ACM*, vol. 30, no. 2, Apr., pp. 360–387.

Gallivan, K. A., R. J. Plemmons, and A. H. Sameh. 1990. Parallel algorithms for dense linear algebra computations. *SIAM Review*, vol. 32, Mar., pp. 54–135.

Garey, M. R., and D. S. Johnson. 1979. *Computers and Intractability: A Guide to the Theory of NP-Completeness*. W. H. Freeman, San Francisco.

Gavril, F. 1975. Merging with parallel processors. *Communications of the ACM*, vol. 18, no. 10, Oct., pp. 588–591.

Gehringer, E. F., A. K. Jones, and Z. Z. Segall. 1982. The Cm* testbed. *Computer*, Oct., pp. 40–53.

Geist, G. A., and M. T. Heath. 1986. Matrix factorization on a hypercube multicomputer. In M. T. Heath, ed., *Hypercube Multiprocessors 1986*, SIAM Press, Philadelphia, pp. 161–180.

Gelernter, D. 1985. Generative communication in Linda. *ACM Transactions on Programming Languages and Systems*, vol. 7, no. 1, pp. 80–112.

Gentleman, W. M. 1978. Some complexity results for matrix computations on parallel computers. *Journal of the ACM*, vol. 25, no. 1, Jan., pp. 112–115.

Ghosh, R. K., and G. P. Bhattacharjee. 1986. Parallel algorithm for shortest paths. *IEE Proceedings, Part E, Computers and Digital Techniques*, vol. 33, Mar., pp. 87–93.

Gibbons, A., and W. Rytter. 1988. *Efficient Parallel Algorithms*. Cambridge University Press, Cambridge.

Gilbert, E. J. 1983. Algorithm partition tools for a high-performance multiprocessor. Ph.D. dissertation, Stanford University, Stanford, CA.

Gillogly, J. 1978. Performance analysis of the technology chess program. Ph.D. dissertation, Carnegie-Mellon University, Pittsburgh, PA.

Gilmore, P. A. 1974. Matrix computations on an associative processor. In *Lecture Notes in Computer Science*, vol. 24, *Parallel Processing*. Springer-Verlag, New York, pp. 272–290.

Glasgow, J., M. Jenkins, C. McCrosky, and H. Meijer. 1989. Expressing parallel algorithms in Nial. *Parallel Computing*, vol. 11, pp. 331–347.

Goldberg, A. V., S. A. Plotkin, and P. M. Vaidya. 1988. Sublinear-time parallel algorithms for matching and related problems. In *Proceedings of the 29th Annual IEEE Symposium on Foundations of Computer Science*, IEEE Computer Society, Washington, DC, pp. 174–185.

Goldberg, M., and T. Spencer. 1989. A new parallel algorithm for the maximal independent set problem. *SIAM Journal on Computing*, vol. 18, Apr., pp. 419–427.

Golden, B., L. Bodin, T. Doyle, and W. Stewart, Jr. 1980. Approximate traveling salesman algorithms. *Operations Research*, vol. 28, no. 3, May–June, part 2, pp. 694–711.

Goldschlager, L. M. 1977. The monotone and planar circuit value problems are log space complete for *P*. *SIGACT News*, vol. 9, no. 2, Summer, pp. 25–29.

Goldschlager, L. M. 1978. A unified approach to models of synchronous parallel machines. In *Proceedings of the 10th Annual ACM Symposium on Theory of Computing*, ACM, New York, May, pp. 89–94.

Goldschlager, L. M. 1982. A universal interconnection pattern for parallel computers. *Journal of the ACM*, vol. 29, no. 4, Oct., pp. 1073–1086.

Goldschlager, L. M., R. A. Shaw, and J. Staples. 1982. The maximum flow problem is log space complete for *P*. *Theoretical Computer Science*, vol. 21, Oct., pp. 105–111.

Goodman, S. E., and S. T. Hedetniemi. 1977. *Introduction to the Design and Analysis of Algorithms*. McGraw-Hill, New York, p. 265.

Gottlieb, A. 1986. An overview of the NYU Ultracomputer project. Ultracomputer Note 100, Ultracomputer Research Laboratory, Div. of Computer Science, Courant Institute of Mathematical Sciences, New York University.

Gottlieb, A., R. Grishman, C. P. Kruskal, K. P. McAuliffe, L. Rudolph, and M. Snir. 1983. The NYU ultracomputer: Designing an MIMD shared memory parallel computer. *IEEE Transactions on Computers*, vol. C-32, no. 2, pp. 175–189.

Graham, R. L. 1966. Bounds for certain multiprocessing anomalies. *The Bell System Technical Journal*, Nov., pp. 1563–1581.

Graham, R. L. 1969. Bounds on multiprocessing timing anomalies. *SIAM Journal on Applied Mathematics*, vol. 17, no. 2, Mar., pp. 416–429.

Graham, R. L. 1972. Bounds on multiprocessing anomalies and packing algorithms. In *Proceedings AFIPS 1972 Spring Joint Computer Conference*, pp. 205–217.

Graunke, G., and S. Thakkar. 1990. Synchronization algorithms for shared-memory multiprocessors. *Computer*, June, pp. 60–69.

Greenberg, D. S. 1987. Optimal expansion embeddings of meshes in hypercubes. Tech. rept. YALEU/CSD/RR-535, Dept. of Computer Science, Yale University, New Haven, CT, Aug.

Gregory, S. 1987. *Parallel Logic Programming in Parlog*. Addison-Wesley, Reading, MA.

Greif, I. 1977. A language for formal problem specifications. *Communications of the ACM*, vol. 20, no. 12, Dec., pp. 931–935.

Gropp, W. D. 1987. Solving PDEs on loosely-coupled parallel processors. *Parallel Computing*, vol. 5, pp. 165–173.

Grosch, H. A. 1953. High speed arithmetic: The digital computer as a research tool. *Journal of the Optical Society of America*, vol. 43, no. 4, Apr., pp. 306–310.

Grosch, H. A. 1975. Grosch's law revisited. *Computerworld*, vol. 8, no. 16, Apr., p. 24.

Gu, Q. P., and T. Takaoka. 1990. A sharper analysis of a parallel algorithm for the all pairs shortest path problem. *Parallel Computing*, vol. 16, pp. 61–67.

Guan, X., and M. A. Langston. 1991. Time-space optimal parallel merging and sorting. *IEEE Transactions on Computers*, vol. C-40, no. 5, May, pp. 596–602.

Guibas, L. J., H. T. Kung, and C. D. Thompson. 1979. Direct VLSI implementation of combinatorial problems. In *Proceedings of the Conference on Very Large Scale Integration: Architecture, Design, Fabrication*, California Institute of Technology, Pasadena, pp. 509–525.

Gupta, A. K., and S. E. Hambrusch. 1991. Embedding complete binary trees into butterfly networks. *IEEE Transactions on Computers*, vol. C-40, no. 7, July, pp. 853–863.

Gupta, A. K., and S. E. Hambrusch. 1992. Load balanced tree embeddings. *Parallel Computing*, vol. 18, pp. 595–614.

Gupta, A., and W. D. Weber. 1992. Cache invalidation patterns in shared-memory multiprocessors. *IEEE Transactions on Computers*, vol. C-41, no. 7, July, pp. 794–810.

Gurd, J. R., C. C. Kirkham, and I. Watson. 1985. The Manchester prototype dataflow computer. *Communications of the ACM*, vol. 28, no. 1, Jan., pp. 34–52.

Gustafson, J. L. 1988. Reevaluating Amdahl's law. *Communications of the ACM*, vol. 21, no. 5, May, pp. 532–533.

Gustafson, J. L., G. R. Montry, and R. E. Benner. 1988. Development of parallel methods for a 1024-processor hypercube. *SIAM Journal on Scientific and Statistical Computing*, vol. 9, no. 4, July, pp. 609–638.

Habermann, A. N. 1972. Parallel neighbor sort. Tech. rept., Carnegie-Mellon University, Pittsburgh, PA.

Hagerup, T. 1990. Planar depth-first search in $O(\log n)$ parallel time. *SIAM Journal on Computing*, vol. 19, no. 4, Aug., pp. 678–704.

Häggvist, R., and P. Hell. 1981. Parallel sorting with constant time for comparisons. *SIAM Journal on Computing*, vol. 10, no. 3, Aug., pp. 465–472.

Halliday, D., and R. Resnick. 1974. *Fundamentals of Physics*. Rev. ed. John Wiley & Sons, New York.

Halstead, R. H., Jr. 1986. Parallel symbolic computing. *Computer*, vol. 19, no. 8, Aug., pp. 35–43.

Hambrusch, S. E. 1982. The complexity of graph problems on VLSI. Ph.D. dissertation, The Pennsylvania State University, University Park.

Hambrusch, S. E. 1983. VLSI algorithms for the connected component problem. *SIAM Journal on Computing*, vol. 12, pp. 354-365.

Han, Y., and R. A. Wagner. 1990. An efficient and fast parallel connected component algorithm. *Journal of the ACM*, vol. 37, July, pp. 626–642.

Händler, W. 1977. The impact of classification schemes on computer architecture. *Proceedings of the 1977 International Conference on Parallel Processing*, IEEE, New York, Aug., pp. 7–15.

Hansen, P., and K. W. Lih. 1992. Improved algorithms for partitioning problems in parallel, pipelined, and distributed computing. *IEEE Transactions on Computers*, vol. C-41, no. 6, June, pp. 769–770.

Harary, F. 1969. *Graph Theory*. Addison-Wesley, Reading, MA.

Harrison, P. G., and N. M. Patel. 1990. The representation of multistage interconnection networks in queuing models of parallel systems. *Journal of the ACM*, vol. 37, no. 4, Oct., pp. 863–898.

Harrison, T. J., and M. W. Wilson. 1983. Special-purpose computers. In A. Ralston, ed., *Encyclopedia of Computer Science and Engineering*, 2d ed. Van Nostrand-Reinhold, New York, pp. 1385–1393.

Hatcher, P. J., and M. J. Quinn. 1991. *Data-Parallel Programming on MIMD Computers*, MIT Press, Cambridge.

Hatcher, P. J., M. J. Quinn, R. J. Anderson, A. J. Lapadula, B. K. Seevers, and A. F. Bennett. 1991a. Architecture-independent scientific programming in Data-parallel C: Three case studies. In *Supercomputing '91*, ACM, New York, NY, pp. 208–217.

Hatcher, P. J., M. J. Quinn, A. J. Lapadula, R. R. Jones, and R. J. Anderson. 1991b. A production-quality C* compiler for a hypercube multicomputer. In *Proceedings of the Third ACM SIGPLAN Symposium on Principles and Practice of Parallel Programming*, pp. 73–82.

Hatcher, P. J., M. J. Quinn, A. J. Lapadula, B. K. Seevers, R. J. Anderson, and R. R. Jones. 1991c. Data-parallel programming on MIMD computers. *IEEE Transactions on Parallel and Distributed Systems*, vol. 2, no. 3, July, pp. 377–383.

Havel, I., and J. Morávek. 1972. B-valuations of graphs. *Czechoslovak Mathematical Journal*, vol. 22, pp. 338–351.

Hayes, J. P. 1988. *Computer Architecture and Organization*, 2d edition. McGraw-Hill, New York.

Haynes, L. S., R. L. Lau, D. P. Siewiorek, and D. Mizell. 1982. A survey of highly parallel computing. *Computer*, vol. 14, no. 1, Jan., pp. 9–24.

He, X., and Y. Yesha. 1988. A nearly optimal parallel algorithm for constructing depth first spanning trees in planar graphs. *SIAM Journal on Computing*, vol. 17, no. 3, June, pp. 486–491.

Heath, L. S., A. L. Rosenberg, and B. T. Smith. 1988. The physical mapping problem for parallel architectures. *Journal of the ACM*, vol. 35, July, pp. 603–634.

Heath, M. T., E. Ng, and B. W. Peyton. 1991. Parallel algorithms for sparse linear systems. *SIAM Review*, vol. 33, Sept., pp. 420–460.

Heidelberger, P., A. Norton, and J. T. Robinson. 1990. Parallel quicksort using fetch-and-add. *IEEE Transactions on Computers*, vol. C-39, no. 1, Jan., pp. 133–138.

Heller, D. 1978. A survey of parallel algorithms in numerical linear algebra. *SIAM Review*, vol. 20, pp. 740–777.

Helman, P., and R. Veroff. 1986. *Intermediate Problem Solving and Data Structures: Walls and Mirrors*. Benjamin/Cummings, Menlo Park, CA.

Helmbold, D., and E. Mayr. 1987. Two processor scheduling is in *NC*. *SIAM Journal on Computing*, vol. 16, no. 4, Aug., pp. 747–759.

Hennessy, J. L., and D. A. Patterson. 1990. *Computer Architecture: A Quantitative Approach*, Morgan Kaufmann, San Mateo, CA.

Herter, C. G., T. M. Warschko, W. F. Tichy, and M. Philippsen. 1993. Triton/1: A massively-parallel mixed-mode computer designed to support high level languages. In *Proceedings of the International Parallel Processing Symposium*.

Higbie, L. C. 1972. The OMEN computers: Associative array processors. In *COMPCON 72 Digest*. IEEE, New York, pp. 287–290.

Hill, M. D., and J. R. Larus. 1990. Cache considerations for multiprocessor programmers. *Communications of the ACM*, vol. 33, no. 8, Aug., pp. 97–102.

Hillis, W. D., and G. L. Steele, Jr. 1986. Data parallel algorithms. *Communications of the ACM*, vol. 29, no. 12, Dec., pp. 1170–1183.

Hillis, W. D., and G. L. Steele, Jr. 1987. Update to Data parallel algorithms. *Communications of the ACM*, vol. 30, no. 1, Jan., p. 78.

Hirschberg, D. S. 1976. Parallel algorithms for the transitive closure and the connected component problem. In *Proceedings of the 8th Annual ACM Symposium on the Theory of Computing*, ACM, New York, May, pp. 55–57.

Hirschberg, D. S. 1978. Fast parallel sorting algorithms. *Communications of the ACM*, vol. 21, no. 8, Aug., pp. 657–666.

Hirschberg, D. S. 1982. Parallel graph algorithms without memory conflicts. In *Proceedings of the 20th Allerton Conference*, Oct., pp. 257–263. University of Illinois, Urbana-Champaign.

Hirschberg, D. S., A. K. Chandra, and D. V. Sarwate. 1979. Computing connected components on parallel computers. *Communications of the ACM*, vol. 22, no. 8, Aug., pp. 461–464.

Ho, C. T., and S. L. Johnsson. 1987. On the embedding of arbitrary meshes in Boolean cubes with expansion two dilation two. In *Proceedings of the International Conference on Parallel Processing*, pp. 188–191.

Hoare, C. A. R. 1962. Quicksort. *The Computer Journal*, vol. 5, pp. 10–15.

Hoare, C. A. R. 1974. Monitors: An operating system structuring concept. *Communications of the ACM*, vol. 17, no. 10, Oct., pp. 549–557.

Hoare, C. A. R. 1978. Communicating sequential processes. *Communications of the ACM*, vol. 21, no. 8, Aug., pp. 666–677.

Hockney, R. W. 1965. A fast direct solution of Poisson's equation using Fourier analysis. *Journal of the ACM*, vol. 12, no. 1, Jan., pp. 95–113.

Hockney, R. W., and C. R. Jesshope. 1981. *Parallel Computers: Architecture, Programming and Algorithms*. Adam Hilger, Bristol, England.

Hoey, D., and C. E. Leiserson. 1980. A layout for the shuffle-exchange network. In *Proceedings of the 1980 International Conference on Parallel Processing*, IEEE, New York, Aug., pp. 329–336.

Holt, R. C., G. S. Graham, E. D. Lazowska, and M. A. Scott. 1978. *Structured Concurrent Programming with Operating System Applications*. Addison-Wesley, Reading, MA.

Hong, J.-W., K. Mehlhorn, and A. Rosenberg. 1983. Cost trade-offs in graph embeddings, with applications. *Journal of the ACM*, vol. 30, no. 4, Oct., pp. 709–728.

Hong, Z., and R. Sedgewick. 1982. Notes on merging networks. *Proceedings of the 14th Annual ACM Symposium on the Theory of Computing*, ACM, New York, May, pp. 296–302.

Hopcroft, J. E., and J. D. Ullman. 1973. Set-merging algorithms. *SIAM Journal on Computing*, vol. 2, pp. 294–303.

Hopcroft, J. E., and J. D. Ullman. 1979. *Introduction to Automata Theory, Languages, and Computation*. Addison-Wesley, Reading, MA.

Hoppe, H. C., and H. Mühlenbein. 1986. Parallel adaptive full-multigrid methods on message-based multiprocessors. *Parallel Computing*, vol. 3, pp. 269–287.

Horowitz, E. 1979. VLSI architectures for matrix computations. In *Proceedings of the 1979 International Conference on Parallel Processing*, IEEE, New York, Aug., pp. 124–127.

Horowitz, E., and S. Sahni. 1978. *Fundamentals of Computer Algorithms*. Computer Science Press, Potomac, MD.

Horowitz, E., and A. Zorat. 1983. Divide and conquer for parallel processing. *IEEE Transactions on Computers*, vol. C-32, no. 6, June, pp. 582–585.

Hsiao, C. C., and L. Snyder. 1983. Omni-sort: A versatile data processing operation for VLSI. In *Proceedings of the 1983 International Conference on Parallel Processing*, IEEE, New York, Aug., pp. 222–225.

Hu, T. Parallel sequencing and assembly line problems. *Operations Research*, vol. 9, pp. 841–848.

Huang, Y., and Y. Paker. 1991. A parallel FFT algorithm for transputer networks. *Parallel Computing*, vol. 17, pp. 895–906.

Hudak, P. 1986. Para-functional programming. *Computer*, vol. 19, no. 8, Aug., pp. 60–70.

Hull, M. E. C. 1984. A parallel view of stable marriages. *Information Processing Letters*, vol. 18, Feb., pp. 63–66.

Huntbach, M. M, and Burton. 1988. Alpha-beta search on virtual tree machines. *Information Sciences*, vol. 44, pp. 3–17.

Hwang, K. 1984. *Supercomputers: Design and Applications*. IEEE Computer Society Press, Silver Spring, MD.

Hwang, K., and F. A. Briggs. 1984. *Computer Architecture and Parallel Processing*. McGraw-Hill, New York.

Hwang, K., and Y. H. Cheng. 1982. Partitioned matrix algorithms for VLSI arithmetic system. *IEEE Transactions on Computers*, vol. C-31, no. 12, Dec., pp. 1215–1224.

Hwang, K., S. P. Su, and L. M. Ni. 1981. Vector computer architecture and processing techniques. In M. Yovits, ed., *Advances in Computers*, vol. 20, Academic Press, New York, pp. 115–197.

Hyafil, L. 1976. Bounds for selection. *SIAM Journal on Computing*, vol. 5, no. 1, Feb., pp. 109–114.

Hyatt, R. M., B. W. Suter, and H. L. Nelson. 1989. A parallel alpha/beta tree searching algorithm. *Parallel Computing*, vol. 10, pp. 299–308.

Ibaraki, T. 1976a. Computational efficiency of approximate branch-and-bound algorithms. *Mathematical Operations Research*, vol. 1, no. 3, pp. 287–298.

Ibaraki, T. 1976b. Theoretical comparisons of search strategies in branch-and-bound algorithms. *International Journal of Computer and Information Science*, vol. 5, no. 4, pp. 315–344.

Ichiyoshi, N., T. Miyazaki, and K. Taki. 1987. A distributed implementation of Flat GHC on the Multi-PSI. In *Proceedings of the Fourth International Conference on Logic Programming*, MIT Press, Cambridge, pp. 257–275.

Imai, M., T. Fukumara, and Y. Yoshida. 1979. A parallelized branch-and-bound algorithm: Implementation and efficiency. *System Computer Controls*, vol. 10, no. 3, pp. 62–70.

Irani, K. B., and K. W. Chen. 1982. Minimization of interprocessor communication for parallel computation. *IEEE Transactions on Computers*, vol. C-31, no. 11, Nov., pp. 1067–1075.

Isloor, S. S., and T. A. Marsland. 1980. The deadlock problem: An overview. *Computer*, Sept., pp. 58–77.

Jacobi, C. G. J. 1845. Über eine Neue Auflösungsart der bei der Methode der Kleinsten Quadrate Vorkommenden Lineären Gleichungen. *Astr. Nachr.*, vol. 22, no. 523, pp. 297–306.

JáJá, J. 1992. *An Introduction to Parallel Algorithms*. Addison-Wesley, Reading, MA.

JáJá, J. and J. Simon. 1982. Parallel algorithms in graph theory: Planarity testing. *SIAM Journal on Computing*, vol. 11, no. 2, May, pp. 314–328.

Jamieson, L. H., D. Gannon, and R. J. Douglass, eds. 1987. *The Characteristics of Parallel Algorithms*. MIT Press, Cambridge, MA.

Janakiram, V. K., D. P. Agrawal, and R. Mehrotra. 1988. A randomized parallel backtracking algorithm. *IEEE Transactions on Computers*, vol. C-37, no. 12, Dec., pp. 1665–1676.

Jess, J. A. G., and H. G. M. Kees. 1982. A data structure for parallel L/U decomposition. *IEEE Transactions on Computers*, vol. C-31, no. 3, Mar., pp. 231–239.

Jesshope, C. R. 1980. Implementation of fast RADIX 2 transforms on array processors. *IEEE Transactions on Computers*, vol. C-29, no. 1, Jan., pp. 20–27.

Johnson, D. S. 1983. The NP-completeness column: An ongoing guide. *Journal of Algorithms*, vol. 4, pp. 189–203.

Johnsson, S. L., and C. T. Ho. 1989. Optimum broadcasting and personalized communications in hypercubes. *IEEE Transactions on Computers*, vol. C-38, no. 9, Sept., pp. 1249–1268.

Jones, A. K., and E. F. Gehringer, eds. 1980. The Cm* multiprocessor project: A research review. Tech. rept. CMU-CS-80-131, Dept. of Computer Science, Carnegie-Mellon University, Pittsburgh.

Jones, A. K., and P. Schwarz. 1980. Experience using multiprocessor systems—A status report. *ACM Computing Surveys*, vol. 12, no. 2, June, pp. 121–165.

Jones, N. D. 1975. Space-bounded reducibility among combinatorial problems. *Journal of Computer Science and System Sciences*, vol. 11, pp. 68–85.

Joseph, M., V. R. Prasad, and N. Natarajan. 1984. *A Multiprocessor Operating System*. Prentice-Hall, Englewood Cliffs, NJ.

Kalé, L. V., and V. A. Saletore. 1990. Parallel state-space search for a first solution with consistent linear speedups. *International Journal of Parallel Programming*, vol. 19, no. 4, pp. 251–293.

Kanevsky, A., and V. Ramachandran. 1987. Improved algorithms for graph four-connectivity. In *Proceedings of the 28th Annual IEEE Symposium on Foundations of Computer Science*, IEEE Computer Society, Washington, D.C., pp. 252–259.

Kang, Y. M., R. B. Miller, and R. A. Pick. 1986. Comments on Grosch's law re-revisited: CPU power and the cost of computation. *Communications of the ACM*, vol. 29, no. 8, Aug., pp. 779–781.

Karlin, A. R., and E. Upfal. 1988. Parallel hashing—an efficient implementation of shared memory. *Journal of the ACM*, vol. 35, no. 4, pp. 876–892.

Karp, A. H. 1987. Programming for parallelism. *Computer*, May, pp. 43–57.

Karp, A. H., and R. G. Babb, II. 1988. A comparison of 12 parallel Fortran dialects. *IEEE Software*, vol. 5, no. 5, Sept., pp. 52–66.

Karp, A. H., and H. P. Flatt. 1990. Measuring parallel processor performance. *Communications of the ACM*, vol. 33, no. 5, May, pp. 539–543.

Karp, A. H., and J. Greenstadt. 1987. An improved parallel Jacobi method for diagonalizing a symmetric matrix. *Parallel Computing*, vol. 5, pp. 281–294.

Karp, R. M., and V. Ramachandran. 1990. Parallel algorithms for shared-memory machines. In J. van Leeuwen, ed., *Handbook of Theoretical Computer Science*, vol. A, Elsevier Science Publishers, North Holland, pp. 869–941.

Karp, R. M., and A. Wigderson. 1985. A fast parallel algorithm for the maximal independent set problem. *Journal of the ACM*, vol. 32, no. 4, Oct., pp. 762–773.

Kasahara, H., and S. Narita. 1984. Practical multiprocessor scheduling algorithms for efficient parallel processing. *IEEE Transactions on Computers*, vol. C-33, no. 11, Nov., pp. 1023–1029.

Kedem, Z. M., and A. Zorat. 1981. On relations between input and communication/comparison in VLSI (preliminary report). In *Proceedings of the 22d Annual Symposium on Foundations of Computer Science*, IEEE, New York, Oct., pp. 37–44.

Keller, R. M. 1976. Formal verification of parallel programs. *Communications of the ACM*, vol. 19, no. 7, July, pp. 371–384.

Khuller, S., and B. Schieber. 1991. Efficient parallel algorithms for testing k-connectivity and finding disjoint s-t paths in graphs. *SIAM Journal on Computing*, vol. 20, Apr., pp. 352–375.

Kim, H. J., and J. G. Lee. 1990. A parallel algorithm solving a tridiagonal Toeplitz linear system. *Parallel Computing*, vol. 13, pp. 289–294.

Klein, P. N., and J. H. Reif. 1986. An efficient parallel algorithm for planarity. In *Proceedings of the 27th Annual IEEE Symposium on the Foundations of Computer Science*, pp. 465–477.

Kleitman, D., F. T. Leighton, M. Lepley, and G. L. Miller. 1981. New layouts for the shuffle-exchange graph. In *Proceedings of the 13th Annual ACM Symposium on Theory of Computing*, ACM, New York, May, pp. 278–292.

Knuth, D. E. 1973. *The Art of Computer Programming*, vol. 3. Addison-Wesley, Reading, MA.

Knuth, D. E. 1976. Big omicron and big omega and big theta. *SIGACT News*, Apr.–June, pp. 18–23.

Knuth, D. E., and R. W. Moore. 1975. An analysis of alpha-beta pruning. *Artificial Intelligence*, vol. 6, pp. 293–326.

Kogge, P. M., and H. S. Stone. 1973. A parallel algorithm for the efficient solution of a general class of recurrence equations. *IEEE Transactions on Computers*, vol. C-22, no. 8, Aug., pp. 786–793.

Kosaraju, S. R. 1979. Fast parallel processing array algorithms for some graph problems. In *Proceedings of the 11th Annual ACM Symposium on Theory of Computing*, ACM, New York, May, pp. 231–236.

Kosaraju, S. R., and M. J. Atallah. 1988. Optimal simulations between mesh-connected arrays of processors. *Journal of the ACM*, vol. 35, no. 3, July, pp. 635–650.

Kowalik, J. S., ed. 1985. *Parallel MIMD Computation: HEP Supercomputer and Its Applications*. MIT Press, Cambridge, MA.

Kowalski, R. 1979. *Logic for Problem Solving*. North-Holland, New York.

Kozen, D. 1977. Complexity of finitely presented algebras. In *Proceedings of the 9th Annual ACM Symposium on Theory of Computing*, ACM, New York, May, pp. 164–177.

Kramer, M. R., and J. van Leeuwen. 1982. Systolic computation and VLSI. Tech. rept. RUU-CS-82-9, Vakgroep Informatica, Rijksuniversiteit Utrecht.

Krechel, A., H. J. Plum, and K. Stüben. 1990. Parallelization and vectorization aspects of the solution of tridiagonal linear systems. *Parallel Computing*, vol. 14, pp. 31–49.

Krumme, D. W., and K. Venkataraman. 1986. On the NP-hardness of a certain construction. Tech. rept. 86-1, Dept. of Computer Science, Tufts Univ., Medford, MA.

Kruskal, C. P. 1982. Results in parallel searching, merging, and sorting. *Proceedings of the 1982 International Conference on Parallel Processing*, IEEE, New York, Aug., pp. 196–198.

Kruskal, C. P. 1983. Searching, merging and sorting in parallel computation. *IEEE Transactions on Computers*, vol. C-32, no. 10, Oct., pp. 942–946.

Kruskal, C. P., and A. Weiss. 1984. Allocating independent subtasks on parallel processors. In *Proceedings of the 1984 International Conference on Parallel Processing*, pp. 183–187.

Kruskal, J. B. 1956. On the shortest subtree of a graph and the traveling salesman problem. *Proceedings of the American Mathematical Society*, vol. 7, Feb., pp. 48–50.

Kučera, L. 1982. Parallel computation and conflicts in memory access. *Information Processing Letters*, vol. 14, no. 2, Apr., pp. 93–96.

Kuck, D. J. 1977. A survey of parallel machine organization and programming. *Computing Surveys*, vol. 9, no. 1, Mar., pp. 29–59.

Kuck, D. J. 1978. *The Structure of Computers and Computations*, vol. 1, Wiley & Sons, New York.

Kuhn, R. H., and D. A. Padua. 1981. *Tutorial on Parallel Processing*. IEEE Computer Society Press, Los Angeles.

Kulkarni, A. V., and D. W. L. Yen. 1982. Systolic processing and an implementation for signal and image processing. *IEEE Transactions on Computers*, vol. C-31, no. 10, Oct., pp. 1000–1009.

Kumar, M., and D. S. Hirschberg. 1983. An efficient implementation of Batcher's odd-even merge algorithm and its application in parallel sorting schemes. *IEEE Transactions on Computers*, vol. C-32, no. 3, Mar., pp. 254–264.

Kumar, S. P., and J. S. Kowalik. 1984. Parallel factorization of a positive definite matrix on an MIMD computer. In *Proceedings of the 1984 International Conference on Parallel Processing*, IEEE, New York, Aug., pp. 417–424.

Kumar, V., and L. Kanal. 1983. A general branch-and-bound formulation for understanding and synthesizing AND/OR tree search procedures. *Artificial Intelligence*, vol. 21, pp. 179–198.

Kumar, V., and L. Kanal. 1984. Parallel branch-and-bound formulations for AND/OR tree search. *IEEE Transactions on Pattern Analysis and Machine Intelligence*, vol. PAMI-6, no. 6, Nov., pp. 768–778.

Kumar, V. P., and S. M. Reddy. 1987. Augmented shuffle-exchange multistage interconnection networks. *Computer*, June, pp. 30–40.

Kung, H. T. 1976. Synchronized and asynchronous parallel algorithms for multiprocessors. In J. F. Traub, ed., *Algorithms and Complexity: New Directions and Recent Results*, Academic Press, New York, pp. 153–200.

Kung, H. T. 1980. The structure of parallel algorithms. In M. Yovits, ed., *Advances in Computers*, vol. 19, Academic Press, New York, pp. 65–112.

Kung, H. T. 1982. Why systolic architectures? *Computer*, vol. 15, no. 1, Jan., pp. 37–46.

Kung, H. T., and P. L. Lehman. 1980. Concurrent manipulation of binary search trees. *ACM Transactions on Database Systems*, vol. 5, Sept., pp. 354–382.

Kung, H. T., and C. E. Leiserson. 1980. Systolic arrays for VLSI. In C. Mead and L. Conway, eds., *Introduction to VLSI Systems*, Addison-Wesley, Reading, MA, pp. 260–292.

Kung, S. Y., K. S. Arun, R. J. Gal-Ezer, and D. V. Bhaskar Rao. 1982. Wavefront array processor: Languages, architecture, and applications. *IEEE Transactions on Computers*, vol. C-31, no. 11, Nov., pp. 1054–1066.

Kutti, S. K. 1985. Taxonomy of parallel processing and definitions. *Parallel Computing*, vol. 2, pp. 353–359.

Ladner, R. E. 1975. The circuit value problem is log space complete for *P*. *SIGACT News*, vol. 7, no. 1, Jan., pp. 18–20.

Lai, T. H., and S. Sahni. 1984. Anomalies in parallel branch-and-bound algorithms. *Communications of the ACM*, vol. 27, no. 6, June, pp. 594–602.

Lakshmivarahan, S., and S. K. Dhall. 1990. *Analysis and Design of Parallel Algorithms: Arithmetic and Matrix Problems.* McGraw-Hill, New York.

Lakshmivarahan, S., S. K. Dhall, and L. L. Miller. 1984. Parallel sorting algorithms. In M. C. Yovitts, ed., *Advances in Computers*, vol. 23, Academic Press, New York, pp. 295–354.

Lambiotte, J. J., Jr., and D. D. Korn. 1979. Computing the fast Fourier transform on a vector computer. *Mathematics of Computation*, vol. 33, July, pp. 977–992.

Lamport, L. 1977. Proving the correctness of multiprocess programs. *IEEE Transactions on Software Engineering*, vol. SE-3, no. 7, Mar., pp. 125–143.

Lang, H. W., M. Schimmler, H. Schmeck, and H. Schröder. 1983. A fast sorting algorithm for VLSI. In *Proceedings of the 10th International Colloquium on Automata, Languages, and Programming*, pp. 408–419.

Lang, T., and H. S. Stone. 1976. A shuffle-exchange network with simplified control. *IEEE Transactions on Computing*, vol. C-25, Jan. pp. 55–56.

Lansdowne, S. T., R. E. Cousins, and D. C. Wilkinson. 1987. Reprogramming the Sieve of Eratosthenes. *Computer*, vol. 20, Aug., pp. 90–91.

Lawrie, D. H. 1975. Access and alignment of data in an array processor. *IEEE Transactions on Computers*, vol. C-24, no. 12, Dec., pp. 1145–1155.

Lea, W. A. 1980. Speech recognition: past, present, and future. In *Trends in Speech Recognition*, Prentice-Hall, Englewood Cliffs, NJ, pp. 39–98.

LeBlanc, T. J. 1986. Shared memory versus message-passing in a tightly-coupled multiprocessor: A case study. Butterfly Proj. rep. 3, Computer Science Dept., University of Rochester, Rochester, NY.

L'Ecuyer, P. 1988. Efficient and portable combined random number generators. *Communications of the ACM*, vol. 31, no. 6, June, pp. 742–749,774.

Lee, C. C., S. Skedzielewski, and J. Feo. 1988. On the implementation of applicative languages on shared-memory, MIMD multiprocessors. *SIGPLAN Notices*, vol. 23, no. 9, Sept., Proceedings of the ACM/SIGPLAN PPEALS 1988—Parallel programming: experience with applications, languages, and systems, pp. 188–197.

Lee, D. T., H. Chang, and C. K. Wong. 1981. An on-chip compare/steer bubble sorter. *IEEE Transactions on Computers*, vol. C-30, no. 6, June, pp. 396–405.

Lee, S.Y., and J. K. Aggarwal. 1987. A mapping strategy for parallel processing. *IEEE Transactions on Computers*, vol. C-36, no. 4, Apr., pp. 433–442.

Lehman, P. L., and S. B. Yao. 1981. Efficient locking for concurrent operations on B-trees. *ACM Transactions on Database Systems*, vol. 6, no. 4, Dec., pp. 650–670.

Leighton, F. T. 1981. New lower bound techniques for VLSI. In *Proceedings of the 22d Annual Symposium on Foundations of Computer Science*, IEEE, New York, Oct., pp. 1–12.

Leighton, F. T. 1983. *Complexity Issues in VLSI*. MIT Press, Cambridge.

Leighton, F. T. 1984. Tight bounds on the complexity of parallel sorting. In *Proceedings of the 16th Annual ACM Symposium on Theory of Computing*, ACM, New York, May, pp. 71–80.

Leighton, F. T. 1992. *Introduction to Parallel Algorithms and Architectures: Arrays • Trees • Hypercubes*. Morgan Kaufmann, San Mateo, CA.

Leighton, F. T., M. J. Newman, A. G. Ranade, and E. J. Schwabe. 1992. Dynamic tree embeddings in butterflies and hypercubes. *SIAM Journal on Computing*, vol. 21, no. 4, Aug., pp. 639–654.

Leiserson, C. E. 1980. Area efficient graph layouts. In *Proceedings of the 21st Annual Symposium on Foundations of Computer Science*, IEEE, New York, Oct., pp. 270–281.

Leiserson, C. E. 1983. *Area-Efficient VLSI Computation*. MIT Press, Cambridge.

Leiserson, C. E., and J. B. Saxe. 1981. Optimizing synchronous systems. In *Proceedings of the 22d Annual Symposium on Foundations of Computer Science*, IEEE, New York, Oct., pp. 23–36.

Leler, W. 1990. Linda meets Unix. *Computer*, Feb., pp. 43–54.

Lenders, P. M. 1988. A generalized message-passing mechanism for communicating sequential processes. *IEEE Transactions on Computers*, vol. C-37, no. 6, June, pp. 646–651.

Levialdi, S. 1972. On shrinking binary picture patterns. *Communications of the ACM*, vol. 15, no. 1, Jan., pp. 2–10.

Levialdi, S. 1985. A pyramid project using integrated technology. In S. Levialdi, ed., *Integrated Technology for Parallel Image Processing*, Academic Press, New York.

Levin, E. 1989. Grand challenges to computational science. *Communications of the ACM*, vol. 32, no. 12, Dec., pp. 1456–1457.

Levine, R. D. 1982. Supercomputers. *Scientific American*, vol. 246, no. 1, Jan., pp. 118–135.

Levitt, K. N., and W. T. Kautz. 1972. Cellular arrays for the solution of graph problems. *Communications of the ACM*, vol. 15, no. 9, Sept., pp. 789–801.

Lewis, T. G., and H. El-Rewini. 1992. *Introduction to Parallel Computing*. Prentice-Hall, Englewood Cliffs, NJ.

Li, G. J., and B. W. Wah. 1984a. How to cope with anomalies in parallel approximate branch-and-bound algorithms. In *Proceedings of the National Conference on Artificial Intelligence*, pp. 212–215.

Li, G. J., and B. W. Wah. 1984b. Computational efficiency of parallel approximate branch-and-bound algorithms. In *Proceedings of the 1984 International Conference on Parallel Processing*, IEEE, New York, Aug., pp. 473–480.

Li, G. J., and B. W. Wah. 1985. MANIP-2: A multicomputer architecture for solving logic programming problems. In *Proceedings of the 1985 International Conference on Parallel Processing*, IEEE, New York, Aug., pp. 123–130.

Li, L. M., and C. T. King. 1988. On partitioning and mapping for hypercube computing. *International Journal of Parallel Programming*.

Li, X., P. Lu, J. Schaeffer, J. Shillington, P. S. Wong, and H. Shi. 1992. On the versatility of parallel sorting by regular sampling. Tech. rept. TR 91–06, Mar., Dept. of Computing Science, University of Alberta, Edmonton, Alberta, Canada.

Lillevik, S. L. 1991. The Touchstone 30 gigaflop DELTA prototype. In *Sixth Distributed Memory Computing Conference Proceedings*, pp. 671–677.

Lin, F. C., and K. L. Chung. 1990. A cost-optimal parallel tridiagonal system solver. *Parallel Computing*, vol. 15, pp. 189–199.

Lin, R., and S. Olariu. 1992. A fast cost-optimal parallel algorithm for the lowest common ancestor problem. *Parallel Computing*, vol. 18, pp. 511–516.

Lin, Y. J., V. Kumar, and C. Leung. 1986. An intelligent backtracking algorithm for parallel execution of logic programs. In *Proceedings of the Third International Conference on Logic Programming*, pp. 55–69.

Lincoln, N. R. 1982. Technology and design trade-offs in the creation of a modern supercomputer. *IEEE Transactions on Computers*, vol. C-31, no. 5, May, pp. 349–362.

Lindstrom, G., and P. Panangaden. 1984. Stream-based execution of logic programs. In *Proceedings of the 1984 International Symposium on Logic Programming*, Feb., pp. 168–176.

Lint, B., and T. Agerwala. 1981. Communication issues in the design and analysis of parallel algorithms. *IEEE Transactions on Software Engineering*, vol. SE-7, no. 2, Mar., pp. 174–188.

Lipovski, G. J., and M. Malek. 1987. *Parallel Computing: Theory and Comparisons.* Wiley & Sons, New York.

Lipton, R. J., and J. Valdes. 1981. Census functions: An approach to VLSI upper bounds (preliminary version). In *Proceedings of the 22d Annual Symposium on Foundations of Computer Science*, IEEE, New York, Oct., pp. 13–22.

Liskov, B. L., and R. Scheifler. 1982. Guardians and actions: Linguistic support for robust, distributed programs. In *Proceedings of the 9th ACM Symposium on Reliability in Distributed Software and Database Systems*, IEEE, New York, pp. 53–60.

Little, J. D. C., K. G. Murty, D. W. Sweeney, and C. Karel. 1963. An algorithm for the traveling salesman problem. *Operations Research*, vol. 11, no. 6, Nov.-Dec., pp. 972–989.

Livingston, M., and Q. F. Stout. 1987. Embeddings in hypercubes. In *Proceedings of the Sixth International Conference on Mathematical Modeling.*

Livny, M. 1983. The study of load balancing algorithms for decentralized distributed processing systems. Ph.D. dissertation, Weizmann Institute of Science.

Lloyd, J. W. 1984. *Foundations of Logic Programming.* Springer-Verlag, New York.

Lo, V. M. 1988. Heuristic algorithms for task assignment in distributed systems. *IEEE Transactions on Computers*, vol. C-37, no. 11, Nov., pp. 1384–1397.

Lord, R. E., J. S. Kowalik, and S. P. Kumar. 1983. Solving linear algebraic equations on an MIMD computer. *Journal of the ACM*, vol. 30, no. 1, Jan., pp. 103–117.

Lorin, H. 1972. *Parallelism in Hardware and Software: Real and Apparent Concurrency.* Prentice-Hall, Englewood Cliffs, NJ.

Lorin, H. 1975. *Sorting and Sort Systems.* Addison-Wesley, Reading, MA.

Loui, M. C. 1984. The complexity of sorting on distributed systems. *Information and Control*, vol. 60, pp. 70–85.

Lubeck, O., J. Moore, and R. Mendez. 1984. A benchmark comparison of three computers: Fujitsu VP-200, Hitachi S810/20 and Cray X-MP/2. Preprint LA-UR-84-3584, Los Alamos National Laboratory, Los Alamos, NM.

Lubeck, O. M. 1988. Supercomputer performance: the theory, practice, and results. In *Advances in Computers*, vol. 27. Academic Press, Orlando, FL, pp. 309–362.

Luby, M. 1986. A simple parallel algorithm for the maximumal independent set problem. *SIAM Journal on Computing*, vol. 15, Nov., pp. 1036–1053.

Lucas, R., T. Blank, and J. Tiemann. 1987. A parallel solution method for large sparse systems of equations. *IEEE Transactions on Computer-Aided Design*, vol. CAD-6, Nov., pp. 981–990.

Luk, F. T. 1980. Computing the singular-value decomposition on the ILLIAC IV. *ACM Transactions on Mathematical Software*, vol. 6, no. 4, Dec., pp. 524–539.

Madala, S., and J. B. Sinclair. 1991. Performance of synchronous parallel algorithms with regular structures. *IEEE Transactions on Parallel and Distributed Systems*, vol. 2, no. 1, Jan., pp. 105–116.

Madnick, S. E., and J. J. Donovan. 1974. *Operating Systems*, McGraw-Hill, New York.

Manber, U., and R. E. Ladner. 1982. Concurrency control in a dynamic search structure. Tech. rept. 82-01-01, Dept. Computer Science, University of Washington, Seattle.

Manoharan, S., and P. Thanisch. 1991. Assigning dependency graphs onto processor networks. *Parallel Computing*, vol. 17, pp. 63–73.

Marrakchi, M., and Y. Robert. 1989. Optimal algorithms for Gaussian elimination on an MIMD computer. *Parallel Computing*, vol. 12, pp. 183–194.

Marsland, T. A., and M. Campbell. 1982. Parallel search of strongly ordered game trees. *Computing Surveys*, vol. 14, no. 4, Dec., pp. 533–551.

Marsland, T. A., and P. G. Rushton. 1974. A study of techniques for game-playing programs. In J. Rose, ed., *Advances in Cybernetics and Systems*, vol. 1, Gordon and Breach, London, pp. 363–371.

Martelli, A., and U. Montanari. 1973. Additive AND/OR graphs. *Proceedings of the International Joint Conference on Artificial Intelligence*, pp. 1–11.

Mashburn, H. H. 1979. The C.mmp/Hydra: An architectural overview. Tech. rept., Dept. of Computer Science, Carnegie-Mellon University, Pittsburgh, PA.

Mateti, P., and N. Deo. 1981. Parallel algorithms for the single source shortest path problem. Tech. rept. CS-81-078, Computer Science Dept., Washington State University, Pullman.

McGraw, J. R., and T. S. Axelrod. 1988. Exploiting multiprocessors: Issues and options. In *Programming Parallel Processors*, pp. 7–25. Addison-Wesley, Reading, MA.

Mead, C., and L. Conway. 1980. *Introduction to VLSI Systems*. Addison-Wesley, Reading, MA.

Mead, C., and M. Rem. 1979. Cost and performance of VLSI computing structures. *IEEE Journal on Solid State Circuits*, vol. SC-14, no. 2, pp. 455–462.

Meertens, L. G. L. T. 1979. Bitonic sort on ultracomputers. Tech. rept. 117/79 Sept., Dept. of Computer Science, The Mathematical Centre, Amsterdam.

Meggido, N. 1983. Applying parallel computation algorithms in the design of serial algorithms. *Journal of the ACM*, vol. 30, no. 4, Oct., pp. 852–865.

Mehlhorn, K., and U. Vishkin. 1984. Randomized and deterministic simulations of PRAMS by parallel machines with restricted granularity of parallel memories. *Acta Informatica*, vol. 21, pp. 339–374.

Mendelson, H. 1987. Economies of scale in computing: Grosch's law revisited. *Communications of the ACM*, vol. 30, no. 12, Dec., pp. 1066–1072.

Metcalf, M., and J. Reid. 1990. *Fortran 90 Explained*. Oxford Science Publications, Oxford, England.

Meurant, G. 1987. Multitasking the conjugate gradient method on the CRAY X-MP/48. *Parallel Computing*, vol. 5, pp. 267–280.

Mierowsky, C., S. Taylor, E. Shapiro, J. Levy, and M. Safra. 1985. The design and implementation of flat Concurrent Prolog. Tech. rept. CS85-09, Weizmann Inst. Science, Rehovot, Israel.

Miller, G. L., and J. H. Reif. 1985. Parallel tree contraction and its application. In *Proceedings of the 26th Annual IEEE Symposium on the Foundations of Computer Science*, pp. 478–489.

Miller, G. L., and J. H. Reif. 1991. Parallel tree contraction part 2: Further applications. *SIAM Journal on Computing*, vol. 20, no. 6, Dec., pp. 1128–1147.

Miller, R., and Q. F. Stout. 1984a. Computational geometry on a mesh-connected computer. In *Proceedings of the 1984 International Conference on Parallel Processing*, IEEE, New York, Aug., pp. 66–73.

Miller, R., and Q. F. Stout. 1984b. Convexity algorithms for pyramid computers. In *Proceedings of the 1984 International Conference on Parallel Processing*, IEEE, New York, Aug., pp. 177–184.

Miller, R., and Q. F. Stout. 1985a. Geometric algorithms for digitized pictures on a mesh-connected computer. *IEEE Transactions on Pattern Analysis and Machine Intelligence*, vol. PAMI-7, pp. 216–228.

Miller, R., and Q. F. Stout. 1985b. Pyramid computer algorithms for determining geometric properties of images. In *Proceedings of the 1985 ACM Symposium on Computational Geometry*, pp. 263–277.

Miller, R., and Q. F. Stout. 1987. Data movement techniques for the pyramid computer. *SIAM Journal on Computing*, vol. 16, no. 1, Feb., pp. 38–60.

Minsky, M., and S. Papert. 1971. On some associative parallel and analog computations. In E. J. Jacks, ed., *Associative Information Techniques*, American Elsevier, New York.

Miranker, G., L. Tang, and C. K. Wong. 1983. A "zero-time" VLSI sorter. *IBM Journal of Research and Development*, vol. 27, no. 2, pp. 140–148.

Missirlis, N. M. 1987. Scheduling parallel iterative methods on multiprocessor systems. *Parallel Computing*, vol. 5, pp. 295–302.

Misra, J., and Chandy, K. M. 1982. A distributed graph algorithm: Knot detection. *ACM Transactions on Programming Languages and Systems*, vol. 4, no. 4, Oct., pp. 678–686.

Mohan, J. 1983. Experience with two parallel programs solving the traveling salesman problem. In *Proceedings of the 1983 International Conference on Parallel Processing*, IEEE, New York, Aug., pp. 191–193.

Moitra, A. 1987. Parallel algorithms for some computational problems. In *Advances in Computers*, vol. 26, Academic Press, Orlando, FL, pp. 93–153.

Moore, E. F. 1959. The shortest path through a maze. In *Proceedings of the International Symposium on the Theory of Switching*, vol. 2, pp. 285–292.

Moravec, H. P. 1979. Fully interconnected multiple computers with pipelined sorting nets. *IEEE Transactions on Computers*, vol. C-28, no. 10, Oct., pp. 795–801.

Moto-oka, T., ed. 1982. *Fifth Generation Computer Systems*. North-Holland, New York.

Mudge, T. N., J. P. Hayes, and D. C. Winsor. 1987. Multiple bus architectures. *Computer*, June, pp. 42–48.

Mukhopadhyay, A. 1981. WEAVESORT—A new sorting algorithm for VLSI. Tech. rept. TR-53-81, University of Central Florida, Orlando.

Mukhopadhyay, A., and T. Ichikawa. 1972. An *n*-step parallel sorting machine. Tech. rept. 72-03, Dept. of Computer Science, University of Iowa.

Muller, D. E., and F. P. Preparata. 1975. Bounds and complexities of networks for sorting and for switching. *Journal of the ACM*, vol. 22, no. 2, Apr., pp. 195–201.

Mundie, D. A., and D. A. Fisher. 1986. Parallel processing in Ada. *Computer*, vol. 19, no. 8, Aug., pp. 20–25.

Naor, J., M. Naor, and A. A. Schaffer. 1989. Fast parallel algorithms for chordal graphs. *SIAM Journal on Computing*, vol. 18, Apr., pp. 327–349.

Nassimi, D., and S. Sahni. 1979. Bitonic sort on a mesh-connected parallel computer. *IEEE Transactions on Computers*, vol. C-28, no. 1, Jan., pp. 2–7.

Nassimi, D., and S. Sahni. 1980a. An optimal routing algorithm for mesh-connected parallel computers. *Journal of the ACM*, vol. 27, no. 1, Jan., pp. 6–29.

Nassimi, D., and S. Sahni. 1980b. Finding connected components and connected ones on a mesh-connected parallel computer. *SIAM Journal on Computing*, vol. 9, no. 4, Nov., pp. 744–757.

Nassimi, D., and S. Sahni. 1981. Data broadcasting in SIMD computers. *IEEE Transactions on Computers*, vol. C-30, no. 2, pp. 101–107.

Nassimi, D., and S. Sahni. 1982. Parallel permutation and sorting algorithms and a new generalized connection network. *Journal of the ACM*, vol. 29, no. 3, July, pp. 642–667.

Nath, D., and S. N. Maheshwari. 1982. Parallel algorithms for the connected components and minimal spanning tree problems. *Information Processing Letters*, vol. 14, no. 1, Mar., pp. 7–11.

Nath, D., S. N. Maheshwari, and P. C. P. Bhatt. 1983. Efficient VLSI networks for parallel processing based on orthogonal trees. *IEEE Transactions on Computers*, vol. C-32, no. 6, June, pp. 569–581.

Nau, D. S. 1982. An investigation of the causes of pathology in games. *Artificial Intelligence*, vol. 19, pp. 257–278.

Nebesky, L. 1974. On cubes and dichotomic trees. *Casopis Pro Pestovani Matematiky*, vol. 99, pp. 164–167.

Newborn, M. 1989. Computer chess: ten years of significant progress. In *Advances in Computers*, vol. 29. Academic Press, Orlando, FL. pp. 197–250.

Ng, K. W., and H. F. Leung. 1988. A competition model for parallel execution of logic programs. In *Proceedings of the Fifth International Conference on Logic Programming*, pp. 55–69.

Nitzberg, B., and V. Lo. 1991. Distributed shared memory: A survey of issues and algorithms. *Computer*, Aug., pp. 52–60.

Norton, A., and A. J. Silberger. 1987. Parallelization and performance analysis of the Cooley-Tukey FFT algorithm for shared-memory architectures. *IEEE Transactions on Computers*, vol. C-36, no. 5, May, pp. 581–591.

Nussbaum, D., and A. Agarwal. 1991. Scalability of parallel machines. *Communications of the ACM*, vol. 34, no. 3, Mar., pp. 56–61.

O'Leary, D. P. 1987. Parallel implementation of the block conjugate gradient algorithm. *Parallel Computing*, vol. 5, pp. 127–139.

Oleinick, P. N. 1982. *Parallel Algorithms on a Multiprocessor*. UMI Research Press, Ann Arbor, MI.

Orcutt, S. E. 1974. Computer organization and algorithms for very high speed computations. Ph.D. dissertation, Stanford University, Stanford, CA.

Orenstein, J. A., T. H. Merrett, and L. Devroye. 1983. Linear sorting with $O(\log n)$ processors. *BIT*, vol. 23, pp. 170–180.

Organick, E. I. 1985. Algorithms, concurrent processors, and computer science education: or, "Think concurrent or capitulate?" *ACM SIGSE Bulletin*, vol. 17, no. 1, Mar.

Ortega, J. M. 1988. The ijk forms of factorization methods I. Vector computers. *Parallel Computing*, vol. 7, pp. 135–147.

Ortega, J. M., and C. H. Romine. 1988. The ijk forms of factorization methods II. Parallel systems. *Parallel Computing*, vol. 7, pp. 149–162.

Ortega, J. M., and R. G. Voigt. 1985. Solution of partial differential equations on vector and parallel computers. *SIAM Review*, vol. 27, no. 2, June, pp. 149–240.

Osterhaug, A. 1986. *Guide to Parallel Programming on Sequent Computer Systems*. Sequent Computer Systems, Beaverton, OR.

Ostlund, N. S., P. G. Hibbard, and R. A. Whiteside. 1982. A case study in the application of a tightly coupled multiprocessor to scientific computations. In G. Rodrigue, ed., *Parallel Computations*, Academic Press, New York, pp. 315–364.

Ottman, T. A., A. L. Rosenberg, and L. J. Stockmeyer. 1982. A dictionary machine (for VLSI). *IEEE Transactions on Computers*, vol. C-31, no. 9, Sept., pp. 892–897.

Owicki, S., and D. Gries. 1976. Verifying properties of parallel programs: An axiomatic approach. *Communications of the ACM*, vol. 19, no. 5, May, pp. 279–285.

Owicki, S., and L. Lamport. 1982. Proving liveness properties of concurrent programs. *ACM Transactions on Programming Languages and Systems*, vol. 4, no. 3, July, pp. 455–495.

Oyama, T., Kitahara, T., and Y. Serizawa. 1990. Parallel processing for power system analysis using band matrix. *IEEE Transactions on Power Systems*, vol. 5, Aug., pp. 1010–1016.

Paige, R. C., and C. P. Kruskal. 1985. Parallel algorithms for shortest path problems. In *Proceedings of the 1985 International Conference on Parallel Processing*, Aug., pp. 14–20. IEEE, New York.

Pancake, C. M., and D. Bergmark. 1990. Do parallel languages respond to the needs of scientific programmers? *Computer*, Dec., pp. 13–23.

Papadimitriou, C. H., and M. Yannakakis. 1990. Towards an architecture-independent analysis of parallel algorithms. *SIAM Journal on Computing*, vol. 19, Apr., pp. 322–328.

Pape, U. 1974. Implementation and efficiency of Moore-algorithms for the shortest route problem. *Mathematical Programming*, vol. 7, no. 2, Oct., pp. 212–222.

Parker, D. S., Jr. 1980. Notes on shuffle/exchange-type switching networks. *IEEE Transactions on Computers*, vol. C-29, no. 3, Mar., pp. 213–222.

Parkinson, D., and M. Wunderlich. 1984. A compact algorithm for Gaussian elimination over GF(2) implemented on highly parallel computers. *Parallel Computing*, vol. 1, pp. 65–73.

Patrick, M. L., D. A. Reed, and R. G. Voigt. 1987. The impact of domain partitioning on the performance of a shared memory multiprocessor. *Parallel Computing*, vol. 5, pp. 211–217.

Paul, G. 1978. Large-scale vector/array processors. IBM Research Report RC 7306, Sept.

Pease, M. C. III. 1968. An adaption of the fast Fourier transform for parallel processing. *Journal of the ACM*, vol. 15, no. 2, Apr., pp. 252–264.

Pease, M. C. III. 1977. The indirect binary n-cube microprocessor array. *IEEE Transactions on Computers*, vol. C-26, no. 5, May, pp. 458–473.

Perl, Y. 1983. Bitonic and odd-even networks are more than merging. Tech. rept., Rutgers University, New Brunswick, NJ.

Perrott, R. H. 1987. *Parallel Programming*. Addison-Wesley, Wokingham, England.

Peters, F. 1981. Tree machine and divide-and-conquer algorithms. In *CONPAR '81, Lecture Notes in Computer Science* 111, Springer-Verlag, pp. 25–35.

Peterson, G. L. 1981. Myths about the mutual exclusion problem. *Information Processing Letters*, vol. 12, no. 3, June, pp. 115–116.

Peterson, G. L. 1982. An $O(n \log n)$ unidirectional algorithm for the circular extrema problem. *ACM Transactions on Programming Language and Systems* vol. 4, no. 4, pp. 758–762.

Piskoulisjski, Pl. Iv. 1992. Error analysis of parallel algorithm for the solution of a tridiagonal Toeplitz linear system of equations. *Parallel Computing*, vol. 18, pp. 431–438.

Polychronopoulos, C. D., and D. J. Kuck. 1987. Guided self-scheduling: A practical scheduling scheme for parallel supercomputers. *IEEE Transactions on Computers*, vol. C-36, no. 12, Dec., pp. 1425–1439.

Potter, J. L. 1985. Programming the MPP. In J. L. Potter, ed., *The Massively Parallel Processor*, MIT Press, Cambridge, pp. 218–229.

Powley, C., Ferguson, C., and R. E. Korf. 1990. Parallel heuristic search: Two approaches. In V. Kumar, P. S. Gopalakrishnan, and L. N. Kanal, eds., *Parallel Algorithms for Machine Intelligence and Vision*. Springer-Verlag, New York, pp. 42–65.

Pradhan, D. K. 1985. Fault-tolerant multiprocessor link and bus network architectures. *IEEE Transactions on Computers*, vol. C-34, no. 1, pp. 33–45.

Preparata, F. P. 1978. New parallel sorting schemes. *IEEE Transactions on Computers*, vol. C-27, no. 7, July, pp. 669–673.

Preparata, F. P., and J. Vuillemin. 1981. The cube-connected cycles: A versatile network for parallel computation. *Communications of the ACM*, vol. 24, no. 5, May, pp. 300–309.

Price, C. C. 1982. A VLSI algorithm for shortest path through a directed acyclic graph. *Congressus Numerantium*, vol. 34, pp. 363–371.

Price, C. C. 1983. Task assignment using a VLSI shortest path algorithm. Tech. rept., Dept. of Computer Science, Stephen F. Austin State University, Nacogdoches, TX.

Prim, R. C. 1957. Shortest connection networks and some generalizations. *Bell System Technical Journal*, vol. 36, pp. 1389–1401.

Quinn, M. J. 1983. The design and analysis of algorithms and data structures for the efficient solution of graph theoretic problems on MIMD computers. Ph.D. dissertation, Computer Science Dept., Washington State University, Pullman.

Quinn, M. J. 1985. A note on two parallel algorithms to solve the stable marriage problem. *BIT*, vol. 25, pp. 473–476.

Quinn, M. J. 1988. Parallel sorting algorithms for tightly coupled multiprocessors. *Parallel Computing*, vol. 6, pp. 349–357.

Quinn, M. J. 1989. Analysis and benchmarking of two parallel sorting algorithms: hyperquicksort and quickmerge. *BIT*, vol. 29, pp. 239–250.

Quinn, M. J. 1990. Analysis and implementation of branch-and-bound algorithms on a hypercube multicomputer. *IEEE Transactions on Computers*, vol. C-39, no. 3, Mar., pp. 384–387.

Quinn, M. J., and N. Deo. 1984. Parallel graph algorithms. *Computing Surveys*, vol. 16, no. 3, Sept., pp. 319–348.

Quinn, M. J., and N. Deo. 1986. An upper bound for the speedup of parallel best-bound branch-and-bound algorithms. *BIT*, vol. 26, no. 1, Mar., pp. 35–43.

Quinn, M. J., and P. J. Hatcher. 1990. Data-parallel programming on multicomputers. *IEEE Software*, vol. 7, no. 5, Sept., pp. 69–76.

Quinn, M. J., and Y. B. Yoo. 1984. Data structures for the efficient solution of graph theoretic problems on tightly-coupled MIMD computers. In *Proceedings of the 1984 International Conference on Parallel Processing*, IEEE, New York, Aug., pp. 431–438.

Quinn, M. J., P. J. Hatcher, and K. C. Jourdenais. 1988. Compiling C* programs for a hypercube multicomputer. In *Proceedings of the ACM/SIGPLAN PPEALS 1988—Parallel Programming: Experience with Applications, Languages, and Systems, SIGPLAN Notices* vol. 23, no. 9, Sept., pp. 57–65.

Radicati di Brozolo, G., and Y. Robert. 1989. Parallel conjugate gradient-like algorithms for solving sparse nonsymmetric linear systems on a vector multiprocessor. *Parallel Computing*, vol. 11, pp. 223–239.

Raghavendra, C. S., and V. K. Prasanna Kumar. 1986. *IEEE Transactions on Computers*, vol. C-35, no. 7, July, pp. 662–669.

Rajasekaran, S., and J. H. Reif. 1989. Optimal and sublogarithmic time randomized parallel sorting algorithms. *SIAM Journal on Computing*, vol. 18, June, pp. 594–607.

Ramakrishnan, I. V., and P. J. Varman. 1984. Modular matrix multiplication on a linear array. *IEEE Transactions on Computers*, vol. C-33, no. 11, Nov., pp. 952–958.

Ramamoorthy, C. V., and L.-C. Chang. 1971. System segmentation for the parallel diagnosis of computers. *IEEE Transactions on Computers*, vol. C-20, no. 2, Feb., pp. 153–161.

Ramamoorthy, C. V., J. L. Turner, and B. W. Wah. 1978. A design of a fast cellular associative memory for ordered retrieval. *IEEE Transactions on Computers*, vol. C-27, no. 9, Sept., pp. 800–815.

Raskin, L. 1978. Performance evaluation of multiple processor systems. Ph.D. dissertation, Carnegie-Mellon University, Pittsburgh, PA.

Reale, F. 1990. A tridiagonal solver for massively parallel computer systems. *Parallel Computing*, no. 16, pp. 361–368.

Reddaway, S. F. 1979. The DAP approach. In C. R. Jesshope and R. W. Hockney, eds., *Infotech State of the Art Report: Supercomputers*, vol. 2, Infotech, Maidenhead, England, pp. 311–329.

Redinbo, G. R. 1979. Finite field arithmetic on an array processor. *IEEE Transactions on Computers*, vol. C-28, no. 7, July, pp. 461–471.

Reed, D. A., L. M. Adams, and M. L. Patrick. 1987. Stencils and problem partitionings: Their influence on the performance of multiple processor systems. *IEEE Transactions on Computers*, vol. C-36, no. 7, July, pp. 845–858.

Reed, D. A., and R. M. Fujimoto. 1987. *Multicomputer Networks: Message-Based Parallel Processing*. MIT Press, Cambridge.

Reed, D. A., and D. C. Grunwald. 1987. The performance of multicomputer interconnection networks. *Computer*, June, pp. 63–73.

Reed, D. A., and M. L. Patrick. 1985. Parallel, iterative solution of sparse linear systems: Models and architectures. *Parallel Computing*, vol. 2, pp. 45–67.

Reghbati, E., and D. G. Corneil. 1978. Parallel computations in graph theory. *SIAM Journal on Computing*, vol. 2, no. 2, May, pp. 230–237.

Reif, J. H. 1982. Symmetric complementation. In *Proceedings of the 14th Annual ACM Symposium on Theory of Computing* ACM, New York, May, pp. 201–214.

Reif, J. 1985. Depth first search is inherently sequential. *Information Processing Letters*, vol. 20, pp. 229–234.

Reif, J. H., and P. Spirakis. 1982. The expected time complexity of parallel graph and digraph algorithms. Tech. rept. TR-11-82, Aiken Computation Laboratory, Harvard University, Cambridge.

Reif, J. H., and L. G. Valiant. 1987. A logarithmic time sort for linear size networks. *Journal of the ACM*, vol. 34, no. 1, Jan., pp. 60–76.

Reingold, E. M., J. Nievergelt, and N. Deo. 1977. *Combinatorial Algorithms: Theory and Practice*. Prentice-Hall, Englewood Cliffs, NJ.

Reischuk, R. 1981. A fast probabilistic parallel sorting algorithm. In *Proceedings of the 22d Annual IEEE Symposium on Foundations of Computer Science*, IEEE, New York, Oct., pp. 212–219.

Ribbens, C. J. 1989. A fast adaptive grid scheme for elliptic partial differential equations. *ACM Transactions on Mathematical Software*, vol. 15, Sept., pp. 179–197.

Ritchie, D. M., and D. Thompson. 1974. The UNIX timesharing system. *Communications of the ACM*, vol. 17, no. 7, July, pp. 365–375.

Robert, Y., and D. Trystram. 1988. Comments on scheduling parallel iterative methods on multiprocessor systems. *Parallel Computing*, vol. 7, pp. 253–255.

Robinson, J. T. 1977. Analysis of asynchronous multiprocessor algorithms with applications to sorting. In *Proceedings of the 1977 International Conference on Parallel Processing*, IEEE, New York, Aug., pp. 128–135.

Robinson, J. T. 1979. Some analysis techniques for asynchronous multiprocessor algorithms. *IEEE Transactions on Software Engineering*, vol. SE-5, no. 1, Jan., pp. 24–30.

Rodeheffer, T. L., and P. G. Hibbard. 1980. Automatic exploitation of parallelism on a homogeneous asynchronous multiprocessor. In *Proceedings of the 1980 International Conference on Parallel Processing*, IEEE, New York, pp. 15–16.

Romine, C. H., and J. M. Ortega. 1988. Parallel solution of triangular systems of equations. *Parallel Computing*, vol. 6, pp. 109–114.

Rosenberg, A. L. 1979. Preserving proximity in arrays. *SIAM Journal on Computing*, pp. 443–460.

Rosenfeld, A. 1985. The prism machine: An alternative to the pyramid. *Journal of Parallel and Distributed Computing*, vol. 2, no. 4, Nov., pp. 404–411.

Rosenkrantz, D., R. Stearns, and P. Lewis. 1974. Approximate algorithms for the traveling salesperson problem. In *Proceedings of the 15th Annual Symposium on Switching and Automata Theory*, IEEE, New York, Oct., pp. 33–42.

Rotem, D., N., Santoro, and J. B. Sidney. 1983. Distributed sorting. Tech. rept. SCS-TR-#34 Dec., School of Computer Science, Carleton University, Ottowa, Ontario.

Roussel, P. 1975. PROLOG: Manuel de reference et d'utilisation. Groupe Intelligence Artificielle, Universite d'Aix-Marseille, Luminy, France, Sept.

Rudolph, L. 1984. A robust sorting network. In *Proceedings of the 1984 Conference on Advanced Research in VLSI*. MIT Press, Cambridge, Jan., pp. 26–33.

Ruzzo, W., and L. Snyder. 1981. Minimum edge length planar embeddings of trees. In H. T. Kung, B. Sproull, and G. Steele, eds. *VLSI Systems and Computations*, Springer-Verlag, New York, pp. 119–123.

Saad, Y., and M. H. Schultz. 1988. Topological properties of hypercubes. *IEEE Transactions on Computers*, vol. C-37, no. 7, July, pp. 867–872.

Saad, Y., and M. H. Schultz. 1989. Data communication in parallel architectures. *Parallel Computing*, vol. 11, pp. 131–150.

Sadayappan, P., and F. Ercal. 1987. Nearest-neighbor mapping of finite element graphs onto processor meshes. *IEEE Transactions on Computers*, vol. C-36, no. 12, Dec., pp. 1408–1424.

Sadayappan, P., F. Ercal, and J. Ramanujam. 1990. Cluster partitioning approaches to mapping parallel programs onto a hypercube. *Parallel Computing*, vol. 13, pp. 1–16.

Sahni, S. 1984. Scheduling multipipeline and multiprocessor computers. *IEEE Transactions on Computers*, C-33, no. 7, July, pp. 637–645.

426

Saltz, J. H., and M. C. Chen. 1987. Automated problem mapping: The Crystal run-time system. In M. T. Heath, ed., *Hypercube Multiprocessors 1987*, SIAM Press, Philadelphia, pp. 130–140.

Samatham, M. R., and D. K. Pradhan. 1989. The De Bruijn multiprocessor network: A versatile parallel processing and sorting network for VLSI. *IEEE Transactions on Computers*, vol. C-38, no. 4, Apr., pp. 567–581.

Samathan, M. R., and D. K. Pradhan. 1991. (Correction) The De Bruijn multiprocessor network: A versatile parallel processing and sorting network for VLSI. *IEEE Transactions on Computers*, vol. C-40, no. 1, Jan., pp. 122-123.

Sameh, A. 1977. Numerical parallel algorithms — A survey. In D. Kuck, D. Lawrie, and A. Sameh, eds. *High Speed Computer and Algorithm Organization*, Academic Press, Orlando, FL, pp. 207–228.

Sameh, A., and D. Kuck. 1978. On stable parallel linear system solvers. *Journal of the ACM*, vol. 25, no. 1, pp. 81–91.

Sang, F. C., and I. H. Sudborough. 1990. Embedding large meshes into small ones. In *Proceedings of the IEEE Symposium on Circuits and Systems.*

Satyanarayanan, M. 1980. Multiprocessing: An annotated bibliography. *Computer*, vol. 13, no. 5, May, pp. 101–116.

Savage, C. 1977. Parallel algorithms for graph theoretic problems. Ph.D. dissertation, University of Illinois, Urbana.

Savage, C. 1981. A systolic data structure chip for connectivity problems. In H. T. Kung, R. F. Sproull, and G. L. Steele, Jr., eds., *VLSI Systems and Computations*, Computer Science Press, Rockville, MD.

Savage, C., and J. JáJá. 1981. Fast, efficient parallel algorithms for some graph problems. *SIAM Journal on Computing*, vol. 10, no. 4, Nov., pp. 682–690.

Savage, J. E. 1981. Planar circuit complexity and the performance of VLSI algorithms. In H. T. Kung, R. F. Sproull, and G. L. Steele, Jr., eds., *VLSI Systems and Computations*, Computer Science Press, Rockville, MD, pp. 61–66.

Schaefer, D. H., and J. R. Fisher. 1982. Beyond the supercomputer. *IEEE Spectrum*, vol. 19, no. 3, Mar., pp. 32–37.

Schaeffer, J. 1989. Distributed game-tree searching. *Journal of Parallel and Distributed Computing*, vol. 6, pp. 90–114.

Schendel, U. 1984. *Introduction to Numerical Methods for Parallel Computers*. Ellis Horwood, Chichester, England.

Schieber, B. S., and U. Vishkin. 1988. On finding lowest common ancestors: Simplification and parallelization. *SIAM Journal on Computing*, vol. 17, no. 6, Dec., pp. 1253–1262.

Schröder, H. 1983. Partition sorts for VLSI. *Informatik Fachberichte*, vol. 73, pp. 101–116.

Schwartz, J. T. 1980. Ultracomputers. *ACM Transactions on Programming Languages and Systems* vol. 2, no. 4, pp. 484–521.

Scott, D. S., and J. Brandenburg. 1988. Minimal mesh embeddings in binary hypercubes. *IEEE Transactions on Computers*, vol. C-37, no. 10, Oct., pp. 1284–1285.

Sedgewick, R. 1988. *Algorithms*. 2d ed., Addison-Wesley, Reading, MA.

Seitz, C. L. 1985. The cosmic cube. *Communications of the ACM*, vol. 28, no. 1, Jan., pp. 22–33.

Shapiro, E. Y. 1983a. The fifth generation project—A trip report. *Communications of the ACM*, vol. 26, no. 9, Sept., pp. 637–641.

Shapiro, E. Y. 1983b. *Algorithmic Program Debugging*. MIT Press, Cambridge.

Shapiro, E. Y. 1983c. The Bagel: A systolic Concurrent Prolog machine (lecture notes). Weizmann Inst. Science, Rehovot, Israel.

Shapiro, E. Y. 1985. Systolic programming: A paradigm of parallel processing. Tech. rept. CS84-16, Weizmann Inst. Science, Rehovot, Israel.

Shapiro, E. Y. 1986. Concurrent Prolog: A progress report. *Computer*, vol. 19, no. 8, Aug., pp. 44–58.

Shaw, A. C. 1974. *The Logical Design of Operating Systems*. Prentice-Hall, Englewood Cliffs, NJ.

Shiloach, Y., and Vishkin, U. 1981. Finding the maximum, merging and sorting in a parallel computation model. *Journal of Algorithms*, vol. 2, no. 1, Mar., pp. 88–102.

Shiloach, Y., and U. Vishkin. 1982a. An $O(\log n)$ parallel connectivity algorithm. *Journal of Algorithms*, vol. 3, no. 1, Mar., pp. 57–67.

Shiloach, Y., and U. Vishkin. 1982b. An $O(n^2 \log n)$ parallel MAX-FLOW algorithm. *Journal of Algorithms*, vol. 3, no. 2, June, pp. 128–146.

Sheu, J.-P., N.-L. Kuo, and G.-H. Chen. 1990. Graph search algorithms and maximum bipartite matching algorithm on the hypercube network model. *Parallel Computing*, vol. 13, pp. 245–251.

Shröder, H. 1983. Partition sorts for VLSI. *Informatik Fachberichte*, vol. 73, pp. 101–116.

Shyu, C.-H. 1990. A parallel algorithm for finding a maximum weight clique of an interval graph. *Parallel Computing*, vol. 13, pp. 253–256.

Siegel, H. J. 1977. The universality of various types of SIMD machine interconnection networks. In *Proceedings of the 4th Annual International Symposium on Computer Architecture*, IEEE, New York, Mar., pp. 70–79.

Siegel, H. J. 1979a. Interconnection networks for SIMD machines. *Computer*, vol. 12, no. 6, June, pp. 57–65.

Siegel, H. J. 1979b. A model of SIMD machines and a comparison of various interconnection networks. *IEEE Transactions on Computers*, vol. C-28, no. 12, Dec., pp. 907–917.

Siegel, H. J. 1985. *Interconnection Networks for Large-Scale Parallel Processing: Theory and Case Studies*. Lexington Books, Lexington, MA.

Simmen, M. 1991. Comments on broadcast algorithms for two-dimensional grids. *Parallel Computing*, vol. 17, pp. 109–112.

Simons, B. B., and M. K. Warmuth. 1989. A fast algorithm for multiprocessor scheduling of unit-length jobs. *SIAM Journal on Computing*, vol. 18, Aug., pp. 690–710.

Singh, V., V. Kumar, G. Agha, and C. Tomlinson. 1991. Efficient algorithms for parallel sorting on mesh multicomputers. *International Journal of Parallel Programming*, vol. 20, no. 2, pp. 95–131.

Singhal, M. 1989. Deadlock detection in distributed systems. *Computer*, Nov., pp. 37–48.

Skillicorn, D. B. 1988. A taxonomy for computer architectures. *Computer*, Nov., pp. 46–57.

Slagle, J. R., and J. K. Dixon. 1969. Experiments with some programs that search game trees. *Journal of the ACM*, vol. 16, no. 2, Apr., pp. 189–207.

Smith, B. J. 1978. A pipelined shared resource MIMD computer. In *Proceedings of the 1978 International Conference on Parallel Processing*, IEEE, New York, Aug., pp. 6–8.

Smith, J. 1986. Parallel algorithms for depth-first searches I: Planar graphs. *SIAM Journal on Computing*, vol. 15, no. 3, pp. 814–830.

Snir, M. 1985. On parallel searching. *SIAM Journal on Computing*, vol. 14, no. 3, Aug., pp. 688–708.

Sollin, M. 1977. An algorithm attributed to Sollin. In S. E. Goodman and S. T. Hedetniemi, eds. *Introduction to the Design and Analysis of Algorithms*, McGraw-Hill, New York, sec. 5.5.

Sridhar, M. A. 1988. On the connectivity of the De Bruijn graph. *Information Processing Letters*, vol. 27, pp. 315–318.

Stenström, P. 1988. Reducing contention in shared-memory multiprocessors. *Computer*, Nov., pp. 26–37.

Stenström, P. 1990. A survey of cache coherence schemes for multiprocessors. *Computer*, June, pp. 12–24.

Stewart, G. W. 1973. *Introduction to Matrix Computations*. Academic Press, New York.

Stockman, G. 1979. A minimax algorithm better than alpha-beta? *Artificial Intelligence*, vol. 12, pp. 179–196.

Stone, H. S. 1971. Parallel processing with the perfect shuffle. *IEEE Transactions on Computers*, vol. C-20, no. 2, Feb., pp. 153–161.

Stone, H. S. 1973. Problems of parallel computation. In J. F. Traub, ed., *Complexity of Sequential and Parallel Numerical Algorithms*, Academic Press, New York, pp. 1–16.

Stone, H. S. 1978. Sorting with STAR. *IEEE Transactions on Software Engineering*, vol. SE-4, no. 2, Feb., pp. 138–146.

Stone, H. S. 1980. Parallel computers. In H.S. Stone, ed., *Introduction to Computer Architecture*, Science Research Associates, Chicago, chap. 8.

Stout, Q. F. 1983a. Sorting, merging, selecting and filtering on tree and pyramid machines. In *Proceedings of the 1983 International Conference on Parallel Processing*, IEEE, New York, Aug., pp. 214–221.

Stout, Q. F. 1983b. Mesh-connected computers with broadcasting. *IEEE Transactions on Computers*, vol. C-32, no. 9, Sept., pp. 826–830.

Stout, Q. F. 1985a. Pyramid computer solutions of the closest pair problem. *Journal of Algorithms*, vol. 6, pp. 200–212.

Stout, Q. F. 1985b. Tree-based graph algorithms for some parallel computers (prelim. ver.). In *Proceedings of the 1985 International Conference on Parallel Processing*, IEEE, New York, Aug., pp. 727–730.

Stumm, M., and S. Zhou. 1990. Algorithms implementing distributed shared memory. *Computer*, May, pp. 54–64.

Sun, X.-H, Zhang, H., and L. M. Ni. 1992. Efficient tridiagonal solvers on multicomputers. *IEEE Transactions on Computers*, vol. C-41, no. 3, Mar., pp. 286–296.

Swan, R. J., A. Bechtolsheim, K.-W. Lai, and J. K. Ousterhout. 1977. The implementation of the Cm* multi-microprocessor. In *Proceedings of the National Computer Conference*. AFIPS Press, Reston, VA, pp. 645–655.

Swarztrauber, P. N. 1987. Multiprocessor FFTs. *Parallel Computing*, vol. 5, pp. 197–210.

Tabak, D. 1990. *Multiprocessors*. Prentice Hall, Englewood Cliffs, NJ.

Tanaka, H. 1986. A parallel inference machine. *Computer*, Aug., pp. 48–54.

Tanaka, Y., Y. Nozaka, and A. Masuyama. 1980. Pipeline searching and sorting modules as components of a data flow database computer. In *Proceedings IFIP Congress: Information Processing*, vol. 80, pp. 427–432.

Tanimoto, S. L. 1981. Towards hierarchical cellular logic: Design considerations for pyramid machines. Tech. rept. 81-02-01, Dep. of Computer Science, University of Washington, Seattle.

Tanimoto, S. L. 1982a. Sorting, histogramming, and other statistical operations on a pyramid machine. Tech. rept. 82-08-02, Dept. of Computer Science, University of Washington, Seattle.

Tanimoto, S. L. 1982b. Programming techniques for hierarchical parallel image processors. In K. Preston and L. Uhr, eds. *Multicomputers and Image Processing Algorithms and Programs*. Academic Press, New York, pp. 421–429.

Tanimoto, S. L., and A. Klinger. 1980. *Structured Computer Vision: Machine Perception through Hierarchical Computation Structures*, Academic Press, New York.

Tantawi, A. N., and D. Towsley. 1985. Optimal load balancing in distributed computer systems. *Journal of the ACM*, vol. 32, no. 2, pp. 445–465.

Tarjan, R. E., and U. Vishkin. 1984. Finding biconnected components and computing tree functions in logarithmic parallel time (extended summary). In *Procedings of the 25th Annual Symposium on Foundations of Computer Science*. IEEE Press, pp. 12–20.

Tarjan, R. E., and U. Vishkin. 1985. An efficient parallel biconnectivity algorithm. *SIAM Journal of Computing*, vol. 14, pp. 862–874.

Taylor, S., S. Safra, and E. Shapiro. 1987. A parallel implementation of Flat Concurrent Prolog. *International Journal of Parallel Programming*, vol. 15, no. 3, pp. 245–275.

Teller, P. J. 1990. Translation-lookaside buffer consistency. *Computer*, June, pp. 26–36.

Thakkar, S., M. Dubois, A. T. Laundrie, and G. S. Sohi. 1990. Scalable shared-memory multiprocessor architectures. *Computer*, June, pp. 71–73.

Thinking Machines Corporation. 1989. *Connection Machine CM-200 Series Technical Summary*. Cambridge, MA.

Thinking Machines Corporation. 1991. *C* Programming Guide*. Version 6.0.2, Cambridge, MA.

Thomasian, A., and P. F. Bay. 1986. Analytic queueing network models for parallel processing of task systems. *IEEE Transactions on Computers*, vol. C-35, no. 12, Dec., pp. 1045–1054.

Thompson, C. D. 1979. Area-time complexity of VLSI. In *Proceedings of the 11th Annual ACM Symposium on Theory of Computing*, ACM, New York, May, pp. 81–88.

Thompson, C. D. 1980. A complexity theory for VLSI. Ph.D. dissertation, Dept. of Computer Science, Carnegie-Mellon University, Pittsburgh, PA.

Thompson, C. D. 1983a. Fourier transforms in VLSI. *IEEE Transactions on Computers*, vol. C-32, no. 11, Nov., pp. 1047–1057.

Thompson, C. D. 1983b. The VLSI complexity of sorting. *IEEE Transactions on Computers*, vol. C-32, no. 12, Dec., pp. 1171–1184.

Thompson, C. D., and H. T. Kung. 1977. Sorting on a mesh-connected parallel computer. *Communications of the ACM*, vol. 20, no. 4, Apr., pp. 263–271.

Thurber, K. J. 1976. *Large Scale Computer Architecture—Parallel and Associative Processors*. Hayden Book Co., Hasbrouck Heights, NJ.

Thurber, K. J. 1979a. Parallel processor architectures—Part I: General purpose systems. *Computer Design*, Jan., pp. 89–97.

Thurber, K. J. 1979b. Parallel processor architectures—Part II: Special purpose systems. *Computer Design*, Feb., pp. 103–114.

Tick, E. 1991. *Parallel Logic Programming*. MIT Press, Cambridge.

Tiwari, P. 1986. An efficient parallel algorithm for shifting the root of a depth first spanning tree. *Journal of Algorithms*, vol. 7, pp. 105–119.

Todd, S. 1978. Algorithms and hardware for a merge sort using multiple processors. *IBM Journal of Research and Development*, vol. 22, no. 5, pp. 509–517.

Tolub, S., and Y. Wallach. 1978. Sorting on an MIMD-type parallel processing system. *Euromicro Journal*, vol. 4, pp. 155–161.

Towsley, D. 1986. Approximate models of multiple bus multiprocessor systems. *IEEE Transactions on Computers*, vol. C-35, no. 3, Mar., pp. 220–228.

Troya, J. M., and M. Ortega. 1989. A study of parallel branch-and-bound algorithms with best-bound-first search. *Parallel Computing*, vol. 11, pp. 121–126.

Tseng, S. S., and R. C. T. Lee. 1984a. A new parallel sorting algorithm based upon min-mid-max operations. *BIT*, vol. 24, pp. 187–195.

Tseng, S. S., and R. C. T. Lee. 1984b. A parallel algorithm to solve the stable marriage problem. *BIT*, vol. 24, pp. 308–316.

Tsin, Y. H. 1986. Finding lowest common ancestors in parallel. *IEEE Transactions on Computers*, vol. C-35, no. 8, Aug., pp. 764–769.

Tsin, Y. H., and F. Y. Chin. 1984. Efficient parallel algorithms for a class of graph theoretic problems. *SIAM Journal on Computing*, vol. 13, Aug., pp. 580–599.

Tucker, A. B. 1988. *Computer Science: A Second Course Using Modula-2*. McGraw-Hill, New York.

Uhr, L. 1972. Layered "recognition cone" networks that preprocess, classify, and describe. *IEEE Transactions on Computers*, vol. C-21, no. 7, July, pp. 758–768.

Uhr, L. 1984. *Algorithm-Structured Computer Arrays and Networks*. Academic Press, Orlando, FL.

Ullman, J. D. 1975. NP-complete scheduling problems. *Journal of Computer and System Sciences* vol. 10, pp. 384–393.

Ullman, J. D. 1984. *Computational Aspects of VLSI*. Computer Science Press, Rockville, MD.

Ullman, J. D., and M. Yannakakis. 1991. High-probability parallel transitive-closure algorithms. *SIAM Journal on Computing*, vol. 20, no. 1, Feb., pp. 100–125.

Ullman, S., and B. Narahiri. 1990. Mapping binary precedence trees into hypercubes and meshes. In *Proceedings of the Second IEEE Symposium on Parallel and Distributed Processing*, pp. 838–841.

Upfal, E. 1984. A probabilistic relation between desirable and feasible models of parallel computation. In *Proceedings of the 16th Annual ACM Symposium on Theory of Computing*, pp. 258–265.

Upfal, E., and A. Wigderson. 1987. How to share memory in a distributed system. *Journal of the ACM*, vol. 34, no. 1, Jan., pp. 116–127.

Üresin, A., and M. Dubois. 1990. Parallel asynchronous algorithms for discrete data. *Journal of the ACM*, vol. 37, no. 3, July, pp. 588–606.

U.S. Department of Defense. 1981. *Programming language Ada: Reference Manual*, vol. 106, *Lecture Notes in Computer Science*. Springer-Verlag, New York.

Valiant, L. G. 1975. Parallelism in comparison problems. *SIAM Journal on Computing*, vol. 4, Sept., pp. 348–355.

Valiant, L. G. 1981. Universality considerations in VLSI circuits. *IEEE Transactions on Computers*, vol. C-30, no. 2, Feb., pp. 135–140.

Valiant, L. G. 1990. A bridging model for parallel computation. *Communications of the ACM*, vol. 33, no. 8, Aug., pp. 103–111.

van der Vorst, H. A. 1987a. Large tridiagonal and block tridiagonal linear systems on vector and parallel computers. *Parallel Computing*, vol. 5, pp. 45–54.

van der Vorst, H. A. 1987b. Analysis of a parallel solution method for tridiagonal linear systems. *Parallel Computing*, vol. 5, pp. 303–311.

van Scoy, F. L. 1976. Parallel algorithms in cellular spaces. Ph.D. dissertation, School of Engineering and Applied Science, University of Virginia, Charlottesville.

van Scoy, F. L. 1980. The parallel recognition of classes of graphs. *IEEE Transactions on Computers*, vol. C-29, no. 7, July, pp. 563–570.

van Voorhis, D. C. 1971. On sorting networks. Ph.D. dissertation, Stanford University, Stanford, CA.

van Wijngaarden, A., B. J. Mailloux, J. L. Peck, C. H. A. Koster, M. Sintzoff, C. H. Lindsey, L. G. L. T. Meertens, and R. G. Fisker. 1975. Revised report on the algorithm language ALGOL68. *Acta Informatica*, vol. 5, nos. 1–3, pp. 1–236.

Varman, P. J., and K. Doshi. 1992. Sorting with linear speedup on a pipelined hypercube. *IEEE Transactions on Computers*, vol. C-41, no. 1, Jan., pp. 97–103.

Vazirani, U., and V. Vazirani. 1985. The two-processor scheduling problem is in *RNC*. In *Proceedings of the 17th Annual ACM Symposium on Theory of Computing*, pp. 11–21.

Vazirani, U. V., and V. V. Vazirani. 1985. The two-processor scheduling problem is in random *NC*. *SIAM Journal on Computing*, vol. 18, no. 6, Dec., pp. 1140–1148.

Vishkin, U. 1983. Implementation of simultaneous memory access in models that forbid it. *Journal of Algorithms*, vol. 4, no. 1, Mar., pp. 45–50.

Vishkin, U., and A. Wigderson, In press. Trade-offs between width and depth in parallel computation. *SIAM Journal on Computing*.

Vitányi, P. M. B. 1988. Locality, communication, and interconnect length in multicomputers. *SIAM Journal on Computing*, vol. 17, no. 4, Aug., pp. 659–672.

Vrsalovic, D., E. F. Gehringer, Z. Z. Segall, and D. P. Siewiorek. 1985. The influence of parallel decomposition strategies on the performance of multiprocessor systems. In *Proceedings of the 12th Annual International Symposium on Computer Architecture, ACM SIGARCH Newsletter*, no. 13, June, pp. 396–405.

Vuillemin, J. E. 1983. A combinatorial limit to the computing power of VLSI circuits. *IEEE Transactions on Computers*, vol. C-32, no. 3, Mar., pp. 294–300.

Wah, B. W., and K. L. Chen. 1984. A partitioning approach to the design of selection networks. *IEEE Transactions on Computers*, vol. C-33, no. 3, Mar., pp. 261–268.

Wah, B. W., and Y. W. Eva Ma. 1984. MANIP—A multicomputer architecture for solving combinatorial extremum-search problems. *IEEE Transactions on Computers*, vol. C-33, no. 5, May, pp. 377–390.

Wah, B. W., G.-J.,Li, and C. F. Yu. 1984. The status of MANIP—A multicomputer architecture for solving combinatorial extremum-search problems. In *Proceedings of the 11th Annual International Symposium on Computer Architecture*, IEEE, New York, Mar., pp. 56–63.

Wah, B. W., G. Li, and C.-F. Yu. 1985. Multiprocessing of combinatorial search problems. *Computer*, vol. 18, no. 6, June, pp. 93–108.

Wah, B. W., G.-J. Li, and C.-F. Yu. 1990. Multiprocessing of combinatorial search problems. In V. Kumar, P. S. Gopalakrishnan, and L. N. Kanal, eds., *Parallel Algorithms for Machine Intelligence and Vision*. Springer-Verlag, New York, pp. 102–145.

Wah, B. W., and E. Y. W. Ma. 1984. MANIP—A multicomputer architecture for solving combinatorial extremum search problems. *IEEE Transactions on Computers*, vol. C-33, no. 5, May, pp. 377–390.

Wah, B. W., and C. F. Yu. 1982. Probabilistic modeling of branch-and-bound algorithms. *Proceedings of COMPSAC*, Nov., pp. 647–653.

Warren, D. H. D., L. M. Pereira, and F. Pereira. 1977. PROLOG—The language and its implementation compared with LISP. *SIGPLAN Notices*, vol. 12, no. 8. Also in *SIGART Newsletter* 64 (August 1977), pp. 109–115.

Warshall, S. 1962. A theorem on Boolean matrices. *Journal of the ACM*, vol. 9, no. 1, Jan., pp. 11–12.

Watson, I., and J. Gurd. 1981. A practical data flow computer. *Computer*, vol. 14, no. 2, Feb., pp. 51–57.

Wagner, A., and D. G. Corneil. 1990. Embedding trees in a hypercube is NP-complete. *SIAM Journal on Computing*, vol. 19, no. 4, June, pp. 570–590.

Weaver, H. J. 1983. *Applications of Discrete and Continuous Fourier Analysis*. John Wiley & Sons, New York.

Wegner, L. M. 1982. Sorting a distributed file in a network. In *Proceedings of the 1982 Conference on Information Science Systems*, Mar., pp. 505–509.

Weide, B. W. 1981. Analytical models to explain anomalous behavior of parallel algorithms. In *Proceedings of the 1981 International Conference on Parallel Processing*, Aug., IEEE, New York, pp. 183–187.

Wheat, M., and D. J. Evans. 1992. An efficient parallel sorting algorithm for shared memory multiprocessors. *Parallel Computing*, vol. 18, pp. 91–102.

Wilson, G. V. 1993. A glossary of parallel computing terminology. *IEEE Parallel & Distributed Technology: Systems and Applications*, vol. 1, no. 1, Feb., pp. 52–67.

Winslow, L. E., and Y.-C. Chow. 1981. Parallel sorting machines: Their speed and efficiency. In *Proceedings of the AFIPS 1981 National Computer Conference*, pp. 163–165.

Winslow, L. E., and Y.-C. Chow. 1983. The analysis and design of some new sorting machines. *IEEE Transactions on Computers*, vol. C-32, no. 7, July, pp. 677–683.

Wirth, N. 1976. *Algorithms + Data Structures = Programs*. Prentice-Hall, Englewood Cliffs, NJ.

Wirth, N. 1977a. Modula: A language for modular multiprogramming. *Software Practice and Experience*, vol. 7, pp. 33–35.

Wirth, N. 1977b. The use of Modula. *Software Practice and Experience*, vol. 7, pp. 37–65.

Wirth, N. 1977c. Design and implementation of Modula. *Software Practice and Experience*, vol. 7, pp. 67–84.

Wold, E. H., and A. M. Despain. 1984. Pipeline and parallel-pipeline FFT processors for VLSI implementations. *IEEE Transactions on Computers*, vol. C-33, no. 5, May, pp. 414–426.

Wolfe, M. J. 1989. *Optimizing Supercompilers for Supercomputers*. Pitman Publishing, Long, England, and MIT Press, Cambridge.

Wolfstahl, Y. 1989. Mapping parallel programs to multicomputers: a dynamic approach. *Parallel Computing*, vol. 10, pp. 45–50.

Wong, C. K., and S.-K. Chang. 1974. Parallel generation of binary search trees. *IEEE Transactions on Computers*, vol. C-23, no. 3, Mar., pp. 268–271.

Wong, F. S., and M. R. Ito. 1984. Parallel sorting on a re-circulating systolic sorter. *The Computer Journal*, vol. 27, no. 3, pp. 260–269.

Wu, A. Y. 1985. Embedding of tree networks into hypercubes. *Journal of Parallel and Distributed Computing*, vol. 2, pp. 238–249.

Wu, C. L., and T. Y. Feng. 1981. Universality of the shuffle exchange network. *IEEE Transactions on Computers*, vol. C-30, no. 5, May, pp. 324–331.

Wulf, W. A., R. Levin, and S. P. Harbison. 1981. *HYDRA/C.mmp: An Experimental Computer System*. Mc-Graw-Hill, New York.

Wyllie, J. C. 1979. The complexity of parallel computations. Ph.D. dissertation, Dept. of Computer Science, Cornell University, Ithaca, NY.

Yadlin, Y., and D. A Caughey, Block multigrid implicit solution of the Euler equations of compressible fluid flow. *AIAA Journal*, vol. 29, May, pp. 712–719.

Yang, C.-B., R. C. T. Lee, and W.-T. Chen. 1990. Parallel graph algorithms based upon broadcast communications. *IEEE Transactions on Computers*, vol. C-39, no. 12, Dec., pp. 1468–1472.

Yang, M. C. K., J. S. Huang, and Y.-C. Chow. 1987. Optimal parallel sorting scheme by order statistics. *SIAM Journal on Computing*, vol. 16, no. 6, Dec., pp. 990–1003.

Yasuura, H., N. Tagaki, and S. Yajima. 1982. The parallel enumeration sorting scheme for VLSI. *IEEE Transactions on Computers*, vol. C-31, no. 12, Dec., pp. 1192–1201.

Yau, S. S., and H. S. Fung. 1977. Associative processor architecture—A survey. *Computing Surveys*, vol. 9, no. 1, Mar., pp. 3–27.

Yoo, Y. B. 1983. Parallel processing for some network optimization problems. Ph.D. dissertation, Computer Science Dept., Washington State University, Pullman.

Yu, C. F., and B. W. Wah. 1983. Virtual-memory support for branch-and-bound algorithms. In *Proceedings Compsac*, Nov., pp. 618–626.

Yu, C. F., and B. W. Wah. 1984. Efficient branch-and-bound algorithms on a two-level memory hierarchy. In *Proceedings Compsac*, Nov., pp. 504–514.

Yu, D. C., and H. Wang. 1990. A new parallel LU decomposition method. *IEEE Transactions on Power Systems*, vol. 5, Feb., pp. 303–310.

Zhang, C. N., and D. Y. Y. Yun. 1984. Multi-dimensional systolic networks for discrete Fourier transform. In *Proceedings of the Eleventh Annual International Symposium on Computer Architecture, SIGARCH Newsletter*, pp. 215–222.

Zima, H., and B. Chapman. 1990. *Supercompilers for Parallel and Vector Computers*. ACM Press, New York.

Znati, T. F., R. G. Melhem, and K. R. Pruhs. 1991. Dilation based bidding schemes for dynamic load balancing on distributed processing systems. In *The Sixth Distributed Memory Computing Conference Proceedings*, pp. 129–136.

INDEX

$\leftarrow$, 31, 123
$\Leftarrow$, 124
β, 172
λ, 14, 172
$\sigma(k)$, 180
χ, 14, 172
Activation steps, 30
Active garbage list, 304
Active operation, 310, 312
Acyclic graph, 368, 376
Adjacency lists, 368
Adjacency matrix, 367, 376
Alfonso X, 255
Algorithm:
   control-parallel (*see* Control parallelism)
   data-parallel (*see* Data parallelism)
   parallel *see* Multicomputer algorithms, Mul-
     tiprocessor algorithms, PRAM algorithms,
     Processor array algorithms)
   sequential *see* Sequential algorithms)
All-pairs shortest-path search, 318–368, 376
Alpha-beta search, 354–365, 376
   parallel, 359–365
   sequential, 354–359
ALT construct, occam, 116–117
Alternation, 116
Amdahl effect, 17, 82, 223, 376
Amdahl's law, 17, 81–82, 376
Ametek, 4
Amplitude, 200
AMT DAP, 54, 86, 213
AND tree, 337–338, 376
AND/OR tree, 337–338, 365, 376
Anomalies, speedup, 80–81, 352–354, 365
ANSI, 95
ARBITRARY PRAM, 28, 376
Architecture:

multicomputer (*see* Multicomputer archi-
   tectures)
multiprocess or (*see* Multiprocessor ar-
   chitectures)
processor array (*see* Processor array ar-
   chitectures)
Arguments against high-level parallelism, 19
Array, processor (*see* Processor array)
Articulation points, 333
Aspiration search, 358–360, 376
Assembly line, 6
Assignment process, occam, 113–115
Associative memory, 118, 307
Associative processor, 334
Astrophysics, 2
Asynchronous algorithm, 159, 253, 376
AVL tree, 297–301, 307, 377
B* tree, 307
Back end, 74, 92
Back substitution algorithm, 220–223
Backtrack, 339
Balance, Sequent (*see* Sequent Balance)
Balanced binary tree, 138
Banded linear system solvers, 252
Bandwidth, 75, 377
   bisection, 88, 377
Bank, 191, 308, 377
Barrier synchronization, 91, 104, 125, 377
Batch search, 294, 307, 377
BBN:
   Butterfly Plus, 365
   TC2000, 57, 70–72, 79, 189, 285
Benchmarking practices, 86
Bennett, A. F., 3
Biconnected components, 333
Binary n-cube network, 57, 377
   (*see also* Hypercube)

Binary semaphore, 151
Binary tree:
    compared to other networks, 61
    embedding in 2-D mesh, 135–136
    embedding in hypercube, 137–138
    fundamental paradigm, 31
    graph defined, 370, 377
    network defined, 54–55
    reasonable model, 86
Binomial tree:
    defined, 370, 377
    embedding in 2-D mesh, 136–137
    embedding in hypercube, 138–139
Biology, 3
Bipartite graph, 138, 333
Bisection bandwidth, 88, 377
Bisection width, 53, 257–258, 377
BIT function, 185–186
Bit reversal, 176
BIT.COMPLEMENT function, 185–186
Bitonic merge, 260–272, 290, 377
Bitonic sequence, 260–265, 377
Bit-parallel arithmetic, 5
Bit-parallel memory, 5
BITS function, 315
Bit-serial processors, 64
Block matrix multiplication, 189–190, 193–
    196, 377
Block-oriented data distribution, 193–196,
    243–244
Bolt, Beranek, and Newman, Inc. (see BBN)
Bound and branch, 363, 377
Branch and bound:
    anomalies, 352–354
    best-first search strategy, 342
    definition, 340–342, 377
    eight-puzzle example, 339–340
    multicomputer implementation, 347–352
    multiprocessor implementation, 346–347
    references in literature to, 364–365
    traveling salesperson example, 342–346
Breadth-depth search, parallel, 311–312
Breadth-first search, parallel, 311–313, 332
Brent's theorem, 44–46, 314, 377
Broadcast:
    2-D mesh, 176
    conjugate gradient, 249
    defined, 31, 377
    gaussian elimination with partial pivot-
        ing, 232, 236
    hypercube, 170–171
BSP model, 49
Buffer deadlock, 151–152, 377
Burroughs Corporation, 4
Bus, common, 68
Busy-waiting, 377
Butterfly:
    compared with other networks, 61
    defined, 57, 377
    fast Fourier transform, 206
    in BBN TC2000, 70–71
    reasonable model, 86
Butterfly network (see Butterfly)

C:
    nCUBE, 109–112
    Sequent, 104–109
C*, 99–103
Cache:
    coherency, 69, 87
    copy-back policy, 70
    memory, 5, 69–70, 377
    write-through policy, 69–70
California Institute of Technology, 4, 87,
    217
Caltech (see California Institute of Technol-
    ogy)
Cancellation lemma, 373–374
Cards, playing, 20
Carnegie-Mellon University, 4, 86–87
Cell modeling, 3
Centralized load balancing algorithm, 143,
    377
Centralized shared memory, 67
Chain, 149, 377
Chaining, 377
Channel, 5, 114–115, 378
Checkers, 354
Cheriton and Tarjan's minimum-cost span-
    ning tree algorithm, 333
Chess, 354, 359–361, 365
Child, 370, 378
Chordal graphs, 334
Chua, B., 3
Circuit problem, 218–219
Circuit value problem, 48
Circuit-switched message routing, 73–74, 132,
    378
Claims adjustors analogy, 158
Classical science, 2
Classifying architectures, 78–80
Classifying MIMD algorithms, 157–159
C-Linda, 118–122
Cm*, 4, 87, 190–191, 346–347, 359
C.mmp, 4, 86
cobegin...coend statement, 149
Coffman-Graham scheduling algorithm, 146–
    149
Cole, R., 201
Color cost problem, 333
Combinatorial search, 336–366
Combining messages, 236
Common bus, 68
COMMON PRAM, 28, 378
Communicating sequential processes, 113
Communication overhead, 360, 378
Communication-computation trade-off, 236–
    237, 360
Comparator, 260–378
Compare-exchange, 260–263, 378
COMPARE-EXCHANGE, 269
Compiler, parallelizing, 128
Complete binary tree, 135–138, 370, 378
Complex nth root of unity, 204, 206, 373–
    374, 378
Component labeling problem, 368, 378
Complex number, 371, 378

Complexity, 26, 27, 295, 378
Computational fluid dynamics, 2
Computational geometry, 255
Computer:
    parallel (*see* Multicomputer architectures,
        Multiprocessor architectures, Processor
        array architectures)
    sequential, 26–27, 62–63, 74, 385
    vector, 61, 387
Computing, high-speed, 1–2
Concurrent Pascal, 106
Concurrent Prolog, 127
Congestion, 133
Conjugate gradient, 248–251, 253
Connected components, 313–318, 368–369,
    378
Connected graph, 368, 378
Connected 1s problem, 368, 378
Connection Machine (*see* Thinking Machines)
Contemporary science, 2
Contention, 321
Control parallelism:
    asynchronous algorithm, 159
    defined, 8, 378
    pipelined algorithm, 8
    scalability, 9
    Sieve of Eratosthenes, 9–13
    when to choose, 159
Convergence criteria, 238, 253
Convolution algorithm, 203–204
Copy-back cache, 70, 378
Corinthians I, 90
Cosmic Cube, 4, 87
Cosmology, 2
Cost, 27, 378
Cost criteria, 27
Cost optimal, 43, 159, 172, 378
Cray X/MP, 4
Cray Y/MP, 5
Cray-1, 61, 80
CRCW PRAM:
    defined, 28, 378
    enumeration sort, 256–257
    lower bounds on sorting, 291
CREW PRAM:
    compared to CRCW PRAM, 256
    connected components, 313–315
    defined, 28, 378
    graph coloring, 42–43
    list ranking algorithm, 34–35
    merging lists, 40–42
    minimum-cost spanning tree, 333
    prefix sums algorithm, 32–34
    preorder tree traversal, 36–40
    reduction, 159
    searching a graph, 309–313
    searching a table, 295
Critical node, 297, 378
Critical section, 91, 106, 321, 327, 379
Crossbar switch, 68
Cube-connected cycles:
    basis for processor arrays, 63
    compared with other networks, 61

defined, 58–59, 379
    reasonable model, 86
    sorting algorithm, 290
Cube-connected network (*see* Hypercube)
Cubical, 137, 379
Cyber-205, 61
Cycle:
    condition of deadlock, 152
    graph theoretic definition, 368, 379
Cyclic reduction, 227, 252, 379
DAP (*see* AMT DAP)
Data flow analysis, 379
Data flow computing, 87
Data flow diagram (*see* Data flow graph)
Data flow graph, 132, 159, 207–210, 226,
    379
Data flow language, 128
Data parallelism:
    becomes SPMD on MIMD machines, 169
    contrasted with pipelining, 7–8
    defined, 6, 379
    indicated by for all statement, 124
    prescheduling versus self-scheduling, 158
    Sieve of Eratosthenes, 12–18
Data pipelining, 5
Data stream, 78, 379
Data-parallel algorithm (*see* Data parallelism)
DataVault, 67
de Bruijn network, 60–61, 85–86, 379
Deadlock, 151–152, 154, 379
Decision problem, 337, 379
Deepness heuristic, 342
Dense linear system solvers, 229–237, 252
Depth, 149, 379
Depth-first search, parallel, 48, 332–333
Deque, 325, 379
Design strategies, parallel (*see* Parallel al-
    gorithm design strategies)
Deterministic model, 144, 379
DFT, 201, 379
    (*See also* Discrete Fourier transform)
Diagonally dominant matrix, 220, 379
Diameter, 53, 379
Dictionary operations, 294–308
Digitized picture input, 368
Dilation, 133, 379
Direct-Connect Module, iPSC/2, 73–74
Directed graph, 367, 379
Discrete Fourier transform,198–202, 373, 379
Discretization stencil, 253
Distributed load balancing algorithms, 143
Distributed memory:
    C* programming model, 100
    multicomputers, 72, 131, 142
    PRAM model, 27
    processor arrays, 62, 131
    pseudocode variables, 122
Distributed shared memory, 67, 70, 87
Distributed sorting, 292
Distributed Tree Search, 361–365
Divide and conquer:
    combinatorial search, 338

defined, 379
fast Fourier transform, 206
pi computation, 119, 121–122
quicksort, 273
represented by binary tree, 31
DMA, 73, 75
Double rotation of AVL tree, 298
DTS (*see* Distributed Tree Search)
Dynamic decomposition, 379
Dynamic load balancing, multicomputer, 142–143
Dynamic programming, 365
Dynamic scheduling, 380
east keyword, pseudocode, 125
Edge, 367, 380
Effective branching factor, 358, 380
Efficiency, 80, 380
    scaled, 83–84
8-puzzle, 339–341
Einstein, A., 217
Elementary parallel algorithms, 157–177
Ellis's algorithm, 297–301
Embedding, 133–142, 380
    2-D mesh into 2-D mesh, 134–135
    binomial tree into 2-D mesh, 136–137
    binomial tree into hypercube, 138–139
    complete binary tree into 2-D mesh, 135–136
    complete binary tree into hypercube, 137–138
    defined, 133
    graphs into hypercubes, 137–138
    grids into hypercubes, 153
    ring into 2-D mesh, 134
    rings and meshes into hypercube, 139–142
Encore Multimax, 68
Enumeration sort, 256–257, 291, 380
Environmental modeling, 3
Enzyme activity, 3
EREW PRAM, 28, 333, 380
eval function, C-Linda, 119–122
Evaluation function, 354
Even-odd exchange, 258, 380
Exchange, 380
exchange keyword, pseudocode, 125
Exhaustive search, 339
Expected space and time complexity, 26, 380
External sorting, parallel, 292
Fact, 380
Fan-in, 31, 249, 252, 380
Fast Fourier transform, 205–213, 380
    iterative algorithm, 208–209
    parallel algorithm, 207–213
    recursive algorithm, 207
Fetch-and-add, 256
FFT (*see* Fast Fourier transform)
15-puzzle, 339
Fifth-generation computer, 128, 380
Filter, low-pass, 214–216
FIND, 326–328
First order recurrence relations, 252

Flat Concurrent Prolog, 129
Flat GHC, 129
Flynn's taxonomy, 78–80
for all statement, pseudocode, 31, 124
for statement, pseudocode, 123
Fork, 380
FORTRAN 77, 93, 95
Fortran 90, 95–99
Forward substitution, 253
Fourier analysis, 198, 380
Frame buffer, 64–67
Frequency, signal, 199, 380
From, 367, 380
Front end:
    multicomputer, 91–93, 380
    processor array, 62–64, 380
Fully distributed load balancing algorithm, 143, 380
Functional units:
    multiple, 158
    pipelined, 5
Gadzooks hypercube multicomputer, 177
Game tree:
    defined, 354, 380
    pathological 365
    perfectly ordered, 361
    searching, 354–359
Gantt chart, 145, 380
Garbage collection, 304
Garbage list, 304
Gaussian elimination, 229–237, 380
    with partial pivoting, 230–237, 380
Gauss-Seidel algorithm, 244–245
Genetic engineering, 3
Genome sequencing, 3
Gigabyte, 380
Gigaflops, 380
Global keyword, pseudocode, 122
Global memory (*see* Shared memory)
Global ocean circulation, 3
Global weather modeling, 3
Go, 354
Goodyear Aerospace Massively Parallel Processor, 54, 86
Graham's list scheduling algorithm, 145–146
Grain size, 188, 236, 380
Grand challenge problems, 2
Graph, 367, 381
Graph algorithms:
    all-pairs shortest path, 318
    connected components, 313–318
    graph coloring, 42–43, 381
    minimum-cost spanning tree, 325–331
    searching, 310–313
    single-source shortest path, 318–325
Graph, bipartite, 138
Graph theoretic terminology, 367–370
Graph theory, relevance of sorting to, 255
Gray code, 140–142, 192, 247–248, 381
Great Seal of the United States, 52
Gregor, J. A., 3

Grosch's law, 19
Halving lemma, 206, 374
Hamiltonian circuit, 134, 155
Heap, parallel, 329–331
Height, 297, 369, 381
Herrick, R., 336
Hexagonal mesh, 155
Heywood, J., 25
High-level languages, 93
High-level parallelism, 4
High-speed computing, 1–2
Hirschberg's algorithm, 313–314, 316, 333
HITECH, 359
Host processor (*see* Front end)
Hot spot, 191, 308, 381
H-tree, 136
Hypercube:
    all-pairs shortest path, 318
    bitonic merge, 271–272
    Connection Machine CM-200, 63
    compared to other networks, 61
    defined, 57–58, 381
    embedding graphs in, 137–142
    fast Fourier transform, 206–213
    graph algorithms, 333
    hyperquicksort, 276–281
    matrix multiplication, 183–186, 191–196
    nCUBE 2, 74–75
    reduction algorithm, 160–163
    traveling salesperson problem, 347–352
Hypercube network (*see* Hypercube)
Hyperquicksort, 276–281
Hypertree:
    compared to other networks, 61
    Connection Machine CM-5, 75
    defined 55–56, 381
    reasonable model, 86
ICL Distributed Array Processor (*see* AMT DAP)
IF construct, occam, 115–117
if...else...endif pseudocode construct, 123
ILLIAC IV, 4, 86
Image processing, 255
Imaginary element, 372, 381
Imaginary part, 371, 381
Immediate predecessor, 147, 381
Immediate successor, 147, 381
in function, C-Linda, 119–122
Independent set of tasks, 147, 381
Index function, 270, 381
Information, 381
Initial tasks, 147, 381
Inmos Limited, 113
INNER.PRODUCT, 249, 251
inp function, C-Linda, 119
Input process, occam, 113–115
Instruction buffering, 5, 381
Instruction cycle, 5
Instruction look-ahead, 5, 381
Instruction pipelining, 5, 381
Instruction prefetching, 5
Instruction stream, 78, 381

Insurance claims adjustors analogy, 158
Intel, 4
    80386/80387 microprocessor, 68–69
    i860 XP microprocessor, 76–78
    iPSC, 73, 213, 363
    iPSC/2, 73–74
    iPSC/860, 73, 285–286
    Paragon XP/S, 5, 54, 72, 76–79
    Touchstone DELTA, 88
Interleaved memory, 5, 381
Internal sort, 255, 381
Interpolation, in multigrid methods, 246
Inverse discrete Fourier transform, 202–203, 381
Inverse Gray code, 140–141
iPSC (*see* Intel iPSC)
Irregular meshes, 142, 154
ISO, 95
Iterative deepening, 359, 381
Iterative methods for solving linear systems, 237–251
Jacobi algorithm, 237–244
Jacobi overrelaxation, 245–246
Jung, C. G., 198
Kasantzakis, N., 157
k-connected components, 333
Key, 294, 381
Knapsack problem, 354, 381
Kruskal's algorithm, 329–331, 333
Landscaping example, 9
Language, parallel (*see* Parallel programming languages)
Lattice, 53
Left subscripting, 124
Length, chain, 149, 381
Level, 149, 381
Level of parallelism, 131
Light, speed of, 5
Light-weight threads 381
Linda, 118, 127
Linear equation, 218, 381
Linear system, 218, 382
Linked array, 323–325, 382
List ranking, 34–35, 382
List scheduling algorithm, Graham's, 145–146
Load, 134, 382
Load balancing algorithms, 143
Local keyword, 122
Local memory (*see* Distributed memory)
Locality of reference, 382
lock function, pseudocode, 125
Lock operation, 151
Logarithmic cost criterion, 27, 382
Logarithmic-time parallel sorting algorithms, 290
Logic programming, 128–129
Loosely coupled multiprocessor (*see* Multiprocessor architectures, non-uniform memory access)
Lower bound, on matrix multiplication, 180–181
Lower bound, on searching, 295–296

Lower bound, on sorting, 257–258, 292
Lower triangular matrix, 219, 382
Lowest common ancestors, 333
Loyd, S., 339
LU decomposition, 252, 382
Luke, 1
Mailbox analogy, 288–289
Mainframe computer performance growth, 4–5
Maintenance processes, 304–306
Manber and Ladner's algorithm, 302–306
Manhattan distance, 340
Manip, 364
Mapping, 132–142, 154
Masking processing elements, 62
MasPar:
    MP-1, 54
    MP-2, 5
Massively Parallel Processor, Goodyear Aerospace, 54, 86
Master/worker algorithm, 119–120
Materials design, 2
Matrix:
    diagonally dominant, 220
    lower triangular, 219
    positive definite, 220
    symmetric, 220
    tridiagonal, 219
    upper triangular, 219
Matrix multiplication, 179–197, 318
    1-D mesh SIMD, 196
    2-D mesh SIMD, 180–184
    block, 189–190, 193–196
    hypercube, 183–187, 191–196
    multicomputers, 191–196
    multiprocessors, 187–191
    NUMA multiprocessor, 189–191
    processor arrays, 180–187
    sequential, 179
    shuffle-exchange, 186–187
    UMA multiprocessor, 188–189
    VLSI algorithms, 196–197
Matrix reduction, 343–344
Matrix transpose, 176
MATRIX.VECTOR.PRODUCT, 249, 251
Maximum-capacity path, 334
Maximum clique, 333
Maximum flow, 48, 334
Maximum independent set, 334
Maximum matching, 333
Max-tournament, 235, 382
MAX.TOURNAMENT, 236
Mechanics, statistical, 2
Medicine, 3
Megabyte, 382
Megaflops, 382
Meiko Computing Surface, 73
Memory bank, 191, 308, 377
Memory, cache (*see* Cache memory)
Memory, distributed (*see* Distributed memory)

Memory, shared (*see* Shared memory)
Memory structure, nonuniform, 132
Mergesort, 291
Merging sorted lists, 40–42
Mesh:
    bitonic merge, 267–271
    compared to other networks, 61
    connected components algorithm, 315–318
    data routing, 176
    defined, 53–54, 382
    embedding graphs in, 134–137
    embedding in hypercube, 139–142
    hexagonal, 155
    lower bounds on matrix multiplication, 180–181
    lower bounds on parallel sorting, 257–258
    matrix multiplication, 181–184
    mergesort, 291
    multidimensional, 140–141
    odd-even merge sort, 290
    odd-even transposition sort, 258–260
    Paragon XP/S, 76
    processor numbering schemes, 270, 291
    reasonable model, 86
    reduction, 162, 164–167
Message latency, 170, 382
Message-passing overhead, 170, 236, 382
Message routing:
    circuit-switched, 73–74, 132
    store-and-forward, 73, 132
m_fork, Sequent C, 105, 108–109
m_get_myid, Sequent C, 105, 109
m_get_numprocs, Sequent C, 105
Microprocessors:
    Intel 80386/80387, 68
    Intel i860 XP, 78
    Motorola 88100/88200, 70
    performance growth, 4–5
Microsecond, 382
Millisecond, 382
MIMD, 79, 382
    (*See also* Multicomputer, Multiprocessor)
Minicomputer performance growth, 4–5
Minimax, 354–355, 358, 382
Minimum-cost spanning forest, 325–326
Minimum-cost spanning tree, 325–331, 333, 369–370, 382
Minsky's conjecture, 19, 382
Min-tournament, 235, 382
MISD, 79, 382
m_kill_procs, Sequent C, 106
m_lock, Sequent C, 106, 109
Modeling, 2–3
Modified hyperquicksort, 281
Modula, 106
Module, memory, 382
    (*See also* Memory bank)
Molecular dynamics, 4
Monitor, 106–107, 382
Moore's algorithm, 319–320
Motorola 88100/88200, 70
MPP, Goodyear Aerospace, 54, 86

m_set_procs, Sequent C, 105, 108–109
Multicomputer algorithms:
  broadcast, 170–171
  fast Fourier transform, 206–213
  graph problems, 333
  hyperquicksort, 276–281
  matrix multiplication, 191–196
  sorting, 292
  traveling salesperson problem, 347–352
  variance computation, 91–94
Multicomputer architectures:
  Connection Machine CM-5, 75–76
  Cosmic Cube, 87
  nCUBE 2, 74–75
  overview, 72–74, 86, 382
  Paragon XP/S, 76–78
Multigrid methods, 246–248, 253
Multilisp, 127
Multimax, Encore, 68
Multiple functional units, 5, 158
Multiple instruction stream, multiple data
  stream, 79, 382
Multiple instruction stream, single data stream,
  79, 382
Multiplexed message routing, 133
Multiplication:
  matrix (*see* Matrix multiplication)
  polynomial, 203–205
Multiprocessing, 5
Multiprocessor algorithms:
  back substitution, 220–223
  batch searching, 296–306
  combinatorial search, 338
  matrix multiplication, 187–191
  minimum-cost spanning tree, 325–331
  odd-even reduction, 224–229
  reduction, 165–170
  single-source shortest path, 318–325
  sorting, 291–292
  traveling salesperson problem, 346–347
  variance computation, 91–92
Multiprocessor architectures:
  cause of superlinear speedup, 81
  Cm*, 87
  C.mmp, 86
  Flynn's taxonomy, 79
  non-uniform memory access, 70, 86–87,
    383
  overview, 67–68, 70
  Paradigm, 87
  Symmetry, 68–70
  TC2000, 70–72
  uniform memory access, 67–68, 86–87,
    387
Multiprogramming, 382
Multistage networks, 85
m_unlock, Sequent C, 106, 109
Muthusamy, Y., 201
Mutual exclusion:
  defined, 383
  implemented via lock and unlock, 125
  implemented via monitors, 106–107
  necessary for deadlock, 151

synchronization method, 91, 104
Nanoinstructions, 64
Nanosecond, 383
$\mathcal{NC}$, 47–48, 50, 383
nCUBE, 4, 58, 74
  C programming language, 93, 109–112
  nCUBE 2, 73–75, 79
  nCUBE 3200: alpha-beta search speedup,
    365
    fast Fourier transform speedup, 210,
      213
    gaussian elimination speedup, 237
    hyperquicksort speedup, 280
    Jacobi algorithm parallelizability, 239–
      240
    matrix multiplication speedup, 193,
      195
    prefix sums speedup, 174–175
    traveling salesperson speedup, 349–
      351
  nCUBE/10, 73
NEC SC-3, 5
Necklace, 60, 383
  short, 60, 385
Network:
  binary n-cube (*see* Hypercube)
  binary tree (*see* Binary tree)
  butterfly (*see* Butterfly)
  cube-connected cycles (*see* Cube-connected
    cycles)
  cube-connected (*see* Hypercube)
  de Bruijn (*see* de Bruijn network)
  hypercube (*see* Hypercube)
  mesh (*see* Mesh)
  omega, 60, 383
  prism, 85–86
  pyramid, 56, 61, 85, 384
  shuffle-exchange (*see* Shuffle-exchange)
Network flow problems, 252
New York University, 68, 86, 256
NEWS grid, 66, 383
Nondeterministic model, 147, 383
Nonlinear problems, 252
Nonlocal variables, 131
Nonnumerical algorithm, 178
Nonpreemption, 152
Nonsimple task graph, 149
Non-uniform memory access multiprocessor, see Multiprocessor
north keyword, pseudocode, 125
Notation, pseudocode, 122–126
$\mathcal{NP}$, 46–48
$\mathcal{NP}$-complete, 46–48, 137, 153–154
$\mathcal{NP}$-hard, 145
nread, nCUBE C, 110, 112, 124
nth roots of unity, complex, 204, 206, 373–
  374, 378
NUMA multiprocessor (*see* Multiprocessor)
Numerical integration, 93–95, 130
Numerical simulation, 2
nwrite, nCUBE C, 110, 112, 124
Oak Ridge National Laboratory, 3
Objective function, 340

Occam, 113–118
Ocean circulation, 3
Odd-even exchange, 258, 383
Odd-even merge sort, 290
Odd-even ordering (*see* Red-black coloring)
Odd-even reduction, 224–229, 252, 383
Odd-even transposition sort, 258–260, 291
Omega network, 60–61, 68, 383
1-D mesh (*see* Mesh)
Optimal schedule, 145, 147, 383
Optimization problem, 337, 383
OR tree, 337–338, 340, 365, 383
Ordinary differential equations, 253
Oregon Graduate Institute of Science and Technology, 201
Oregon State University, 3
Othello, 363–364
out function, C-Linda, 118
Output process, occam, 113–115
Overhead, communication, 360
Overhead, search, 360
$\mathcal{P}$, 46–48
P operation on binary semaphore, 151
Pape-d'Esopo's algorithm, 325
PAR construct, occam, 115–117
Paradigm, 87
Para-functional programming, 127
Paragon XP/S (*see* Intel Paragon XP/S)
Parallel algorithm design strategies, 375
    #1, find cost-optimal PRAM algorithm, 159
    #2, consider data parallelism first, 168
    #3, make best use of resources, 171
    #4, use best sequential algorithm, 172
    #5, maximize grain size, 188, 320, 326
    #6, increase locality, 190
    #7, change temporal order of data accesses, 191
    #8, change data structures, 321
Parallel algorithms (*see* Control parallelism, Data parallelism, Multicomputer algorithms, Multiprocessor algorithms, PRAM algorithms, Processor array algorithms)
Parallel aspiration search, 359–360
Parallel computation thesis, 47, 383
Parallel computer, 6, 383
    (*See also* Multicomputer architectures, Multiprocessor architectures, Processor array architecture)
Parallel computing, 6, 383
Parallel data distribution, 132
Parallel languages:
    high-level, 93
    issues, 91
    (*See also* Parallel programming languages)
Parallel prefix, 33, 383
    (*See also* Prefix sums)
Parallel processing:
    defined, 6, 383
    practical, 4–5
Parallel processing unit, 63–64
Parallel program development system, 132

Parallel programming languages, 90–130
    C*, 99–103
    C-Linda, 118–122
    Fortran 90, 95–99
    nCUBE C, 109–112
    occam, 113–118
    pseudocode, 122–127
    Sequent C, 104–109
Parallel sorting by regular sampling, 281–286
Parallel subtree evaluation, 359–360
Parallelism, 4, 383
    control (*see* Control parallelism)
    data (*see* Data parallelism)
    level, 131
Parallelizability, 80, 383
Parallelization, 383
Parallelizing compilers, 128
Parameter keyword, 122
Parent, 370, 383
Paris, 64
Parlog, 129
Parsytec SuperCluster, 73
Partial differential equations, 142, 239–241, 246, 253
Partial pivoting, 230
Partial sum, 383
Particle-in-cell simulation, 142
Partitioned algorithm (*see* Data parallelism)
Path, 368, 383
Pathological game trees, 365
Pattern recognition, 200
$\mathcal{P}$-complete, 47–48, 310, 332, 383
pcoord function, C*, 101
P-depth search, parallel, 310–312
Perfect shuffle, 59, 176, 265, 267, 384
    (*See also* Shuffle-exchange)
Perfectly ordered game tree, 358, 383
Performance growth, computer, 4–5
Permutation, 208–210, 214, 255, 286–288
Pharmacology, 3
Phonemes, 200
Photocopier example, 6
Physics, relativistic, 2
Pi computation:
    C* implementation, 103
    C-Linda implementations, 120–121
    description of algorithm, 93–95
    Fortran 90 implementation, 99
    nCUBE C implementation, 111–112
    occam implementation, 117
    pseudocode implementations, 126–127
    Sequent C implementation, 108
Picosecond, 384
Pipelined algorithm, 6, 157, 384
Pipelined functional units, 5
Pipelined vector processor, 61, 75, 384
Pipelining, 6–8, 384
Pivot row, 230, 384
Planarity testing, 333
Playing cards, 20
Plus-min multiplication, 313

Ply, 359, 384
Pointer jumping, 34–35, 38, 384
Polylogarithmic function, 47, 384
Polylogarithmic time complexity, 47, 54, 260, 264, 384
Polynomial multiplication, 203–205
Polynomial time, 47
Positive definite matrix, 220, 248, 384
PP-PRAM, 49
PRAM:
  models, 27–30, 384
  pronunciation, 25
  spawning processes, 30
PRAM algorithms:
  connected components, 313–315
  enumeration sort, 256–257
  graph coloring, 42–43
  list ranking, 34–35
  merging two sorted lists, 40–42
  minimum-cost spanning tree, 333
  prefix sums, 32–34
  preorder tree traversal, 36–40
  reduction, 31–32, 159
  searching a graph, 309–313
  searching a table, 295
  sorting, 290–291
Precedence synchronization, 91, 125
Predecessor keyword, 124
Prefix sums, 32–33, 45–46, 172–175, 384
Preorder tree traversal algorithm, 36–40
Prescheduled data-parallel algorithm, 158, 384
Primality testing, 9–10
Prim-Dijkstra's algorithm, 333
Primitive root of unity, 201–203
Principal nth root of unity, 373, 384
Principal variation splitting, 365
PRIORITY PRAM, 28, 384
Priority queue, 349–351
Prism network, 85–86
Private memory (see Local memory)
Process creation and coordination, 91
Process creation time, 150
Processor array algorithms:
  bitonic merge, 267–271
  bitonic merge, 271–272
  broadcast, 170–171
  connected components, 315–318
  matrix multiplication, 181–186
  mergesort, 291
  odd-even merge sort, 290
  odd-even transposition sort, 258–260
  reduction, 160–167
Processor array architectures:
  classified in Flynn's taxonomy, 79–80
  Connection Machine CM-200, 63–67
  overview, 61–63, 384
  references in literature to, 86
Processor, bit-serial, 64
Processor organizations, 53–61
Production systems, 129
Projection, in multigrid methods, 247

Prolog, 128
  Concurrent, 127
Protein folding, 3
Proust, M., 178
Pruning, alpha-beta, 355
Pseudocode description, 122–127
Ptolemaic system, 255
PVS, 365
Pyramid network, 56, 61, 85–86, 384
QIX, 128
QR factorization, 252
Quantum chemistry, 2
Queuing models, 154
Quicksort, parallel, 272–286, 292
RAM (see Random access machine)
Random access machine, 26, 384
Random read, 286–289, 315, 384
RANDOM.READ, 315, 317
Random uniform game tree, 384
Random write, 286–288, 315, 384
RANDOM.WRITE, 315, 317
Randomized parallel algorithms, 290–291
Rank, 385
rd function, C-Linda, 119
rdp function, C-Linda, 119
Ready list (ready queue), 132, 144, 150
Real part of a complex number, 371, 385
Reasonable parallel model, 86, 385
Rebound sorter, 291
Receiver initiated load balancing algorithms, 143, 385
Recurrence relation, first-order, 252
Red-black coloring, 245
REDUCE, 316–317
Reduction
  2-D mesh, 162, 164–167
  CREW PRAM, 31–32, 44–45
  defined, 31, 385
  hypercube, 160–163
  Little et al.'s algorithm, 343–344
  shuffle-exchange, 160–161, 164–165
  UMA multiprocessor, 165–170
Reference keyword, 122
Relativistic physics, 2
Relaxation, in multigrid methods, 246
Relaxed algorithm (see Asynchronous algorithm)
Replicator construct, occam, 116
Resource waiting, 152
Ring, 134, 139–142, 191–195
$\mathcal{RNC}$, 154, 332
Roethke, T., 309
Rogers, S., 131
Root, 369, 385
Root of unity, primitive, 201
Rotation in AVL trees, 298
Routing:
  circuit-switched, 132
  store-and-forward, 132
Routing algorithms, 176
Row-major order, 270, 291

Row-oriented data distribution, 241, 243–244
RP-RAM, 49
Rule-based expert systems, 129
Scalability, 9, 87
Scalable algorithms and architectures, 9, 87, 385
Scaled efficiency, 83–84, 385
Scaled speedup, 81–84, 385
Scan, 33, 67, 385
Schedule, 145, 385
  optimal, 145, 147
Scheduling algorithm:
  Coffman-Graham, 146–148
  Graham, 145–146
Science, classical vs. contemporary, 2
Scientific Computing Associates, 120–121
Search:
  breadth-depth, 311–312
  breadth-first, 311–313
  depth-first, 48, 332–333
  p-depth, 310–312
  strong, 303
  weak, 303
Search overhead, 360, 385
Search tree, 296
Searching on multiprocessors, 296–306
Seevers, B. K., 169, 175
Segment, 6, 385
Self-scheduled data-parallel algorithm, 158, 385
Semaphore, 151
Semi-distributed load balancing algorithms, 143, 385
Sender initiated load balancing algorithm, 143, 385
SEQ construct, occam, 115–117
Sequence, bitonic, 260–265, 377
Sequent:
  Balance, 69, 167–169, 365
  C programming language, 93, 104–109
  Symmetry: architecture, 68–71
    back substitution speedup, 223
    matrix multiplication speedup, 189
    MIMD category, 79
    odd-even reduction speedup, 227, 229
    quicksort speedup, 275, 277
    Sollin's algorithm speedup, 329
  System Bus, 68–70
Sequential algorithm:
  alpha-beta search, 356
  Back substitution, 221
  Coffman-Graham scheduling algorithm, 146–148
  conjugate gradient, 250–251
  defined, 385
  fast Fourier transform (FFT), 207–208
  gaussian elimination, 231
  Graham's list scheduling algorithm, 145–146
  heap construction, 331
  Jacobi algorithm, 239, 242

heap construction, 331
Matrix multiplication, 179
minimum-cost spanning tree, 328
Moore's algorithm, 320
odd-even reduction, 228
shortest path, 320
Sieve of Eratosthenes, 9–10
Sollin's algorithm, 328
traveling salesperson, 345
tridiagonal system solver, 225
Sequential computer, 26–27, 62–63, 74, 385
Sequential programs, 93
Serial, 385
shape, C*, 100, 385
Shared address space, 70
Shared data, language support for, 104, 106
Shared memory:
  Fortran 90 model, 96
  hot spot, 191, 308, 381
  Linda model, 118
  NUMA multiprocessor, 67
  PRAM model, 27–28
  Pseudocode constructs, 122, 124–125
  ready list stored in, 144
  role in reduction algorithm, 165
  Sequent C model, 104
  Sequent Symmetry, 68
  UMA multiprocessor, 67
Shared variables, contention for, 150, 308
Shell sort, parallel, 292
Short necklace, 60, 385
Shortest path problems, 252, 318, 334, 368–369
shuffle keyword, pseudocode, 125
Shuffle:
  defined, 385
  (See also Shuffle-exchange)
Shuffled row-major order, 270, 291
Shuffle-exchange:
  all-pairs shortest path, 318
  basis for processor arrays, 63
  bitonic merge, 264–269
  compared to other networks, 61
  defined, 59–60, 385
  lower bounds on sorting, 258
  matrix multiplication, 186–187
  pseudocode support for, 124
  reasonable model, 86
  reduction, 160–161, 164–165
  relation to omega network, 85
Sieve of Eratosthenes:
  control-parallel algorithm, 10–13
  data-parallel algorithms, 12–18
  sequential algorithm, 9–10
Signal frequency, 199–200
Signal strength, 199
SIMD, 79, 385
  (See also Processor array)
SIMDAG, 49
SIMD-SM model, 49
Simple task graph, 149, 386
Simpson's Rule, 130

Single instruction stream, multiple data stream (*see* Processor array)
Single instruction stream, single data stream (*see* Sequential algorithm, Sequential computer)
Single Program, Multiple Data, 109, 169
Single rotation of AVL tree, 298
Single-source shortest-path problem, 318, 334, 368, 386
Sinusoidal functions, 198–200
SISD, 79, 386
(*See also* Sequential algorithm, Sequential computer)
s_lock, Sequent C, 106–107
Slotnick, D., 4
SM SIMD model, 49
Snakelike row-major order, 270, 291
Sollin's algorithm, 326–329, 333
Solomon, 4
Solution to a linear system, 218, 386
SOR (*see* Successive overrelaxation)
Sorting, parallel:
    bitonic merge, 260–272
    enumeration sort, 256–257
    hyperquicksort, 276–281
    lower bounds, 257–258
    odd-even transposition sort, 258–260
    parallel sorting by regular sampling, 281–286
    quicksort, 273–277
    random read and random write, 286–290
Sorting networks, 267, 291
Source vertex, 318, 386
south keyword, pseudocode, 125
Space complexity, 26, 386
Spanning tree, 369, 386
SPARC CPU, 75
Sparse linear system solvers, 237–251, 253
Spatial locality, 386
Spawning PRAM processes, 30
Spectral analysis, 199
Spectral decomposition, 214
Speech analysis, 199–201
Speed of light limitations, 5
Speedup, 6, 80, 87, 386
    anomalies, 80–81, 352–354, 365
    scaled, 81–84, 385
    superlinear, 80–81, 353–354, 387
Spin lock, 386
Spinning, 386
Split-and-merge, 277
SPMD, 109, 169, 386
SP-RAM, 49
Spread, 67, 386
SSB, 68
SSS*, 365
Stable-marriage problem, 334
Stack monitor, Sequent C, 107
Stage, 6, 386
Stanford University, 87
State space tree, 339–340, 342, 345, 386
Static scheduling, 143–150

deterministic models, 144–147
nondeterministic models, 147–150
Statistical mechanics, 2
Steady-state temperature distribution, 219–220, 239–241, 244–245
Stencil, 253
Store-and-forward routing, 73, 132, 386
Strassen's algorithm, 179, 196
Stream, data or instruction, 79
Strong search, 303, 386
Strongly connected components, 333
Strongly ordered game trees, 365
Subgraph, 368, 386
Subtree evaluation, parallel, 360
Successive overrelaxation, 245–246, 253, 386
Successor keyword, pseudocode, 124
Suffix sums, 34, 386
Summation (*see* Reduction)
Sun workstation, 63
s_unlock, Sequent C, 106–107
Supercomputer, 6, 80, 386
    performance growth of, 4–5
Superconductivity, 2–3
Superlinear speedup, 80–81, 353–354, 387
Symmetric matrix, 220, 387
Symmetry, Sequent (*see* Sequent Symmetry)
Synchronization, barrier, 91, 104, 125, 377
System Link and Interrupt Controller, Sequent, 69
System of linear equations, 218, 387
Systolic array, 79
T414 Transputer, 113
T800 Transputer, 73
Table, 294, 387
Task graph, 144, 149, 387
Task scheduling, 145–148
Taylor series, 373
Temporal locality, 387
Terabyte, 387
Terminology, parallel processing, 5–9
Test and Control System, TC2000, 72
Thinking Machines, 63, 99
    Connection Machine CM-200, 58, 63–67, 79
    Connection Machine CM-5, 5, 56, 73, 75–76, 78–79
Throughput, 6, 387
Tightly coupled multiprocessor (*see* Multiprocessor architectures, uniform memory access)
Time complexity, 26, 387
To, 367, 387
Toeplitz linear systems, 252
Touchstone DELTA (*see* Intel, Touchstone DELTA)
Tournament, 235, 387
Transitive closure, 313
Transputer, 73, 113, 213
Traveling salesperson problem, 333, 342–346, 365, 387
Tree:, 369, 387

AND, 337–338, 376
AND/OR, 337–338, 365, 376
binary (see Binary tree)
complete binary (see Complete binary tree)
defined, 369, 387
OR, 337–338, 340, 365, 383
search, 296
state space, 339–340, 342, 345, 386
Tree sorter, 291
Tridiagonal linear system solvers, 224–229,
    252
Tridiagonal matrix, 219, 387
Triton/1, 61
Truth table, 64–65
TSP, see Traveling salesperson problem
Tuple space, 118, 387
Turbulence, 2
2-D mesh (see Mesh)
Two-processor unit time scheduling, 154
Ultracomputer, 68, 86, 256
UMA multiprocessor (see Multiprocessor)
Undirected graph, 367, 387
Uniform cost criterion, 27, 387
Uniform memory access multiprocessor (see
    Multiprocessor)
UNION, 326–328
Unit element, 372, 387
Unit time scheduling, two-processor, 154
Universal computer, 86
University of Illinois, 4
University of Karlsruhe, 61
University of Manchester, 87
UNIX, 76, 104
unlock function, pseudocode, 125
Unlock operation, 151
Upper bounds:
    searching, 295–296
    sorting, 292
Upper triangular matrix, 219, 387
Upper triangular system solvers, 220–223
Utilization, 145, 387
V operation on binary semaphore, 151
VAL, 128
Value keyword, pseudocode, 122
Variance computation, 91–94
Vector computer, 61, 387
    (See also Pipelined vector processor, Pro-
    cessor array architectures)
Vector reversal, 176
Vectorizing compiler, 128
Vertex, 367, 387
Vertex collapse, 313
Virtual memory, 25, 78
Virtual processor, 64–65, 67, 100, 387
Virtual tree machine, 365
VLSI algorithms, 87, 291, 307
VME bus, 70, 72
von Neumann model of computing, 25
Weak search, 303, 387
Weakly connected components, 333
Weight, 367, 369, 387
Weight matrix, 367, 387

Weighted graph, 367, 387
Weitek WTL 1167, 68
west keyword, pseudocode, 125
Westinghouse Electric Company, 4
where statement, C*, 101–102
while construct, pseudocode, 123
White House, 294
whoami, nCUBE C, 110–112
Widget machine example, 7–8
Width, 149, 388
with statement, C*, 100–102
Worst-case space and time complexity, 26,
    388
Write, random, 286–288, 315, 384
Write-through cache, 69, 388
X3J3 committee, ANSI, 95
Zero element, 371, 388
0-1 knapsack problem, 354
Zero-sum game, 354

DATE DUE

AUG 0 7 2001			
GAYLORD			PRINTED IN U.S.A.